ALSO BY GEOFFREY PERRET

NONFICTION

Days of Sadness, Years of Triumph
A Dream of Greatness
America in the Twenties
A Country Made by War
There's a War to Be Won
Winged Victory
Old Soldiers Never Die
Ulysses S. Grant

FICTION

Executive Privilege

EISENHOWER

★ ★ ★ ★ ★

EISENHOWER

GEOFFREY PERRET

RANDOM HOUSE
NEW YORK

All photographs courtesy of the Dwight D. Eisenhower Library

Library of Congress Cataloging-in-Publication Data
Perret, Geoffrey.
Eisenhower / Geoffrey Perret.
p.   cm.
Includes bibliographical references and index.
ISBN 0-375-50046-4 (hardcover : alk. paper)
1. Eisenhower, Dwight D. (Dwight David), 1890–1969.
2. Presidents—United States Biography. 3. Generals—United States.
Biography.   I. Title.
E836.P47   1999
973.921′092—dc21
[B]   99-20101

Random House website address: www.atrandom.com

Printed in the United States of America on acid-free paper

2 4 6 8 9 7 5 3

First Edition

Book design by Mercedes Everett

This book is dedicated to

John and Carol Nalbandian
Hank and Jo Royer
Victoria Paige and Earl Levine

Kansas wouldn't be the same without them

ACKNOWLEDGMENTS

My debts begin with Stephen Ambrose, whose two-volume biography of Dwight Eisenhower, published in 1983, was a landmark work. This was the first scholarly and authoritative account of Eisenhower's life and, for me, an inspiration. Since its publication, however, a great deal of new primary material has become available. Moreover, there are by now dozens of scholarly studies that have provided, in nearly every instance, valuable new insights into Eisenhower's extraordinary abilities as both a military commander and as a President. These, combined with the new primary material, justify a fresh look at a man whom Americans trusted as they have trusted no President since.

It has been my great good fortune to have been able to talk at length with John S. D. Eisenhower, who has been as gracious as he has been helpful. His dispassionate yet affectionate insights into his father's life have been invaluable.

I would also like to thank two members of Eisenhower's White House staff, General Andrew J. Goodpaster and Henry Roemer McPhee, both of whom found the time to talk to me despite being remarkably busy men.

I am deeply indebted to the staff at the Eisenhower Library in Abilene, and especially to its director, Dan Holt; to the deputy director,

Matthew Teasley; and to the archivist assigned to help me on my numerous visits there, Herb Pankratz. At the Truman Library, in Independence, Missouri, Dennis Bilger, a man famous for his encyclopedic knowledge of that library's holdings, was a tremendous help.

At the Manuscript Division of the Library of Congress, I have benefited from the skills and knowledge of Mary Wolfskill and Jeffrey M. Flannery. In researching this book, as in researching others, I was helped at the U.S. Military Academy by Alan Aimone, Judith Sibley and Suzanne Kristoff, leaving me in their debt once again.

I was aided, too, by Dr. Richard Summers and his assistant, David Keogh, at the U.S. Army Military Institute, a truly unique institution.

To Dr. Daun van Ee, one of the editors of the superb *Papers of Dwight D. Eisenhower,* I owe an immense debt of gratitude. He provided me with an invaluable insight into the forthcoming final volumes and, as if that were not enough, he read the entire manuscript for accuracy, thereby enabling me to correct various errors.

Finally, if not redundantly, I must express my gratitude yet again to my editor, Robert D. Loomis. I know that I am not alone in my admiration. Nearly everyone who has had the benefit of his skills seems to have arrived at the same conclusion—we are immeasurably lucky to have Bob Loomis edit our work.

CONTENTS

EISENHOWER

D. Dwight Eisenhower

Under a starless sky that heaved and cracked, every crash of thunder that broke over Denison, Texas, that October night rolled down the broad valley of the Red River, shaking the cheap little clapboard houses plunked down beside the steel tracks that followed the river's course. Typical homes of the working poor—the gandy dancers and engine wipers—they were as deficient in plumbing as they were in charm, infernally hot in the summer, grimy with soot, their white paint scarred by cinders. On the Denison side of the fast-flowing Red stretched the monotonously dull landscape of northern Texas. Across the river was an even bleaker expanse of southern Oklahoma, scoured year round by strong winds that stunted the trees and blew the topsoil away. And inside one of the dingy houses, Ida Stover Eisenhower was giving birth as lightning flashed to Earth. The sound of thunder and the pelting rain drowned the mewling of the baby as it emerged into the world and the umbilical cord was cut.

Even as she cradled the helpless pink creature in her arms, Ida couldn't help fearing for what might become of him, her third son. A deeply religious woman, she saw meaning all around her. There had to be something different about a life that began in the melodrama of such a tremendous storm. She asked herself, Wouldn't a child born to lightning flashes and cataclysmic thunder be drawn, as it grew, into a life of violence?[1]

Several days later she opened the family Bible, pen in hand. Birth certificates were rare in frontier towns. The usual record of a new birth was kept by the family, and Ida now wrote a fresh entry: "D. Dwight Eisenhower, born October 14, 1890."

This should have been a joyous moment, for her and for her husband, David Jacob Eisenhower, but whatever joy there was in it was clouded not only by Ida's anxieties about the meaning of the storm but by the failure of their early prospects and youthful hopes. Since their marriage five years earlier, this young couple had fallen a long way to find themselves living in this cramped house, this dull blue-collar town.

The first Eisenhowers had arrived in America more than 150 years earlier, as members of the Mennonite sect. They had settled in and around Lancaster, Pennsylvania, the domain of the Amish. Sects breed more sects, and after a while there was an offshoot of the Mennonites who opted for total immersion and took to baptizing believers in the Susquehanna River. They became known as the River Brethren. Like their Mennonite forebears, they were pious and industrious farmers. The men made the decisions, handled the money, wore patriarchal beards and went bareheaded, because men were "the glory of God." That made women inglorious in comparison, a point reinforced by making them wear large black bonnets when they left the house.[2]

In 1878 most of the River Brethren, who by this time numbered around five hundred, decided to move west and resettle in Kansas. Just why they chose to move a thousand miles isn't altogether clear, but Kansas was bound to appeal to people like them. It was a firmly moral place, and about to set a moral standard for the nation, if not the world.

Kansas Territory had been settled by New England abolitionists in the 1850s to prevent it entering the Union as a slave state. The slavocracy fought back by sending in its own settlers. Fanaticism on both sides rehearsed the slaughter of the Civil War, making "Bloody Kansas" a name synonymous with terrorism, even if it was in a good cause.

After the Civil War, with slavery finally defeated, Kansas remained different. Being more moral than the rest is a habit hard to shake, and it didn't take long for a new struggle to emerge. Kansas became the cradle of the Prohibition movement and its doughtiest champion was Carry Nation, a small, bespectacled, middle-aged divorcée formerly married to a drunk.

This firebrand from Enterprise, a hamlet a few miles from Abilene, was a direct action, antidrink crusader who cast fear into the hearts of burly barkeepers, the kind of men who could throw even the biggest, most aggressive drunks into the street without bothering to untie their aprons first. She liked to show up unannounced, dressed in black—like a widow—brandishing a hatchet in one hand and a Bible in the other, usually at an hour when the saloon was likely to be filled with sinners bellying up to the bar, clutching heavy glasses, puffing on three-cent stogies and pausing now and then to wipe the beer foam from their whiskers.

Going after the beer barrels with her hatchet and the souls of the soused with choice quotations from the Good Book, Carry Nation held Kansas politicians in thrall, inspired right-thinking editors to extol her as morality on the march and made baffled workingmen complain they were being picked on by tub-thumping old maids who were too ugly to catch a man.[3]

Across Kansas, county after county voted itself dry and it became only the second state (Maine was the first) to enact Prohibition. Here, then, was a haven of right thinking and right living. There was still plenty of Homestead Act land to be had there for nothing. And there were also failing homesteads that could be bought for next to nothing, homesteads where there was at least some kind of dwelling to live in and a start had been made on plowing the plains. So for the River Brethren, looking for a new beginning, dry, moral Kansas and cheap—even free—land made a magnet.

The sect leaders who organized the move included two pastors, one of whom was Jacob Eisenhower, able to preach fluently in both English and German. Jacob bought a typical plains farm of 160 acres in a village called Hope, in Dickinson County. Typical because when the nation was surveyed beyond the Mississippi, it was divided into sections of 640 acres. A homestead was a quarter section, or 160 acres, the amount of land the government thought a family needed to operate a successful, self-sustaining farm.

When Jacob and his family moved to felicitously named Hope, the seat of Dickinson County was Abilene, twenty miles to the northeast. Abilene, with a population of around eight thousand, was the railhead at the northern end of the Chisholm Trail. Up the trail from Texas in the early 1870s came more than ten thousand head of cattle each week, to be shipped on to Chicago by rail. Abilene in those heady days was as wild, rough and dangerous a town as could be found anywhere on the grass-covered plains, its streets filled with roistering cowboys prepared to spend an entire year's wages in a single weekend on whores who promised quick satisfaction and whiskey that guaranteed oblivion.

The town hired Wild Bill Hickok as sheriff, but what really ended the rootin' tootin' shootin' days in Abilene was the extension of the railroad to Dodge City in 1875, so the cattle didn't have to plod so far and lose so much weight—muscle was money—before getting their free ride to the stockyards and a fatal encounter with Poles and Lithuanians wielding stun hammers and large knives. By the time the Eisenhowers arrived in Kansas, Abilene was fast becoming a tame, respectable kind of place, as moral and staid as the rest of eastern Kansas.

Meanwhile, Jacob's son David was approaching manhood. There are only two fully approved occupations in the Bible—fishing and farming—and David had the good fortune to be living in one of the best farming areas in the known universe. Jacob hoped—probably expected—that his son would become a sod buster. David worked on his father's farm, as a dutiful son should, but his passion turned out to be machinery, not crops.

David told his father emphatically that he wanted to become an engineer and Jacob tried to dissuade him, but David wouldn't be talked out of it. With a heavy heart, Jacob at last agreed to support him, possibly because a number of River Brethren families were allowing their sons and daughters to enroll at Lane University in Lecompton, a small town a few miles from Abilene. A son with a college education conferred tremendous prestige on a family in an era when barely 2 percent of the population had any exposure to college.

Even so, Lane was probably less challenging than some of the better high schools in Boston and Philadelphia. The campus consisted of four recitation rooms and a one-room laboratory in a modest three-story building. The curriculum emphasized religion, instructors in nonreligious subjects lacked advanced degrees and Lane was on the road to nowhere: it never achieved accredited university status in its brief existence. Founded in 1865, it folded in 1903.

David enrolled in September 1883, at the age of twenty, probably expecting he would get an education that would serve as the foundation stone of a life as a professional engineer, a man who built things and commanded respect. At the start of his second year, he met a young woman with a soft Virginia accent, Ida Stover, who had just enrolled. She was a Lutheran, not River Brethren, but her ancestors, too, were German. They had spelled the name Stoever and emigrated to the colonies in the mid-eighteenth century, settling in Virginia. Ida was born in the village of Mount Sidney in the Shenandoah in 1862. She was just old enough to have traumatic memories of Sheridan's soldiers laying waste the rich valley, the granary of the Confederacy. Ida grew up knowing only one thing about the military—it was "of Satan."[4]

Adding immeasurably to the anguish of her childhood was the death of her mother shortly before her fifth birthday. Her father, with seven sons and four daughters to raise, decided it was too much of a challenge and parceled them out among his and his wife's relations. Ida grew up in the care of her maternal grandparents and, later, an uncle.[5]

For all her sorrows, she turned out to be a lively, intelligent young woman. At sixteen she began earning her living as a housekeeper, before finding work as a teacher in a one-room country school near Staunton, Virginia. Her great joy in life was music and when she came into her inheritance at the age of twenty-one, she bought a black ebony upright piano for six hundred dollars, which was more money than most working Americans earned in a year. At about this time, two of her brothers moved to Topeka. Soon after buying her piano, Ida traveled west to join them.[6]

She had barely arrived in Kansas before deciding to enroll at Lane, mainly because it offered classes in music. Besides which, she would have been well aware that at almost any college there would be the chance to meet presentable young men, the ambitious, upwardly mobile kind who came from good families.

There were few female students at Lane to compete with for male attention, but Ida would have stood out had there been hundreds. She was five feet six, which was tall for a woman then, gracefully slender and pretty. Ida had light brown hair and deep blue eyes, a small nose, a wide, generous mouth with exceptionally full lips. During the course of a long life, Ida was photographed many times, either alone or in a group. It is obvious in the group photos that while most of those around her are making an effort to smile, she is struggling not to break into an earsplitting grin. Even pictures of her in old age convey the irresistible charm of someone in whom the flame of life burns with passionate intensity.

Poor David Jacob Eisenhower, a serious, not to say solemn, young man; he didn't stand a chance. Ida would have gotten him confused and excited in ways he could never have comprehended. She had tremendous sex appeal. Not that he or she would have ever confronted that elemental force directly or attempted to consider it coolly. But David was soon so far gone that he had to have her, and there was only one way to do that. Within a few months of meeting her, he asked her to marry him, and Ida, whose passion was music, not college, said yes.

Jacob Eisenhower had three children and he gave the same wedding gift to each: two thousand dollars in cash and a 160-acre farm. David, having abandoned college in favor of Ida, still rejected farming. He had no mercantile experience or aptitude, but with the two thousand dollars his father promised to give him when he married, he'd be able to open a business of his own, a general store.

In March 1885, with a wedding date set for September, David formed a business partnership, with Milton D. Good, a young man who had spent two years working in a dry goods store in Abilene. Unable to give David a farm, Jacob mortgaged it instead. With the money, he erected a two-story building on a vacant lot he owned in Hope. This building would not only house David's store; it also included two small apartments.

On September 23, David's twenty-second birthday, he and Ida were married in the chapel at Lane. Ida was a year older than her husband. They moved into one of the small apartments above the store. Milton Good and his wife lived in the other, and for a time at least the two couples socialized regularly.[7]

After a year or so, it was evident that the store was in trouble. David was a difficult, emotionally volatile young man trying to get along with a partner who, it turned out, wasn't completely committed to the business. Good was pinning his hopes on perfecting a new type of floor clamp that he expected to make his fortune on once he got it perfected and patented. And all the while the Great Plains were descending into the kind of turmoil that could drive otherwise responsible, stable people to kill themselves.

Kansas farmers were producing as never before, thanks to the introduction of the first generation of modern farm machinery. Even so, their crops were as vulnerable to droughts and infestations as ever. In other words, they could go vertiginously into debt to modernize their farms with gleaming McCormick harvesters one year, only to find themselves wiped out the next. Farmers, those industrious pillars of small-town life on the plains, really were betting the farm. It was as scary as a no-limit poker game, yet local banks and general stores were expected to carry them through the rough times, as they had done in the past, and could count on going down with them if the farms failed. The businesses that survived would be those that were well capitalized and run with ruthless efficiency. The new general store in Hope, Kansas, was neither.

As the unpaid bills mounted and the stock of working capital evaporated, the two partners began bickering. David finally decided to settle the issue—he would buy Good out. Jacob provided the money and in November 1886, after only eighteen months, the partnership was dissolved. David got a new partner—his brother, Abraham, who had recently qualified as a veterinarian. Abraham established his veterinary practice in part of the building, and when he wasn't dosing gargety cows or helping sheep at lambing time, he gave David a hand behind the counter.

The business staggered along for another two years, but the weight of carrying local farmers through a long spell of drought proved too much. David's store spiraled on down until, in the fall of 1888, it finally went bust.

David was in trouble so deep he may have despaired of ever seeing daylight again. He and his father had lost a lot of money on a failed business and now he not only had a child to provide for—Arthur, born in November 1886—but Ida was pregnant again. Shortly after the store folded, he did what many another man has done in similar circumstances: he lit out, leaving his family behind.

David drifted down to Texas looking for work and, ironically, ended up as an engine wiper in Denison. Ironic because two railroads ran through Abilene. He could have done the same mediocre job for the same mediocre wages without ever leaving Dickinson County. On the other hand, here he was a stranger; in Abilene people would know who he was and either laugh at him behind his back for getting too big for his britches or pity him as a foolish and unlucky young man.

In Texas he was living in self-imposed exile, but at least he had a job now, one with a regular paycheck. He could provide for his family. And as he got into his overalls and walked to the railroad roundhouse each morning David may, on good days, have fancied he was at last satisfying his lifelong interest in machinery.

In January 1889, Ida had her second child, Edgar, and prepared to join David in Texas once the infant could travel. In the meantime David rented the small clapboard house alongside the railroad tracks. He had to take in a roomer, though, to help cover the rent. When Ida eventually set off that spring she probably had mixed feelings about what lay ahead, but behind her, like a promise of eventual return, she left the black ebony piano. It was a gesture that told its own story: Texas was for now, but Kansas was forever. In early 1890 she became pregnant again, news that only deepened David's depression.

He continued to work at his lowly twelve-hour-a-day, ten-dollar-a-week job, cleaning the grease and soot off dirty locomotives; an unsmiling man with not a lot to smile about. At home, he retreated into pyramidology, drawing a huge chart of the Great Pyramid of Giza, in which he hoped to find the answers to the fundamental questions of human existence and the cruel workings of implacable fate. The chart was lovingly drawn and eventually grew into a massive object, ten feet by six, that his children gaped at in amazement.[8]

In early 1892, when Dwight Eisenhower was little more than one year old, Ida found she was pregnant for the fourth time. The tiny house was already swamped with humanity, and another mouth to feed would be a crisis. A few months earlier, however, Jacob had written, gently urging David to come back to Kansas. David ignored the old man's request. The prospect of returning was still humiliating.

In March 1892 Jacob tried again. David's father had not only lost all the money he had invested in his son's failed store, but he had also invested heavily in a Hope bank, and the bank had gone bust. His beloved wife, David's mother, had died shortly after the store failed. Now, facing a lonely and possibly straitened old age, Jacob craved the emotional support of his eldest son and his grandchildren. He found David a job to come back to.[9]

While the Eisenhower clan was struggling, Christian Musser, who had married David's sister Amanda, was prospering. The River Brethren had established a major business in Abilene, the Belle Springs Creamery, which provided milk and other dairy products for much of eastern Kansas. Chris was the butter maker and plant foreman. He was holding a position open for someone to look after the refrigeration machinery. Did David want it?[10]

David had only twenty-four dollars to his name when he got the letter from his father offering him a job working for Chris at the creamery. He was too poor to move his wife, children and few possessions back to Kansas. Swallowing his pride, he borrowed the money for rail fares from his brother-in-law. He was eager, though, to get away from Denison, away from the shack built almost on top of the tracks, away from the noisy, dirty roundhouse. Less than two weeks after being offered the creamery job, he went on the Belle Springs payroll. He, Ida and their three sons were in Abilene at last, the place where Dwight always felt he ought, by rights, to have been born. Instead, he'd drawn his first breath in Texas: born in the wrong place, at a bad time, to the crashes and flashes of an earth-shaking storm.

As a boy made his way through the predictable stages of life on the rocky road to manhood, he was expected to pay careful attention to his father, for it was the father above all who would show him what it was to be a man. Yet in Ike's case something was missing. When the young Dwight Eisenhower was growing up in Abilene, his father managed to be absent even when he was present.

David rose at around five in the morning and set off for work at the creamery at six. He never came home for lunch, although the creamery was just a few blocks away. He reappeared at six in the evening, to say grace at the start of supper, eat silently through it, then hole up in a room with a book. David had no amusements or hobbies. "Work was his recreation," said his eldest son, Arthur. Most weeks he worked six days; some weeks he worked seven.[11]

He shunned alcohol and cards, did not take any of his sons hunting or fishing or horseback riding, and showed no interest in their schooling, their friends or anything else that was important to them. Yet what was important to him was thrust upon them, and what was important to him was the Bible. Because he liked to read it, they had to read it. He liked to discuss it, so they had to discuss it, too. His religious opinions were, like the man, narrow and rigid. "He was an inflexible man," thought his second son, Edgar, "with a stern code." The result was that none of his sons grew up with any interest in religion. They had done that, been there and been bored half to death.[12]

David Eisenhower meanwhile remained fascinated by the Great

Pyramid and could study his chart for hours, lost in a fantasy world of his own creation. His sons were taught that if you understood the Great Pyramid, you could see how it corroborated the prophecies contained in the Bible, but not one of them, young as they were, ever believed it. In his quest for certainty, a certainty that he never found, David drifted from one faith to another—from the River Brethren to the Baptists, then on to Methodism, and finally to Jehovah's Witnesses, and before he died he broke away even from them. He remained true only to his belief in the mystical power of pyramids.[13]

Ike's father was at heart a restless man, always seeking, never finding. His spiritual wanderings were only one manifestation of the itch; his absorption in the literature of travel and exploration was another. That restlessness, however, was never yoked to a spirit strong enough to take him farther from Abilene than Texas or into physical or moral danger. He voyaged safely, within his own circumscribed imagination, and from his normally dour expression he didn't seem to land often, if at all, on sunny shores.

By nearly all accounts, David had little or no sense of humor. The only joke he is known to have made in the course of a lifetime was to threaten to pack his suitcase and leave when his seventh and last child, Milton, was born. He'd been determined that this time, he said, he was going to have a daughter.[14]

David had grown up speaking both German and English, but he chose not to pass on his knowledge of German to his sons. They told people this was because he wanted them to be 100 percent American and speak English perfectly, but this isn't persuasive, seeing that his own English was fluent. The truth is almost certainly that because Ida didn't speak German, the entire burden of teaching them the language would have fallen on him. To do it, he would have to spend many hours every week with each of his sons, encouraging them, talking to them. That was never going to happen.

Given his early defeat and the bewildered efforts to make sense of his life, it is hardly surprising that David's anger, which was never hard to arouse, turned readily to rage. There was an emotional force within him in the years when Dwight was growing up that could be terrifying. Whenever Ida reported some serious transgression by one of the boys, David was swift and energetic with his belt. He inflicted pain on those who could not fight back with a zeal close to gladness or madness.

On one memorable occasion, David discovered that his second son, Edgar, was playing truant from school. Grabbing a leather harness, he began flaying the boy without mercy. Dwight, who was twelve at the time, was shocked at the fury of his father's assault on his brother. Bursting into tears, he begged his father to stop. When that failed to work, he tried to grab his father's arms. "I don't think anyone ought to be whipped like that—not even a dog!"[15]

Ike later tried to portray his father's frenzied wielding of leather as a positive influence that kept Edgar from growing up to become the town handyman, but David did not limit his beatings to his own children. In 1896 he was arrested on charges of assault and battery for attacking a neighbor's boy. He pleaded guilty, was convicted and fined before being let out of the Abilene jail.[16]

In respectable families, the more flawed the father, the more important it becomes to obscure the truth. David's status as head of the household had to be propped up if he was to hold his sons' respect. So the story of the failed store was told as a morality tale, in which the evil Milton D. Good had swindled the honest David Eisenhower, run off with the inventory and ruined the business, a wicked deed made even worse by a crooked lawyer by the name of Mahan, who had grabbed whatever Good didn't get his hands on. The story was completely untrue, but it was a necessary fiction, and the Eisenhower sons accepted it without question, as loyal offspring will.[17]

Their father's decision to quit college after only a year was offset by yet another family myth—that despite his lack of a degree, he was an innately brilliant man, someone so clever that he was fluent in ancient Greek. The boys were taught, in effect, that a blue collar does not restrict the flow of blood to the brain, that their taciturn, withdrawn father read the Bible in Greek for relaxation, and they believed it without question. Yet David Eisenhower had studied Greek only during his short time at Lane, and no one learns a language as challenging as ancient Greek in the eight or nine months of a freshman's academic year, plus a couple of months as a sophomore.

While David no doubt liked to be seen poring over his copy of the Bible in Greek and to give the impression that he was reading it as if it were the *Abilene Daily Reflector,* this was the only book in Greek in the house when he died. There was *The Alpha Greek Primer,* by W. G. Frost, from his time at Lane. There were also three Latin primers, probably accumulated by the boys during their years in high school. There was no Greek dictionary or Latin dictionary, yet as anyone who has seriously studied foreign languages knows, mastery is impossible without a comprehensive dictionary. When it comes to tackling a major work in an ancient language, the small dictionary section of a primer will never be remotely adequate. It is unavoidable, too, that in mastering a foreign language, a student accumulates other books in that tongue—biographies, histories, memoirs—and doesn't read just a single work, even if it is the Bible.[18]

Every family has its myths and legends, its secrets and lies. The effect of these particular legends—of David the cheated and David the brain—is to highlight the impression of Dwight Eisenhower's father as a weak man, not a strong one; of someone who attempted to tackle the Bible in Greek only to be defeated again, the Jude the Obscure of Dickinson County.

The result of David Eisenhower's limitations was inescapable. The most important formative influence on young Dwight Eisenhower was not going to be his father. It would be his mother.

When they moved to Abilene, David and Ida rented a small house on South Second Street, a few blocks from the creamery. Although the new house wasn't any bigger than the one in Denison, there was no roomer this time taking up valuable space, which was just as well, because Ida had her fourth child, another son, Roy, in August 1892, only five months after the return. And yet another child was born, Paul, in May 1894. Paul lived for less than a year before dying from diphtheria.

The family was able to scrape along mainly because Ida had a gift for managing a household on a meager budget. She was a talented seamstress, knitter and embroiderer and a wizard with a sewing machine. Ida made most of the boys' clothes, could run up cushions and bedspreads and tablecloths for the house and cut and sewed dresses for herself and shirts for her husband.[19]

While some women would have found the scrimping and the lack of creature comforts depressing, she cheerfully ignored the ineluctable hardships of family life among the working poor. Even so, no sensible person wants trouble with the neighbors. The biggest problem with the Second Street house, thought Ida, wasn't that it was cramped, which it certainly was, but that it had no yard. And as her three sons got older, they were proving energetic and boisterous, especially Edgar and Dwight. "I spend all my time trying to keep the boys quiet and out of other people's yards," she told David one day, exasperated.[20]

There was not much, though, that David could do about it. His salary at the creamery was thirty-five dollars a month, which was what high school students who worked there in the summer were paid. The job of refrigeration mechanic did not call for much knowledge or skill. It was rewarded accordingly.[21]

Then, in 1898, he and Ida were rescued once again by his father. David's brother, Abraham Lincoln Eisenhower, decided to sell his veterinary practice, move to Oklahoma and become a religious missionary. Abraham owned a house, with three acres of land, at South East Fourth Street. The property had been bought by Jacob Eisenhower in a bankruptcy sale back in 1892, as an investment, but then he sold it to Abraham in 1894. And now Abraham was willing to let David have it for a thousand dollars, on condition that Jacob would be allowed to live there if he ever wanted to do so.

David wouldn't risk it. He preferred the safety of renting. Ida had other ideas. They had to move, she insisted—she was pregnant again. So move they did. It is hard to believe that David had saved a thousand dollars, yet the house soon changed hands. Jacob probably put up most—maybe even all—of the money. What's more, David wasn't registered as the new owner. The house was in Ida's name, probably in case debtors from the failed store emerged if David became a man of property. Ten years later, when this threat had receded to the vanishing point, Ida sold the home to David. Price—one dollar.

Ida was overjoyed. The new home, a white-frame two-story structure, had a reasonable number of rooms, even if they were on the small side, but best of all were those three inviting acres, as much space as a mother with a brood of lively children could ask for. There was also a huge two-story barn at the back, with a horse operating table, a hayloft and a big sign on the roof that announced A. L. EISENHOWER—VETERINARY SURGEON. The boys would finally be able to engage in their rough-and-tumble games without straying into the neighbors' yards.[22]

Boys needed to be noisy and energetic, to get dirty and fight one another and have adventures. Having grown up with seven brothers and been a tomboy until her teens, rearing sons was something else that Ida Eisenhower knew how to do.

201 South East Fourth Street

To Abilene, and then to an entire country, and eventually to half the world, he was going to be Ike, but Ida did not want it to be that way. She loathed nicknames, such as Art for Arthur and Ed for Edgar. A real person had a proper name, the one he or she was given when born or baptized. Nicknames were frivolous and silly and unnecessary, seeing as there was always a perfectly good, to say nothing of correct, alternative. Besides, nicknames smacked of laziness and carelessness. So, having failed with her first two sons, Ida was determined that the third would bear a name that had no abbreviated version, one that defied being twisted into a nickname. Dwight seemed perfect.

That part worked as planned. There never was a variant form of Dwight. It was people ruining her project by calling him Ike that she hadn't foreseen. If anyone said Ike around her, Ida snapped back, "Ike? Who's Ike?"[1]

Nor did she ever call him David. The Bible entry marking his birth—D. Dwight Eisenhower—indicates the child was supposed to be called David, after his father, but at the point where she had to write it out for posterity, Ida balked. It was simply inviting confusion to have two Davids in the same household, so she simply gave him the initial, not the name. To her, he was and would always be Dwight and nobody else.[2]

With the move to the new house, Dwight, or as the rest of us say, Ike, was about to learn the second most important article of the Protestant faith. He already had picked up the first, from his hymn-singing mother and regularly praying father—the lesson that even though all people are sinners, everyone can be saved. The second article of faith—and from the way this family lived, it was nearly in a dead heat with the first—was the Protestant ethic: life is work and work is life. Not even childhood offered a chance to opt out. For an eight-year-old, which is what Dwight was in 1898, the number of chores must have seemed endless.

Within a year of so of moving, Ida had the three acres of land planted with a dozen kinds of vegetables, including several varieties of corn. There were also an apple orchard, some cherry trees and pear trees, and maple trees oozing syrup ringed the property. Ida had always loved flowers, especially madonna lilies, so there was a flower garden that demanded regular weeding. And there were the animals to take care of, too—a couple of horses, a cow, plenty of chickens, a few pigs, even some ducks. What the Eisenhowers had at 201 South East Fourth Street was a small farm. But David, who had never cared for farming, was free to ignore that fact. He didn't work the land; his sons did.[3]

The Eisenhowers were almost self-sufficient when it came to groceries. That was a big savings in itself. There were also no utility bills to worry about—kerosene lamps instead of electricity, a wood-burning stove for cooking and heating and no indoor plumbing, just an outdoor toilet and a huge water tank on stilts looming somberly over the eastern end of the house. Within a year or two of their moving, David's workman's wages covered the family's cash needs.[4]

As in a lot of small towns, the railroad tracks marked Abilene's great divide. The town lies almost, but not quite, flat on the prairie. The ground rises noticeably as you walk from the southern to the northern side, and all over the world, the better-off prefer the higher ground. This was where the majority of the more prosperous and influential citizens lived, north of the Union Pacific tracks, while most of the rest, like the Eisenhowers, lived on the lower ground to the south.

That did not make the south-siders poor white trash or anything like it. Ike's rise from obscurity to power and fame was spectacular by any standard, a testament to the meritocracy that sustains and in each generation reinvigorates a democracy in good working order. But journalists who spread his fame during World War II—and, later, serious biographers—could not resist the temptation to lower the family's status, to make the ascent even more awe-inspiring. The years in Abilene were usually presented as a triumph over grinding poverty and social prejudice.[5]

The hard times, though, were in Denison, of which Ike had no memory—for years, in fact, he thought he had been born in Tyler, Texas. Life was only a little better in the first home the Eisenhowers owned in Abilene. When they moved into the house and three acres on South East Fourth Street, however, the place that became known as *the* Eisenhower home, Ike had reached the age where children begin to become aware of their surroundings, and at this point in the lives of David and Ida and their sons the days of poverty were behind them.

There was always plenty to eat, a secure roof over Ike's small blond head, and although Ida was handy with home remedies—such as making the boys swallow gunpowder to prevent iron deficiency—when they really needed it, there was enough money to pay for a doctor.[6]

The fact that each son in turn wore an older brother's hand-me-downs, and that both Ike and Edgar for a time wore their mother's high button shoes, is often stressed but is really neither here nor there. Plenty of children reared in thrifty, not poor, homes endured similar experiences up to World War II, a tradition doomed by the rise of the teenager.[7]

What was truly different was the amount of work that had to be done on this small farm, and Ida, going about her daily routine cheerfully humming to herself or singing a hymn, supervised her sons with the brio of a circus ringmaster. There were indoor chores, such as washing the dishes, which everyone hated. And Ike, in the first couple of years in the new house, made it plain that he loathed having to do chores of any kind. Ida, however, made sure he did them, and simply refused to pay any attention to his sulking and tantrums.[8]

The absolute worst as far as Ike was concerned was having to get up on a winter's morning at half past four, go downstairs in the freezing darkness and start the fire in the kitchen stove, usually with dried corn cobs soaked in kerosene. It would be a shocking start to anyone's day.

For him, and for his brothers, the outdoor tasks were a lot more popular than anything that had to be done indoors, except that at some point Ike developed a love of cooking. He was the only one of Ida's sons wise enough to discover the happiness that can be found in a kitchen.

To keep them from growing bored, and to preclude anyone from developing ideas about monopolizing one of the easier tasks, Ida rotated the chores. Each boy found himself with a different schedule every week. Dwight not only learned to cook but to clean the house, do the laundry, including the ironing, raise vegetables, tend the flowers, collect eggs—putting china eggs under poor layers, to encourage them to make a better effort—wash the dishes without breaking them, feed the horses and pigs, milk the cow, hoe the vegetable plots, pick apples and cherries and pears from the trees and tap maple syrup into a small bucket.[9]

Ida herself was energy unleashed. Keeping an eye on the boys' efforts was only a small part of her work. She mended, cleaned, baked nearly every day, cooked most of the meals, planted and weeded, but when she felt she really needed it, she found the time to sit at her beloved ebony upright and, as she described it, "Play myself rested."[10]

One of the reasons Ida had been so determined to buy this house was that she was pregnant again when the offer was made. Although she and David prayed for a girl, they got another boy, Earl, who was born shortly before the family moved. The last child, Milton, was born in September 1899. To his dismay and disgust, Dwight had to wash diapers, first for Earl and later for Milton.

To earn a little pocket money, Ike and Edgar from time to time loaded some of the produce they had grown onto the family's spring wagon, hitched up one of the horses and plodded across the railroad tracks to the north side of town. One boy held the horse while the other went knocking on doors, asking people to buy their fruits and vegetables. Edgar, who was two years older than Dwight, found the business of door-to-door selling humiliating. He was convinced the north-siders deliberately handled their produce disdainfully, hinting that it was inferior stuff, as if to say the Eisenhowers were inferior people. Even after he became a millionaire attorney, Edgar seethed at the memory of north-side snobbery, while Ike more sensibly ignored it.[11]

As they went about their chores, Ida talked to her sons, chatting easily with them. Unlike silent David, she always had something to say. Ida was not a clever or intellectual person. Her interests did not reach beyond her family, her friends, her house and her religion. And the lessons she imparted to Ike and the other boys were little more than the predictable apothegms and clichés of generations of ordinary Protestant toilers and believers.

Ida had few idle moments in the day, but she kept a deck of cards in a drawer. She liked to distract herself with a couple of hands of solitaire on long winter evenings. "The Lord deals the cards," she earnestly told Ike. "And you play them." Whenever he got into trouble or seemed to be looking for a way of avoiding something he didn't want to face up to, his mother was likely to tell him bluntly: "Sink or swim. Survive or perish." Another favorite was the inverted compliment that good people liked to pay to themselves—"There's no rest for the wicked." Above all, "Nothing comes easy in life."[12]

At Halloween in 1900, Ike had just passed his tenth birthday and insisted he was old enough to go trick-or-treating with his big brothers, Arthur and Ed. His father told him he was too young and that was all there was to it. Dwight threw a tantrum, rushed into the yard and attacked the stump of an old apple tree, hitting it until his little fists were raw and bloody. He screamed against the injustice of the adult world until David came out, gave him a whipping and ordered him to go straight to bed.

He sobbed in futile rage on his bed for the best part of an hour. Then his mother came into the room, sat in the rocking chair next to the bed and after a while wiped the dirt from his red, abraded hands, gently rubbing some salve into them before wrapping them in bandages. She talked as she did so about how easy it was to lose one's temper sometimes, but it was never right to hate anyone.

"He that conquers his own soul is greater than he that conquers a city," she said. Besides, who had he hurt by being so angry? Only himself.

For much of his life thereafter, Ike, who had inherited something of his father's capacity for rage, tried to remember what his mother had told him when he felt his anger rising. It didn't always work, of course, but these little homilies, absorbed in childhood not as lectures but as pure love, become part of the architecture of our lives. In moments like this Ike, the confused and angry boy, was on the receiving end of what a modern philosopher, Bernard Williams, calls "moral luck."[13]

While her love for Dwight was intense, Ida never played favorites. In 1945, when Ike was named Chief of Staff of the Army, a journalist phoned and said she must be very proud of her son. She gave the perfect reply—"Which one?"[14]

Even so, there was something about Ike that convinced people he was more like his mother than any of his five brothers. Partly it was a matter of the grin. Nobody else in the family grinned like Ike, except his mother. It was also something innately cheerful in his temperament, a trait he shared with Ida. "Dwight—you'd hear him coming two blocks away, whistling and singing," according to Ida's niece, Nettie Stover Jackson.[15]

Ike never had much to say about his father. He talked about his mother a lot more and readily acknowledged the importance of what she had taught him. It is striking, too, that when he wrote his memoir *At Ease: Stories I Tell to Friends,* there was a chapter called "Life with Mother." There was no "Life with Father." His feelings about his parents were almost certainly the same as Edgar's, who wrote in his own memoir, "Our love for our father was based on respect. Our love for our mother was rooted in something deeper."[16]

For all the debt to his mother—and maybe even because of it—Eisenhower sometimes liked to talk as though his approach to people and problems was the product of a rugged frontier code of manly courage and fair play, epitomized by two men out in the open, facing each other and ready to draw. He was fascinated by the Wild West his whole life—not because he had experienced it directly, but because he had just missed out on it, like a child who grows up in the shadow of a great war. Yet the truth is, he really got most of his ideas of right and wrong, of what was good and what was bad, from a middle-aged, graying woman in the clean and orderly setting of a neat little house, not out in the streets of a brawling frontier town.

In many ways, Ike's childhood was not all that different from growing up in a modern white-bread suburb—apart, that is, from the never-ending farm work. Turn-of-the-century Abilene was really a tame place, with churches all over town, and saloons were banned. Drinking was a furtive, underground, almost subversive activity. Abilene's wild days had ended more than a decade before David and Ida moved there. The burg was so buttoned-up and carefully controlled that when Ike was a boy, children couldn't even play ball games on Sundays. The only approved activity for them was going to Sunday School. Abilene was just the kind of dull but decent place that a lively and intelligent young man was likely to think about leaving.

Pacifism was blood of her blood, bone of her bone. It was therefore bound to distress Ida when she found that boys are going to play at being soldiers, especially when there's a war going on. In the summer

of 1898, the United States went to war with Spain and REMEMBER
THE MAINE! screamed from windows, lapel buttons, banners and newspapers.

That was all the inspiration eight-year-old Ike and his brothers
needed. They bushwhacked make-believe Spaniards all over south Abilene. A modest knoll became San Juan Hill, begging to be seized in repeated heroic charges. For the Eisenhower boys, as for boys all over
town that summer, there were fantasy corpses and gunsmoke all around.
But when Ida caught her sons playing soldier, she was horrified, and
gave them a lecture on war, a lecture that was probably wasted.[17]

Yet much as she deplored war and make-believe violence, Ida
thought there was a lot to be said for a real scrap. Her hymn-singing, religious neighbors and various pacifistic Eisenhower relatives were astonished. A relative visiting the house one day heard a fight erupt in the
yard between Ike and Edgar and called, "Ida! They're fighting."

"They have to get it out of their system," said Ida philosophically.
"You can't keep healthy boys from scrapping. It isn't good to interfere
too much."[18]

That doesn't mean there weren't limits. There was another day, for
instance, when Ida was entertaining some visitors and Ike and Edgar
started throwing punches in another room. One of her guests grew
alarmed at the noise of battle. "Mrs. Eisenhower, aren't you going to
stop it? They're going to get hurt."

"Just ignore them," advised Ida. "Let them solve their own problems and things will be better for them both." Then she shouted to the
combatants, in a commanding voice, "You boys know the rule about
fighting in the house. Get outside—*fast!*"[19]

Most of Ike's fights were with Edgar, who was bigger, older and
heavier. That meant he suffered the usual fate of the overmatched
pugilist—he got thrashed—but the fierce sibling rivalry between him
and Edgar meant they were forever fighting, and constantly dared one
another to do dangerous things, always looking for some weakness in
the other that could be exploited for purposes of humiliation.[20]

For instance, there was that tempting big sign that Uncle Abe the
veterinarian had erected on top of the two-story barn. There was no way
they could ignore it, and what began as a game of tag on the roof turned
into dare—Dare you to sit on top of the sign. Double-dare you. So they
both ended up on top of the sign, forty feet above the ground. But that

wasn't enough. They dared each other into hanging upside down from it, knowing that one slip and they would fall far enough to break their necks.

Like his fights, many, possibly most, of Ike's boyhood adventures involved Ed in some way, like the time they found a full bottle of beer. Instead of drinking it themselves, they grabbed hold of a hen, held her beak open and poured the beer down her throat. The chicken got drunk, which two adolescent boys were bound to think was hilarious, but the poor hen was turned into a neurotic wreck—she never laid another egg.[21]

In 1903 the part of Abilene that borders Mud Creek was flooded, as were the ditches running alongside the town's principal streets. Ike and Ed were making their way through ankle-deep mud to the creamery, carrying their father's lunch, when they spotted a rowboat floating in one of the overflowing ditches, climbed aboard and set off through the town, at one point getting out of the boat to lift it across the railroad tracks as they headed for deeper, fast-flowing water. Paddling along, the two boys tunelessly but exuberantly belted out "Marching Through Georgia." This was great fun, and they began picking up passengers as they navigated their way through downtown. Eventually, the small boat took on so many of their friends it cracked open and sank.

At that point a neighbor, Mr. Volkman, appeared on top of the bank along Mud Creek, shouting that their mother was looking for them. "Gee!" cried Edgar. "We forgot to take Dad's lunch to him!"

"Well, it's too late to do anything about it now," said Dwight. "It's past two o'clock."

The two boys made their way home, fearfully. Ida was waiting. "You boys go to the back porch and strip." While they got out of their wet clothes, she cut a switch from a maple tree and proceeded to give them a thrashing they never forgot. She didn't only believe in the therapeutic value of boyhood scraps. Ida also believed in the education potential of corporal punishment, swiftly applied and in moderation. The eternal subtext to "Life is work" is "Life is duty."[22]

The next year brought more floods. This time the boys saw a piece of wooden sidewalk that had been ripped away by the rising waters floating down the street. They waded over to this impromptu raft, climbed aboard and let the current carry them merrily along, until they realized they were about to be swept into the raging torrent that used to be Mud Creek. Several adults intervened just in time and pulled the raft back onto solid ground before anyone was drowned. Ida was waiting again. They had to strip off again. Another piece of maple was wielded again.

Ike seems to have been a robustly healthy child, missing out on a wide range of typical childhood ailments. Even so, he came close to dying at the age of fourteen. He fell and skinned his left knee one afternoon, running home from school. The knee became swollen, the leg below the knee turned an ominously dark shade—blood poisoning. The doctor examined Ike's leg and was metaphorically reaching for the saw. He drew a line just above the knee. "If we do it now, we can save the rest of the leg. The longer we wait, the more we'll have to take off."

Ike shook his head. Death seemed better. "You won't take any off." The doctor went downstairs and talked, sotto voce, with David and Ida in the small hallway, urging them to give permission to start cutting.

When Edgar came home from school shortly afterward, he found his brother crying, frightened but determined. "You've got to promise you won't let 'em do it. I'd rather be dead than crippled and not be able to play ball."[23]

Ed gave his promise, but he was too bright not to realize that he was not going to be able to stop the doctor if his father told him to stand aside. For two days and nights, Ed loyally remained outside the bedroom door, while on the other side Ike was biting on a fork to keep from screaming out loud. The pain from his leg, swelling up like a balloon about to burst, was agonizing. Ida acted as Ike's day nurse. A family friend came in each evening to stay with him throughout the night.

David and Ida refused to give the doctor permission to cut. They did not want to see their son mutilated and embittered, blaming them for the rest of his life for turning him into a cripple. Besides, whatever power the doctor possessed was as nothing compared to the will of God. If it was the Lord's will for Dwight to die, not even the sharp scalpel and singing bone saw could save him.

The doctor painted a band of carbolic acid around his body; more gesture than barrier. Dwight lapsed into unconsciousness and his breathing became labored. Death seemed about to take him, only to tiptoe away. His breathing began to improve, the swelling began to go down, the fever subsided. He would live after all, saved not by Ed, not by the doctor but, David and Ida were certain, by God's will and goodness.[24]

If nothing else, Ike's near-death ordeal showed that he was a strong and healthy young man, with a powerful immune system in excellent working order. He possessed the kind of innate physical resilience that is acquired mainly in youth, if it is acquired at all. Far down the road it was going to save him again. For now, though, all he could think of doing with it was play football.

Little Ike

Dwight Eisenhower was born when immigration into the United States was at its peak. Before the 1880s, immigrants came mainly from the British Isles and from Germany. Culturally and ethnically, they had little trouble adjusting to American life. The new immigration was different. Most of those arriving after 1880 came from southern and eastern Europe, fluent in Polish or Italian but unable to speak English; used to living in poverty and fear but not used to casting a ballot or reading a book.

One reaction to the new immigration was to introduce laws to stem the tide of pinched, anonymous faces shuffling daily through Ellis Island, an ever-changing, never-changing panorama—scuffed shoes, pathetic bundles, cheap headscarves. Another was to build a lot of new schools. Few of the adults were likely to achieve anything much, but the children might be saved, if they were turned into Americans first; and in the homes of the immigrant poor, parents said amen to that in a dozen tongues.

With this unexpected shift in the zeitgeist giving power to educational reformers who had been arguing for years that the country had to provide a free secondary education for all, in the space of a generation new high schools arose not just in the East Coast cities but in nearly every American town. Before the 1890s, most people got no more than a grade school education. High school was a privilege enjoyed by roughly 10 percent of the population, usually the offspring of aspirational families living in the big cities. It suddenly became available to everyone, even the poorest—except, of course, in the South.

Providing a free high-quality secondary education for Ike's generation was a watershed, socially, culturally and economically. It was seen, in the long lens of History, as the single most important factor in making the U.S. the most economically productive country in the world. Although he was completely unaware of it, the young Dwight Eisenhower was part of a new and lucky generation, riding the crest of a reforming wave into the new century.[1]

The first school he attended in Abilene was a grade school just across the street from the house his parents rented when they returned from Texas. For the seventh and eighth grades, he had to go to Garfield, a school north of the Union Pacific tracks.

In the fall of 1902, Ike started classes at Garfield. School tradition demanded that the honor of the south side be upheld each year in a fight against a battler representing the north side. Edgar fought and won on behalf of the area south of the tracks that year. A year later, when he started the eighth grade, Ike more or less inherited the mantle, and his opponent, a boy named Wes Merrifield, was expected to beat him easily.

The ensuing fight plays a crucial role in early Ike lore. It has been written about in more detail and with more enthusiasm than some heavyweight championship bouts. This fight was said to have lasted more than two hours and been a knock-down, drag-'em-out slugfest that left both opponents covered in gore, their faces and bodies little more than an oozing collection of cuts and bruises. It is pretty incredible, as Ike at this time was a slightly built thirteen-year-old weighing about 115 pounds. Merrifield, who was roughly the same height, was a stocky youth and somewhat heavier.[2]

Most accounts of this fight, compiled decades after the event, were stretched and embroidered until they became big enough to fit a five-star commander. Yet all that happened was that a pair of boys from decent homes ineffectually threw punches at one another for what seemed like an eternity. To a pair of thirteen-year-olds, half an hour is a long time. In the end, they had to settle for a draw, because neither one of them knew how to fight seriously. But this was Abilene and an honorable draw, without scarring, was good enough.

Besides, the important thing was not who won or lost. It was that even though Ike knew from the start that he could not beat Merrifield, he didn't duck the fight, and once it got going, he wouldn't quit, either.

He arrived home with a face that was puffy and bruised. One eye was almost shut. But Ida only wanted to know one thing: "Was it a fair fight?"

"Yes," said Ike. "It was a fair fight and neither of us won."[3]

When most of his classmates finished at Garfield, that was the end of formal education for them, but Ike was going to continue his education. In September 1904 he enrolled in what passed for a high school—a handful of cramped rooms on the first floor of city hall. The town jail was just below, in the basement. The fire department was installed on the same floor and male high school students were considered volunteer firemen. When the fire bell clanged into life, they rushed out of the classroom, hauled the two-wheel fire cart out onto the street and pulled it through town, heading in the direction of the blaze.[4]

Classes weren't interrupted only by fires. There was one memorable day when a prisoner managed to set off a stick of dynamite and got out of jail free. Even without these dramas, Ike and his classmates, said one of the teachers, "received their education midst the howling of dogs, the wailing of prisoners, and the odor of onions being cooked for the fire marshal's dinner."[5]

It was during his first semester that Ike nearly lost his leg. His recovery was so slow that he missed most of the year and would have to repeat it. While he was recovering, Abilene was building a new high school, a real one, a spacious structure whose imposing red-brick walls announced that secondary education was something important to the town and to its young people. The adult volunteer firemen would have to haul the cart from now on.

Graduating from high school had never been taken seriously in Abilene and many parents, and even more children, still didn't see the point. A teenage boy was considered almost a man in small-town America, ready—and probably eager—to put schoolbooks aside and start earning a living.[6]

Unless they intended to go to college, there was no obvious reason at this stage of Abilene's development for most teenage boys to spend four years in high school. The establishment of the new school nevertheless helped spark a fresh interest in education, and Ike enrolled there in the fall of 1905.

The school remained small in terms of numbers. It had four female faculty members and one male. Ike's class was also overwhelmingly female—twenty-two girls and only nine boys. Not, you might think, a promising milieu for a budding jock.

Ike got a thrill from danger, probably more so than Edgar. The barn at the back of the Eisenhower house had a large hayloft and Ike liked to climb up to the roof beam, balance himself for a moment, then fall, head first, toward the piles of hay. He always managed to pull off a somersault in midair and land feet first. Ike had taught himself how to perform this stunt and tried to teach it to his younger brother Earl, but Earl, lacking Ike's natural athleticism, landed on his head, knocking himself out.[7]

That natural ability and an ingrained competitiveness, kept razor-sharp by the never-ending rivalry with Edgar, made it inevitable that he would grow up with a passion for sports. Ike shared the love of baseball common to boys all over the country. His sporting idol during his high school years was Honus Wagner, the legendary Pittsburgh Pirates shortstop who led the National League in batting for eight seasons.[8]

Ike made the Abilene High School baseball team at the start of his junior year, but the outcome was pretty dismal: the team won two games and lost four. What really got him excited, though, was making the football team that year, which was the first year the school adopted the forward pass. Until then, football was really rugby, rather than American football as most people know it now.

He was not simply competitive: he liked the raw physical challenge of a contact sport. Playing conditions were about as basic as it gets. The school contributed nothing toward coaching or equipment. A football uniform was something the players improvised—light-colored duck pants with some quilting stitched on at appropriate points; old sweaters, with horses' sweat pads cut up and sewn into the shoulders; a pair of worn-out dress shoes with a V-shaped cleat nailed hopefully to each sole for traction; no helmet, but a woman's stocking pulled over the head and a few rags tucked underneath.

The team had only two footballs: a battered, almost round object that was used for practice, and a newer, more oval ball that was used only for scheduled games. The rules were enforced by the coach, a local farmer by the name of Orin Snider, a high school football hero who had just graduated from AHS in 1906. He was unpaid, untrained and the same age as some of his players.[9]

During Ike's first season AHS ran wild: played seven, won seven, scored 127 points and gave up only nine. Ike, Edgar and the rest of the jocks got together at the start of the next school year and organized the AHS Athletic Association, to try to raise enough money to buy some halfway decent equipment. The association elected Dwight Eisenhower president, and the first decision taken under his leadership was to forget about other sports that fall. Everything would be devoted to football.

Ike, who still didn't weigh more than 140 pounds, played right end on offense and wherever he was needed on defense; in those days, you played both ways, as it is still done in rugby. Edgar was two years older but was in the same class, having quit school for two years after finishing the eighth grade at Garfield. With the opening of the new high school, Ed returned to education and as the biggest, strongest boy in the Class of 1909 he was the team's fullback. To Ike's dismay, other schools were reluctant to be run over by invincible Abilene High following its perfect season. Only four football games were played during his senior year.[10]

In February 1909, his thoughts turned to the upcoming baseball season. Something had to be done about the pitching. The previous year's pitcher had graduated. Ike detected hidden talent in one of the infielders, a pal of his called "Six" McDonnell. Ike's suggestion was instantly rejected.

"I'm no pitcher," McDonnell protested, but Dwight was president of the athletic association, which counted for a lot in these matters. He was backed up, too, by Edgar, who was one of the school's star athletes. Edgar was known, formidably, as Big Ike. (That meant that Dwight had to endure being called Little Ike, a cross to bear for someone almost desperate not to live in the shadow of his big brother.) With both Eisenhowers insisting he had a fine pitching arm if he only cared to discover it, McDonnell caved in.[11]

He was the team's one and only pitcher, and put in a creditable performance. His first season on the mound he won five and lost five, which was a big improvement over the previous year. And Ike was convinced AHS would have finished six and four had it not been for him.

In the final game, the high school was up against the University of Kansas freshman team, and was leading 1–0 in the seventh and final inning when a screaming line drive was belted in his direction. He misjudged the ball and ran under it, allowing KU to score two runs. What upset him more than the loss, though, was a conviction that had Six pitched a winner, KU would have recruited him for its baseball team.

"I lost you a possible athletic scholarship," he told Six apologetically. "Forget it," said McDonnell, but Ike was upset about that misjudged ball for years afterward. He had been right, though, about Six's natural ability, because McDonnell went on to play semipro baseball for nine years.[12]

The Class of 1909 would graduate in May. Looking at their pictures in *The Helianthus,* the male seniors, such as Ed, and most of the girls, look outgoing and eager, ready to get on with their lives. Edgar Eisenhower is described in the yearbook as the school's best football player. "Also on his head," runs the description, "there is a depression due to the non-development of the conscious and over-development of the unconscious brain." A cute way of saying that Ed was egotistical, outgoing and ambitious. His future was extrapolated from his forceful, argumentative character: Ed would be a two-term President of the United States.

The picture of Dwight, or Little Ike, does not show the rough-and-tumble jock that he yearned to be. It is the image of a sensitive, watchful youth, a pouting and good-looking teenager who seems alert and intelligent. The caption under his picture says, "Best Historian and Mathematician."

Although David and Ida had gone to Lane, their precollege education did not amount to anything much. Lane itself was more like a high school than a college. In 1904 David had completed a correspondence course in refrigeration engineering and proudly hung his certificate on his bedroom wall. What David and Ida had derived from a haphazard exposure to formal education was an interest in books, beginning with but not completely restricted to religious works. The house at South East Fourth Street contained several hundred books, including dozens on history and more than a score of novels, of a suitably uplifting kind. For the time and the place, this was a bookish home.

Not surprisingly, then, Dwight Eisenhower developed a love of reading before he even went to high school. He claimed it was having to read the Bible out loud that made him better at reading than his classmates, but it wasn't the Bible that stimulated his interest in books. It was history that did it, especially history that involved war and military heroes. His interest was sparked by a book on Hannibal, which led him to read widely in the history of ancient Greece and Rome. Battles such as Marathon and Cannae and Salamis provided thrilling reading, as they have done for countless boys over many generations.

When his teachers found that he was by far the best history student they had, he was given different and more challenging assignments than his classmates. This only gave him a chance to show his superiority in yet another field, English. He had a natural gift for writing clear, effective prose.

Ike found he had a talent for math, too, especially geometry. Unlike algebra, which has a remote, almost surreal quality, geometry, with its demands on spatial reasoning, is the branch of math that develops skills in real-life problem solving. When he encountered plane geometry for the first time, Ike was enthralled. He had such natural ability that after a while his teachers decided he was finding geometry too easy. They gave him problems to solve that were not in the textbook. It was for him to come up with his own original solutions.[13]

His imagination was, meanwhile, being stretched down at the office of the *Dickinson County News.* His friend Six McDonnell was the kind of teenager who could go either way—settle down and turn out all right or become one of the town's bad boys. The newspaper editor, Joe Howe, had no children of his own but took an interest in youngsters. He was a member of the school board and created a boys' club, the Knights of Honor. In a room at the back of the newspaper office, he provided a haven for potentially wayward lads such as Six to hang out, let off steam in supervised boxing matches and play pool in a place where there was no risk of their being lured into drinking, smoking or other bad habits. Dwight took to stopping by the newspaper office to meet Six and found the country, and much of the world, stacked up and yellowing underneath Howe's windows.

Before World War II, newspapers across America sent copies of their latest edition to one another. The papers were scanned by journalists at the other end, and Howe dumped his in piles by the windows. Ike got in the habit of sitting in Howe's office, waiting for Six to finish playing pool and reading stories from New York and Kansas City, St. Louis and Chicago, handling papers from New England, papers from the South. America as a moving, thrilling pageant, teeming in its unstoppable vitality and variety, was there in his hands, in narrative form, but not as a tale of something that had happened fifty years ago or even last year. Here, said the newspaper stories, is what is happening now. And this is what might happen tomorrow.

He had found the world beyond Abilene—a bigger, more exciting place than Kansas could ever hope to be, and Ike, utterly fascinated, talked about it with Joe Howe, an interesting man who knew things and had been places. "I like to read what's going on outside of Kansas," he told Howe one day. "Makes me realize that Kansas isn't the whole world."[14]

Other parts of his education were picked up elsewhere. In the course of fishing the local rivers for catfish, he became friendly with a poker-playing hunter and fisherman by the name of Bob Davis. Ida approved of her son's hero-worshipping friendship with Davis, probably sensing that this illiterate, childless bachelor in his fifties, a lonely but good-hearted man with a passion to teach the things he'd spent a life learning, could be the father to him that David Eisenhower had never been and would never be.

It was Bob Davis who taught Ike how to use a shotgun, trap muskrat and mink, paddle a flatboat, handle a trout rod and, above all, how to play poker. The Bob Davis secret was to figure out the percentages and play your hand accordingly.

He and Ike played for matches. Each player began with a full box and Davis dealt each of them five cards. "Okay, bub. Do you have a pair?"

"Yes, nines," said Ike.

"All right. How many nines are there out of the forty-seven cards you haven't seen?"

"Two."

"Well, then. The chances of your drawing a nine as you take each card is two out of forty-seven. Since you are drawing three cards, you have six chances out of fourty-seven of catching another nine."

Ike, with his aptitude for math, learned to calculate percentages in his head and played accordingly, but once he'd lost his whole box of matches, this session of poker school was over.[15]

On the weekends, Ike and his surrogate dad trapped, hunted, fished and played cards together and he discovered the joy there is in catching some trout, cooking them over an open fire under the stars and eating them in the company of a good friend. He probably never had a happier time in his life than some of those evenings in the woods that covered the Smoky Hills.

Thanks to his mother, the able and committed teachers at Abilene High School, friendly Joe Howe and unlettered Bob Davis, young Dwight Eisenhower got as rounded an education as any teenager in town, possibly in the whole state, but he was not aware of that yet. Nor were his friends or his family. To him as to them, growing up like this seemed natural and ordinary.

As for the future, that inescapable void into which he was expected to pitch his hopes and shape his dreams, it remained stubbornly remote. His one concrete hope was that it might bring more chances to play baseball and football. He hardly noticed, or placed much value on, what his AHS classmates rightly saw as his truly distinctive elements. What stood out as far as they were concerned wasn't the athlete he wanted to be but the thinker he was.

"Whenever the teachers called on Dwight he could always recite," said one classmate, Winifred Williams. "I never heard him say, 'I don't know.' " Even Edgar conceded there was something unusual in his brother's intellect. "His curiosity is inexhaustible. It always was."[16]

When the time came to put the Class of '09 yearbook together, the *Helianthus* editors weighed him up, in the half-solemn, half-joky way that yearbook editors still do. Dwight Eisenhower, they prophesied, would become a professor of history at Yale. They could not have known anything much about Ivy League professors. And they surely knew Yale only by its reputation as one of the best universities in the United States. But in a sensible world, he could flower into an intellectually brilliant man, move far away from Abilene to live and work among other intellectually gifted people.

Their prophecy was an indirect acknowledgment, cautious and opaque, that Little Ike was the smartest student at the new AHS, with its faintly defensive school motto: "Not at the top, but climbing."

✫✫✫✫✫

4

The Appointment

What made him decide to go to college? Ed, probably. And the possibility of playing more football would have exerted its own leathery allure. Although Ida and David liked to think they had encouraged their boys to be educationally ambitious, there's as much evidence against it as for it.

For instance, Arthur, the eldest son, didn't even finish high school. He quit after a year and shortly afterward headed for Kansas City, where he got a job as a bank messenger and rented a room in a house where one of his fellow boarders was a young man named Harry S Truman. And there was Roy, who finished high school and went to work in a drugstore. He eventually qualified as a pharmacist, but in those days someone could do that on the basis of on-the-job training and passing a practical exam, which was what Roy did.

At first, Edgar looked determined to follow Arthur's example. He quit school when he finished the eighth grade at Garfield. For the next two years he worked desultorily at various jobs, before deciding to give high school a chance. Just why he made that decision isn't clear, but in his case, too, it was as likely to be the chance to play football as anything his parents had to say.

Behind high achievers there is usually at least one teacher who has made a difference. There definitely was in Edgar's rise to riches. He was never one to give his admiration quickly or easily, but at Abilene High School he came to admire one of his teachers, a young woman who had graduated from the University of Michigan.[1] And as his junior year drew to a close, he began thinking of what he would do once he had his diploma, and she started him thinking about going to the University of Michigan. Its appeal was no doubt amplified by the fact that this was the era of the legendary coach "Pop" Warner, who turned Michigan into a football powerhouse. Ed had hopes of making the team. But what would he study? For someone as argumentative and egotistical as Ed, the choice seems obvious from this distance: he was going to become a lawyer.

When he informed his parents, David was appalled. A college education was a good thing; he regretted he hadn't finished college, and Ida, too, regretted not seeing the course at Lane through to the end. But lawyers, David was certain, were chiselers. That, he told his wife and sons, was what he had learned from the aftermath of the failed business venture in Hope, when a crooked lawyer moved in and picked the bones clean. "Listen, Edgar, if you'll change your mind and go to the University of Kansas and take medicine, I'll help you through. If you go to Michigan to study law, you'll go on your own."[2]

It did no good. Edgar's mind was made up. And while he was deciding to go to college, so was Ike. It is open to question whether Ike would have set his sights any higher than AHS had Edgar skipped college. The rivalry between them was so intense, however, that once Edgar started talking about getting a college education, Ike became interested in the same thing. Where would he go? Kansas. What would he study? Hadn't a clue. The main thing was keeping up with Ed. It is one thing for a brother to get ahead, something else for him to get out of sight.

If they were going to college, though, they had to finance it themselves. Ike had an idea. "We both want to go," he told Edgar. "But you know what you want to do, and I don't. Besides, you're the oldest, so you ought to go first." He would work for a year, send as much money as he could to Ed, then Ed would work for a year while Ike hit the books and so on, until, after eight years, the Eisenhower family would boast two college graduates. So while Edgar set about being a big man on campus in sylvan Ann Arbor, Ike was toiling at the Belle Springs

Creamery in Abilene and going to the Western Union office to send money by wire.[3]

Becoming a regular worker for modest wages seems to have brought an identification with people who were destined to spend their entire lives like this, or maybe that was already there. Either way, in November 1909, a few weeks after he turned nineteen, Ike addressed a gathering of local Democrats at Workman Hall in Abilene. His speech was titled "The Student in Politics," but it was mainly an attack on the Republican party. He characterized it as an organization devoted to securing the privileges of the well-off. Democrats, on the other hand, were devoted to the welfare of the ordinary working people, and any student who thought carefully about what he was doing would vote Democrat every time.[4]

Ike had worked at the creamery before, during summer vacations. He had also worked on a local farm, and for a few weeks he had worked for a local manufacturer of grain bins. Handling sheets of galvanized metal under the Kansas sun in August was an open invitation to sunstroke and burns. He only did it once.[5]

When he went to work full-time at the creamery, he pulled three-hundred-pound blocks of ice out of a tank, using a chain and pulley, and put them onto a chute that guided them down into the ice room. It was heavy work that did wonders for developing his chest, shoulders and arms. He did not put on any weight to speak of, but from the waist up he began to assume a wedge shape. When he wasn't pulling ice, he made butter, clop-clopping across the treacherous butter-room floor in wooden-soled shoes that he had to pay for out of his wages. During the course of Ed's nine months at Michigan, Ike was able to send him two hundred dollars and David, relenting, sent some money, too.[6]

In June 1910, at the point where Ike should have been making his own plans to start college in the fall, an acquaintance from Garfield grade school came back to Abilene, a big blond fellow by the name of Everett "Swede" Hazlett. The son of a doctor, Hazlett had left Abilene some years earlier to enroll at a private military school in Wisconsin. He had done well enough there to secure a congressional appointment to the naval academy, but that was only the first hurdle to overcome. An appointment to either West Point or Annapolis—and whether it was offered by a congressman or the President himself—did not guarantee admission. It merely gave a young man the chance to take the academy's entrance exam, and Swede had failed the math section. He came home to Abilene to work on his math before tackling the entrance exam again.

Swede began hanging around the creamery, because in Ike there was someone of his own age and intelligence. Ike told him he was thinking of going to KU but still didn't know what he wanted to study. There was also the problem of finding a way to pay for four years of college. "Look, Ike," said Swede, in a sudden burst of enthusiasm. "Why don't you come with me?"[7]

That was it—go to Annapolis, become a naval officer, get a free college education and a ready-made career. Old ideas, half-forgotten images—grainy pictures of soldiers boarding ships in Tampa Bay, on their way to fight in Cuba, the stories he had read about Hannibal and Napoleon and Washington—had planted the seeds of unsuspected ambitions for a soldier's life.[8]

There was a problem, though—that speech at Workman Hall. It had pleased Joe Howe, who was chairman of the Kansas Democratic central committee. But the only military academy appointment available was in the gift of Senator Joseph Bristow—a Republican! He went to Joe Howe and asked what he should do and Howe told him in so many words to swallow his pride and make his peace with the local Republican notables, starting with the one who counted most in Abilene—Charles Moreau Harger, editor of the *Abilene Daily Reflector.*[9]

Harger was a Harvard graduate, a Theodore Roosevelt stalwart, a man who wrote articles for *The Atlantic Monthly,* irritatingly sure of himself, a bit of a snob, a big intellectual fish in an exiguous pond. He overreached himself when he ran for Congress. The ordinary folk got a chance to bring him down a peg, and couldn't resist. Had it not been for the people of Abilene voting for his opponent, Harger would have won the election.[10]

He was a fundamentally decent man, though, above seeking revenge on a youngster who, in the ignorance of his tender years, had failed to see the merits of Republicanism. Harger said he would support Ike's application, but it probably wouldn't do much good, seeing as how he had supported Bristow's opponent in the Republican senatorial primary. He and the senator were not on good terms. The person to see was the town postmaster, Philip Heath, who was a friend of Bristow's.

When Ike showed up and told Heath he was hoping to secure an appointment to Annapolis, the postmaster was encouraging, but there was one thing that he wondered about: Kansas was a long way from salt water. "Aren't you afraid of getting seasick?"

Ike grinned. "I guess I can stand it if I do."[11]

On August 10, 1910, he wrote Bristow. "I would very much like to enter either the school at Annapolis, or the one at West Point. . . . I have graduated from high school and will be nineteen years of age in the fall." This simply was not true. Dwight Eisenhower would be twenty in October 1910. Even though Ida never baked a birthday cake—it was against her religion—he surely knew how old he was. Yet he was claiming to be younger than he was, inverting the time-honored practice of young men trying to get into the military by exaggerating their years.[12]

He probably knew from talking to Swede that there were age limits for entrants to both academies, and he might be too old to get into Annapolis. He could still get into West Point, though, because it had a different age limit. It may have seemed to him like a mistake to waste time on getting the age issue clarified when the urgent need was to take and pass the senator's exam.

If he passed, he could wrestle with the eligibility question later. Anyway, whatever the limit, there might be exemptions or exceptions. And if he did not pass, the whole business would be academic anyway. This, or something like it, may have been the reason he misstated his true age. Nor was he likely to be caught out. There was no birth certificate to trip him up. The only documentary proof of his age was Ida's entry in the family Bible.

While he waited to hear from Bristow, he launched his campaign to win the appointment. He enrolled at Abilene High School again for further study. One happy spin-off from this was that he got to play football again. The team was so desperate for players that the lone male teacher was sometimes drafted into service, along with the coach. Not that this infusion of maturity made much difference. The team compiled a three-and-three record during Ike's "postgraduate" year, against mediocre opposition.[13]

Swede wasn't the only person he knew who was trying to get into Annapolis. Ike's friend John H. Long had applied a year earlier but failed an exam that would have secured him a congressional appointment. Long had done well in school, yet fell at the first obstacle. He told Ike plainly, "Don't take Bristow's exam until you're well prepared."[14]

Although neither David nor Ida was happy about their son's sudden enthusiasm for a military career, David did his part by getting his son onto the night shift. There was a lot less work to do at night. Ike's duties consisted mainly of looking after the three boilers, which took about ten minutes out of each hour. That gave him fifty minutes an hour for studying.[15]

Swede was, meanwhile, cramming hard, and each afternoon he and Ike got together and tested one another or jointly worked out solutions to difficult math problems. So this was the structure of his day: Ike went to the high school each morning, studied with Swede in the afternoon and read for most of the night. He tore himself away now and then to go fishing or play football, and to his immense delight, he found a friendly stray terrier, a little dog that could do so many tricks Ike concluded he must have run away from, or been abandoned by, a circus. Amused by its tricks, admiring its eagerness to win his affection by brazenly showing off, he gave it a name redolent of daring. He called his dog Flip.[16]

Weeks went by and there was still no reply from Bristow, even though Eisenhower had followed up his inquiry with an impressive letter writing campaign. Twenty of Dickinson County's leading citizens wrote the senator urging Ike's appointment to Annapolis.

In later life, he convinced himself that he had received this backing because of his father's sterling reputation, which came about not because he had accomplished anything but because he paid his bills promptly. But in a place like Abilene, that was probably what at least 95 percent of the population did at the turn of the century. Being a deadbeat was not the norm, or even commonplace. Even today people are not praised for meeting their obligations to local stores and tradesmen. The fact that Ike unconsciously distorted something so matter-of-fact to make his father appear a crucial player only underlined a painful truth: David Eisenhower probably counted for little when it came to winning support for Ike's application.

In mid-September, the *Abilene Reflector* announced that Senator Joseph Bristow would hold a competitive examination in Topeka on October 4 and 5 for aspirants to West Point and Annapolis. Eisenhower wrote to him immediately, reminding the senator that he had sent a letter some weeks earlier. "Now, if you find it impossible to give me an appointment outright to one of those places, would I have the right to enter this competitive examination?" The senator wrote back and told him he was welcome to do exactly that.[17]

This was the exam that Eisenhower had studied so hard for and it took two days to complete it. When the results were announced, they inverted all his expectations. He had scored poorly in two of his best subjects—history and geometry—only to do well in algebra, which bored him. He had been saved from disaster by scoring a 99 in English, the subject in which he excelled throughout his life. Overall, he had placed second.

As a rule, that would only get him on the senator's list as an alternate to the young man—George Pulsifer, Jr.—who placed first. Ike, however, was second by less than one point. He was also older, and maybe a little more mature, than Pulsifer, and might therefore be better able to stand the competitive grind at West Point. And, of course, there were those twenty supportive letters from prominent citizens.[18]

There was something else working in his favor, too. Normally, Ike and the third-highest scorer would be named as alternates while Pulsifer received the principal appointment. But Bristow could in good conscience give the principal appointment to Ike because Pulsifer stood an excellent chance of securing a presidential appointment (which, in fact, came through shortly afterward) while for Ike this would almost certainly be his only chance.

Bristow wrote offering him the principal appointment, but asked just how old he was and how long he had been a resident of Kansas. The dreaded eligibility question had just reared its unwelcome head. Ike promptly replied, on October 25, "I am just nineteen years old and eleven days of age, and have been a resident of Abilene, Kansas, for eighteen years." Yet the truth was otherwise—on October 14 Ike had reached his twentieth birthday.

He was probably disappointed not to receive an appointment to Annapolis but thrilled all the same to get one to West Point. And having misrepresented his age in his first letter to the senator, he was in no hurry to set matters straight. After all, he was well within the age limit for West Point, which took candidates up to the age of twenty-two.[19]

There was still a major hurdle to clear: the West Point entrance exam, which had a failure rate of 25 percent. Ike only had to think of Swede to know this test was no mere formality. It was because Swede had failed the Annapolis equivalent that he had been working so hard to improve his math.

For the next ten weeks, Ike continued his punishing schedule of reading and revising. Then, in January 1911, he took the train to St. Louis and reported to Jefferson Barracks. St. Louis seemed so big, so bustling, so alive, it stunned his senses and created a rush of excitement and wonder and something like helplessness, which he had never experienced in small, predictable Abilene. He remembered in old age the sensation as the city, embracing the ocherous moving highway of the mile-wide Mississippi, carelessly placed its machine-tool and big-money grip on a fresh-faced youngster's burgeoning awareness of the wider world and made him blink in astonishment.[20]

He and another young hopeful decided to see the sights one night, got lost when fog swirled up from the river, blanketing downtown, and did not get back to the barracks until one in the morning. As they hadn't been authorized to leave, reporting at the gate seemed unwise. They scaled the wall and sneaked back to their bunks undetected.

Ike passed the physical exam easily; he was healthy but as lean as a post—five feet eleven, all of 150 pounds. There was no news of how he had done on the written exam for seven or eight agonizing weeks after he returned to Abilene. Then, at the beginning of spring, he received a letter from the secretary of war ordering him to report to West Point.

It was close to midnight on a warm night in early June and his mother, Milton and Flip were waiting on the side porch when he came downstairs carrying a small cheap suitcase. "You take care of yourself, Dwight, and be a good boy," said Ida, looking up at him.

"Sure, Mother, I will."

Then something extraordinary happened, something that surprised and embarrassed them both: tears began sliding in silvery rivulets into the cobweb of fine creases that reached from her bright eyes to her rounded, high-boned cheeks. Ike had never seen his mother cry, not even at the worst times, such as the day a knife had fallen into two-year-old Earl's right eye out in the barn and Ike, screaming, had picked him up and run into the kitchen carrying his little brother, the blinding wound shocking and fresh. Nor had there been tears when Arthur left home or when Edgar departed for Ann Arbor. But here was his mother, this figure of indomitable sureness and strength, weeping almost as if she had gone into mourning.

Ike extended an arm and placed it around her shoulders. He hugged her awkwardly, diffidently, for this wasn't a hugging age, a hugging place or a hugging family. "I'll be back before you know it, Mother. And I'll write you often while I'm gone."

He tried to calm things down by telling his twelve-year-old brother, man to man, "Milton, I'm counting on you to look after Mother," but Milton let him down by bursting into tears. "Aw, for goodness' sake!"

Ike picked up his bag, told Flip, "Stay home!" went out to the street, looked back one last time and called, "Good-bye." With a loping, youthful stride, he faded into the darkness, heading for the creamery three blocks away.[21]

There was someone else tending the boilers at night now, his friend Les Asper. Ike sat and chatted with Les, waiting for the early morning train to Kansas City to pull into the depot. A little before three, its whistle blew as it rumbled across the still and dusty streets of the little town. Time to go.[22]

5

The Cadet

He walked into a dream colored gray and cut from granite, like an assertion of timelessness less friable than the marble of the Parthenon and turning a more obdurate face to eternity than the striated sandstone gaze of the Sphinx. It was a place where fabulous beings—"Stonewall" Jackson and Winfield Scott, Ulysses S. Grant and Robert E. Lee, "Yellow Hair" Custer, grizzled "Cump" Sherman and little Phil Sheridan—shared those same dreams.

Some of the men whose character had been shaped here were even greater than their legends; some of the legends were greater than their men. Whichever they were, they could at times be a discomfiting presence, for too much awareness of giants can oppress.

As he reported in on June 14, 1911, he signed his name in the adjutant's register as Dwight D. Eisenhower, reversing what was in the family Bible. Shortly afterward, he changed into a tight gray jacket and white duck pants and packed his cheap, ill-fitting civilian coat, slacks and cloth cap into his one suitcase, and as he did so a question was insinuating itself into his life: How long would it take for him to make this dream in stone truly his own? Not all do so. Some reject it and walk away to lives of a different kind; others simply find its demands impossible and are dismissed.

Many more arrive at West Point already entranced, submitting to the romance long before their eager feet tread the forty-acre grass parade ground, the Plain, or glimpse the magnificent "million-dollar view" from Trophy Point for the first time. This, though, is the ardor of youth. Nearly twenty-one, Ike was more mature, more cautious in his temperament. He was also a practical-minded young man, someone who delighted in using his large, powerful hands and accustomed to finding whatever excitement he needed in the immediate and tangible world. He wasn't given to living inside his own head or to tormenting himself, as his father did, with metaphysics. Yet this gray, granitic ideal—of duty, sacrifice and an eternal brotherhood—was a writ-large version of happiness as he had learned it at home. So Ike's submission would come.

In the closing months of his life, when he was dying at Walter Reed Army Hospital, connected to drips and monitors, weak and skeletal, his old friend General Mark "Wayne" Clark went to see him often. Clark was surprised to discover, sitting next to the bed that Ike would never rise from, that "all he wanted to talk about was West Point. Not about being President, not about being Supreme Commander, not about D-Day, none of that. West Point was all, ever."[1]

What it meant to him had been signaled, too, in the way he structured his memoirs, published shortly before he died. The first chapter is about West Point, an indirect way of saying that *here* was where his life really began—not in Abilene but at the Academy. He leaves Abilene till later; it becomes a flashback to the ritual and drama of the Point, a spell that began to work its magic that first day as a cadet.

From the moment they reported in, Ike and 246 other plebes were ordered to collect their uniforms, collect their bedding, collect various pieces of equipment and do it double-time, Mister! Struggling under mountains of uniforms and bedding, they rushed in and out of doors like people fleeing a fire, took the stairs two at a time, hurried along narrow corridors and across echoing courtyards, screamed at by yearlings (i.e., sophomores) every step of the way. They were ridiculed and insulted and harassed, and whatever they were doing, they were doing it wrong.[2]

That was how the first day of "Beast Barracks" had always been, and it was nothing compared to the days that followed. Ike couldn't take it completely seriously, anyway. He was older, after all, and more worldly-wise than most of the self-important yearlings who were doing all this strutting and bellowing. And then, at five P.M., the frenzy suddenly stopped.

The plebes assembled on one side of the Plain. The Corps of Cadets, looking magnificent as only confident youth on the threshold of full manhood can look, stepped onto the grass and paraded under glossy black ostrich feathers and fluttering flags, as the West Point band pumped out thrilling patriotic and martial tunes.

Still awestruck to the point of reverie, the new arrivals were ordered to raise their right hands and repeat, as American soldiers had done since the Civil War, "I do solemnly swear that I will support the Constitution of the United States of America and bear true allegiance to the national government . . ."

A strange sensation came over Dwight Eisenhower as, for the first time, he gave his undying loyalty, publicly and firmly, to "the United States of America." Whatever he had been expecting to happen this first day, he could never have anticipated that overpowering feeling of devotion to something far bigger than himself, something greater even than those giants whose ghostly shadows blended imperceptibly with the gray granite that was already reaching out to embrace him.[3]

The three weeks of Beast Barracks were an introduction to the Point designed to weed out the unready and the uncommitted. Hazing had long been a public embarrassment to the faculty and the superintendent, not because they saw much wrong with it but because there were always congressmen who were keen to criticize the military and some threatened to cut the Academy's money if something wasn't done about the tormenting of plebes. The West Point staff, particularly the tactical officers, who were responsible for cadet discipline, nevertheless tacitly encouraged it, making complete abolition impossible.

The worst forms of hazing—making plebes perform dangerous stunts or forcing them to fight one another until someone was knocked out—had nonetheless been eradicated. What remained was almost childish, such as making plebes assume contorted postures while eating or forcing them to stretch out on a narrow beam six feet above the ground and pretend they were "swimming to Newburgh." Some cadets took it all too seriously, as Ike's roommate, Henry Dykes, did. They had been paired simply because room assignments were made alphabetically, and the last of the D's, Dykes, came just before the first of the E's, Eisenhower.

Dykes was seventeen years old, an earnest youngster from a small town in Kansas. The Army was considered a dead end for most young men, but getting into West Point was a chance to join a national elite. When Dykes left for the Academy, the town band serenaded him to the train station—something that happened to other Academy entrants in small towns across the country. The burden of his hometown's expectations only added to Dykes's fears about not surviving Beast. He huddled on his Army cot at the end of each exhausting, frazzled day weeping in frustration. Ike told him to look to the future—"It won't always be like this." Dykes, to his credit, stuck it out, but five plebes quit before the three weeks of Beast ended and the survivors moved into summer camp with the rest of the Corps of Cadets. In the meantime, other plebes arrived, mainly "turnbacks"—cadets, that is, who had been required to repeat the plebe year. Altogether, the Class of 1915 began with 276 members, making it the Point's biggest class up to that time.

When the regular academic year began in September, the Corps broke summer camp and everyone moved into barracks. Ike was assigned to F Company, which probably thrilled him, because the average height in this outfit was six feet. Having many of the biggest men, F Company boasted a higher proportion of athletes than any of the other five companies. Ike and another Kansan in F Company, Paul A. Hodgson, became roommates. Hodgson was unusually bright and had already completed a year of college.

The West Point curriculum, which was based squarely on math and related subjects, such as physics, held no terrors for either Ike or his roommate. They gave little thought to the classroom; what interested them far more was the football field. Both went out for the plebe football team, which played as "Cullum Hall." It played other college freshman teams and even high school squads.

Cullum Hall had a good season, and Hodgson showed so much ability that he made the varsity team before it ended. While Ike was glad for his friend, his own prospects seemed paltry in comparison. He stood no chance of making the varsity unless he did something about his weight. At 152 pounds, he was too light for varsity football, especially when it came to playing defense. Ike's most important project his plebe year turned out to be a pursuit of greater avoirdupois.

He tucked in with a will, eating voraciously, exercising vigorously, adding muscle to his chest, his thighs and his arms. He got his weight up to 174 pounds without losing any of his quickness. In the meantime, the harassment of plebes by upperclassmen continued and he had to put up with it as everyone else did, until the day when he and a classmate, Layson Enslow Atkins, were caught in a minor infraction of the Academy's mind-bogglingly strict rules for appearance, demeanor and housekeeping by a cadet corporal, Elmer E. Adler. He ordered them to report to his room in their full dress coats. Adler evidently had some hazing in mind.

Ike and Atkins walked into his room shortly afterward, in their full dress coats . . . and nothing else. As the coat was a cutaway, each forward step brought full exposure. Adler, stunned, let out a bellow of rage. The two miscreants were ordered to report back after taps, in complete uniform and carrying their rifles. They spent much of that evening pressed against a wall in Adler's room. The granite, when they were finally released, was black with the sweaty imprint of their bodies. It was worth it, though: Ike was never hazed again after that.[4]

As the spring of 1912 drew near, he tried out for baseball. The West Point coach thought highly of his fielding but deplored his batting style. At Abilene High School he had learned to be a chop hitter, picking a spot where he wanted the ball to go before he swung the bat. The coach at West Point had no time for that kind of fancy-dan stuff. What he wanted was belters, young men who would hit the ball as hard as they could as far as they could. "Practice hitting my way for a year," he told a bitterly disappointed Ike, "and you'll be on my squad next spring."[5]

When June came around, he was promoted to cadet corporal and became a yearling, authorized, even expected, to torment Beast Barracks plebes as he had been tormented. It was a diversion that he indulged in only once.

An inattentive, hurrying plebe ran into him, literally, and fell over. "Mr. Dumgard," Ike bellowed. "What was your PCS?" (or, "previous condition of servitude," meaning, What did you do in civilian life?). To rub it in, Ike grasped for something that would seem belittling—some menial, even ridiculous, trade. "You look like a barber!"

The plebe picked himself up, his embarrassment written in scarlet across his youthful face. "I *was* a barber, sir."

Ike walked away ashamed. He had pulled ice in a creamery at nights and made grain bins from galvanized metal in the midday sun. The plebe was like him, a working stiff who had gotten here the hard way. Back in his room, he told Hodgson, "I'm never going to crawl another plebe as long as I live. I've just done something that was stupid and unforgivable." Half a century later, it still bothered him that he hadn't apologized.[6]

At the end of summer camp that year, he played in a practice game of cadets against serving soldiers and, with his increased weight, made an impression on the head football coach, Captain Ernest Graves. Ike started the season as a varsity player, but spent the entire first game warming the bench. In the next five games, however, he got a chance to show what he could do, carrying the ball on offense, playing linebacker on defense. The press began to take notice. *The New York Times* called him "one of the most promising backs in Eastern football."[7]

Opposing players noticed him, too. During one game, a player on the opposing side said to the referee, "Watch that man," indicating he meant Eisenhower.

"Why?" replied the ref. "Has he slugged you or roughed you up in any way?"

"No, but he's going to!"[8]

On November 16, a week before the grand climacteric—Army v. Navy—West Point was playing Tufts, and Ike plunged effectively into the opposing line time and again until, late in the second half, he twisted his right knee severely. He spent the next five days in the Academy dispensary before being allowed to limp back to his room.

Although he wouldn't be able to play in the Navy game, he did not ask to be excused from reporting to the riding hall with his fellow cadets for mounted gymnastics, which involved repeated mounting and dismounting, something likely to aggravate the damage to his right knee. Graves could have had him excused, but lacked the sense to do it. Anyone who has ridden knows that controlling a horse calls for using the knees and Eisenhower simply lost control of his. It shied up, throwing him onto the tanbark, and he landed on his right leg.[9]

He spent the next four days in agony as Army doctors worked to get the leg straight again. They allowed him out long enough to watch the Army-Navy game, on crutches, before returning to the dispensary. It was December 29 before he was finally discharged, still limping heavily. He became a familiar face at the dispensary in the months that followed. His sole consolation was the award of his football letter in March 1913.[10]

Ike's busted knee not only put an end to his dreams of football glory; it also ruled out any chance of his making the baseball team. This was a bitter blow. Failing to play baseball at the Point and for the Point ranked as one of the great setbacks in his life; it bothered Eisenhower even after he became President.[11]

In June 1913 Ike and his classmates got a ten-week break, their first chance to go home in two years. He arrived back in Abilene to be feted and admired, especially when he walked through town in his form-fitting West Point uniform. He looked terrific and he knew it. His old friends, like Six McDonnell, were thrilled to see him.[12]

Part of the unfinished business of Ike's life was to be big enough and strong enough one day to whip his brother Edgar, to end a losing series with a spectacular win that erased a score of humiliations. He had hoped the extra muscle he'd added at West Point would do that for him, but Edgar wasn't at home that summer.

When he ran into Wes Merrifield, though, he couldn't resist asking him if he remembered their epic battle in the eighth grade. "Do I!" said Merrifield.

Ike admitted that while he'd called it a draw at the time, Wes had had the best of it. "You really licked me," he said. "But what I want to know is whether you have any ambitions now."

Merrifield surveyed the muscular form and held up his hands. "Ike, I'm the most unambitious man in town."[13]

He did get one fight, though. There was a black porter working at a local barber shop by the name of Dirk Tyler, and Tyler had gained a reputation as a bully. Unless someone took him down a peg, said Ike's friends, Dirk was going to end up in serious trouble one day. And when Ike went to get his hair cut, Dirk said bluntly he was ready— "Anywhere, anytime." After that, Ike had to fight him.

They met in a nearby basement, stripped to the waist, pulled on some boxing gloves and agreed to slug it out in two-minute rounds, under the watchful eye of a referee. Dirk was big and Dirk was strong, but Dirk was a barroom brawler who rushed at his opponent, arms flailing. Easy meat for a strong young man with a cool head. Ike parried, planted his feet and took advantage of the huge exposed expanse of brown chest in front of him and delivered the second most effective punch the sweet science knows, the hammer blow to the heart. When it works, it's nearly as good as the hammer blow on the point of the chin. When it's done well, it causes what feels like arrhythmia—the onset of a heart attack. Dirk Tyler folded up like a punctured balloon. He collapsed at Ike's feet, completely winded, unable to rise.

"Honestly," said Ike later, whenever this fight was brought up, "I've never been particularly proud of that scrap." And he'd grin.[14]

Physically strong and blessed with a fighter's heart, Eisenhower was nevertheless a sensitive young man. Late at night, when the rest of the family was asleep, he'd tiptoe out of the house, then walk for miles in the Flint Hills, musing to himself about the fundamental questions of human existence while looking at the stars. He'd arrive back in Abilene at dawn as the town came to life once again.[15]

This leave also saw the first stirring of romantic love, when Ike finally got to date the prettiest girl in town, Gladys Harding. He had never been serious about a girl before and he wasn't entirely comfortable when it came to dealing with women, ever. He saw himself as a man's man, a figure of strong actions and few words. What's more, Ida was a hard act to follow.

Between graduation from high school and his departure for West Point, Ike had dated a girl called Myrtle Hoffman, but when she made it clear she was still playing the field, Ike promptly lost interest. There was also Ruby Norman, whom he saw as a friend rather than a romantic interest. With Ruby it was more a case of palling around than dating.

Gladys was different. Although she lived south of the tracks, her father was a well-to-do livestock dealer. The Hardings were socially and economically on a more elevated plane than the Eisenhowers. Given her looks and her social standing, Gladys was Abilene's golden girl. She had talent, too, as a pianist, and was aiming at a theatrical career.[16]

So Ike returned to the Academy if not in love certainly infatuated. But Gladys rarely wrote. The one who kept in touch was Ruby Norman, who was studying piano in Chicago. Ike had spent a couple of days looking around the city with her in 1911, on his way to West Point. It was Ruby, not Gladys, who bore the burden of his loneliness and heartache, both of which became acute during the 1913 football season, when other cadets with better luck and stronger knees performed the gridiron heroics that meant so much to him.

Writing to her in November, he told Ruby she had to root for Army "if you don't want your head pounded off." He gave her the scores of the eight games Army had played so far that season. The tone of his letter is one of bleak, unrelieved loneliness. Ike was discovering something about himself, and it was painful: he needed a girl to write to him, to notice him, to care. Ida's mother love was no longer enough.[17]

Two weeks later he wrote again, telling her he had written Gladys some time before but still hadn't received a reply. Even so, "That girl is just <u>crazy</u> about me." He urges Ruby to go home for Christmas instead of coming to New York, as she was thinking of doing. "If you'd spend your vacation in N.Y., we don't know <u>what might</u> happen."[18]

Only two days later, he wrote again: "Seems I'm never cheerful any more," blaming his depression on his wrecked knee. And only two days after this, he wrote yet again—"Everything has gone wrong . . ." Then, on November 30, after Army beat Navy, his spirits soared and he wrote to tell her, "Some game! Some game! . . . I feel my reason toppling."[19]

The itch was still there, but it was beginning to mature into something more than holding his own against Ed or trying to impress Abilene or an expression of youthful high spirits. Far from home and old friends, Ike yearned as much as ever to be daring and different. Like all who break away from the ready-made certainties of a safe, conventional existence, he needed answers to some basic questions: Who was he? What was he? What he wasn't, any longer, was an athlete. Saturdays wouldn't be the glory days after all.

Sometimes he thought about quitting. Just walk away. Go to Argentina, maybe, and become a gaucho. Or how about the stage? Gladys was fascinated by it. So was Ruby. He might even have a talent for it. When he and Ed and the rest of '09 put on the school play just before graduation, they had taken *Othello* and turned it into a farcical parody of Shakespeare that set Abilene rocking with laughter. His part was, naturally, a lot smaller than Ed's. His brother got the star role, but people had praised Ike's performance as "Launcelot Gobbo, servant to the Duke."

It was a lot to walk away from, though—a college education that was better than free: the government paid the cadets. At the end of four years Ike would graduate with hundreds of dollars in savings, savings that he was steadily augmenting with his poker winnings. He'd stick it out.[20]

The logical thing to do, he saw years later, would have been to hit the books. That never occurred to him during his grieving days of disappointment as he rubbed his aching knee. Being more studious would have broadened and deepened his education, a good thing in itself. But he had wasted too much time chasing leather mirages for two years to improve his class standing significantly. He was never going to be among the top 3 percent who would be offered commissions in the Corps of Engineers. Besides, he had no desire for a career in engineering.

He could not hope, either, to make the tranche below the engineers, the part of the class with grades good enough to get commissions in the field artillery. Whatever he did now, he was almost certain to slot into the 85 percent of his class that would be commissioned in the lowly and indispensable infantry—"The infantry, the infantry," it chanted along country roads, "with mud behind the ears. The infantry, the infantry that drinks up all the beers. The cavalry, artillery and goddamned engineers—they couldn't beat the infantry in a hundred million years!"

When, at the end of 1913, Ike looked to the future he saw only an invitation to hang on and plod through the next eighteen months and he was sure to graduate somewhere around the middle of his class—the Point's equivalent of the gentleman's C.

That didn't allow for the itch, however—to be daring, to test his limitations and the boundaries of the world around him, to prove in some way that he was bigger than the dull curriculum, the tedious routines, the uninspiring faculty. Cadet regulations treated men like himself— old enough to vote and get married and sign legally binding contracts— as if they were incorrigibly shallow and dim.

As Ida's son, able to cook, sew, do laundry and iron it, Ike had been a chore-meister since childhood, unlike most of his classmates. He could probably have set the West Point all-time record for housekeeping. Instead, virtually from the day he arrived he had neglected his dusting and polishing, made an untidy bed, left his gloves negligently on the mantelpiece and accumulated an above-average number of demerits for infractions of petty rules.

After his busted knee ended his ball-carrying, line-plunging fall afternoons as one of the most promising backs in eastern football, he still ate among the athletes. He was an assistant coach now for Cullum Hall and cheerleader for the varsity team. Beat Navy!

He also found another way to get involved in sports—he was selected for the honor guard and carried the national colors. The honor guard paraded at every game. Long after he left West Point, it still gave him a thrill to recall the enormous patriotic pride he'd felt when he carried Old Glory.

Ike had been spared having to eat the regulation fare from the day he was picked to play for Cullum Hall in his plebe year. As an athlete he ate at the training table, where gray jocks shoveled up the carbohydrates at an altar where muscle was worshipped. Better food, more of it, sloppily and eagerly consumed; a man's way with table manners. Despite the gustatory riches of the training table and the sense of privilege a good steak leaves as an aftertaste, Eisenhower nonetheless organized the most daring boodle caper the Point had ever seen.

Illicit foodstuffs were bought in nearby Highland Falls, brought by boat to a cove at the foot of a bluff within the Academy grounds and surreptitiously hand-carried to a latrine at the top. The smugglers got themselves and the boodle in and out of the latrine by carefully unscrewing the wire-mesh screen that covered the window facing the river. Ike devised and directed the operation while other cadets handled the boat, the latrine and the boodle; risky activities but comparatively simple. What Ike provided was the most important element—the leadership.

West Point was hog-tied by a nineteenth-century conception of its mission to provide the Army with men capable of leading other men in peace and war. It was a conception that relied so much on unquestioned authority backed up by draconian punishments that leadership was no more than an aspect of command.

Ike represented something else, even at this early stage in his career. Within his character were the germs of a new approach, the modern one, which makes command but one aspect of leadership. It was an approach that could be traced back to Ulysses S. Grant, and the more he learned about the Army, Ike became one of Grant's greatest admirers.

Eisenhower would prove to be a pioneer of the modern military style, but for now he could develop his leadership skills only by mounting sub-rosa challenges to the West Point system, something that most of his classmates avoided. Long afterward, when he heard that one of them had just been promoted to a star, Ike was disgusted. "How did *he* ever make general? He never broke a regulation in his life!"[21]

The need to dare, to be different, expressed itself not only in sloppy housekeeping and boodle smuggling but in the way he danced at the rare hops organized to help cadets develop their social skills. Dancing was strictly regulated, like everything else. Ike showed what he thought of that at his first hop by turning his partner so quickly that her skirt rose higher than her ankles. He was reprimanded for "improper dancing." At the next hop he did it again, and was reprimanded again.

West Point allowed cadets to smoke now and then, provided they stuck to the smoking materials of the well bred—cigars and pipes. Cigarettes, the dreadful weed puffed on by laborers and farmhands, were forbidden. Defying the rules yet again, Ike began smoking cigarettes and didn't stop for more than forty years.

During their last year at the Point, Ike's roommate, P. A. Hodgson, was dating an attractive eighteen-year-old called Dorothy Mills. When P.A. was confined to their room by illness in March 1915, Eisenhower made a play for Dorothy, trying to sweep her off her feet with impassioned letters and ardent requests for dates. She told him he was going too fast, and would he please stop calling her "Dearest Girl" in his overheated correspondence? He replied defiantly: "I don't intend to be ruled by convention in writing letters to you." It did no good. Dorothy wasn't interested in starting a romance, and nothing would change her mind.[22]

As graduation day drew near, the question of what to do about Eisenhower and his ruined knee rattled around in the upper reaches of the War Department, but he knew nothing of that. An Army medical board decided his knee was so bad he was unfit for active service, which ruled out a commission.

The board chairman, Colonel Henry Shaw, disagreed, and Shaw was the post surgeon at West Point. He knew and liked Cadet Eisenhower, who was, Shaw insisted, "a good gamble." Back at the Academy, the colonel solicited recommendations in support of Ike from instructors and tactical officers. Armed with these, he persuaded the War Department to overrule the board.[23]

So Ike would receive his commission, and Shaw urged him to apply for service with the coast artillery, the easiest duty there was. Ike refused to consider it—"routine chores and a minimum of excitement," he said later. When he completed the form that asked for his preferred branch of service, he wrote "Infantry" as his first, second and third choices.[24]

When he saw Ike's list, Shaw may well have sighed at its youthful foolishness and bravado, the outright rejection of common sense, and wondered why he had taken so much trouble over this cadet. The infantry sleeps in the mud, marches till it drops and carries heavy loads on its back.

On June 11, 1914, the secretary of war, Lindley Garrison, handed Second Lieutenant Dwight D. Eisenhower his commission in the infantry in front of a sea of upturned faces, pink and glowing with the love of parental pride, but it was the pride of other people's parents, and he was merely walking through quickly, a stranger at someone else's feast. Neither David nor Ida was there, nor any of his brothers, nor Ruby nor Gladys. As his classmates and their families embraced all around him, wiping away tears of joy and relief and exultation, he started his journey into the world that he had to conquer, the world of the Army, alone.

Miss Mamie

It was a three-day journey from New York back to Abilene, plenty of time to gaze out from the railroad car rocking him westward and think about his life. First came perspectives on the dark green, densely timbered slopes of the Alleghenies, up, then down. Beyond stretched the rich, uninteresting farmland of the Midwest, with neat little towns every few miles. Then, on the other side of the Mississippi, with dramatic suddenness, he entered a different atmosphere—thinner air, a landscape gashed by the dried beds of long-vanished rivers, a geology of shale and limestone covered with the eternally agitated, hardy grasses of the empty, echoing prairie. Home.

The topography of his youth seemed so open it was like a public invitation to walk in, but stretching to distant horizons under those yawning skies it was a reminder, too, of the loneliness of life in the West, a reminder that could only have stirred the inchoate compulsions of his young man's heart. After he'd tried and failed to turn his flirtation with "Dearest Girl" Dorothy Mills into a romance, Ike had rebounded by writing a jokey ad for the West Point yearbook, *The Howitzer:* "Wanted—a wife. Modest young man of gentle disposition and refined (?) nature desires to try matrimony with any coy damsel willing to take the chance. Retiring but affectionate. Prefer girl with money. Eisenhower."

Cracking jokes about love is often youth's wary way with life's most important subject, but there was no escaping its demands. Anyway, there was hope. Gladys, with her golden beauty, respected family and musical talent, the Gladys whom he had been so ready to disavow interest in if that was the price of winning the affections of Dorothy Mills, Gladys, too, would be home for the summer. Hardly had he greeted his parents and brothers and unpacked his suitcase before Ike laid siege to the Harding home. Gladys's father, one of Abilene's more prosperous citizens, grew irritated. He couldn't go into the parlor, it seemed, without finding the Eisenhower boy there, either waiting to collect Gladys or bringing Gladys home or simply sitting there making eyes at his daughter. He hoped Gladys wasn't falling for a soldier, because the Army was not a suitable place for his vivacious and artistic child.

Ike virtually monopolized her time during the day and in the evenings took her to the movies or band concerts in the city park or borrowed an automobile and took her on long drives through the Flint Hills. Sometimes, to impress her, he dressed in his fanciest uniform, a dazzling white outfit with shiny gold buttons and pants with creases so sharp you could almost cut bread with them.

For the first month or so after he came back, Ike tried to pretend he and Gladys were simply good friends and he and Gladys and redheaded Ruby Norman sometimes made a threesome, old pals laughing and joking together. But when July gave way to August, he was fast running out of time. The concert season, when Gladys would go on tour with her "pianologs"—whimsical little monologues interspersed with piano pieces—would resume in the fall and Gladys was scheduled to head east September 1. Ike abruptly quit pretending his interest was nothing more than an old friendship. On August 5 he came out with it: he was in love with her, he told Gladys, and wanted to marry her.[1]

He was never any good at expressing his feelings to a woman; he remained tongue-tied and foot-shufflingly self-conscious where overt expressions of love were concerned throughout his life. Ike had a high color, especially when he was young. It is easy to imagine him turning vermilion as, driven by a force he did not understand and may even have been annoyed to find taking over his life, he felt compelled to act. Nothing he had learned at the Point was of much use here. At a guess, he may well have barked out his declaration of love as if it were a football play.

Or did he make it sound like a confession? He may even have tried to pass it off as a kind of joke. However he did it, chances are he kept what he had to say as brief as possible.[2]

Gladys had never encouraged him in his hopes of love and marriage. She didn't do so now. After twelve days had passed without a response to his proposal, he wrote her a long, impassioned letter. "More than ever now, I want to hear you say *the* three words. . . . For girl I do love you. . . . Sept 1st seems so fearfully close. . . . I love you as a man does the one woman, whom in his most cherished dreams, he hopes some day to call his wife." It made no difference. Gladys departed as planned.

He convinced himself it was only a temporary separation. "I know that you love me—me! And oh girl! That knowledge is the great and wondrous influence that will help me through this coming year and bring me to you again—to claim you forever . . ." Shortly after this, he left Abilene to join his regiment, the 19th Infantry, in Galveston. On arrival there, he found the regiment had moved to Fort Sam Houston, the Army's biggest post, straddling the city boundary of San Antonio, Texas.

At about the time he reported in, Gladys wrote to tell him her career came first. She was letting Ike down the best way she could, shading the brutal truth. Her career was not the unyielding element in her existence that she made it out to be, for it wasn't long after this that she returned to Abilene to marry a widower, a local businessman named Cecil Brooks, and soon gave up touring her pianologs through small-town America. Gladys hadn't accepted Ike's proposal of marriage for the best reason in the world—she did not love him.

He reacted to rejection like many another young man, with a show of bravado. When Ike moved into the junior officers' quarters on the infantry post at Fort Sam, he informed two new acquaintances, Leonard "Gee" Gerow and Wade Haislip, shavetails like himself, that he had no—meaning nugatory in the extreme—interest in women. He had sworn off the species for good.

On Sunday October 3, three weeks after reporting in at Fort Sam, Ike was Officer of the Day. And he looked it—a beautiful young man, calf-length boots and golden bars glinting in the Texas sunshine, the rakishly tilted campaign cap on his large blond head insouciantly telling the world to get the hell out of his way. It was late afternoon when he walked out of his quarters, strapping on a large belt heavy with the deadly weight of the Army's latest sidearm, a big, black Colt .45.[3]

Gee was across the street, on the lawn of the house occupied by a major named Harris, chatting with the major's wife, Lulu, and on this pleasant fall afternoon there were deck chairs clustered on the grass, most of them occupied by civilians dressed in their Sunday best and sipping grape juice.[4]

"Hey, Ike! Come over here!" Gee had just been talking about Ike, who was, as Gerow described him, a very handsome fellow who happened to hate women. This, of course, only intrigued the females present, including eighteen-year-old Mamie Doud of Denver. Ike strolled onto the lawn with the characteristic long-legged stride of the West Point cadet.

Mamie was impressed. "He's a bruiser," she thought, looking up at him. In the demotic of a later day, "What a hunk!"

After introductions, chitchat and grape juice, Ike said he really had to leave. He had probably noticed the impression he had made on Mamie Doud, who was wearing a high-waisted floral print skirt and a large black hat. She had, he thought, "a saucy look." Nothing to lose. "I've got to inspect the guard," said Ike. "Would you like to walk post with me, Miss Mamie?"

She replied that she would have to say no—she had a date that evening. Another young man was coming to pick her up at eight o'clock. Ike assured her she would be back in good time. So they set off on what was a three-mile hike through the infantry post. Nothing to him, of course, but to her, trying to keep up in a pair of tightly laced, snugly fitting, brand-new and fashionable beige high boots, it soon became a test of how well Miss Mamie could pretend her feet weren't killing her. She had been raised, though, to appear endlessly charming and pleasant, especially toward men. Having agreed to a stroll, she would not turn back.

Passing one of the barracks, Ike noticed soldiers inside, changing out of uniform and into something more casual for Sunday night. "Don't look up," he said. "The boys aren't too careful about pulling down the shades." Mamie's china blue eyes instantly raked the row of windows. Ike roared with laughter. "If that isn't just like a woman!"[5]

Mamie hobbled back onto the Harrises' lawn in time to go home and change for her date. The next day, Ike launched the siege of the

Doud family's San Antonio home. Mamie had recently made her debut into society. Eligible young men from San Antonio and its environs were expected to meet her and date her, and they did. She had dates for weeks ahead. Ike was dismayed to find she had so many prior engagements, but while he waited for her to work her way through them, he astutely paid court to her family, especially to Mamie's mother, Elivera, and her two lively sisters, Buster and Mike.

Nor did he neglect her father, John Sheldon Doud. The two of them spent many evening hours on the wide veranda discussing the Civil War. Although he had never served in the military, Doud had read widely on the struggle for the Union and considered himself something of an expert.[6]

Mamie's father interested Ike, possibly because he was in nearly every respect the antithesis of David Eisenhower. Doud possessed genuine intellectual attainments, having earned a degree in math at the University of Chicago in an era when only 1 percent of the population graduated from college. He was also a success in business. His father, Royal Doud, had made and lost a fortune. John Sheldon Doud had repaired the family's finances by making a fortune in the meat-packing business in Iowa. He was rich enough to retire before he reached forty, secure in the knowledge that he would be able to provide handsomely for himself and his family for the rest of his life.

His wife, the charming Elivera, was the daughter of Swedish immigrants. She was both good-looking and motherly. Mamie, however, did not have her mother's looks. She bore a much stronger resemblance to her Swedish grandmother, with a fine complexion, beautiful eyes and the high, rounded cheekbones typical of Northern European peasantry.

Mamie had been born in Boone, Iowa, but the harsh Iowa winters and scorching summers proved too hard on Elivera, who was known to her daughters as Nana. John Doud moved his family to Colorado, thinking the climate there would be kinder to her. Rocky Mountain winters soon disabused him of that idea, so he bought a second house, in San Antonio, and there the Douds lived from September until spring each year.

Elivera bore four children, all daughters, one of whom died in 1912. As offspring of the haute bourgeoisie of a provincial, essentially working class town, the Doud girls led lives that were as physically comfortable as they were intellectually narrow. The Denver house, at 750

Lafayette Street, was a large and ugly structure, maintained by four servants and crammed with heavy, dark furniture and an abundance of ghastly knick-knackery that was easy to collide with in its poorly lighted, airless rooms. For all its creature comforts, this four-story dwelling was something of a cliché in gray brick, a reaffirmation that new money left to its own devices has only an accidental connection with good taste.[7]

It was the children and their mother who infused the house with liveliness and warmth. When John Sheldon Doud—affectionately called Pupah—descended for breakfast, Elivera and the girls were already waiting for him, immaculately coiffed and well dressed. Theirs was the kind of life depicted and damned as early as 1879, in Henrik Ibsen's masterpiece *A Doll's House.* But the clarion call to a feminist future, the famous slamming of the front door as Ibsen's questioning heroine, Nora, shuns its certainties, its comforts and its repression, never reached either 750 Lafayette Street in Denver or the Doud's *résidence secondaire* on McCullough Street in San Antonio.

Ike hung around the San Antonio home whenever he wasn't on duty. He was there to make his presence only too obvious when Mamie's dates arrived. He was still there when they brought her home. Meantime, Ike was not falling in love so much with Mamie as with her entire family. The warmth the Doud women generated was irresistible. When one of the girls went into town, her sisters kissed her good-bye, then rushed to the window to wave to her as she went down the steps. This was a world removed from family life as he had known it in Abilene.[8]

In his loneliness and need for love, Ike probably wanted to be a part of this life beyond anything he would ever be able to put into words, even to himself, yet Mamie seemed reluctant to date him. Maybe it was an understandable dread of being dragooned into another exhausting hike. Eventually, Pupah had to intervene. "Stop this flighty nonsense," he told Mamie sternly, "or the Army boy will give up in disgust."[9]

Ike courted her over one-dollar dinners in local Mexican restaurants and took her to the movies. At Christmas, he blew his poker winnings on an expensive heart-shaped silver jewelry box. Mamie's parents pointedly reminded her that this side of an engagement, a young man was not allowed to give a young woman anything but flowers or candy. But Ike seems to have foreseen that—he'd had the box engraved with Mamie's initials. It was, in effect, unreturnable to the jewelry store and, short of her parents demanding that their daughter terminate her relationship with "the Army boy," it was equally unreturnable to him. Anyway, Mamie informed them, "we're practically engaged."[10]

Ike was not aware of that yet. Early in the New Year, he wrote to Ruby: "The girl I run around with is named Miss Doud, from Denver. Pretty nice—but awful strong for society—but we get along well together—and I'm at her house whenever I'm off duty—whether it's morning, noon or night."[11]

Sometime shortly thereafter, he and Mamie started talking about marriage without his making a formal proposal. He had tried that with Gladys, only to be crushed. Ike seems to have secured some kind of commitment from Mamie without having to declare his hand first. On Valentine's Day, February 14, they agreed to become engaged and informed Mamie's parents. Elivera seemed willing to accept Ike as a prospective son-in-law, but Mamie's father had his doubts. Mamie was so young, too innocent for Army life, but when he saw how determined she was to go through with it, John Doud accepted the inevitable.

Shortly afterward, Ike applied for a transfer to the aviation section of the Signal Corps. As an aviator, his salary would increase by 50 percent, but his chances of dying young would rise even more. Pupah was shocked. He could not allow his daughter to marry anyone so crazy as to become a pilot, he said, and Mamie agreed with him. She gave Ike an ultimatum: "Choose—flying or me." When Ike's transfer came through, he turned it down. He was sticking with marriage and Mamie.[12]

John Doud had given his blessing on the understanding that there would be no wedding before November, when Mamie reached her twentieth birthday. Ike had no intention of waiting that long and the zeitgeist was a hurricane blowing in his favor. War and threats of war screamed daily from newspaper headlines.

Only weeks after Ike and Mamie got engaged, Pancho Villa raided Columbus, New Mexico, killing eight soldiers and nine civilians. A punitive expedition was mounted, under Brigadier General John J. Pershing. While Pershing chased Villa, with little chance of catching him, Second Lieutenant Eisenhower was applying, just as vainly, for assignment to the pursuit. Meanwhile, the United States looked increasingly likely to be drawn into World War I, despite Woodrow Wilson's efforts to stay out. While publicly trumpeting the necessity of neutrality, Wilson expected neutrality to fail and the Army, with no encouragement from him, was preparing plans for a wartime draft because it had reached the same conclusion.

The War Department, meanwhile, issued a directive that leaves and furloughs were not to be granted except in cases of emergency. Undeterred, Ike applied for a twenty-day leave. Getting married *was* an emergency as far as he was concerned. While his application wound its way through the Army bureaucracy, the Douds returned to Denver.

The colonel commanding Ike's regiment could have approved his application but chose not to. Nor did he have the honesty to reject it and provoke muttering among the junior officers. He did what weak officers always do: he passed the paperwork upward, in this case all the way to the commander of the Western Department, Major General Frederick Funston. The colonel probably expected the general's staff would kill it.

Eisenhower was in luck, though. "Fighting Fred" was the most unusual officer in the Army. He had begun his military career as a civilian volunteer, fighting with Cuban guerrillas against the Spanish army in Cuba before the Spanish-American War. After the war came, he was awarded a commission and went on to win the Medal of Honor during the Philippine Insurgency, when he captured the most important of the Filipino leaders, Emilio Aguinaldo. Funston had a fundamentally romantic nature, so when Ike appealed to Funston for love to have its way despite the imminence of war—and despite the War Department's directive—Fighting Fred replied, "You may have ten days."[13]

Ike then told Mamie that the military situation was so uncertain the only thing to do was to get married at once. Her parents were shocked. What about the rest of the family and the neighbors—they'd think she *had* to get married! Mamie brushed that aside. Let them think whatever they wanted. "Ike is on his way."[14]

At the stroke of noon on July 1, 1916, Ike married Mamie in her parents' house, dressed in his fancy white tropical uniform and the shiny silver bars of a brand-new first lieutenant. "Repeat after me," said a visiting English Episcopalian minister named William Williamson, and Ike and Mamie duly repeated the words of the traditional Anglican marriage service, with its practical emphasis on sex ("With my body, I thee worship") and its idealistic emphasis on love ("Till death us do part").[15]

After a two-day honeymoon at Eldorado Springs, a resort just outside of Denver—a honeymoon marred by the sudden and unwelcome appearance of Mamie's parents—they set off for Kansas. They spent two days in Manhattan, visiting Ike's brother Milton, who was a student at Kansas State. Then they headed for Abilene. Their train arrived at four A.M. Ida cooked a fried-chicken breakfast to welcome her daughter-in-law, and at eleven A.M. Ike and Mamie boarded another train, heading this time for Texas.[16]

Short of moving into a cave, it was as brutal an introduction to home-making as a young bride from a sheltered background was likely to get. Mamie knew there were no married quarters for lowly lieutenants, but this place was simply horrible. There were only two small rooms, with grubby walls, chipped woodwork, peeling paint, a tiny bathroom and exactly one closet, which was already filled with Ike's uniforms. Even a seasoned Army wife would have been downcast trying to make a home out of the shabby Fort Sam officer's billet that Ike had occupied on his own. Marriage meant two fully grown people had to live in something that was hardly big enough for one. Like Ida, Mamie created a refuge from her home within it. She rented a piano for five dollars a month, an extravagance that was also a necessity, and escaped into music.

Having forced the pace and gotten his own way, Ike may have begun to wonder just what it was that had made marriage seem so urgent. His new bride couldn't cook or clean. About all she could make was mayonnaise and fudge. They would have to eat out most of the time, something they really couldn't afford. John Doud had told him plainly that Mamie was not going to get an allowance: they would have to live on Ike's salary, which currently amounted to $151 a month. On the other hand, Pupah had given Mamie a large check before they left Denver, allowing her to buy not only some furniture for the already cramped apartment but also a secondhand automobile for Ike to drive.

A month or so after he returned to Fort Sam with Mamie, Ike came home one day and started packing uniforms and equipment. The 19th Infantry was going to march to Camp Wilson, a new post established near Austin, more than two hundred miles away. He would be gone about two weeks. "You're not going to leave me here so soon after our wedding day?" protested Mamie.

"There's one thing you must understand," said Ike. "My country comes first and always will. You come second."[17]

In the spring of 1917, dozens of officers from the 19th Infantry were transferred to Camp Wilson, where they were to form the nucleus of a new regiment, the 57th Infantry. Eisenhower was dismayed to find his name on the list of officers being transferred. Like most infantrymen, he loved his first regiment above all others and leaving it was a wrench. Ike set off for Camp Wilson on April 1. The next day, Woodrow Wilson asked Congress to declare war on Germany.

Shortly after this, Ike was promoted to captain. Like one of his heroes, Ulysses S. Grant, he was appointed regimental supply officer. One afternoon, as he stood under some trees during a thunderstorm and gave a lecture on supply in the field, Ike was so absorbed in what he had to say that he didn't notice he was brushing up against a long piece of telephone wire that had been strung between the branches. A bolt of lightning sizzled overhead and, seeking the most direct way to earth, coursed along the wire. Fire seemed to explode inside his brain, then the world went black. A minute or so later, Ike regained consciousness. He was wet from lying in the mud, and the white, alarmed faces of other officers looming over him swam into view. His head felt as if it had been split with an ax.[18]

The War Department was under intense pressure to ship American troops to France and as the half-trained 57th prepared to go overseas Ike, naturally, expected to go with it. He had proven too good an instructor, however. He possessed a talent for teaching, and when the regiment moved out, he was ordered to Camp Oglethorpe, Georgia, to instruct officer candidates, mockingly known in the Old Army as "ninety-day wonders."

While he was teaching bayonet drill and other rudiments of the military arts to prospective lieutenants, Mamie returned to Denver, to have their first child, in September 1917, in the comforting and familiar surroundings of the house on Lafayette Street. The baby, a boy, was baptised Doud Dwight. At first, Mamie called him Little Ike, then she called him Ikey for a time, before settling finally on Ikky. He was a blond, blue-eyed, pink and miniature version of his father. Pupah was so thrilled to have a grandson that he relented and gave Mamie an allowance of a hundred dollars a month.[19]

Ike had applied to the War Department several times for overseas duty, without success, but he probably half expected that he would get his wish once his Georgia assignment came to a close. Instead, he received orders to head for Fort Leavenworth, Kansas, and train yet another batch of ninety-day wonders. The only good part about it was the chance to stop off in San Antonio to see Mamie and put his arms around his infant son. He probably felt overjoyed, like most new fathers, but we will never know for sure. Ike was silent on that first encounter with Ikky.

Shortly after reporting in at Fort Leavenworth, he was summoned to see the post commandant, Colonel Harvey Miller. The Adjutant General had written a letter, Miller told him, in which the War Department formally expressed its disapproval of Lieutenant Eisenhower's repeated requests for overseas service. Miller proceeded to add a rebuke of his own. Eisenhower's face turned scarlet.

"Sir," he said, forcing himself to keep his temper in check. "This offense—if it *is* an offense—was committed before I came under your jurisdiction. If there is punishment to be given out, I think it should be given by the War Department and not by yourself, with all due respect."

To his astonishment, Miller said, "I think you're right. And I respect you for standing up for your convictions."[20]

That winter, he received yet another training assignment, this time at Camp Meade, Maryland, where the 65th Engineer Regiment was about to start training men for service in tanks. The officer in charge of tank training, Lieutenant Colonel Ira Welborn, was a Medal of Honor winner from the Spanish-American War and had seen him training officer candidates in Georgia. He specifically requested Eisenhower's services.[21]

For all Ike's frustration at not going to France, the fact was that training was the Army's most urgent need and assignment to tanks was an accolade, for this was the newest weapon of war. His task at Camp Meade was to help get the 301st Tank Battalion ready to deploy overseas. It was desperately short of both training and equipment. The men were eager to learn—every one of them had volunteered for tanks. And in March 1918 he was told that all his soldier dreams were about to come true: when the 301st Tank Battalion deployed to France for combat on the western front, he would command it.

Hardly had his spirits been sent into the stratosphere, though, than they were brought crashing down. Eisenhower, Welborn decided, was just too good at training men to be spared. While the 301st packed to go overseas, Ike was sent to command Camp Colt, Pennsylvania, a small post on the edge of the battlefield at Gettysburg. The War Department created the Tank Corps, and Camp Colt was where future tankers would be trained. It meant another promotion. Ike became a major in June 1918. He was now senior to nearly everyone in the Class of 1915, including those who had graduated at the top of his class.

He and Mamie moved into a deserted fraternity house on the campus of Gettysburg College. Shortly after they arrived, there was a tremendous spring snowstorm. Ike worried constantly about his trainees, freezing under canvas. He bought up every portable stove he could find in Gettysburg. Apart from that, there was little he could do except pray for better weather.[22]

For months after he arrived at Camp Colt he didn't have a single tank, just thousands of young men who expected "the old man" to have all the answers. He improvised brilliantly. When the Army failed to provide him with tank guns for training, he managed to wangle some three-pounders out of the Navy. To improve battlefield communications in the Tank Corps, he established his own telegraphers' school. He scrounged vehicles and created his own driving school, believing that a man who could drive a truck skillfully over difficult terrain would soon learn how to drive a tank well. He trained men to become tank machine-gunners by bolting machine guns to flatbed trucks, and had them practice firing at targets on Little Round Top while the trucks jolted over the rough ground below. By August 1918 he had ten thousand men under his command, keeping them busy, well disciplined and enthusiastic.

Eisenhower succeeded, too, by refusing to be satisfied with his own efforts. There was always something that could be done better. When one lieutenant began marveling at how smoothly the camp was running, Ike told him abruptly, "Get out and find something wrong with this camp! It's not *that* good."[23]

Camp Colt's proximity to the Gettysburg battlefield was inspiring. When the bitter cold of winter yielded to scorching summer weather, he and Mamie drove around the battlefield some evenings in a battered Dodge that the Army provided, just trying to cool off. And there were times when he visited the cemetery alone, to sit and pensively reread the Gettysburg Address.[24]

On June 6 Ike finally received his first tank, a small French Renault, which made the training more realistic. He taught himself how to operate it, in order to train other officers, who in turn would train the men. Two British Army officers visited for a few weeks and tried to inject some realism into the proceedings, based on their experience of tank combat on the western front, but Ike would have had few illusions about how much even the best stateside training could achieve. For his trainees, as for most soldiers who served with the American Expeditionary Forces (AEF), their real instruction would come in France, and much of it would prove to be on-the-job training at the hands of the Germans.[25]

And gnawing at him, daily if not hourly, was an unshakable sense that in time of war there was really only one place for a twenty-seven-year-old infantry officer with a West Point education to be, and it wasn't in Pennsylvania.

Ike longed for battle as youth yearns to grow up, to earn its own money, make its own decisions, live its own life. Welborn had assured him that he would recommend him for overseas service if Ike succeeded in training these neophyte tankers. When the moment came, however, Welborn recommended him not for France but for promotion. In October 1918, on his twenty-eighth birthday, Eisenhower became one of the youngest lieutenant colonels in the Army.

A week or so later, he returned home one evening carrying an order from the War Department in his hand. "I've made it!" he announced. "My orders for France have come!"

"It's grand, Ike," Mamie replied loyally. "I'm truly happy. When do you go?"

He handed her the War Department order, which read, "You will proceed to Camp Dix, New Jersey, for embarkation on November 18, 1918."[26]

Welborn tried to talk him out of it. If he applied to stay on at Camp Colt, said Welborn, he would put him in for a colonelcy. Ike told him bluntly he wasn't interested in rank. "I'm ready to take a reduction in rank," he said, if that was what it took to go to France.[27]

This was nonetheless a sad and stressful time. The Spanish influenza pandemic that circled the world and killed more people than the war was taking a heavy toll in stateside training camps. By acting quickly to isolate men who came down with any hint of colds or flu, Eisenhower managed to keep the illness from decimating his command. Even so, nearly two hundred men died from Spanish influenza at Camp Colt in the space of a couple of months.[28]

Meanwhile, Mamie's sister Buster fell seriously ill with nephritis and went blind. On November 9 her suffering ended. Ike was nearly as devastated as Mamie, who set off for Denver the next day, taking Ikky with her.[29]

Over the following days there came rumors, then stories, that the Germans were seeking an armistice. Late on November 10, the news came through: the war would end at eleven A.M. on the morning of November 11—five A.M. in Gettysburg. When Ike went to his office that morning, the guns had already fallen silent. Ike and one of his West Point classmates, Captain Norman Randolph, talked desultorily about what the future might hold. "I suppose we'll spend the rest of our lives explaining why we didn't get into this war," Ike said bitterly. It seemed all wrong somehow. He had been cheated out of the chance to prove himself. As his spirits sank, they collided with something deep and hard—the bedrock of pride—and ricocheted back up. "By God!" he expostulated, not so much to Randolph as to the whole small world that is the Army, the world that had denied him his chance. "From now on I'm cutting myself a swath that will make up for this!"[30]

★★★★★

7

Ikky

The happy sounds of Camp Colt—of crackling bonfires, of trumpets and drums, of exultant choruses that warned Kaiser Bill "the tanks are coming"—would all quickly fade, leaving only black circles of dead ashes on the ground and, for those like Ike who had a sense of history, a haunting echo that mingled with the long-lost Rebel yells and Union "hurrahs" among the encircling trees of the Peach Orchard, the Devil's Den, Cemetery Ridge. Singing was almost as much a part of soldier life as saluting and he loved belting out "It's a long way to Tipperary" and "Hail! Hail! The gang's all here!" despite being tone-deaf. His contribution to music was volume.

Shortly after taking command at Camp Colt, Ike had encouraged some men from Company C, 303rd Tank Battalion who wanted to compile a songbook—*Tank Tunes: Songs for Camp and March*. He may have heard about officers over in France who scornfully claimed that the only part of soldiering that units fresh off the boat from training camps in the United States had mastered was community singing, but what of it? Voices together mean people together. That was his real contribution to the war: he had turned thousands of civilians into soldiers, eager not as individuals but as a team to face battle and its inevitable dangers and sorrows as brothers might. What had Camp Colt given him in return? A cruel taste of the joys of troop command—cruel because he had learned to love it so yet it would be many long years before this kind of happiness came his way again.[1]

With the Armistice, the camp came to a jolting halt, almost as if a bullet had been put in it. No more parades. No more singing around huge campfires. While fall rains washed away the dead ashes, men were demobilized or dispersed. The gang wasn't here anymore, and Tipperary was farther away than ever. There were no permanent barracks at Colt, and to keep the men in tents through the winter would kill many of them. Three weeks after the Armistice, Ike closed down Colt and departed for Camp Dix, New Jersey, with the six thousand men still under his command. Once there, 95 percent of them were discharged from the Army.

Ike took those who wanted to remain in uniform, roughly 250 men, down to Fort Benning, Georgia. He also took three Renault tanks for the Infantry School. At Benning, the Infantry School would try to figure out how to integrate armor into future infantry operations.

In March 1919, Ike found himself back at Camp Meade, commanding a tank battalion. He had come full circle, he reflected ruefully—"Meade to Meade within one year." Nor was there any chance of Mamie and Ikky joining him anytime soon. Only quarters for bachelor officers were available at Meade. There was nothing for a family.[2]

At times, he grew so discouraged that he thought about quitting, and a businessman from Indiana who had served under him at Colt offered him a well-paid job. Ike's uncertain mood was much like that of the country as a whole. America itself seemed to be plunging into a long, dark tunnel; no way out, no hope yet of seeing the slanting shaft of light that reveals the distance to the end and no turning around. That's how it is when a major war ends and people have to return to what they think of as normal life, even though they know without saying it that this is really going to be a new normality. The old one died in the war.

Naturally, there were a few certainties—the nation would go dry, women would get the vote, two million doughboys would come back from France different from when they left and women would surrender their jobs to provide work for the men. And for Ike, there was something he could bet on more confidently than on any poker hand he'd ever held. He, like nearly every officer in the Regular Army, was going to lose his present rank. The only question was how far down he would go. Ike was a temporary lieutenant colonel; his permanent rank was captain. He might have to be a captain again.

That almost surely galled him, knowing that he could handle a general's command. His responsibilities at Colt had been those of a brigadier, as Welborn noted in one of Ike's efficiency reports.[3] In terms both of duties discharged and rank achieved, he had surpassed all his classmates. Three years out of West Point and he had proven he could manage troops like a general officer. The ultimate military skill is leadership, and he had a talent for it. No doubt about that. Welborn had even recommended him for the Distinguished Service Medal, the highest decoration any officer who did not go overseas could receive.

The DSM usually went to generals, sometimes went to colonels, but almost never went to lieutenant colonels. He couldn't resist sending his father a copy of Welborn's recommendation. "There is no chance of getting one of the medals," he assured him, "but it shows Colonel Welborn's opinion of me." So while the immediate future wasn't promising, things might still work out.[4]

There may have been times when he considered himself lucky that he could still have a military career. When the professor-President had said this was "the war to end wars," millions had believed it. And now the War Department was thrashing around looking for a way to convince those same people that they still needed an Army, by showing them that the Army wasn't a creature of the past but a modern-minded organization that was looking to America's future. A young officer, Captain Bernard McMahon, dreamed up a clever publicity stunt—send an Army truck convoy from coast to coast. The point wasn't that a cross-country road journey was easy but that it was damn difficult. While there were adequate roads up and down the eastern seaboard, across the Mississippi, the highways changed from tarmac to sand.

Not surprisingly, industrialists such as Harvey Firestone, the tire baron, and companies such as Portland Cement Company thought this was a terrific idea and supported it. So did the Lincoln Highway Association, which had been lobbying for better highways for years. And the Army was a natural choice. The West had been opened up not by hardy pioneers in wagon trains but by Army surveying parties and Army engineers building military roads. The pioneers followed where the Army had already gone.[5]

The War Department organized a transcontinental truck convoy and decided that as it involved a test of mobility, two officers from the Tank Corps could go along as observers. Ike immediately applied for one of these assignments and nominated his assistant, Major Sereno Brett, a highly decorated veteran of the western front, for the other.

The convoy was a heterogeneous America on wheels. There were all kinds of trucks, staff cars and vans, including two motorized kitchens, more than a dozen motorcycles, an ambulance, some engineer vehicles, a water truck, a gasoline truck, a wrecker, a caterpillar tractor, a pair of rolling machine shops and a small Renault "Whippet" tank lashed to a flatbed trailer. All told, there were seventy-two vehicles and roughly 280 officers and enlisted men. On July 7, this motley assortment was parked around the Zero Milestone, a pink granite object that stands almost unnoticed only yards from the fence at the bottom of the South Lawn of the White House. President Wilson strolled down with his pint-sized secretary of defense, the very able Newton D. Baker, and Army Chief of Staff Peyton C. March, to wish the convoy Godspeed and good luck.

By the time permission came through for them to take part, Ike and Brett had missed the ceremonial send-off. They joined the convoy two days later, when it reached Frederick, Maryland, en route to Gettysburg, where it parked across the battlefield. Like most ad hoc formations, made up of people who did not know one another and would disperse once the present mission ended, the truck convoy was not particularly efficient and discipline was poor. Ike was appalled. "The Expedition Train Commander"—Lieutenant Colonel C. W. McClure—"should pay more attention to disciplinary drills for officers and men, and all should be intelligent, snappy soldiers before giving them the responsibility of operating trucks," he pointedly remarked at journey's end.[6] For now, though, he had to put up with it.

As it made its way slowly across the U.S., the truck convoy followed a course that prefigured what later became Interstate 80, aiming for San Francisco Bay. In Ohio, Harvey Firestone welcomed the convoy crew to his huge and luxurious estate, Harbel Manor, and treated his visitors to a lavish picnic. From Indiana, Ike sent Mamie a postcard. One side showed a picture of part of the convoy. On the other, he scribbled in his cramped, hard-to-read hand, "Dearest, I am not in this picture—but I thought you'd like to see it. Love you heaps and heaps. Your lover."[7]

When the "truck train," as Ike called it, reached Boone, Iowa, Mamie's aunt and uncle were there to give him a personal welcome to the town where Mamie was born. Best of all, however, when the convoy pulled into North Platte, Nebraska, the midpoint of the journey and only two hundred miles from Denver, there was Mamie, with Ikky, Pupah and Nana. She had come to see him, Mamie said, to tell him she was going to live with him at Camp Meade "if I have to live in a tent." She expected Ike to try talking her out of it, but he didn't. She could come, he told her, but it was no place for an infant. Ikky would have to stay with his grandparents until they had adequate quarters. Mamie and her folks tagged along with the convoy for the next four days, until it reached Laramie, Wyoming, where they peeled off and drove back to Denver.[8]

The convoy was feted royally when it reached Salt Lake City. It seemed that half of Mormonism had turned out to greet it. The officers and men were treated to dinner and a dance when they reached Stockton, California, and when the convoy rolled to a halt at its final destination, Oakland, the city welcomed them with a civic banquet. They were two days behind schedule, but that was shrugged off as the result of weather that had made the roads impassible in some places.[9]

An estimated 3.25 million people had watched and waved as the truck train rolled past on its two-month hegira. It had covered thirty-two hundred miles, at an average speed of six miles an hour. Ike told stories about this adventure for years afterward, especially about the pranks he and Sereno Brett had played on the rest of the crew. "Difficult, tiring and fun," was how he summarized it in his memoirs, but it had also been a revelation for him. He had seen a different America: the world's richest country slowed down by some of the world's worst roads.[10]

He wasn't happy about having a football thrust into his hands again, but what could he do? An order was an order and Ike wasn't about to have a fight with his new boss, Colonel Samuel D. Rockenbach. Pershing's AEF headquarters in France had included a "tank office," and Rockenbach, a cavalryman like Black Jack Pershing himself, ran it. Rockenbach had sat in a big office at Chaumont and managed the organization and logistics, while Colonel George S. Patton led the tank units in the field. Patton soon learned to loathe Rockenbach—"The most contrary old cuss I ever worked with." He was too limited, too slow to grasp new ideas.[11]

When Rockenbach returned from overseas, he displaced Welborn, who was junior in rank, and proceeded to make his weight felt at

Meade, which was still the home of the Tank Corps. One of the first people to feel it was Eisenhower, who was bluntly told by Rocky that he was going to coach the Meade team.[12]

Being a football coach did nothing for an ambitious officer's career and was always likely to prompt a damaging question: Why would a truly able field grade officer waste his time on sport when all his energies ought to be spent on preparing to fight the wars of the future? Even so, Eisenhower knew better than to risk any head-to-head clash with a superior as emotionally volatile as Rocky. He took charge of the team, telling himself it would help keep his leadership skills sharp.

He needn't have worried about that, though—he still had the gift. Eisenhower was demanding yet remained scrupulously fair, instinctively friendly and good-natured. One reason he was a remarkably successful leader was that young though he was, he took a genuine interest in other people and their problems. His approach to troop leadership brought out both the natural teacher and someone who didn't run his unit by the book. He relied instead on his intelligence and his imagination. There was, for example, the case of two men in his battalion who simply loathed one another. Eisenhower assigned them to clean all the windows in a barracks, one man working on the inside, the other on the outside, and they were to clean each window together. They hadn't gone far before they started sneering and pulling faces at one another, to express their disdain, then one of them laughed, and so did the other, and by the time the last window was cleaned, mutual antipathy had dissolved in the solvent of mutual laughter.[13]

Meanwhile, he was looking for a place where he and Mamie might create a home, and eventually found an apartment in Laurel, Maryland. It was too small and crude, though, to raise a baby. Mamie arrived alone but hopeful, only to be seized by despair. The apartment was a dingy one-room walk-up and she had it virtually to herself. Ike was almost never there. He left early each morning, came home long after dark each night. She was still, in effect, living apart from him rather than with him, only now she was also separated from her little boy. After a month Mamie told him bluntly, "I can't live this way, Ike." She was returning to Denver.[14]

A few weeks later, the Army went ahead and reduced nearly every officer below the rank of general. For Ike, dropping down to a major's rank meant that his salary was lowered from $290 a month to $220. On the other hand, things weren't as desperate as he and Mamie liked to believe. They still received $100 a month from Pupah, which gave them a household income not far short of a colonel's.[15]

At the same time it was reducing Ike in rank, the Army made some run-down barracks at Camp Meade available as married quarters. That was all it took to bring Mamie back. The quarters they were assigned were primitive, but Ike spent eight hundred dollars—which probably exhausted their savings—fixing the place up. They slept on surplus Army cots. For the rest, Mamie did what she could. When Ike came home one day, he found a battered octagonal table and dismal-looking rattan chaise occupying the living room.

"Oh my God. Mamie, you're not going to keep that?" he said, incredulous.

"Yes," replied Mamie emphatically. "I like it. I got it off the dump heap." He would learn to live with Mamie's *trouvées* just as he'd had to learn to live with being a football coach again. Anyway, they felt they could now send for Ikky. Not only was there enough room for a child, but they could afford to hire a servant girl who would do most of the housework and help Mamie look after their son.[16]

Shortly after this, Woodrow Wilson and Newton Baker visited Camp Meade and decided they'd like to talk to some Army wives. Ike was with his battalion, getting it ready for the presidential inspection. Mamie heard a knock at the door, and she opened it to find the President standing there with the secretary of war. They chatted amicably for a few minutes, then Baker asked Mamie, "And what does your husband do best?"

"He plays an awfully good game of poker," Mamie answered brightly.

When Ike heard about it that evening, he was not exactly thrilled to learn that Baker had probably returned to the War Department thinking the most outstanding trait about young Major Eisenhower wasn't his way with men or with tanks but knowing how to play a poker hand.[17]

He and Mamie had spent so little time together, they were still getting to know one another, still forging the foundations of an enduring and happy marriage. Ikky, though, was something else. Ike adored Ikky. With Mamie, he didn't know how to express his affections physically except by pinching her now and then, the way a teenage farm boy might act with a girl. With Ikky, it was different. He could hug him and kiss him without feeling self-conscious, get down on all fours, make ridiculous growling noises, roll over on his back, wave his legs in the air and try to make Ikky laugh.

The men of Ike's battalion had a little uniform made for Ikky, complete with an overcoat and an overseas cap, and the blond cherub loved to stand at attention and salute when the colors went by during parades. To his chortling delight, he got taken for rides on the roaring, smoke-shrouded tanks and was fussed over like a little hero. In the innocent yet somehow wise way of small children, he won the affection of the entire camp.

As Christmas 1920 drew near, Ike put up a tree and spread Ikky's carefully wrapped presents beneath it. On December 23 Mamie returned from shopping in Baltimore to find that Ikky was running a temperature. At first, it seemed to be influenza, but on Christmas Day the child was too sick even to open his presents. Ikky had scarlet fever.[18]

He was moved to the post hospital, but there was no hope of saving him. Mamie remained at home, quarantined in case she had contracted this highly infectious illness. It was Ike who bore the burden of the death watch, but this grim ritual was made even more traumatic by the fact that all visitors were barred from the hospital, to prevent them catching the disease. Forced to remain outside, Eisenhower desperately pulled himself up to the window of his son's room countless times, gripping the window ledge to gaze upon his dying child until, strength failing, he fell to the ground. On January 2, 1921, Ikky died.

Time heals all wounds? If only. Some steal too much love from us ever to heal. Those wounds hurt right to the end. People get used to the pain, but it is never more than an inward glance away, still bleeding. Losing Ikky hurt Eisenhower as nothing else ever could. "The greatest disappointment and disaster of my life," he called it. For a time, he thought he'd go crazy. "I was on the ragged edges of a breakdown," he admitted later. And in writing to a friend in 1948, someone whose twin girls had just died, he offered his heartfelt sympathy, recalling "the very great grief that then seemed unsurmountable" after Ikky's death. "I cannot think of it without experiencing it again."[19]

There was no one else like him—not in the Army, not in the country. Lusting for military glory and eternal fame, he was driven by a spirit so huge, so intense, that many who met him were thrilled to stand in its glow and boasted in old age, "I rolled with Patton!" The more perceptive may have sensed, too, that if anything like that fierce spirit ever took root in their suburban souls, it would destroy them.

To his critics, he sometimes appeared almost insane. Over the years he had fallen from many a horse and struck his head on the ground where he fell, but he wasn't mad in any certifiable sense. Instead, he possessed something of the divine lunacy of some great painters and poets; or maybe the truth was, it possessed him. His critics also liked to think he was none too bright, because it had taken him five years to get through West Point, yet Patton was one of the most studious officers of his time and knew his profession as well as any man in the Army. In France, he had been wounded in the backside, been recommended for the Distinguished Service Cross and threatened to resign if he didn't get it. The medal was awarded, but it seems a small thing compared to the reputation Patton had made within the Tank Corps for courage and dash.

When he arrived at Camp Meade on returning from France, he and his wife moved into the house next door to the Eisenhowers and he and Ike became fast friends. Mamie and Bea, however, never gelled, possibly because Bea Patton was one of the Ayers of Boston, who were far richer and grander than the provincial Douds of Denver.[20]

Ike and "Georgie" enjoyed riding horses, pistol shooting and playing poker together twice a week, but the real common bond was a passionate belief in the tank. They looked on these noisy, stinking metallic beasts and came close to falling in love with them as other men fall under the spell of old airplanes or rebuilt Duesenbergs. To them, the tank wasn't so much metal in motion as a messenger from that troubling, mysterious realm, the future. Here I am, announced this messenger in steel diapers, a being freshly created, yet I will shake the world and bring nations to their knees. My tracks are destiny. Where they go, humanity will follow and water them with its tears.

This message was wasted, of course, on men too blind or deaf to see or hear it. But to Eisenhower and Patton, it might as well have been written in ball lightning across the night sky. Once they had been favored by this revelation, it became their mission to defend the tank from its critics, conjure up its terrifying and thrilling possibilities and get the Army to reshape itself around the potency of tank tracks and tank guns.

Like all believers, they sought to penetrate to the heart of the mysterious power before them—and also, because they were regular guys who liked getting grease on their hands, they took a light Renault tank apart, right down to the last nut and bolt. Then they put it back together and got it running again. By the time they'd finished, they knew that Renault as well as the French workers who'd built it.

Patton commanded a battalion of Renaults. The battalion Ike commanded comprised American-made medium tanks powered by airplane engines and when Patton's light tanks got bogged down, something they almost seemed designed to do, they used the mediums to haul them out. One day, as they supervised an experiment to see whether a medium tank could pull two Renaults up a slope using a one-inch steel cable, the cable groaned, then snapped with a gunshot *crack!* A long section of steel cable whipped through the air, passing less than a foot from the two officers' heads before dancing like a wrathful snake across the ground, leveling the shrubbery over a large area. The danger had passed before Ike and Patton had any chance to feel afraid. Seconds later, as it struck them that sudden death had just passed by, they stared at one another, their faces pale from shock, and then the fear hit them, leaving both too shaken to speak.[21]

They continued their experiments, and thought about what tanks might be able to do with better engines, better suspensions, better tracks, bigger guns. Here were two of the most intelligent officers in the Army, each sparking ideas in the other. They studied the problems that were given to students at the Command and General Staff School and took a close look at the approved solutions. They added a few tanks to the mix, and in every instance, the force supported by tanks won the battle.

This was news they couldn't wait to share. Both Ike and Patton wrote articles for the *Infantry Journal*. Patton's called for an independent tank arm, one free from the plodding three-miles-per-hour pace of the infantry. Ike's contribution, published in November 1920, was much more cautious. He modestly entitled his article "A Tank Discussion." First, he spelled out the merits of the tank as an instrument of war, stressing its mobility, its ability to smash through barbed wire and the protection it offered its crew. The tank could not hold ground taken, he conceded, and there were serious problems with reliability, but most of its faults were those of an immature technology. Over time, these problems would be solved and he conjured up a bigger, more powerful tank than anything currently in production.

He did not press for massing tanks into huge formations. Nor did he urge the separation of tanks from the infantry. In later years, various biographers had Ike arguing, heroically and in vain, for tank forces that would smash through enemy lines and plunge deep into the rear, creating havoc and devastation: the blitzkrieg scenario.[22]

There is no such argument in the documentary record from the time, including his article, which merely asserts, "There must always be a large unit of tanks as army troops which can be used at the points most desired," and that's it. There is nothing compared to Patton's call for armor to operate independently. On the contrary, Ike suggests that "in future wars tanks will be a profitable adjunct to the Infantry." And far from arguing that armor had unlimited offensive potential, he challenged what he called the "axiom that tanks are of use only on the offensive" and praised their defensive capabilities, "In making local counterattacks . . ."[23]

The heart of Ike's piece was a proposal to replace the machine-gun battalion of the infantry division with a company of Mark VIII tanks. It didn't look like a lot to ask for. To his amazement, he was summoned to see the chief of infantry and told that his ideas were "not only wrong but dangerous" and that he was to keep them to himself. If he didn't, he would face a court-martial.[24]

He was appalled, and remained appalled long after at what seemed to him an acute case of head-in-the-sandism. During World War II, there would be a tank battalion attached to nearly every infantry division the Army fielded. There would be, in fact, more tanks supporting the infantry than assigned to the armored divisions.

Nevertheless, proposing to dispense with the machine-gun battalion was absurd. There were a lot of things wrong with the "square" infantry division of World War I, an organization that was carried over into the 1920s and 1930s. Each division contained twenty-eight thousand men and was dogged in combat by a lack of mobility and firepower. The machine-gun battalion not only provided supporting fire but was one of the few motorized elements in the division. Ike was right in thinking that a company of tanks would provide heavier support and at least as much mobility, but the difference wasn't going to be remotely enough to justify throwing away the machine-gun battalion.

Had he left the machine-gun battalion alone and added a tank company by subtracting something else, such as some of the engineer troops (on the grounds that much of the demolition and obstacle clearing work they did wouldn't be necessary in a division with an organic company of tanks), his proposal might have been tolerated, even if it wasn't accepted. In the context of Army organization of the time, however, the chief of infantry was right: Eisenhower's proposed abolition of the machine-gun battalion *was* wrong and dangerous. At the time of Pearl Harbor, an American infantry regiment had twice as many machine guns as its World War I equivalent. In modern combat, however, even this wasn't enough. The number doubled again before World War II ended. Infatuated by tanks, Ike had missed the future importance of the machine gun. As a visionary, he still needed glasses.

With his career in tanks crashing around him, Eisenhower applied for a transfer to the Infantry School, which had been established at Fort Benning in the closing days of World War I. However, Rocky refused to endorse his application. Ike had produced winning seasons in 1919 and 1920. Rocky wasn't going to surrender a coach who got results.

This was bad, but far worse was the fact that he was now facing the prospect of a court-martial. In 1920, he had applied for a housing allowance for Ikky, but at the time he made this application, Ikky was still living with his grandparents. All told, Ike had collected $250.67 in housing benefits. Although he had made the application believing he was entitled to the money, the acting Inspector General of the Army, Brigadier General Eli A. Helmick, had conducted an investigation and thought Eisenhower deserved to be punished.

Eisenhower freely admitted that he had made a mistake and offered to repay the amount immediately. Helmick would not be placated and cast doubt on Eisenhower's integrity. It wasn't credible, he insisted, that a West Point graduate with command experience should be as unaware of *Army Regulations* as Eisenhower claimed. In truth, however, Ike was proud of the fact that he had never read the regulations. Even after he rose to five stars, he advised at least one young officer to do the same. He had always relied on common sense, Ike told him, and his own idea of what was right. The inspector general may never have been born who would understand, or approve of, that. Helmick certainly wouldn't, and was pressing for a court-martial.[25]

What saved Ike from probable disgrace and resignation from the Army was a chance encounter. Pershing's AEF headquarters in France contained a fair number of burned-out volcanoes, men who had once been inspiring fountains of energy but now were stale and rigid. Yet it also had its rising stars, men such as Colonel George C. Marshall and Brigadier General Fox Conner, who were the brains behind the AEF's operations. Patton had known Conner before the war, and their friendship had only become deeper in France. One day in the fall of 1920, Ike met Fox Conner over Sunday lunch at the Pattons'. When the meal ended, Eisenhower and Patton showed Conner their camp and their tanks. He took a close interest and quizzed them extensively about the possibilities of the tank in future wars. It was nearly dark when the discussion ended.[26]

Conner was currently serving as Pershing's chief of staff. Black Jack had come back from the war thinking he might run for President, only to fall flat on his face. For the moment, he didn't have anything much to do, but by remaining on active duty he was in line to become Chief of Staff of the Army on July 1, 1921, when Peyton March's tenure ended. Shortly after that, Conner would get an assignment with troops, commanding an infantry brigade in Panama. Sometime around February 1921, Conner informed Ike he was going to need an executive officer to help him run the brigade. Was he interested? Ike immediately applied for the Panama assignment.

Colonel Rockenbach refused to approve his application. The colonel had no intention of losing his football coach with the 1921 football season rapidly approaching. Ike's despair only deepened as he was caught fast, it seemed, between coaching and a court-martial.

Yet he was about to make an amazing escape. By meeting and making a favorable impression on Conner, Ike was now plugged into the upper echelon of the Army. In the fall of 1921, as Conner prepared to leave for Panama, Helmick learned that a memo had gone from the Adjutant General to Pershing concerning Major Dwight D. Eisenhower, whose services Conner had requested: "He desires the detail of this particular man because he knows his efficiency and because he is due for foreign service." Pershing would not have been involved in a lowly major's assignment had there not been a problem, and the problem was Helmick's effort to get Ike court-martialed.[27]

Spinning around so fast that he nearly tied himself into a slipknot, Helmick hurriedly recommended that Eisenhower shouldn't face a court-martial after all. Repayment and a formal reprimand would do. In December 1921, at the conclusion of another winning season, Ike was packing for Panama.[28]

Number One

Ferdinand de Lesseps thought big. He built a canal at Suez that transformed the world's trade. Then he tried building an even bigger canal across Panama, and persuaded the local government to pass a law protecting bats, because bats ate insects and killed rodents. Malaria and yellow fever nonetheless slowed the construction of the canal. The French ran out of money and De Lesseps gave up, leaving some big wet rectangles deep in the jungle but nothing you could call a canal.

Some years later, the U.S. Army moved in and an Army doctor, William C. Gorgas, attacked the mosquitos' breeding grounds with a tar-based spray, virtually eradicating yellow fever. Army engineers, meanwhile, designed an even bigger and better canal, based on the rudimentary efforts of the French, and in 1914 the Panama Canal opened to traffic, a triumph of military medicine and Army engineering. Not only did the world's commerce profit once again, but the Atlantic was finally joined with the Pacific and the United States could move its warships rapidly between the two great oceans in time of war.[1]

When Ike and Mamie set sail from New York on January 7, 1922, aboard the Army transport *St. Mihiel,* they ought to have been looking forward to Panama, but the timing was all wrong. At more or less the moment Ike's orders for Panama finally came through, Mamie had become pregnant. She probably realized it shortly before they departed.

Having another child was the right, the brave, the defiant response to the loss of Ikky. But Mamie had led too sheltered an existence to face giving birth far from home, at an Army base surrounded by jungle, with anything that resembled equanimity.

Ike's new posting was at Camp Gaillard, home of the 20th Infantry Brigade, on the Pacific side of the isthmus. To reach it, they took a train across Panama, but the last few hundred yards required walking across the locks of the Culebra Cut, clinging to a rope. The steam heat of the tropics was enervating and the sight of the muddy waters of the Cut swirling beneath her feet did nothing to soothe Mamie's jangled nerves.[2]

The house they had been assigned had been built for one of the French engineers involved in de Lesseps's failed attempt to build the Canal. It had stood empty for a long time. Positioned against the side of a hill above the Cut, it loomed out of the shadows like an alien presence, a large two-story building with wide verandas on all four sides. There was no glass in the windows, just lattices and wire screens that thick vines curled around. Thrust deep into the dense foliage, sunlight rarely penetrated its spacious rooms. In its dilapidated state it had a mildewed Gothic spookiness. The roof, made of sheet metal, caught the sun, only to transfer its heat into the house below. During tropical downpours, which occurred regularly, the roof reverberated like a half-empty steel drum and leaked water like a sieve. Ike tried to tell her the house would be all right once they had fixed it up, but Mamie was almost in shock.[3]

The Conners lived next door, and Ike and Mamie had barely arrived before they pushed their way through the hibiscus hedge that separated the two properties. Fox Conner's wife, Virginia, greeted them warmly and told Mamie not to fret. This house, she told Mamie as she showed her around the Conner home, was just as bad as yours when we arrived a couple of months ago. But look at it now. Isn't it wonderful what some paint and elbow grease will do?[4]

Mamie resigned herself to her fate, but that night as she and Ike got into bed under the cover of their mosquito net, she sat bolt upright. A rasping noise had just erupted somewhere in the darkened room. "What's that? Something's eating the house!"

"Probably a rat. We've got to ignore these things or we won't get any sleep at all," said Ike. Mamie listened to the rat gnaw industriously at a chair leg for most for the night.[5]

A week or so later, she heard a different sound—flapping and darting. She turned on the bedside light. Something was flitting around the room. Pulling the sheet over her head, she screamed, "Ike! There's a bat in the room. Kill it!"

He grinned at her. "I can't do that, honey. It's against the law."

"Law or no law, kill that bloody bat!"[6]

Ike got out of bed to see to his mission—a silent killing. He was an expert with a pistol or rifle, but gunshot would be heard all over the post. Dress sword—that ought to do it. For half and hour he and the bat danced a life-or-death duet. He leapt on and off chairs and tables, lunged furiously at movement in dark corners, rushed from window to window flailing with his sword. Mamie, peeking out from under the bedsheet, rocked with suppressed laughter. A sudden thrust and an exultant cry, "Got him!" The tiny carcass of a bat in its death throes twitched on the point of Ike's blade.[7]

Mamie never got used to the cacophony of the jungle at night, to the Turkish-bath heat of the day, to the huge cockroaches that leapt out at her from their hiding places when she ventured near. She learned to cope, putting the legs of the furniture in pans of kerosene to keep the insect life somewhere near floor level. She stripped the bed each week and ignited paper on it to heat the metal and toast the vermin that bred in the springs.[8]

In June, seven months pregnant, she returned to Denver. There was a post hospital at Gaillard and other officers' wives had their babies there, but Mamie wasn't taking any chances. Her second child, John Sheldon Doud Eisenhower, was born in Denver General Hospital, on August 3, 1922. And Ike, who had not been present when Ikky was born, was present this time. Mamie returned to Panama that fall, taking a nurse from Denver General, Kathryn Herrick, with her. To Ike's immense delight, his new son was as blond and pink as Ikky had been. He looked, that is, a lot like Ike.[9]

While Mamie never pretended to want anything from Panama but the chance to leave it, Ike paid little heed to the hardships of life at Camp Gaillard. A soldier, especially an infantryman, expects hardship. To him, this was turning into the place where he would finally learn to think broadly and deeply about his profession, and maybe about his life, under a teacher he came to admire and love. Ike had always been exceptionally intelligent. What had been lacking until now was the time to read and the chance to talk over ideas with someone who was both a true intellectual and an accomplished soldier.

Being a brigade adjutant made no unusual demands on his time. The 20th Brigade contained only one regiment, the 42nd Infantry, whose officers were Americans but whose troops were Puerto Ricans. The postwar Army was holding on to a large number of officers. They represented its most priceless asset—combat experience. But it was being forced by lack of money to cut back on enlisted personnel. The brigade had plenty of gold braid and nowhere near enough riflemen.

Here, then, was an unexpected opportunity to study his profession. Ike had increasingly felt embarrassed at how little reading he had done at West Point. But there had been something lacking going back as far as Abilene—someone who would guide and encourage him. There had never been anyone he could admire sufficiently to fill the hole his distant father had left in his life. In the entire Army there probably wasn't anyone who could have satisfied his need better than Fox Conner, who was regarded throughout the Army as the brains of Pershing's AEF headquarters. A wealthy Mississippian with a drawl that charmed, Conner had graduated from West Point in 1898 and been commissioned in the field artillery. Shortly after the General Staff was created, he was assigned to it. Had he not been such a brilliant staff officer, he would probably have held a combat command in France.

Almost the first thing that Eisenhower noticed about the Conner home was that it was a lot like walking into a library. Here, said Conner, no doubt pleased to see Eisenhower's reaction to a house that was a monument to the power to knowledge, take this, and this, and this. What he gave him were three historical novels with military themes, including the classic fictional treatment of Napoleonic warfare, *The Adventures of Brigadier Gerard*. Like any good teacher, he made lesson one pure pleasure.

Eisenhower established a study on the second floor of his house, tacked up some campaign maps, erected some bookshelves and began reading seriously about the history of war. Mamie was astonished that he could spend a day in the field, come home, eat dinner, read until two in the morning, get up four hours later to go to work and return at night to do it all over again.[10]

Under Conner's tutelage, key works that Ike had already tackled and failed to digest—such as Clausewitz's *On War*—were read again, and discussed at length. He read the memoirs of great soldiers, such as Grant and Sherman. He studied Napoleon's life and campaigns. He stretched his intellectual awareness by tackling philosophical writers, such as Plato and Cicero, and read the Federalist Papers twice, but had to give up on Nietzsche—not, one suspects, because the work was too deep but because Nietzsche's trenchant criticisms of bourgeois morality would have made uncomfortable reading for someone who believed in it as deeply as Eisenhower.[11]

Many of his conversations with Conner took place when they rode around the camp on horseback. The Conners had a tennis court, and Ike played tennis there. They also had a swimming pool, and Ike swam in it. Mamie neither swam nor played tennis, but she and Virginia Conner became as good friends as the twenty-year gap in their ages allowed. Mamie became even better friends with the Conners' two daughters, who were nearer her own age.

Eisenhower's closeness to Conner led, inevitably, to jealousy and resentment among other officers in the brigade. The brigade adjutant seemed to them no more than a yes man, the general's glove puppet. Even some of Ike's old friends were dismayed by the change in him.[12]

Conner was determined, for example, to get at least 90 percent of the brigade qualified as marksmen. During rifle qualification, the normal practice was that officers from one company would oversee the shooting of another company to ensure there was no cheating. Conner said he was doing away with that. "Too much supervision. It makes the men nervous."

Some 20th Brigade officers, including Ike's West Point classmate Bradford "Chen" Chynoweth, were disgusted. You know what will happen, he said to Ike. The best shot in each company is going to shoot for all the men who couldn't hit a barn door. He'll appear on the qualification form as Private Lopez, Private Hernandez, Private Santiago . . .

According to Chynoweth, Ike replied, "Well, Chen, I'll tell you my guiding philosophy. When I go to a new station, I look to see who is the strongest and ablest man on the post. I forget my own ideas and do everything in my power to promote what *he* says is right." The first part of this is not credible, given Ike's known disagreements with superiors at other posts. What Chynoweth elevated and embellished into an Ike "philosophy" was the core, nonetheless, of Ike's relationship with Fox Conner: whatever Conner said was right. But that was because it came from Conner, not because Conner was his boss.[13]

One of the most often repeated stories about Ike's experience with Conner is that the general told him there would be another world war in fifteen to twenty years and Ike was shocked and incredulous. Yet in Ike's own copy of Kennett Davis's *Soldier of Democracy,* which first related this tale, he scribbled in the margin, "Hardly true!"[14]

This marginal scrawl suggests that Ike had already arrived at this conclusion. If so, he had plenty of company. By 1922, many thoughtful people were convinced that the Treaty of Versailles had sown the seeds of another war. Ike's determination to master his profession now had a motive that lifted it onto a plane higher than personal ambition. In the normal course of events, he could expect to retire on his sixtieth birthday, in October 1950. Somewhere between Panama and retirement, he was convinced, there was going to be another war. His duty was obvious.

One thing Fox Conner did tell him was that the United States would have to fight that war as part of a coalition of nations. "George Marshall," he added, "knows more about the techniques of arranging allied commands than any man I know. He is nothing short of a genius."[15]

In October 1922, Ike's Distinguished Service Medal came through. The War Department was disgracefully slow in rewarding people for their service in World War I. Eisenhower's long wait for recognition was typical. A few weeks later, the 20th Brigade paraded in Ike's honor and Conner pinned the medal to his broad chest. Eisenhower had not only achieved the highest rank of anyone in his class, but he was the only one to have received the DSM for service in the Great War. The view of most historians and biographers—that he was plodding along in the 1920s—is mistaken. As Army officers measured such matters, he had already compiled a record few majors could equal.[16]

In the summer of 1924, Eisenhower was asked what his preference was for his next assignment, and he replied firmly that he would like to go to the Infantry School at Fort Benning, Georgia. Meanwhile, Conner's assignment to Panama was coming to a close. Before leaving, he made out Eisenhower's "efficiency report." He lauded his protégé: "One of the most capable, efficient and loyal officers I have ever met." Conner pointedly added, "Upon completion of his foreign service tour he should be sent to take the course at the Army Service Schools at Ft. Leavenworth." He was saying, in effect, that Eisenhower was ready for the Command and General Staff School, a place much more exalted than Benning.[17]

The 1920 National Defense Act had authorized an Army of two hundred thousand men, but year by year Congress failed to provide the money either to maintain it at that level or to modernize it. The Army's strength dropped steadily, its bases fell into disrepair and its combat units continued to train with worn-out, obsolescent equipment. Unable to arm for wars to come, the Army could only prepare for them mentally, and that is just what it did. The beating heart of the Army became its school system, where officers who had served in France passed on what they had learned.

The school system was integrated into an officer's career development. As a lieutenant or a captain he would attend his branch school, such as the Infantry School at Benning; the Artillery School at Fort Sill, Oklahoma; the Engineer School at Fort Belvoir, Virginia; or the Cavalry School at Fort Riley, Kansas. If he did well there, he could expect that when he rose to major or lieutenant colonel, he would attend the Command and General Staff School at Fort Leavenworth, Kansas. And then, when he reached colonel, he might be sent to the Army War College in Washington, D.C.

Assuming he did not make a mess of his career, the general pattern to an officer's peacetime duty was a staff assignment, followed by a school, followed by service with troops, over and over until he retired or became a general. There were some variations, but by the summer of 1924, when Eisenhower still had nearly six months to go before his assignment in Panama would come to an end, he was ordered to report to Camp Meade. He soon found out why—football season would be starting soon, and the team needed a coach. He was amazed, but resolved to do his best. It was a mistake, all the same, to try creating a Notre Dame offense with Podunk personnel. That way there was only grief. A season of defeats wound its weary course.

Meanwhile, Ike received orders putting him in command once again of the heavy-tank battalion he had commanded three years earlier at Meade. No one would ever imagine from reading his account of this development that it was perfectly logical.

In his memoir *At Ease,* he treats his assignment to Meade as if he had been singled out for harsh treatment. In fact, however, he was being asked to follow much the same pattern as everyone else. He had already attended a service school, the Tank School at Meade, in 1921. After that came three years on a brigade staff, and he was now being given service with troops. In another two or three years he would probably be sent to the Infantry School, and if he did well there, he would still be young enough to attend the Command and General Staff School at Leavenworth, which routinely took students up to the age of forty-seven.

At thirty-four, however, Ike was a young man in a hurry. Some of his friends and contemporaries had already graduated from the Infantry School. His own completion of the Tank School course didn't count for much. The school was tiny and its curriculum was limited to practical tasks such as tank driving. Besides, the future of the tank itself was in doubt. To progress in the Army, he had to get back into the infantry mainstream. As he puts it in his memoirs, he needed to attend "one of the *established* Army schools [my emphasis]." He does not even mention the Tank School he'd attended. He went to Washington and made his pitch directly to the chief of infantry, Frank L. Sheets, who promptly turned him down. He would go to Benning sometime in the future, said Sheets, but not yet.[18]

Fox Conner was currently the deputy Chief of Staff of the Army, under Pershing's successor as Chief of Staff, Major General John L. Hines. It seems probable that after his depressing interview with Sheets, Eisenhower talked to Conner about it. He returned to Meade engulfed in gloom and despondency. A few days later Ike received a telegram from Conner that read, "No matter what orders you receive from the War Department, make no protest. Accept them without question."[19]

Barely had he digested this gnomic missive than fresh orders arrived. His permanent assignment had been changed after all; he would not have to command the tank battalion again. He had just been ordered to Fort Logan, Colorado, as the post recruiting officer! It was hardly credible. Commanding a battalion, almost any battalion, was fabulous compared to recruiting. Recruiting is what you did when you were no good at staff work and had failed with troops.

Conner explained the mystery in a letter that arrived a few days later: Ike could not attend the Infantry School without the agreement of the chief of infantry. As a recruiting officer, however, he would be attached to the office of the Adjutant General, and that opened up an even better possibility than Benning—there were two openings at Fort Leavenworth for officers assigned to the Adjutant General. He could have one of them.

He was both thrilled beyond words and apprehensive as hell. To graduate from Leavenworth could put him squarely on the inside track for future assignments. Promotions were so slow these days that rank had lost much of its importance. What mattered in the interwar Army was the kind of assignment an officer got. Many of the most interesting and rewarding posts were held by majors and lieutenant colonels, while many a dull, paper-shuffling job was held down by a bored colonel or a yawning brigadier general with his mind on a golfing retirement. Here, then, was a great and unexpected opportunity. The best assignments for field grade officers almost invariably went to Leavenworth graduates.

But could he measure up to the famously demanding Leavenworth course? He had not attended his service school at Benning yet would be plunged into a ferocious competition against other officers who had, virtually without exception, not only attended their service schools but excelled there. That was how nearly every officer got one of the coveted places at the Command and General Staff School. Most would also be older than he was, with more experience of Army staff work.

Conner told him not to worry about that. "You may not know it, but because of your three years' work in Panama, you are far better trained and ready for Leavenworth than anyone I know. . . . You became so well acquainted with the technics [sic] and routine of preparing plans and orders of operations that included their logistics that they will be second nature to you . . ."[20]

Ike and Mamie arrived at Leavenworth, which sits almost exactly on the Kansas-Missouri border twenty-five miles northwest of Kansas City, Missouri, in August 1925 and by September he was ahead of most of the competition. First, instead of being housed in the huge, noisy housing complex known as the Beehive, where most student officers and their families lived, he was in Otis Hall, which consisted of comfortable and quiet apartments. Second, he teamed up with Gee Gerow, the officer who had called out, "Hey, Ike. Come over here," that afternoon at Fort Sam when he had met Mamie. Not only was Gee a good friend, but two months earlier he had graduated first in his class at the Infantry School. Whatever Gee had learned at Benning, Ike was going to get the benefit of it. They agreed to study the Leavenworth problems together. And, finally, Patton had completed the Leavenworth course in

1924, with grades high enough for "Hon. Grad." to be placed in his entry in the *Army Register*. That meant he was eligible for service on the War Department General Staff, the brain of the Army. Patton was a diligent student and had compiled a hundred pages of detailed notes on the best way to tackle the 126 problems that were the core of the Leavenworth course. Ike brought Patton's notes with him to Leavenworth.[21]

The biggest weakness of senior officers in France had been an unwillingness to act decisively. The unstated point behind the Leavenworth problems was to force students to make firm decisions, often in light of information that was fragmentary or, conversely, when they were swamped with more information than they could possibly digest. Nor were these the kind of problems that majors and lieutenant colonels could expect to face in the course of their duties. These were problems at the division, corps and army level—decisions, that is, that were the responsibility of two- and three-star commanders.

There were school-approved solutions to all of the problems, but learning them was only one part of what the students were there for. The essential thing was to absorb the major principles behind the Army approach to combat, and the most important of these was that only the offensive is decisive in war. The long and bloody stalemate that had characterized the war in Europe before the U.S. moved 2 million men to France seemed vindication enough of that aggressive approach. Students whose solutions emphasized maneuver, avoided frontal assaults and refused to be drawn into trench warfare got the highest grades.[22]

The course was famous for being difficult and rumors flourished about student suicides, even though there hadn't been any. Everyone who stayed with the course, in fact, graduated. It was like being at Harvard—people dropped out, but nobody flunked out.

Some of the problems were daunting nonetheless. While there were problems that could be tackled in a few hours, others took several days. The question every student faced was, Should I be a solo operator, should I form a study partnership or should I be involved in a study committee? Having opted for the partnership method, Ike never regretted it. His friendship with Gerow was strengthened, deepened and enriched by their nine months studying maps and dreaming up solutions to tactical problems such as this: You are moving your division across a river; half of your force is across; the enemy appears in strength on one flank and contests the crossing. Do you withdraw, regroup or attack?

There would, of course, be a lot of detail about roads, logistics, communications, the weather, the terrain, the width of the river and so forth, and these factors might have some bearing, or none, on the decision.

The toughest assignments had strict time limits, such as twelve hours or twenty-four hours or two days. These were known as the pay problems, because this was where a student really earned his money. At such times, Ike, like everyone else, stayed up all night if necessary. Students were expected to show they could be decisive and issue clear, firm instructions at a time when they were tired and, in the demotic of a later day, stressed-out.[23]

Conner was right. When it came to technique—writing a five-paragraph field order, a report, a memo, an operations plan—Eisenhower did not have much to learn. What he got from Leavenworth was something different: a memorable education in the rewards of remaining calm as the pressure increases, a reaffirmation of the importance in a large organization of common sense over cleverness and an appreciation that even at the higher levels of command nothing could be accomplished without first creating a team.

Other students noticed that he spent a lot of time talking to the instructors, which encouraged one of his West Point classmates who was at Leavenworth that year, Roscoe B. Woodruff, to suggest long afterward that Eisenhower improved his grades by brownnosing the staff. The truth was, Eisenhower had discovered something that Woodruff and others had failed to put to the test: The instructors *wanted* students to talk to them about the problems. Too few students did that. Ike's innate friendliness and interest in other people paid off throughout his Army career.[24]

He claimed, in an article that he wrote for the *Infantry Journal* in June 1927, that there was no point worrying about grades at Leavenworth. They weren't given out until the end of the course, so there was no way of knowing how you were doing.[25]

It isn't credible, though, that Eisenhower was ever indifferent to his class standing. His friend and West Point classmate John Leonard said Ike had told people he intended to graduate number one at Leavenworth. That sounds like an exaggeration, but he almost certainly intended to finish high enough to get "Hon. Grad." after his name in the *Army Register,* as Patton had done.[26]

Students generally have a good sense of whether they are in the top

10 to 15 percent of a class, and he would have been aware that he was doing well almost from the first just by talking to some of the 244 other students at Leavenworth that year. At the end of the first month, he was rated fourteenth in the class. Throughout the winter, Ike inched his way forward. By May 1926, he was up to third place. In the last few weeks, he closed the gap. In June, when final grades were posted, Eisenhower had just beaten his West Point classmate Charles M. Busbee in a tight finish for the number-one spot. Gerow was number eleven.[27]

Ike threw a party at the Muelbach Hotel in Kansas City for himself and his Leavenworth friends. While bootleg liquor flowed and Mamie rejoiced, an exultant Ike bellowed out fifty-one off-key verses of "Abdul the Bulbul Amir." For once in his life, nobody tried to stop him.

☆☆☆☆☆

9

Guidebook Ike

Abilene hadn't changed much, except now there was a hangout run by a boyhood friend, Joner Callaghan, where a fellow could play poker and reminisce about the old days—the fights, the pranks, the football games. Ike had a memorable time when he went back to Abilene for a few days that summer of 1926. The soldier ascendant in a home filled with pacifists, the south-side boy who was fast going places. Arthur, the Kansas City banker, balding Edgar, shy Roy, intellectual Milton and rufous Earl—they all came home, too. One Sunday afternoon all six Eisenhower brothers went up Buckeye Street, arm in arm, pretending they were looking for Henry Engle, the sheriff, to pay off some old scores, but it was really a way of showing off to the town, a gesture that told the people on the north side that the south-side Eisenhowers had made something of themselves. It was their answer to hometown snobbery, the kind that wounds most.[1]

There are a number of other well-known stories about this visit. According to Kenneth Davis's 1945 biography, *Soldier of Democracy,* Ike challenged his father to a wrestling match in the yard and let middle-aged David win. But in the margin of his copy of the book, Ike wrote an emphatic "This is not true."[2]

There is also a story, repeated in many accounts, that during Mamie's first visit to Abilene in 1916, on the honeymoon trip, Ike and

Mamie had the biggest fight of their marriage. When Ike went into town one evening to play cards at Joner Callaghan's, the hours passed and Mamie thought he ought to come home. "I'm going to call him," she told Ida.

"That wouldn't be a good idea," Ida warned her.

Mamie wasn't impressed and called Ike at Joner's place, demanding he come home immediately. It was nearly midnight.

"I can't come home now," said Eisenhower. "I'm still behind."

"You come home right this minute!" Mamie responded, and slammed the phone down.

Ike showed up several hours later, having won back all he'd lost and more besides. Mamie was waiting up for him. The little house at 201 South East Fourth Street rocked as he bawled her out for meddling in something she didn't understand (and the macho mystique of a marathon poker session *is* inexplicable to anyone who hasn't been involved in one), while she berated him—rightly—for being so inconsiderate, for thinking only of himself.[3]

This actually occurred, but Ike and Mamie were in Abilene for only seven hours during the 1916 visit, and Joner Callaghan's hangout wasn't in business until about 1921. Next to Davis's version, Ike wrote, "Much later." In all likelihood, the famous "battle of Abilene" occurred during the 1926 visit.

Abilene, Ike knew by now, would always be a good place to return to, but it was his young, exuberant self that was there, not his future—a future that was still ripe only with promises, not certainties. The commandant at Leavenworth, Brigadier General Edward King, wanted him to remain at the Command and General Staff School as an instructor. That was what often happened with students who proved outstanding, and by teaching others for a year or two, they would widen and deepen their grasp of what the course offered.

There was also the opportunity, he was informed by the War Department, of becoming professor of military science and tactics at a major university in the Pacific Northwest, and he could augment his salary, if he wished, by coaching the university football team for an extra thirty-five hundred dollars a year. He turned this job down and by the time he heard about King's wish to keep him at Leavenworth, orders had already been cut sending him to Fort Benning to command an infantry battalion.[4]

When he arrived at Benning in September 1926 he was disgusted to be asked—again!—to coach the football team. He could not do two full-time jobs properly, he insisted. One—probably both—would suffer. He agreed to serve as backfield coach, but the head-coach position was out of the question. The Benning team had a miserable season, but he probably foresaw that.

When the whistle blew on the last play of the last game, he applied for admission to the Army War College class that would enter in September 1927. It was an application that Mamie was sure to favor, if only because the War College was located in Washington. The commandant at Fort Benning resoundingly endorsed Ike's application—"Major Eisenhower has force, character and energy as well as knowledge . . . his loss to this command will be regretted."[5]

The only question now was, What would he do for the next eight months? Fox Conner had the answer—come to Washington right away and write a guidebook. The American Battlefield Monuments Commission had been created to build and maintain cemeteries for those Americans whose bodies would be buried overseas, following the wishes of their families. The cemeteries were bound to attract—indeed, were intended to attract—both the families and many of the American tourists who visited France each year. Pershing, who was the chairman of the commission, wanted a guidebook to the battlefields available for the benefit of the tourists.[6]

Ike arrived in Washington in January 1927, and he and Mamie leased a two-bedroom apartment at the Wyoming, near Dupont Circle. The Wyoming, which boasted imposing marble corridors and lofty Corinthian columns, was one of the District's more prestigious addresses. It was well within walking distance of the State-War-Navy Building, next to the White House, and had the added charm of being the home of his closest friend in the Army, Gee Gerow.

Before long, Ike and Mamie moved into a three-bedroom apartment, with a huge if antiquated kitchen. The fact that they took out a lease for several years reflects his expectation that following graduation from the War College, he would be assigned to the General Staff.

First, though, he had to write the guidebook. In only six months, he produced a detailed but highly readable work that ran to 282 pages. Pershing's executive officer, Major Xenophon Price, who had known Ike at West Point, was impressed. He gave Ike a rating of superior on his efficiency report. Pershing, meanwhile, wrote to the chief of infantry. As a rule, Black Jack doled out praise in tiny doses or not at all. Here was an exception: "What he [Eisenhower] has done was accomplished only by the exercise of unusual intelligence and constant devotion to duty." Ike was so thrilled that he sent it to his parents, scribbling at the bottom in his wayward scrawl, "To my mother and father, with love and devotion."[7]

Price tried to convince Ike that he ought to stay with the commission, and pompously assured him, "Every officer attached to the Commission is going to be known as a man of special merit." Eisenhower was not going to turn down a place at the War College, however.[8]

The Army War College (AWC) did not study organization or tactics but considered issues of war and peace from a national perspective. It was also the place where Army doctrine was formulated, unlike Leavenworth, which taught what the doctrine was. It was also a place where elderly colonels on the verge of retirement could spend a pleasant year in Washington on their way out. The important work was more likely to be accomplished by the younger officers than by their seniors and Ike, at thirty-six, was one of the youngest students ever admitted to the AWC.

The heart of a student's work was the production of a paper on some self-selected topic. Eisenhower's paper was titled "An Enlisted Reserve for the Regular Army." The Army had never had a proper reserve of its own. In World War I, the government had been obliged to federalize the National Guard in order to create a force big enough to fight in France, and found that Guardsmen needed just as much training as draftees.

The strength of the Army's enlisted reserve when Ike wrote his paper stood at six thousand men. Yet there were, he pointed out, 4 million men who had served during World War I. There was a pool of experience available for the nation to draw upon to create an enlisted reserve that was already trained by the Army to meet its own needs and standards. By spending a few weeks on refresher training each year, many men would remain fit for service long after leaving active duty in the Army.

In his paper, Ike anticipated that the Army might once again have to provide "an expeditionary force" to fight overseas, paying no attention to the national consensus of the 1920s that American entry into the war had been a major mistake. The commandant of the War College, Major General William D. Connor, noted in the margin next to the expeditionary-force reference, "Trouble would arise from any use of this term." Connor can hardly be blamed, though, for failing to foresee that one day Eisenhower would have the last word on this point. Anyway, Connor wasn't blind to the merits of Ike's contribution. He wrote a special letter of commendation to be placed in Ike's official file, praising Ike's paper for demonstrating "exceptional merit" and noting that the Chief of Staff had directed that it be circulated within the War Department.[9]

Ike would have realized there was no realistic chance of his program being implemented in the 1920s. It was adopted, though. The kind of large enlisted reserve Eisenhower foresaw, one based upon men with recent military service, eventually became a reality . . . in 1953.

In June 1928 he graduated from the War College—once again, the number-one man in his class. And with graduation from the War College, he was offered an assignment on the General Staff. Pershing, however, urged him to produce a revised and expanded version of the guidebook, based on firsthand study of the battlefields in France. Eisenhower wanted to accept the assignment to the General Staff. Mamie, however, was drawn by the irresistible lure of Paris in the twenties. She had no appreciation of serious literature or art, did not speak French and knew almost nothing about French culture. What she did know was that Paris was the most glamorous and exciting city in the whole world circa 1928. She would have been aware, too, that a dollar went a long way in France. The fight over Ike's next assignment may have been as great as the one over the poker game, but this time Mamie won.[10]

Eisenhower felt aggrieved about this for a long time, convinced he had damaged his career by turning down a place on the General Staff. In truth, though, Mamie had just saved him from a terrible mistake.

The Chief of Staff at the time was Charles Summerall, a small-minded, mean-spirited and vindictive man. He trusted a handful of cronies, not the General Staff, and was mentally stuck around October 1918, when he had commanded a corps in action during the Meuse-Argonne offensive. His command style was to use divisions like battering rams, call his soldiers "bodies," and expend them like cartridges in frontal assaults on some of the toughest defenses in the world.[11]

Summerall seemed to have learned little from his experience of war. The Infantry School, under George C. Marshall, began experimenting with a new organization for the infantry division, making it smaller and giving it more mobility and firepower. When he heard about it, Summerall demanded that the experiments be stopped immediately, and they were.

Had Eisenhower accepted an assignment to the General Staff in 1928, he would have found himself serving under a Chief of Staff who was a mental bully and a military reactionary. He missed nothing by letting Mamie have her way and heading for Paris in August 1928 except the chance to be miserable.[12]

"Mort pour la France"—"Died for France." There was no getting away from it. This laconic, chilling phrase was everywhere, chiseled into marble or granite or limestone, like a new national motto, one more immediate and convincing than *"Liberté, Egalité, Fraternité,"* those three revolutionary promises carved in gold on public buildings for more than a century only to prove to be more than France, in its fundamentally conservative soul, could deliver. You could go to a village in Provence and stand in the little *place* where the narrow, crooked streets met in the shadows of the cypress trees, and there, hundreds of miles from any of the Great War battlefields, would be a column or a plaque with a list of fifty names, or even a hundred, carved on it, the names of local men *mort pour la France,* and it hardly seemed credible that so many had died from this one tiny place. But they had, and the pain of their loss seemed to shriek from the white stone walls and blood red tiles of the silent, shuttered houses. Ike had missed seeing action in the war, but that legacy of grief was the not-so-secret heart of the France he traveled through.

There were other lessons, too, lessons that a soldier's mind and imagination would thrill to. Nearly the whole of France is an outdoor classroom. In this valley, Caesar fought the Gauls. Here the Moors were turned back by Charles Martel—"the Hammer"—in the eighth century. There, a tiny English army, trapped but trusting to its long bows, destroyed the gorgeously caparisoned flower of fifteenth-century France. This gray city, its granite walls mottled and made charming by three centuries of lichen, was built by Vauban and resisted every siege. Over there is the road that Napoleon took to Italy, and that way is a highway that goes north to Belgium and a crossroads called Waterloo. Follow the winding Marne and among fields so flat and open they seem almost like central Kansas stands a granite marker showing how close the Germans got to Paris in August 1914. In France's open-air classroom for soldiers, war was ever present, as both suffering and romance, as two thousand years of legend and history, and with it went a Homeric metatext of sacrifice and heroism, the original tale of soldier life.

Years later, Ike talked to people about how he had learned about the French road system and railroads during his assignment in France. Useful information, he suggested, for what came after. He didn't have much to say about how it advanced his understanding of the history and art of war. Yet he had arrived prepared for that. All those books he had read, all those late-night talks with Fox Conner, had their place in his education, of course. But in France he got more memorable lessons, for there is nothing like walking over the ground to make a battle come alive in the mind. Many years later, when he was asked which military assignment he had enjoyed most, Eisenhower replied without hesitation, "The year in France."[13]

For twelve busy months he traveled up and down the roads with a French-speaking driver. They ate simple picnic lunches by the roadside on pleasant days and went into ordinary cafés when the weather was bad. Ike liked to exchange pleasantries with road workers and local farmers in halting, heavily accented French. He never managed to get a real purchase on the language, but a few phrases and a winning smile go a long way in brief encounters in foreign parts.

Mamie wasn't keen to travel with him at first. She preferred to stay in their apartment at 111 quai d'Auteil, with its view of the Seine, or go shopping with friends. In the spring of 1929, however, she and John went on some of Ike's trips and she found she enjoyed them. Ike had studied the photographs and the maps so closely that his knowledge of the countryside seemed encyclopedic. He could describe in detail places he had never seen. One day, on a trip to the Argonne forest, he told Mamie and John, "Now, just over the next rise there should be a small stream. The land is swampy on this side and goes up in a V-shaped hill on the other. The 42nd Division lost fifteen hundred men taking that hill." He was about to show her, that is, the Côte de Chatillon, where a young brigadier general in the Rainbow Division, Douglas MacArthur, had performed one of the greatest feats of combat leadership of the war, taking a position that Summerall had tried, and failed, to take with massive frontal assaults that bled the famous 1st Infantry Division white.[14]

For Mamie, Paris turned out to be as interesting and enjoyable as she had hoped it would be. She was naturally gregarious and fun-loving, regularly having members of the staff over for dinner or cards and always ready to throw a party or help someone else put one together. It wasn't only Ike's brother officers who warmed to her charm and liveliness. Her greatest triumph was in winning the friendship of other Army wives. In the hothouse world of Army wives, petty jealousies and resentments spring up like weeds. But Mamie was one of the most popular Americans in Paris. A quartermaster captain on the commission, George Horkan, dubbed the Eisenhower residence the Club Eisenhower and the nearby Pont D'Alma became the Pont Mamie. For the rest of their time in the Army, wherever Ike and Mamie lived was known as Club Eisenhower, a place where there was always a good time to be had.[15]

Eisenhower got on well with everyone on the small Paris staff of the Battle Monuments Commission except for his immediate boss, Xenophon Price. In his diary, he called Price "old maidish," and there was no doubt what Price thought of him, because the efficiency reports Price filed on Ike were increasingly dismissive. Price, who had graduated from West Point a year ahead of Eisenhower, may have been motivated somewhat by jealousy, for he had not attended Leavenworth, still less the War College. Contrary to his assumption that service with the commission was the highway to stars, Price, in fact, was going to rise no higher than colonel.[16]

That, however, was all in the darkness of the future. When Ike headed back to Washington in September 1929, those efficiency reports could only have added to his feeling that the guidebook assignment had blighted his career.

Ike and Mamie landed in New York on September 24, 1929, on the brink of a new era in American history. Four weeks after they returned to the U.S., the stock market crashed spectacularly, the prelude to the Great Depression. Having sublet their Wyoming apartment while they were abroad, they now reclaimed it and moved back in.

During the late fall and winter of 1929, Ike finished working on the revised version of the battlefield guidebook and tried to help Pershing with his war memoirs. Pershing was taking the easy way to produce a book, doing little more than amplify what he had already written in his diaries. The result was a thousand-page work that consisted almost entirely of details, presented in a disjointed format, with little sense of the larger picture. Eisenhower told Pershing bluntly, "Everything in that war, as far as the Army is concerned, pointed up to the two great battles, Saint-Mihiel and the Argonne. Now, I don't believe you should tell the story in those two chapters in the form of a diary. It takes the reader's attention away from the development of the battles and just follows your own actions, your own decisions and your own travels."

He advised Pershing to adopt a more thematic approach, at least for the major battles, and rewrote some of the book, but Pershing was unhappy at seeing his turgid prose interfered with. He asked his protégé, George C. Marshall, what he thought and Marshall told the general the book was fine as it was, although he was too astute not to realize that the work was almost unreadable. Still, when it was published in 1931, that didn't stop it from winning the Pulitzer Prize, publishing's Medal of Honor. In the meantime, Marshall, who had just taken control of the Infantry School, wanted Eisenhower to join his staff there, but Ike's next assignment had already been arranged.[17]

The Flaming Pen

Class after class of German Army officers at the fabled Kriegsakademie in Berlin in the 1920s and 1930s studied what had gone wrong in the Great War. Germany had seemed to have victory in its grasp again and again, only to be doomed to defeat in 1918. Why? The answer, they learned, was "pitiless American production." All those factories, belching smoke into the vast American skies, had crushed the kaiser's warrior-heroes. Mortal flesh and matchless courage could never overcome mountains of implacable steel, an infinite supply of high explosive.[1]

If there were prizes given for those myths of consolation that have the least connection with reality, this explanation for Germany's defeat would be a contender. American industrial production had been pitiful, not pitiless. The high-minded Woodrow Wilson had chased the chimera of neutrality with such myopic enthusiasm—myopic because he never believed the U.S. would be able to stay out of the war—that the government had wasted the twenty-eight months between the onset of hostilities and the American declaration of war on Germany. A warship program was begun in 1916, but Wilson did nothing to create an American arms industry that would be capable of supporting an American Army in France.

When the 2 million men of the American Expeditionary Forces arrived in Europe they were desperate for planes, tanks and artillery. The British and French had to arm the Americans. Tens of thousands of Americans were forced, for want of anything better, to fight in British uniforms. American officers had to fill their holsters, which flapped lightly for want of real sidearms, with toilet-paper rolls. Such were the fruits of Wilson's mistake.

While the graduates of the Kriegsakademie were spared these truths, U.S. Army officers couldn't afford to forget them. The 1920 National Defense Act created a new position, assistant secretary of war. The role of the assistant secretary was to manage procurement and make industry aware of the Army's needs. Four years later, in 1924, the Army dipped into its limited funds to create the Army Industrial College, which would train Army officers in the mysterious business of procurement. The "college" consisted of one room in the Munitions Building, a temporary structure erected during the war.

The assistant secretary was not himself expected to be an expert in this field. That didn't matter, provided he had an Army officer who understood logistics as his executive assistant. In the fall of 1929, the executive assistant was Brigadier General George Van Horn Moseley, West Point 1899, a cavalry officer who had supervised the AEF's supply system in France in 1918, and Moseley was looking for an able, intelligent young officer to work in his office. Two of Ike's oldest and closest Army friends, Gee Gerow and Wade Haislip, were already working for Moseley. They probably suggested Eisenhower to him.[2]

Ike was delighted to be working with Gerow and Haislip, and he took an instant liking to Moseley, who impressed him as "alert and energetic." Ike was less enamored of the assistant secretary, a New England industrialist by the name of Frederick Payne, but had no trouble getting along with him. The trouble with Payne was that he was avid for attention and laughably self-important.[3]

Eisenhower was put to work studying industrial mobilization. Moseley was moving the Army's approach to procurement in a bold new direction. The politicians and businessmen had failed to provide the weapons needed to fight World War I. In future wars it might have to count on itself, or face defeat. Under Moseley, the Army began drawing up plans to mobilize the economy for war. Eisenhower was thrilled to find he was in at the start of something new and important.

In the spring of 1930, as part of this effort, he and an engineer officer, Major Gilbert Wilkes, made a personal, and uncomfortable, journey through Texas and northern Mexico to study the prospects of
getting rubber, one of the most important strategic raw materials, from
the guayule plant. Ike returned convinced that guayule might be able to
supplant, or at least supplement, the more traditional sources, in Southeast Asia. He was wrong about that. Guayule rubber wasn't robust
enough.[4]

He and Wilkes were also visiting factories and asking industrialists
what they expected to be able to contribute in the event of another war.
The industrialists were baffled. *Another* war?[5]

In retrospect, it seems almost perverse that Moseley would have
chosen this moment to launch the Army into planning for economic
mobilization. There was a steady outpouring of books in the 1920s that
purported to reveal the secret history of World War I. By 1930, Americans were convinced they had been conned out of neutrality—and
morality—into taking part in an unnecessary conflict produced by arms
manufacturers pursuing ever greater profits. To Americans in 1930 *military* meant *militaristic* until proven otherwise and arms manufacturers
were known as "the merchants of death."

In June 1930 Congress created a War Policies Commission to consider ways of taking the profit out of war and to decide whether the
Constitution ought to be amended so the President could seize private
property—i.e., the arms factories—if he deemed it necessary to do so
in wartime. Eisenhower, Wilkes and Moseley's contribution to the commission's deliberations was a revolutionary new document, *Industrial
Mobilization Plan—1930.*

Eisenhower helped prepare the way with an article entitled "Funda-
mentals of Industrial Mobilization," which was published under
Payne's name in *Army Ordnance* in the summer of 1930. Ike's article
justified the new plan as little more than a method of streamlining procurement and making it more efficient.

While working on the industrial mobilization plan, Ike had astutely
sought the advice of Bernard Baruch, the Wall Street operator who had
been the head of the War Industries Board in 1917–1918. Out of their
meetings came a lifelong friendship. Baruch's support for the Army's
new initiative gave it credibility when it came under congressional
scrutiny.[6]

In the fall of 1930, Summerall's tenure as Chief of Staff came to an end. There was a mood close to rejoicing when the new Chief of Staff, Douglas MacArthur, was sworn in. Overnight, the War Department seemed like a different—and better—place. Under Summerall, Moseley had been allowed to start something important simply because Summerall, fighting man that he saw himself to be, could not bend so far as to take any interest in the lowly business of procurement.

MacArthur was different. Not only was he a much greater combat commander than Summerall, but he had a more realistic idea of what the Army's mission was in peacetime: to get ready for war. That was true whether there was plenty of money or very little, whether public opinion was favorable or not, whether Congress understood or not. And the whole of the Army had to get ready, down to and including supply. MacArthur was so impressed by Moseley's initiative and determination that he made him deputy Chief of Staff.

Payne and Moseley in turn had no doubt about who ought to be the new executive assistant to the assistant secretary of war—Major Eisenhower—and urged that Eisenhower be promoted to brigadier general immediately. MacArthur, however, would not alter the current promotion system, which was based entirely on seniority—no exceptions. So Ike remained a major, and continued working on industrial mobilization.[7]

In 1931, he enrolled as a student at the Army Industrial College. Each student was required to turn in a special study and Eisenhower's was a seventeen-page report entitled "Brief History of Planning for Procurement and Industrial Mobilization Since the World War," which provided both a context and a strong justification for Moseley's industrial mobilization plan. So, too, did "War Policies," an article he published in the *Cavalry Journal* that fall. Ike insisted that there was no conflict between the Army's plans for industrial mobilization and the determination of the War Policies Commission to control the "merchants of death."

His remarkable writing ability was, meanwhile, keeping his pen busy on other projects. Summerall had no gift for self-expression and had put a young captain named Tom Betts to work as his speechwriter. Payne decided he needed something similar and asked Eisenhower to write his speeches and his annual report. The War Department did not need a Hemingway or a poet laureate, but at a time when the public was hostile to the military and its budget shrank from year to year, it desperately needed people who could explain what it was doing in language free from the irritating pomposity and irrelevant details that serve as mental props for the typical military bureaucrat. Ike, like Ulysses S. Grant, could write a speech, a letter, an official report, plan or memo with enviable limpidity and vigor.

He was so talented that MacArthur, a man with literary skills of his own, had him write his annual report as Chief of Staff in 1931. MacArthur was sufficiently impressed to write Eisenhower a special letter of commendation, thanking him for his "excellent work," and noted that he had undertaken this task in addition to his normal duties. "I write you this commendation," MacArthur added, "so that you may fully realize that your outstanding talents . . . are fully appreciated." Ike was astonished and informed his diary, "Mamie had it framed!!!"[8]

Despite such successes, Eisenhower never felt completely comfortable in Washington. Early in 1932 he was hoping to get away from the War Department. The appeal it had once exerted was exhausted when his work on economic mobilization came to an end. Writing speeches and official reports was demanding but boring. It was during his War Department service that he began keeping a diary, something he had never done before. Diaries mean loneliness, isolation, unhappiness; keeping one is a form of self-help. For a busy middle-aged man to keep one was not a good sign. It was a pattern that would recur. In future years, whenever Eisenhower felt depressed, he put his thoughts and, more important, his feelings, into a diary.

What he yearned for now was service with troops, to lose himself once more in the unit pride, the outdoor life, the marching and shooting, the mud on the boots and the camaraderie of field soldiering. During these years in Washington, John Eisenhower noticed how his father "writhed in frustration [and] worked like a slave."[9]

He suffered, too, from a succession of ailments that were almost certainly brought on by stress—mysterious pains in the back and stomach, diarrhea, excruciating headaches. Physical examinations showed nothing seriously wrong and to people such as Moseley he seemed a powerfully built man who was energetic and strong. There was the Ike who showed up smiling for work each morning and his twilight twin, the Ike who went home looking drawn each evening, complaining to Mamie that he felt unwell.[10]

He hinted to the chief of infantry that he'd like a battalion at Fort

Sam Houston. The heat of Texas, he knew, would be as unpleasant as ever, but Mamie's parents still spent half the year in San Antonio and she and they were urging him to ask for Fort Sam. Besides which, living expenses would be lower in Texas, something worth thinking about after Hoover cut Army salaries by 10 percent. Hoover was convinced that reducing government spending would help beat the Depression. All that did was make it worse.

MacArthur, however, had no intention of letting Eisenhower and his "flaming pen" get away. On February 13, Ike was summoned to the Chief of Staff's splendiferous office. Behind the huge desk was a floor-to-ceiling mirror that MacArthur used mainly to nourish his romantic imagination with the reversed image of himself. He had a habit of pacing back and forth in front of the mirror, flourishing a huge, ornately carved ivory cigarette holder while dressed in a Japanese robe, giving his visitor the oratorical works. It was the best free show in town. And if Ike didn't get the full treatment on this particular day, he would have had the benefit of it on other occasions. What it came down to, said MacArthur, was that he wanted Eisenhower to remain in Washington. He had so much to contribute to the department.

The chief of infantry's office was working on Ike's next assignment by counting his departure from France in August 1928 as the beginning of four years of staff duty, and decided he was therefore eligible for troop duty at the end of July 1932. But, said MacArthur, War Department assignments were normally for a period of four years, and Eisenhower would not complete four years' duty at the War Department until September 1933.

This was a somewhat specious argument, but such considerations never deterred MacArthur when he was intent on getting his own way. Ike could have countered MacArthur with various arguments, insisted on returning to service with troops or appealed to the Adjutant General for a ruling. He did none of those things.

To mollify him, MacArthur offered him command of Fort Washington in September 1933 if he agreed to remain in the War Department until then. Ike acceded to MacArthur's wishes without a murmur of protest, even though he did not believe for a minute that he was going to get command of the fort. That was a colonel's job, not a major's.[11]

As he walked back to the Wyoming that evening to give Mamie the news that they wouldn't be going to Fort Sam after all, the streets around the Capitol were agitated by the shouts and singing of shabby figures. Out of work, down-on-their-luck former doughboys were streaming into Washington to demand a bonus for their contribution to winning the war.

Walter W. Waters was a slender young man with wavy blond hair and piercing blue eyes when he went overseas with the 146th Field Artillery in 1918. He served as a medic and by the time of the Armistice had risen to the rank of sergeant. After his discharge from the Army in June 1919, Waters drifted from town to town and job to job until, in 1925, he got married and settled down in Portland, Oregon. He got a job at a cannery and worked his way up to assistant superintendent. By December 1929 he had saved a thousand dollars. In December 1930 the cannery laid off half its employees, including Waters. In December 1931 he was destitute: no job, no savings, no future. All he had left was a government certificate, which he could cash in for about a thousand dollars in 1945. That same month, December 1931, Wright Patman, a congressman from Texas, introduced legislation that would authorize early payment of the World War I soldiers' bonus.

Several hundred AEF veterans from Portland, including Walter Waters, decided to make their way to Washington and lobby on behalf of Patman's bill. They marched out of Portland in May 1931 behind a bugler, rode the rails at times, hitched rides when they could, and long before they reached the District, their numbers had grown into the thousands and Waters had become the leader of the Bonus Expeditionary Force, better known as the Bonus Army. By July, pathetic camps had sprung up in various parts of the District where the members of the self-styled Bonus Expeditionary Force lived in squalor and argued vehemently among themselves late into the night.[12]

Moseley's reaction when the first group of marchers arrived was to advise MacArthur to plan on using troops to maintain order in the District. MacArthur brushed the idea aside. If these really were former soldiers, they would know how to conduct themselves properly, he said. Besides, the police would deal with any trouble.[13]

While Congress debated the bonus bill, however, the number of bonus marchers grew until it reached fifteen thousand. The mass protest of so many disgruntled unemployed men was simply irresistible to Communist party organizers, who tried to wrest leadership away from Walter Waters. Moseley and others were convinced the Communists had taken over, but Waters managed to retain his leadership of most of the Bonus Army.[14]

In early July, the House passed the bonus bill, but the Senate swiftly rejected it. Hoover expected the marchers to take their disappointment stoically and go home. Many did so, aided by the Veterans Administration. By late July the number still in the District had fallen to roughly five thousand. Things seemed to be going much as Hoover had expected, but small groups of marchers suddenly took over several buildings that were scheduled for demolition. Attempts by the police to evict them, on July 28, led to a shower of bricks, leaving several policemen, including the chief of police, Pelham D. Glassford, with serious head injuries. One of the rioters was shot dead and another was wounded by police gunfire.

At this point the District commissioners demanded Hoover's help. A little before noon Secretary of War Patrick J. Hurley gave MacArthur a written order: "Proceed immediately to the scene of disorder. . . . Surround the affected area and clear it without delay." Hoover, well aware of how easily public opinion could be inflamed by the use of troops against civilians, told MacArthur he expected him to oversee the operation in person.[15]

Eisenhower received a summons to the Chief of Staff's office. Go home and get into uniform, MacArthur told him. The President has ordered the use of troops. I am going to accompany them and you will go with me. At which point, Eisenhower claimed in his memoir, *At Ease,* "I told him that the matter could easily become a riot and I thought it highly inappropriate for the Chief of Staff of the Army to be involved in anything like a local or street-corner embroilment."[16]

The chances that Eisenhower told the Chief of Staff to his face that he was making a serious mistake are close to zero. First, the gap between a major and a four-star general is simply too big. Second, if Eisenhower had been capable of standing up to MacArthur, he would have done it a month earlier, over his assignment. In his diary, he had scoffed at the idea that commanding Fort Washington would be counted as service with troops, but he didn't dare say that to MacArthur's face. Instead, his response to MacArthur had been to cave in without a murmur. Third, had he really told MacArthur he was making a mistake, MacArthur might well have told him that it wasn't his idea but the President's. Ike remained ignorant of that fact. He did not know nearly as much about what was happening between Hoover, Hurley and MacArthur as his memoir suggests. It is possible that he thought MacArthur ought not to go out on the streets, but even that isn't certain. There is no mention of this famous rebuke to MacArthur in Ike's diary, a document so frank that much of it remained under wraps until 1998.

After talking to MacArthur, Ike rushed back to the Wyoming. He scattered hangers and boxes all over his bedroom floor as he hurriedly changed into uniform, sprinkled a generous amount of talcum powder into his rarely worn boots, then wrestled them over his feet and up his calves.[17]

Hurrying over to the Munitions Building, he met up again with MacArthur and MacArthur's aide, Captain Thomas Jefferson Davis. The commander of the 16th Brigade, Brigadier General Perry L. Miles, arrived in his staff car and MacArthur climbed aboard. The six hundred infantrymen who would clear the streets were under Miles's command.

Miles, who was an old friend, expressed surprise at seeing MacArthur there. MacArthur was wearing his fanciest dress uniform and every badge, medal, pin and piece of gold braid he was entitled to, along with a couple of medals he wasn't entitled to wear that had been won by his father, Lieutenant General Arthur MacArthur, in the Philippines. He told Miles his presence was all Hoover's idea. "I'm here to take the rap," he said, "if there should be any unfavorable or critical repercussions."[18]

Eisenhower and Davis climbed into another staff car and the two vehicles proceeded down Pennsylvania Avenue, following the troops, who advanced in gas masks and with bayonets fixed. Five small Renault tanks commanded by Patton were also assigned to this operation, but the tanks broke down long before they reached Capitol Hill.

By five P.M., the infantry had dispersed the Bonus Marchers. The troops continued to advance, heading toward the principal Bonus Army camp, at Anacostia Flats. By this time, however, the head of the White House Secret Service detail, Edmund Starling, had warned Hoover that there were still women and children in the camp at Anacostia and the troops were using tear gas freely. Hoover promptly wrote out an order to MacArthur not to allow the troops to cross the Anacostia Bridge. They were to stay out of the camp.[19]

Hurley entrusted this order to Moseley. Meanwhile, a couple of

Bonus Marchers had emerged from the camp and asked MacArthur for time to allow the people still inside the camp to leave. MacArthur replied this would be a good time for the troops to eat dinner, and Ike, along with the rest, spent the next two hours eating and chatting, while dozens of people, clutching their pathetic possessions, emerged from the Anacostia camp and walked away.

Moseley arrived and had a word with MacArthur but did not pass on Hoover's order, although in his memoir he claims he did so. In truth, though, he—and Payne—wanted to see the Bonus Marchers driven out of Washington and taught a lesson they would never forget.

Hoover became anxious when the hours passed and there was no word from MacArthur. He wrote out the order again, and Hurley gave this to Colonel Esmund White, the secretary of the General Staff. Moseley, however, delayed Wright's departure until he was sure the order would be a dead letter, as it turned out to be. When it finally reached MacArthur, the troops were across the bridge and entering the camp, which Miles and MacArthur believed was now deserted. They were wrong. There were up to fifty people still refusing to leave their pestilential shacks. The troops fired more tear gas and drove them out of the camp. At this point the police took over and ordered the troops to set fire to the shacks, which the D.C. public health department wanted destroyed.

Moseley covered up his role masterfully, by writing a wholly false account of what had happened, and ensured that it was not published until after MacArthur's death. He thereby hoped to preserve his own reputation, at the cost of destroying MacArthur's.

The plan worked. MacArthur was excoriated, then and later, for allowing the troops to cross the Anacostia Bridge in defiance of Hoover's orders when, in fact, he did not receive any such order until it was too late to be implemented.

Eisenhower wrote the Chief of Staff's report, and could do so with a certain authority simply from having been present. But when he came to write *At Ease,* he appears to have been influenced by the vehement criticism of these events. Ike expressed far more opposition in retrospect than he ever did at the time. He also got salient details wrong. In one often-quoted passage, for example, he says MacArthur refused to see Moseley and describes Moseley as being Payne's assistant, when in fact he had been deputy Chief of Staff for eighteen months. He also says that someone came from Colonel Wright, when the man in question *was* Colonel Wright, who happened to be an important member of MacArthur's own staff. Nevertheless, Eisenhower claims that MacArthur said he did not want "either himself or his staff bothered by people coming down and pretending to bring orders." This could hardly apply to Wright, who was already on that staff. As for refusing to see Moseley, his own deputy—that is simply unbelievable.[20]

Had Eisenhower felt as strongly about the eviction of the Bonus Marchers as he later claimed, it seems likely that he would have made some such remark in his diary. The sole reference to it, however, runs as follows: "As Gen. MacA's aide took part in Bonus Incident of July 28. A lot of furor has been stirred up but mostly to make political capital. I wrote the general's report, which is as accurate as I could make it."[21]

Ike's report was moderate in tone, easy to follow and cogently expressed. Even so, it didn't make one iota of difference. MacArthur's reputation was in tatters and Lou Henry Hoover, the gray-haired and formidably intelligent First Lady, might as well start packing.

In February 1933, with Franklin D. Roosevelt's inauguration only a few weeks away, Payne resigned as assistant secretary of war and went back to Connecticut. MacArthur promptly had Eisenhower assigned to the General Staff and installed him in what amounted to a cubicle separated from his own imposing office by a slatted door. In the confines of his cubicle, arriving early, departing late, Ike worked as hard as ever.[22]

When Roosevelt was sworn in as President, MacArthur led the new President's inaugural parade riding a handsome gray gelding. Many a New Dealer came to Washington still disgusted and angry at the Army for the forcible eviction of the Bonus Marchers. MacArthur expected Roosevelt, to whom he was distantly related, to replace him as Chief of Staff.

That did not happen, mainly because MacArthur turned Roosevelt's first major pubic works project, the Civilian Conservation Corps, into the New Deal's first major success. Under the guidance of Army officers, more than two hundred thousand unemployed young men were put to work cutting fire trails, clearing streams, planting trees and doing other useful outdoor work within six months of Roosevelt's inauguration. It was the kind of bold, practical initiative that won the acclaim of the people and historians.

Eisenhower had chosen not to vote in any election, convinced that the line between the military and the political shouldn't be blurred. Even so, he took a close interest in the New Deal. He tended to look on an America prostrated by the Depression as if it were a poorly run battalion ruined by its former commander. During the first couple of years of Roosevelt's presidency, left and right alike feared that the country was sliding into dictatorship, while Ike worried that Roosevelt was dragging America into socialism.[23]

He was dismayed, too, at the way the Army's budget was slashed and slashed again. These were stressful times for anyone who believed, as Eisenhower did, that another major war came closer with each passing day. Many congressmen who had to approve military appropriations were convinced that the Army should be buying new tanks and airplanes, even if that meant getting rid of many of its officers.

MacArthur appeared before Congress regularly and kept up a large correspondence with politicians and publishers to argue that well-trained, highly experienced officers *were* the Army. Ike wrote many of the letters, the reports and the documents that MacArthur used to press the Army's case. One of Ike's old friends from West Point and Panama, Bradford Chynoweth, was directly involved in these budget battles and concluded late in life that the three years he spent fighting them were incomparably worse than the three years he spent as a Japanese prisoner of war.[24]

Hoover had already cut military pay by 10 percent, and when Roosevelt's budget director proposed cutting it by another 10 percent, Ike told Mamie he might just have to ask for relief from his current assignment, on the grounds that he couldn't afford to live in Washington any longer. When the cut went through, however, he did nothing.[25]

Throughout his life, Ike's relationship with money was more like that of the born aristocrat, someone like Roosevelt, than the stereotypically ambitious poor boy. Eisenhower always liked to live well and appreciated expensive possessions, yet he couldn't chase a dollar if it begged him. He was inclined to be envious of people who were rich, yet didn't mix that envy with the stuff of his soul. While Ike was still slaving in the War Department, William Randolph Hearst saw in the advent of Hitler and the militarism of Japan that another war was coming. He wanted to hire a military correspondent and his first choice was Eisenhower, an expert on military subjects but with more writing ability than most journalists possessed. Ike was offered the job. Salary—fifteen thousand dollars a year.[26]

This was three times what he was earning in the Army. He turned it down without hesitation. Moments such as this are the defining acts in a man's life, and his was the kind of reaction nearly everyone would want to be judged by.

Although Mamie was notoriously parsimonious, the Eisenhowers still lived comfortably, mainly because Mamie's father continued paying for Mamie's maid (who also doubled as a cook) and bought her a new car, a Plymouth she fondly called Pete. Besides which, the pay cut was partly offset when the Wyoming went into receivership. Many tenants had lost their jobs and could no longer pay their rent. Under the new owners, rents were reduced.[27]

Having shifted from Paris to Washington, Club Eisenhower was as lively as ever. There were card parties nearly every week, and Mamie was the resident pianist. Old friends such as the Gerows were invited for dinner regularly, and so were new ones, such as Major Everett Hughes, an ordnance officer with whom Ike had become friendly at the War College. And while Ike did not much care for living in Washington, it had one major advantage over all other cities: he could see his brother Milton almost every day.

Milton, who was rising rapidly in the Department of Agriculture, had married the daughter of the owner of the biggest department store in Manhattan, Kansas. His father-in-law had since become a major property developer in the Washington area and provided Milton and his wife, Helen, with a large, gracious home in Falls Church, Virginia, only a twenty-minute drive from the Wyoming. Ike and Milton talked about everything, including politics. Milton defended and explained the New Deal and Ike criticized it.[28]

Among the six Eisenhower brothers, there was only one truly close, deep friendship, and this was it. Ike and Milton were intellectually and temperamentally alike and both were devoted to public service. Their disagreements were cheerful rather than combative, unlike Ike's arguments with his big brother Edgar.

Milton also widened Ike's circle of Washington acquaintances, expanding it beyond the inward-looking world of the ever-shrinking peacetime military. Among those he introduced Ike to was a young journalist named Harry C. Butcher, editor of *The Fertilizer Review* but clearly destined for grander outlets. Eisenhower astonished Butcher soon after they met by standing almost in a trance for a moment with his hands at his side, his body going as rigid as a board. He then leaned forward and kept on leaning until he toppled over, falling straight toward a face-smashing collision with the floor. Butcher gasped, but at the last moment, Eisenhower brought his large, powerful hands up to his chest, and when he stopped falling, his nose was virtually touching the ground.[29]

While Ike's friendships with contemporaries were flourishing, the relationship with John was always problematic. Possibly because David Jacob Eisenhower had been quick to beat his sons, or more probably because he saw this as yet another test of leadership ability, Ike never laid a hand on John, to his son's lasting regret. A dad who spanked you looked to him like a dad who really cared. It is also the case that a spanking is a form of physical contact, something he yearned for. Instead, Ike used his leadership skills to make Johnny do what he wanted. John Eisenhower admired his father, ached to please him, sought to be a good son and hoped to be loved in return. Eisenhower had trouble expressing such feelings to his wife; expressing them to his son was even harder.

They did father-and-son things together, such as using the bathroom at the same time, and sometimes even shared a bath. Such experiences were both charming and fleeting. Ike left home early most days, came back late. He worked so hard that he sometimes disappeared in the middle of parties at Club Eisenhower to work on a memo or a report or a staff study. Most of what time Ike spent with his wife and son was wedged into the hollow crepuscular hours of early breakfasts and late dinners. The one day of the week he spent much time at home was Sunday, when he and Mamie were likely to spend the whole morning in bed, and then pay social calls—something Ike loathed—on his superiors in the afternoon.[30]

From the time little Johnny learned to read, Ike began inducting him into the cult of West Point. The Point had been his entrée into the world of public service and solid achievement; he intended it to be Johnny's, too. His son spent hours poring over *The Howitzer,* Ike's West Point yearbook, until he knew the names and faces of nearly all his father's classmates.[31]

Having failed to escape from Washington in 1932, neither did Ike get away when September 1933 rolled around and he had put in four years at the War Department. Nor did he get service with troops, still less command of Fort Washington. What he got was more staff work for MacArthur. If Ike made any protest, there is no record of it, not even a hint. He seems to have resigned himself to staying with MacArthur until MacArthur left town. The general was scheduled to step down as Chief of Staff in the fall of 1934.

By then, though, MacArthur had turned the tide in Congress, secured an increase in the Army's budget and launched a number of important reforms. To many officers, he was a miracle worker, the man who had saved the Army from virtual destruction.

No one was more in awe of MacArthur than the secretary of war, George Dern. He convinced Roosevelt that MacArthur's tenure as Chief of Staff should be extended indefinitely. Eisenhower thereby found himself still working ridiculously long hours, with no date certain set for his release.

While Congress was buzzing with the news that MacArthur was going to remain as Chief of Staff for an unprecedented fifth year, it was also enacting a bill that would lead to Philippine independence around 1946. As an interim measure, it would become a semiautonomous commonwealth in late 1935, under the presidency of the principal leader of the Philippine independence movement, Manuel Quezon. In the spring of 1935, Quezon invited MacArthur to come to Manila and help build up the defenses of the Philippines before it achieved full independence.

MacArthur began working on a plan. Or, rather, he told Eisenhower he needed a plan and Ike drew up an outline. The details, however, would take up too much of his time. His solution was to find some free help. One of Ike's West Point classmates, Major James Ord, was presently a student at the War College. Ord had been born in Mexico and grew up speaking Spanish. He was also the first man in the Class of 1915 to win an award for bravery. Recommended for the Medal of Honor during the Pershing expedition into Mexico in 1916, Ord had received the Distinguished Service Cross. He was, that is, the kind of officer MacArthur was almost certain to trust. Ike's suggestion was that Ord and some of his classmates at the War College could form a committee and devise a plan and submit the plan as meeting the requirement that every AWC student must write a special report.

MacArthur was delighted with the result. It could only have reinforced his determination to take the inky armature of Ike's "flaming pen" with him to Manila. He was also going to need the major's other great gift, the ability to bring him solutions rather than problems. So one day in the summer of 1935 when MacArthur called out, "Major Eisenhower, I'd like to speak to you," Ike stepped through the slatted door and got the general's specialty, the stirring, quasi-operatic harangue.

It is our loss that Eisenhower never left a detailed account of this encounter, but it isn't hard to imagine the architecture: the sonorous appeal to duty, the patriotic mood music, the almost painfully dramatic pauses, the assertion of absolute trust in Ike's future, the fulsome expression of gratitude for services already rendered, mention of the extra remuneration that the government of the commonwealth was prepared to pay, the understated but emotional appeal to manly friendship, at least one hint that helping the Filipinos survive as a people was part of God's plan, the whole delivered as MacArthur paced furiously around the room swinging a small gold football at the end of a slender gold chain.

Eisenhower later said he felt dismayed, but "I was in no position to argue with the Chief of Staff." He still didn't know how to say no to MacArthur. In the Philippines he would become an expert.[32]

The House on the Wall

Back in 1915, Cadet Eisenhower had applied for service in the Philippines, even though there was a war in Europe and if the U.S. got involved in that—which a lot of people expected—he could find himself sitting it out under a palm tree when his classmates were winning medals and promotions on the battlefields of France. What he had his mind on, though, wasn't gore and glory but enjoying himself.

He was going to look as swell as swell could be when he got to the Philippines. No doubt about that. The Army's handsomest uniform was the tropical whites. With the equatorial sun glinting on the five big brass buttons down the front of the jacket, the crossed muskets of the infantry on each side of the high, neck-choking collar and the gold bars of a second lieutenant shining on the shoulders, he'd be a treat for the eyes of almost any girl. He wanted it so badly, he'd taken a chance and ordered the tropical whites before learning whether his application had been approved.[1]

Ike was more than ready to travel. A posting to the Philippines meant seeing something of the world—Hawaii, Japan, Shanghai, maybe even Singapore—on the voyage out and back. As he told Dorothy Mills, the girl he'd met six months before graduation, "I've had wanderlust since the day I learned to walk." Applying for duty in the Philippines, he gave the Army the chance to help those itchy feet on their eager way. But when cadet assignments came through, he got Texas, not Manila.[2]

Life disappoints us all. Besides, the uniform hadn't been wasted. Ike wowed the girls with it when he returned to Abilene, and when he got to Fort Sam, it made a big impression on Mamie. He'd also gotten married in it.

It would be 1935 before he got to see what the Philippines was like, and he was going to arrive as a married lieutenant colonel, not a bachelor second lieutenant. Mamie, however, wasn't going with him, so neither was John. She insisted that it was essential for John to complete the eighth grade in Washington and not be uprooted. Moving would seriously harm his education, said Mamie. This argument couldn't have carried much weight, not after all the pressure she had put on Ike to get a transfer to Texas.

Wounded, Ike reacted as if he didn't care whether she went to Manila with him. He did such a good job of it that she became convinced he didn't want her to go. The truth was, he hated the idea of being apart from his family. He tried to tell himself it wasn't so bad, that he wouldn't be gone more than a year, but it still hurt. Ike and Mamie endured, with the stoicism of a military family of the time, a separation made doubly painful by suppressed doubts, wounded feelings and mutual misunderstanding.[3]

The whole venture had an air of make-believe, anyway. As Chief of Staff, MacArthur was a temporary full general, with four stars. The moment he ceased to be Chief of Staff, he would revert to a major general, with only two white stars gracing the red silk flag in his office. Because he would be representing the Army at the inauguration of Manuel Quezon as president of the Philippines, however, he made a personal appeal to Roosevelt to allow him do so as Chief of Staff. What he didn't say was that this would also postpone the awful moment when he had to yield two of his stars.

MacArthur was convinced there had been an agreement, although Roosevelt being Roosevelt, the President probably didn't make any categorical commitment. In all likelihood there would have been some qualification—i.e., it would be all right so long as nobody objected. MacArthur tried to nail things down by having his travel orders read, "He will stand relieved from duty on the General Staff and as Chief of Staff as of date Dec. 15, 1935."[4]

The morning of October 1, Eisenhower boarded the train heading for San Francisco along with the general; the general's ailing mother, Mary "Pinky" MacArthur; the general's widowed sister-in-law, Mary McCalla MacArthur; the general's aide, Captain Thomas Jefferson Davis; and Ike's old friend Major James Basevi Ord. The company of Jimmy Ord was probably the only enjoyable prospect that Ike could glimpse on the distant equatorial horizon. At least Jimmy would be there.

On the portly side and slightly owlish in heavy horn-rimmed spectacles, Ord looked like central casting's idea of a small-town bank manager. Yet he was, in fact, a lively, fun-loving character who brought to everything he did extraordinary charm and remarkable intelligence. As the DSC on his dress uniform showed, he also possessed physical courage.

The train whistled and rumbled into Cheyenne, Wyoming, the night of October 2. There was a telegram waiting for the general. MacArthur read it rapidly, emotions churning. FDR had just named Major General Malin Craig to be Chief of Staff, effective immediately. Eisenhower was taken aback as MacArthur ranted and raved, launching into an "explosive denunciation of politics, bad manners, bad judgment, broken promises, unconstitutionality, insensitivity . . ."[5]

In truth, what MacArthur had proposed to Roosevelt was unworkable. The secretary of war handled the political side of the Army, but the Chief of Staff fielded the crucial questions—about personnel, weapons, training, promotion, planning, relations with the Navy and so forth—that came up nearly every day. To put the powers of Chief of Staff on ice for ten weeks would undermine the War Department's ability to act quickly and effectively. Someone was bound to point this out to Roosevelt. Besides, Craig's appointment would remind MacArthur of just who was boss, lest he was tempted to forget while so far away.

MacArthur was high-strung, sensitive to the least slight, rarely governed by what others thought of him, but guided instead by an inflexible sense of his own worth and dignity. And at that remote railroad station he blazed like a bonfire. Ike had never seen him like this—the unbridled rage, the utter contempt for his Commander in Chief, the stricken pride. He had just had a glimpse of another MacArthur. For some time, Eisenhower had been slightly awestruck by MacArthur, but here was someone else, a man engulfed not just by rage against what he saw as an injustice but someone overwhelmed by self-pity, on a Wagnerian scale. All that was lacking was the chorus, and if he expected his entourage to provide it, he was going to be disappointed in Eisenhower and Ord.

The offices of the Philippine defense mission were housed in 1 Calle Victoria, a large and picturesque building atop the huge medieval stone wall the Spanish had built in the seventeenth century when they fortified Manila. Known to the local people as the House on the Wall, it had a large, round Chinese-style front door. Ike, Ord and the rest of the staff had to mount a flight of steps just inside the door to reach their offices. The rooms were spacious, with high ceilings and stunning views of the bay on one side, downtown Manila on the other. Ceiling fans hummed high above, stirring the blue haze of cigarette smoke. The well-buffed corridors echoed to the ubiquitous clatter of heavy black Army typewriters being pounded into submission.[6]

MacArthur managed to build up a staff that numbered around fifteen officers and enlisted personnel to plan for the defense of the Philippines as of July 4, 1946, the day the archipelago would achieve its independence. In the meantime, though, the U.S. Army and Navy had that responsibility, and neither had a plan to discharge it.

The War Department had long been convinced that acquiring the Philippines was a national blunder. The islands conferred no strategic or economic advantage on the United States. Rather, they seemed likely to embroil it in a war with an ever expanding, increasingly militaristic Japan. They could be defended only at a cost that no American government would ever willingly pay. Even so, the Army had to dig in and do its best, knowing it faced inevitable defeat.

The Navy, meanwhile, drew up a plan that was faultless in its logic and bold in its conception: If the Japanese invaded, or even looked poised to invade, the Navy would sail away. When the United States built a fleet big enough for a rematch, the Navy would go back and fight.

It was against this background that Quezon had asked MacArthur, "Do you think the Philippines can be defended after they shall have become independent?"

MacArthur answered, "I know they can! The islands can be protected, provided of course that you have the money which will be required." According to Quezon, the money involved was modest; according to MacArthur, he said no such thing.[7]

One thing was certain—the commonwealth could not afford to raise, train and maintain a large standing army. However, when MacArthur looked at the Philippines, he saw something most people could hardly imagine. He saw Switzerland. That small nation had protected its independence over four centuries by arming and training every able-bodied male. The reputation that Swiss soldiers had made in their struggle for independence led their more powerful and aggressive neighbors to conclude that even Swiss militia, fighting in the mountain passes, would make the price of conquest so exorbitant that it just wasn't worth taking Switzerland when there were easier pickings elsewhere.

MacArthur was hoping that he could achieve something similar in the Philippines and left it to Ike and Ord to work out the structure. Neither MacArthur nor his staff ever looked up from wrestling with the intractable details to confront the design principle of their plan and acknowledge that Switzerland was a rich, modern country with a highly educated and technically skilled population. They were trying to create Swiss defenses without the Swiss.

Giving themselves a cable address that was almost like a marriage announcement—telegrams to either one were addressed to JIMIKE, MANILA—they began calculating costs, manpower, training schedules, tables of organization, tables of equipment and so on. They had little choice but to base the Philippine Army on the paramilitary Philippine Constabulary, whose proud motto was "Outnumbered, always—outfought, never." The Philippine Army would comprise a regular force of 920 officers and 7,000 enlisted men. This tiny professional component—the size of two American regiments—would attempt to train up to 40,000 reservists, aged eighteen to twenty-one, each year.

"Jimike" proposed to build up gradually. The first year would go into turning the constabulary into a military force, establishing a network of training sites and building up a corps of trained noncommissioned officers, who would become instructors. Reservists reporting for duty would get five and a half months of training their first year, then return for a six-week refresher course in subsequent years. At the end of ten years, the Philippine Army would boast ten reserve divisions, with the small regular army serving as its spearhead. A military academy at Baguio, a hundred miles north of Manila, and an ROTC unit at the University of the Philippines would provide a small but steady stream of trained officers.[8]

The defense plan was based on some crucial assumptions, such as getting the War Department to sell the Philippines obsolescent rifles at four dollars each. They also expected help with training from the Philippine Department, which commanded the fifteen thousand U.S. Army troops in the archipelago and was completely separate from MacArthur's operation. The War Department proved a grudging source of weapons, however, and charged nine dollars for each rifle, and the commander of the Philippine Department was willing to cooperate, but his own command was so impoverished that he could not offer much.

The worst problem, though, was MacArthur. To sell the plan to Quezon, he kept producing impossibly low figures for what it would cost. He had originally told Eisenhower and Ord to work on the basis of a budget of 22 million pesos a year, which was $11 million. But when they produced a detailed plan, he then told them they couldn't spend more than $8 million a year. Out went the planned artillery corps. Out went trucks. Out went engineering equipment. And when he told them they had to train tens of thousands of reservists the first year and aim to have thirty divisions by 1946 rather than the ten the plan called for, Eisenhower was incredulous and angry.

"We have no officer corps," he protested to the general. "We have no comprehensive supply system." There were only going to be ten training sites available that first year. At its peak, there would be 128, and "each needs water, roads, lights, drainage." They had not even decided where all 128 would be built. MacArthur could not refute Ike's assertions. He fell back instead on seigneurial scorn.[9]

Once again, Eisenhower began keeping a diary. This one was so full and frank that it would be many years before it saw the light of day. It recounted the dramatic story of two highly capable and strong-willed men savaging each other over a project so flawed that it barely merited their attention. Both men were too intelligent not to know the plan would never work, yet each, for his own reasons, found himself helpless to acknowledge that fact openly—not to each other, still less to Quezon. They were situational victims—of the Army, of their own temperaments and ambitions, of American history and the world's mad rush toward World War II. Helplessness could only infuriate them and play its part in turning what by rights were shared anxieties into increasingly bitter trials of intellectual strength and unyielding pride.

They also clashed fiercely over MacArthur's intention of becoming a field marshal in the Philippine Army. To cover himself, MacArthur wanted Ike and Ord to accept rank in it as brigadier generals. Ike was appalled. To be a general in an army that existed mainly on paper was simply absurd. It would not only invite ridicule within the U.S. Army but would compromise their position as a source of independent, objective advice to the commonwealth.[10]

MacArthur's sudden excursion into fantasy land, that wonderful place where divisions could be conjured out of wishes and the cost of defense went down as the number of troops increased, was bizarre. There was a reason for it all the same. The more Quezon learned about the defense plan, the less Don Manuel liked it.

Eisenhower was dismayed at how rarely MacArthur got together with Quezon. It seemed to him only common sense that MacArthur should see the *presidente* at least once a week, but MacArthur loftily maintained that now he was "an elder statesman," he could not report each week to the Malacañan Palace as if he were some kind of subordinate.[11]

When the first batch of reservists reported for training in the summer of 1936, Ike may have had less faith in the plan than almost anyone involved in it and he had lost whatever reservations he once had about telling MacArthur he was wrong. Mamie had recently told her parents that Ike was "under MacArthur's thumb" when in truth he was finally wriggling free.[12]

John Sheldon Doud Eisenhower finished the eighth grade in June 1936, shortly before he reached fourteen. He was a bright, shy, sensitive youth, tall for his age, almost painfully thin. After a year apart from Ike, Mamie was at last willing to travel to Manila, although she still dreaded the idea of living in the tropics again. The year apart had been hard on Ike, too. The bruising clashes with MacArthur only served to make him miss his family more, and however deep his friendship with Jimmy Ord, male friendship is never a complete substitute for the happiness of marriage.

That September Mamie and John arrived at the Manila docks to be reunited with Ike, who stood there in a white linen suit slightly crumpled by the steam heat. To embrace his wife, Ike removed his panama hat, and Mamie shrieked. His head was as shiny and smooth as a ball on a pool table. "Ike! What have you done with your hair?"

He flashed his dazzling grin, a tactic that usually charmed and dis-armed. "It's so hot out here I shave my head whenever I shave my face. Can't be bothered with hair."

"You haven't had much to bother with for some time," Mamie countered wryly.

The Eisenhowers moved into a spacious apartment in the Manila Hotel, with fine views but lacking air-conditioning. Only MacArthur, up in the penthouse, had air-conditioned quarters, a luxury that was wasted on him. He throve on high temperatures and had the heat turned on whenever the thermometer dropped below eighty. Club Eisenhower was soon in business again, and after MacArthur married Jean Faircloth in May 1937, Mamie and Jean became good friends.

John was enrolled at an American school in Baguio, where he turned into a star pupil. He saw his parents mainly during vacations; even then, he did not see much of his father. Ike was nonetheless a lot happier to have his family with him, but the struggle to inject realism into the Philippine defense plan wasn't getting any easier. If anything, the general was becoming more difficult.

When Roosevelt ran for reelection in November 1936, MacArthur wanted desperately to see him beaten—to know what it felt like to be publicly humiliated, to be brutally cast aside by people he had served loyally. So when the *Literary Digest* polled its readers on who they would vote for and they said Governor Alf Landon of Kansas was their man, MacArthur just knew the *Digest* had to be right. Justice was at hand. He told Quezon that Roosevelt was going to be ousted by Landon.

To Ike, this was nonsense. He showed MacArthur some letters from Art Hurd, an old friend in Topeka, who said Landon wouldn't even carry Kansas. "Don't be so damned certain," Ike advised MacArthur, "and don't go out on a limb unnecessarily." He pointed out that the *Literary Digest* was read mainly by people who had nice homes and secure employment despite the Depression. They weren't remotely representative of ordinary Americans. MacArthur got mad at him all over again.

After Roosevelt thrashed Landon—and Landon failed, as Art Hurd had foreseen, even to carry Kansas—the general had to hurry over to the Malacañan Palace to see Quezon and try to restore his credibility as a political soothsayer. He was frightened, too, that somehow word would get back to the White House that he had foreseen, even welcomed, a Roosevelt defeat. In medieval times, foretelling the death of the king was known as misprision of treason and was the path to the scaffold. The world had moved on since then, but openly willing the President's defeat invited retribution.

As if to prove it, in the summer of 1937 Malin Craig informed MacArthur that he would be returning to the United States for reassignment. His foolish support for Landon may have played some part in this decision. More important was the fact that MacArthur had thoroughly alienated Frank Murphy, a New Deal heavyweight who had recently returned to the U.S. after serving as high commissioner of the Philippines. Murphy disliked MacArthur personally and was certain the defense plan would never work.[13]

Craig warned Roosevelt that trying to force MacArthur to come home was the wrong approach. MacArthur, he said, would apply for retirement and remain in Manila as Quezon's military adviser, and would then be free from War Department control. Roosevelt did not take Craig's warning seriously, and MacArthur acted exactly as Craig had anticipated.[14]

Even though Quezon retained MacArthur as his military adviser, that did not mean he was now wholeheartedly behind the effort to create a Philippine Army. Whenever MacArthur tried to talk to him about Philippine defense, Don Manuel talked about Philippine poverty. The thing to do, MacArthur decided, was to put on a demonstration. What patriot could not thrill to the sight of a new army marching through the streets of Manila, forty thousand strong, behind fluttering flags and braying brass, with some snappy saluting and "Eyes right!" for the *presidente*? MacArthur had Ike and Ord start planning for the big parade.

Someone leaked the news to Quezon, and he was shocked. How was his impoverished government going to cover the cost of bringing forty thousand soldiers to Manila, housing and feeding them in the city for up to a week, then transporting them back to their homes, scattered over the far-flung archipelago? He sent for MacArthur and told him this was an idiotic idea and had to be called off immediately. MacArthur coolly agreed with him. Eisenhower and Ord had simply gotten carried away, he explained. He would put a stop to this nonsense.

When Ike heard what had happened, he was outraged. "General, all you are saying is that I'm a liar, and I am not a liar. So I'd like to go back to the United States right away."

MacArthur put an arm around his shoulder. "It's just fun to see that

Dutch temper take over. It's just a misunderstanding, and let's let it go at that."

Some members of MacArthur's staff so idolized the general that they did not mind being used, may even have told themselves it showed how valuable they were to the great man, but Eisenhower would never let MacArthur take him for granted or lie about his actions. He had too strong a sense of his own worth to let it go at that. "Never again," he wrote years later, "were we on the same warm and cordial terms."[15]

In January 1938, Ike checked into the hospital for treatment of one of his many minor ailments, bursitis. Ord stopped by the next morning to say he was flying up to Baguio. Ike had been taking flying lessons from two U.S. Army pilots, William Lee and Hugh Parker, and advised him to get one of them to take him. Ord said no, he thought he'd get one of the Filipino flyers Lee and Parker had been instructing. He was evidently determined to demonstrate his confidence in their students.

That evening, Mamie came to the hospital. She told him that Jimmy was dead. Two days later, Ike wrote to Ord's widow, Emily, to tell her just what had happened. Jimmy had told the pilot to fly low and slow over the home of some friends in Baguio, so he could drop a note to them. The plane stalled and crashed into a tree in the yard. The pilot survived with minor cuts and bruises, but Ord died two hours later from internal bleeding.[16]

The loss of Jimmy Ord was one of the greatest blows of Eisenhower's life. For months thereafter, he sat in his office each morning wanting only to hear the familiar footfall in the corridor, wait for the cheery greeting, "Top of the morning, Comra-a-ade!" then look up and see Jimmy stride into the room. He was isolated and grieving in a place that seemed empty without his friend.[17]

To fill Jimmy's vacancy on the staff, Eisenhower recommended that the general apply for Major Richard K. Sutherland, serving in China with the 15th Infantry Regiment. When Sutherland arrived and took up his duties, Ike was impressed by his ability, energy and intelligence.[18]

Ike was due to return to the U.S. in the fall, but MacArthur urged him to apply for a one-year extension. When John came home for the Easter break, Ike talked it over with his wife and son. Pacing the living room floor, he thought out loud about leaving Manila. "The only reason left for me to stay in this place is the extra money the Philippine government is giving me," he told them. "Other than that, there's not much to keep me here." In his current mood, he could resist any appeal that came from MacArthur, but he liked Quezon. Eisenhower also found it hard to admit failure, and the defense plan as it stood was a mess. So when Don Manuel begged him to apply for an extension, he agreed. He also applied for leave, and MacArthur granted it.[19]

Ike spent four months that summer and fall in the United States. Mamie stayed most of the time in Denver, recuperating from surgery for fibroids. John was in Abilene, with David and Ida. As for Ike, the only part of the trip that could be called a vacation was a week or so at Yellowstone. Otherwise, his energies went into begging equipment from the War Department and looking at airplanes—MacArthur had decided the Philippines needed a 250-plane air force. There was no money for 250 planes, of course. He was also planning to have a flotilla of torpedo boats. There was no money for them, either.[20]

In September, Hitler swallowed peaceful, democratic Czechoslovakia without firing a shot. Britain and France stood aside, feeling too weak militarily to intervene. Eisenhower was disgusted. "Things are so bad right now," he told John, "something, anything, might happen. Maybe this son of a bitch Hitler will get shot."[21]

When Ike returned to Manila, he found that MacArthur had made some changes in his absence. Sutherland had been promoted to lieutenant colonel and MacArthur reorganized the office. He made Sutherland his chief of staff and gave Ike responsibility for plans and training. Sutherland now had Ike's old job, and Ike had Ord's. He felt humiliated.

Outwardly unruffled, he seethed. "I will not give him the satisfaction of showing any resentment," he told his diary, but he was so wounded by the change in his status that he convinced himself MacArthur had done it to force him to leave, which did not make any sense. The more likely explanation is that MacArthur needed a miracle. The defense plan could not be implemented on a budget, over ten years, of $80 million. It was going to cost more than $100 million, and MacArthur knew that Quezon would never pay that much. If Eisenhower were to devote all his efforts to plans and training, however, the flaming pen would be free from routine chief of staff responsibilities—free, that is, to concentrate on making a miracle.[22]

Eisenhower was also convinced that MacArthur had made this change to stop him going to the Malacañan and talking to Quezon. There was a flaw in this reasoning, too. Quezon regularly asked him to stop by, and no one prevented Eisenhower from going. Quezon was a fixer and a lounge lizard, a statesman only in his dreams, but he knew there was something wrong with the defense plan and looked to Eisenhower, not MacArthur, for honest answers. Their relationship was cemented not only in these têtes-à-tête but also over bridge games aboard the *presidente*'s luxurious yacht, the *Cassiano,* whose spar-varnished decks MacArthur never trod. Eisenhower's increasing closeness to Quezon worried and annoyed MacArthur, but he couldn't stop Ike from meeting with Don Manuel, supreme master of the commonwealth's checkbook.

Torn between the *presidente* and the general, however, Ike was in an intolerable position. He was being pushed into being disloyal to one of them—or both—by two men who were no longer on speaking terms. The only thing to do was get out. He would not apply for another extension of his tour of duty. Ike contacted an old friend, Jimmy Ulio, who was now Adjutant General of the Army, and made clear his willingness to depart.

Quezon once again begged him to stay. He told Ike to name his own price—the commonwealth would meet it. MacArthur, too, urged him not to go. Despite their acrimonious disputes, MacArthur knew that Eisenhower stood head and shoulders above the rest of the staff. His efficiency reports on Eisenhower praised him without reservation. MacArthur wrote in one of them, "A brilliant officer . . . in time of war [he] should be promoted to general officer rank immediately."[23]

Eisenhower stood firm and orders were cut for him to report to Fort Lewis, Washington. He'd had enough, and then some, of what he called "the comic opera wars" between the House on the Wall and the Malacañan. There was an Army transport out of Manila four times a year. He, Mamie and John were given passage on the sailing in the fall.

Ike and Mamie began counting the days. Only John was reluctant to leave. He liked the Philippines and had done well in school. This, though, was a good time to leave. The war in Europe that Ike had long expected was now inevitable and at the end of August 1939 Hitler's troops marched into Poland. The evening of September 3, Ike, Mamie and John went downstairs to the apartment of Colonel Howard Smith, an Army doctor with whom Ike occasionally played cards. Smith had a shortwave radio. Crackling over it from half a world away came the funereal tones of Prime Minister Neville Chamberlain announcing, "This country is now at war with Germany."

When they went back upstairs, Ike sat down at the typewriter he had recently acquired after discovering he couldn't read his own diary. He pounded the keys, trying to come to terms with these momentous events. Ike expected that this war would last as long as World War I, but it would be far more devastating. "Hundreds of millions will suffer . . . because one man so wills it. He is one of the criminally insane. . . . Germany will have to be dismembered and destroyed."[24]

Working in the Philippines had been the most bruising time of Ike's life, but it wasn't all bad. In the summer of 1939 he finally achieved something he had longed for since 1916—he became a pilot. Mamie had nipped his aerial ambitions in the bud back then, but in the Philippines he was able to argue—rightly—that transportation was so primitive he needed to be able to fly just to get his job done. He had gotten up early to fly before going to work, and came home in the evening to put a knife between his knees at dinner and pretend it was a joystick.[25]

Bill Lee and Hugh Parker had paced their middle-aged aspirant carefully. It had taken him two and a half years to accumulate 181 hours—about four times as long as a twenty-one-year-old aviation cadet would need to reach the same level of skill—but he could take the test for his private pilot's license with complete confidence. He was thrilled and delighted when he passed, and at the age of forty-eight wrote an autobiographical short story, unpublished until 1998, called "Fledgling at Fifty."[26]

It recorded a near disaster in the air, but there was a subtext, a tale of happiness a mile high in the sky, of escape into the freedom of flight, of soaring away from the demands of MacArthur, the pleas of Quezon and the impossibility of miracles. There in the cockpit of a chrome yellow trainer with a big star on each wing, his huge hands lightly grasping the controls, watching the verdant mountains and fetid jungles of Luzon glide below and behind, Ike had realized at last that haunting cadet dream, of fun in the sun of the exotic Philippines.

12

Star Bright

There was a staff car and a major waiting at the Fort Mason dock for Eisenhower when the Army transport *Cleveland* arrived in San Francisco on January 5, 1940. Once through customs, he was driven to the Presidio to meet Lieutenant General John DeWitt, commander of the Fourth Army. DeWitt said he had altered Ike's orders because he needed his help. Ike responded by telling him he hadn't come home to do more staff work. For the sake of his career, he absolutely had to have an assignment with troops.[1]

Ike says nothing about this episode in his memoirs, but every chief of infantry had the same policy—no one became a general in the infantry without commanding a regiment first. Ike had never expected to be a general in peacetime. Colonel was the most he could hope for, he told Mamie and John. But, "In case of war—no question: I'll be a general." This was a time of war, and although the United States wasn't involved yet, he knew it was only a matter of time. "We're going to fight," he told his old friend Everett Hughes. That being so, the only thing that could stop him getting a star was lack of service with troops.[2]

DeWitt cajoled him—just a temporary job, a month at the most, but he had to have Ike's help because there was an emergency. George Marshall, who was now the Chief of Staff, seemed to think the Army was not only going to get into this new war but unlike the last time, when it simply marched into Europe after getting off ships in the ports of western France, it might have to fight its way ashore, mount a massive invasion. Hitler's tanks were still churning up the beet fields of Poland in September 1939 when Marshall had gotten together with the chief of naval operations, Admiral Harold "Betty" Stark, and got the Navy to agree to ship the 3rd Infantry Division down from Fort Lewis, Washington, so it could make an amphibious assault against a National Guard division that would be dug in at Monterey Bay. This was the kind of thing that would normally take up to a year to plan and organize, but Marshall was in a hurry. His timetable made the logistics of this operation so difficult that the first casualty was the 3rd Division's supply officer, who had a nervous breakdown.

DeWitt could only sympathize. Although he had an army to run, he'd been Pershing's quartermaster expert in World War I and had spent most of the years since then in supply. As a high-level logistics planner, he would have been well aware of Ike's work as a staff officer in Washington in the early 1930s, first for George Van Horn Moseley and then for MacArthur. That awareness probably accounts for his decision to intervene and change Eisenhower's orders as the good ship *Cleveland* steamed toward the Golden Gate.

As a rule, the War Department did not look kindly on field commanders who interfered with assignments once a decision had been made and orders cut. But in this instance DeWitt could, if he had to, defend his decision all the way to the Chief of Staff. The Fourth Army's troops were spread from Southern California to Minnesota. Ike's job was to figure out a way of concentrating both the regulars and the guard units quickly enough to mount Marshall's maneuver. DeWitt's plans and operations officer couldn't figure out how to do it, but Eisenhower did.[3]

Walking along the designated invasion beach at Monterey Bay a couple of days before the 3rd Division arrived, Ike saw coming toward him the bald and bustling figure of DeWitt, who wore rimless spectacles and often had the air of an overexcited clerk. Striding along with DeWitt and towering over him was the slightly gawky, unmilitary figure of George Marshall.

If there was one reason why Army officers—and especially their wives—liked service in the Philippines, it was the availability of inexpensive but attentive servants. So Marshall, who had a much livelier sense of humor than would ever be guessed from his mournful blood-hound features, couldn't resist saying, "Have you learned to tie your own shoes again since coming back, Eisenhower?"

Ike grinned at him. "Yes, sir. I am capable of that chore anyhow."[4]

When the maneuver was mounted, its success was attributed not to Eisenhower, still less to DeWitt, but to the 3rd Division's operations officer, Major Mark Clark, an old acquaintance who had been instrumental in getting Ike assigned to one of the 3rd Division's regiments before DeWitt pulled rank and grabbed him. Clark had graduated from West Point in 1917. Because he stood six feet four, he was assigned to the same cadet company as Eisenhower, the one, that is, with the tallest and most athletic men. Even without that distinction, though, as an exceptionally handsome and half-Jewish cadet, Clark was always going to stand out. Although they had not seen each other for twenty years, the two men had kept in regular contact through a shared interest in first-issue airmail stamps.[5]

Clark had hired local pilots to photograph the Monterey beach defenses, and handed out the photographs to regimental and battalion commanders. It had never been done before. They could see from the photographs where the defenses were strongest and Clark had been even more helpful—he'd marked which routes to take to outflank them. When the 3rd Division hit the beaches, it turned both flanks of the defending National Guard division, completely routing the guardsmen. The aggressive, well-planned attack by the 3rd Division provided an inspiriting start to Marshall's program of maneuvers.[6]

DeWitt reluctantly let Eisenhower go. Instead of returning to Fort Lewis, however, the 3rd Division moved into Camp Ord (named after Jimmy's grandfather, the Civil War hero Major General E.O.C. Ord), on the northern shore of Monterey Bay. Ike joined the division there, to serve as executive officer of the 15th Infantry Regiment and command the regiment's 1st Battalion. He soon made an impression on Major General Walter C. Sweeney, the division commander. Sweeney and members of the division headquarters staff played poker once a week. Clark arranged the poker sessions and one night found he was short a man. He asked Ike if he'd like to sit in. Late that night, Eisenhower had won handsomely from everyone at the table, including the general. As the other players wandered back to their homes, Sweeney accosted Clark. "What do you mean by bringing a ringer into the game?"[7]

While Ike and the division were floundering in a sea of mud produced by torrential winter rains, Mamie decided this was no place for John. He was sent off to Tacoma, Washington, not far from Fort Lewis, to stay with his uncle Edgar, who was practicing law there.[8]

Ike, meanwhile, was commanding 1st Battalion, 15th Infantry in a state of controlled rapture. He was like a starving man falling on food and gorging himself, or a thirsty one gulping rather than drinking. Command at this level was a constant study of human psychology. There was rain and mud day after day during the winter months at Camp Ord, but learning to bear miserable conditions together without becoming miserable human beings is an essential part of infantry life. "I belonged with troops," he wrote some years later. "With them I was always happy."[9]

As winter drew to a close, Ike and Mamie finally got away to Fort Lewis. Mamie wasn't too excited about moving there. She couldn't help thinking about how much she would have preferred to be back in Washington, D.C., instead of Washington state, living in the Wyoming. Fort Lewis was the boondocks, a rough and isolated Army post, all bugle calls and tramp, tramp, tramp of marching feet. Still, the Eisenhowers were assigned a comfortable four-bedroom house and she soon made friends with the other 3rd Division wives.[10]

Whenever Ike was at Fort Lewis and had a Sunday free, he went to Tacoma and played golf with Edgar. The old sibling rivalry proved itself as unyielding as ever, but now it assumed an almost humiliating guise: Edgar regularly shot in the low to mid-70s, while Ike never broke 80. Even so, he couldn't resist playing Ed. There was something faintly masochistic about Ike's refusal to acknowledge his big brother's superiority in a game that he loved, but like most golfers, he believed in miracles. Not that he ever got the benefit of one.

The competition between them was so intractable that it even cast a shadow over John. He was seventeen going on eighteen in the spring of 1940, and it was time for John to start thinking about his future. What would he do; what would he be? Ike had saved ten thousand dollars in the Philippines, but that was peanuts compared to what his brother was worth. If Edgar wasn't a millionaire yet, he was well on his way. He ran one of the most prosperous law firms in the Pacific Northwest. Ed offered to pay for John's education, provided he studied law.

Ike was not going to have his son turned into an Ed clone. That would have been unbearable, the ultimate admission that Ed, in his choice of career, all gray suits and moneymaking, had been right while Ike, in his fancy uniforms and medals and contact with heroes like MacArthur and Pershing, had gone down the wrong road. For years, he had made it clear that he wanted John to go to West Point. He wasn't going to relent now. John, dutiful son that he was, understood, obeyed, probably hoping that cadet gray would bring his father close at last. In the fall of 1940, he sat the competitive exam of Senator Arthur Capper of Kansas, and to Ike's immense delight racked up the highest score among the senator's many hopefuls. John was then sent to Washington, to prepare himself for the West Point entrance exam.[11]

That spring the division returned to California for maneuvers at the Hunter Liggett military reservation, fifty miles south of Monterey. Sweeney made Ike chief umpire and, when the maneuvers ended, placed a letter of commendation in his official file, but Eisenhower would almost certainly have swapped a world of praise for a chance to lead his battalion like an infantry officer ready for war.[12]

The division returned to Fort Lewis for corps-level maneuvers near Centralia that summer. Temperatures broke a hundred degrees during the day but fell to forty after sundown. There was an outbreak of dysentery, poison oak was rife, rattlesnakes slithered into the tents at night and gophers snuggled up to the troops in their foxholes, giving them the mange. Much of the terrain was rugged cut-over land, choked with fallen timbers and stumps. Rugged is considered good for the infantry; on that basis, this exercise was close to ideal.[13]

When the maneuvers ended, a tired but exultant Ike wrote to his old friend Gee Gerow, now serving as Marshall's executive officer. This time, instead of umpiring, he had led his battalion in one attack after another. It was, he said, "a lot of fun. I froze at night, never had, in any one stretch, more than 1¾ hours of sleep, and at times was really fagged out." He was bursting with pride at his battalion's performance. "My youngsters," he told another old friend, Everett Hughes, "kept on going and delivering handsomely after five days of almost no sleep!"[14]

Shortly after this, Ike heard from Georgie Patton, who wrote to say that he expected to get command of an armored brigade. How would Ike like to return to his old love, tanks? "*I think* I could do a good job commanding a regiment," Ike replied enthusiastically.[15]

Patton then wrote back to say he expected to get command of one of the two armored divisions that were about to be created. He wanted

Ike to come and join him as his chief of staff, but if Ike wanted a regiment, he could have one. "No matter how we get together we will go PLACES." He closed with a warrior's wish—"hoping we are together in a long and BLOODY War."[16]

The Army had been starved of money and attention for twenty years. Now it was getting a lot more of both than it could handle without making mistakes. There were waste, inefficiency, public relations disasters. Even so, the groundwork that Ike had helped create for mobilizing the economy was paying off. The War Department placed hundreds of "educational" orders in 1940, small-scale purchases that were not simply designed to procure essential items but were intended to prod companies into learning how to manufacture military materiel to the Army's unique and exacting standards.

The mobilization plan that had been little more than a rough sketch in 1932 had grown from year to year. By 1940 it amounted to a detailed blueprint of America's manufacturing capacity. The Army had a clearer view of industry's innate wartime potential—of who could turn plowshares most effectively into swords—than the National Association of Manufacturers or government economists possessed. The United States had gone to war in 1917 and tried to create an arms industry later. This time, the Army was breaking its back to create an arms industry before any declaration of war.

Congress was not only providing billions for defense, but it also enacted a peacetime draft for the first time. Draftees began to arrive in September 1940, conscripted for one year. They would put flesh on the new divisions the Army was creating. Maneuvers had become the focal point of the training program, but they were suspended that winter. The Army was at full stretch simply processing the draftees, feeding them and building new camps to house them.

Still waiting to hear whether he would get to command one of Patton's regiments, Eisenhower got a frightening cable from Gerow. It began, "I need you in War Plans Division . . ."

He responded with a long, detailed and frank letter. "Your telegram sent me into a tail spin," he began. The chief of infantry had turned down requests from various corps commanders for Ike to serve on their staffs, "on the ground that I needed duty with troops." Not only did he need it, but he enjoyed "the fascinating work of handling soldiers." He told Gee that he had often asked MacArthur to place his requests for troop duty in his official file, but MacArthur had invariably refused to do so.

Having made his point about wanting to remain with troops, Ike more or less resigned himself to being called back to a desk in the War Department. He wanted to know if there was any chance of getting an apartment in the building where Gerow now lived. He concluded, "If war starts, I expect to see you raise the roof to get a command, and *I go along!*"[17]

A few days later, orders arrived giving Eisenhower an unusual status: He was now assigned to the General Staff, but "with troops." In other words, he could remain where he was for the time being, but the long arm of military bureaucracy might reach out without warning and yank him back to a desk in Washington at any moment.

While he continued commanding his battalion, Eisenhower was also reading every report from the British Ministry of Defence that he could get his hands on, the student still, determined to discover just how the German Army had deployed its forces when it invaded Poland, overran the Low Countries, conquered France. What tactics did it use? What was the role of tanks? How did the Germans coordinate air and ground operations, something the U.S. Army hadn't even begun to get right?[18]

On February 17, 1941, he could mark up a year with troops, and shortly after this he was appointed chief of staff of the IX Corps, commanded by Major General Kenyon P. Joyce, a former cavalryman who had commanded the 3rd Division for a while and whose legacy was to infuse the division with some of the traditional horse soldier's panache. Ike himself had made a lasting contribution by getting the band to add the joyous, lively and decidedly unmilitary "Beer Barrel Polka" to its repertoire.

Service with the 3rd Division had given Eisenhower the happiest year he'd had since returning from France in 1929 after revising the battlefield guidebook. For the rest of his military career, he took a close interest in the 3rd, convinced it was the best division in the Army and proud to have served with it.

On March 12, 1941, Ike was promoted to colonel, with date of rank as of March 6. The corps staff, the division staff and his old battalion staff, plus numerous assorted friends and admirers, made a huge fuss. But you watch, some of them said. You'll be a general soon!

He was as sure of that as they were, but Ike wanted to savor the moment. "Damn it!" he complained to John. "As soon as you get a promotion, they start talking about another one. Why can't they let a guy be happy with what he has? They take all the joy out of it."[19]

By June, the Army was preparing for the biggest maneuver in its history. There had been division maneuvers and corps maneuvers, and now that it numbered 1.5 million men, it was ready to have entire armies engage in mock combat. The Second Army, commanded by Lieutenant General Ben Lear, would slug it out with the Third Army, commanded by Lieutenant General Walter Krueger, in Louisiana in September. Krueger went looking for a first-rate chief of staff, and his first choice was Brigadier General William D. Simpson, a rawboned, highly intelligent and aggressive Texan. Simpson turned him down. He was hoping to get command of a division. Krueger's second choice was Eisenhower.

The scale of the maneuver was exciting in itself, but so was the fact that the Third Army had its headquarters at Fort Sam. Mamie moved back to San Antonio gladly, although she was dismayed to find the house they were assigned, on the artillery post, was cramped compared to what she had left behind at Fort Lewis and the street it was on was busy and noisy.[20]

A week or so after arriving at Fort Sam, Ike learned that Mark Clark had been promoted to brigadier general. Having demonstrated his talents during the 1940 maneuvers, Clark had become the right-hand man of Lieutenant General Lesley J. McNair, commander of the Army's General Headquarters. McNair was responsible for training the Army and creating the new divisions. Clark proved to be decisive, imaginative and clever. His friend's first star nevertheless made Ike impatient for a star of his own. The table of organization for a field-army headquarters made the chief-of-staff slot a brigadier general's assignment. Ike and Clark talked on the phone nearly every day about some aspect of training and the forthcoming Louisiana maneuvers. Why haven't I been promoted? Ike regularly wanted to know. "It's in the works," Clark replied just as regularly.[21]

The plan for the maneuvers was that Lear's Second Army would cross the Red River and attack Krueger's Third Army, while the Third Army would move toward the Red River and block the Second Army's advance. The Germans had devastated one opponent after another by using tanks advancing under the cover of dive bombers and fighters to punch holes in their defenses that the infantry could pour through, while the tanks went on to wreak havoc deep in the rear. In a word, blitzkrieg.

McNair and Clark had devised a maneuver to see whether tanks could be stopped by infantry. Lear's army had only 130,000 men it, but they were mainly regulars and they had nearly all the tanks and most of the airplanes. Krueger had 270,000 troops, but they were mostly guardsmen, desperately short of training and in regiments commanded by elderly gents unfit for field soldiering.

When the maneuver opened on September 15, the Third Army did not simply advance as expected but rushed forward, and instead of fighting a defensive battle, Krueger seized the initiative from Lear and attacked. His leading units pinned the Second Army's spearhead units against the Red River. With bottlenecks at the bridges, Lear found it almost impossible to get the bulk of his force into action. Having stopped the Second Army, the Third proceeded to destroy it. After three days, the maneuver ended prematurely, thanks to a bold plan well executed. Another maneuver was hurriedly improvised, but it too was ended quickly by a successful Third Army attack. The point had been made: Resolute troops, properly handled, could stop an armored attack.

The press gave Eisenhower much of the credit for Krueger's success. Important journalists from all over the country had come to cover the maneuvers. They soon learned to like and trust this smiling, approachable colonel who had a gift for explaining, in terms any civilian could grasp, just what was going on in these swamps and bayous. The newshounds had trouble spelling his name right but no trouble at all in presenting him as the attractive face of the transformed United States Army.

They exaggerated Ike's contribution to the Third Army's success, but their grasp of the essentials was more or less right. Krueger was a slow, methodical, cautious commander, as his later career in the Pacific would show. The kind of daring that characterized the Third Army in Louisiana was never Krueger's style. His main contribution was to be found in the details; the boldness was Ike's.[22]

Clark conducted the final critique. These maneuvers had shown up a lot of weakness and faults in commanders, in organization, in training and in equipment, but they had gone a long way toward proving that tanks could be stopped, provided the infantry had plenty of antitank guns. To conclude things, Clark took out a sheet of paper. The following officers, he announced, had just been promoted to brigadier general. He read out the names of more than a dozen colonels. "That's all." Officers got up to leave and the new brigadiers, glowing with pleasure, had their hands shaken, their backs slapped. Suddenly, above the hubbub, Clark's gavel came down hard. *Bang!* Men froze in position and the room fell silent. "I forgot one name," said Clark. "Dwight D. Eisenhower."

Ike was almost out the door and Clark couldn't see him, but he heard the familiar laugh, followed by a cheerful threat—"I'll get you for this, you sonofabitch!"[23]

A star meant a move. There was a leap in magnitude between a colonel's house on the artillery post and a residence fit for a general over on the infantry post at Fort Sam. "We have a house as big as a barn," Ike jubilantly informed his old friend and West Point roommate P. A. Hodgson, urging him to bring his wife for a visit. In the lengthening evenings, when the new general came home from work, he developed a habit of stopping dramatically once inside his front door, casting an admiring eye over the huge hallway and staircase, putting his briefcase down and flinging both arms wide in the gesture of all-embracing delight that would one day be known to half the people in the world. Then he'd shout, "Isn't it wonderful!" and wait for Mamie to appear.[24]

On Sunday, December 7, Eisenhower did what he did most Sundays that hectic fall—he went to the office. The United States had been edging closer to direct involvement in the war. The Navy was tracking German U-boats, attacking them and being attacked in return. British and American officers were holding earnest discussions on how best to defeat Germany and Japan. Roosevelt was using all his enormous powers of persuasion to wear down and chip away at isolationism. Most people now felt as Ike had done when the war began, that American entry was inevitable. The Depression had ended, wiped out by a defense boom that was spreading munitions factories across the land. The Army was not training for an if but for a when—*when* we fight, not *if* we fight.

After wading through a pile of paperwork that morning, Ike grabbed a bite to eat at lunchtime. He felt exhausted. "I'm dead beat," he told a captain and a major who were on duty with him that day. "I'm going to take a nap. Call me if anything happens."

He had just dozed off, stretched out on an Army cot in a back room, when they came in and woke him up. "General," the major announced. "The Japs have just bombed Pearl Harbor."

Ike got up from the cot wide awake, almost serene. "Well, boys, it's come."[25]

13

War Plans

The night of December 11, a weather front unleashed a storm across the Rockies. In the darkness and lashing rain a B-17 carrying Colonel Harvey W. Bundy of the War Plans Division (WPD) crashed into the mountains south of Denver. Bundy was on his way to Hawaii, to ask a thousand questions on behalf of George Marshall, who wanted to know just what part the Army had played that disastrous Sunday at Pearl Harbor. Bundy's sudden death created a vacant slot at WPD. Marshall made a quick decision. He told his executive officer, Colonel Walter Bedell Smith, to call Krueger's Third Army headquarters at Fort Sam.[1]

Eisenhower picked up the phone. "Is that you, Ike?" said Smith.

"Yes."

"The chief says for you to hop on a plane and get up here right away."

Eisenhower felt a sense of dread. The great fear of his life stirred once more, but he calmly told Smith he would be there as soon as possible. He then called the house and told Mamie to have his orderly, Sergeant Mickey McKeogh, pack a small duffel bag. He would pick it up on his way to Randolph Field, the Army Air Forces (AAF) base adjacent to Fort Sam.

"I'll be back in a few days," he assured Mamie. He didn't tell her what he really thought—that it could as easily be a few years as a few days. He had missed out on the last war. Once he got to Washington, there was a danger he'd miss out on this one, too.[2]

A little before noon, Ike clambered aboard a C-47 at Randolph Field clutching his duffel bag. The pilot soon ran into the huge storms now sweeping across north Texas from the Rocky Mountains and made a hurried landing. Meanwhile, Third Army headquarters contacted the Kansas and Texas Railroad to ask that it hold the Blue Bonnet Express, which had pulled out of Dallas a short while before, and pick up a general officer on a top-priority mission to Washington.

Raindrops were bouncing off the tracks like bullets in the early afternoon as the express unexpectedly slowed to a halt in Plano, Texas. Sid Richardson, one of the richest oilmen in the Lone Star state, looked out of his compartment window, puzzled. The train was crowded and nearly everybody aboard was heading for Washington on important win-the-war business. So why the holdup? He stared in bemusement at the rain gusting and billowing like a gray spinnaker while, beyond the muddy streets and huddled buildings of the drab small town, lightning danced an electric waltz across the horizon.

Sid Richardson glanced impatiently at his watch. The train had been halted nearly half an hour, panting in the steam cloud of its own scalding breath. Just then an Army staff car came splashing down Plano's main street throwing out huge sheets of spray before stopping next to the halted train. Eisenhower, still hugging his bag, jumped out and ran to an open carriage door.

The oilman stepped into the doorway of his compartment to get a better look, to see just who this military big shot was that was important enough to make the "Katy" Railroad hold an express in the middle of a war. He heard the conductor telling Ike there wasn't a berth left. "There's not even an upper available," he said apologetically. "I'm terribly sorry, General." Richardson half expected the officer to start throwing his weight around, try impressing the conductor with what an important man he was, but he didn't. Instead, Ike removed his cap, shook the water from it and smiled equably. "Looks like I'll have to sit up."

To his surprise, Richardson found himself saying, "Would you like to share my drawing room, General?" So began a lifelong friendship.[3]

The train pulled into Union Station at seven A.M. on Sunday, December 14, just one week after Pearl Harbor. Milton Eisenhower was waiting to welcome his brother and drove him over to the Munitions Building, on 20th Street, N.W. As Eisenhower walked into the section of the War Department that housed the War Plans Division, a young AAF major named Samuel Anderson came up to him, holding a piece of paper. The word had already gone around that Ike was going to take Bundy's place as chief of the plans group in the WPD and this was a paper that only a few days earlier would have gone to Bundy for his signature. It recommended handing millions of dollars of AAF equipment over to the British even though America was now in the war.

"Would you sign this pleasc, General?"

Ike looked at Anderson, barely glancing at the paper he was holding. "Does it seem right to you?" he asked Anderson.

"Yes, sir. It does."

Eisenhower took the paper, put it on a nearby desk, bent over and signed. He hadn't read it, hadn't even taken his raincoat off, but this major was probably the WPD expert on whatever the paper involved. No time to waste. This was war.[4]

Marshall was waiting for him and gave him the news, all of it bad. The Navy had taken such a clobbering that it wouldn't be able to do anything for months. The Philippines was in danger of going under. The Japanese were attacking across the western Pacific. The U.S. and its allies lacked planes, ships, trained soldiers. The situation was grim, and getting worse by the day, if not by the hour. He concluded, "We have got to do our best in the Pacific and we've got to win this whole war. Now, how are we going to do it?"

Ike was taken aback, but quickly covered his surprise. "Give me a few hours."[5]

His old friend Gee Gerow, the chief of the WPD, provided him with an office and a desk to sit at while he pondered Marshall's question. It was late afternoon and the short winter's day was shading into dusk before he returned to Marshall's office holding several sheets of yellow copy paper on which he had set out his thoughts. At the top of page one Ike had typed, "Steps to Be Taken."

The most important step, he told Marshall, was to secure the sea and air routes to Australia. In time, Australia would become the base from which the Allies could fight back. For the present, it could be used to funnel reinforcements into the Philippines. Ike said he did not expect the archipelago to withstand the Japanese onslaught, but the United

States had a duty to the people of the Philippines not to abandon them. Besides, Allied nations, such as China and the Netherlands, were watching closely. The U.S. had to show that it would not cut and run, whatever the odds. "I agree with you," said Marshall. "Do what you can to save them."

The Chief of Staff then leaned toward him across the large, highly polished desk, and as Eisenhower looked into Marshall's pale blue eyes, he had an impression of coldness and distance. He was looking into an inner world, one with a crystalline atmosphere that allowed high intelligence to operate free of emotion. There was also, in Marshall's words, an echo from the aerie of command at this level, a hint of isolation. "Eisenhower, this department is filled with able men who analyze their problems well but always feel compelled to bring them to me for final solution. I must have assistants who will solve their own problems and tell me later what they have done." Ike went back to his office slightly disconcerted. There was such remoteness about the man that Marshall seemed almost unfathomable.[6]

Eisenhower moved into his brother Milton's spacious home in Falls Church, Virginia, and soon came to regret it. He got the benefit of his brother's company for only a few minutes each morning, yet it took half an hour to get to the War Department from Falls Church and another thirty minutes to get home each night. He did not have an hour a day to waste on commuting. In early February, however, Mamie came to Washington and they took an apartment in the Wardman Park Hotel, near the War Department.[7]

Shortly after this, Gerow left the WPD. He had been a superb peacetime planner, but with the responsibilities of war, the job became too big. It crushed the confidence out of him. Ike told him, "Gee, you have got to quit bothering the chief with this stuff."

"I can't help it, Ike. These decisions are too important. He's got to make them himself," Gerow replied. It was bitterly ironic that having reached his level of incompetence, Gerow now moved on to command the 29th Infantry Division—a ticket straight into battle. "I really envy him," groaned Ike.[8]

He took over from Gerow as chief of the War Plans Division and his days became more hectic than ever. Eisenhower went to work before the sun rose, left long after it set. Lunch consisted of a hotdog washed down with a glass of milk. "I am fast becoming an appendage to my desk," he informed an old friend, "and I don't like it."[9]

Once again, as at other stressful periods, he began keeping a diary. It may seem surprising that a man so tired and busy would even find time to keep a diary, but the fact that he kept one was both a symptom of that stress and a way of dealing with it. Eisenhower never kept a diary when he was happy.

On March 10, his father died. Ike was stricken with guilt that he could not go back to Abilene and comfort his mother. He didn't really have time to grieve. Two days later, his father was buried. He closed his office door and gave orders that he wasn't to be disturbed for half an hour. In that time, Ike focused his thoughts on the life and character of David Jacob Eisenhower, dead at the age of seventy-nine. A surging tide of emotion brought a sudden sense of profound and tender love, but this overflowing heart was, in truth, for someone who existed only in his dreams—a father who was strong and just, an intellectual and scholar, a figure of exemplary integrity, someone known and admired across the state of Kansas. The stern, remote small-town failure went out of life and into the blinding mists of filial grief. More than anything, though, Ike felt a wrenching regret that he and his father had never been close, that the happiness and friendship he yearned for had never arisen between them, and he blamed himself for that irrecoverable loss.[10]

To a later age, the exaltation of his father in death, a father with whom he chose to have almost no contact after leaving home thirty years before, must look like an obvious example of emotional denial and self-deception. And yet, to Ike and his contemporaries, his attitude would have seemed stoic and Roman. *De mortuis, nil nisi bonum*—"Of the dead, speak nothing but good." Emotionally and physically exhausted, Ike opened his office door and continued doing his best at a job he would joyfully have shunned.

He remained determined to live up to his belief that in his life, duty would always rule over wishes, a belief that Marshall would soon test to the limits. On March 20, when Eisenhower was sitting next to the Chief of Staff's desk dealing with various important matters, they got into a discussion on promotion policy in the rapidly expanding Army.

As Ike already knew, the Chief of Staff had served in France in World War I and never rose higher than colonel despite Pershing's repeated efforts to get him promoted to a star. What rankled wasn't so much missing out on that star as the knowledge that paper-shufflers back home had become generals without ever hearing a shot fired in anger. "In this war," said Marshall, "the commanders are going to be promoted and not the staff officers." To illustrate his point, he added, "General Krueger said you should have a corps command. But you are not going to get any promotion. You are going to stay right here on this job and you'll probably never move. While this may seem a sacrifice to you, that's the way it must be."

Eisenhower's face turned red. He had tried for years to control his temper, but this was too much. The general almost surely realized that he was blasting and burning Ike's picture of himself as an infantry officer, a man of courage and spirit, a leader of men. Marshall's brutally casual declaration made the old terror flare up, but now it had such a definite shape that it was almost palpable—he wouldn't get a division, wouldn't command a corps, would never lead men in battle. The role he had prepared himself for, dreamed of since Camp Colt, shriveled as if dead. The swath he had vowed to cut petered out in a trail of dusty ashes. All those sacrifices of money, of energy, of status, of hope had been for what—a typewriter, an in tray and a Dictaphone?

"General, I'm interested in what you say, but I want you to know that I don't give a damn about your promotion plans as far as I'm concerned!" Ike responded fiercely. "I came into this office from the field and I am trying to do my duty. If that locks me to a desk for the rest of the war . . . so be it!" Raging inwardly, he got up quickly before he said anything he might regret and headed for the door, obviously stricken. Marshall said nothing, but as Eisenhower half turned to close the door behind him, he glimpsed a vellicative movement at the corners of Marshall's thin-lipped mouth—the hint of a shadow of a smile. Satisfaction, perhaps, at touching the core of Ike's being.[11]

Back in his own office, he was angrier than he had felt since those epic rows with MacArthur back in Manila. Taking his diary, Ike wrote an incandescent page of protest, a bitter outburst against Marshall and the Army, read it, then tore it up. The next day, a Saturday, he made a quick visit to West Point to spend a few hours with John. He told his son—more or less apologizing for it—that it looked as if he'd spend the whole war in Washington and never rise higher than a single star. John, a lowly plebe, was bemused. Being a brigadier general and a member of the inner circle of men who would make the big decisions in the war . . . wasn't that success?[12]

Several days later, a copy of a memo from Marshall to Roosevelt crossed Ike's desk. It recommended Eisenhower for promotion to major general.

* * * * *

General Henry H. "Hap" Arnold knew his limits. At times he seemed the living proof of the Army's conviction that the airmen were a slovenly, undisciplined bunch. Arnold ran the Army Air Forces with his blouse unbuttoned, his head lost in cigarette smoke and his right foot buried in the bottom drawer of his desk. Yet he was, in truth, both an exceptionally able man and a modest one.

With American entry into the war, the world became a much more complicated place. He would have to go to meetings with Marshall and Admiral King and the British chiefs and they would talk strategy. The British had a huge empire that they claimed the sun never set on, and they knew their way around the globe, as did the Navy. But Arnold was likely to get flummoxed when the British and the sailors started talking in that irritatingly knowledgeable way they had about faraway places with outlandish names. That would only embarrass him, Marshall and the Army Air Forces.

So for an hour or two every Sunday morning during the first few months after Pearl Harbor, Hap Arnold went to his office and spun a huge globe this way and that, peering at it closely through his reading glasses, memorizing the names of towns and seas, mountains and lakes, and calculating the distances between them. When Ike heard about what Hap was doing, he joined him. He needed that grounding, too.[13]

At Christmas 1941, Churchill and his military chiefs arrived in Washington and stayed for nearly three weeks talking strategy. Eisenhower was a peripheral figure at these discussions, known as the Arcadia Conference, a name out of Greek mythology, redolent of harmony and happiness. The two nations endorsed the tentative agreement they had reached during informal discussions the previous fall—that they would wage a strategic defensive in the Pacific, which would free them to concentrate on defeating Germany first. Obvious as the wisdom of this strategy was to Army and AAF planners, it would nevertheless have to be sold to the Congress, to the Navy and to the people.[14]

Tall and bald Admiral Ernest J. King, the hard-bitten, hard-driving chief of naval operations, had no intention of remaining on the defensive until German defeat. The Capitol dome, meanwhile, reverberated with demands for revenge against Japanese "treachery." Ordinary Americans, too, were filled with an anger against Japan that they simply did not have against Germany. And day by day, the situation in the Philippines grew increasingly grim. As it did so, MacArthur's stature as the nation's hero, the one ray of defiant hope on a canvas black with defeat, cast a shadow that stretched from malodorous Malinta Tunnel on Corregidor to the oak desk made from warship timbers where Roosevelt sat in the Oval Office, surrounded by charming naval prints.

During those early months, the U.S. and its allies tried to stem the onrushing Japanese by creating an American, British, Dutch and Australian command—ABDA—that pooled its meager military resources and tried, in vain, to hold the Malay Barrier; the two thousand miles of territory (mostly islands) that stretched from Singapore to Papua New Guinea.

Most of Eisenhower's efforts were devoted not to ABDA, however, but to the Philippines. His knowledge of its defenses and terrain were useful, but above all there was his knowledge of MacArthur. It has often been stated that this was why he was brought in to the WPD after Pearl Harbor, but Gerow had him earmarked for a WPD slot long before that, as had Marshall. The other myth is that Mark Clark was the one who had brought Ike to Marshall's notice and urged his assignment to the WPD, but this idea was spread by Clark, prompted by his gigantesque view of the Clark role in History.[15]

At Christmas, MacArthur's forces pulled back into the Bataan Peninsula and MacArthur moved his headquarters to the small island of Corregidor in Manila Bay. Over ensuing months, Eisenhower tried to push the Navy into running the Japanese blockade of the Philippines with submarines loaded with food, ammo and medical supplies. The Navy ran in a few boats, but not enough to make any difference. Ike flew $10 million in cash out to Australia to hire seamen willing to try sneaking through the blockade in merchant vessels. Only three ships got through, and not one made a second voyage.[16]

MacArthur sent long, hectoring messages to Marshall demanding every man, ship and plane be devoted to the western Pacific. Ike drafted most of the replies, his patience worn as thin as the copy paper he typed on. MacArthur, he told his diary, was "as big a baby as ever . . . is losing his nerve . . . he's jittery." And when MacArthur designated Sutherland as his successor "in the event of my death," Eisenhower's contempt was withering: "He still likes his boot lickers."[17]

Marshall and Roosevelt decided to bring MacArthur out of the

Philippines rather than risk having him fall into enemy hands. Eisenhower privately disagreed with them. MacArthur had played out on the screen of his own imagination how it should end—in the Tunnel, face to the enemy, Colt .45 in hand, dying with his face to the foe, his bullets expended. Eisenhower was thinking along the same lines, as if some telepathic connection joined them still. And there was a lot to be said for it, provided MacArthur did die a hero's death and didn't end up as a propaganda pawn in the hands of the Japanese. Lacking any assurance of that, the only thing to do was to order him to leave.[18]

Eisenhower's fulminations against MacArthur expressed frustrations that went back a long way, to arguments unfinished, anger unappeased, resentments long suppressed. Even so, these days he was lashing out in every direction. He excoriated the British for refusing to call on the fighting power of the Chinese Army to save Burma—not that Ike had a clue about the Chinese Army's military capabilities, which were close to zero. He damned his colleagues in the War Department for being great talkers and poor "doers." He tore into the Navy—"One thing that would help us win this war is to get someone to shoot King." He berated the AAF for lacking "men that will do things." He poured scorn on his fellow citizens for seeming to think America could "buy victory." Wherever he looked, he saw ineptitude and inertia.

There is a slightly hysterical note to many of Ike's diary entries in the first four months he was back in the War Department. As often as not, the planning papers he worked on were marked by intellectual confusion and dubious assumptions. Sometimes the Far East was critical, and sometimes it wasn't. Eisenhower scoffed at British efforts to secure the Middle East and thought they ought to abandon Libya. After they destroyed the Italian army that was defending Libya, he began preaching the crucial importance of the Middle East. Holding Australia was essential, he argued, then began worrying about deploying major resources there. He failed to see that once they captured the Philippines, the Japanese would continue pushing south. He was slow to accept that the first priority in Allied strategy had to be keeping the Soviet Union fighting. He ridiculed efforts to build up forces in the United Kingdom for an eventual invasion of France and pinned absurdly great hopes on the striking power of American bombers. Ike wanted the U.S. to pressure the Soviets into providing air bases for attacks on Japan, ignoring the fact that Stalin would do almost anything to avoid provoking the

Japanese, who had two field armies in Manchuria. The Soviets had a big enough war just fighting Hitler.

It was inevitable, though, that there would be little consistency or clarity to Ike's ideas on strategy before the end of March 1942, when the campaign in the Philippines moved toward its grim conclusion. It was asking too much of the War Department to expect it to function in a completely rational and sensible way so long as Bataan and Corregidor distracted attention from "Germany First." It was especially hard on Ike. Old Army friends and acquaintances, people he had known for many years, were facing violent death or mutilating wounds. The best they might hope for was prolonged captivity, with every prospect of torture. He felt close to despair. "For many weeks—it seems years—I've been searching everywhere to find any feasible way of giving more help to the Philippine Islands. . . . I'll go on trying, but daily the situation grows more desperate," he wrote on March 31.[19]

This, however, was more an expression of guilt at failure as the heartbreaking end came in sight than any kind of pledge for the future. With MacArthur safe in Australia and the endgame reached on Bataan and Corregidor, Ike was at last free to devote all his energies to Germany First.

Black Jack Pershing, bracing himself even in old age like a West Point cadet, was convinced he had always been the most obedient, most loyal of soldiers, ever mindful of his superiors, punctilious in the fulfillment of any order. All the same, when he was in France commanding the AEF, he found it impossible to admit that the Chief of Staff back in Washington, Peyton D. March, was his superior. He loathed Peyton D. March and manufactured casuistic arguments to support his claim to be free to fight the war any way he chose and to hell with the Chief of Staff.[20]

Marshall had served in Pershing's headquarters and seen how a field commander had successfully defied the authority of the Chief of Staff, flouting both the law and Army regulations. That wasn't going to happen again.

The problem did not really begin with Pershing. He had added immensely to the burden of being Chief of Staff, but even before World

War I, the chiefs of the combat arms—infantry, artillery, cavalry and coast artillery—had been able to limit the Chief's control over them. There were other powerful figures, too—the Adjutant General and the Quartermaster General—who ran what amounted to independent fiefdoms. When Marshall became Chief of Staff in 1939, he found that whenever he wanted to do anything important, he had to seek the concurrence of the heads of all those arms and branches that might be affected by his action. Any one of them could stop him by filing a nonconcurrence.

This was the system Marshall inherited and had to get rid of if he was to have any chance of solving the Pershing problem. He was careful not to say anything about Pershing, however, as he set about his task. Black Jack, his longtime mentor, a man he loved and admired, was still alive, still alert. Instead, Marshall dwelt on the obvious fact that following Pearl Harbor he was overwhelmed by demands from the twenty-seven heads of the various arms and branches, asserting their right to see him at any time even though he now had a war to fight.

The shockwave rippling through Washington in the aftermath of Pearl Harbor gave him his chance and Marshall seized it. Two of the combat arms chiefs were retired and the other two were reassigned. In this vacuum, the Army was reorganized on March 9, 1942, into three major commands—Army Ground Forces, Army Air Forces, and the Service of Supply. The system of concurrences was abolished. The General Headquarters, which supervised training, was swept away. The number of people who had direct access to Marshall was reduced to a handful. The key move was the abolition of the War Plans Division—ironically, the one part of the department he completely controlled. In its place arose a much larger entity, numbering more than a hundred officers, the Operations Division—or OPD—under Eisenhower.[21]

The world was going to be divided into theaters of operations, each of which would be in constant communication with the OPD. The relevant theater officers in Washington represented to Marshall the needs and views of that theater's commander, and transmitted in turn Marshall's orders and advice to them. Marshall told them, "You gentlemen are not my staff officers. You are the representatives of those theater commanders and you'd better satisfy *them*."[22]

It would be the summer of 1942 before this system was operating smoothly. Once it did, the Chief of Staff would control the entire Army, safe from having his authority challenged by a strong-willed commander in the field.

Eisenhower had comparatively little to do with the reorganization of the War Department, but he played a crucial role in establishing the working methods of the OPD. He would not allow anyone to reject a proposed line of action by saying it wouldn't work. An officer could put his negative on a proposal only if he offered a solution to the problem he claimed to have identified. And as if there wasn't enough pressure on OPD officers already, he introduced a top-priority system—"the Green Hornet." Anything important enough to go to Marshall went in a green folder. On the cover was the name of the action officer designated to deal with whatever was in that folder. Marshall received a copy, every section of OPD that was affected by the folder got a copy and the action officer got twenty-four hours to come up with an answer. He could not even leave the building until he produced a reply to the Green Hornet and drew its sting.[23]

The OPD was Marshall's command post, allowing him to direct American armies in combat. It was, in effect, the equivalent of a field headquarters. Its paradigm was Pershing's AEF headquarters in France. Now, though, the field of battle encompassed the entire globe, and Washington was the rear area. The atmosphere in which Eisenhower and the OPD staff worked had much of the tension, the drama, the electricity of a field headquarters just beyond the sound of the guns. Pershing problem solved.[24]

Even before the OPD was up and running, Ike had one of his assistants, Colonel John E. Hull, at work on a project he had described to Marshall as "a definite plan for operations against Northwest Europe." Shortly after the OPD was established, Hull showed him what he had come up with—a projected invasion of the Continent. Hull said he calculated that there would be enough shipping to deploy thirty divisions and fifty-eight hundred combat aircraft to the United Kingdom by the spring of 1943. This force, combined with the striking power of the RAF and up to eighteen British divisions, would be able to land on the French coast about May 1. The American buildup might even progress rapidly enough, Hull argued, to seize a beachhead in northern France in late

1942 and hold it through the winter. The beachhead would then become the springboard for a breakout in 1943. Ike decided Hull's plan was worth showing to Marshall.[25]

Hull explained the plan to the Chief of Staff, who accepted it with only minor changes. Once these refinements had been worked in, Marshall managed to sell it to a reluctant Roosevelt, who told him to take it to London, show it to the British and win their approval. Marshall set off on April 7, accompanied by the President's closest adviser, Harry Hopkins.

The proposed invasion of France in May 1943 was code-named Roundup; the subsidiary operation, a landing to seize a bridgehead in the fall, was called Sledgehammer. Marshall presented Sledgehammer as an emergency operation to be mounted if Soviet resistance threatened to collapse. Alternatively, the Germans might be so heavily engaged on the eastern front by the fall that France would be open to an attack, making it possible to grab and hold a beachhead. Either way, Marshall said, the Allies had to be ready to act.

Many American officers had been irritated by the British officers they met in the early months of 1942. They criticized them for what they saw as arrogance in dealing with Americans and timidity in dealing with the Germans. The War Department was half convinced the British had no intention of ever attacking the Continent, overlooking the fact that long before Pearl Harbor, the British had been designing landing ships and landing craft for an eventual invasion and tried, unsuccessfully, to get the United States to build them under Lend Lease.

What the British were hoping for was that Germany and the Soviets would bleed each other white. Only when that happened would any landing in France be likely to lead to the defeat of the Germans. Until then, they were satisfied to concentrate their military power on fighting the Germans and Japanese for control of strategic objectives such as Gibraltar, the Suez Canal and India, doing all they could to keep the Soviets fighting and fighting on the periphery of German-held territory.

No doubt aware of American complaints about British haughtiness and inertia, the British strove to appear cooperative and positive as Marshall presented Roundup and Sledgehammer. They committed themselves in principle to an invasion in 1943, but Marshall noticed the lack of enthusiasm, the numerous reservations, some stated openly, others to be read between the lines. As for grabbing a beachhead, the British were appalled. It seemed suicidal to make any landing in 1942. They expressed their complete rejection of Sledgehammer to one another and to their diaries, however, not to Marshall.[26]

While Marshall was in London, Ike was working on a plan for deploying the airplanes, men and supplies needed for an invasion of France. This deployment was code-named Bolero, from the composition by Ravel—the simple theme, the relentless build-up, the crashing finale, seemed artistically, maybe inspiringly, appropriate. Hardly had Marshall returned from London, though, before messages about Bolero flashing between the OPD and the American headquarters in London produced discordant notes and dying falls. "Either we do not understand our own commanding general [James E. Chaney, an AAF major general] and his staff in England or they don't understand us," Ike concluded. Marshall told him to go to London and find out what changes were needed there.[27]

On May 23, Eisenhower departed, accompanied by Clark, whom he always called Wayne. If Ike was the War Department's number-one planner, Clark qualified as its most outstanding trainer of troops. He had masterminded a simple and effective system for creating new divisions. Many of them would have to complete their training in Britain before fighting their way into France.

Ike was dismayed and angry when he visited Chaney's headquarters. The general and his staff were, he decided, "completely at a loss" as to just what they ought to be doing. While no doubt true, this wasn't entirely Chaney's fault.[28]

The headquarters in London had been established before Pearl Harbor in 1941 as the U.S. Special Observer Group. Its role was to report back to Washington on how the British were fighting the war so that lessons could be learned back home, and to ensure cooperation with the British Army. A month after Pearl Harbor, an American division was moved to Northern Ireland. With the arrival of American troops, Chaney's headquarters became USAFBI, or U.S. Army Forces, British Isles.[29]

Even after the War Department reorganization of March 1942, no one told Chaney and his staff to start operating like a theater headquarters engaged in a race against time to get ready for an invasion of France in May 1943. As far as Chaney was aware, there was no rapid build-up in the pipeline. The British, too, had no idea that Chaney's headquarters had been transformed. One of the questions they put to Ike was, Where is the American headquarters that is preparing for Roundup? So it wasn't surprising that Chaney's staff continued as before, coming to work in civilian clothes and taking off on the weekends.

While Chaney was a great disappointment to Eisenhower, he was thrilled to meet Winston Churchill, and pleased to meet Sir Alan Brooke, the Chief of the Imperial General Staff. He and Brooke talked at length about command arrangements for Roundup. Brooke wanted a supreme commander to be named for the operation, and soon. At that point, it would almost certainly have been a British officer. Ike balked at that, arguing there was no need yet to name anyone. They also sparred, gently, over which type of organization should be employed—the British, which allowed widespread consultation and discussion, or the American, which put nearly everything in the hands of one man and his immediate staff.[30]

Eisenhower went to watch a major training exercise directed by the British Army's most renowned trainer of troops, General Bernard Law Montgomery. He liked Montgomery's vigorous, energetic style and evident self-confidence. The person who made the biggest impression, however, was Lord Louis Mountbatten, the youthful commander of Combined Operations headquarters.

Mountbatten was only thirty-eight, handsome in the approved equine style of the British aristocracy, related to the royal family and irresistibly charming. He had spent twenty years in the Royal Navy and possessed a pugnacious streak that seemed to make him ache for a scrap. Lord Louis was also frank and open-minded and seemed to adore Americans. They tended to adore him right back.

His command was new and untested, but Mountbatten had been among the first people on either side of the Atlantic to push for the development of landing ships and landing craft. Combined Operations' mission was to develop the doctrine and techniques for getting men and equipment onto landing ships and landing craft and decanting them, ready to fight, onto a hostile shore.

Eisenhower returned to the United States with two recommendations for Marshall. The first was that Major General Joseph T. McNarney should replace Chaney. McNarney was someone Ike had known for thirty years; they had graduated together from West Point. During World War I, McNarney had been an infantry officer in France, but in the 1920s he switched to the Air Corps and became a pilot. Later, he proved to be a talented military administrator and had overseen the War Department reorganization in March 1942. Ike's second recommendation was that a corps headquarters be established for the American combat units that would spearhead the U.S. role in Roundup. He urged Marshall to give this command to "Wayne" Clark. Marshall was amused by this, because shortly afterward, Clark came to him to recommend Eisenhower for the same assignment. One of Marshall's rare, wintry smiles blossomed. "It looks to me as if you boys got together on this."[31]

On June 8, Ike gave Marshall the draft of a proposal to create a European Theater of Operations in London and asked him to take a good look at it. "I certainly do want to read it," said Marshall. "You may be the man who executes it. If that's the case, when can you leave?"[32] Marshall had just made McNarney his deputy chief of staff, and intended to keep him where he was.

Three days later, Marshall told Eisenhower that he would be the theater commander in Europe. Clark would get command of the ground-force troops in England, under a new combat headquarters, II Corps.

Shortly after this meeting, the new West Point superintendent, Major General Francis B. Wilby, encountered Ike coming down the stairs in the Munitions Building and thought he seemed strangely somber. No grin, not even the usual smile. "How are things, Ike?"

"Brother," Eisenhower replied. "What do you think they've done to me now?" He shook his head as if in a daze. "They're sending me over there to command the whole shebang!"[33]

Wilby granted John a weekend leave so he could see his father before Ike left for Europe. Father and son felt a strong, rare bond as they said farewell, but Mamie's mood was grim. A Signal Corps photographer snapped them on the large screened porch of Quarters No. 7 at Fort Myer. Ike looks serious and confident. The drama of the picture is provided by Mamie, who sits on a rattan couch and glares at the camera—a woman as angry as she is helpless.[34]

On Monday morning, June 23, the sky over Washington was black with thunderstorms. Ike and Mamie said their farewells at home; she couldn't bear to go out to Bolling Field and watch him depart. When Ike arrived at Bolling, Clark was embracing his wife, Maurine. Ike said good-bye to Maurine Clark, then he and Wayne headed for the C-54 that would take them across the Atlantic. Clark climbed the steps to the open door of the airplane. Ike, following behind, watched Maurine walk away, her body language a tale of sorrow. He suddenly ran after her, caught her in his arms and kissed her fondly on the cheek. "Don't worry about Wayne. I'll take good care of him." Then he hurried away through the rain.[35]

Change of Plan

They had been waiting a long time for him; nearly three years, in fact. The British never expected to destroy Nazi Germany on their own. It would take the mightiest coalition in history to do that. But there were two related thoughts that sustained them through the darkest times: Hitler would never defeat them, and the United States could not stay out of the war indefinitely. One day, an American general would arrive as an avatar in khaki, brass buttons and a rainbow smear of medal ribbons, the manifest form of the assurance of victory, with all the power of America at his back, and the forces of democracy would then possess the amassed strength that would save the world.

Ike also brought something else with him, something more prosaic but almost as welcome—a crate of fresh fruit. The British, he knew from his earlier visit, not only craved the downfall of Hitler but yearned, too, for oranges, bananas and grapes, which had been unobtainable almost since the war began. Bearing these gifts, he landed in Britain on June 24, to intense, openly expressed curiosity and an understood but understated sense of relief.[1]

Ike moved into a suite at Claridge's, the most fashionable hotel in London, with his naval aide and longtime friend Harry C. Butcher, a lieutenant commander in the Navy Reserve. When they had first met,

Butcher was editor of *The Fertilizer Review;* he had since risen to a vice-presidency at CBS.

Ike had also brought to London another old friend, Thomas Jefferson Davis. Once Ike's strongest supporter in many a fierce argument with MacArthur, Davis was now Ike's adjutant general.

Eisenhower felt uneasy in the luxurious, upper-crust atmosphere of Claridge's, a place where anything that doesn't move is likely to be gilded and anything that does is likely to carry an aroma of snobbery. "I feel like I'm living in sin," he told Butcher. Eisenhower's chief of staff, Brigadier General Charles Bolté, gave him another good reason to move. "Claridge's is like a hunk of sugar," said Bolté. "One bomb and the whole building will dissolve." He urged him to come and live where he did, in the Dorchester, which was built of concrete and steel. The Dorchester also had a more modern, almost American, atmosphere. Two weeks after his arrival, Ike moved with something like a sigh of relief. The Dorchester faced Hyde Park and was only a brisk five-block walk to his ETO headquarters at 20 Grosvenor Square.[2]

As the word spread that he was in London, invitations flooded in—to speak, to receive awards, to be feted and toasted, to open this or inaugurate that. He turned nearly all of them down, including a dinner hosted by the lord mayor of London. He also rejected, to Butcher's dismay, a chance to meet George Bernard Shaw. "To hell with it," said Ike. "I've got work to do!"[3]

Almost from the moment he arrived, Ike missed Mamie intensely. He wrote to her three or four times a week. He apologized for not being able to tell her anything specific about what he was doing but tried to give her a rough idea: "In a place like this, the Commanding General must be a bit of a diplomat—lawyer—promoter—salesman—social hound—*liar* (at least to get out of social affairs)—mountebank, actor—Simon Legree—humanitarian—orator and incidentally (sometimes I think most damnably incidentally) a soldier!" The main thing in his letters to Mamie wasn't what little news they contained but the constant reassurance that he was all right; that, and the warrior's eternal plea: "Lots of love—don't forget me."[4]

He also agonized over keeping in touch with John. "He's on my mind all the time," Ike told Mamie. Before he left for London, Ike had told John how much it would mean to him to get a letter, however brief, once a week, but like most young men his age, John was shy and self-

conscious when it came to correspondence. After he had been in England six weeks and received nothing but a short note from his son, Ike
became exasperated and couldn't help comparing his own upbringing
with Johnny's: "Sometimes I worry that he may be just a bit spoiled. . . .
Things have been easy for him. . . . After all—suppose he'd have had to
start at 13 or 14 getting up at 4 or 5 in the morning working through a
hot summer day to 9:00 at night—day after day—or doing his winter
work with cold chapped hands and not even gloves—maybe he'd think
writing a letter wasn't so terribly difficult!"[5]

It almost never occurred to Eisenhower that he might be responsible for the emotional distance between them. He was doubtless handi-
capped by the daunting self-control essential to any military career.
More important, though, was the distant, emotionally stiff relationship
with his own father. Ike frequently wrote to old friends and sent them
his love or told them just how much they meant to him. No matter how
far he traveled or how long they were parted, he did not do that with his
own son.

Even after he had shunned all but a minimal effort on what he called
"the Social Front," Eisenhower found the city too crowded, too noisy.
Besides, the headquarters at 20 Grosvenor Street was in a building that
the Navy owned, not the Army. He told Bolté he wanted to move out of
the city—about fifty miles away, preferably. Bolté said that was impossible. He had to be within easy reach of the Ministry of Defence, the Air
Ministry, Downing Street and so on. As for fifty miles, "You can't even
drive at 20 miles an hour in the blackout," Bolté warned him.[6]

Despite this, his determination to get away from Grosvenor Square
grew stronger. It was terrible to withstand the incessant demands imposed on him by two governments and make life-or-death decisions all
day and then have nothing but a hotel to go home to at night. "I want to
get the hell out of London," he told Butcher. The British generals and
politicians he was dealing with nearly all had a place in the country to
retreat to on the weekends where they could relax. Why shouldn't he do
the same?

Butcher found the ideal place: a two-story, five-bedroom house
called Telegraph Cottage built in mock-Tudor style. It was in the heart
of London's stockbroker belt, near Kingston on Thames, a forty-minute
drive from Grosvenor Square. Telegraph Cottage was set back from the
main road at the end of a long driveway, had a large garden at the front

and ten acres of woodland at the back. Best of all, perhaps, it was adjacent to a golf course.

At first, Ike spent only weekends at Telegraph Cottage, but by the fall he was there for half the week. In London, up to twenty people a day came to see him. Between visitors, he wrestled with mountains of plans and correspondence and there were dozens of telephone calls. At the cottage, he could play a few rounds of golf with Butcher, weather permitting, and think. Or stroll around in his wood, and think. Or plant a vegetable garden, and think.

Telegraph Cottage soon had something like a family atmosphere. Ike, Butcher, Ike's Army aide Major "Tex" Lee, his stenographer, Warrant Officer Walter Marshall, and his orderly, Sergeant Mickey McKeogh, shared the house. Ike's secretaries and female drivers were billeted with families living nearby, but they came to the cottage most evenings when he was in residence to watch a movie, play cards or simply chat.

There was only one thing missing, Ike decided. He asked Lee one day if Army regulations prevented him from having a pet. Lee said he wasn't aware of one. A few days later, Ike called Butcher into his office and told him, "I'm going to get a dog." He already had the ETO Service of Supply looking for one, preferably a Scottie. Butcher tried to persuade him to embrace a more exotic breed, but Eisenhower's mind was made up. "I like the independent attitude of a strutting Scottie." A week later, he had his dog, a black bundle of fur that he named Telek. It sounded like a cable address for Telegraph Cottage, but it amused him to tell curious journalists that the dog's strange name was "a military secret."[7]

From the moment Eisenhower arrived, the British were more than eager to learn all they could about this American general come to command the European Theater of Operations, the main theater of war. So, too, were many millions of Americans. He was almost as obscure a figure to his countrymen as he was to the British. The first morning he went to work at 20 Grosvenor Square, he had to carve a path, smiling and nodding, through a crowd of jostling, bulb-popping photographers.

Ike's predecessor in London, Lieutenant General James Chaney, had imposed a wide range of restrictions on the press, and many journalists came to feel the Army disdained, if not despised, them. Eisenhower changed all that. Three weeks after he arrived in London, he held

what he called "a conference with the press," instead of a press conference. The point wasn't to give them news but to establish a working relationship. He talked about how well he'd gotten along with journalists
during his nine years working with and for MacArthur. "I have only
been double crossed by one newspaperman in my life," he said, shrug-
ging it off as one of those things.[8]

They disliked the strict censorship rules, they said, and complained
about how long it took to get photographs and stories through censorship. Ike told them he'd relax the rules immediately and would hire
more censors to speed things up. They said they weren't allowed to give
the names of any but the two highest-ranking American generals, himself and Carl Spaatz, commander of the Eighth Air Force. That rule is
now abolished, Ike replied. And there was the subject of race. Reporters
weren't allowed to file copy on racial friction between American troops
or submit stories on black soldiers dating English women. Ike said the
ban was lifted as of now.

The journalists left dazzled. It was like emerging from a tunnel into
sunshine. "I don't think he needs a public relations adviser," wrote an
astonished Butcher, who had arrived in England convinced that Ike
would need his extensive experience with newspapers and radio sta-
tions back home to help get the press on his side. "He is tops."[9]

Ike's first weekend in England was spent at Mountbatten's magnificent
country house, Broadlands. His second was spent at Chequers, the even
more magnificent seventeenth-century country residence of British
prime ministers. Churchill asked him to bring anyone he wished, and
Clark accompanied Ike.

Churchill greeted them wreathed in smiles and dressed in carpet
slippers and his specially tailored "rompers," a baggy one-piece construction in light blue with a huge zipper down the front. Smiling and
voluble, he led them down the driveway and into the woods until they
reached a bench set in a pleasant spot. He proceeded to tell Ike that he
couldn't go along with Sledgehammer, the proposed emergency landing in France that fall. It was certain to fail.[10]

Although Eisenhower disagreed with Churchill, and said so, this
weekend marked the beginning of what would rapidly become a close

relationship, based on mutual admiration and mutual trust. No doubt it helped that Churchill's mother was Jenny Jerome from Indiana. So too did Churchill's extraordinary charm. He could be as funny as a professional comedian, as moving as a great actor, witty if the occasion was ripe for wit, nostalgic to the point of tears when in a reminiscent mood, and armed with both a memory for poetry and an orator's gift for the inspirational utterance. He had led a life crammed with drama and incident, and was a romantic even at his most calculating and manipulative. Bald, pink and cherubic, in his siren suit he looked like an overgrown baby who had somehow picked up a cigar. Ike did not even try to resist the charm. He chose to enjoy it instead, called it "the sun lamp" and remained careful not to be so lulled by its warmth that it affected his judgment.[11]

Ike was guided, too, by something his mentor Fox Conner had told him twenty years earlier—"We cannot escape another great war. When we go into that war it will be in company with allies . . . leaders will have to learn how to overcome nationalistic considerations in the conduct of campaigns."[12]

Eisenhower remained convinced of the need for Sledgehammer. The Germans' summer offensive in Russia was driving inexorably toward Stalingrad and, beyond, to the oilfields of the Caucasus. As the Red Army fell back, Ike became alarmed. If Stalin was forced to make peace with Hitler, it might become impossible to mount a successful invasion of the Continent in 1943, or any other year.

Churchill, however, was convinced that the Soviet Union would hold out, that the Red Army was not about to collapse. The Russians were doing what they had done often before—trading space for time and praying for "General Winter" to arrive early. The Germans, meanwhile, had enough strength available in Western Europe to destroy any small-scale invasion. A failed landing would do nothing to aid the Soviet Union. On the contrary, it would demoralize the British, possibly make the U.S. shift the focus of its efforts to the Pacific and might help convince Stalin that he had to reach an accommodation with Hitler.

The modesty of Sledgehammer was a good reason not to attempt it. It called for putting only one division into the initial assault and feeding more divisions in once a beachhead was established. Moreover, the Germans had air superiority over the beaches of France in 1942, even though most of the Luftwaffe was assigned to the eastern front. At this stage of events, Eisenhower had only a hazy grasp of the requirements of a successful air war and took AAF propaganda seriously. He discounted British arguments that without Allied air superiority there could never be a successful amphibious assault. Ike had no inkling yet that the struggle for air superiority in Europe would be one of the longest, costliest and most bitterly contested campaigns of World War II.

One British general, hearing Ike espousing the case for Sledgehammer, told his colleagues, "This man has dangerous ideas!"[13] Churchill used all his eloquence to talk him out of them and tried to get him to accept instead a landing in North Africa. But however strongly Churchill opposed Sledgehammer, Eisenhower just as strongly supported it. Deadlock. Two weeks after Ike's first visit to Chequers, George Marshall and Admiral King flew to London to support him.

Marshall counted on Ike to produce a plan that would prove to the British that Sledgehammer was feasible. Ike's ideas were certainly daring, the kind that might have wowed the instructors at Leavenworth, because while he argued his case with tremendous conviction, he held out no false hopes. He did not rate the chance of getting a division ashore as better than 50 percent, and there was only a 20 percent chance of building up the beachhead to a force of six divisions. In short, there was an 80 percent chance of failure, because a small beachhead held by only three or four divisions was going to be wiped out.[14]

After a long and heated argument with the British, Marshall informed Roosevelt that the Anglo-American Combined Chiefs of Staff remained deadlocked. The only operation the British were prepared to mount was a North African landing. Eisenhower was angry and depressed. He expected the Soviet Union to be out of the war in a few months. When that happened, the Allies would stand forever condemned for lacking the guts and vision to put every soldier they could on the Continent in an attempt—even a failed attempt—to take some of the pressure off the Red Army. July 22, 1942, he grimly told Butcher, could well be "the blackest day in history."[15]

On July 23, the Combined Chiefs held a long and exhausting conference, during which they finally agreed to make a landing in North Africa. A delighted Churchill gave the operation a code name intended to make it shine like a beacon of hope. He called it Torch.

Next morning, Eisenhower was summoned to Claridge's to see Marshall. Ushered into Marshall's suite, he found that the Chief of Staff was taking a bath. Through the open door, Marshall told him he would be the chief planner for Torch, and, for now, its "Deputy Allied Commander." A commander would be chosen later. "It will probably be you."[16]

The Allies had promised the Soviets they would open a second front in 1942. Torch could just about be presented as such to Stalin, and to public opinion in the U.S. and Britain. More important, perhaps, Roosevelt had pledged shortly after Pearl Harbor that American soldiers would be fighting the Germans by the end of 1942, a promise he hoped to make good before the midterm elections that November.

The military situation in North Africa when Ike began planning Torch was precarious. Earlier in the year, a British offensive had come close to destroying the Italian Army in Libya and ended with the capture of the crucial port of Tobruk. Hitler's response to that had been to send one of his best generals, Erwin Rommel, and two panzer divisions, to stop the Italian retreat turning into a rout. The thirty-five thousand British troops holding Tobruk soon found themselves besieged by the Germans and Italians, and on June 20, only four days before Eisenhower arrived in Britain to establish the ETO headquarters, the defenders of Tobruk surrendered.

This was a staggering blow to British morale and forced the British Army to pull back to the Egyptian border. The British hold on the Middle East suddenly appeared in jeopardy. Three hundred American tanks, a hundred self-propelled artillery pieces and more than a hundred American combat planes were rushed to Egypt to help make good the matériel losses at Tobruk. The strategic initiative was nonetheless firmly in Axis hands. A successful North African landing in what amounted to Rommel's rear should go a long way toward getting it back.

Although he continued to command the ETO from his headquarters on Grosvenor Square, Ike created a separate entity—the Allied Force Headquarters, or AFHQ—nearly a mile away to plan Torch. He also got a new chief of staff.

Even before he set off for London, Ike had told Marshall he would like to have the services of Brigadier General Walter Bedell Smith, the secretary of the Combined Chiefs, formerly Marshall's executive officer. Marshall turned him down. Almost from the moment he reached England, however, Ike decided to get rid of the chief of staff he inherited there, Charles Bolté. It wasn't that Bolté was a dud. On the contrary. Before the war ended, he would prove to be one of the best combat commanders the Army possessed. In London, however, Bolté had grown used to doing things the British way, starting work late, having a leisurely lunch, then working until midnight. People might toil on a Saturday, but short of Germans goose-stepping up the beach at Dover some Sunday morning, Sunday was a day of rest, a day to be spent in the country. That was the way Churchill operated, so it became the way the British high command did business, and Bolté followed suit.

Ike couldn't stand it. He believed in going to work early, eating at his desk if necessary and going to the office Sunday morning for at least a few hours of drudgery. Bolté had to go, and once he got command of Torch, Eisenhower insisted yet again that he had to have the services of Beetle Smith. Marshall finally relented and sent Smith to London.

Meanwhile, Ike had made it part of his routine to see Churchill at least twice a week, at the Cabinet War Rooms, at 10 Downing Street or at Chequers. The Downing Street meetings often involved dinner, and it was his misfortune that the PM was likely to dine around nine o'clock and still be holding forth at two in the morning. For Ike, who was invariably at his desk before eight A.M., such evenings were as punishing as they were fascinating.

Eisenhower saw Torch less as a military operation than as a political move undertaken for short-term gains. He thought it made no sense strategically. Nevertheless, he intended to make it work.

Apart from Spanish Morocco, North Africa from the Atlantic coast of Morocco to the western border of Libya consisted of French colonial territory, ruled by the government of Vichy France. As Ike got down to planning Torch, it was clear from the start that the essential objectives were the port cities of Oran, Algiers and Bône. The greatest prizes, though, were Tunis, the capital of Tunisia, and the nearby port city of Bizerte. Tunis and Bizerte both had excellent harbors and both possessed large, all-weather airfields.

There was no point, Churchill argued, in making a landing that was not aimed at the capture of Tunisia before the Germans could move in. It wasn't possible to make a direct assault on Bizerte or Tunis, because they were well within the range of Axis airfields in Sicily. A successful landing at Bône, a hundred miles to the west of Bizerte, however, was feasible if risky, and from there it should be possible to race to Tunisia overland and grab it before the Germans could react, especially if the Vichy forces in Tunisia came over to the Allied side. The British from Churchill down argued for this strategy.

At the end of the war, Ike recalled, "I came to favor, personally, taking the entire force inside the Mediterranean. I believed that Tunis was so great a prize that we should land initially as far east as Bône."[17] At the time, though, he never spelled this out, never once urged boldness on Marshall. Instead, he was content to set out the options available and leave it for Marshall to choose between caution and daring.

Marshall refused to take risks. Whenever he thought about Spanish Morocco, Marshall had visions of the Spanish dictator, Francisco Franco, attacking Gibraltar and knocking out its airfield with long-range artillery, and without that airfield, landings at Oran and Algiers would be almost impossible. Even if that didn't happen, he reasoned, when winter fell on the eastern front, Hitler could shift large forces to Spain and seize Gibraltar.

The British considered this absurd. Spain's economy had been shattered by the Spanish Civil War, which had ended only months before World War II began. Nearly 5 percent of the population had been killed; 10 percent had been wounded. Spain was too traumatized to pick a fight with anyone.

Even so, the Chief of Staff insisted that most of the American troops committed to Torch must land at Casablanca, one hundred miles west of Gibraltar, on the Atlantic coast of Morocco. When the British chiefs dissented from this plan, Roosevelt backed Marshall and that settled the issue. There would be a landing at Casablanca and none at Bône, a mistaken decision that ruled out any swift capture of Tunis.

The entire operation had to be presented as an American venture and not a British one. This was so important that Churchill even offered to put British soldiers into American uniforms to help ensure success. The French Army, Churchill believed, would mount a halfhearted show of defiance to save *l'honneur* while looking for a white bedsheet to run up a flagpole, and they would find it a lot easier to capitulate to Americans than to the British.[18]

When France surrendered in June 1940, the British had hoped the French Navy might sail to British ports, to continue the fight along with those French airmen and soldiers who had escaped the occupation of their homeland. The French Navy, however, was largely the creation of a pint-sized, moon-faced admiral, Jean François Darlan, who had persuaded French governments of the 1930s that France should become a world-class naval power. The French fleet of 1940 had new battleships and battle cruisers, thanks to Darlan, with more under construction.

Following the fall of France, Darlan believed that a different and better France would emerge within a Europe under Hitler's rule. A crypto-fascist, he swore loyalty to Vichy France and its head of state, Maréchal Philippe Pétain, a man who had watched the Nazis destroy his country and then traveled to Montelimar to shake Hitler's hand. Darlan became Pétain's designated successor and the defense minister of Vichy.[19]

In July 1940, to prevent the collaborationist Darlan from making the French fleet available to Hitler, Churchill ordered the Royal Navy to attack the units at anchor in Oran. The result was twenty-five hundred dead French sailors and thousands more seriously injured. If there was any serious resistance to Torch, the British knew it would come from the French Navy, not the French Army.

As Torch planning progressed, Eisenhower was appointed commanding general of AFHQ. He decided that one of the first things he should do was appoint a deputy commanding general to step into his shoes should anything happen to him. His choice fell on Mark Clark, who was appalled. Clark had established his II Corps headquarters at Longford Castle, on the edge of Salisbury Plain, almost within sight of Stonehenge. He was absorbed in training his troops to spearhead Roundup, the invasion of France in the spring of 1943. Hanging around AFHQ waiting to discover whether he would have to take over from Ike was nothing compared to a combat command. Roundup, however, was not going to happen. Torch meant there would be at least half a million Allied troops in North Africa by early 1943, and keeping them supplied would tie up too much shipping for any invasion of France in the spring. When Clark tried to beg off becoming his deputy, Ike told him bluntly, "The question is, do you want to stay at Longford Castle and sit on a dead fish."[20]

When it was put like that, Clark reluctantly agreed to be Ike's deputy commander, but as the planning for Torch unfolded, he became restive and began demanding command of one of the task forces assigned to seize Casablanca, Oran or Algiers. Ike would not agree.

The State Department's expert on the French military in North Africa was Robert Murphy, a career diplomat who had represented the United States in Algeria in recent years. Murphy arrived in England in mid-September in an Army uniform, as "Lieutenant Colonel McGowan." Marshall had decided what rank he would have for his disguise. He told Murphy, "I've observed that nobody pays any attention to a lieutenant colonel."[21]

Sitting on the lawn at Telegraph Cottage one sunny afternoon, Murphy briefed Ike and Clark on the leading figures among the French colonial forces, overtly loyal to Vichy but in fact divided into numerous mutually antagonistic factions. The only man who could get them to join the Allied side, Murphy said confidently, was not Charles de Gaulle, who had fled to England in May 1940 just before France surrendered, but General Henri Giraud.

No one doubted that Giraud was a resolute patriot. In World War I he had escaped from a German POW camp. Rising to four-star rank during the interwar years, he had commanded the French Seventh Army and been captured by the Germans in 1940. Imprisoned in a castle in Saxony, he had made his second escape, in April 1942, at the age of sixty-three. Making his way south for five hundred miles, he reached Vichy France and found refuge there.[22] Murphy claimed that the commander of the Algerian Division, Major General Charles Mast, had assured him that virtually all the troops in North Africa would rally to Giraud.

This was encouraging, but Ike wasn't completely convinced by Murphy, who claimed, for example, that he had organized a strong but secret anti-German resistance movement in North Africa that was waiting to spring into action. He wanted Ike to arm these putative resistance fighters. Eisenhower did not know much about Vichy France or North Africa, but he knew the dismal truth: the overwhelming majority of the French were not and would not become involved in any act of resistance until German defeat seemed certain.

For more than two years, there had been nothing that could be seriously termed a French resistance movement, despite the efforts of de Gaulle and the British to create one. In fact, when de Gaulle had called in 1940 for French men and women to rally to him, only twelve hundred had responded—out of a nation of 45 million. The situation had not changed much since then. There was a minority that collaborated unhesitatingly, and many more who collaborated through their support of the Vichy government. If Eisenhower did as Murphy wanted and armed French civilians, they were more likely to use them against one another to settle old scores than to fight the Germans.

Murphy's meeting with Ike was conducted in the deepest secrecy—not to keep the Germans in the dark, but to prevent de Gaulle from finding out that a North African operation was being planned. Free French headquarters had a bad record for security. Anyway, Murphy emphasized, the man who mattered wasn't de Gaulle but Giraud, and because he outranked Eisenhower, he would expect to take command of Torch. This was too ridiculous for comment, so Eisenhower let it pass.

Even though he had not swallowed everything Murphy had told him, Ike nevertheless believed he had learned much from their interview. He informed Marshall that he had "the utmost confidence" in Murphy. "I will be able to work with him in perfect harmony."[23]

Three days after the meeting with Murphy, Ike was at his Grosvenor Square office saying farewell to Brigadier General Lucian K. Truscott, who was returning to the U.S. to take command of part of the force committed to Torch. They were interrupted by the arrival of de Gaulle's chief of staff.

Politely declining Ike's invitation to sit down, the French general said he preferred to stand. Then, in flawless English, he declared with stiff dignity, "Sir, I am directed by General de Gaulle to inform General Eisenhower that General de Gaulle understands that the Americans and British are planning to invade French North Africa. General de Gaulle wishes to say that in such a case he expects to be designated as Commander in Chief. Any invasion of French territory that is not under French command is bound to fail." While the Frenchman spoke, Eisenhower put on his poker face, and when he had finished, Ike merely said, "Thank you," in a tone of voice that betrayed nothing. The French general saluted and left.[24]

Murphy had returned to Algeria and a month later, Saturday, October 16, Ike received a sensational message from him: Darlan's son, who was badly crippled with polio and hoped to travel to the United States for treatment, had told him that his father was willing to throw his support to the Allies. While that might take care of the French Navy, Mast didn't think the French Army would follow Darlan. Only Giraud would do, in which case, "Mast asserts we can gain entry practically without firing a shot." Something else that Mast asserted was that the Americans had to send someone to Algeria immediately for discussions.

Ike showed the message to Clark, who asked, with obvious excitement, "When do I go?"

"Probably right away."

First, though, Ike set off for Chequers, taking Clark with him. This was as much a political matter as a military one. When Ike showed Churchill the message, the PM responded, "Kiss Darlan's stern if you have to, but get the French Navy." As for sending a delegation from AFHQ to meet with Mast and his coconspirators, Churchill said, "This is great!" He gave orders for a Royal Navy submarine to be made ready at Gibraltar at once to take Clark to Algeria, shook Clark's hand and assured him, "The entire resources of the British Empire are at your disposal!" By midnight, Clark and four other AFHQ officers were in the air, headed for Gibraltar.[25]

Clark returned on October 25 with a tale of adventure to relate, and that was about all. He and the rest of his party had nearly been captured by the local police and had been forced to hide in a wine cellar. He had deliberately misled Mast about Torch, and Mast had given him no useful information about what would happen when the landings were made. As Eisenhower acknowledged after the war, while Clark had picked up various interesting details, "these did not compel any material change in our planned operation."[26]

Ike intended to fly to Gibraltar on November 2, but the weather was too bad for flying that day. Three days later, the British Isles were still shrouded in fog and the rain continued to fall. Ike and his staff were driven down to the south coast, to an airfield near Bournemouth, where six B-17's were ready to fly them to Gibraltar. Major Paul Tibbets, who would lead the flight, told Ike the situation was still bad—"ceiling zero." In other words, the weather was unflyable. It was up to Ike. "I have to go," he said.

Tibbets decided to stay under the clouds. If he ever got into them, he was almost certain to get lost. The six Fortresses took off, with Ike in the lead aircraft, *Red Gremlin,* piloted by Tibbets, a brilliant flier who would one day drop an atomic bomb on Hiroshima. A piece of two-by-four, covered with a folded brown Army blanket, had been wedged into the narrow gap between the pilot and copilot's seats. Eisenhower settled onto the blanket, shoulder to shoulder with the two fliers, peering intently ahead, probably willing the mist away.[27]

One B-17 turned back, but the other five flew on, a hundred feet above the whitecaps that covered the gray, churning Channel and, farther south, the Bay of Biscay. After an eight-hour flight, the Rock of Gibraltar loomed up through the mist. Tibbets pulled back on the controls, remarking wryly, "This is the first time I ever had to climb to get into landing traffic!"[28]

As Ike got out of the bomber, he saw signs of Torch in every direction. The airfield was covered with planes, wings overlapping, as if they were parked on an aircraft carrier, and more were landing. In the hangars, British "aircraft erectors" were busily unpacking crates and rapidly assembling Spitfires.

All that stood between Gibraltar and Spain was a fence consisting of three strands of barbed wire. Anyone could walk up to the fence on the Spanish side with a pair of binoculars and count the ever-increasing number of planes. The Germans had to know that a landing was imminent . . . somewhere.

Ignition

In the Gibraltar operations center, beneath eighteen hundred feet of solid rock and half a mile from daylight, Ike touched his six "lucky coins" whenever he thrust those huge, bony hands into his pants pockets. He was carrying a small coin for every country represented at Allied Force Headquarters—the U.S., Britain, Canada, Australia, South Africa and New Zealand. Like all card players and golfers, his preferred companion at crucial moments was Lady Luck. He could use her favors now. Torch might push two neutral countries—Spain and France—into the Axis. And if it failed, any invasion of Europe might be ruled out for years, until after Japan surrendered.

Ike was thrilled to see the Rock of Gibraltar but repelled as he walked into it, his echoing footsteps taking him ever deeper into an underworld of mold and dankness, a skin-crawling place where water seeped eternally through the solid rock to form puddles where it could, a maze of long, dimly lighted tunnels fetid with stale air that remained stubbornly unmoved by underpowered fans turning listlessly in the dripping roofs. He got away whenever he had the chance, to eat or hold conferences at Government House, a short stroll from the tunnel entrance.

At night, he and Clark slept in simple cots set up in a small room they shared deep inside the noisome tunnel. At other times, Ike worked inside the Rock at the operations center, which had walls thirty feet high. Against one of them was a huge map of North Africa, with the three principal objectives of Torch clearly marked—Casablanca, Oran and Algiers.[1]

The big decisions had been made even before he left England. Ships were already heading from Britain and the United States to put men and vehicles on the designated landing beaches. What Ike was doing now was tinkering with the final details and waiting for Giraud. The old hero was to be taken off a beach on the French Riviera by a British submarine, transferred to a flying boat and brought to AFHQ at Gibraltar.

That first evening in Gibraltar, Ike played bridge with Clark, Butcher and Brigadier General Al Gruenther, one of the principal planners of the operation. Gruenther was already on his way to becoming one of the best bridge players in the world and was Ike's favorite partner. As the four men chatted, Ike said he would rather be commanding a division now than a major headquarters. And if he had to lead an invasion anywhere, it would be an invasion of France.

Messages arrived from Robert Murphy, demanding attacks on Norway, the Channel coast, the eastern front and southern France to divert German attention from North Africa. Murphy wasn't simply being unrealistic, Ike informed Marshall; he was showing signs of hysteria.[2]

At dusk on November 7, he walked up to a point high on the Rock. Down below he could make out sleek, dark shapes gliding across the water, passing easily from the Atlantic into the Mediterranean—the leading ships of the task force heading for Algiers.[3]

Giraud arrived, with the landings little more than twelve hours away. Eisenhower showed him into the small room he shared with Clark, and Giraud began by demanding to take command. Holding himself erect, looking and sounding like a character from a Gilbert and Sullivan operetta, the tall, thin, elderly Frenchman produced a memorandum listing what he would require, such as "good radio transmitters and rapid means of transport" and "qualified representatives of the American General Staff." Ike scanned the list and put question marks next to nearly everything Giraud demanded, then gave it to Clark, to see if he could make sense of any of it.[4]

Eisenhower and Giraud argued, with the aid of an interpreter. Then Clark took over and argued with Giraud. After a while, Ike took over from Clark, and so it went on, for four hours. During this discussion,

Giraud pointedly remarked that he was the equivalent of a five-star commander, a remark that only annoyed the three-star Eisenhower. When he took command, Giraud loftily suggested in his stiff, staccato way of speaking, he wouldn't waste his time on Torch. He intended to set new objectives—the conquest of Sardinia and an invasion of southern France.

As Giraud stood in the small, cramped room, stiff and proud in a crumpled, travel-stained uniform, imperiously barking out demands, his pale blue eyes flashing scorn, Ike recognized what he was up against—Gallic posturing, the cynical act camouflaged by windy rhetoric. Giraud didn't mean a word of what he was saying.

The banal reality was that he was not going to commit himself to Torch because there were certain to be French casualties. And suppose the operation failed? He would then be doubly damned as someone with French blood on his hands and a general who'd tied himself to a lost cause. Giraud was biding his time, and bluffing up a storm, until the Americans and British were securely ashore, looking like winners. If French resistance cracked, he would immediately offer himself as the peacemaker, the one man to whom both sides would feel beholden. "His method of gaining time is to insist upon a point which he as a soldier he is well aware the Allies cannot accept," Ike told Marshall. "Clark and I are bitterly disappointed."[5]

The hours of argument concluded on an anticlimactic note. Giraud, obviously exhausted by his dramatic journey and this heated debate, headed for Government House, remarking melodramatically, "Giraud will be a spectator in this affair!" The invasion craft were already closing on the beaches. Aircraft filled with paratroopers were droning south over the Bay of Biscay.[6]

The Western Task Force, heading for Casablanca, was commanded by Patton and would put fifty thousand men ashore on the Atlantic coast of Morocco. The Center Task Force, commanded by Major General Lloyd Fredendall, would seize Oran. Fredendall had no combat experience. He had made his reputation as a trainer of troops during maneuvers in 1940–1941. The Eastern Task Force, steaming toward Algiers, had the most important objective of all—the one closest to Tunisia. It was entrusted to Major General Charles "Doc" Ryder, one of the most highly decorated American soldiers of World War I, one of Ike's West Point classmates and a fellow Kansan.

When the landings were made, it was not yet first light on November 8. After a few hours' sleep, Ike was up and eager for news, but there was none. Not yet. While he waited and wondered and worried, he took a piece of paper and wrote across the top, "Worries of a Commander." Then he started listing them. The first item began, "Spain is so ominously quiet . . ." He listed ten worries, and number ten was the key to the rest: "We cannot find out anything."[7]

As news trickled in, though, nearly all of it was good, and late in the afternoon a message arrived that Darlan was in Algiers. Darlan had been visiting his polio-stricken son when the Americans landed. The little admiral, said the message, wanted to negotiate. Ike read it in astonishment. How could he deal with Darlan? The man was virtually a Nazi. But how could he avoid it if Darlan wanted to talk? "Jee . . . zus Kee . . . rist!" he moaned. "Then what do I do with Giraud? What I need around here is a damned good assassin!"[8]

By the morning of November 9, it was clear that both Oran and Algiers would soon be in American hands. Clark and Giraud flew off to Algiers—Clark to talk to Darlan, Giraud to appeal to his countrymen to cease fighting. Meanwhile, Ike chain-smoked his way through a pack of Camels and wrote a cable to Marshall: "I am so impatient to get eastward and seize the ground in the Tunisian area that I find myself getting absolutely furious with these stupid Frogs."[9]

He cheered himself up by reflecting that he was now in command of a piece of history more than two thousand years old. "I have operational command of the Rock of Gibraltar!! The symbol of the solidity of the British Empire—the hallmark of safety and security at home . . . I simply must have a grandchild or I'll never have the fun of telling this when I'm fishing, grey-bearded, on the banks of a quiet bayou in the deep south."[10]

Later that day, Giraud made his radio broadcast and was ignored from one end of North Africa to the other. Mast had been wrong: Giraud counted for nothing. Darlan was pressured into ordering a cease-fire, but although the fighting died down, it did not end, and the next morning Pétain repudiated Darlan's order. French resistance seemed about to flare up again.[11]

By noon on November 10, Oran and Algiers were almost under Allied control, but Patton was still trying to take Casablanca. Ike scribbled a brief message: "Dear Georgie—Algiers has been ours for two days. Oran defenses crumbling rapidly with Navy and shore batteries surrendering. The only tough nut left is in your hands. Crack it open quickly and ask for what you want." He knew just how Georgie was going to react to this. Ike scribbled at the bottom of the page on which he'd written this message, "Will he burn!"[12]

While he waited for Casablanca to fall and Algiers and Oran to be completely secured, he was itching to shift forces eastward, toward Tunisia. But with Pétain repudiating Darlan, he couldn't risk it. Then, on November 11, the Germans moved into Vichy France, to secure the beaches of southern France, despite Pétain's assurance to Hitler that the French troops in North Africa would resist the Allies.

Darlan then announced that he and Pétain had agreed two years earlier that he would act in Pétain's place should the *maréchal* ever became a prisoner of the Germans, and that was what he was now, a prisoner.[13]

Meanwhile, Pétain was trying to convince Hitler that he had ordered all French forces in North Africa to resist the Allies. Darlan's authority to act otherwise was certainly open to doubt, but what mattered was *l'honneur,* not *l'exactitude.* The fighting stopped at once.[14]

Ike knew that there would be a reaction to any deal he made with Darlan, but he did not foresee just how virulent it would be. Even if he had done so, he would have acted as he did. He intended to use the admiral so he could get on with the war. On November 12, Ike instructed Clark to install Darlan as the head of the French administration in North Africa. The next day, he flew to Algiers to meet with the admiral and work out the details. Giraud would become commander of the French armed forces.

There was an outcry in the U.S. and British press at the "Darlan Deal." Darlan was virtually a fascist and an overt anti-Semite. He was the embodiment of much that the Allies were fighting against. Even so, the outrage in the press was less the thunder of moral outrage than the carping of moral confusion. The Allies had formed a partnership with Stalin on grounds of expediency; the Darlan Deal was justifiable on exactly the same shabby but inescapable basis.

Ike had three good reasons for putting Darlan in charge in North Africa. First, it had taken the French decades to pacify the many tribes that made up the Arab population of North Africa, but the war had brought hunger and hardship to millions. There was also constant friction between Arabs and Jews. "Many things done here," Ike told Mamie, "are just to keep the Arabs from blazing into revolt. We sit on a boiling kettle!!"[15]

For the moment, the French had the situation under control, but this was a French administration that still felt its loyalty was to Pétain and Darlan. Giraud counted for nothing with these people. Nor were they going to follow de Gaulle—who was anathema, anyway, to Roosevelt. Who, then, was going to govern North Africa if not Darlan? The United States couldn't do it, nor could the British.

Second, Ike wanted Darlan to get the French fleet at Toulon to sail across the Mediterranean and join the Allies. This hope came to nothing. Rather than let the Germans have their ships, however, the French sailors at Toulon took their ships out to deep water outside the harbor and scuttled them, sending more than a hundred warships, including a new battleship and two new battle cruisers, to the bottom.

The third reason Ike had for making Darlan governor of North Africa was that this was his best—probably only—chance of taking the port cities of Bizerte and Tunis, which were only a hundred miles from Sicily. Both Bizerte and Tunis boasted all-weather airfields. If the French troops holding those airfields would accept Darlan's authority and deny them to the Germans, Allied troops could be flown into them and seize control of Tunisia.[16]

The press outcry against the Darlan Deal was wounding. "I'm no reactionary," Ike protested to Churchill's representative in North Africa, Harold Macmillan. "Christ on the Mountain, I'm as idealistic as Hell!"[17]

Ike's brother Milton was sent to Algiers to help repair his public relations. Milton was currently one of the highest-ranking officials in the Office of War Information, a federal agency created to help win the propaganda battles. The company of his brother for a couple of weeks helped sustain Ike's morale at a testing time, although when Milton arrived, the Darlan Deal was not the most pressing problem Ike faced. It was the dismaying realization that he was going to have to fight for Tunisia. The highest hopes he had for the Darlan Deal had already come to nothing.

Following the fall of Tobruk in June 1942, Rommel had moved east, toward Cairo, forcing the British Eighth Army to pull back three hundred miles. The British dug in near El Alamein, on the Egyptian border. Rommel attacked twice, was stopped twice. Thanks to Ultra, their intelligence system for cracking German codes, the British could track nearly every vessel carrying fuel for Rommel's army, and sank most of them. Rommel was attacking even though he could not advance any farther, like a man maddened by excessive insolation and lashing out blindly at his enemies.

The Eighth Army, meanwhile, got a new commander, General Sir Bernard Montgomery. While he rebuilt the morale of the defeated Eighth Army and restored its confidence, the arrival of American tanks, self-propelled artillery and aircraft restored its firepower and mobility. On October 23, Montgomery attacked. After ten days of hammering, the German position cracked and Rommel was forced to retreat, although it was several days before he informed Berlin of the fact.

Given the rate at which Rommel was retreating, the British would soon hold every port in Libya, including Tobruk. As Hitler pondered that fact, there came the news that Torch was putting a hundred thousand Allied troops ashore in Morocco and Algeria. There was only one place now where the Führer could secure ports and airfields to get supplies and reinforcements to Rommel's Afrika Korps, and that was Tunisia.

Hitler and the German high command had followed the buildup of shipping and aircraft at Gibraltar and concluded that it presaged an attempt to run a large convoy to Malta. The German supreme commander in the Mediterranean, Field Marshal Alfred Kesselring, arrived at a different conclusion—that the Allies would make major landings in North Africa. As a Luftwaffe officer, he was sure of something else, too—the key to North Africa was airpower. The Luftwaffe had fifteen hundred combat aircraft deployed in Western Europe in the fall of 1942. Kesselring built up a force of four hundred fighters and bombers in Sicily and Sardinia as his own prelude to Torch.[18]

On November 9, forty German dive-bombers landed at Bizerte airfield. More German aircraft were on the way, carrying paratroopers. Without orders to resist, the colonel commanding the airfield had done nothing to deny the runways to incoming German aircraft.[19]

It was another four days before the Darlan Deal was sealed, and by then, the Germans had a secure grip on the airfields at Bizerte and Tunis. A sealift was bringing in tanks and artillery. When Darlan appealed to the French forces in Tunisia to join the Allies, it was too late to keep the Germans out.[20]

There was a floating reserve for Torch, a British infantry brigade numbering five thousand men of the 78th Division, and Ike was later criticized for not using this force to sail four hundred miles eastward and seize Bizerte before the Germans took it. From Bône eastward, however, there was no Allied air cover. Thanks to Kesselring's foresight, the Luftwaffe not only possessed air superiority but beneath that aerial umbrella, Axis submarines, torpedo boats and destroyers patrolled Tunisian coastal waters. A seaborne thrust toward Bizerte would have been suicidal.[21]

The Combined Chiefs of Staff, meanwhile, urged Eisenhower to consider using the floating reserve to scoop up Sardinia. This idea was no more realistic than trying to grab Bizerte. He had his planners work out what it would take to seize Sardinia. The answer was a huge fleet of battleships and cruisers, seven aircraft carriers, more than thirteen hundred aircraft, five divisions (roughly seventy-five thousand men) and three hundred tanks. The earliest date it could be done, he informed the Chiefs, was March 1943.[22]

The floating reserve was used instead to seize Bougie, a small port more than a hundred miles east of Algiers. As reports of movement to the east came in, Ike's hopes rose. "This business of battle is just rush and rush," he informed his chief of staff, Beetle Smith, who was still in London. "But I like it."[23]

Ferocious German air attacks sank four of the floating reserve's ships, which left the troops who landed at Bougie with few vehicles and little artillery. On November 12, a British paratroop battalion grabbed the airfield at Bône, while commandos landed and took the port.

The forces advancing on Tunisia were now consolidated under a new headquarters, the British First Army, commanded by Lieutenant General Kenneth Anderson. On November 15, Anderson's troops reached the Tunisian border. They were now only sixty miles from Bizerte and Tunis. And that same day, a battalion of American paratroopers seized the airfield at Tebessa, which was also on the Tunisian border. Anderson nevertheless lacked the firepower and mobility to mount a successful offensive, something that was inevitable given the Torch plan.

Ike had made Clark the chief planner for this operation and Clark had made a major mistake. The original plan had been to put one hundred thousand fully equipped troops ashore, with plenty of trucks and tanks, jeeps and self-propelled guns. However, Clark thought the more men who landed, the more impressed the French would be, so he got rid of nearly all the vehicles and crammed the invasion fleet with 167,000 men.[24]

On November 25, Anderson attacked. He sent two armored columns—one American, one British—toward Tunis. The Americans overran an airfield and got to within nine miles of Tunis before being mauled. The Germans had shipped twenty of their new Mark VI panzers, better known as Tiger tanks, to Tunisia for combat testing. The Tiger carried an 88-millimeter gun that ripped American Grants and British Crusaders apart. Anderson's armor was trounced. Meanwhile, Stuka dive bombers strafed Anderson's infantry remorselessly. Seizing the initiative, the Germans launched a counterattack that drove Anderson's troops back until they dug in twenty miles southwest of Tunis.[25]

For a day or so, Ike thought Anderson's troops might have to pull back to Algeria. He wrote to his old friend Tom Handy at the Operations Division about the failed advance on Tunisia. "I think the best way to describe our operations to date is that they have violated every recognized principle of war, are in conflict with all operational and logistic methods laid down in textbooks, and will be condemned, in their entirety, by all Leavenworth and War College classes for the next twenty-five years."[26]

Even allowing for the nightmarish problems of getting men and supplies up to the front, he told Churchill, everything depended "on our ability to build up fighter cover over our ground troops." Anderson was trying to advance in the teeth of German air superiority and the presence of Tiger tanks. His airfields were poorly drained grass strips in valleys. When it rained, the strips turned to mud. His only paved runways were at Bône, more than a hundred miles away, but even there the lack of hard standings meant that planes parked next to the runways sank into the mud and couldn't be pulled out without being damaged. The Germans, on the other hand, possessed paved runways and ample hard standings at Bizerte and Tunis. They also had the new FW-190, a plane far superior to any Allied fighter.[27]

In a logical world, the lack of air cover and the torrential winter rains ruled out any further attempt to advance, but Eisenhower sanctioned a new offensive. Anderson planned to launch an assault on Longstop Hill, nine hundred feet high and dominating the roads between Bizerte and Tunis. To nullify German air superiority, the attack would be made at night, on December 22.

At first light on the twenty-third, Ike set off from Algiers in his armored Cadillac to be driven the 380 miles to Anderson's command post. His cavalcade included a Daimler, a three-quarter-ton truck and a jeep. He arrived at the front the afternoon of Christmas Eve. The news wasn't good, Anderson told him. Part of the hill had been taken, but the Germans were bringing up troops. Anderson was planning to renew his attack.[28]

Eisenhower and Anderson went to visit an American armored unit that had been involved in the fighting. Rain was falling heavily, and the Cadillac drove slowly past four men trying to wrestle a motorcycle out of the mud and get it back onto the road. The mire was getting more liquid all the time. Their efforts were completely in vain. Anderson's offensive would have to be called off. Even so, Ike intended to keep pressure on the Germans, by pounding their lines with heavy artillery and probing their lightly held positions farther south. Anderson, however, didn't provide much encouragement even for this limited offensive effort. He said he had consulted the local people and they claimed that once the winter rains arrived, it rained like this for at least six weeks.[29]

Back at Anderson's command post, Ike was talking to a French general, Alphonse Juin, when a call came through from Mark Clark. Something important had happened in Algiers, said Clark, something so serious that Ike simply had to come back right away. Within an hour, the armored Cadillac was rolling westward. Ike told Butcher that Wayne had been so guarded in what he said but so urgent in the way he said it that he thought Darlan had been shot. When Ike's little caravan stopped at Constantine for breakfast on Christmas Day, he learned that his guess was right.[30]

He reached Algiers at nightfall and scribbled a note of condolence to Madame Berthe Darlan—"I feel we have lost a most valuable ally . . . I extend my heartfelt sympathies . . ." After a brief conference with his staff, he headed for Beetle Smith's to have Christmas dinner. Smith, recently arrived from London, had moved into a huge, luxurious villa overlooking Algiers and Patton had sent him two turkeys. Ike put on his grin and entered his chief of staff's villa singing, "God rest ye, merry gentlemen! Let nothing you dismay!"[31]

Smith had some news for him—the President wanted to award him the Medal of Honor, for the success of Torch. Eisenhower felt affronted. The Medal of Honor was for the fighting men, the kind of junior officers and NCOs who were clinging to the frozen earth of the Tunisian hills, cold, wet, miserable and under fire. It was an insult to such men to give the Army's most important medal to a general safe in a headquarters—or a warm villa—far to the rear.

He told Smith he had a message for Roosevelt: "I don't want it and if it is awarded I won't wear it. I won't even keep it."[32]

AFHQ

He was running Allied Force Headquarters from a corner suite in the St. Georges Hotel, sitting in front of a small, smoky fireplace, sneezing and coughing, with a cigarette in one hand and a long pointer in the other, moving the tip of the pointer over the situation maps that covered the walls, looking for places where he could make an attack. Two or three nights each week, Ike stood on the balcony outside his office, wearing a helmet and watching sheets of flame erupt along the quay, less than a mile away. Huge geysers of turbulent water rose up like ghostly pillars from the harbor as, high in the darkness, German bombers attacked the docks. The waterfront at Algiers was so crowded with Allied shipping that the Germans could bomb blind and still be sure of striking something worthwhile. For an hour or more, antiaircraft guns pumped exploding shells three miles high and a hard rain of small metal fragments crepitated on the roofs, streets and helmeted onlookers far below. Red tracer bursts arced into the blackness of the night, before tumbling back, their bright tails spent, to splash unseen into the blackness of the sea.

On these pyrotechnical nights, Ike got only a few hours of sleep, but he was invariably back in his office before eight, weariness dimming the light in his prominent blue eyes, his pallor ashen, that cough more rasping than ever. He had suffered from colds ever since Gibraltar; in fact, he blamed them on that godawful tunnel. But in early January the colds gave way to something much worse—"a murderous case of flu," he called it. Forced to spend four days in bed, Eisenhower finally confronted the truth behind the illness—working himself to death was not going to help the Allies defeat Hitler. He resolved to pace himself hereafter.[1]

The St. Georges was the best hotel in Algiers and conveniently located for the Maison Blanche airfield. Other than that, though, it made an unlikely setting for a major headquarters. Each day, a steady flow of visitors left muddy footprints on the mosaic floors of the cold, echoing corridors. In the morning Ike walked into his office past barefoot Arab women wielding twig brooms, sweeping up the now-dried mud in a cloud of dust.

Home was the Villa dar el Ouad (House of the Family), spacious and white, set amid the hills south of the city. "A sprawly affair and gloomy," Ike informed Mamie, "but it has a nice living room and my bedroom is quite comfortable. Lighting, heating and all facilities are typically French and you know what that means."[2]

During that dreary winter, Butcher and the rest of the staff were able to make both the AFHQ offices and the home in the hills pleasant places to work and live. Even so, Ike wanted something cozier, something like Telegraph Cottage. Butcher found the nearest thing that Algeria had to offer, a small farmhouse ten miles away, at Guyotville. It offered a tennis court, stables and a view of the Mediterranean. Ike's staff found four magnificent Arab stallions for him to ride, even though it wasn't a good place for riding; too rocky. The horses provided relaxation nonetheless and he went out there two or three times a week to ride them or play tennis with Butcher or just knock a few golf balls around. In the evenings he played bridge, before getting into bed and reading himself to sleep with Western stories or the novels of C. S. Forester. He was keeping his New Year resolution to pace himself from now on, and it worked. He never had a serious illness for the rest of the war.[3]

Ike gave up something important to be Allied commander in chief—his right to privacy, and there were times when a burr of resentment stirred. He was never alone now. Wherever Eisenhower went, there were armed guards. He complained about living in a goldfish bowl, but resigned himself to the necessity.

In the month following his departure from London, he discovered that he missed something else, too—the presence of women. Eisenhower had never been a ladies' man, but what he discovered, first on Gibraltar and then in Algiers, was how much he liked—needed, in fact—to have women around him. "I think I have learned more about the value of feminine companionship in the last month than I ever knew in my life," he informed an old friend. It meant a lot to him "to be around someone whose outlook is purely feminine and whose daily problems are so much different from my own."[4]

Shortly before Christmas, six Women's Army Corps (WAC) officers who had served at his ETO headquarters in London reached Algiers, after being torpedoed off Gibraltar. Ike suffered an unpleasant few hours before news arrived that all of the women had been rescued. One of the six was Ike's favorite driver, Mrs. Kay Summersby, a former Worth model now in her mid-thirties and still an exceptionally beautiful woman. With her auburn hair, piercing green-eyed gaze, long, slender legs and flawless skin, she made an impression on everyone who met her, men especially.

Kay Summersby was not the only driver at AFHQ assigned to drive the general, but she considered herself first among equals. Ike was more or less willing to go along with this much of the time, but on the long drives to and from the front, Eisenhower was driven by Sergeant Leonard Dry and Kay remained in Algiers.

When she wasn't driving "the Boss" around—and everyone on the staff called him the Boss by now—Kay was in a small office next to his, handling his mail. She saw a lot more of him than did the rest of the staff at AFHQ. The only person who seems to have seen more of Ike each week was Harry Butcher. Kay was not only a good driver and a competent personal assistant, but she possessed two abilities that Mamie had never managed to acquire, despite Ike's encouragement: she was an excellent bridge player and a fine horsewoman. Whenever Ike headed for the little farmhouse to ride the horses, Kay was likely to go with him.

It was inevitable, then, that rumors would begin to circulate about Ike and Mrs. Summersby, but the speculation was groundless. In England she had fallen in love with Lieutenant Colonel Richard Arnold. Both already married, they filed for divorces in order to marry each other.

Arnold left hurriedly for Washington in the early fall of 1942. Shortly thereafter, he was assigned to a Torch task force. He could not tell her anything about that, but when news of the Torch landings broke, Kay guessed that he was either in North Africa now or would soon be on his way. She applied for a transfer as soon as AFHQ moved to Algiers.

It was a good guess, because Arnold was already in North Africa, about to take command of an engineer regiment. As soon as their divorces came through, Arnold applied for permission to marry Kay "on or about 22 June 1943, or at the conclusion of the Tunisian campaign if the latter be delayed beyond that date." Ike approved the request the day it reached him.[5]

While Eisenhower's spirits brightened at having women around his headquarters again, their absence had only deepened his longing for Mamie's company. After Ike left for Europe, Mamie and Ruth Butcher had rented an apartment together at the Wardman Park, a comfortable but not particularly luxurious establishment close to downtown Washington.

At the end of 1942, AFHQ established a teleprinter link with the War Department. Almost the first outgoing message was from Ike, asking the duty officer at the Operations Division to call the Wardman Park, speak to Mrs. Eisenhower and ask her if everything was all right. It had been more than a week since he'd received a letter and he was starting to worry. Twenty minutes later the teleprinter clattered reassurance—Mrs. Eisenhower was fine. It eased his mind thereafter to know that he could get a message to Mamie in a hurry and she could just as quickly get in touch with him.

Mail, however, remained the main form of communication, and in those early months in Algiers he became, for him, exceptionally passionate toward his wife. "I'm old," he told her, "my days of romance may be all behind me—but I swear I think I miss you more and love you more than I ever did." She knew that by now there were women at AFHQ and she doubtless had heard about Kay. "Don't forget I love—all the time—always," he reassured her. "You're the only woman I could ever live with." In another letter, he told her that although there were WAC secretaries in his office, he relied on Warrant Officer Walter Marshall, "the best secretary anyone ever had," and dictated to a female secretary only when Marshall was busy with something else.[6]

This wasn't strictly true, but he was right about Marshall's abilities.

Marshall remained with Ike until the end of 1943, when he was suddenly dropped from the staff, possibly because Eisenhower—or, more likely, military intelligence—decided, rightly or wrongly, that Marshall was gay.[7]

During the war, Eisenhower wrote to Mamie on average every three days. With other people, including John, he told her, he had to wait for the right mood to strike him before he could think of what to put in a letter. With her, it was different. She was on his mind all the time; the time was always right. And while he dictated virtually all his correspondence, including letters to his son, nearly every letter to Mamie was written by hand. Ike wrote to her this way even when his hand was swollen and painful. It was a direct link from him to her. She insisted on it. Mamie did not want any secretary, even a male one, standing on the paper ribbon that bound them across an ocean.

Roosevelt and Churchill couldn't stay away. The Allies had taken most of North Africa and were on their way to liberating the rest. They decided to meet in Casablanca and work on strategy for 1943. Eisenhower, barely recovered from the flu, was summoned to attend.

He had a feeling that his job was on the line when he headed for Casablanca on January 15, 1943. The failure to capture Tunisia still nettled and dismayed him. The political gyrations and rearrangements following Darlan's death were depressing. There were criticism and second-guessing across North Africa and at home. He had developed a habit of groaning, "Anybody who wants the job of Allied commander in chief can have it!" He didn't mean it, but Butcher was worried that it might get back to Roosevelt and Marshall and they could take him up on his offer.[8]

The Casablanca Conference turned into a drama before Eisenhower even got there. As his B-17 droned westward, crossing the Atlas Mountains, he was looking out a window when he noticed a black haze whipping around one of the starboard engines before coalescing into a shiny black stream of oil that ran along the rear edge of the wing. Ike informed the pilot and the engine was shut down.

The pilot then ordered him, Butcher and the rest of the passengers to put on their parachutes and prepare to bail out. As Ike wrestled his way into the parachute harness, one of his stars came off. While Butcher scrambled to retrieve it and pin it back on, Ike huddled by a hatch in the floor of the fuselage, wondering how his weak knee was going to cope with a jump.

The Fortress droned on, but just as the danger seemed to pass, the propeller shaft on another engine broke. It was possible to fly a B-17 on three engines, but with only two, it was bail out, crash-land or glide and pray. The pilot chose not to risk Ike's life in a jump or a crash landing. The Fortress's nose dipped and it glided the last fifty miles to Casablanca.[9]

Patton drove Ike to the Anfa Hotel, where Roosevelt, Churchill and the Combined Chiefs were staying. After lunch with Marshall, King and Arnold, Eisenhower gave the Combined Chiefs a long, detailed account of everything that had happened since the landings on November 8, concluding with the stalemate in rugged and rain-swept Tunisia.

As he described the logistical horrors of being tied to a rickety railroad that took ten days to move a tank from Casablanca to the front, pent-up frustration began to get the better of him. Marshall thought he was about to burst into tears. He had to have trucks, said Ike, plenty of them, and soon, if he was going to mount an offensive when the winter rains stopped.[10]

It was Ike's luck that the exceptionally able chief of the Army's Service of Supply, Brehon "Bill" Somervell, was also at Casablanca. Ike and Somervell had been at West Point together and were old friends. Ike urged—almost begged—him to ship fifty-four hundred trucks to North Africa, and quickly.

Marshall had come to Casablanca to argue that once operations had reached a conclusion in Tunisia, the next objective had to be Roundup, the landing in France. Marshall said it could still be done in 1943, even if they had to wait until September. Ike told him that Roundup simply wasn't a possibility before 1944. To mount an invasion of France with any realistic hope of success was going to take twice as many landing craft as the staff in OPD had been calculating. It would also require far more shipping than was available to support a large beachhead. It was a bitter disappointment to Marshall, but he accepted what Ike said.[11]

The issue was going to come down, then, to objectives in the Mediterranean. The British had arrived in Casablanca with a six-thousand-ton cruise ship crammed with planners and filing cabinets to argue the case for a landing in Sicily. From a purely military perspective, the correct objectives were Sardinia, for its airfields, and Corsica, for its ports. Sicily made sense only as part of a strategy to invade the Italian mainland, which consists mainly of mountains. That rocky spine, all goat tracks and vertiginous forested slopes, is the topographical dreamscape of any army prepared to dig in, pour some reinforced concrete and fight to the death.

Airfields on Corsica and Sardinia, on the other hand, would put Axis territory from the naval shipyards at Bordeaux to tank factories in Hungary within the range of heavy bombers. Corsican ports were so close to the beaches of southern France that taking them was guaranteed to tie down a huge number of Germans, who would otherwise be guarding the Channel coast. Corsica could even be the key to pulling German troops out of Russia. But such a strategy accepted there would be no Allied divisions in combat against the Germans on the European mainland until 1944, something that was intolerable to Roosevelt, Churchill and Allied public opinion.[12]

Before dinner, Roosevelt had Ike come for a talk. The President spoke expansively about what would happen after the war. Ike was taken aback. It seemed wrong to him to be talking like this when there was so much fighting still to do. Roosevelt sounded as though the campaign for Tunisia was virtually over. Eisenhower made it plain he disagreed, so Roosevelt challenged him to say when the campaign would end. Ike replied, "May 15," just four months away.[13]

At dinner with the President and the Combined Chiefs, he noticed that no one congratulated him on Torch. That was annoying, but he didn't let it show. The President, the PM and the Chiefs seemed to be blaming the Tunisian disappointment on him, yet he had done everything he could to win that race.

Of course, assuming he captured Tunisia, they would throw their arms around him, and congratulate themselves on their foresight in choosing Eisenhower to command AFHQ. But if it all went wrong, they would dump him without compunction and do what they could to make sure the history books read that the failure was Eisenhower's and his alone.[14]

At dawn the next day, he flew back to Algiers. Five days later Marshall arrived, unannounced, at AFHQ. The Chief of Staff was worried about Eisenhower's health, especially reports that he had high blood pressure. Marshall told him bluntly, "You're trying to do too much." What Ike needed, said Marshall, was a couple of able young generals to act as his "eyes and ears." They could travel around and unearth those truths that didn't appear in the message traffic or official reports and bring them to him, freeing him to concentrate on the big decisions.[15]

Marshall also told him, "You ought to have a masseur. They're great for relaxing you before you go to bed." Pershing had always had a masseur available in World War I. To Eisenhower, there were few physical experiences more repellent than having another man touching his naked flesh. Even as a football player, he had gritted his teeth and submitted unwillingly to postgame rubdowns. After Marshall left, he dutifully hired a masseur, submitted to a massage and didn't have another one for a decade.[16]

Before Christmas 1942, Ike's staff started betting on just when he would get his fourth star. They expected it to happen any day now, and were puzzled when it didn't. AFHQ was an aberration, a major headquarters where the boss was outranked by some of his subordinates. It seems to have taken the visit to North Africa to convince Marshall and Roosevelt to put this right. On February 10, Ike became a four-star general.

It gave him an enormous thrill to know that he was only the twelfth person in American history to wear four stars. This was as high as he could go. He had reached the top of his profession, and in the best way possible. He had gotten there by the path that only Grant and Pershing had followed before him—as a commander and not as the others, including MacArthur, had done, by becoming Chief of Staff.

No one understood coalition warfare better than the British. The United Kingdom was itself a permanent coalition of three nations—England, Scotland and Wales—with an Irish element mixed in. It was that combination that had enabled the British to create the largest empire in the history of the world, but Britain never had a large army. When it fought on the Continent—against Louis XIV or Napoleon or the kaiser—it had to form alliances and coalitions. Its talent for managing these was as important as its naval skills and its far-flung empire in preserving the security of the British Isles.

That was the context in which Eisenhower had set up Allied Force Headquarters in London in the summer of 1942. The U.S. wasn't used to coalition warfare and the British were used to little else. It was for him to create an architecture that would bring out the best that both parties had to offer, while minimizing the inevitable friction. His solution was something that had never been attempted before in the long history of war, and like all elegant ideas, it was simplicity itself.

Eisenhower took the U.S. chain of command and the British chain of command apart and put them back together to form a single chain. Where there was an American link, the one above would be British and so would the one below; similarly, a British officer would find an American above him and another American below. At the very top of the chain was the Combined Chiefs of Staff, which was itself an Anglo-American entity and, in effect, the headquarters that Ike reported to.

There were anomalies galore in this structure during the early months and there was strong resistance, especially from the airmen, who insisted that American public opinion would never tolerate putting AAF units under a British commander. Ike had been willing to go along with that because the AAF provided most of the planes deployed to North Africa, including the only heavy bombers at the disposal of AFHQ.

There were teething problems, too, as Eisenhower pulled together two different military styles. American officers, himself included, disparaged the British approach, which relied on committees and conferences to coordinate ground, air and naval operations. That wasn't how it had been done by Pershing and the AEF. Pershing had operated through a small staff under his direct control. Army officers like Ike were trained accordingly, and it took them a long time to get used to the committee system. "Life is one long conference!" he complained to Mamie.[17]

Time-consuming as it was, however, the use of coordinating committees was going to take combined arms to a level that no one had ever imagined before World War II. It went beyond anything the Germans developed to produce their version of blitzkrieg. If anyone practiced total war, it was going to be Eisenhower, not Hitler. To get there, he would have to overcome many of his most cherished theories of how war was waged, and the place where he learned to do it was North Africa.

During the tense early days of Torch, Ike had kept his spirits up by marveling at what he had already wrought. "What soldier ever took the trouble to contemplate the possibility of holding an Allied command," he mused. "And of all things, an Allied Command of ground, air and naval forces . . . I am proud of this British-U.S. command!"[18]

It wasn't perfect yet, however, and by early 1943 the forces it commanded were so widely scattered and problems of coordination were becoming so acute that a new system was imperative. At Casablanca, the Combined Chiefs created a command structure that provided Eisenhower with three deputies, all British, all military knights. Air Chief Marshal Sir Arthur Tedder, presently in Cairo and commanding the Eastern Air Command, would become his air commander; General Sir Harold Alexander would command the ground forces; and Admiral Sir Andrew B. Cunningham would oversee naval operations.

The Chief of the Imperial General Staff, Field Marshal Sir Alan Brooke, later made a supercilious boast that the British "were pushing Eisenhower up into the stratosphere and rarified atmosphere of a Supreme Commander, where he would be free to devote his time to the political and inter-allied problems . . . whilst we inserted our own commanders to deal with the military situations."[19]

Yet Eisenhower was never as far removed from "the military situations" as Brooke liked to imagine. Besides, although Torch had an American face, the fight to capture Tunisia was going to be waged mainly by the British, who would provide 80 percent of the troops, 90 percent of the ships, nearly 100 percent of the signals intelligence and much of the airpower. Giving Ike three British deputies for the advance into Tunisia was neither a sellout nor a clever British ploy.

Alexander's selection could not have been more welcome to Ike. When he had met Alexander for the first time, in London in the summer of 1942, he had been profoundly impressed. Alexander was a handsome, aristocratic man with some impressive decorations for heroism in World War I. He had an even bigger collection of gongs for his success in high-command assignments since. Alexander had also done something that was bound to get Ike's respect: he had put his reputation at risk in order to accept an assignment that was bound to bring him nothing but criticism and end ingloriously.

Early in 1942 Alexander had gone to Burma, not to make a do-or-die stand against the oncoming Japanese but to save what could be saved while defenses were hurriedly created along the eastern borders of India. Burma could be sacrificed if the result was to retain India, and Alexander could be sacrificed if that too was needed. He had accepted this assignment on that basis and had done well enough for Churchill to make him commander in chief of British forces in the Middle East. In the summer of 1942, after listening to Alexander talk about the kind of Anglo-American command that would be needed to fight the Germans, Ike told Butcher, "That guy's good! He ought to be Commander-in-Chief instead of me!"[20]

As for Cunningham, Ike described him as "the Nelsonian type of admiral. He always thought in terms of attack, never defense. He was vigorous, hardy, intelligent and straightforward." All those who served under Cunningham, of whatever rank or nationality, had nothing but affection for him, Ike added. "He was a real sea dog."[21]

Ike met Tedder for the first time at Casablanca. For the moment, he had to take Tedder on reputation, but what a reputation. It was Tedder who had masterminded the eventual victory of the Western Desert Air Force over the Luftwaffe in North Africa.

The Germans had sought air superiority by sending many of their best planes and pilots to North Africa. Tedder saw that the real key was the dull business of maintenance. Whoever beat the sand and kept its planes flying would win. Besides that, he was the absolute master of coordinating air, ground and naval operations. Tedder had a quicksilver mind, seeming to know almost intuitively what to do day by day with his limited resources: Should he provide close air support to the soldiers or attack shipping or hit Luftwaffe bases or bomb enemy fuel and ammo dumps or do something else? That gift—to get the most out of the inherent flexibility of airpower—was one of the rarest skills in the world, and Tedder—whom Churchill mistakenly thought was really a mechanic, not a warrior—possessed it in spades. Ike recognized from the first that Tedder, with his narrow, intelligent face, ever-present pipe and the thoughtful demeanor of a scholar, was one of the outstanding air commanders of the war.[22]

Allied Force Headquarters had no precedent; it was itself the precedent for interallied commands ever since. The defense of the free world throughout the Cold War can be traced back to what Ike wrought in North Africa. It worked because Eisenhower overcame the provincialism and narrow nationalism that a life like his—small-town boyhood, military career—was almost designed to cultivate. There was in his mind and spirit a force that was nearly always bigger than his circumstances.

In this, he stood in stark contrast to Patton, for whom being a good American involved despising foreigners, and he despised none so fiercely as the British, whom he considered stuffy, arrogant and cold. When he met Ike at Casablanca, he was appalled at his old friend's Anglophilia. For the rest of the war, Patton made biting comments about Eisenhower selling out to the British.

Ike had himself tried to preclude such accusations. When AFHQ was established in London, he instructed its American personnel to avoid using British expressions. By the time he got to North Africa, though, he was, to Patton's disgust, saying *petrol* for *gasoline* and *tiffin* for *lunch.* "London has conquered Abilene," Patton grimly reported to his wife.[23]

Eisenhower was well aware of accusations that he had defected to the old colonial oppressor, and they were bound to reach back to the War Department. Shortly after the Casablanca Conference, he wrote to his old friend Tom Handy at the OPD, assuring him he was well aware that the British "instinctively approach every military problem from the viewpoint of the Empire, just as we approach them from the viewpoint of American interests. [But] the second anyone brings up an idea that sounds to me as if it represented a purely national attitude or viewpoint, I challenge him openly on the spot."[24]

What he meant was typified by what was probably the most famous anecdote about Ike's approach to Anglo-American relations. An American colonel got into an argument with a British officer and called him a "British son of a bitch." Ike, hearing about it, sent for the colonel and told him that he was right about the point in dispute "and you might be excused for calling him a son of a bitch. But you called him a *British* son of a bitch. For that, I'm sending you home!"[25]

Eisenhower was so determined to make the Allied internationalist principle on which AFHQ worked a success that he told Churchill one day, "When I am acting as Allied commander-in-chief, I feel I am half British," but added that he did not want this to be repeated back home.[26]

The ultimate version of AFHQ combined a structure that satisfied the American idea of how a military staff should be organized, but planning and administration were along British lines. Ike's revamped headquarters became operational in February 1943, just as the rains petered out in Tunisia and Rommel attacked.[27]

Tunisgrad

When Ike received Marshall's order summoning him to Casablanca, he thought his job was on the line. Not only had he lost the race for Tunisia, but Brooke and other British generals were damning him for not controlling the course of battle. They saw in him not so much a supreme commander as a weak one. The subtext was inevitability—this is what happens when great ventures are in the care of a man who has never been shot at, an officer never entrusted before this with anything bigger than a battalion.

Churchill paid no attention to his generals' sniping. If anything, he was relieved that Tunisian setbacks were occurring under an American commander. Had a British general commanded AFHQ, Churchill told King George VI, such failures would have created an outcry in the United States that would have harmed the Allied cause. So long as he had Churchill and Marshall behind him, Ike's position was safe.[1]

No one—not him, not his critics, not his admirers—could yet penetrate to the heart of the struggle for Tunisia and tease out its true meaning in the six-year exploration of the law of unintended consequences that was World War II. It became clear after it concluded, though, that Eisenhower had done more for Allied victory by failing to win the race for Tunisia than he could have achieved by winning it. As General Walter Warlimont, one of the most cerebral members of the German high command, acknowledged in 1948, the fight for Tunisia was "decisive for the conduct of the whole war."[2]

Torch was mounted just as the Soviets launched a winter offensive to surround the German Sixth Army at Stalingrad. There was only one move for Hitler to make at this juncture—deploy the best twelve to fifteen divisions in Western Europe, along with six to seven hundred combat aircraft, to Stalingrad at once. Air and ground reinforcements on that scale would have given Hitler the margin needed to take the city and prevent the encirclement. Capturing Stalingrad would easily have negated any potential Allied gain in North Africa, given him the oilfields of the Caucasus and might have forced a general Soviet withdrawal all the way to the Urals.

Instead, Hitler moved into southern France, to plant soldiers on the beaches, and began funneling well-trained, well-equipped, full-strength divisions into Tunisia. He also sent the 150 torpedo aircraft based in Norway that had devastated convoys taking Lend Lease supplies to the Russians; 250 bombers that had been supporting the Sixth Army; plus 400 Junkers trimotor transports that had been flying supplies to the Sixth Army. The diversion of troops and aircraft on this scale doomed the Sixth Army to encirclement, starvation and eventual surrender. The hidden side of Ike's lamented "failure" in Tunisia in December was the Soviet victory at Stalingrad in February.[3]

After returning from Casablanca, Eisenhower resumed his intense study of the situation maps at AFHQ, still searching for a way to go on the offensive. A front 180 miles long had taken shape during the rainy season. At the northern end, close to Bizerte and Tunis, was General Kenneth Anderson's British First Army. In the center was the French XIX Corps, consisting of two understrength, poorly armed French divisions. The southern half of the line was assigned to the II Corps, commanded by Major General Lloyd Fredendall.

Short, foul-mouthed and cantankerous, Fredendall had made a reputation as an effective trainer of troops in the year before Pearl Harbor and shortly afterward was rewarded with command of the II Corps. When the corps was assigned to the ETO, however, Fredendall remained in the U.S., because Marshall did not think that someone of fifty-nine was suited to command a corps in combat. The II Corps was given to Clark instead.

When, only a few months later, Clark became Ike's deputy commander for Torch, Eisenhower chose Fredendall to take command of the II Corps again, and skipped over several other generals offered him by Marshall. The presence of Fredendall at the front would not, in itself, be enough for Ike to get a grip on events there.

To achieve that, he established an advanced command post at Constantine in mid-January. The advanced CP would be run by an able and aggressive cavalryman, Brigadier General Lucian K. Truscott. Here was one of the most gifted soldiers of the World War II army. Truscott was a suave and handsome man who wore a red leather jacket, highly polished cavalry boots and a yellow cavalry scarf, but beneath the style was steel. He arrived in Constantine fresh from performing superbly in Patton's conquest of Morocco. The CP at Constantine would help, but until Alexander took over as his deputy for ground forces—which was scheduled to happen once the British Eighth Army advanced into Tunisia—Eisenhower was his own ground commander.

The topography of Tunisia, as the situation maps all too clearly showed, was as discouraging to his offensive desires as the miserable weather. The dominant terrain features of central Tunisia are north-south lines of treeless hills, some more than two thousand feet high. The British held fifty miles of hills and ridges and were nearest to Bizerte and Tunis. To the south of them, the French held twenty-five miles of low hills and passes. And south of the French, in more open country, was Fredendall's II Corps, thinly stretched over seventy-five miles.

Eisenhower intended to use the British and French to put pressure on the Germans in the north while making a strike toward the Tunisian coast with II Corps, a move that would help the British Eighth Army as it advanced into eastern Tunisia from Libya. This idea had to be shelved when Montgomery's advance slowed down. Meanwhile, Alexander advised Ike that the II Corps wasn't ready anyway for a major offensive move. "Americans require experience and French require arms," Alexander told Churchill. The French positions amounted, in effect, to penetrations waiting to happen.[4]

Even as the rain continued to fall, the German commander in Tunisia, Jurgen von Arnim, a battle-hardened veteran of the eastern front, began probing the French positions, which crumbled under pressure. Eisenhower was forced to break up his American divisions to reinforce the British in the north and support the collapsing French-held center.

Von Arnim and Rommel were debating not whether but where and when to make an attack. Should they strike in the north, to drive the British back from Bizerte and Tunis, or aim south, and cripple the II Corps while its units were still dispersed and its troops bright green?

This debate was no secret to Ike. Every day, sometimes several times a day, Ike's chief intelligence officer, a British brigadier named Eric Mockler-Ferryman, came into his office at the St. Georges Hotel and briefed him, mainly on what Ultra intelligence had intercepted. It wasn't clear, though, whether von Arnim or Rommel was winning the argument.[5]

On January 30, von Arnim's Fifth Panzer Army attacked Faid Pass, more or less in the center of the Allied line. The Germans took the pass in a two-day battle and, after a pause for bringing up reinforcements, advanced toward a crossroads village called Sidi-bou-Zid.

The question of where the main blow would fall was still being debated. Von Arnim wanted to make only a spoiling attack; Rommel wanted an offensive that would drive Ike's forces out of Tunisia and back into Algeria. On February 11, Mockler-Ferryman advised Eisenhower that the issue had been decided: the main German attack would strike the First Army. Half of the U.S. 1st Armored Division was hurriedly moved north to assist the British.

Mockler-Ferryman was relying entirely on Ultra, which was always right but often ambiguous. It was right in that it really did reflect what the Germans were communicating to one another. The meaning, however, was not always clear. Normally, an impending German attack would be monitored not only by signal intelligence but also by aerial tactical reconnaissance, or Tac R. At this time, however, there was no Tac R for either the First Army or the II Corps. Without this crucial supplementary source of information Mockler-Ferryman was forced to make a guess.[6]

At dawn on Friday, February 13, Eisenhower set off from Algiers and at dusk the armored Cadillac pulled up at Fredendall's command post, some forty miles behind the front lines. To Ike's amazement, the air was filled not with the sound of artillery or tanks but of jackhammers and drills. Fredendall had Army engineers blasting into the sides of a ravine to create a bomb-proof bunker. "It was the only time during the war that I ever saw a divisional or higher headquarters so concerned over its own safety," Ike commented years later, still disgusted.[7]

Late that night, the Cadillac arrived up at the forward CP of the commander of 1st Armored Division, Major General Orlando Ward. Half the division's tanks were still in the north, with the British First Army, waiting for the Germans to attack. The other half of the division's combat strength was here, defending Sidi-bou-Zid. After talking to Ward, Ike headed back to Fredendall's construction site command post. Several hours later, von Arnim launched his attack, and it was aimed not at the First Army but at the II Corps.

One panzer division headed straight through Faid Pass toward Sidi-bou-Zid while a second one moved through the low hills twenty miles farther south, then turned north, to strike Ward's position in the flank and rear. Over the next twenty-four hours, Ward lost more than a hundred tanks, and three thousand American soldiers were killed, wounded or captured. He pulled the survivors back thirty miles, toward Kasserine Pass.[8]

Sidi-bou-Zid was an unmitigated defeat for Fredendall and enough of a victory for von Arnim. Not only had he shattered half of the 1st Armored Division, but his troops had overrun the AAF airfields at Thelepte, which had provided air cover for Allied troops across the Tunisian front. Ike was dismayed at losing a battle but, he told Marshall, "the real tragedy is the loss of the Thelepte airfields."[9]

Rommel had been denied the huge offensive he wanted but was authorized to capitalize on von Arnim's success. His fabled Afrika Korps was currently holding a strong defensive position known as the Mareth Line on the border between Tunisia and Libya, waiting for Montgomery to advance. Montgomery's slowness gave Rommel enough time to pull a division of the Afrika Korps out of the Mareth Line and hurry westward, to join up with one of von Arnim's panzer divisions. With two veteran divisions, Rommel believed he had enough muscle to brush the stunned and bleeding II Corps aside and break through into Eisenhower's rear positions, where he would loot and then burn the huge supply dump that U.S. quartermasters had created at Le Kef.

To reach Le Kef, Rommel had to push through Kasserine Pass. His troops thrust through the lightly held pass but failed to seize the high ground. That was held instead by American troops, who had scrambled up the slopes and began installing mortars and artillery along the ridge.

American losses in the fighting at Kasserine were light—roughly six hundred men. This conflict was, in fact, more of a skirmish than a battle. Kasserine bore no serious comparison to the disaster at Sidi-bou-Zid. But the presence of the glamorous figure of Rommel ensured that

Sidi-bou-Zid was virtually ignored by the press, while Kasserine Pass was portrayed as both an epic fight, something like Waterloo, and a military catastrophe, like Custer's Last Stand. In fact, though, Rommel hurried through the pass hoping he wouldn't have to come this way again, because he did not hold it; the U.S. II Corps did.[10]

Ike sent the commander of the 2nd Armored Division, a short, feisty and chubby cavalryman, Major General Ernest Harmon, to report on the situation. He arrived just as Fredendall had a nervous collapse and didn't get out of bed for the next twenty-four hours. While Fredendall took cover in his bunker, Harmon took control in the field. He organized a defensive position on the road to Le Kef and more or less ambushed Rommel, whose troops suddenly found they were up against the massed artillery of the U.S. 9th Division. The Germans were on the road to annihilation. They promptly scrambled back the way they had come. Rommel's only ambition now was to escape.[11]

Ike made the long journey to the front in the armored Cadillac again. With Rommel in full retreat, Eisenhower intended to destroy him. He told Fredendall to counterattack. Fredendall lacked the courage even to try. Rommel scurried away, aided by the craven timidity of a failed corps commander and several days of bad weather that foiled every attempt to punish him from the air.

Ike took out his frustration by firing Mockler-Ferryman, but even now he tried to protect Fredendall, telling Marshall that he was "a good fighter" and blaming the problems of the II Corps on Fredendall's staff. He even claimed, "Alexander likes him," which was simply untrue. The trouble was that not only had Ike passed over some abler men to choose Fredendall (almost certainly on Clark's advice) but that he had only recently recommended him for a third star—as good as saying that Fredendall deserved command of an army. Ike had made a monumental misjudgment, one all the harder to admit when it had ended in a major defeat, but on the evening of March 4, Alexander visited Ike and talked to him about Fredendall—"I'm sure you must have better men than that." The next morning, Ike fired Fredendall.[12]

Several days before the battle of Sidi-bou-Zid, Eisenhower had finally acted on Marshall's suggestion at Casablanca that he appoint a couple of officers to act as his "eyes and ears" and untangle his logistics and the endemic problems of discipline. He sent Marshall a list of names, and like all such lists it ranked people in order of preference. The third name on his list was Omar Bradley, who was first on Marshall's mental list of potential combat commanders. Marshall's protégé had never been Eisenhower; it had always been Bradley. Marshall sent him Bradley, as if to say he could do the work of two men.[13]

With his maps, pointer, rumpled appearance and homely visage, he looked like a straitlaced country schoolteacher, which was what his adored father had been back in southern Missouri, where the only other occupation open to a young man at the turn of the century was hard-scrabble farming. Encouraged and inspired by his father, Bradley had managed to get into West Point, where Eisenhower had envied him for his football feats on fall afternoons and his springtime successes at baseball. When they graduated in 1915, it was Ike who wrote the ad-miring pen portrait of Bradley for *The Howitzer,* with its confident, prophetic conclusion, "One day we'll be able to say, yeah, sure, I know General Bradley."

Since then, Bradley had become the Army's leading expert on in-fantry tactics. To him, war was not an arena for egotism, nor a holy cru-sade, still less a romantic adventure. War meant the professional management of socially acceptable violence, a responsibility that had to be discharged dispassionately and systematically. Although he had shown that he could train and lead troops effectively, Bradley's greatest skill was battle management—pulling supply, intelligence, transporta-tion and communications together in a way that got the most out of the fighting skills of his infantry. Bradley arrived in North Africa during the fighting around Kasserine Pass. Marshall's protégé had finally reached the war.[14]

Shortly after this, Ike asked Clark to take over the II Corps, but Clark refused. In January 1943 he had been given a new command, the Fifth Army, whose mission was to make sure the Spanish did not use Spanish Morocco to mount any kind of threat to the long, tenuous lines of communication running the six hundred miles from Casablanca to the front in Tunisia.[15] The fact that Ike needed his help, and needed it right now, didn't carry any weight with Clark. Moving from command-ing an army in the rear to a corps in combat was, in the Clark-centric mind, a demotion, not an opportunity and certainly not a duty.

Since they had arrived in North Africa, Ike had discovered the ex-

cessive ambition and craving for acclaim that motivated, if not dominated, his old friend. Clark courted publicity shamelessly. He even got
the head of Twentieth Century–Fox, Darryl F. Zanuck, into the theater,
in defiance of Ike's instructions, so that Zanuck might immortalize his
exploits on film. When he discovered that Zanuck had reached North
Africa, Ike promptly shipped him home. That did nothing, however, to
discourage Clark. Wherever he traveled, a military band preceded him,
as if he were an Oriental potentate.[16]

Patton, who was about to get his third star and was preparing to
command an army in the invasion of Sicily, took the II Corps without a
murmur of protest. What he wouldn't accept was having Bradley ("one
of Ike's goddamn spies," Patton snorted) come around from time to
time snooping on him.[17] He asked Ike to make Bradley his deputy corps
commander. Ike readily did so, because by this time his logistical problems were well on their way to solution. Somervell had not only managed to scrape up nearly six thousand trucks but found shipping for
them, at a time when there was supposed to be no spare shipping anywhere. Three weeks after Ike made his plea to Somervell, the trucks
were in North Africa. By March 1943 the supply dumps at Le Kef were
growing prodigiously, the rains were petering out and Montgomery was
coming up to the Mareth Line.[18]

Those long drives across gray, sodden landscapes were journeys of la-
tent drama. There was always a chance that a pair of Me-109s might
come flashing down toward the little convoy—the armored Cadillac
with a scout car in front and a weapons carrier behind, a spare limousine in case the Caddy broke down and a second scout car bringing up
the rear. Together, they made a large, slow-moving target and everybody
knew what to do: at the first sight of a strafer, stop the vehicles and run
like hell for about fifty yards, then lie flat on the ground and watch the
Caddy and the rest get shot to blazes.[19]

That never happened, but Ike might have welcomed some strafing
as a break from another drama, the one that was played out on the exhausting road journeys to the front. His driver, glancing from time to
time in the rearview mirror, caught glimpses of that expansive brow
furrowed into a pattern of wavy lines. Ike slumped slightly in the back-

seat, stared out of the window, silent for hours at a time, his thoughts playing across that mobile, expressive face with every jolting mile, absorbed in a general's soliloquy.[20]

Eisenhower worried about everything, great and small, personal or military. He had trained himself to appear calm, no matter what, in front of subordinates, yet he was a powerfully emotional man. He couldn't help that. Nor could he stop his mind from racing from care to care.

Why, for instance, when congratulations poured in from all over the world on his getting his fourth star, was there no message from Johnny? Something was wrong there. And Mamie . . . did she think he was getting involved with Kay or some other WAC? Wayne Clark was his friend and he owed a lot to him, but shouldn't he do something to curb Wayne's inordinate ambition? And how was he going to keep someone as volatile as Patton out of trouble? He had to convince Alexander that American soldiers would fight well once they got some experience, but Alexander was trying to keep them out of the heavy fighting, denying them the experience they needed. Why did so few junior officers arrive from the States able to lead their men in combat? And why were American troops so damned sloppy? They didn't seem to care what they looked like, while the British had a distinctive "battle dress" that made them look smart and military even in the field. He would have to devise something similar, some kind of snug-fitting jacket for American soldiers. And saluting. Why in the hell didn't Army officers make their men salute? He couldn't care less as a personal matter, but there was something seriously wrong when he could drive through Algiers with that big red plate on the front of the Cadillac, its four white stars as plain as day, and most soldiers he passed pretended not to notice. Failing to salute was always a sign of poor discipline. It was never going to be possible to beat the Hun without discipline. The airmen were the worst, though. He could walk across Maison Blanche airfield and not a single airman or AAF officer was likely to salute. Yet Spaatz never stopped pestering him about promoting AAF officers, and Jimmy Doolittle, commanding the Twelfth Air Force, acted more like a teenage fighter pilot than a general. When was he going to grow up? Then there were the damned French, refusing to operate under Anderson and the British First Army. Not that Anderson was any kind of military genius. Behind his back, Alexander called him "a good plain cook." But the French, who lacked the guts to fight as well as the British, wouldn't take orders

from any Britisher. They said they'd only take orders from him. So he'd
caved in to their whims, only for Giraud to start accusing him of reneg-
ing on the agreement to rearm the French, as if he were to blame for the
shortage of shipping. Marshall had backed him solidly at Casablanca,
but would he hold it against him that he had picked Fredendall to lead
II Corps in battle and the man turned out to be a coward? Brooke obviously despised him, and Brooke and Montgomery were old friends.
How was he going to get on with Monty? And even before this Tunisian
business was finished, he was having to plan Husky, the invasion of
Sicily. From what he'd seen of the Germans, they might be able to beat
an invasion if they had anything more than a couple of divisions well
dug in on the high ground overlooking the beaches. It could be like December in Tunisia all over again. And he simply had to get more sleep
and stop waking at four-thirty each morning, mind churning. Was it a
sign he was becoming weak-minded? Isn't that what happened when a
man began losing his grip?[21]

Montgomery and the Eighth Army had crossed the Libyan border during the fighting around the Kasserine Pass, and approached the tough
defenses of the Mareth Line. Rommel got back safely and prepared to
make a spoiling attack. Montgomery was following these preparations
closely. Ultra revealed every move, every intention this time, and Tac R
played its confirming role. When the Afrika Korps struck, on March 6,
it was ambushed by six hundred well-concealed antitank guns. Shortly
afterward, Rommel was flown out of North Africa, never to return.[22]

Von Arnim finally had undisputed command of the Italo-German
army defending Tunisia. His task was hopeless. Ultra exposed every attempt to ship fuel and ammunition to him, and most of the supply ships
and oil tankers trying to make a dash from Sicilian ports were sunk.
When Hitler tried to create an air bridge, Ultra exposed that, too. Hundreds of trimotor Junkers transports—many of them manned by Luftwaffe flying instructors and veteran bomber pilots—were shot down in
aerial ambushes. The loss of so many skilled multiengine pilots was a
blow from which the Luftwaffe's bomber arm never recovered. By April
1943, von Arnim's panzers, his sole offensive threat, were so short of
fuel they were virtually immobilized.[23]

On April 2, Ike received a phone call from Tedder. Patton's aide, Captain Richard Jenson, had been killed in a German air attack the previous day. Distraught and tearful, Patton had vented his grief by amending an official report to read, "Total lack of air cover [allows] German air forces to operate almost at will." The commander of the Allied tactical air units, an outspoken New Zealander, Air Vice Marshal "Mary" Coningham, had promptly struck back, calling American soldiers "not battleworthy" in an official report.

Eisenhower was plunged into fury and despair. He dictated a letter of resignation to the Combined Chiefs, telling them that if he could not win the cooperation of important subordinates such as Patton and Coningham, he could not serve as a supreme commander. Beetle Smith talked Ike out of sending it, but whether he really intended to send it isn't certain. Tedder told Coningham to apologize to Patton, which he did, and Ike rebuked Patton.[24]

When his aide was killed, Patton was pushing the II Corps toward the Tunisian coast, putting pressure on the Mareth Line from the rear. On April 7, a cable landed on Ike's desk that said patrols from the II Corps had linked up with British patrols from the Eighth Army. He felt an immense sense of relief. There was now a single Allied battle line across central and southern Tunisia and the II Corps had been transformed under Patton's leadership. With the II Corps problem solved, Ike released Patton to return to planning the invasion of Sicily. Bradley took command of the II Corps.[25]

Alexander, meanwhile, was drawing up a directive to have the First and Eighth armies converge on Tunis. The II Corps would come under the control of General Anderson, and its mission would be to support Monty's advance from the Mareth Line, which he was about to attack. Bradley protested vehemently to Ike that his troops were being squeezed out. The British would march into Tunis in triumph while the Americans looked on from somewhere in the hills. Eisenhower agreed with him, and told Alexander that it would do immeasurable harm if people in the U.S. got the idea that American soldiers were denied their share of the glory. Bradley urged that all American ground units in Tunisia should be brought together under II Corps and given a mission of their own—capturing Bizerte.[26]

Alexander amended the plan to satisfy Ike and Bradley, but he remained deeply skeptical about the fighting ability of American troops, with some justification. The four U.S. divisions in Tunisia—the 1st, 9th and 34th Infantry, plus the 1st Armored Division—had been shipped overseas long before they completed the divisional training cycle. The 34th had been the first to depart for Europe, because Eisenhower knew, liked and trusted its commander. Back in 1911, Ike had gone to St. Louis to take the West Point entrance exam and met a gangling, tow-headed Kansas farm boy, someone much like himself, by the name of Charles "Doc" Ryder. They had become friends at West Point and Ryder had won two DSCs and two Purple Hearts in World War I.

In February 1942, when Ike was at the War Plans Division, the question of which division should be deployed to Britain first had to be settled, and quickly. It was a remarkable coincidence that the choice fell on the 34th, which had not done much to distinguish itself in maneuvers but happened to be commanded by Ike's old friend Doc Ryder. The 34th paid heavily for the honor of leading the way to Europe. No division was sent overseas with so little training in World War II, and now its amateurs were fighting German pros.

On April 22, the First and Eighth armies began their drive on Tunis. Next day, the II Corps made its attack, spearheaded by the 34th Division, which had to capture a two-thousand-foot peak called Hill 609. It tried three times, failed three times, but Ike supported Doc Ryder and defended the division against its critics. On its fourth attempt, the 34th triumphed. By May 2, the hill was secured and the road to Bizerte was open for the II Corps.[27]

On May 7, the 9th Infantry Division marched into Bizerte—mission accomplished. That same afternoon, the British captured Tunis. There was more fighting to do, but on May 15 it ended, exactly as Ike had told Roosevelt it would. He couldn't help feeling slightly astonished that the pinpoint accuracy of his own prediction had been so resoundingly vindicated.

Germans and Italians poured out of bunkers and trenches, arms raised overhead, in *feldgrau* uniforms that were ragged and dirty, and he was flabbergasted. Ike had told Marshall there were 150,000 enemy troops opposing his armies. There were, instead, more than 250,000, two-thirds of them German. He had nearly twice as many prisoners as the Soviets had taken into captivity at Stalingrad. German generals bitterly called this strategic and avoidable debacle "Tunisgrad."[28]

Alexander and Monty were planning a victory parade, an idea that

Eisenhower privately disparaged. It seemed anachronistic somehow. So did the request from his defeated foe, von Arnim, to be allowed to pay a courtesy call. He turned von Arnim down. But Ike was not all high-mindedness at close of battle. The French, ran a joke common in North Africa, fought for glory; the British fought for the king; and the Americans were fighting for souvenirs. Eisenhower told Monty, "A couple of Luger pistols represent all the loot I want to take back from this war." Could the Eighth Army help him out? It did so.[29]

On May 20 the Americans, British and Free French marched through Tunis, beneath fat palm trees whose exuberant curving fronds cast a web of shadows over rhythmically moving bayonets winking under an African sun. The men were tanned and sinewy and in their confident stride and on their uptilted faces was the unshakeable will of the conquering soldier; in their stern young eyes was the pride of battle won that seeks yet other fields of glory.

As they marched past the crowded reviewing stand to braying brass that mingled with the sound of marching boots and groaning tank treads and bellowed, "Eyes right!" Ike felt a surge of unexpected emotion. "I could never have believed it possible even to dream of such an honor as to command an army like this!" he told the generals clustered around him. He was in a state close to rapture, as if this day were a dream.[30]

★★★★★

18

Missed Chances

When the Tunisian campaign ended, Kay Summersby and her fiancé, Colonel Richard Arnold, were still hoping to get married on June 22, but there was no news yet that her husband's divorce suit had been finalized. While Kay was waiting, impatiently we have to assume, to hear that she was at last free to marry, Ike received a message from Lucian Truscott: "Colonel Richard E. Arnold, Commanding Officer 20th Engineers, killed instantly about 1100 hours, June 6, while on inspection of mine clearing work, being carried out by elements of his command. Death resulted from his tripping on trip wire that set off concrete mine." Ike ordered that "special care be taken in marking and caring for Arnold's grave." Then he called the villa and told his orderly, Sergeant Mickey McKeogh, to place a dozen clean handkerchiefs on a small table in the living room.[1]

He waited until they were back at the villa that evening before he told her. "Kay, I am going to give this to you straight," he said. "Dick has been killed." They were now in the living room and she collapsed onto the sofa, weeping and distraught. Putting a comforting arm around her shoulders, Ike reached with his free hand for one of the clean handkerchiefs. "There, there. Blow your nose." By the time she stopped weeping, there was a pile of crumpled, soggy handkerchiefs at their feet. He gave her some advice. "Activity helps. I've learned that my-self," he said, thinking, inevitably, of Ikky.[2]

Over the weeks that followed, he found plenty of things for her to do. She became so much a presence that Bradley called her "Ike's shadow." Wherever Ike went so, it seemed, did Kay. She drove him nearly everywhere now, and at AFHQ he put her to work in a small room adjoining his office and let her tackle the tidal wave of fan mail that followed victory in Tunisia. Able to imitate his signature to perfection, Kay sent out thousands of photographs and thank-you notes convincingly counterfeited "Dwight D. Eisenhower."

According to Kay Summersby, the weeks immediately after Arnold's death brought a mutual recognition that she and Ike were hopelessly in love. She had never really loved Arnold, she decided. How could she? They had barely known one another. It was a relationship based on a few snatched moments in the middle of a war. With Ike, though, it was different. They were together all the time, holding hands, kissing, exchanging meaningful glances, passionately involved even if their affair was never consummated physically.

What she claims might be true; no one will ever know for certain. The fact is, however, that not one of the half dozen people who were part of Ike's wartime "family" believed then or later that there was any kind of romance between Ike and Kay. Butcher, McKeogh and the WACs on the staff with whom Kay shared rooms and forged friendships that lasted until her death in 1976 all poured scorn on her claim. Nor could she produce a single piece of material evidence to confirm it. Her memoir *Past Forgetting* reproduces a small card on which Eisenhower had scribbled, "Good luck to Kay," and another card that reads, "Good night. There are lots of things I could wish to say. You know them." Such anodyne souvenirs are but frail reeds bending, before ultimately collapsing, under the enormous weight she placed on them.

Besides, her story is riddled with holes, beginning with Telek, the incontinent black Scottie. According to Kay, Ike got the dog not for himself but for the two of them, as a surrogate child, and its name was a combination of Telegraph Cottage and Kay. "Two parts of my life that make me very happy," Ike is supposed to have told her. Yet this occurred when she was simply one of several people who drove him around London.[3]

Shortly before he acquired a dog, Ike was looking for a way to dismiss the British women drivers. "I prefer men drivers," he'd told Butcher. Besides, he added, being driven around by an attractive red-

head didn't look right; it was open to misunderstanding and sure to provoke gossip. It was only after he concluded, reluctantly, that it would
take Americans too long to learn their way around London, especially
in the blackouts, that Ike abandoned the idea. Rather than seeking a way
to bring the two of them closer, Ike had been looking for a chance to get
rid of her.[4]

As for Telek's name, it makes perfect sense without Kay. It was
either an abbreviated version of Telegraph Cottage, concocted at a time
when *k* was often used as substitute for *c* in cable addresses. Or, more
likely, it was simply a name that combined Telegraph Cottage and Ike.
And although he brushed aside journalists' questions as to what Telek
meant, the existence of Telegraph Cottage as his country hideaway *was*
a wartime military secret.

"All we had needed to complete our little wartime family and make
Telegraph Cottage a real home was a child. And Telek, for us, was a reasonable facsimile," claimed Kay in *Past Forgetting*, published in 1976.
She ignores the fact that the supposed surrogate child was being acquired at a time when she had begun sleeping with Richard Arnold. Her
version of events was that she and Arnold had met, fallen hopelessly,
head-over-heels in love and done the decent thing by asking their re-
spective spouses to divorce them. The truth, however, was that she had
begun an affair with Arnold while still married. Her husband had discovered it and sued for divorce on the grounds of her adultery. Mrs.
Arnold had then learned of her husband's affair with Kay and sued for
divorce on the same grounds. In *Past Forgetting*, Kay claimed she had
divorced her husband because they had drifted apart. This was a lie, told
by a woman who'd cheated on her husband when he was India, serving
in the British Army.[5]

In *Eisenhower Was My Boss*, published in 1948, Kay said that when
Ike went back to London in June 1942, following his brief trip to England in May, he brought a crate of fresh fruit with him to distribute
among various people he had met on the earlier visit. But in *Past Forgetting*, written nearly thirty years later, she becomes the sole recipient
of the gift of fresh fruit. She becomes, that is, someone he specially
wanted to please, and this small gift is where he first signals that she
was on his mind while he was away and that he was eager to please her
on his return. This scenario works only if no one else shares in the
bounty, so in *Past Forgetting*, no one else does.[6]

There is much else besides in Kay's account that doesn't add up.

She says it was Roosevelt who intervened to get her commissioned in the Women's Army Corps, despite the fact that she was a British subject. In truth, however, she got her commission because MacArthur's chief of staff, Richard K. Sutherland, and two other generals in MacArthur's command had obtained WAC commissions for their Australian girlfriends. When Ike asked about getting a commission for Kay, Marshall could only sigh and let it go through.

It is telling, too, that in describing Ike's character, she damages her own case for a clandestine romance that was conducted with a kind of perfection. Subterfuge, she says, "was not in keeping with his character. Dwight D. Eisenhower was a man of the utmost integrity."[7]

Finally, it is worth noting that in *Eisenhower Was My Boss,* there is an explicit acknowledgment that she had a ghostwriter, Michael Kearns. *Past Forgetting,* on the other hand, is presented as being written entirely by Kay and Kay alone. In fact, though, she had a ghostwriter, Barbara Wyden.

The back story to *Past Forgetting* was that Kay was dying of cancer and, in the grip of certain death, was reviewing a life that was a tale of failure and disappointment. She had wasted so many opportunities and privileges that her life almost cried out for a redeeming experience, something powerful enough, dramatic enough, to lift it above the dismal truth. As a young woman, Kay Summersby had attracted a wide choice of suitors. Married twice, both of her marriages failed. She tried to make a career in the postwar military, and gave up. Trying to earn a living at various civilian jobs, she failed at all of them. She had mingled with presidents, prime ministers and generals, but ended her days broke and alone.

Even so, she was not simply trying to cash in by inventing fiction and calling it a memoir. It seems unlikely that either Kay or Ike could ever have given a clear, objective account of the nature of their relationship. The likeliest explanation is that Eisenhower needed her and he indirectly admitted as much and that she read into his admission a passion that was not there and never would be. She read love into opaque utterances that to him were merely words of gratitude or fondness.

Eisenhower was like many another strong man with a weakness for which there is neither armor nor cure: he needed to see the sustaining reflection of himself that shines only in a woman's eyes. MacArthur had his wife with him to provide it. Marshall went home each night to

Mrs. Marshall. Churchill had Clementine, and Roosevelt had Lucy Rutherford. Ike was in North Africa, far from a wife he had not seen for a year. Mamie wasn't there to gaze at him with her stunning china blue eyes, listen to him with that slightly amused expression playing at the corners of her mouth or slip a tiny hand within one of his huge, powerful paws.

Eisenhower was using Kay, in a one-sided relationship that was exploitative and manipulative. To some extent, it was an old story— "Man's love is of man's life a thing apart/'Tis woman's whole existence," says Byron's Don Juan. Even the war could be invoked as justification. A general has a staff not to provide him with friends or a make-believe family but to provide him with people who will help him win battles. Kay was a member of his staff, and if she hadn't been a civilian looking for love in all the wrong places, she would have realized that and, at thirty-four, seen it for what it was, accepted it or walked away.

She wanted so much to believe that Ike loved her, but the space between fondness and true love is immense. She never managed to bridge it with any man—not with her two husbands, not with Dick Arnold, still less with Ike. For all that Kay Summersby wrote about love, she knew little about it, for throughout her unhappy life it eluded her.

When Ike went to Casablanca in January 1943, he was given the outline plan for Operation Husky, the invasion of Sicily, produced by the Joint Planning Staff in London. He wasn't impressed. It seemed to him that it lacked punch in the assault and dispersed the invading forces too widely. He thought it would be better to concentrate the assault against the island's southeastern coast. The logistics experts told him that wouldn't work. There wouldn't be enough LSTs to put both Montgomery's Eighth Army and Patton's Seventh Army ashore in one sealift with all the tanks, trucks and artillery they were going to need.[8]

In mid-February, Alexander came into the picture as Ike's deputy for ground forces and took over as the chief planner for Husky. Sicily was going to be a huge and complex operation, bigger than any amphibious assault ever attempted. Assault units would be sailing from Egypt and Malta, Algeria and Tunisia, Morocco and Gibraltar, England

and Virginia. Choreographing so many complex naval movements with the operational sorties of several thousand aircraft, the amphibious assaults of seven divisions, plus the air assault of two airborne divisions—one American, one British—was so difficult that it seemed to rule out proper concentration or coordination. The planners, in effect, threw up their hands and proposed to land these forces piecemeal, in stages, even though that carried a high risk of defeat in detail. Alexander, however, was so preoccupied with coordinating the operations of two British armies and the U.S. II Corps in Tunisia that he made few changes.

The strategic objective on Sicily was the port of Messina, on the northeast coast. Messina controls communications with the Italian mainland, only three miles away. The outline plan called for the British Eighth Army to take Syracuse, eighty miles south of Messina, while Patton's Seventh Army took Palermo, 150 miles west of Messina. This would give each army its own port and put each in a position to seize some of Sicily's best airfields within days of going ashore. Patton and Monty would then converge on Messina, with the British skirting the eastern side of Mount Etna and the Americans passing across the volcano's northern flank. Although the plan involved dividing Allied forces in the assault, it offered a better chance of success than did making a single thrust on one side or the other of Mount Etna. The topography around the volcano would allow a determined defender to concentrate his forces on a narrow front in mountainous terrain. Facing two widely dispersed thrusts, on the other hand, would force him to spread his forces, thinning them out and increasing the chances of an Allied breakthrough.

The outline plan anticipated the presence of up to six Italian and two German divisions on Sicily. By April 1943, Ike had seen enough of German fighting ability to conclude that if the planners were right, Husky was probably doomed. It was hard to see how the weak first echelon could survive a strong counterattack by two German panzer divisions.[9]

Churchill was aghast at such pessimism. "If the presence of two divisions is held to be decisive against any operations of an offensive or amphibious character open to the million men now in French North Africa, it is difficult to see how the war can be carried on."[10]

By late April, it was finally possible for Alexander, Tedder and Cunningham to take a close look at the plan and they were soon completely deadlocked. Nobody was satisfied with it. And when Montgomery studied the plan, he derided it as "a dog's breakfast." Certainly, there were some serious flaws in the plan. Landing in echelons was a bad idea, and the assault in southeastern Sicily simply had to be made stronger in case the opposition it faced proved to be German rather than Italian.

Monty, however, wasn't interested in improvements or modifications. He was demanding that Patton and the Seventh Army be limited to defending his left flank, not heading for Messina by way of Palermo—in effect, a different plan, one that minimized the American role and maximized his own.[11]

This approach threw out the best part of the outline plan—its strategic design: it sought to trap large numbers of Germans and Italians by the rapid capture of Messina. Montgomery's plan, even if it worked perfectly, would do nothing more than push them out of Sicily and over to the Italian mainland.

He was also slighting the need to seize major airfields quickly, was denying the Seventh Army a port and forcing Patton to rely on over-the-beach supply. He seemed blithely indifferent to the fact that he was expecting the Allied naval force to concentrate in waters likely to be heavily mined, and assumed it would remain well within the range of enemy airpower without any assurance of adequate air cover. Not surprisingly, naval planners expected to lose up to three hundred ships if Montgomery got his way.

Part of Ike's difficulties with Monty sprang from Monty's prickly personality, but far more important was that Montgomery's misfortune was to reach the top of his profession just as it reached the threshold of a magnitude leap in combined operations.

There was a paradigm shift under way in military operations in 1943–1945, a shift that went far beyond the much-vaunted concept of blitzkrieg. The future of war was henceforth going to be defined by two words—*combined* and *joint.* Eisenhower was almost the first among senior Allied commanders to accept that fact without hesitation, equivocation or qualification. By the time World War II ended, he wanted to abolish the separate services and put all military personnel into the same uniform. Monty, by comparison with Eisenhower's grasp of the evolution of modern warfare, was and would remain a generation behind.

He might have ridden the shifting tide had it not been for an unyielding sense of being always in the right, which is not the same thing as confidence. With Monty becoming a stranger in a military world that was moving inexorably toward the multiplied combat power of combined and joint, it was no surprise, then, that from Husky onward, Allied air and naval commanders increasingly, and scathingly, disparaged his abilities. So too, before the war ended, would many senior British generals and war correspondents.[12]

On May 2, Monty cornered Beetle Smith in one of the bathrooms at the St. Georges Hotel, steamed up a mirror over one of the basins and with his right forefinger made a crude triangular shape to represent Sicily, then drew a couple of arrows pointing at the southeastern corner. Mass is what matters, Monty told Smith, and we have to put it all here. Smith agreed with him, and told Ike so. Smith's conversion broke the deadlock between Alexander, Cunningham and Tedder. Monty would get his way. At the very least, it would do what Eisenhower had wanted from the beginning—focus the assault on the southeastern corner.

Meanwhile, the biggest weakness—having to make an assault in echelons—was going to be eliminated. One of the bright lieutenant colonels on the Joint Planning Staff, a Rhodes scholar by the name of Charles H. Bonesteel III, had worked on the outline plan and been profoundly troubled by the acute shortage of LSTs (see pages 256–57). He also found another problem, nearly as bad. A mile or so out from the invasion beaches were long lines of sandbars. Bonesteel went to see the head of the War Production Board, Donald Nelson, and told him Husky would probably fail for want of LSTs. Nelson issued an emergency top priority rating for production of landing ships and landing craft. The attack would not have to be made in echelons: all seven divisions in the amphibious assault would land at the same time.

That left the sandbars. But Bonesteel had heard about an experimental amphibious two-and-a-half-ton truck called the DUKW that had rescued the crew of a naval vessel in distress off Cape Cod one stormy night in December 1942. He had a feeling this odd amphibian was the key to unlocking the sandbars.[13]

He went to Algiers and told Ike about the DUKW. Bonesteel had never seen one. Neither had Ike, but he had a feeling Bonesteel was right. In his mind's eye he could see LSTs bellying up to the line of sandbars that screened the invasion beaches and disgorging DUKWs loaded with troops, rations and artillery. The DUKWs would chug across the sandbars, slide into the water on the other side, unload on the invasion beaches a mile or so distant, then go back to the LSTs for more. Ike sent a message to the War Department demanding that all DUKW production be committed to Husky.[14]

In the immediate aftermath of the Tunisian campaign, the Combined Chiefs met in Washington to try and decide where to go after Sicily. It was unthinkable that a million Allied soldiers, sailors and airmen in the Mediterranean would rest on their laurels from mid-1943 until spring 1944. Churchill had no doubts—Italy was "the first objective . . . the great prize" that drew his gaze across the Strait of Messina.

Five Italian divisions were occupying southwestern France. There were twenty-nine divisions occupying the Balkans. Knocking Italy out of the war would force German soldiers to take their place.

To Marshall, however, the Italian mainland was a trap. His mind and heart were set on a landing in northern France in the spring of 1944. Italy looked like a sideshow to him, an invitation not to success but to stalemate.

The Combined Chiefs sanctioned a cross-Channel attack in 1944, but left it to Ike to decide where he would strike after Sicily. He was told only to look for a way of forcing an Italian capitulation and to try to pin down the maximum number of Germans. He was free, that is, to mount an Italian campaign in the fall of 1943, provided it would help pave the way for an invasion of France in spring 1944.[15]

From Washington, Churchill headed for Algiers, shrewdly getting Roosevelt to order Marshall to go with him. Eisenhower was always pleased to see Churchill. Their mutual admiration and trust was becoming the bedrock on which a truly Allied command could be built. Even so, the PM could be wearing. If he had a case to make—and he usually did—he was as unrelenting as a salesman with a foot wedged in your front door. Churchill arrived in Algiers to sell Ike on Italy and dangle before him the mirage of strategic riches beyond. Churchill made his pitch at breakfast, lunch and dinner, his volubility distracting attention from table manners of the insouciant variety best left to truckers and aristocrats. During his long soak in a hot tub daily during his week and a half in Algiers, he summoned Ike into the bathroom, to perch on the toilet and talk strategy amid cigar smoke and mirrors.[16]

During a formal session with Churchill and his military advisers, including General Sir Alan Brooke, Eisenhower grew so confident about Allied prospects in the Mediterranean that he unwisely remarked that an invasion of France in 1944 might prove "unnecessary . . . a drop in the bucket." Churchill's riposte was, "Both the British people and the British Army are anxious to fight across the Channel"—an extraordinary claim in view of the fact that Churchill had come all this way to make the case for an open-ended commitment in the Mediterranean.[17]

When Brooke later managed to talk to Ike alone, he tried to tell him he was right. An invasion of France wouldn't be necessary, provided the Allies pursued the correct strategy. With Italy out of the war, Allied air bombing the Reich around the clock and Allied navies destroying Hitler's U-boats, all that remained was to let the Red Army grind the German Army into the dust.

By the time of this conversation, Eisenhower had already changed his mind. "How," Ike said to Brooke, "would you like conduct a war on the plan you've just outlined and then find that all of Central and Western Europe has been overrun by the Russians? How do you think we could deal with the Soviets?" Oh, said Brooke, the Soviets will obviously pull back to Russia; Stalin won't want to hold on to anything beyond Russia's borders. Eisenhower could only marvel at the political innocence of Britain's senior soldier.[18]

While he was wrangling with Churchill and Brooke, Ike was also having to deal with de Gaulle, who had arrived from London. Roosevelt made it clear that he didn't want Eisenhower to have anything to do with de Gaulle and was still backing Giraud, but Churchill knew that de Gaulle could sway the French and Giraud could not. He had no illusions, though, describing de Gaulle to Eisenhower as "an egomaniac."[19]

De Gaulle and Giraud agreed to establish a French "committee of national liberation" (FCNL) in Algiers, under their joint leadership. On June 4, Ike hosted a luncheon for the two Frenchmen, an event that cemented their new partnership and allowed them to pledge mutual cooperation, through fixed smiles and bristling mustaches. In the weeks and months that followed, de Gaulle and his followers gradually took over the committee, to Roosevelt's dismay. But Eisenhower, like Churchill, had come to accept the inevitable rise of *le Grand Charles,* who would not only push Giraud aside but was already turning the FCNL into a provisional government.[20]

Churchill left for London on June 5, and three days later, Ike went to take a look at Pantelleria. This small island, strategically placed between Sicily and Tunisia, had for years been touted as an Italian Gibraltar, an impregnable fortress. There was a lot to be said for trying to take it, if only for its large, modern airfield, which would allow the enemy to launch strong air attacks against the convoys sailing for Sicily if left alone. But there was no beach on which to land an invading force. Any landing would have to be made within the small harbor, and would be exposed to the fire of eighty large coastal guns.

Eisenhower would later forget that his first inclination was to avoid any attack on Pantelleria, but a message from Marshall in the closing days of the Tunisian campaign had indirectly criticized him for being too conservative and suggested he "lacked adaptability." Pantelleria, this supposed Gibraltar, was his chance to show Marshall he was wrong. Besides, if he could seize it, that huge airfield would provide air cover for Husky's convoys and allow him to launch a big air campaign against Sicily ahead of the assault.[21]

The British 1st Division was available and had trained for amphibious warfare. It was assigned to take Pantelleria, but its commander, Major General Walter Clutterbuck, came to see Eisenhower and told him he expected his division would be slaughtered. Alexander and Brooke agreed with Clutterbuck.

Even so, a British scientist, Solly Zuckerman, thought it was possible to neutralize strong, fixed defenses such as heavy coastal guns by intensive air attack. Eisenhower turned Pantelleria into an experiment to see if Zuckerman was right. The island was pounded for three weeks in an air campaign that built to a climax on June 8, when Ike and Cunningham looked on from the deck of a Royal Navy cruiser, HMS *Aurora*. Cunningham remarked casually that the seas around Pantelleria had been heavily mined, but they were now inside a channel that had been swept. "Are there no floating mines about?" asked Eisenhower.

"Oh, yes," said Cunningham, as if that were the most obvious thing in the world. "But at this speed the bow wave will throw them away from the ship. It would be just bad luck if we should strike one."[22]

American and British air crews put on a maximum effort that day, drenching the small island with high explosive. Eisenhower thrilled at the precision of the air attack. As the heavy bombers flew away at twenty thousand feet, the mediums arrived, flying below radar coverage, and as the mediums finished, the light bombers came in, flashing low over the water, bombing the smaller targets and dropping leaflets that demanded surrender. Fighter-bombers flew in after the light bombers left, to strafe the barracks and other installations. Throughout the four-hour attack, Italian antiaircraft fire was weak and ineffectual. The feared coastal batteries barked fitfully, then fell silent, their crews dead, wounded or paralyzed with fear.[23]

Ike turned to Cunningham as Pantelleria shook and boiled and thick pillars of smoke curled thousands of feet into the high summer sky. "Andrew, if you and I got into a small boat, we could capture the place ourselves."[24]

After two more days of air and naval bombardment, the British 1st Division made its assault, on June 11. The Italians rushed toward the invaders, waving surrender leaflets. The only casualty was a British soldier bitten by a jackass. Scattered around the airfield was the wreckage of nearly a thousand German and Italian aircraft.[25]

For the rest of his life, whenever Ike met anyone who so much as hinted that he had been a cautious, conservative commander, his answer was, "Pantelleria," a place they couldn't remember but one he could never forget.[26]

With this success, a ferocious counter–air campaign was launched from the modern all-weather airfields of Bizerte, Tunis and Pantelleria to drive the German and Italian air forces out of their airfields on Sicily. Holding a three-to-one advantage in combat aircraft, Ike's air commanders had the upper hand and used it like a club. Heavy bombers hit the ports and the marshaling yards while mediums attacked enemy airfields day after day. Axis air units had lost both the will and the mass to put up a serious defense. They were driven out of the best airfields of central and eastern Sicily. Humiliated, Hermann Göring ordered the courts-martial of dozens of Luftwaffe fighter pilots for cowardice.[27]

Shortly before the invasion, Eisenhower went to visit the 3rd Infantry Division, commanded now by Lucian K. Truscott. Visiting his old division again—especially to meet up with his old regiment, the 15th Infantry—stirred his emotions, awoke dormant memories of field-soldiering in the Cascades, the excitement of leading men in mock battles through rain and the mud, baking heat and rattling snakes. There were scores of officers and NCOs to greet him whom he remembered from those hectic days and sleepless nights at Fort Lewis, three years earlier. "There is no better division in the Army than the 3rd," he told them. "And no better regiment in any division than the 15th." What he didn't tell them, but almost surely thought, was that he would have gladly yielded all that the Army had given him since then—rank, status, medals, fame—to go with them to Sicily, to be, just once, the complete soldier, an infantry officer leading men into battle.[28]

On July 8, with Husky less than forty-eight hours away, Ike flew to Malta with Alexander and Cunningham. The Royal Navy had an excellent, modern communications center there. His quarters, though, were in a tunnel nearly as squalid as the one on Gibraltar—a small room so damp it was impossible to light a cigarette and so cold he had to wear his overcoat while he worked. It was located next to a stairway that led down to a dungeon used for centuries to confine prisoners guilty of the traditional sailor sins—mutiny, drunkenness, sodomy.[29]

The next morning, the huge Allied armada for Husky assembled in the waters off Malta. German reconnaissance planes flew high overhead, as expected, but six weeks earlier the body of a British major had been dropped from a British submarine off the Spanish coast. The dead major was carrying a letter to Alexander that referred to a planned Allied landing, code name Husky, that was going to be mounted in July against beaches in Greece. The invasion fleet, said the letter, would feint north toward Sicily, before heading east.[30]

Hitler fell for it, and sent reinforcements to the Balkans and Greece. Kesselring, however, was convinced the letter was a fake and did what Eisenhower feared most—he built up German forces on Sicily from five thousand men until, by early July, he had two divisions there, the 15th Panzer Grenadier Division and the Hermann Göring Parachute Panzer Division, both elite formations. The Husky invaders would enjoy no benefit of surprise.[31]

The afternoon of July 9, as the invasion fleet began steaming toward the beaches of Sicily, Ike walked from his dank quarters over to the communications center and noticed the sails on the windmills that dotted the nearby hills rotating into a blur. The barometer fell, the wind howled, the sea rose. Unless the wind slackened, Eisenhower would have to call the invasion off. When the sun went down, there was still no improvement. He could only hope his weather forecasters were right when they said that night would bring an improvement.[32]

The airborne troops would reach Sicily first, landing in the early hours of July 10 to seize key objectives. More than three hundred C-47's carrying paratroopers and towing gliders crammed with men of the U.S. 82nd and British 1st Airborne divisions took off from bases in Tunisia, and when darkness fell they were droning toward Malta, where they would turn northwest for Sicily. Ike, Butcher, Mountbatten and Cunningham climbed a hill surmounted by a lighthouse to watch the passage of their obsidian silhouettes across the purple satin of the night. Back in his small, damp room, Ike rubbed his six lucky coins, climbed into bed and fell asleep.[33]

At dawn, fourteen hundred warships and troop transports—loaded with 160,000 men and eleven hundred landing craft—closed on the beaches of southeastern Sicily. The gale had given the men going ashore a nauseating night. Seven Allied divisions staggered onto the beaches of Sicily retching. Even so, the breaks were already evening out—an American air attack had wiped out the communications center of the Axis defense headquarters on Sicily. It would be nearly midnight before it was back in operation.

The next day, the Germans and Italians launched a strong counter-attack against the Seventh Army, but there were enough men ashore and, with naval gunnery, enough firepower to crush it. That night, a reinforcement of two thousand American paratroopers flew toward Sicily. In the darkness and confusion, Navy gunners opened up, shooting down twenty-three C-47's and damaging dozens more.[34]

In the early hours of July 12, Ike boarded a Royal Navy destroyer, HMS *Petard.* Next morning he met up with Patton aboard a U.S. Navy cruiser and rebuked him for not sending back adequate reports during the July 11 fighting. Patton noted in disgust: "Ike is now wearing suede shoes, à la British."[35]

Eisenhower returned to the *Petard,* and shortly afterward a well-concealed Italian coastal battery opened fire on the vessel. The destroyer's commander insisted that Eisenhower wear a helmet, and he tried it on, but it was absurdly small. "If I use this," Eisenhower grumbled to John Gunther, who was writing a book on the invasion, "I'll need two men to hold it on!" A couple of hours later, he hailed a passing DUKW and went ashore in the British sector for a brief visit. By evening, he was back in Malta, thrilled and excited.[36]

With the beachhead secure, Montgomery began pushing north, but after only five days the Germans had him blocked on the southeastern slopes of Mount Etna. He relaunched his offensive, but the Germans brought in two more divisions and stopped him again. Meanwhile, Patton became restive. There was no threat against the British Eighth Army's left flank, which meant there was little or nothing for his army to do. He began probing westward, then struck north, toward Palermo. With the 3rd Infantry in the lead, the Seventh Army began outflanking Mount Etna and headed toward Messina. Patton was, in effect, following the strategy of the discarded outline plan, the strategy that Monty had called "a dog's breakfast."

On July 19, five hundred B-17's of Jimmy Doolittle's Twelfth Air Force mounted one of the heaviest raids of the war to date with an attack on the railroad yards of Rome. For three years, Mussolini, King Victor Emmanuel III and the military high command had, in common with the ordinary Roman in the via, convinced themselves that no matter what happened, their beautiful and historic Rome, the cradle of Western civilization, a place holy before Christianity existed, was too precious ever to be bombed. When this myth of inviolability was blown apart, it demoralized and terrified them. Six days later, the king and his generals forced Mussolini out of office and placed him under arrest. Italy wasn't out of the war yet, but the first step toward its exit had just been taken. Eisenhower, meanwhile, rode out the storm of protest from Catholic opinion at home for sanctioning a heavy bombing within the boundaries of Rome. Fortunately, there were few stray bombs and damage to religious sites was slight.[37]

Even as the reverberations from this mission died away, the commander of the Ninth Air Force, Major General Lewis Brereton, was preparing to launch one of the most controversial air operations in history—a low-level attack with B-24's on the huge oil complex at Ploeşti, in central Romania. Eisenhower and Tedder knew that Ploeşti was operating at only 50 percent of its capacity. The most the raid could hope to achieve was to reduce spare capacity; it stood no chance of reducing oil output. Ike tried to talk Brereton out of mounting this attack, but when he failed to dissuade him, Eisenhower loyally supported Brereton.[38]

The attack, launched on August 1, was a disaster. Of the 164 bombers that reached Ploeşti, seventy-three were lost, a fact that was concealed for many years. Instead, the AAF made much of the extraordinary courage shown by its air crews in one of the most daring, vigorously pressed bombing attacks of the war. Five Medals of Honor were awarded for Ploeşti. It would have been possible to justify a dozen.

Back on June 11, the day Pantelleria was captured, Eisenhower had reminded Marshall that "today marks the completion of my twenty-eighth year of commissioned service and I believe I am legally eligible for promotion to colonel." Although he currently wore four stars, his rank as general was temporary. He was still just a light colonel in the Regular Army.[39]

Marshall was more than willing to promote him, but Ike had to pass a physical first. It was August 10, as the Sicilian campaign was drawing to a close, before he could find the time for it, and the results were alarming. His blood pressure was so high that the doctors who examined him told him to go to bed for a week. He complied to the extent of not leaving his bedroom for two days, during which he worked almost as hard as ever. When the doctors reported that Ike had passed his physical, Marshall had him promoted to permanent brigadier general, skipping the rank of permanent colonel.

During his two days of "rest," Eisenhower thought back over the past year, looking at the things he'd done wrong, or at least might have done better. The worst mistakes, he told Butcher, were failing to make a landing in Tunisia the first day of Torch, as Cunningham had urged him to do, and he should not have attacked the southeastern tip of Sicily—he should have landed on the beaches of Messina, cutting Sicily off from the mainland and trapping nearly 250,000 German and Italian troops.[40]

Even as he objectively dissected his Sicilian failure, resolving to learn from it, Truscott was advancing into the outskirts of Messina with the 3rd Infantry Division. But the Germans were nearly gone by now. They had improvised a ferry system and over the past ten days and nights had moved more than fifty thousand men and their tanks and artillery the three miles across the strait of Messina, despite Allied superiority in the air and at sea.[41]

It was not until August 13, when nearly all the Germans had escaped—as had seventy-five thousand Italians—that AFHQ intelligence officers woke up to what had happened. It was one of the worst intelligence failures of the war, one that would cost Allied troops dearly in months to come as they tried to dig those four German divisions out of the Italian mountains.[42]

On August 15, as the last of the retreating Germans reached the Italian mainland, Truscott's patrols advanced into Messina. City officials offered to surrender to Truscott next day. On the morning of the sixteenth, however, Truscott received an order from Patton's headquarters: stop right there. Patton would take the surrender; it would be Patton, not Truscott, who beat Monty into Messina. Two hours later Patton arrived, in a cloud of dust, sirens blazing. The Sicilian campaign really ended there, with Monty still twelve miles away, stymied by defeated Italians.[43]

One Down

When Eisenhower arrived at his office on the morning of August 17, his old friend and adjutant, T. J. Davis, told him that the chief surgeon at AFHQ, Brigadier General Frederick A. S. Blessé, wanted to see him. Patton was in serious trouble. Blessé entered Ike's office shortly after this and handed him a report from the chief surgeon of the II Corps, Colonel Richard T. Arnest.

According to Arnest, on August 3 Patton had visited an evacuation hospital filled with men brought in recent days from the battlefield, many of them suffering terrible wounds. Encountering a soldier without any evident injury, Patton had called the man a coward, slapped him across the face with his gloves and kicked him in the backside. A week later, visiting another evacuation hospital, he had met yet another soldier who claimed he was suffering from combat fatigue. "It's my nerves," said the soldier. "I can't stand the shelling anymore." Patton had called him "a yellow bastard," threatened to shoot him, waved his Colt .45 in the man's face, slapped him, walked away, then gone back and slapped him again, hard enough this time to send his helmet liner flying.[1]

Of all a general's burdens, visiting wounded men was both one of the worst and one of the most important. Nobody liked doing it. Walking into a hospital ward, with wounded men, rusty bloodstains seeping through their bandages, men who stoically stifled their groans despite agonizing pain and terrifying fears, would tear at the emotions of almost anyone. A few commanders, such as MacArthur, almost never visited the wounded, to their lasting discredit. Eisenhower and Bradley did it occasionally, but Patton and Truscott did it regularly, steeling themselves to look into the faces of men who had lost eyes or limbs as a result of their decisions . . . and their mistakes. Truscott had the emotional ballast to keep control of his emotions, hard though that was, but Patton was too volatile, too given to anger and tears.

"I guess I'll have to give George Patton a jacking up," Eisenhower said as he finished Arnest's report. "But if this thing ever gets out, they'll be howling for Patton's scalp, and that will be the end of Patton's services in this war. I simply cannot let that happen. Patton is indispensable to the war effort—one of the guarantors of our victory."[2]

Then he wrote out, in longhand, a stiff, personal letter to Patton. "It is *not* my present intention," he wrote, "to institute any formal investigation [but] if there is a very considerable element of truth in [these] allegations, I must so seriously question your good judgment and your self-discipline as to raise serious doubt in my mind as to your future usefulness. . . . I strongly advise that you make, in the form of apology or otherwise, such personal amends to the individuals concerned as may be within your power. . . . No letter I have been called upon to write in my military career has caused me the mental anguish of this one . . ." Eisenhower told Blessé to go to Sicily, conduct an investigation—a quiet one—and deliver this letter to Patton.[3]

Over the days and nights that followed, there was little rejoicing for Eisenhower over the Sicilian campaign. The escape of so many Germans and Italians cast a shadow over victory; so too did the shadow of Patton, arm raised, gloves in hand. Word of what Patton had done had already spread among the troops. And, as Ike soon discovered, American war correspondents knew about it, too. Three of them made their own report to him, on August 19, and suggested they would sit on the story provided that he relieved Patton.

One of the journalists, Quentin Reynolds, told him, "General, there are at least fifty thousand American soldiers on Sicily who would shoot Patton if they had the chance." This was ridiculous, as Eisenhower was doubtless aware; he knew soldiers a lot better than Reynolds could ever hope to do, but he tactfully did not dispute anything the journalists said. Instead, he told them just how valuable Patton was. The war wasn't over yet, he said, and "in any army, one third of the soldiers are natural fighters and brave. Two thirds are cowards and skulkers." Patton could get even the skulkers to fight. "His method is deplorable, but the result is excellent." He implored the journalists not to bring Patton down. Not one of them filed a story on the slapping incidents. Their restraint owed nothing to Patton and everything to their admiration for Ike.[4]

And still Eisenhower agonized. Getting the journalists on board was one thing. He had to tell Marshall, but how? He spent hours thinking out loud in front of Butcher, unsure of how much—or how little— Marshall needed to know. It was a week before he finally figured out how to do it. On August 24, he sent a cable on a subject that Marshall had not yet raised. "Foreseeing a future need of yours for senior U.S. commanders who have been tested in battle, I have been watching very closely and earnestly the performance of American commanders here," he began. "*First, Patton.* He has conducted a campaign where the brilliant successes scored must be attributed directly to his energy, determination and unflagging aggressiveness. The operations of the Seventh Army are going to be classed as a model of swift conquest by future classes in the War College [but] in spite of all this—George Patton continues to exhibit some of those unfortunate personal traits of which you and I have always known and which during this campaign caused me some uncomfortable days. His habit of bawling out subordinates, extending even to personal abuse of individuals, was noted in at least two specific cases." He then went on to discuss Bradley ("running absolutely true to form all the time") and Clark ("the best organizer, planner and trainer of troops that I have met").[5]

He left it up to Marshall to ask for further details on Patton, no doubt praying the Chief of Staff wouldn't be curious enough to know them. As the days passed so, it seemed, did the crisis. Eisenhower had saved Patton's career. Maybe.

The Combined Chiefs were so pleased with the rapid establishment of a strong beachhead on Sicily that as early as July 16, they urged Eisenhower to consider making a landing on the Italian mainland, close to

Naples. He was being advised, that is, not to bother with a slow, safe crawl up the Italian boot. Although the decision on where to go after Sicily had ostensibly been left to him, the Combined Chiefs were in fact urging him to forget about other possibilities, such as Sardinia, and pressing him not only to strike quickly at Italy but to take half the peninsula at a stroke.[6]

He responded two days later. "I recommend carrying the war to the mainland of Italy immediately Sicily has been captured." Eisenhower downplayed the possibilities of a landing near Naples—"It would be unlikely to succeed." He hinted, instead, that he was already thinking of taking the cautious road to Rome, pushing up the peninsula from the toe once Messina had fallen.[7]

As Eisenhower worked on plans for knocking Italy out of the war, he continued to hope that an Italian capitulation would spare him having to fight this campaign. The Combined Chiefs were already building up forces for a cross-Channel attack and seven battle-hardened divisions were going to be redeployed to the British Isles once Sicily was conquered, leaving him to tackle Italy with much smaller forces than he commanded now.

Anyway, he had good reason to think that even if Italy did not capitulate, the campaign would be over quickly. The eagerness with which Italian soldiers were surrendering on Sicily showed that the fight had gone out of all but the best units of the Italian Army. The overthrow and arrest of Mussolini at the end of July was another promising sign. It was only a matter of time, he became convinced, before the Italians started to negotiate.[8]

He didn't have to wait long. On August 4, an Italian diplomat approached the British embassy in Lisbon, and a week later a second Italian diplomat contacted the British embassy in Tangier. Both posed the same question: What terms would the Allies offer? Both got the same reply: No terms but unconditional surrender.[9]

That was the position of both Washington and London, but Eisenhower drafted a demand for an armistice—not a surrender—and sent it to the Combined Chiefs for their endorsement. Roosevelt and Churchill wouldn't budge and the Combined Chiefs picked his proposal apart. Fuming at this rejection, he was, he told Mamie, "a slave rather than a master," unlike the great commanders he had read about and envied as a young officer.[10]

Then, on August 15, one of the Italian generals who had organized the coup that ousted Mussolini, General Giuseppe Castellano, arrived in Madrid. He told the British ambassador that he was authorized by the new Italian government, headed by Marshal Pietro Badoglio, to say that in exchange for an armistice, Italy would join the war against Germany. To demonstrate his sincerity, he provided information on the thirteen German divisions currently deployed in Italy and said that three more were on their way.[11]

With the approval of Roosevelt, Churchill and the Combined Chiefs, who were meeting in Quebec, Eisenhower sent his G-2, Brigadier Kenneth Strong, and his chief of staff, Beetle Smith, to Lisbon, to meet with Castellano. By this time, the realization that the Germans were going to have up to sixteen well-equipped, veteran divisions in Italy by the time of any Allied landing had given the conferees in Quebec pause. So they threw together a new set of demands, known as the Quebec Memorandum. It began with an assertion that Italy was offering unconditional surrender, which was untrue, and granted Eisenhower the authority to accept that imaginary surrender. It would not take a literary critic to realize there was something fishy about the memorandum. It contained exactly one reference to unconditional surrender and numerous and detailed references such as "the Italian government must proclaim the Armistice immediately . . ." It also slighted the fact that if a country has surrendered, hostilities automatically cease, so an armistice, which is an agreed and temporary suspension of hostilities, is unnecessary.[12]

Nor were the terms in the memorandum the end of the matter. Eisenhower was to tell the Italians that even after they had agreed to these conditions, they would have to accept an even longer list of conditions—dealing with political and economic arrangements—at some future date.

Castellano was plainly discomfited by the reference to unconditional surrender and it also became obvious in his nine-hour conversation with Ike's two emissaries that the Italians were expecting the Allies to land in Italy with enough force to drive the Germans out and save Rome from Teutonic revenge. Strong and Smith said nothing that might have disabused him of this idea.

Believing that the Allies were going to put up to eighteen divisions ashore and that they would seize and protect Rome the moment the armistice went into effect, the Italian government agreed to accept the armistice offered by the Quebec Memorandum, and ignored the demand for unconditional surrender. Castellano flew to Sicily on September 2, where he met Beetle Smith.

In the early hours of September 3, Montgomery pushed two British divisions across the Strait of Messina and that afternoon Eisenhower flew to Sicily from Algiers. Several hours later, after a small ceremony had been arranged, Ike looked on as Castellano signed a secret armistice agreement on behalf of Badoglio and Smith signed on behalf of AFHQ. Afterward, the participants drank some whiskey, tore some olive branches from a nearby tree as souvenirs and had their photographs taken. And then Smith handed Castellano the list of additional conditions the Allies would attach to the agreement just signed. The list began, "The Italian Land, Sea and Air Forces hereby surrender unconditionally." Castellano had been tricked, and Ike couldn't help feeling embarrassed at the shabby way the Italians had been treated. It was "a crooked deal," he told Butcher that night, adding that it reflected so badly on the Allies that it would probably be a long time after the war before the details were revealed.[13]

His discomfiture would have been even greater had he known that the Germans were following these developments closely. They had tapped into the transatlantic telephone cable and cracked the scrambler telephone code used by Roosevelt and Churchill. They were well aware that Badoglio was about to take Italy out of the war. What Hitler had not yet decided was what he would do about it. He was inclined to write off most of Italy, withdraw all the way to the wide, almost unbridgeable Po River and dig in.[14]

Castellano repeatedly emphasized the importance of seizing and protecting Rome from German fury. He pointed out that there were already thousands of SS troops stationed in the city, and both a panzer division and a German parachute division were on the outskirts. They could take Rome within hours, unless Allied units got there first. Eisenhower turned his mind to ways of capturing Rome in conjunction with the Allied landing, code-named Avalanche, which was only five days away when the secret armistice was signed.

The limited range of Allied fighters ruled out the landing in the Bay of Naples that the Combined Chiefs had recommended. The farthest north Ike could strike was the beaches of Salerno, forty miles south of

Naples. The assault would be made by the Fifth Army, commanded by Mark Clark. His experience of combat consisted of three days in France in World War I, an experience cut short when he was seriously wounded. He owed his three stars and an army command almost entirely to Eisenhower.

Clark's amphibious assault consisted of only three divisions—one U.S., the other two British—with a follow-up force of two more divisions. His attack was going to hit Italy not so much with the impact of an avalanche as that of a snowball. Clark diluted its impact even more by deciding to attack across a thirty-six-mile front, and his beachhead would be split by the fast flowing Sele River. The British would land north of the Sele, the Americans south of it.

Clark had chosen to be strong nowhere and weak everywhere. The Germans might as well have done his planning. Eisenhower's judgment of Clark as a brilliant planner was a serious misjudgment, one doubtless influenced by his immense gratitude for the way Clark had helped reshape his career following the return to the U.S. after spending seven stressful years working for Douglas MacArthur.

Eisenhower intended to take Rome when Clark went ashore at Salerno. The 82nd Airborne Division would be dropped onto the city's main airfields. The commander of the 82nd, Major General Matthew Ridgway, protested that his division was going to be wiped out. There were forty thousand Germans, with two hundred tanks and hundreds of artillery pieces capable of being deployed rapidly in any fight for Rome. In the first phase of the airborne operation, there would be only enough airlift for a single regiment, numbering twenty-five hundred paratroopers. A second regiment would be inserted twenty-four hours later. Unless large numbers of Italians were able to fight effectively and promptly alongside the Americans, the operation could not possibly succeed. Eisenhower sent Brigadier General Maxwell Taylor, commander of the 82nd's artillery, into Rome, disguised as a captured American pilot, to assay the chances of success.[15]

The morning of September 8, with Avalanche less than twenty-four hours away, Eisenhower flew to his advanced command post at Amilcar, on the outskirts of Bizerte, to meet with Castellano and monitor the landing. When he arrived, there was a message from Taylor. Badoglio, said Taylor, was repudiating the secret armistice because there were too many Germans in and around Rome and the Allies couldn't protect the city.[16]

Scarlet with rage, Eisenhower started writing a reply to Badoglio, but was so angry he broke his pencil. He took another pencil. That too shattered. He resorted to dictation: "From Allied Commander in Chief to Marshal Badoglio. I intend to broadcast the existence of the Armistice at the hour originally planned. . . . Today is X day and I expect you to do your part. I do not accept your message of this morning . . ." He then summoned Castellano and read the message to him, his anger only too obvious.[17]

In midafternoon, a second message came from Taylor. The Germans were already occupying the airfields that the 82nd was going to try landing on. Taylor's signal read, "Innocuous"—a code word that meant the airborne operation would fail. There were C-47's already loaded with paratroopers taking off. Eisenhower cancelled the operation and the planes turned back.

He went to have a late lunch with Bradley, who was about to leave for England, where he would assume command of an army training for the cross-Channel attack. After Bradley departed, Eisenhower made a radio broadcast: "This is General Dwight D. Eisenhower, commander in chief of the Allied forces. The Italian government has surrendered its armed forces unconditionally. . . . Hostilities between the armed forces of the United Nations and those of Italy terminate at once . . ." He fretted and chain-smoked, waiting for Badoglio's response. It came at eight P.M. The marshal ordered all Italian military operations against the Allies to cease. Ike's mood changed to jubilation. "One down—and two to go!" he joyfully announced to Kay.[18]

There wasn't much left for him to do now. The Avalanche assault would go ahead in the early hours of September 9. He dictated a letter to John, telling him, "Today was a very full one for me and crowded with anxiety [but] I am probably the most optimistic person in this whole world." Then he dictated a letter to Mamie, apologizing to his wife for being "too worn down to start writing . . . long before you get this note you will have read in the papers enough that will show you why . . ."[19]

American and British soldiers making the Salerno assault heard Eisenhower's announcement that Italy had surrendered over the loudspeakers of the ships that were carrying them to the beaches in the early hours of

September 9. They expected a cakewalk, but what they got was a fight. German resistance was fierce, fueled by a sense of betrayal, but it was not well organized. The Germans made nothing but sporadic, piecemeal counterattacks for the first few days, when Clark's army was at its most vulnerable.

Then, on September 13, they drove into a five-mile gap between the Americans and the British and began attacking Clark's inner flank. For a few hours, they seemed about to drive the invaders into the sea. Clark grew alarmed and, in a moment of desperation, began planning a withdrawal.

When reports of Clark's evacuation plans reached AFHQ there was, in Ike's word, "consternation." He wondered out loud whether he'd made a mistake in giving Clark an army, and among his staff there was a widespread feeling that he had. Patton, they said to one another, would have died on the beaches and never thought for a moment of pulling out.[20]

By nightfall, however, the situation stabilized, thanks mainly to the intervention of the warships offshore, whose huge guns shattered oncoming panzers like tin cans hit with sledgehammers. The Germans had no answer to the power and accuracy of naval gunnery, and the closer they were to the beach, the more of it they got. In the fight for the beachhead, the fleet offshore dumped eleven thousand tons of shells on the Germans, far exceeding the three thousand tons of bombs dropped by Allied aircraft or the fire of American artillery.[21]

On September 16, Ike went to Salerno to take a look at the situation for himself. As he and Clark sat in a grove of trees, with the sounds of artillery exchanges and the rattle of machine gun fire in the background, a stray shell flew through the trees and exploded nearby. They were so engrossed in discussion that they didn't even notice it. Clark was blaming the near disaster not on his faulty plans—which had been drawn up by his chief of staff, Ike's old friend Al Gruenther—but on his corps commander, Major General Michael Dawley. Alexander had paid a visit to the beachhead the previous day and Dawley had been so jumpy that Alexander concluded he was "a broken reed."[22]

Clark made the most of this. He did not tell Ike the whole truth, which was that Dawley had protested vehemently against any suggestion of pulling out and that it was he, not Clark, who had managed to form American units into a defense line, under intense German pressure. What Clark did tell Eisenhower was that Dawley had been a dithering, nervous wreck at critical moments. Yet it emerged after the war that the three division commanders who had seen Dawley in action thought Dawley had performed at least as well as Clark. Ike busted Dawley to colonel and sent him home.[23]

Eisenhower repeatedly lectured senior commanders that they must be ruthless with officers who had failed and put friendship aside, yet he was deaf to his own advice when it came to Mark Clark. No one doubted Clark's physical courage. On the beaches of Salerno he rallied men under fire like a Napoleonic general, armed a band and gave it a hill to defend, moved platoons around. All very brave, but in modern war, that was the work of a lieutenant, not a lieutenant general. He was taking unnecessary risks with his own life and thereby jeopardizing the outcome of the battle. Nor did his troops see him as an inspired combat commander. In old age, men liked to boast, "I rolled with Patton!" Hardly anyone claimed with comparable pride, "I fought under Clark!"

Yet he might as well have been Ike's brother for all the second chances he got. Clark had done nothing to curb his overweening vanity, but Eisenhower looked the other way. His Salerno plan was abysmal and courted disaster. Ike ignored that. Under pressure, Clark had shown terrible misjudgment. That, too, was ignored. If Dawley deserved to be relieved, so did Clark.

On September 27, Montgomery's soldiers captured the huge complex of airbases at Foggia, in southern Italy. Possession of Foggia put war industries in southern Germany and across much of Central Europe within range at last of American heavy bombers. It also made possible a sustained, year-long campaign against the oilfields of Ploeşti. Clark's Fifth Army was, meanwhile, advancing on Naples, and entered the city on October 1.

When Naples fell, Hitler still had not made up his mind about Italy. The sensible, logical action in light of the fact that the Allies were almost certain to make a landing in northern France sometime in 1944 was to pull his divisions in Italy back to the Po. It would be almost as hard for the Allies to push armies across the Po as it would be to push them across the Channel. He might be able to contain more than a dozen Allied divisions in Italy at comparatively little cost. But what power does logic have against a sunny disposition, easy, practiced charm and a sharp mind?

Albert Kesselring, otherwise known as Smiling Al, was both a Luft-waffe general and a highly skilled commander of ground forces. He was also a strong contender for Ike's self-awarded title of most optimistic person in the world. Kesselring had urged Hitler to fight in Tunisia, confident that the supply problems could be solved. He was just as optimistic about the strategic benefits to be gained from defending Sicily. "Third time lucky" is the eternal optimist's creed, and Kesselring told Hitler it would be possible to hold Italy south of Rome. On October 4, Hitler decided to fight an Italian campaign.[24]

Ultra was monitoring much of the German debate but was slow to reveal Hitler's October 4 decision. So early October found Churchill firmly convinced that the Germans were about to withdraw to the Po. Eisenhower was confident that the Germans would continue to withdraw, but for a different reason—Allied airpower, he believed, was so devastating that the Germans would not be able to stand and fight. He looked forward to taking Rome before the end of October and expected to be fighting a huge "Battle of the Po" around Christmas 1943. It was a serious misjudgment.[25]

Although Italy was no longer part of the Axis, it was not yet a member of the coalition against Germany. To bring it completely into the fold, Eisenhower met with Badoglio in Malta at the end of September. Badoglio had only one point to make: he could not publicly stand by any document that said Italy had submitted to "unconditional surrender." It was too humiliating for the Italian people to understand or accept. Eisenhower had never favored unconditional surrender anyway, and after talking to Badoglio he finally persuaded Roosevelt and Churchill to drop the phrase. All that Italy agreed to in the end was an armistice, which Eisenhower had pushed for from the beginning. With that settled, the Italians became cobelligerents.[26]

While he was dealing with Badoglio, Eisenhower was also receiving messages from Churchill, communications that had the urgency of a ransom note, demanding an invasion of the island of Rhodes. The Prime Minister believed that taking it would push the Turkish government into declaring war on Germany. Eisenhower was appalled. Any attempt to capture Rhodes, he told the Combined Chiefs, would be "a diversion highly prejudicial to the success of Italian operations [and] these operations will probably assume the aspect of a major bitter battle."[27]

Just to nail the matter down, though, Ike convened a conference with his three British deputies at AFHQ on October 9. Not one of them thought Rhodes was worth fighting for, and certainly not at the cost of taking forces away from Italy, where at present the Germans had twenty divisions to the Allies' nineteen. Ike later said "It was the simplest, most unargumentative" commanders' conference he attended during the war.[28]

The autumn leaves were beginning to fall back home, and with the November 1944 election barely a year away, the first Ike-for-President movement was stirring into life. In late October, he opened a letter from an old friend—and lifelong Democrat—George Allen and out slid a clipping from *The Washington Post* with a headline that read, EISENHOWER URGED FOR PRESIDENT. His old pals in the Tank Corps were promoting the idea. The letter from Allen read, in its entirety, "How does it feel to be a candidate?"

Ike scribbled a prompt and heated reply in pencil. "Baloney! Why can't a simple soldier be left alone to carry out his orders? And I furiously object to the word 'candidate'—I ain't and won't!"[29]

To his dismay, in mid-October he lost the services of Andrew Cunningham. The First Sea Lord, Admiral Sir Dudley Pound, was dying, and Cunningham was the officer best qualified to replace him. Eisenhower told Cunningham that if the post was offered to him, it was his duty to take it. Shortly after this, Cunningham was summoned back to London to take Pound's place. As Cunningham departed, Eisenhower expressed his "profound sense of loss. . . . No words of mine can ever adequately express my gratitude for your unfailing support, your wisdom in counsel and your brilliant leadership . . ."[30]

After Cunningham's departure, Eisenhower went to Naples, to see conditions for himself. Airpower was doing nothing to prevent the Germans from creating bunkers with reinforced concrete in the Italian mountains. And when Allied air was unleashed against Italian railroad depots, the Germans assembled their trains in Germany and Austria and ran them through the night into Italy. It was a grim prospect, but Italy was turning into the battle Eisenhower had feared. He went back to take another look in November. There was no doubt about it now—Clark and the Fifth Army were in for a hard, miserable winter campaign, one that couldn't be supervised from distant North Africa. He told Beetle Smith to move AFHQ to Naples.[31]

By this time, the Patton story seemed to be safely buried, but it rose from the dead when Drew Pearson visited the theater and heard about it. He wasn't party to Ike's agreement with other journalists, and on November 22, he talked about it on his weekly radio show. Marshall was caught unawares. To make things worse, Beetle Smith held a press conference the day after the story broke and said that Eisenhower had not reprimanded Patton, which made it appear that Ike had treated it as a trivial incident.[32]

Eisenhower finally, and belatedly, sent Marshall a long and detailed account of what had happened and how he had handled it. What Smith ought to have said, but didn't, was that there was no *official* reprimand. The letter Ike had send Patton, ordering him to apologize to the men he had slapped, was a stiff rebuke even if it had not gone into Patton's official file. Marshall agreed with Ike that Patton was too valuable a commander to lose, and Eisenhower sent a reassuring message to his old friend Georgie—"this storm will blow over."[33]

In early October, the secretary of the Navy, Frank Knox, visited Eisenhower and told him command of the cross-Channel attack had been settled. During the Quebec Conference, Roosevelt had insisted that it must go to an American, because the United States would provide most of the forces. This embarrassed Churchill, who had already promised Brooke that he would have what was the most coveted command of the war. Churchill, however, quickly accepted both the logic of Roosevelt's argument and the near certainty that the command would go to Marshall. The decision, Knox claimed, would be announced to coincide with a major victory, such as the capture of Rome. Ike would go home and become Chief of Staff.[34]

Eisenhower had been expecting something like this, and he told Butcher that if it came to pass, he was going to tell Roosevelt he was making a big mistake. The Chief of Staff had to devote a lot of time and energy to dealing with Congress. "I'm not temperamentally fitted for the job," he fumed. He simply loathed politicians. If they made him Chief of Staff, he said, "They'll have to carry me up to Arlington in six months." What he wanted was to remain in the Mediterranean and command the fighting there. There was even a possibility that once the Germans were drawn into big battles in northern France, he might be able to thrust rapidly northward from the Po and get into Germany first. He might even capture Berlin that way.[35]

Shortly after Knox's visit, Eisenhower saw the outline plan for the cross-Channel attack, code-named Overlord. He wasn't impressed. "Not enough wallop in the attack," he told Butcher. It stood such a good chance of failing that he wasn't sure he'd even want to command it.[36]

Despite what Knox had told Eisenhower, the question of command had still not been settled by the time Roosevelt, Churchill, Chiang Kai-shek and the Combined Chiefs met in Cairo on November 26. Although Roosevelt expected Marshall would command Overlord, he had not gotten around to offering it. In his presentation to the Combined Chiefs, Ike emphasized the need for strategic bombing from bases in Britain and Italy. That meant the drive toward the Po had to continue. "In no other area could we so well threaten the whole German structure, including France, the Balkans and the Reich itself."[37] As Marshall watched him, he thought Eisenhower looked exhausted and, when the conference ended, ordered him to take two or three days off. Tedder suggested he might enjoy visiting the Pyramids, Luxor and Karnak and told him about a British major, Walter Bryan Emery, who was a prominent Egyptologist.[38]

Eisenhower and four members of the AFHQ staff—including Kay Summersby—had two wonderful days, with Emery as their guide. Ike was able to indulge once again his fascination with ancient history. It was thrilling to him to reflect that not far from his advanced CP at Amilcar he had a cottage that stood on the ruins of Carthage, home of his boyhood hero, Hannibal. To gaze upon the Pyramids and to wander through the columns of the great temple at Karnak was to feel the sweep of history move in his soul. It surely awoke, too, strong memories of his father and the ten-foot chart that David Jacob Eisenhower had drawn of the Pyramids, convinced that within their geometry lay the answers to the eternal questions of human existence: Who are we? What are we? Why are we here? When he returned to Cairo, Eisenhower looked healthier and happier than he'd looked for months.

Roosevelt and Churchill had, meanwhile, gone to Teheran, to meet with Stalin. When they told him about Overlord, he wanted to know who would command it. Until they could answer that question, Stalin was unlikely to take what they said seriously, yet it was crucial to Overlord's chances of success that the Red Army launch an offensive in conjunction with the cross-Channel attack and pin down as many Germans as possible.

Roosevelt returned to Cairo, unable to postpone the decision any longer. He felt strongly that Marshall deserved command of Overlord, if only to secure his place in history. But even now the President was reluctant to act. Marshall was the dominant figure on the Combined Chiefs. Even if he became Chief of Staff, Eisenhower could not possibly have Marshall's clout among the Combined Chiefs—not after being their subordinate for eighteen months.

Back in Cairo, Roosevelt had Marshall join him for lunch and asked him what he wanted to do. He was more or less inviting Marshall to say that everything he had done so far was a preparation for command of Overlord, which would have been no more than a simple statement of fact. Marshall, however, told him that in other wars, individual considerations had been allowed to take precedence over the good of the country. That must not happen now. The President must have an entirely free hand in deciding what was best for the success of Overlord.

"Well," said Roosevelt, plainly relieved, "I don't feel I could sleep at ease if you were out of Washington."

In terms of selflessness and love of country, Marshall's action was one of the most heroic feats of the war, one that he proceeded to cap with an act of singular graciousness and dignity. After Roosevelt had announced his decision to the Combined Chiefs, Marshall wrote out a brief message for Stalin. In his distinctive backward-sloping hand, he scribbled: "The immediate appointment of General Eisenhower to command of OVERLORD operation has been decided upon." The President then signed it, "Roosevelt."[39]

By this time Eisenhower was back in Amilcar. On December 6, he was informed that Roosevelt would be stopping off to see him on his way to Malta. He had a feeling the President intended to tell him that Marshall would command Overlord and he would become Chief of Staff. He started thinking about making a trip around the world on his way back to Washington, visiting Mountbatten in India and MacArthur in Australia along the way. But the next morning a cable from Marshall about future administrative arrangements seemed to assume that Eisenhower was going to England. Hope flared, but he wisely kept it in check.[40]

Roosevelt arrived a few hours later and when Eisenhower climbed into the armored Cadillac to join him in the back seat, the President said, in his patrician, offhand way, "Well, Ike, you are going to command Overlord."[41]

★★★★★

20

Time Out

In Tunisia, Eisenhower was living in a modest white villa—known locally as La Maison Blanche, and to Ike's staff as the White House—and that December, it looked as if Churchill was going to die on him, in his house, as his guest. It was a prospect that Churchill viewed stoically. Eisenhower could not have contemplated the PM's sudden death with anything like the same equanimity, even though he had been given a grim warning almost the moment Churchill arrived on December 10.

The PM had flown in from Cairo less than twenty-four hours after Roosevelt departed for home. He looked ghastly. His normally pink, cherubic features were gray and puffy. Ike ushered him into the armored Cadillac, and as they drove away from the airfield, Churchill told him, in a shaky voice, "I am afraid I shall have to stay with you longer than I had planned. I am completely at the end of my tether."[1]

An X ray next day showed the PM had pneumonia. Three days after arriving, Churchill was so ill that his doctor, Lord Moran, expected him to die. The PM's daughter, Sarah Churchill, was traveling with him, and he offered her a battler's reassurance: "If I die, don't worry—the war is won."[2]

All Eisenhower could do was pace downstairs and worry, smoke furiously and exude an optimism double-distilled through doubt. Then things got worse. On December 15, Churchill sent a telegram to Roosevelt: "Am stranded amid the ruins of Carthage . . ." Shortly afterward, his heart began to beat erratically, fluttering furiously like a terrified bird in a very small cage. He was having a heart attack. Churchill slipped to the very edge of death's frontier with life and hovered there through four agonizing hours.[3]

Within a few days health and strength returned, but slowly and fitfully. With the first stirring of renewed life, Churchill began to press Eisenhower to agree to another landing, this time at Anzio, which was not far from Rome and deep in the German rear. A grim stalemate had descended on the Italian front, which snaked across the peninsula from coast to coast a hundred miles south of Rome. By landing near Rome and threatening to cut off the German divisions far to the south, Churchill said, the Allies could force a general withdrawal, breaking that stalemate and forestalling a protracted winter campaign in the mountains.

Ike himself had been thinking along the same lines only a few weeks earlier, but an Anzio operation could not succeed unless it was at least as big as the Salerno assault, which had three divisions in it, plus a two-division follow-up, and that had been barely enough to prevail against an enemy who at that time was preparing to abandon most of Italy. As things stood now, there were only enough LSTs for a two-division assault at Anzio, with a one-and-a-half-division follow-up. Given that paucity of resources, he told Churchill, the proposed Anzio assault would probably fail.[4]

As they debated the issue, Eisenhower was rapidly making the mental transition from commander in chief of AFHQ to Supreme Commander, Allied Expeditionary Force. And to his mind now, what limited shipping was available for another amphibious assault in the Mediterranean would be better employed in an attempt to capture a major port in the south of France, preferably Marseilles, to improve the chances of victory in Overlord.

Even so, Eisenhower finally and grudgingly allowed the fifty-six LSTs that were still in the Mediterranean but due to be redeployed to England for participation in Overlord to be assigned to an Anzio assault. That did not mean, though, that he had changed his mind about its prospects for success.

One of Eisenhower's earliest decisions on learning that he would command Overlord was that he would take Tedder and Alexander with him. One person he didn't want was Montgomery, who was too slow, too unenterprising. During the Sicilian campaign, Ike had grumbled repeatedly to his staff, "Why doesn't Monty get going? What's the matter with him?" And as if to vindicate Ike's doubts, once Montgomery crossed to the Italian mainland, he had plodded up to Foggia, not seized it.[5]

When Eisenhower talked with Churchill about taking Alexander to England, however, the PM insisted that he take Montgomery instead. Following El Alamein, the British press, starstruck by Rommel and therefore rapturous at what it perceived as the military genius of the British general who had defeated him, virtually deified Monty. Churchill cared little about Montgomery's limited military abilities and a lot about his unlimited popular appeal back home. Eisenhower would have to take Montgomery, like it or not, and he liked it not.[6]

Once satisfied that Churchill would survive, Eisenhower went to Italy shortly before Christmas to see Clark, tour the battle front and take a look at AFHQ, which had just transferred to Caserta, a small town ten miles north of Naples. Rain fell in torrents, reducing his planned tour of the front to the Fifth Army's American units. Beetle Smith had moved AFHQ into the Caserta Palace, on Clark's advice, but the palace turned out to be as cold as it was filthy. It seemed to consist mainly of enormous, echoing rooms decorated with huge terra-cotta tubs from which rose overgrown plants that created a sinister, oppressive atmosphere.[7]

Butcher took Ike to spend a night in a hunting lodge that belonged to the Italian royal family. And here occurred what Kay called Eisenhower's "Battle with the Rat," after his orderly, Sergeant Mickey McKeogh, reported that Telek had just found a rat in the general's bathroom. Eisenhower put on his reading glasses, took up his Colt .45 and headed for the bathroom, with the staff crowding close behind him as he opened the door. The rat hadn't moved. The first shot plowed a furrow in the seat, while the roar of the Colt boomed deafeningly from the tiled walls. The rat jumped onto a pipe. Eisenhower shot again. Missed. And again. This time he nicked the tail. His fourth shot hit the rodent, but it was twitching too furiously to be dead. Despite the marksmanship of "General Dwight D. Eisenhower of the straightest-shooting army in the world, things were so bad that someone else had to come in and club the poor animal to death," using a log from the fireplace.[8]

Some weeks earlier, Eisenhower had directed that the fabled isle of

Capri in Naples Bay be set aside as a rest and recreation area. On Christmas Eve, the sun decided to shine and he took a ride on a Navy destroyer to see how the troops were enjoying Capri. But there were no parties of enlisted men to be seen wandering among the pastel-colored pretty little villas set among dark green cypress trees. He noticed a large villa, much bigger than those around it. "Whose is that?"

"Yours, sir," replied the naval officer who was acting as his guide.

Ike's face went from its normal pink to a deep red. "And that one?" he asked, pointing out another grand construction.

"That one belongs to General Spaatz, sir."

"Goddamn it! That is *not* my villa. And that's not General Spaatz's villa! This is supposed to be a rest center—for combat men—not a playground for the brass!"[9]

He sent a sent a rebuke to Spaatz and told Spaatz to meet his plane when he got back to Tunisia.[10]

Returning to Tunisia on Christmas Day, he began to give Spaatz a chewing out, only to discover that the R&R situation in Italy was worse than he thought: Spaatz and Clark had agreed to ignore his instructions about R&R. Capri, they'd decided, would be reserved for the use of Air Force officers, while Sorrento (another designated R&R center) would be reserved for the officers of the Fifth Army. And the enlisted men? Spaatz and Clark evidently thought it was enough to allow them the run of the back streets of Naples and the chance for five minutes with a cheap whore.

The details of the Capri-Sorrento deal made Eisenhower livid with rage. The good infantry officer's first principle of leadership is always to look after your men. Despite the many years he had served on high-powered staffs, that was still as natural to him as breathing. Being with soldiers, the kind who carried rifles and lived in holes in the ground and closed with the enemy, was his idea of happiness. Nothing cheered Eisenhower more than to go down the road in a jeep and see the troops he passed half turn, curious to see who was going by, and break into smiles, shout, "Hey, it's Ike!" and wave at him, while he saluted them, not so much unable as unwilling to suppress his ear-to-ear grin. To treat the men who suffered all the hardships of war with such disdain outraged him as a man and as an officer.[11]

Back at La Maison Blanche, Eisenhower had Christmas dinner with his three deputy commanders and Churchill. It was the first time

Churchill had felt strong enough to get out of bed and eat at the dinner table for two weeks. The PM raised his glass and toasted the King, the President, Stalin, Ike and the Combined Chiefs before offering toasts for the success of the two big operations ahead—Anzio and Overlord.[12]

Four days later, a cable arrived from Marshall, informing Eisenhower that with Overlord now his responsibility, "you need to be fresh mentally. . . . Now come on home and see your wife . . ."[13]

Ike's C-54 touched down in Washington in the early hours of January 2, 1944, a Sunday. Mamie had been alerted a few hours earlier. She and Ruth Butcher had forged a close friendship while their husbands were away and lived in modest apartments that faced each other in the annex of the Wardman Park Hotel. Both women were no doubt eager to see their husbands again, but they were probably apprehensive, too. Would Ike be the same old Ike? Would Butch be the same old Butch? So much had happened to them in the eighteen months they had been overseas. These days they rubbed shoulders with Roosevelt and Churchill. They were living at the heart of the greatest drama of the twentieth century. They were part of History now.

Ike and Butcher arrived at two in the morning, each holding an excited small Scottie. The puppies were Telek's offspring. Each was attached to a Scotch-plaid leash, and around their necks, in an excess of cuteness, were Scotch-plaid collars. Not yet house-trained, they proceeded to defecate on one of Mamie's blue Chinese rugs, bought during the years in Manila. Not the most auspicious beginning. They later did the same in the Butchers' apartment. Within days of setting paw on American soil, both Scotties were under new ownership.[14]

The Ike who came home looked and sounded like a slightly different man. What remained of his hair had gone gray. Still powerfully built, he had nonetheless grown thicker around the middle and his face had rounded out. His voice was gravelly and noticeably deeper, the result of four packs of cigarettes a day and countless conferences. Half of what he did these days consisted of thinking. Most of the other half consisted of talking. Used to being the man in charge, he terminated conversations abruptly and expressed himself bluntly, with the confident, assertive manner appropriate to a general who had won two major campaigns.

After a few hours of sleep, Eisenhower was up early to cook himself eggs and bacon. At 7:45 Marshall's aide, Colonel Frank McCarthy (in civilian life a major Hollywood producer), arrived in a black sedan to take him to the Pentagon. Eisenhower got into a trench coat to cover up his stars and a plain overseas cap to hide his distinctive, nearly bald head and slipped out of the Wardman Park through the service elevator, trying not to look too conspicuous. The black sedan had drawn curtains across its windows. Eisenhower's presence in the United States was top-secret.[15]

Although Marshall intended this visit to be a vacation, there was serious business to be discussed. Ironically, Eisenhower probably didn't mind talking business. It was the vacation part of it he disliked. He considered that an intrusion. His place, he had no doubt, was in England now. Every minute in the day belonged to Overlord. But much as he felt that way, he couldn't tell Marshall that.[16]

What Marshall wanted to talk about was the invasion of southern France, code-named Anvil. From the message traffic, it appeared to Marshall that Eisenhower was weakening under British pressure. Churchill and Brooke were completely opposed to Anvil, which they saw as a diversion from Italy and an obstacle to a possible advance into the Balkans. Marshall told Eisenhower that Anvil was indispensable. The Army needed Marseilles in order to feed the maximum number of American divisions into Europe, to get the French divisions it had trained and equipped into the fight and to draw German forces away from northern France. Besides which, Roosevelt had assured Stalin at Teheran that Anvil would take place. Whatever happened, he had to save Anvil from the British.[17]

Once the word got around the Operations Division that Eisenhower was in the building, almost everyone who dealt with Europe or the Mediterranean wanted to see him. They had a hundred questions needing answers and expected him to provide them. There was also a stack of cables from London they would like him to take a look at. Eisenhower's vacation began with a full day at work.[18]

That evening, there was a party in the Butchers' apartment for their and Ike's old friends. In the morning, Frank McCarthy was back with the black sedan, to take Eisenhower to the White House to see the President. Roosevelt was propped up in a huge bed, supported by a pile of pillows, gray in the face and prostrated by the flu. Eisenhower told him about Churchill's way with doctors. Whenever one attempted to take the

PM's temperature, Churchill whipped out the thermometer, squinted at it, then announced a temperature that suited him. "I always do that," Churchill had told him. "I believe these doctors are trying to keep me in bed."

Roosevelt responded, "I've been doing that for years. I don't trust those fellows either."[19]

They talked about de Gaulle and the French Committee of National Liberation. Eisenhower thought the FCNL would be valuable to Overlord in fomenting French resistance. Roosevelt, however, still had nothing but disdain for de Gaulle. He was deaf to Eisenhower's assertions that de Gaulle would command the loyalty of millions once Allied troops landed in France.[20]

That evening, Marshall hosted a party for Eisenhower. The guests included generals, admirals and politicians who sat on congressional committees dealing with the military. Eisenhower talked about various incidents from Torch, Husky and Avalanche. It was late when he set off with Mamie for Union Station. They rumbled northward through the night and after breakfast next morning arrived at West Point. There, next to a siding at the little East Shore Station stood the tall, thin, blond figure of Cadet Sergeant John S. D. Eisenhower.

Ike couldn't leave the train and hope to keep his presence secret. But as he grew older, simply being at West Point ignited feelings of satisfaction, pride and identity that no other place, not even Abilene, quite managed. He and Mamie remained at the siding for six hours, talking to John and hosting a small lunch for him and several of his cadet friends.[21]

For months now he had tried repeatedly to persuade John to apply for the field artillery and stay out of the infantry. Eisenhower had the normal anxieties of a father, and knew as well as anyone the odds against survival of an infantry second lieutenant serving in a war zone in 1944. He knew, though, that John would see frontline service as the rightful place of any infantryman in time of war. Nevertheless, the country and the Army could not accept the risk of John's being captured. John, however, would not be dissuaded. Perhaps Ike had done too good a job of portraying the infantry as where the real soldiers were found. John was going to graduate in June and, he told his father, he still intended to take his commission in the infantry.[22]

This reunion of father and son was slightly awkward for both of them. Eisenhower was all too obviously impatient to be on his way to England. His mind was on Overlord, and Mamie and John were being squeezed into the interstices between his thoughts, rather than being foremost in them. And when Mamie rebuked him for being so abrupt with people, he responded, "Hell, I'm going back to my theater where I can do what I want." He smiled, as if to say he was joking, but that *was* his desire.[23]

He and Mamie were back in Washington that night, and next day he returned to the White House. Roosevelt showed him a message from Churchill asking him to hand over AFHQ to a British general, Maitland "Jumbo" Wilson as of January 8, and Ike readily agreed. With the change of command settled, there was no point now in returning to the Mediterranean, not even to say goodbye.

Four days after arriving in Washington, Ike and Mamie headed—on Marshall's orders and in Marshall's railroad car—for White Sulphur Springs, a stuffy resort in West Virginia favored by the haute bourgeoisie. They spent two days together, in a small cottage, and do not appear to have had a good time.

It may have been at White Sulphur Springs that Ike called her Kay. More than thirty years later, Kay Summersby claimed that when he arrived in England from his visit to the U.S., he told her that he and Mamie had argued furiously. "I kept calling her Kay. Every time I opened my mouth to say something to Mamie, I'd call her Kay." There may well have been such a lapse, but only once. Eisenhower would one day stop smoking simply by giving himself an order to quit. To claim that someone with that kind of self-control, acquired while young and reinforced over a lifetime, could not stop himself from blurting out "Kay" is ridiculous. What is certain is that Kay cast a shadow over the reunion with Mamie, whether her name was mentioned or not.[24]

The best part of the visit was probably January 8, when Ike flew, alone, to Fort Riley, Kansas. A staff car drove him to Manhattan, to the home of his brother Milton, recently installed as president of Kansas State. His brothers Edgar and Arthur were there, waiting to see him. So, too, were Mamie's parents. Best of all, though, Ida was there. He had been warned that at eighty-one, her mind was so erratic she might not even recognize him, but she did. "Why, it's Dwight!" she said, laughing with joy as tears ran into the deep lines that crosshatched her cheeks. She seemed as full of life as ever. Yet even now, as he embraced his adored mother, his mind was churning, his nerves tightly drawn, his new responsibilities opening a vast gulf between Supreme Commander and people who loved him. He could not help himself, but there was the same impatience he'd felt with Mamie and John, the same urgent need to get out of here, be somewhere else, do something else. In the empyrean, the pull of duty was so damn strong it was a kind of slavery.[25]

Returning to White Sulphur Springs the next morning, he rejoined Mamie, and they had another couple of days together. Then they went back to Washington. On January 12 he had his third and, as things turned out, final meeting with Roosevelt, who was still flat on his back.

During his visits to North Africa, Roosevelt had met Kay and been driven around by her. Eisenhower had wanted to award her the Legion of Merit but was advised against it. So he had a request for Roosevelt: Could he have an autographed photograph to give to Kay? Roosevelt signed one gladly.

He tried to talk to Roosevelt again about de Gaulle, but got nowhere. What the President wanted to talk about was Germany. There was, he said, a debate going on within the administration. Some of his advisers wanted Germany to be broken up into three zones, one each being assigned to the U.S., Britain and the Soviet Union. He was inclined to agree with the demands for a hard peace and large reparations.

Eisenhower said he thought it would be a serious mistake to carve Germany into zones of occupation. Far better, in his view, was a military government consisting of the three major allies running an occupied, and undivided, Germany for a short time, then handing over to civilian administrators. But whatever arrangement was made, he did not trust the Soviets.

Roosevelt impatiently dismissed his fears and changed the subject. How did Ike like his new title, Supreme Commander? Eisenhower said wryly, "It has the ring of importance . . . like 'Sultan.' "[26]

As the interview ended and Eisenhower departed, he said, "I sincerely hope you will quickly recover from your indisposition, Mr. President."

"Oh," replied Roosevelt breezily, "I have not felt better for years. I'm in bed only because the doctors are afraid I might have a relapse if I get up too soon." In truth, though, he looked deathly ill, much as Churchill had looked just before he suffered his heart attack.[27]

The next morning, Eisenhower had a final meeting with Marshall. Back at the Wardman Park, he packed his bags. As they said their farewells, Mamie was almost distraught, her anguish only too evident. "Don't come back again till it's over, Ike. I can't stand losing you again." At seven P.M. the C-54 lifted off into the night sky, swinging eastward across the Atlantic. Back to the war.[28]

Craftsmanship

Eisenhower arrived in London late at night on January 13 and was greeted by his British aide, Colonel James Gault, who had found a house for him near Berkeley Square. London was so blanketed by fog that night it was possible to get lost just walking from the staff car to the front door. In the morning, he arrived at Norfolk House, the European Theater headquarters, finally free to turn all his energies to Overlord. For a man who had been chafing to do so ever since Roosevelt had given him the word, that came as something of a relief.

Even so, Overlord did not really begin with Eisenhower, and in its tangled origins lay all its problems, and its possibilities. In the summer of 1941, when Ike was still Third Army chief of staff and planning for the Louisiana maneuvers, a Royal Navy captain was in Washington knocking on doors at the Munitions Building and over at the Navy Yard. The Englishman spread drawings on people's desks and talked about a new kind of vessel, called a Landing Ship, Tank (LST). Having been kicked off the continent of Europe at Dunkirk, the British were planning to go back. When? They couldn't say. Just how? Not sure. But one thing was certain: if they were going to put troops ashore and keep them there, they would have to land armor with them.

After Dunkirk, the Royal Navy had conducted some experiments with three converted oil tankers and soon had a good idea of what was needed—a flat-bottomed ship that could be grounded on a beach, with a ramp that could be lowered and enough carrying capacity for up to twenty tanks. Besides drawings of LSTs, the captain also had some drawings of a Landing Ship, Dock (LSD). This vessel would be built around a massive hold, one big enough to take twenty-five landing craft. An LSD would carry its landing craft through rough waters, flood the hold a mile or so offshore and discharge the landing craft, loaded with nearly a thousand infantrymen, close to the beach. What the Royal Navy officer wanted to know was, Would the United States be willing to build some LSTs and LSDs under Lend Lease?[1]

These were no small ships. At four thousand tons, they were the size of light cruisers, and the Navy's answer was a firm, clear no. It was already embarked on the biggest construction program in its history to turn out dozens of new aircraft carriers and scores of fleet submarines for a probable war with Japan. But Marshall was interested in the LST and LSD. He had been wondering for nearly two years just how he was going to put American divisions ashore in Europe if the U.S. got into the war. So he had Army engineers take a look at the drawings and build a wooden mock-up of an LST at Fort Knox, Kentucky, home of the Armored Command, and tank crews practiced with it, far from any hostile shore—except, that is, those already casting long shadows across Marshall's visionary mind.[2]

Even after Pearl Harbor, the Navy continued to disdain landing ships. Admiral Ernie King's priorities remained carriers and submarines for the war in the Pacific, plus destroyer-escorts to fight the U-boat menace in the Atlantic. After an initial burst of landing-ship and landing-craft construction to meet the requirements for Torch, output was actually falling in January 1943, when the commitment was made at Casablanca to mount an invasion of France in the spring of 1944.

Brooke chose one of the youngest lieutenant generals in the British Army, Frederick E. Morgan, to serve as chief of staff to the Supreme Allied Commander (designate), or COSSAC, and begin planning. Morgan, a highly decorated soldier, had a reputation as a thinker. Within little more than a month, COSSAC had an outline plan, and Morgan had gotten the most important thing right—the scale of the operation. The Allies would have to be prepared to put around forty divisions into Normandy to fight and win a campaign there.

The operation would break into two distinct parts: first, an amphibious assault to seize a beachhead, followed by a rapid buildup of the beachhead to put Allied divisions into Normandy faster than the Germans could rush reinforcements there.

COSSAC said that the Supreme Allied Commander, whoever he turned out to be, would need eighty-five hundred ships and landing craft to carry ten divisions into the amphibious assault, plus enough airlift for a simultaneous two-division paratroop and glider assault. Ultra was currently showing twenty-nine German divisions in France. By the time of the invasion, there were certain to be more, and beach defenses would be much stronger, because right now, there was virtually nothing beyond a few coastal guns and barbed wire.

The Joint Chiefs threw out Morgan's plan. The huge fleet of warships the Navy had begun building in 1941 was about to go into the water in the second half of 1943. It would spearhead a central-Pacific offensive aimed at destroying the Imperial Japanese Navy and putting Japanese cities within range of American bombers. King could not agree to provide landing ships and landing craft on the scale COSSAC was demanding without some reduction in production for the Navy's central-Pacific drive. Besides, Marshall, King and Hap Arnold told one another, Morgan had probably cooked up this impossible figure because the British really didn't want to land in northern France. By getting the Joint Chiefs of Staff (JCS) to reject it, they could wriggle off the hook and let the Yanks take the blame. Morgan was informed that he would have the services of four thousand ships and landing craft—barely enough, that is, for a three-division assault—with a two-division floating reserve that would come ashore on the next tide.[3]

This meant COSSAC had to draw up a new plan, one that committed the Allies to invading France on a scale that was barely half the size of the Husky operation against Sicily and not much bigger than the assault at Salerno. Yet this was supposed to be the most important single operation of the war!

A landing in France on this exiguous scale, with the Germans able to throw as many as a dozen divisions into a swift counterattack, was little more than a glorified version of the Dieppe raid of 1942, yet Morgan and his staff plugged away, trying to salvage something. What could they get for small change? A port, maybe. His planners concentrated on mounting an operation to seize Caen, in Normandy, on the first day and try to build up a beachhead around it. Given the fact that by late 1943 Ultra was showing the number of German divisions in France rising steadily and a program for constructing beach defenses had just begun, this was an open invitation to disaster. Eisenhower was hardly called upon to demonstrate military genius when he was shown the outline plan in October 1943. One glance told him it would fail.

Two months later, he was the designated Supreme Allied Commander, and when he headed for Washington to see Marshall and Mamie, his C-54 landed at Marrakesh to refuel. Churchill was there, recuperating from his heart attack, and by sheer chance so was Montgomery, who had just been shown the outline plan. Montgomery's immediate reaction was exactly the same as Ike's—the assault lacked weight and was on too narrow a front. As Monty's chief of staff, Major General Francis de Guingand, dryly noted, "any trained soldier" would have seen as much.[4]

Monty and Ike conferred briefly, then went their different ways—Ike to Washington and Monty to London. While Eisenhower was in Washington, he received a message from Montgomery, who had begun working with Beetle Smith on revisions to the plan. "Will you hurl yourself into the contest," Monty cabled Eisenhower, in the tone of an equal, not a subordinate, "and what we want, get for us?"[5]

According to Nigel Hamilton, Montgomery's authorized biographer and family friend, Montgomery's arrival in London that January was "a miracle," because nothing less could save Overlord and no man alive could do it but Monty. But if anyone could be said to have saved Overlord, Charles Bonesteel III had a better claim, because it was he who had gotten Donald Nelson to issue an AAA emergency rating for LST production in the spring of 1943, despite Admiral King's objections.[6]

When Ike reached London in January 1944, nearly every weakness in the plan could be traced to the same source—a shortage of LSTs. There were not enough for the Navy to drive across the central Pacific, for MacArthur to advance along the northern shore of New Guinea, for the imminent landing at Anzio to succeed, for Overlord to mount a five-division amphibious assault against Normandy and for Anvil, the three-division amphibious assault in southern France that Marshall wanted Ike to launch in conjunction with Overlord. Churchill grew so exasperated by the constant talk of LSTs that he protested feelingly to John McCloy, the assistant secretary of war, "The destinies of two great empires seem to be tied up in some god-damned things called LSTs whose engines themselves have to be tickled on by LST experts . . . of which there is [also] a great shortage!"[7]

On January 21, Eisenhower met with Morgan, Montgomery, his air commander, Air Marshal Sir Trafford Leigh-Mallory, and his naval commander, Admiral Sir Bertram Ramsay. Everyone agreed that the amphibious assault should be made with at least five divisions, with a two-division follow-up and an airborne division securing the western flank.[8]

Eisenhower and Smith drafted a long and detailed message to the Combined Chiefs. It amounted to a supreme commander's wish list. There was a precise breakdown of the number and types of additional landing ships and landing craft he needed for a five-division assault. If you give me these, Ike said in effect, and if we play our part by cutting the number of vehicles each division takes over to France, I will put five divisions ashore. The Combined Chiefs more or less ignored him, because assault shipping was almost completely controlled by Admiral King, and he was unrelenting. Only after Roosevelt urged him to make a concession did he finally release an extra seven LSTs for Overlord. Eisenhower seethed at what he bitingly called "the Navy's private war" in the Pacific, but if he wanted more assault shipping, he'd have to find it.[9]

Montgomery and Smith proceeded to work on what to do if no more shipping was found. Monty wanted to get ashore in early May, to maximize the amount of time for fighting in good weather. By cutting the floating reserve from two divisions to one, a four-division assault could be mounted in May. But that would leave him one division short in the amphibious assault, and he could not be sure of having enough airlift to put an entire airborne division into the fight. This attack would therefore have only a little more weight than COSSAC's much-derided proposal.[10]

Churchill, Brooke, Montgomery and Beetle Smith had a simple solution to the LST problem: cancel Anvil, the proposed assault in southern France. Eisenhower was deeply reluctant to do that, for various reasons, including the fact that Marshall had stressed the importance of Anvil during his visit to Washington. Even so, the ineluctable LST shortage was wearing him down. He told his diary on February 7, "It looks like Anvil is doomed. I hate this . . ."[11]

Once it became evident that the Combined Chiefs were not going to ride to the rescue of Overlord, Eisenhower postponed the operation from May 1 to May 31. That would give him an extra month's output of ninety-six tank landing craft from British shipyards. He also recommended that the Combined Chiefs cancel Anvil. That would release assault shipping from the Mediterranean. Marshall refused to accept cancellation, however, and the operation was postponed instead. A postponement had the same assault shipping benefits as a cancellation: an extra twenty-six LSTs, plus another forty landing craft for infantry, now became available for Overlord.[12]

Eisenhower took a close and critical look at the number of LSTs the Royal Navy said it had available. In response to his probing questions, the Royal Navy did a recount—and found it had ten more than it had originally calculated.

Delaying D-Day by a month, postponing Anvil, cutting the number of vehicles each division took to France, getting seven more LSTs from King and unearthing the extra British LSTs made a five-division assault possible, with another division as a floating reserve to be landed on the next tide in case of a crisis or, more hopefully, used to reinforce success. Eisenhower would also have enough airlift to carry three airborne divisions into the battle within twenty-four hours. Overlord would be only two-thirds as strong as Morgan had originally hoped, but it might have just enough wallop to work.

Throughout all the revisions and refinements to Overlord, two important elements in the COSSAC design were never challenged. First, the attack would be made in Normandy and not against the Pas de Calais, which was the shortest, quickest route and the place the Germans would defend the most effectively. And, second, British units would land east of Bayeux—that is, on the beaches closest to Paris—with the Americans landing to the west of Bayeux. This was dictated by shipping—American units were based in Northern Ireland and southwestern England; most British units were deployed in or close to southeastern England.

A five-division assault meant that the front could be widened from twenty-five miles to forty miles, much as Morgan had originally proposed to the Washington Conference. This made it possible to seize the beaches on the southeastern corner of the Cotentin peninsula. The Cotentin was strategically valuable for two reasons: the rivers flowing

across its base make it virtually an island, aiding its defense once captured, and on the northern shore of the peninsula stands Cherbourg, a
much bigger port than Caen. The two American airborne divisions—the
82nd and 101st—would be dropped into the Cotentin to protect Overlord's western flank and speed the capture of Cherbourg. The 6th British
Airborne Division would be dropped to protect the eastern flank and
speed the capture of Caen.

While Montgomery worked on the details of command and control,
of securing the beachhead and putting the troops ashore with clearly defined objectives to aim for, it was Eisenhower more than anyone who
was turning a doomed three-division assault from the sea, plus one from
the air, into a five-division assault from the sea plus three from the air,
thereby doubling its weight and more than doubling its chances. Although Monty himself believed that he had raised Overlord from the
land of the dead and brought it, reborn and pink with health, into the
realm of the living, there wasn't much scope for a Monty miracle, because there would have been the same amount of assault shipping available by June 1944 had Alexander gone to England and Montgomery
been left in Italy—the same five-division amphibious assault; the same
airborne drop on each flank; the same beaches assaulted; the same arrangement, with the Americans in the west and the British in the east;
the same corps and division commanders and the same deception operation that convinced Hitler the invasion would be made in the Pas de
Calais. It was Ike who had found extra assault shipping, and that was
what brought Overlord to life.

Soon after Eisenhower moved into Norfolk House, where he had begun planning Torch eighteen months before, he established Supreme
Headquarters, Allied Expeditionary Force, better known as SHAEF. Its
symbol was a flaming sword pointing assertively upward against a deep
blue background surmounted by a rainbow. The people who wore that
patch would, in time, be as proud of it as any infantryman was of his
division shoulder patch.

The lessons learned at AFHQ were applied at SHAEF. From the
start, Eisenhower put his new headquarters on a three-shift basis. It
would operate around the clock and have plenty of staff. In time,

SHAEF grew to number nearly sixteen thousand people, which made it bigger than an infantry division, and it was so complex, some people complained, that dealing with it was as hard as trying to deal with the Pentagon.[13]

In a perfect world, Eisenhower would have had Cunningham as his naval commander, Tedder in command of the air forces and Alexander commanding the ground forces. Instead, his naval commander was Admiral Sir Bertram Ramsay, and Ike simply couldn't help comparing him to Cunningham, whom he considered the world's greatest sailor. For his air commander, Eisenhower got Air Marshal Sir Trafford Leigh-Mallory, a man with a lot of combat experience, but it was all in fighter units. He knew nothing about strategic bombing. Eisenhower wanted Tedder, not Leigh-Mallory, but the British had insisted on making Tedder the deputy supreme commander, to Tedder's frustration. He had almost nothing to do.

Eisenhower chose not to have a ground-force commander, because the man he wanted for that assignment, Alexander, had been denied him. Montgomery would serve as ground-force commander only for Overlord, but once SHAEF moved to the Continent, Monty would assume command of the British army group in France, Bradley would command the American army group, and Eisenhower would become, in effect, his own ground-force commander, directing the operations of Bradley and Montgomery. This was not an arrangement that Monty was ever going to accept without protest.

In creating a truly Allied command at SHAEF, Eisenhower applied the interleaving principle he had introduced at AFHQ—an American section chief would have a British deputy; a British section chief would have an American deputy and people would be in constant communication with those above and below them. His second principle was that only cheerful, positive and optimistic attitudes were permitted. The third was that doubts and reservations must be freely and fully expressed, but once a decision was made, it had to be supported to the hilt.[14]

The principle of unity of command that Eisenhower had found so difficult to establish at AFHQ was, if anything, harder than ever to achieve. Roosevelt and Churchill were supposed to tell the Combined Chiefs of Staff what they wanted and the CCS turned their wishes into orders to Eisenhower. The President and the PM were too confident of their standing as military experts to refrain from dealing directly with senior commanders, short-circuiting the system. Of the two, Churchill was by far the worst, unable to restrain himself from telling British commanders ostensibly answerable to Eisenhower that they ought to do this or avoid doing that. Nothing annoyed Eisenhower more, but Churchill was incorrigible.

To make things even worse, Ramsay and Leigh-Mallory were wedded to outmoded, doctrinaire attitudes. World War II was really two wars in one. The first, which ran from the fall of 1939 to the fall of 1942, was a struggle in which the Germans held the initiative and taught the lessons. The second, from the fall of 1942 to the fall of 1945, amounted to a different conflict in the way it was fought, even though it remained the same in its purposes. The Allies not only held the initiative but were superior in nearly every department. Ramsay and Leigh-Mallory hadn't fathomed the implications of that change, yet Eisenhower's ideas were based on the new realities of combined operations and joint operations, on maximizing firepower and flexibility, whatever established doctrine said. The manual could be rewritten later. This was a form of warfare that reached out to embrace emergent technologies and an increasingly managerial approach to the application of state-sanctioned violence. Men like Ramsay and Leigh-Mallory, for all their dedication and bravery, were passé.[15]

With the creation of SHAEF, COSSAC came to an end, and Morgan was offered command of a corps, but Ike was so impressed by Morgan's work and manner that he persuaded him to turn it down. Morgan became Beetle Smith's deputy instead.

It was a shrewd move. Beetle was good at making quick decisions, but that owed something to the fact that he often didn't bother to think about the implications. Smith was also an abrasive man, his natural irascibility made worse by his martyrdom to duodenal ulcers. Many SHAEF officers feared him and counted that day good when they managed to keep out of his way.

Morgan not only did not fear him but could handle him better than anyone else—including, at times, Eisenhower, with whom Beetle had occasional shouting matches. Morgan's technique was to tell Beetle that he had just made a splendid decision or that his current way of handling problems was the right one. Then he'd start wondering aloud about whether it was possible to make even that splendid decision better or if Beetle's excellent way of doing things couldn't be made still more effective by introducing a few adjustments. It wasn't flattery but shrewdness, and there was little glory or praise or chance of promotion in it. But many a SHAEF officer antagonized by Beetle Smith's abruptness was likely to get a visit soon thereafter from Morgan, who would couch what Beetle *really* thought in kinder, gentler terms than Beetle ever imagined.[16]

Morgan and Smith were a perfect good cop/bad cop team and it was largely through them that Ike was able to impose himself on his huge, sprawling headquarters without being drawn into the dense, snagging bracken of bureaucratic detail, a world that he dreaded more than the enemy waiting, preparing, on the other side of the Channel.

Without air superiority Overlord would be impossible. Even with it, there was no guarantee of success. At Anzio, the Allies had control of the skies yet were unable to break out even though they had the Germans outnumbered. And when Eisenhower arrived in London, he found the Eighth Air Force in crisis. In June 1943 the Combined Chiefs had issued a directive known as Pointblank, which made the destruction of the German fighter arm the Eighth's number-one priority. It was ordered, in effect, to bomb the German aviation industry out of business and blast Göring's fighters out of the skies.

By December 1943, however, German fighter production had increased and the Eighth Air Force had recently cut back on the frequency of its attacks to reduce the scale of its losses. As for the highly vaunted, heavily publicized practice of precision bombing, that was a steel-clad myth. More USAAF bombs landed in fields and killed cows than hit German factories. The long-cherished theory of the airmen that a vigorously pressed bombing attack would always get through and strike its target was in ruins.

Pointblank's objectives could never be achieved without long-range fighter escorts for the bombers, yet fighter escort was something the AAF had not so much neglected as scorned. Not until the fall of 1943 did it finally begin to take the subject seriously. The Eighth's failure nevertheless provoked Hap Arnold into firing the commander of the Eighth, Lieutenant General Ira C. Eaker, and sending him to Italy in December 1943.

Eaker was replaced by Jimmy Doolittle, who had gotten off to a terrible start with Eisenhower in North Africa but had since redeemed himself. The brash Jimmy Doolittle who had gone brothel-crawling with his air crews and flown along on the most dangerous raids had changed. He was, Eisenhower informed Marshall, the Allied officer who had improved the most in North Africa.[17]

At one of the earliest conferences on Overlord, Leigh-Mallory said he did not expect to win air superiority this side of D-Day. It would be achieved, he told Eisenhower, only over the invasion beaches. For the sake of Allied harmony, he did not criticize Pointblank, but what he said meant it had failed.[18]

Leigh-Mallory's forecast put Overlord itself in doubt, because the old rules still applied—ground units needed a manpower advantage of around three to one to prevail over an entrenched enemy. The Red Army planned on a basis of four to one. Eisenhower was going to be fighting the German Army in France on a basis of roughly 1.25 to 1. On that calculation, he didn't stand a chance. SHAEF's strategy was a bet that the difference would be made up by superior firepower and superior mobility—command of the air, command of the sea, jeeps, C-47's, DUKWs, two-and-a-half-ton trucks, more and better artillery, more (even if inferior) tanks and the world's first semiautomatic rifles. Of all these, command of the air mattered most in the campaign ahead. Eisenhower wrote to retired Major General Herbert Jay Brees, who had been in charge of the curriculum at the Command and General Staff School when he was a student there. Ike told Brees he would change only two parts of the Leavenworth course. One would be to treat war "as the drama it is," instead of trying to reduce it to a science. "The second would be a greater emphasis upon the Air Arm . . ."[19]

Leigh-Mallory considered Pointblank such a failure that he was eager to suspend it and try something else. Tedder's civilian expert, Solly Zuckerman, the mastermind behind the bombing of Pantelleria, had come up with a plan that he claimed would ensure the success of Overlord: a prolonged, intensive bombing of the French railroad network, culminating with a massive bridge-busting campaign on the eve of D day. Zuckerman's "Transportation Plan" was aimed at isolating the battlefield and making it impossible for the Germans to move toward the beachhead in sufficient strength to drive the invaders back into the sea.[20]

Spaatz emphatically rejected it. He did not believe the Luftwaffe would come up to defend French railroads, and if they did not come up, they couldn't be shot down. Only by shooting down German fighters could air superiority be won. He argued instead for attacks on Germany's synthetic oil plants and rubber factories. And one thing he would not accept was having Doolittle's heavy bombers put under the control of Leigh-Mallory, a man who knew nothing about strategic bombing and was likely to use heavy bombers against tactical rather than strategic targets. Air Marshall Arthur Harris, who ran the RAF's Bomber Command, also refused to put his command under Leigh-Mallory's control.

Churchill, too, had objections to the Transportation Plan. It might result in the deaths of tens of thousands of French people and cast the Allies not as liberators but callous butchers. De Gaulle, consulted, said if that was the price of French liberation, it would be paid without regret or complaint.[21]

Eisenhower became increasingly angry and frustrated at the refusal of Spaatz, Harris and Leigh-Mallory to cooperate with one another. "Now, listen, Arthur," he told Tedder. "I am tired of dealing with a lot of prima donnas. By God, you tell that bunch that if they can't get together and stop quarrelling like children, I will tell the Prime Minister to get someone else to run this damned war!" As well as anger, there was memory—George Marshall saying that had he been named supreme commander, he would have demanded control of the air forces. Ike knew Marshall would back him on this one, and he did.[22]

At the end of March, Eisenhower secured the authority to do what he had wanted from the beginning—he inserted Tedder over Spaatz, Harris and Leigh-Mallory. There were some brain-numbing quibbles over wording that were almost theological in their turgidity. Nevertheless, Eisenhower finally got control of the heavy bombers, with Tedder acting as "my Executive."[23]

Tedder had backed the Transportation Plan from the start because, as Spaatz himself acknowledged, it would be six months before his Oil Plan had any real impact on the German war machine. The head of the RAF, Charles Portal, supported the Transportation Plan, for the same reason, and Portal sat on the Combined Chiefs of Staff.[24]

The oil-versus-transportation debate consumed much of Eisenhower's time in February and March 1944, and while it rumbled on, the heavy bombers were continuing their Pointblank attacks. The difference now was that in December and January, P-47's with droppable fuel tanks had escorted the bombers into western Germany and wiped out the cream of German fighter pilots. In March and early April, P-51's were escorting B-17's all the way to Berlin, and each week shot down scores of inexperienced, undertrained Luftwaffe pilots who rose to defend Hitler's capital. On April 14, Eisenhower declared that the mission set out in the Pointblank directive had been fulfilled. Air superiority had finally been won. In four months, nearly seventeen hundred German fighter pilots had perished. It hardly mattered that Germany was producing more planes than ever, that the precision-bombing side of Pointblank had failed.[25]

At this point, Tedder came close to throwing away all that had been gained. Instead of unleashing the Transportation Plan, he gave priority to hitting the German V-1 sites springing up along the Channel coast. Tedder was under tremendous pressure from Churchill, who feared for British morale. Thousands of sorties were flown, in complete futility, against these sites. So long as the Germans knew how to pour concrete and assemble a steel ramp, there was no way such targets could be bombed out of existence. Spaatz protested strenuously, and this time Ike upheld Spaatz.[26]

Zuckerman's Transportation Plan was finally unleashed against northern France. The Pas de Calais was hit as hard as Normandy, to keep the Germans guessing. There was no air opposition to speak of. The Luftwaffe would count for nothing on D-Day.[27]

Overlord called for putting a total of thirty-seven divisions ashore, with more to follow once a breakout from Normandy had been achieved. Eisenhower wanted to visit all thirty-seven divisions before the operation was launched. It was a goal he did not meet, but he managed to visit twenty-six divisions—both U.S. and British—plus numerous warships and airfields. Many a day found him rocking gently across the green landscape of Britain aboard his private railroad car, *Bayonet,* to visit units in training.[28]

He believed he could judge the quality of a division from taking a good look at its commander, and although he had the authority to remove any of the American division commanders, he kept all of them. The quality of the fully trained, fully equipped divisions shipped to

Britain was high, with few exceptions. The Army school system of which he was himself a notable product had produced dozens of able, aggressive young generals to lead them.

Happy as he was with what he saw of the divisions, there was a question mark over his corps commanders—Roscoe B. Woodruff, Willis D. Crittenberger and Ike's old friend Leonard T. Gerow. Not one of them had any combat experience. Much of what a division commander did came down to problems of supply and personnel. It was the corps commanders who concentrated on tactics, using divisions much as a surgeon uses scalpels and clamps. One of his earliest requests as supreme commander was for Truscott, whom he would have made a corps commander. But Truscott had just been given command of a corps in Italy and was fighting desperately at Anzio.[29]

Marshall sent Eisenhower two generals who had performed superbly in the Pacific, J. Lawton Collins and Charles Corlett, as potential corps commanders. Eisenhower and Bradley grilled Collins on how he had handled the 25th Infantry Division on Guadalcanal. Collins said every time he attacked, it was to seize the high ground. "He talks our language," said Bradley. Woodruff was one of Ike's West Point classmates; Collins nevertheless got Woodruff's VII Corps. Woodruff ended up commanding a division in the Pacific.[30]

Had experience been the overriding criterion, Corlett would have been given command of Gerow's V Corps. Besides, Gerow was defeatist about his Overlord assignment. The 1st Infantry Division, which would be leading the V Corps attack in Normandy, had been assigned to seize a beach called Omaha. Photographs taken from submarines showed Omaha to consist of a long, narrow strip of sand at the bottom of a 110-foot cliff defended by huge coastal guns and machine gun nests, and there was no evident way of getting off the beach and up to the top of the cliff.

Eisenhower tried to brush aside Gee's worries. "You should be optimistic and cheerful. Behind you will be the greatest fire power ever assembled." He then described the huge armada that would provide naval gunfire from just offshore, but Gerow wasn't impressed. And why should he be? Gerow hadn't seen the awesome tank killing power of the fleet at Salerno.[31]

His pessimism and inexperience more than justified giving his corps to Corlett, but that was something that Eisenhower could never contemplate doing. Gee Gerow was so close to Ike's heart that he might as well have been one of his brothers. Corlett would have command of Crittenberger's XIX Corps, which contained the floating reserve. Crittenberger was transferred to Italy.

Although visiting troops in training helped buoy him up, Eisenhower nevertheless found the burden of supreme command crushing. He seemed almost to dread having to decide when to launch Overlord. "Someone has to make the decision and I suppose I'm it," he remarked glumly.[32]

Eisenhower tried to pace himself. At least one day a week, he did not go to the office and went riding in Richmond Great Park instead. He took immense pleasure in seeing the day-to-day drama of the countryside bursting into life to the rhythms of an English spring. Meanwhile, he persuaded Tedder, who was living at Telegraph Cottage when Ike arrived in January, to swap it for the large, imposing house that had been thought appropriate for the supreme commander.

Back at Telegraph Cottage, Ike was able to re-create the family atmosphere that had made such a difference to his happiness during his six months in England in 1942. And it was in the living room at Telegraph Cottage that, according to Kay Summersby, they twice stripped naked in front of the fire and tried to consummate their love affair.

If she is to be believed, they failed each time because Eisenhower was impotent. Yet, given the number of people living in the house, the almost total lack of privacy and the regularity with which important messages arrived during the night, what she describes was akin to making love in a doorway on a busy street. It was the kind of reckless act a pair of college students might attempt in a spirit of lust, defiance and bravado but something that no one with any common sense or maturity would even consider. Adults with copulation in mind would have found a room with a lock on the door. On the balance of probabilities, Kay's claim is not so much unlikely as slightly sad, slightly pathetic.[33]

By May, Eisenhower was troubled by a host of minor ailments. A sore left eye, a persistent cough, insomnia, tinnitus and a general feeling of being out of sorts. His unhealthy pallor and obvious weariness had Butcher worried. "Ike looks worn and tired," thought Butcher. "The strain is telling on him. He looks older now than at any time since I have been with him."[34]

Not only had he felt obliged to remove his classmate Roscoe Woodruff from command of a corps, but another classmate, Major General Henry J. Miller, had compromised Overlord. On April 18,

Miller, commander of the Ninth Air Force Service Command, was in the dining room of a prominent London hotel, and complained in a voice loud enough for people at nearby tables to hear, that it was hell getting supplies from the U.S. Then he cheered up. His problems would be over by June 15, he announced, because the invasion of France would have taken place by then. Eisenhower busted Miller to colonel and sent him home. It was a depressing episode.[35]

Even worse, however, was another Patton crisis. Patton had arrived in England shortly after Eisenhower and he reminded him that he had to behave himself. Patton had responded with some outrageous flattery. "Ike, as you are now the most powerful man in the world, it is foolish to contest your views." Eisenhower paid no attention to that, but for good measure Patton poured honeyed words into Butcher's ear, confident of their eventual destination. "He is on the threshold of becoming the greatest general of all time," Patton confided to the war's number-one naval aide. "Including Napoleon!"[36]

Patton had come to take command of the Third Army, which would be activated when the Overlord forces broke out from the beachhead. Eisenhower was counting on Patton to lead the charge into Brittany that would secure badly needed ports for a summer offensive in France. For now, however, Patton would play a central role in the most ambitious deception plan of the war, Operation Fortitude, which sought to convince the Germans that any landing in Normandy was only a feint designed to make them shift their tanks away from the Pas de Calais, where Patton was going to lead an army group ashore.[37]

Eisenhower put no faith at all in Fortitude. He did not believe that deception plans made any difference in war, and the more ambitious they were, the more likely to fail. Meanwhile the airwaves crackled with signal traffic generated by Patton's fictitious army group headquarters.

Then, on April 25, Patton went to Knutsford, a pleasant small town in northwestern England, to open a "welcome club" operated by women from the town for the thousands of American servicemen stationed at army bases nearby. Asked to make a few remarks, he went on to quote George Bernard Shaw's comical chestnut about Americans and the British being "two people separated by a common language," and couldn't resist adding that "since it is the evident destiny of the British and Americans, and of course the Russians, to rule the world, the better we know each other, the better job we will do."[38]

Poor Patton. To him, what he had said was unremarkable, but in the

United States it unleashed a storm of hostile publicity. It was portrayed in *The Washington Post* and in Congress as an insult to the United Nations. The Allies were fighting under the umbrella of the UN and their most important war aim was to prevent anyone from dominating the world. The Allies were supposed to be liberators, not the crafty masterminds of an updated version of colonialism.

Patton's latest foolishness wasn't as bad as slapping a soldier, but it came close. "I'm just about fed up," Eisenhower told Bradley. "If I have to apologize publicly for Georgie once more, I'm going to have to let him go, valuable as he is. I'm getting sick and tired of having to protect him."[39]

Eisenhower composed a scathing letter of rebuke, the kind an angry parent might produce: "I have warned you time and again against your impulsiveness. . . . I have always been fully aware of your habit of dramatizing yourself and of committing indiscretions. . . . I am thoroughly weary of your failure to control your tongue . . ." And if there was just one more incident, "I will relieve you instantly from command."[40]

As reports of criticism in Congress and the press continued to flow in, Eisenhower decided to let Patton go. He told Butcher, "George's goose is cooked," and informed Marshall, "On the evidence available, I will relieve him from command and send him home unless some new and unforeseen information should be developed in the case. [I] believe that disciplinary action must be taken."[41]

Patton was summoned to SHAEF, and reported to Eisenhower the morning of May 1. The previous day, Eisenhower had talked to Churchill, who dismissed it as a trifling affair. Churchill didn't say so, but given his own perspective on the postwar world, Patton's remarks would have been no more than a glimpse of the obvious.

Patton, suitably contrite and apologetic when he greeted Eisenhower, tried to deflect him by talking about Overlord. The assault was too small, he said. Eisenhower ignored that, confident that Overlord would work now that he had air superiority. He hinted to Patton that disciplinary action was likely. If reduced to colonel, Patton replied, he would ask for command of a regiment assigned to the D-Day assault. Ike wouldn't promise him that, although he surely knew that being sent home, even without being busted, was a fate Patton feared more than death. Better to be a colonel in combat than a three-star sitting in retirement and reading about other men fighting the war.[42]

Eisenhower couldn't quite bring himself to act even now. Patton was still the best man for the breakout from Overlord, and if he did depart, who would take command of the Third Army? Had Truscott been available, this story might have had a different ending, but Truscott was still in Italy, defending the Anzio beachhead. He may also have hesitated because Patton had a powerful patron in Henry Stimson, the secretary of war, and for every congressman who damned him, another admired him. But the main reason he hesitated was that he had not yet heard from Marshall. Patton was dismissed, looking thoroughly miserable, left in suspense, to twist in the wind.

The next day a cable arrived from Marshall—"The decision is entirely yours. . . . Do not consider the War Department position in this matter. Consider only Overlord. . . . Everything else is of minor importance."[43]

In his anger and frustration, Eisenhower had not been thinking clearly. No doubt he felt that Patton had betrayed his trust and part of him craved to punish that betrayal. Throughout his life, Eisenhower could be adamantly unforgiving toward anyone who he felt had failed him. Marshall, thinking more coolly, took a detached win-the-war-and-to-hell-with-everything-else approach. Applying that yardstick, Ike had no choice about keeping Patton to command the Third Army. Eisenhower also had the assurance that Marshall would support his decision not to sack Patton.

In *Crusade in Europe*, he claimed he told Patton at their meeting on May 1 that he was not going to fire him. The documentary record clearly shows, though, that he did not inform Patton until the day after Marshall's cable arrived and two days after the May 1 meeting. Like all memoirs, Eisenhower's *Crusade* is not a perfect record of what actually happened. It is, instead, a perfect record of how someone remembers the great events in his life and the feelings those memories evoke. In that, Eisenhower was no different from other great soldiers who produced best-selling memoirs, such as Douglas MacArthur and Ulysses S. Grant.[44]

Montgomery was a Pauline, a former student—or "old boy"—at one of England's most prestigious private schools, St. Paul's, adjacent to St.

Paul's Cathedral. He took over part of the school for his headquarters when he got down to work on planning for Overlord. On May 15, 1944, one of its pine-paneled lecture rooms became the venue for the most impressive commanders' conference of the war, when the final plan was presented to Churchill, King George VI and 150 force commanders and senior staff officers.

A row of armchairs was provided for Ike, Churchill, the King and the British chiefs of staff. The rest sat in a balcony, on hard wooden benches used by students. Nearly everyone wore an overcoat. It was a bitterly cold day for May and whatever antiquated heating the school possessed had been turned off weeks earlier. They looked down on a low stage on which was placed a huge relief map of northern France, slightly tilted so those in the balcony could see it clearly. There were phase lines, reaching inexorably inland, marking anticipated progress from D-Day to the breakout, until, on D+90, Allied forces reached the Seine. The relief map also showed dozens of German divisions along or close to the invasion beaches.

Precisely at nine A.M., the King stammered out a few opening remarks. He was followed by Eisenhower, only to be interrupted by ferocious hammering on the double doors, which had just been locked. Patton. Late as usual.[45]

Resuming, Eisenhower described the general design of the plan and concluded, "Here we are, on the eve of a great battle. . . . I consider it to be the duty of anyone who sees a flaw in the plan not to hesitate to say so. I have no sympathy with anyone, whatever his station, who will not brook criticism. We are here to get the best possible results."

Montgomery then began his presentation, speaking in his brisk, clipped manner, punctuated by his odd habit of repeating himself—"It is intended to move towards Caen. *Towards Caen.*" He described how divisions would move quickly inland, and said he expected British tanks would be "knocking about" Caen by nightfall on D-Day. Every time Montgomery got into his stride, Churchill interrupted to make some point about strategy or tactics, not so much to improve the plan as to show that he approved of the plan.[46]

Ramsay gave a brief presentation following Montgomery's. The man who really held forth was Leigh-Mallory, who talked for forty minutes. Allied aircraft would fly eleven thousand sorties on D-Day, he said, and the Germans wouldn't be able to do anything about it. Having complete and unbreakable superiority in the air, he spoke as if his Overlord mission had already been fulfilled.

One after another, men in stars and gold braid, crowns and crossed batons, stood up and talked about the role their forces would play in the fighting ahead. Some were better speakers than others, but nearly all exuded the kind of calm confidence Eisenhower was looking for.

Churchill then got up to speak. Dressed in an Edwardian frock coat and brandishing a double corona, he looked and sounded like a figure from an earlier age, yet his mind and heart were in the present. He spoke for half an hour, rousing, martial stuff, about millions of men poised for the attack, ardor for battle stirring their souls, waiting only for the officers here assembled to lead them boldly into the fight. He was well aware that everyone in the room knew of his long-held doubts about a cross-Channel attack, but he waved all that away. "Gentlemen," he growled, grasping the lapels of his frock coat. "I am *now* hardening to this enterprise!"[47]

The King departed, and as Eisenhower saw him to the door, he reminded him of the huge naval armada (George VI was a sailor, after all) and the eleven thousand sorties Leigh-Mallory had promised. "Your Majesty, it will not fail."[48]

It was late in the afternoon when Ike closed the proceedings, standing in front of the gathering in his now-famous Ike jacket, hands on hips in a typical pose. "A few minutes from now," he told his audience, "Hitler will have missed his last chance to wipe out the entire leadership of this operation with a single, well-placed bomb!" That made them smile. Then he said quietly, "I want everyone here to see himself as being part of a staff college for the future. This will be a college in which there is neither Army or Navy or Air Force; not British or American; but a college consisting of nothing but fighting men who are there to learn, and to teach others, the art of future wars."[49]

Two days later, on May 17, Eisenhower gave the commanders who had attended the St. Paul's conference the one remaining piece of information they needed. D-Day would be June 5.

22

The Day

Eisenhower had a personal plan for D-Day—he would watch the amphibious assault go in. He might even go ashore once the troops had secured a beachhead, to visit them under fire. When his staff discovered what he had in mind, they were appalled. Suppose he got killed? Oh, that, responded Eisenhower. Hardly worth worrying about. Tedder could fill in long enough to get Marshall over to take command at SHAEF.[1]

With D-Day a week away, Leigh-Mallory put the whole operation in doubt. Leigh-Mallory was a likable man who, having reached his level of incompetence early in the war, continued to float upward thereafter. There were people much like him in the USAAF, such as Lewis Brereton, old-time aviators who had stuck with the service during the lean years of the 1930s, shown their loyalty and dedication but, when the war came upon them, failed at the first test, only to be saved by having the right friends in the right places.

The RAF had won the Battle of Britain largely thanks to Air Vice Marshal Hugh Dowding, who saw the battle unfold in his mind years before the war, and prepared RAF Fighter Command to win it. Leigh-Mallory had weakened Dowding's brilliant plan by trying, in his sector of the Fighter Command network, to assemble huge fighter formations that he hoped to hurl at the Germans. The trouble was, the Luftwaffe could bomb London and be back across the Channel before Leigh-Mallory's "Big Wing" formations were ready.

He was never completely honest about what he was doing and Dowding found him a difficult, wayward subordinate—something excusable in a man of great ability, but nothing but a pain in anyone else. As his performance in the Battle of Britain had shown, Leigh-Mallory was too rigid in his ideas and too unpredictable to be a suitable commander of the Allied Expeditionary Air Forces.[2]

On May 29, Leigh-Mallory visited Eisenhower, his normally mournful mien growing even more depressing as he said the two U.S. airborne divisions assigned to land in the Cotentin peninsula were going to be slaughtered. Ultra showed that an elite German division had just moved into the section of the Cotentin where the 82nd Airborne Division had its D-Day drop zones. Besides which, there were glider units scheduled to attempt a landing that night. In his judgment, the gliders were likely to lose more than 50 percent of their troops due to ground fire, collisions with trees, landings in swamps and other accidents before the glidermen were engaged in battle with the enemy.

The amphibious assault against the southeastern Cotentin, where the 4th Infantry Division would go ashore at a beach called Utah, depended on the success of the paratroopers and the glidermen. But according to Leigh-Mallory, there was not going to be an airborne success.

Eisenhower put a call through on his scrambler telephone to Bradley, who said, No airborne, no Utah. Matthew Ridgway, commander of the 82nd Airborne Division, agreed with Bradley, and made it clear that come what may, this operation was so important, he would risk the survival of his division.

Even if the situation was as bad as portrayed, Eisenhower reasoned, he could not call Overlord off now. He seethed that Leigh-Mallory had not raised these issues sooner. Back in January, Leigh-Mallory had said that some of the people on his staff were doubtful about airborne operations in the Cotentin, but his own view was that "parachutists can be dropped in that area without difficulty." Having changed his mind, why hadn't he spoken up earlier? The conference at St. Paul's was the right place to do it, not here, not as the invasion fleet prepared to sail. Eisenhower called Leigh-Mallory late that night and told him the plan would

be modified. He was shifting the drop zones of the 82nd so that Ridgway's paratroopers would land closer to Utah and would order the glider
assaults to be limited to daylight hours. At noon the next day, a courier
arrived from Leigh-Mallory with a two-page letter. He was putting his
objections on record in case it all went wrong. Eisenhower was disgusted. So much for Leigh-Mallory's loyalty to his commander.[3]

The next day, Ramsay phoned from his headquarters in Portsmouth
to inform Ike that Churchill intended to go along with the invasion fleet.
The PM had made similar demands before, and Eisenhower had done
what he could to discourage him, but Churchill was now arguing that
the Supreme Allied Commander did not have the power to make personnel decisions about the complement of Royal Navy ships. Ike told
Ramsay to say to Churchill that his plan had just been "disapproved" by
SHAEF, but he knew the PM would simply ignore his objections.
Somewhere along the way, Eisenhower had realized that he couldn't go,
and he was hoping Churchill might come to the same realization.
Churchill, however, was not going to give up easily.[4]

On June 1 Eisenhower moved down to Portsmouth, where his advanced command post had been set up in the extensive grounds of
Ramsay's headquarters at Southwick House, a splendiferous eighteenth-century Palladian construction that was almost a palace in size
and architectural ambition. His own command post consisted of half a
dozen trailers and tents. Ike's trailer contained a chemical toilet, a
shower and washbasin, a desk with three telephones on it (one connected to Number 10, one connected to the War Department, the third
for communication with SHAEF), a tiny bedroom (with a stack of western magazines on a table next to a narrow bunk bed), a minuscule sitting room and a glassed-in observation deck. This trailer and the tents
in which his immediate staff lived and worked were placed in a stand of
trees, making them invisible from the air. A cinder path wound nearly a
mile from the trees and trailers to imposing Southwick House.[5]

There was some good news waiting for Eisenhower when he arrived: the King had told Churchill that he would accompany him on the
trip to watch the D-Day assault. Churchill had then replied that he could
not allow the King to take such risks. To which the King responded
that maybe neither one of them should go. The PM finally yielded to his
sovereign.

Churchill came down to Southwick House on June 2, sulking at missing out on the great adventure. He sat in the mess more or less ig-noring the dazzling array of brass taking dinner there, devoting himself instead to playing with Shaef, the headquarters cat, and feeding it milk from a saucer.[6]

Once dinner concluded, Eisenhower, Churchill, Tedder, Mont-gomery, Ramsay, Leigh-Mallory and Beetle Smith trooped into the paneled library and spread themselves on the sofas and easy chairs to hear what SHAEF's chief meteorologist, Group Captain John Stagg of the RAF, had to say. Overlord was little more than forty-eight hours away. The weather, Stagg told them, was "untrustworthy" but "finely balanced." When the meeting broke up, Eisenhower dictated a memo-randum, damning the British climate. "The weather in this country is practically unpredictable."[7]

The next day, the skies were clear, but when Stagg came into the li-brary that evening, he did not have to tell them what the forecast was. They could read it on his face. Ships from as far away as Scotland were already making their way out to sea for the invasion, but the barometer was dropping like a stone. Thick, low cloud was rolling in rapidly from the west. The weather on June 5 would be unflyable. Eisenhower could hardly stand it. When Stagg finished his forecast, he asked, almost pleaded, "Is there just a chance you might be more optimistic tomor-row?" Stagg said there was no chance of a major development over-night.[8]

They would meet again, said Eisenhower, seven hours from now, at four-thirty on the morning of June 4. When Eisenhower and the others reconvened, Stagg said, "No change, sir." Ramsay wanted to go ahead. The seas wouldn't be too rough either to put troops ashore or provide naval bombardment. Leigh-Mallory, however, said the air plan couldn't be implemented. The weather wasn't flyable. Montgomery brushed that aside. "We must go," he said.[9]

Tedder strongly disagreed. He was amazed, if not aghast, that Montgomery would even think of going ashore without the three air-borne divisions to secure his flanks and without close air support. Eisenhower pointedly remarked that this operation was only possible because of air superiority. It wasn't overwhelmingly powerful in ground units. He couldn't risk it without a maximum effort from the AEAF. The ships at sea were ordered to return to port and refuel.[10]

Later that morning, de Gaulle arrived, at Eisenhower's request.

Eisenhower gave him a tour of Southwick House, showing him the huge situation maps hung from the walls of the war room, where he explained, in broad outline, the Overlord plan. He then flattered de Gaulle by asking him, "What do you think of it?" De Gaulle responded that the sooner it could be implemented, the better; delay would only exhaust the nervous energies of those involved and increase the risk of a security failure.[11]

Eisenhower then handed him the text of an address he would be making at the time of the invasion. De Gaulle's face froze as he read what amounted to a summons to the people of France to obey instructions from SHAEF and follow Eisenhower's orders. There was nothing about de Gaulle, nothing about the French Committee of National Liberation, which de Gaulle now dominated completely, having forced Giraud to resign two months earlier.

They took a walk in the rain along the cinder path outside Southwick House. De Gaulle, gesticulating vehemently, explained that he could not endorse Eisenhower's speech, which more or less treated France as a country destined to come under the occupation of SHAEF, and in the meantime seemed to accept the continued rule of pro-German officials.

To mollify de Gaulle, Eisenhower told him he was ready to listen to any suggestions he had to offer, which de Gaulle mistakenly assumed meant changes to the speech, when what Ike meant was that he would consider changes to implementation of the policy once the Allies had liberated France. During the night, de Gaulle rewrote Ike's text, turning it into an instruction to the French to "follow the orders of the legitimate French authorities"—i.e., himself and the FCNL.

There was another evening session with Stagg in the library. Eisenhower was the last to enter the room, and his mood was grim, but as ever, he was careful not to appear despondent. Stagg, however, seemed to have cheered up. "I think I have found a gleam of hope for you, sir," he said, addressing Eisenhower directly. Although the situation was bad now—and it was terrible: the wind was so strong that the rain that lashed the windows and tugged at the roof tiles was traveling in horizontal streaks—the weather was going to break later in the day. The small, tired group of middle-aged men who carried half a world on their shoulders broke into a cheer. When they regained their composure, Stagg explained that from the afternoon of June 5—and only for about thirty-six hours—the wind would diminish to a stiff breeze, the rain would stop and there would be large breaks in the cloud as the barometer rose.[12]

A decision would have to be made now for a June 6 D-Day. Leigh-Mallory was irresolute, even though Stagg said he thought visual bombing would be possible. Tedder twice said it would be "chancy" to go ahead, but Ramsay was strongly in favor. Eisenhower turned to Montgomery. "Do you see any reason why we should not go on Tuesday?"

Monty replied emphatically, "No. I would say—go!"[13]

"It's a hell of a gamble," mused Beetle Smith. "But it's the best possible gamble."

No one said anything while Eisenhower turned the decision over and over in his mind. If the assault was postponed, it would be June 19 before the tides would once again favor an invasion, but there would be no moon to aid the airborne then. The Germans had fallen for the deception plan but could wise up any day now. The troops were keyed up and ready for action.

"The question is," he said at last, "how long can you allow this thing to just kind of hang there out on a limb?" He paused for a moment. No turning back now. "I'm quite positive the order must be given. I don't like it, but there it is."[14]

When he left the room, Kay was waiting for him outside the tall, ornately carved double doors. He told her, "D-Day's June 6."[15]

There was another meeting, even so, at four A.M. on June 5. Stagg was almost smiling this time. There were some changes in the forecast but all were "in the direction of optimism." The cloud cover was lifting even as they met, and the pelting rain had slackened. It was falling vertically now. "Okay," said Eisenhower. "We'll go."[16]

In the morning, de Gaulle submitted his rewritten version of Eisenhower's message to the people of France. Eisenhower then had to explain to him that his speech had already been recorded and a million copies of the text had been printed. They would be dropped over France on D-Day. De Gaulle, feeling he had been lied to when Ike said he would consider making changes, grew huffier than ever and said he wouldn't broadcast the message Ike wanted.[17]

Eisenhower tried to relax by playing checkers with Butcher before lunch. Afterward, he talked to a small group of reporters, and when they had left, he took a message pad and wrote, in his crabbed, spidery hand,

"Our landings in the Cherbourg–Le Havre area have failed to gain a satisfactory foothold and I have withdrawn the troops. My decision to attack at this time and place was based on the best information available. The troops, the air and the navy did all that bravery and devotion to duty could do. If any blame or fault attaches to the attempt, it is mine alone." He put it in his pants pocket, just in case.[18]

Sometime later, oppressed by the dismal predictions of Leigh-Mallory, Eisenhower called for Kay to fetch his car. He was going to visit the men of the 101st Airborne Division as they prepared to make their first combat jump. It was a long, slow drive along roads clogged with traffic heading for the Channel ports before he reached the 101st's base, at Newbury. He moved among paratroopers who were putting on their packs and smearing each other's faces with cocoa or burnt cork. Ike asked them where they were from, did they feel ready, anybody here from Abilene? He exuded a calm confidence and offered a guarantee: "If you see airplanes overhead, they will be ours."

When the C-47's were fully loaded—each bearing a "stick" of sixteen paratroopers—they began taxiing for takeoff. Ike, Kay, Smith, Butcher and Jimmy Gault climbed up to the roof of the division headquarters building. They watched impassively, their feelings under tight control, as C-47's with white "invasion stripes" painted on their fuselages and wings began lifting into the darkening sky. The vibrant hum of their engines drifted sweetly back over the field as they headed south, on a bearing for France.

Eisenhower walked back to the car with Kay. "Well," he said. "It's on." In the dim light, she saw, there were tears shining in his eyes.[19]

It was late in the evening on June 5 when Gerd von Rundstedt, commander of the German armies defending Normandy and the Pas de Calais, sent a reassuring message to his forces in the field: "There is no immediate prospect of the invasion."[20]

A few hours later, American and British paratroopers jumped into Normandy, nearly eighteen thousand of them tumbling out of the low, thin clouds that forced C-47 pilots to guess where they were and drop the troops even though they knew they had missed the drop zones. Paratroopers landed in fields among surprised cows rudely awakened from ruminative sleep; they landed in thorny hedgerows tended since before Joan of Arc's birth; they landed in apple orchards fragrant with fruit and blossom; they landed in marshes and flooded rivers, to drown in their harnesses; they landed in farmyards, frightening the chickens; they landed to be greeted by wary Frenchmen with pitchforks; they landed in trees, at the cost of cut faces and necks; one snagged on a church steeple; others landed on low stone walls, breaking ankles and legs; they landed terrified and jubilant on a country that ached for them like an old wound. And few landed where they were supposed to be.

Besides the real parachutists, there were also six thousand dummies, standing about three feet high and festooned with firecrackers. The scattered drop of so many parachutists and exploding dummies led German headquarters to inform one another that up to ninety-six thousand Allied paratroopers had just landed in Normandy. One load of dummies fortuitously dropped between Omaha and Utah pushed the Germans into a serious mistake. A few weeks earlier, the Germans had moved the 352nd Infantry Division to Omaha Beach. Eisenhower heard about it from Ultra, but he had chosen not to tell Gerow, who was already pessimistic about the 1st Division's chances there. As reports came in of hundreds of paratroopers landing between Omaha and Utah, one of the 352nd's regiments was sent to launch a counterattack, crucially weakening Omaha's defenses.

At first light, the sea mists cleared to reveal more than four thousand Allied warships offshore, just as thirty-five hundred heavy bombers thundered overhead to bomb coastal defenses. The bombers, however, were above the clouds and dropped their loads blind. Bombardiers hesitated a few seconds to avoid killing the men of the underwater demolition teams, emerging from the water about now after clearing paths through beach obstacles for the incoming landing craft. As a result, thousands of bombs fell up to half a mile inland, slaughtering cows, not Germans, and leaving the bunkers along the cliffs unscathed. Then fifteen hundred medium bombers flashed over Normandy, flying just below the clouds, bombing visually, and striking their targets. Meanwhile more than five thousand Allied fighters began flying huge circular patrols over the invasion beaches, but there was no air opposition.

The fight for Omaha provided the biggest drama of the day, a fight that was narrowly and heroically won by the battle-hardened 1st Division, making its third amphibious assault of the war. The other great drama was in the British sector, where the British 3rd Division attempted to advance on Caen, a small port five miles inland. The capture of Caen was intended to be the centerpiece of the Overlord assault, an objective so important that it called for using a spearhead division, a unit comparable, that is, to the 82nd Airborne or the 1st Infantry Division.

Montgomery had made a major mistake. The unit that was assigned to advance on Caen was the British 3rd Infantry Division, a run-of-the-mill outfit and one that was remarkably short of experience for an army that had five years of hard fighting behind it. Its last appearance under fire had been in 1940, when it was evacuated from Dunkirk by its commander—Major General Bernard Law Montgomery. In a sentimental gesture, he had given his old command the chance of returning to the Continent in a blaze of glory.

The division waded ashore virtually unopposed, then spent the morning making frontal attacks on strongpoints that it could have bypassed and left to other units to tackle. It was midafternoon before the 3rd Division moved toward Caen, where it collided with a battalion of tanks from the 21st Panzer Division. Ten tanks were knocked out quickly by antitank guns and the Germans faltered. There were four hours of daylight left and an armored regiment was coming to support the advance, but the 3rd was already digging in. Once stopped, the 3rd stayed stopped. Monty wouldn't have his tanks "knocking about" Caen on D-Day after all.

Eisenhower slept fitfully during the night of June 5 and awoke early. He was propped up in bed, reading a western magazine at 6:45 A.M. when the telephone next to the bed rang. It was Ramsay. All was going according to plan. Then came the sound of footsteps on the cinder path. The door of the trailer opened and there stood Butcher, in flannel pajamas and a dressing gown. Leigh-Mallory had just called to say that losses among the airborne were light. There had been no slaughter of American paratroopers. Eisenhower grinned and lit another cigarette.[21]

After these initial reports, the morning dragged in an agony of suspense. He sat in the trailer most of the time, smoking his way through entire packs of cigarettes and gulping cup after cup of scalding black coffee, until Churchill arrived in midafternoon, accompanied by the King.

Eisenhower went with them to look at the situation maps in the war room, but reports from Bradley and Montgomery were still fragmentary and the brief bulletins about Omaha were ominous. Eisenhower ordered Leigh-Mallory to have the mediums bomb the Omaha position through the clouds if necessary, even though blind bombing was certain to produce some casualties in the 1st Division. Better that, though, than a defeat.[22]

It was late at night, some hours after Churchill and George VI departed, before Eisenhower could count the assault a success. He didn't have Caen, but the airborne hadn't been slaughtered and the 1st Division had finally captured Omaha in one of the epic battles of the war. There were 156,000 men ashore in France, along with tanks and artillery. Casualties came to roughly ten thousand—less than half the figure expected. He had rubbed his lucky coins, gambled on the weather and won.

Blitzkrieg, American-style

On D-Day, he could only smoke and worry, hope and pray. An operation on this scale was beyond any individual's power; no chance there to control events. Yet his relationship to this triumph of Allied planning, of Allied skill, of decent and courageous men and women united against a great evil, even at the cost of their lives, was beyond dispute—he was the embodiment of all that they were risking, all that they had won. It was History reduced to a broad grin and one man's name: Eisenhower. If a single individual was going to be remembered from this huge enterprise a hundred years from now, it would be him. Unjust? Of course. But inescapable, and even defensible, for he had grown into his role as supreme commander, become big enough to carry it. That didn't necessarily make him more likable as a man, but it made him more credible as a historic figure.

With his rocketing ascent to high-level command, Eisenhower had rapidly assumed an air of authority, without which he could hardly have argued with presidents and prime ministers. The projection of power was what had struck John most when he saw his father briefly in January 1944—the timbre of authority was there in his voice; it informed his gestures; it flashed from his large blue eyes. The difference between being a major general in the War Department and being the commander of a wartime theater of operations was of a magnitude almost beyond description, and it had a transforming effect on his already outgoing personality and shrewd, probing mind.

That transformation showed in small things as well as large. When he set up AFHQ in the summer of 1942, Eisenhower virtually gave up wearing the ever-growing acreage of decorations he was entitled to flaunt. When a man has that much power, the trappings of authority are almost irrelevant. Like Napoleon, who dressed more plainly than any of his marshals, Eisenhower had discovered that when a man reaches a point where nearly all other men have to please him and he needs to please few, the appropriate aesthetic of command is the Bauhausian axiom that says less is more.

With exponentially growing authority had come something else— an increased irritability. Eisenhower had always been able to balance his fierce competitiveness with that irresistible grin and a natural small-town friendliness. But beneath the charm, an urgent—sometimes angry —spirit had always been at work, and the pressures of high command could only exacerbate it.

On D+1, he was not relishing success but seething. The buildup was already running into trouble, thanks to poor coordination between soldiers and sailors, and by nightfall it was going to be two tides behind schedule; in other words, almost nothing got unloaded that day except extra troops. The flow of crucial supplies, such as artillery ammunition, was already problematic.

Eisenhower was an expert on logistics and knew that if the situation was bad now, it was almost certain to get worse, because the U.S. Army's Service of Supply in Europe was run by John C. H. Lee, an ineffectual, vainglorious character whom Marshall had unwisely elevated to high rank in the ETO while Ike was in North Africa. After arriving in London in January 1944, Eisenhower discovered he could neither fire nor fire up the infuriating Lee, who much preferred riding around England in his own private train—one bigger and more sumptuous than the King's—to the tedious business of managing supply.[1]

At dawn on June 7, Eisenhower boarded a British minelayer and shortly before noon reached the American command ship, the cruiser *Augusta,* a few miles off Omaha Beach. Someone was going to feel the edge of Ike's anger, and that someone turned out to be Bradley, his tall, homely classmate whose praises he had sung from North Africa and

Sicily. Now, though, he ripped into Bradley. Why hadn't Bradley sent him regular reports throughout D-Day? How could he justify neglecting his responsibilities so? Bradley was amazed, and explained that he had sent reports almost hourly, via Monty's message center, where they appeared to have vanished.[2]

Bradley then explained that only a couple of hours earlier he had talked to Montgomery about linking up the landing sites. In the American sector, there was a five-mile gap between the V Corps and the VII Corps, and there was another five-mile gap between the American sector and the British. They had worked out ways of closing the two gaps quickly, he assured Eisenhower.

The minelayer sped east, taking Ike to the British command ship, HMS *Faulknor*. Hardly had he been piped aboard before Monty started complaining bitterly about the air commanders. Throughout much of northern France, major roads tend to meet up in small towns and villages, where they wind sinuously between stone buildings. Monty wanted the bombers—mainly B-17's and B-24's—to bomb the village crossroads and choke them with huge piles of rubble from the shattered houses, to slow the German advance. But Leigh-Mallory and Tooey Spaatz refused to cooperate, he fumed, and Ike had to intervene.

Back aboard the minelayer, Eisenhower asked its commander to go in closer. He wanted to get a better look at the beaches. The vessel struck a sandbar, then damaged its propeller and the propeller shaft as it struggled to break free. Eisenhower transferred to another British ship, and arrived back in Portsmouth at ten P.M., to go straight into a meeting with Leigh-Mallory and Spaatz. He told them bluntly that they had to isolate the battlefield. The bridges along the Loire would be bombed; so would railroad yards, village crossroads, airfields and depots.

Behind the reluctance of the airmen was a contempt for Montgomery that was going to grow more profound the longer the war lasted. It was a contempt that Monty repaid with interest. His attitude toward air commanders and the proper use of airpower had been memorably exposed at the June 3 meeting when Leigh-Mallory said the weather would be too bad for flying on June 5. Monty brushed that aside, saying, "We must go." It was Eisenhower who had been obliged to point out that without SHAEF's eleven thousand planes in action, a cross-Channel attack was likely to fail.[3]

There were fierce disagreements between Montgomery and the airmen right up to D-Day, as he tried to convince them that their only proper role was close air support and they, guardians of a different and zealously held faith, dug in their heels and refused to comply. Like many another ground commander, the only air power Monty recognized was the airplane he could see attacking an enemy position in close support of his frontline units. Counter-air, deep interdiction, strategic bombing, photo recon and much else that air forces did were mysteries to him.

He was unable to accept that anything he did not control could possibly play a proper role in his operations. Monty therefore made no more than token attempts to integrate them with ground operations. The Allied armies that landed in Normandy did so without an effective system of ground-air cooperation. Montgomery wasn't alone to blame for this. Before D-Day, Bradley was almost as clueless as Monty when it came to integrating airpower with the ground, but in France, Bradley proved more than willing to learn.

Montgomery had also made a bad mistake in making what sounded like a promise to American and British air commanders during the famous conference at St. Paul's School, when he said he would seize the level ground southeast of Caen by the end of D-Day. They badly needed that terrain to carve out forward airfields. Because he failed to take ground for forward airfields, up to 80 percent of the tactical airpower committed to ground support—the fighters, fighter-bombers, light and medium bombers—was more or less out of the battle, tied to airfields up to two hundred miles away, in southern England. Trying to make up for that blunder by using heavy bombers to fill village crossroads with rubble was absurd. It had been attempted in Sicily and in Italy, and failed miserably. All it had done was kill or cripple thousands of harmless farm workers. Eisenhower had little choice, though, but to order Spaatz to do what Monty demanded.

What made this decision doubly indefensible was the fact that the Transportation Plan had virtually isolated the battlefield already. What was needed now was to concentrate the AEAF's efforts on dropping the bridges over the Loire and continue attacking German movements by rail and road on days when the weather proved flyable, which was only about four days a week, and this was, legend had it, summertime.

On June 8, Eisenhower held a press conference, but going into it, he told Butcher, "I hardly know what to say to them." He couldn't talk about the operation being a great success in case people back home decided the war was over just as it went into high gear. But if he talked about the tough road ahead, they might think the landing was in trouble. In a listless monotone that betrayed his underlying weariness, Eisenhower talked about the current state of fighting in the beachhead. Then he started talking about the weather, about how cloud cover was hindering bombing operations. What he wanted most, he told the journalists, was good weather. He was praying for it. "You fellows pray for it, too."[4]

Unfortunately, the weather gods were not on the Allied side. The year 1944 was turning into one of the wettest and coldest in the twentieth century. He grew weary, and exasperated, at hearing reports of how the weather had just set a new record for awfulness. Eisenhower's soldiers would devote much of their energies that summer, fall and winter to fighting not one but two formidable foes—the German Army and General Mud.

What had him even more worried at the moment, though, was the race to expand the beachhead. "The buildup is good," he told Kay, "but it isn't fast enough." It stayed that way.[5]

On D+3 Marshall, Arnold and King arrived in London, eager to visit France and see the epic battleground along the Normandy beaches for themselves. Eisenhower briefed them, then Marshall gave him some good news. On D-Day, John Eisenhower had graduated from West Point. Ike had been able only to lament the law of physics that says it is impossible to be present in two places at once. Marshall had arranged for Second Lieutenant John Eisenhower to spend his two-week graduation leave with his father. John would arrive in a few days. "How I look forward to seeing Johnny," he wrote to Mamie. "It will be odd to see him as an *officer of the Army!* I'll burst with pride!"[6]

On June 12, the Joint Chiefs, with Ike as their guide, headed for Omaha Beach—and Bradley's CP—aboard a U.S. Navy destroyer. The sun was shining, the sky was blue and the linkup of all five invasion beaches would be completed that day. Even so, the bridgehead was still disquietingly shallow, making it difficult to funnel men and munitions into France. Bradley provided a C-ration lunch, impatient to get his VIPs back to England. Omaha was still under fire from German artillery.[7]

As the destroyer carried Ike and his starry charges back across the

Channel that evening, Marshall told him that he would no doubt become Chief of Staff when the war ended. He would reach, that is, the very pinnacle of his profession. Eisenhower was so dismayed at the prospect of going from commanding armies in war to commanding in-trays in peace that he brusquely protested, "General, I'm hoping to have a long rest!"[8]

In the morning, he dashed off a letter to Mamie. John would be arriving in a few hours. "I'm really as excited as a bride," he told her. That afternoon, John walked into Ike's office, embraced him and, in a rare, spontaneous gesture of filial devotion, kissed his father on the cheek.

Over the next two weeks, father and son were constant companions, but there were always undercurrents flowing between them. John, a thoughtful, highly intelligent young man with artistic and literary sensibilities, was facing a future that was, paradoxically, both privileged and unenviable. With his father's ascent to world fame and immense power his likely fate was a total eclipse of the son, something that already created tension. Yet by complying with his father's wishes and seeking a career in the Army, he had made it even harder to carve out a life that was truly his own and not a footnote to Ike's.

Eisenhower was too shrewd not to understand all of that, but probably the most serious problem for him in dealing with his son was his lifelong inability to express his deepest feelings freely. What came to the fore instead were irritability and impatience. When John offered comments that amounted to little more than pat observations from military textbooks, Eisenhower was likely to snap, "Oh, for God's sake!"

On June 15, Eisenhower took his son with him on a quick trip to see Montgomery. John was astonished. The roads were crowded with military traffic, moving insouciantly in broad daylight. "You'd never get away with this without air supremacy," he said. His father replied curtly, "If I didn't have air supremacy, I wouldn't even be here!" This was a chance to explain how air supremacy had been won, or to comment on the problems of integrating air attacks with ground operations, to include Johnny in his vision of Normandy as a classroom for studying the future of war, but Ike lacked the patience to explain this triumph to a bright young officer who happened to be his son.[9]

That night, back in England, Eisenhower renewed the pressure on Spaatz to use his strategic bombers to help get the British Second Army moving. So what if doctrine said heavies shouldn't be used for close support, said Eisenhower. "We need to exercise our full imagination in the employment of forces." Spaatz was not impressed.[10]

Several evenings during his stay at Telegraph Cottage, John played bridge with his father, Harry Butcher and Kay. Even here, Eisenhower bore down hard on his son, criticizing John's bidding mistakes in a peremptory way, embarrassing him in front of his new acquaintances. For his part John, in his youthful eagerness to impress his father, overdid the military punctilio. That kiss on the cheek was atypical; after that came a lot of bracing, snappy saluting and barked "Yes, sir!" "No, sir!" responses.[11]

Beneath Ike's brusqueness, however, was a man who ached for his son's company. As John's two weeks drew to a close, he begged his father for assignment to an infantry company in France, yet that was out of the question. First, if he were to be killed, the effects on his father's judgment might well be disastrous. Second, he might be captured—which was unthinkable. Ike's own preferred solution was equally impossible: to have John remain with him until the end of the war. "If you weren't an officer in the Regular Army, I'd keep you here," he said. But blatant favoritism—assigning his son to an interesting and safe job at SHAEF—could only damage John's career. It would create nothing but resentment and jealousy. So John went home, to be a student at the Infantry School, like many other second johns fresh from the Point.[12]

Hitler had two cards left to play: jet fighters and cruise missiles. He had hoped to have hundreds of jet aircraft ready to contest the invasion, but there were too many problems developing the engines for that. Nor was the world's first cruise missile, the V-1, ready in time. On June 15, however, three hundred V-1's were fired in the direction of London.

They exploded in and all around the city, doing little serious damage but spreading alarm. Churchill was at first so worried that he seriously contemplated dropping poison gas on German cities, but the British chiefs of staff flatly refused to countenance any Allied first use of such weapons.[13]

Sending for Eisenhower, Churchill demanded that V-1 sites be designated the highest-priority target for Allied air forces. Eisenhower wouldn't give him that. What he did, though, was make the V-1 sites second in importance only to air operations in support of the ground battle. Meanwhile, Eisenhower was forced to make up to a dozen visits a night to the humpbacked bomb shelter that looked like a sinister growth on the lawn of Telegraph Cottage. Grumbling, sometimes clutching a western and his reading glasses, he could only curse German science as the air-raid alarms wailed.

The diversion of Allied airpower from strategic bombing of targets such as German aviation plants and oil facilities to attack V-1 sites achieved nothing. Far more effective was the use of deception to convince the Germans that their missiles were landing north of London. They reduced the fuel supply of V-1's accordingly, and close to 90 percent were thereafter shot down by flak and fighters, flew into balloon barrages and exploded or simply ran out of fuel and plowed up farmland between the Channel and London.

Even so, Londoners remained tense and frightened and several hundred were killed or wounded each week by these "buzz bombs." The only sure way of putting the V-1 sites out of business was to reach the Pas de Calais, where most of them were located, as soon as possible. Unfortunately, Montgomery was in no hurry to get there.

At the St. Paul's conference, the huge relief map of France had clearly shown the area southeast of Caen being in Allied hands by June 20. When it wasn't, Tedder's patience ran dry. He told Eisenhower that if he wanted to sack Monty, he would have his—Tedder's—complete support. Even so, Montgomery's tactical approach to Caen was sound. Following his D-Day failure, he proposed to take it by envelopment, not by frontal assault. He was so fearful of heavy casualties, however, that he was overly cautious.

It was not as if the Germans posed much of a threat. They had managed to push enough troops forward to contain the beachhead, but it had taken an enormous effort to get them there. German commanders had planned to move most of their troops by rail, but the Transportation Plan had shattered the railroads. Ultra also provided a steady flow of information on the movement of German truck convoys, which were attacked from the air. Many thousands of German troops were obliged to move to the beachhead at night and on foot.

It was June 29 before Hitler had enough men and tanks available to mount a counterattack, and that was a modest three-division affair. They advanced into a well-prepared killing ground, thanks to Ultra, and the attack was called off only a few hours after it was launched.

Nevertheless, the Germans were well dug in across the hedgerow country of Normandy. Digging them out was proving to be exasperatingly time-consuming. Buying Normandy a hedgerow at a time could take the rest of 1944 to accomplish. A stalemate seemed to be settling over the beachhead, which was far smaller than Montgomery had projected. There was a huge backlog of men, vehicles and supplies still on the English shore, with nowhere to put it in France.

Montgomery, however, seemed oblivious to all that. He talked about drawing the Germans onto his front so that Bradley could expand the American sector and capture Cherbourg. But while Eisenhower agreed with the broad outline of Monty's strategy, he thought the way to pin down the Germans was by putting the pressure on them. Monty seemed satisfied to keep them occupied by letting them put the pressure on him. That, however, left the Germans with the initiative, and whenever they feared that the U.S. First Army was preparing to break out from the Cotentin, they moved panzer divisions from Montgomery's front to Bradley's, aided by the unseasonable weather that grounded Allied air units.

On July 1, Eisenhower flew to France and spent the next four days at Bradley's headquarters, with a side visit to Montgomery that resolved nothing. He took advantage of this trip to tour the front, driving his own jeep on visits to corps and division headquarters. He may, at one point, have been behind German lines, but there was nothing within sight or hearing to indicate as much. Eisenhower stopped on his travels to talk to ordinary soldiers, who cheered him or shouted greetings whenever he came in view. Being with infantrymen fresh from battle, or advancing up to the front line, inspirited and excited him as almost nothing else could. He thrilled to the phenomenology of war as if it were both a spectacle for the eye and solace for the soul. In tanks and guns and marching men and fighters darting overhead was the material manifestation not only of great powers but of great truths. There was something eternal and profound in an army's ability to make young men court death rather than fail one another. It was the stuff of Homer, and he did not need to know much about epic poetry to respond to the lure of a life that offered self-sacrifice, comradeship and courage.

Ike and Bradley spent hours in Bradley's paneled trailer, looking at the situation maps that covered one wall. Bradley was in the habit of sitting in front of the maps for hours, thinking, while clutching a blue crayon in one hand, a red crayon in the other. All the time he was looking for a key piece of terrain—a ridge, a hill, a river line, a crossroads—that would weaken German defenses if he could take it from them. Sometimes what he wanted seemed to jump from the map; more often, he had to look closely and debate the issue with his staff. With Ike there, he could debate it with his boss, friend and classmate, too. And as the two of them sat in the cramped trailer looking at the maps, talking in their flat, slightly nasal border-state accents, two balding middle-aged men with reading glasses perched at the ends of their noses, they were America the ordinary transmuted into something else.[14]

The weather was so miserable that it reminded Eisenhower of Tunisia. The one bright moment in this Normandy sojourn came on July 4. Pete Quesada, commander of IX Tactical Air Command, offered to take him on a tour of the front jammed into an improvised seat in a P-51 Mustang. Bradley was appalled, and his homely features grew longer than ever as Ike made light of his worries: "Don't worry, Brad. I'm not going to fly to Berlin!"[15]

Eisenhower treated this escapade as a spur-of-the-moment idea, but he also liked to claim that it added to his understanding of the situation at the front. One thing it wasn't, though, was a momentary inspiration. The P-51 had been prepared for the flight two days earlier, when the large radio behind the pilot's seat was removed and a seat wedged in its place.

Crouched behind Quesada, his helmet scraping the canopy, Eisenhower's 45-minute sortie over German lines had the seductive sapidity of forbidden fruit, the boyish joy of playing hooky at twelve thousand feet and the thrill of seeing a theater of war as only a flier—and Ike *was* a pilot, after all—sees it. When Marshall heard of it he was, predictably, annoyed, and Eisenhower, knowing Mamie was sure to hear about it, sent a preemptive reassurance: "I'm most careful—and I'm not talking for effect." What he didn't say was that a moment of irresponsibility made crushing responsibility more bearable.[16]

When he returned to England, Eisenhower complained so passionately about Montgomery to Churchill that the PM hinted he would remove Monty if Ike insisted on it. Eisenhower couldn't fire Monty, but the PM could. He could even disguise it, somewhat, by promoting him to the House of Lords and claim that Montgomery had been obliged to retire on grounds of poor health.

Sir Alan Brooke intervened and in a furious four-hour argument with Churchill won a reprieve for his protégé. But Monty's position remained precarious, because although Eisenhower could not fire him, he had all the authority he needed to move an advanced HQ to France and take over as his own ground commander. Monty would then command only the British troops in France. This would be an obvious slap, wounding not only Montgomery but British pride. Even so, Eisenhower's patience was wearing thin.[17]

Within days of Brooke's intervention, Montgomery mounted his biggest attack since D-Day, yet instead of enveloping Caen, as he had talked about for weeks, he suddenly lunged straight at it. At midnight on July 7, the RAF's Bomber Command dropped six thousand tons of bombs on the town. When the British Second Army advanced at first light on July 8, it found Caen reduced to a network of contiguous craters, not one of which was less then twenty feet across, and nearly all were choked with huge mounds of rubble. As the troops picked their way through the carcass of what had only hours before been an attractive medieval town, Monty issued a bulletin announcing he'd taken Caen, and then, beyond the craters and rubble, the British reached the German defenses—still intact. Even now, Monty did not have the terrain needed to establish forward airfields. Caen's military value was zero. Its value as a neck saver, however, was incalculable.

Butcher had seen it all before—the bone-weariness, the niggling little health problems that were slow to clear up, the insomnia, the tinnitus, the endless succession of cigarettes deeply inhaled, the furrowed brow. The last time Eisenhower had been like this was in Tunisia in early 1943, when nothing seemed to be going right.

As if he hadn't enough worries, Henry Stimson, the geriatric but still pugnacious secretary of war, arrived in Britain in July 1944, only a week before the Democratic convention, to tell Eisenhower how the Normandy campaign looked back home. It didn't look good, said Stimson. Nearly two thirds of the troops in France were Americans, and so were two thirds of the casualties. Such losses would be acceptable if there were some sense that the campaign was succeeding. Instead, it was turning into a stalemate. No one in the U.S. now had any confidence in Montgomery. The sooner Eisenhower took personal control of the land battle, said Stimson, the better.[18]

Following his hollow success in taking Caen, Montgomery wasted little time in coming up with yet another frontal attack. He proposed to have the heavies mount another carpet bombing, and this time he would thrust three armored divisions straight at the Germans. "My whole eastern flank will burst into flames on Saturday!" Monty exuberantly informed Eisenhower.[19]

This operation, code-named Goodwood, was launched on July 18. Some seven hundred British tanks rumbled through the ruins of Caen and tried to get across the Orne River, where the Germans had dug in to block access to the Falaise plain. Montgomery issued a bulletin, claiming the British Second Army had "broken through." In truth, though, it ground to a halt two miles short of its objective. It had barely dented the German line, at the cost of more than four hundred tanks.[20]

While Caen was the major obstacle in the British sector, its equivalent for Bradley was the town of Saint-Lô. Just taking it had cost the First Army forty thousand casualties. To move beyond Saint-Lô, Eisenhower suggested to Bradley that he, too, try carpet bombing, followed by a powerful armored thrust. Bradley didn't like the idea. He was a ground soldier to the marrow, and if a hole had to be punched, he preferred heavy artillery to do it. Even so, Bradley was desperately short of artillery ammunition, particularly the large calibers. This problem dogged American divisions in Europe to the end of the war. Bradley reluctantly accepted Eisenhower's idea, which became Operation Cobra.

Cobra was supposed to follow only twenty-four hours after Goodwood, when the Germans were expected to be reeling from Monty's attack. Bad weather forced Cobra to be delayed until July 25. Eisenhower flew to France that morning. Watching the bombing through his binoculars from five miles away, he was impressed once again by what airpower could do when unleashed in mass. In the space of several hours, nearly twenty-five hundred bombers and fighter bombers dropped four thousand tons of high explosive and napalm on the Panzer Lehr Division and more or less blew it out of existence.[21]

That didn't become evident for another couple of days, though, and even before the bombing ended, reports were coming in that American bombs were falling short of German positions. Nearly five hundred American soldiers had been killed or wounded. Among the dead was Lieutenant General Lesley J. McNair, the head of Army Ground Forces. Angry and grief-stricken, Ike told Bradley he would never use heavies to support ground troops again. "That's a job for artillery. I gave them a green light this time. But I promise you it's the last." He seemed to forget that Spaatz had always opposed this kind of bombing and that it was he who had initiated Cobra.[22]

When he got back to England that night, Eisenhower was profoundly depressed, but the next day he bounced back, telling Tedder he had drawn two lessons from witnessing Cobra: "We possess the power of a breakthrough, and we must learn how to use it."[23] The two carpet bombings in the British sector had produced meager results and Eisenhower feared that Cobra, too, might turn out to be a missed opportunity. Yet even as he wondered and doubted and hoped, new techniques that could turn a bombing into a breakthrough were about to be applied.

One of the biggest defects of the U.S. Army in Normandy had been a wretched lack of cooperation between ground and air, but Pete Quesada had pitched his tent next to Bradley's and had breakfast with him nearly every day and the two of them worked on ground-air cooperation with completely open minds. Starting in mid-July, they began putting pilots with the ground units and gave them radios that allowed direct two-way communication between air and ground.

Cobra was the first serious attempt to put this system to the test. Armored columns with flights of fighter bombers above and ahead of them, providing both tactical reconnaissance and accurate, instantly available flying artillery, proved a devastating combination. As French fields still steamed and smoked from Cobra, tank battalions with column cover began probing the crust of what remained of the German position. The next day, they punched holes in it, and the day after that it fell apart.[24]

Unable to move as quickly as he liked, the commander of the VII Corps, J. Lawton Collins, made a scapegoat of the commander of the 3rd Armored Division, Leroy H. Watson. Collins had to be careful, however, about how he got rid of Watson, because "Wop" Watson was a West Point classmate of both Eisenhower and Bradley. He talked to Eisenhower, who then informed Watson, "Wop, we're sending you home, but without reduction in rank."

"The hell you are!" Watson protested. "I came over here to fight and can fight as good as a colonel as I did as a general." Eisenhower obligingly busted Watson to colonel, and Bradley sent him to the 29th Infantry Division. Watson ended the war commanding the division, retired as a major general and became mayor of Beverly Hills.[25]

On August 1, Eisenhower activated the Third Army, with Patton in command, and elevated Bradley to command the 12th Army Group. Patton gave the Germans no chance to recover. Instead of grinding their way forward, as Montgomery expected, the Americans were racing out of the beachhead.[26]

The Germans had nearly four hundred thousand Allied troops stymied in Italy through the winter and early spring of 1944, but on June 4, Rome fell to Mark Clark's Fifth Army. As far as Marshall was concerned, that ought to have been the end of the Italian campaign, and it might have been had not Ultra intercepted a signal two weeks later that began, "The Führer has ordered the Apennine position as the final blocking line, since the enemy's entry into the Po plain would have incalculable military and political consequences." It went on to say that current reports of strong defenses in the Apennines were a bluff. Defenses would have to be created while the Germans fought a prolonged delaying action between Rome and the Po.[27]

Almost from the moment on June 27 when the decryption of this message was handed to Churchill, Eisenhower came under intense, unremitting pressure from the PM to cancel Operation Anvil, the landing on the French Riviera. The thing to do, Churchill told Eisenhower, was to maintain maximum strength in Italy, break into the Po valley before the Germans could organize strong defenses in the Apennines and seize Trieste. From there it would be possible to thrust into the Ljubljana gap, in the mountains of northern Yugoslavia. On the other side of the gap was the Danube basin and nothing but a hundred miles of level ground to Vienna.

This was map-pointer strategy, blissfully oblivious to considerations of topography, logistics or the need to cooperate with the Soviets. Eisenhower saw Churchill's proposal as a move to block the Red Army from getting into the Balkans, and possibly keep it out of Germany, too. Stalin would have seen it the same way, and rejected it. Marshall didn't think it would work anyway. He was convinced that a descent into the Danube basin wasn't going to happen before the spring of 1945, and even that wasn't certain, because there were virtually no modern roads and only a small, obsolescent single-track narrow-gauge railroad in the whole of northern Yugoslavia.

Both the Operations Division in Washington and the mainly British

Joint Planning Staff in London looked at Churchill's proposed strategy. They arrived at the same conclusion: It could only be done at the expense of the campaign in France, which amounted to rejecting the agreed strategy for defeating Germany.[28]

Nevertheless, Churchill continued trying to get Anvil canceled, and the theater commander in the Mediterranean, General Sir Henry Maitland Wilson, supported the PM. Anvil, said Wilson, could never succeed. It would be vigorously resisted by the Germans and could not possibly lead to the swift capture of a major port. Nor would it contribute anything to the campaign in Normandy, because it would take three months for Allied troops to fight their way up the Rhone valley to northern France. Eisenhower nevertheless insisted that Anvil had to be mounted, even though it meant taking troops and equipment away from the Italian front.

Hardly was the breakout from Normandy under way, however, than he was summoned to 10 Downing Street for yet another talk about Anvil. By now, though, Ike was in a jubilant mood. "If the intercepts are right," he told Butcher shortly before going to see the PM, "we are hell and gone in Brittany and slicing 'em up in Normandy."[29]

During the day, he dictated a cable to Marshall, telling him that maybe Anvil wouldn't be necessary after all: "It is my hope that once we have secured the Brittany peninsula we will find that our total capacity for receiving and maintaining additional divisions has been increased and that all that can be brought . . . to Europe should come in here rather than through the gateway of the Mediterranean." In that mood, he went to Downing Street for dinner, where he and Churchill debated Anvil for three hours.[30]

He briefly considered shifting the Anvil assault from southern France to Brittany, to help ensure the capture of the Breton ports. It was an idea that Churchill was pressing and Beetle Smith agreed with the PM. Yet Eisenhower still had doubts, and they wouldn't go away. Suppose the ports weren't captured quickly? Suppose, even when captured, they were so badly wrecked they proved useless for months? Cherbourg, taken on June 26, was still not in full operation, and even when it was, it would be able to handle little more than half the tonnage Bradley needed just to maintain his two armies.

Three days after the Anvil dinner, Churchill came down to Portsmouth to talk about the operation some more, and this time Eisenhower said flatly that Anvil must go ahead as planned. Churchill was almost bereft. For six hours he pleaded with Ike, in vain. Rebuffed, he rebounded like a rubber ball. With Anvil only five days away, he invited Eisenhower to Downing Street and tried again. At one point he even threatened to resign—"to lay down the mantle of my high office," as he expressed it—if Anvil wasn't abandoned, but Eisenhower stood up once again to poetry, personality and prime ministerial tears.[31]

Churchill accused him of using the great power of the United States to pursue American interests and damage those of the British, an assertion that wounded Eisenhower twice—as a man who had the deepest respect and affection for Churchill and as the Supreme Allied Commander. He insisted that Anvil was justified solely on military grounds. It had nothing to do with national interests or throwing America's weight around within the alliance.[32]

There were dozens of American divisions available now; more would be available in coming months; all had to be put into the fight. Taking Marseilles, with its capacity to handle twenty thousand tons a day, was the only way to be sure of doing so. There were also six French divisions that the United States had trained and equipped. De Gaulle was adamant that they would fight in France but not in Italy.

Not only was Marseilles bigger than all the Breton ports combined, but Brest didn't fall until September 15, by which time it was so comprehensively wrecked that it would take at least six months to get it back in working condition.[33] The Allies gained nothing from capturing Brest. The Germans would doubtless turn a fight for Saint-Nazaire and Lorient into an opportunity to wreck them, too, so they were sealed off and remained in enemy hands until the end of the war.

Anvil wasn't canceled, but it got a new code name—Dragoon—because the Germans had discovered that Anvil was the code name of an impending attack. The Seventh Army, commanded by Lieutenant General Alexander Patch, mounted the amphibious assault against the south of France on August 15 with three veteran infantry divisions. A provisional airborne division was dropped inland, and four thousand aircraft supported the invasion. On August 28 Marseilles fell, virtually intact, to a French armored division.

Two weeks later, the Seventh Army linked up with the Third Army, which had roared across central France in an epic of lightning war. Eisenhower's decision to take Marseilles was vindicated by the swift fall of Marseilles. Not that he ever convinced Churchill of that. When his war memoirs were published, Churchill still insisted that Anvil was a big mistake, that the Allies should have concentrated on Italy and advanced on Vienna through "the soft underbelly of Europe." No Allied soldier who fought in the Italian mountains, however, is known to have described his experience as "soft."[34]

On August 1, the U.S. 12th Army Group was activated, with Bradley in command, directing the operations of the First Army, now under Courtney Hodges, and the Third Army, under Patton. From that moment, Monty's days as Eisenhower's ground commander were numbered, and the number of days was exactly six, because on August 7 Eisenhower established a forward SHAEF headquarters in Normandy. Butcher wasn't sure just what the command situation was at this point, so Eisenhower explained it to him: Bradley was now in complete command of the American ground units, making him Monty's "coequal" under the supreme commander.

Butcher unwisely explained this to a friend, Wes Gallagher, who worked for the Associated Press, and Gallagher wrote it up as a story. The British press exploded in fury. Monty, British headlines screamed, had just been demoted by the bullying, amateurish Americans. From then on, Ike saw comparatively little of and unburdened himself hardly at all to his old friend, loose-lipped confidant and diarist. Butcher spent most of the rest of the war in England, at SHAEF rear. The cost to Eisenhower of this rupture isn't hard to guess. He had just lost the one person with whom he thought he could talk about everything. Butcher's fall from grace made Kay more important than ever as an emotional prop.[35]

As American troops broke out from the Normandy beachhead, the VIII Corps headed west into Brittany and the VII Corps thrust southeastward. A gap was opening between the two corps, a gap centered on the small town of Mortain, in the southeastern corner of the Cotentin peninsula. Hitler thought he saw a great opportunity. If he mounted a strong counterattack toward Mortain, took it and then drove twenty miles west to Avranches, at the southwestern corner of the peninsula, he would cut the supply lines of the American divisions driving into Brittany. Force them to pull back, and Bradley might have to retreat into the Cotentin, reversing the breakout.

The German counterattack began on August 7, the day Eisenhower established a field headquarters in France. Ultra provided a detailed picture of German plans and operations throughout this battle. The Germans seized Mortain, but the 30th Infantry Division held the 325-foot hill that dominated it. From the top of the hill, it was possible to see twenty miles in every direction. Meanwhile, the Germans were being clobbered by heavy artillery up to fifteen miles away and fighter-bombers swarmed overhead, guided by Ultra. Hitler nevertheless kept feeding divisions into the fight until the bulk of the German Seventh Army and the elite Fifth Panzer Army were committed to it.[36]

Bradley had six divisions available to meet this attack. How best to deploy them? Eisenhower thought that if Bradley held at Mortain with three, he could send the other three, which were already moving south, down to Le Mans, then swing them north into the German rear. It was risky, of course. If the Germans did manage to break through, they could find themselves cut off.

Eisenhower went to see Bradley and found Bradley was already acting along exactly the lines he had anticipated. Bradley's one reservation was, How could he keep the three divisions south of Mortain supplied if the Germans broke through? Eisenhower had already thought of the answer: "We could give them 2,000 tons a day by air."[37]

It was a bold plan, but Bradley was probably too cautious in its execution. He chose to minimize the risk by making a comparatively short loop, which reduced the potential gains. As Canadian and Polish troops pressed southward from Caen, they took the town of Argentan. Meanwhile, the three-division corps that took Le Mans came northward and seized Falaise, only fifteen miles from Argentan. By August 14, the Germans were trapped in a pocket that looked on Eisenhower's situation maps like a *U* tipped on its side. Eisenhower issued an Order of the Day, calling on Allied soldiers and airmen to make this "a brilliant and fruitful week."[38] But at that point Bradley became even more cautious. The Argentan-Falaise pocket was closed slowly, not quickly, to minimize the chances of Allied forces firing on each other as they advanced.

Even so, up to seventy-five thousand Germans were killed, wounded or captured. Another fifty thousand managed to escape to the Seine and cross it, despite Allied air supremacy and more Ultra material than at any other time in the war. There were recriminations that the enemy had not been annihilated, but no one could gainsay the fact that the two German armies defending Normandy had been destroyed. Eisenhower could now liberate the whole of France and advance on the last great barrier, the Rhine.

24

Broad Thrust

Paris. He didn't need it, didn't want it, and whatever he did, he couldn't be drawn into fighting a street battle. The city was an expression of the civilized values that the Allies were fighting to preserve in the face of Nazi barbarism. Destroying it was unthinkable. Toward the end of the Normandy campaign, Eisenhower told his staff he wasn't going to take Paris if it could be avoided. Allied armies would move around it. He wanted to reach Rheims, nearly halfway between Paris and the German border, before he had to move into the city. Frontline units were already running out of gasoline and if he took Paris, he would have to supply it.[1]

Even so, less than a week later, on the night of August 19, the 79th Infantry Division reached the river Seine and started across in torrential rain. Throughout August 20, the entire division crossed over to the other side. There was nothing but fifty miles of gently undulating countryside between its bridgehead and the city.

Even as the 79th Division crossed the Seine, Bradley was advising Eisenhower that the Germans would not give up Paris without a fight and Hitler was issuing a stark order to the commander of the Paris garrison, Colonel General Dietrich von Choltitz. It was impossible to hold France, said Hitler, without holding Paris. Von Choltitz must not allow it to fall into Allied hands, even if that meant fighting a battle and reducing Paris to "a field of ruins."[2]

The French had only one card to play in this dangerous game—themselves. The Gaullists had created the French Forces of the Interior (or FFI), a coalition of Resistance groups that embraced everything from monarchists to Stalinists. One of de Gaulle's staff, a distinguished soldier, noted Arabist and best-selling novelist, General Pierre Joseph Koenig, was the commander of the FFI. Koenig joined the SHAEF staff, ostensibly bringing the Resistance into Eisenhower's command structure, yet without giving him anything that resembled control.

Just as Allied soldiers crossing the Seine could sense Paris, so Paris sensed them, and the emotions of Parisians were suddenly inflamed until they became suffocating. The mood in the city was beyond the reach of reason. Anything might now ignite a confrontation with the Germans, and no one could foresee the result. Freedom, massacre, battle, a German retreat, mutual destruction—all seemed equally possible.

Koenig ordered the FFI in the city not to start a battle with the Germans, but Parisian resistants nevertheless started taking over public buildings. The French police, who had collaborated enthusiastically throughout four years of German occupation, went on strike, a cynical ploy to distance themselves from their masters.

Had he yielded to the dynamics of this feverish situation, von Choltitz would have sent his troops out to reclaim the streets, a move certain to destroy the wonder that was Paris and kill the thing he could not hold. He had five thousand troops within the city and twenty thousand more in the suburbs. His engineers could easily blow up every bridge across the Seine, as it flows through the city, and fill the broad thoroughfares with the rubble of demolished buildings and monuments. They possessed enough incendiary munitions to burn the heart out of the city if he ordered it.

Von Choltitz looked capable of giving the order, almost a cartoon version of the nihilistic Nazi thug—close-cropped blond hair, unblinking moon face, bucket-shaped head, a pale and paunchy figure with small blue eyes sullenly regarding a world that mocked fat men dressed up as soldiers, his thin, bloodless lips suggesting a costive fascination with cruelty. Yet von Choltitz suddenly made a discovery. Forced to choose between his oath of loyalty to the Führer and the romantic atmosphere that seemed to blow in through the open windows of his office on the second floor of the Hotel Meurice these lovely summer afternoons, he found he did not command the city's fate—Paris commanded his.

Von Choltitz declared a seventy-two-hour truce with the main Resistance groups, hoping they would turn on one another and leave his troops alone. Having arranged the truce, he tore a piece of paper from a notebook and scrawled in High Gothic script, "Paris will *not* be destroyed. Von Choltitz," then put it in a desk drawer.[3]

While these dramas were being played out in the city, de Gaulle arrived at Eisenhower's forward headquarters in Normandy that same afternoon. A few weeks earlier, de Gaulle had visited Washington, but Roosevelt still refused to recognize the French Committee of National Liberation, which de Gaulle headed, as the de facto government of a liberated France. Eisenhower now advised him that the only thing that could make Roosevelt change his mind was a pledge of elections in the near future, something de Gaulle was reluctant to give until all of France, and especially Paris, was free.

Eisenhower then showed him the situation maps: the British Second Army was moving along the Channel coast toward Belgium, the U.S. First Army was advancing on a line that would take it northeast of Paris, while Patton's Third Army, driving rapidly east, was already passing south of the city. Unfortunately, said Eisenhower, "the Resistance is fighting too soon."

"Too soon?" De Gaulle was astonished. How could it be too soon when there were Allied soldiers only thirty miles away?

He didn't want a battle for the city, Eisenhower explained, but de Gaulle was not impressed by that. What Eisenhower could not tell him was that Ultra had reported the sudden redeployment of two panzer grenadier divisions from Italy to France. One, maybe both, might be headed for Paris.

When Eisenhower refused to commit himself to a rapid move into the city, de Gaulle said he would order the French 2nd Armored Division to take it. Eisenhower had to suppress a smile. He had created the French 2nd Armored Division and it was so dependent on U.S. Army mechanics, spare parts and gasoline that it could not move a kilometer without his approval.[4]

Although he and de Gaulle were going to clash sharply over military and political questions during the year ahead, their relationship was now one of mutual respect rather than mutual mistrust. In North Africa, Eisenhower had come to recognize that in this vain, mercurial, difficult man was the embodiment of French courage and pride, that it was de Gaulle who, by saving his country's honor in that black hour when most

Frenchmen seemed dead to honor, had ensured its place among the Allies and was now its guarantor of a democratic future in the postwar world. Before leaving North Africa in December 1943, Eisenhower had visited de Gaulle to tell him, "I was wrong about you."

De Gaulle had responded warmly, "You are a man."

Eisenhower had then told him that although he couldn't vouch for the attitude of the U.S. government once Allied troops landed in France, he knew he would have to rely on de Gaulle and his followers if the Allies were going to win the support of the French people. De Gaulle assured him of his complete cooperation, but added, "Don't go into Paris without French troops!"[5]

"You may be certain that I wouldn't dream of taking Paris without French soldiers," Eisenhower had said. One of his first steps after arriving in London in January 1944 was to create the 2nd French Armored Division (or 2ème Division Blindée), for that purpose. Commanded by an ardent Gaullist, General Philippe Leclerc, the division was assigned to the V Corps, commanded by the French-descended Gee Gerow (originally Giraud). Yet even with Paris within his grasp, Eisenhower hesitated to act.

The day following their August 20 meeting, de Gaulle wrote to tell him that the Germans were pulling out of Paris and the city was running short of food. If Paris fell into chaos, it would be much harder to get the situation under control than it would be if he acted swiftly now. This message was delivered to Eisenhower by Koenig, whom de Gaulle had just named military governor of Paris. The Germans were not, in fact, abandoning Paris; von Choltitz was merely redeploying his men and trying to keep them out of sight. Unaware of that, Eisenhower wrote a note to Beetle Smith in the margin of de Gaulle's letter: "I talked verbally with Koenig on this. It looks now as if we'd be compelled to go into Paris."[6]

Bradley ordered Leclerc to advance on the city and had the U.S. 4th Infantry Division move just behind the French troops. Eisenhower insisted that a British contingent be ordered into the city, too. He wanted to be sure that the liberation of Paris would be a triumph of Allied arms, symbolizing shared sacrifices, shared glories, albeit a triumph with Leclerc at its head.[7]

The sight of French soldiers drove the French half crazy with joy. Leclerc's men were dragged from their tanks and into sidewalk cafes, to be kissed, caressed, toasted, propositioned, offered cigarettes and invited to drink all the champagne and cognac they could manage. Even more than they could manage. The armored dash into the city turned into a festive crawl through the outer suburbs. Bradley became so angry that he ordered the 4th Division to liberate Paris at once, "and to hell with prestige." This order sobered up Leclerc's division faster than any detox method known to modern medicine. The French rolled through the streets of Paris on the evening of August 24 and at midnight their tanks and half-tracks pulled up outside the Hôtel de Ville. By dawn, most of the German garrison had melted away.[8]

De Gaulle couldn't resist having Leclerc's division put on a parade two days later, despite warnings from Gerow, who said that German sympathizers would open fire on it. The parade went ahead, and shooting broke out. Eisenhower decided he and Bradley ought to take a look at the situation for themselves and invited Monty to join them. Monty predictably declined, as if to say he was too busy fighting the war to indulge in tourism.

When Eisenhower's armored Cadillac arrived on a beautiful Sunday morning, August 27, de Gaulle had installed his command post at the Prefecture of Police. Picking up Gerow on a street corner, the Cadillac moved toward the Prefecture, but that broad Ike grin thrusting out from a car window was soon recognized by the delirious crowds. He was mobbed, to his immense delight and bright-red blushes.[9]

At the Prefecture, de Gaulle told him that the Resistance was already breaking apart, split between the third who followed Stalin and the two-thirds who did not. He asked Eisenhower for a show of force, to impress the Communists with the fact that American power was firmly on the Gaullist side.[10]

To provide it, Eisenhower had the 28th Infantry Division parade down the Champs-Elysées on August 29, followed by elements of the 5th Armored Division. Continuing its line of march, the 28th Division made an attack on German positions east of the city that afternoon.[11]

Taking Paris, Eisenhower knew, would add a crushing logistical burden to a supply system that was already creaking and stumbling. His armies were going to run short of crucial supplies in a week, two at the most. Yet now that he had Paris in his hands, he had to find four thousand tons of food and coal each day to keep its people fed and ensure the lights didn't go out in the *ville lumière*. That was enough tonnage to keep seven American, or eight British, divisions moving and shooting. How many divisions could he immobilize and still hope to win the war? Being pushed and prodded into this move had been less a strategy than a gamble. But what was the French word for bets? *Paris.*

A month before D-Day, Eisenhower had met with the SHAEF planning staff to decide on his strategy for destroying the German war machine. The planners had done what high-level staffs are expected to do—spell out the options. Germany had, in effect, not one heart but two, they said. The political heart was Berlin, but the heart of its war economy was the Ruhr. It was for him to decide, but the planners felt that of the two, the Ruhr was the better objective. Berlin was not only more distant, but taking it would not necessarily destroy Germany's ability to fight. Seize the industries of the Ruhr and the adjacent Saar, however, and Germany could not resist. The Ruhr was so important, in fact, that it would give Allied armies their best opportunity to bring the enemy to battle and destroy him. Eisenhower agreed with the planning staff and ruled out Berlin.[12]

While the planners were laying out the options, he had been bent over a map, holding a pencil. How best to tackle the Ruhr and the Saar—frontal assault or envelopment? That one was easy, even predictable, for someone who had graduated first in his class at the Command and General Staff School.

Most Western armies had entire manuals devoted to tactics, but in the 1920s, the U.S. Army had opted for one tactic simple enough for citizen soldiers to learn quickly. It also had the merits of drawing maximum advantage from the superiority of American infantry and artillery weapons and superior American mobility. That tactic was, from the level of an infantry platoon to a division, known as the holding attack, in which part of a commander's force moves toward the objective and pins the defender in place, while the other part of his force maneuvers to strike the enemy in a flank or the rear. At the level above a division, that same tactic was employed but called the wide envelopment. Such a plan of maneuver was employed by the Allies to liberate Kuwait in 1991.

Eisenhower drew two long black lines. One, beginning near Caen, went across northern France, through Belgium, ran north of the Ardennes and ended in the area where the Ruhr flows into the Rhine, near Düsseldorf. The second line, beginning at the base of the Cotentin peninsula, went eastward following the Loire River, then turned north, skirted Paris, passed south of the Ardennes and ended at Cologne, the gateway to the southern Ruhr. From Cologne he marked a third line, thrusting into the Saar, Germany's second most important industrial area.

What he was aiming for was the ultimate in envelopment strategies—the double envelopment that produces a battle of annihilation. It was redolent of the most famous of all double envelopments, mounted by his boyhood hero, Hannibal, at Cannae in 216 B.C.[13]

Armies moving along the three axes of advance that he had drawn would find themselves able to provide increasingly effective mutual support the nearer they drew to their objectives. This design was simple, feasible and negated the defender's traditional advantage of operating on interior lines. Long before D-Day, this was Eisenhower's strategy for the advance into Germany. It bore a strong resemblance to Grant's April 1864 plan for destroying the South.[14]

The attempt to assassinate Hitler on July 20, which had failed to kill him but left him seriously injured, and the breakout from Normandy and the rapid drive to the Seine combined to create a dangerous mood of euphoria in the United States and Britain. People began saying confidently that the end of the war was at hand. Irritated and frustrated, Eisenhower flew back to London on August 15 to hold one of his increasingly rare press conferences. Recent success, he said emphatically, did not mean the end was near. "Hitler and his gang have nothing to lose by enforcing prosecution of the war," he said grimly. If they fell into Allied hands, their fate was a length of rope, and they knew it.[15]

Hardly had he returned to France before Montgomery began demanding revisions to Eisenhower's strategy for enveloping the Ruhr. As a rule, Monty sought to avoid face-to-face meetings with Eisenhower, but he was now so desperate that he insisted on having one—only at his HQ, not Ike's, and alone.

No one else treated Eisenhower with such disdain, yet according to Nigel Hamilton, Montgomery's biographer, Eisenhower's problems with Montgomery had less to do with Monty's shortcomings than with Ike's—"Eisenhower at bottom was frightened by Montgomery's military expertise." It is certainly true that Eisenhower was envious of Montgomery's extensive combat experience, which had seen him command everything from a company to an army group. He may even have envied Monty his wound scar from World War I. Yet what troubled Eisenhower about Montgomery was not a sense of being intimidated by Monty's experience of war but that success had dulled rather than whetted whatever lust for battle he had once possessed.[16]

At the end of the Tunisian campaign he had sent this appraisal of Montgomery to Marshall—"very conceited [and] so proud of his success to date that he will never willingly make a single move until he is absolutely certain of success—in other words, until he has concentrated enough resources that anybody could practically guarantee the outcome."[17] Nothing that had happened since—in Sicily, in Italy or in Normandy—had made him alter that opinion.

The conceit had, if anything, become more nauseating. Montgomery avidly collected photographs, flattering portraits and favorable press clippings. When he became a field marshal, he immediately arranged for a new portrait to be painted and had a well-known British painter installed at his headquarters for two weeks. To friends, he boasted that the new portrait was "the cat's whiskers. It will without doubt be the great picture of the year . . ." Not Ike's kind of soldier, still less his kind of man.[18]

At the meeting in Condé, Montgomery told Eisenhower that if the war was going to be won, he simply must be retained as ground commander, that Patton's Third Army must be immobilized, that the U.S. First Army must be assigned to the British 21st Army Group, that all available supplies must be given to him and Eisenhower's strategy must be scrapped. Instead, "a solid mass of forty divisions, with nothing to fear," should drive straight for the Ruhr, under his command, to end the war.

He said he would willingly serve under Bradley if Eisenhower would only adopt this strategy. Eisenhower must have been obliged to assume his best poker face at moments such as this. Alexander hadn't been able to control Monty and Montgomery never showed any loyalty to Eisenhower. On the contrary, he reported regularly to Brooke on what a stupid and ridiculous person Eisenhower was. His contempt was so wide and so deep that even in Eisenhower's presence he found it impossible at times to conceal it. Any suggestion that he would be

Bradley's loyal and willing subordinate was risible. Monty had no more respect for Bradley than he ever had for Ike.[19]

At Condé, Monty made a fool of himself. If the eight divisions assigned to Patton were immobilized as he demanded and those that had recently landed on the French Riviera were discounted, SHAEF had only twenty-seven divisions in France available for frontline service. Some of those, however, such as the French 2nd Armored Division, would have to be committed to rear-area security. There were, at most, only twenty-two divisions available for Monty's plan. It would be the end of October before SHAEF would have enough divisions to thrust forty of them at the Ruhr, but by then German defenses would be strong and autumnal rains, mist and fog would rule out any rapid movement. The huge, fearless beast of forty divisions that Monty conjured up at Condé for his single-thrust strategy was a fantasy. Eisenhower didn't waste time discussing it.

Nonetheless, as supreme commander, he had to make what use he could of Montgomery, and the 21st Army Group was, under the strategy he had decided on back in May, going to conduct the main thrust toward the Ruhr. For one thing, the thrust to the north of the Ruhr would be easier to support, thanks to the Channel ports. For another, once it crossed the Rhine it would be in open country, suitable for the kind of combined arms operations in which Allied forces excelled. Eisenhower therefore assigned one corps of the First Army to Montgomery's command, gave him priority of supplies and cut back on deliveries to Patton.

Some historians have argued that what really lay behind Monty's forty-division proposal was not, in truth, a dispute over strategy but an argument over command. It is likely that it was both. He was plainly unhappy that since the American breakout from the Cotentin peninsula his role as ground commander had been more nominal than real, and even that pretense was set to end on September 1. On the evening of August 31, Churchill promoted him to field marshal, to cushion the blow and provide a sop to British public opinion.[20]

The British press, and Montgomery himself, consoled themselves that Monty now outranked Eisenhower, that he had the equivalent of five stars to Ike's four. Eisenhower refused to see it that way. At AFHQ in North Africa and, later, at SHAEF he compared ranks from the top down, not the bottom up. This meant that for all practical purposes, his four stars made him the equivalent of a field marshal.[21]

While getting his portrait painted, Montgomery was planning an advance on Arnhem, a small town on the lower Rhine in central Holland, when he heard that Courtney Hodges and the First Army were planning to use the recently created First Allied Airborne Army (FAAA) to seize key terrain in the Aachen gap, thereby speeding Hodges's advance on the Rhine.

It was Marshall who had pushed for the creation of an airborne army, at a time when Bradley was trying to find a way of getting rid of the commander of the Ninth Air Force, the indolent and uncooperative Lewis Brereton, the driving force behind the disastrous Ploeşti raid. The FAAA comprised four divisions—two British, two American. Eisenhower gladly approved Hodges's proposal for a three-division drop near Aachen. Afraid that the Americans might beat him to the Rhine, Montgomery immediately demanded that Eisenhower rescind his approval, and Eisenhower complied. Monty seemed to consider that the FAAA had been created for his benefit and insisted that it be employed to speed his advance and presented a daring and elaborate plan, code-named Market-Garden, which, he claimed, would achieve exactly that.[22]

Even though he had given Monty's advance priority, Eisenhower would have been justified in giving Market-Garden the thumbs-down, because to okay it meant delaying the attempt to get the crucial port of Antwerp open. But Market-Garden carried with it an irresistible possibility: If it worked, it might speed the end of the war.

A lightning stroke that produced a bridgehead at Arnhem would outflank the Siegfried Line defenses that the Germans were hurriedly strengthening along the length of Rhine. It was an operation that in some ways resembled Anzio—make an outflanking assault, using superior Allied mobility, to seize a bridgehead, then build up that bridgehead to a point where Allied troops could break out. When the breakout came, Montgomery would be able to attack the Ruhr from the north or drive east, toward Berlin. "I'll tell you what I'll do, Monty," said Eisenhower. "I'll give you whatever you ask to get over the Rhine, because I want a bridgehead . . . but let's get over the Rhine before we discuss anything else."[23]

Montgomery's plan was to drop the British 1st Airborne Division and the Polish Parachute Brigade at Arnhem. Once they had secured an airhead, an infantry division would be flown in. Meanwhile, the elite Guards Armoured Division would make a two-day, sixty-five-mile dash from Belgium. The U.S. 82nd and 101st Airborne divisions would be dropped between Arnhem and Belgium to secure vital bridges that the British tanks had to cross on their way north. It was one of the most daring plans of the war, and only the best, most experienced troops could have pulled it off.

Just as Market-Garden seemed about to be launched, Montgomery grew cautious again and said it would have to be postponed. On September 11, Eisenhower sent Beetle Smith to tell him that he could have all the supplies that were currently available if he would only grab a bridgehead over the Rhine. Montgomery responded by fixing a firm date for Market-Garden—September 17.

Even so, Montgomery's chief of staff, Major General Francis de Guingand, didn't think it would work; neither did his chief of operations. He brushed their protests aside. The only person who might have convinced Montgomery to change his mind was his chief of intelligence, a young Oxford don, Brigadier Edgar T. Williams, but Williams possessed cleverness, not judgment. In the five days preceding Market-Garden, Ultra code breakers decrypted German signals that showed three panzer divisions and an assault gun regiment were in Arnhem, receiving new equipment. To confirm it, there were oblique-angle photographs provided by aerial reconnaissance showing tanks under camouflage netting on the outskirts of the town. Williams refused to take this material seriously and Montgomery supported him. It was rare for high-grade Ultra, confirmed by photo recon, to be dismissed because it happened to be inconvenient.[24]

On September 17, Market-Garden was launched. The small, lightly armed British 1st Airborne Division (it was two-thirds the size of its American equivalent) lacked the muscle to fight its way past the tanks outside the town. The division suffered 75 percent casualties and was never rebuilt. Only the much bigger, battle-hardened 82nd and 101st Airborne divisions secured their objectives, but the Guards Armoured Division moved out late, before advancing slowly toward Arnhem. The battle ended, with the withdrawal of the British paratroopers, before it arrived.[25]

Montgomery liked to talk about how he fought in a "balanced" way, unlike the impetuous Americans, who seemed to prefer attacking everywhere at once. Yet Eisenhower surely found little "balance" in Arnhem, where Monty had handed the retreating, demoralized Germans a major victory at the end of a field marshal's baton.

Eisenhower had established his headquarters in Granville, a small coastal town near the southwestern corner of the Cotentin peninsula. As far as communications went, Granville was a poor location, but that was true of everywhere in France outside Paris, and Paris had not yet been liberated when he moved his advanced CP to French soil. He compensated by traveling extensively by air and by road and spoke to Bradley on the scrambler telephone several times a day, but he had few such conversations with Montgomery.

On September 2 he flew to Chartres in his B-25 to meet with Bradley and Patton, who were indignant that just as American divisions began running out of gasoline, he had given priority to Montgomery's advance. Patton insisted that if he got priority, "We could push on to the German frontier and rupture that goddamned Siegfried Line. I'm willing to stake my reputation on it!"

Eisenhower was amused. "Careful, George. That reputation of yours hasn't been worth very much."

"Pretty good now," said Patton, having just crossed the breadth of France in one of the most brilliant campaigns of the war.[26]

Even so, what Patton was demanding was much the same as Montgomery demanded—absolute priority—on a promise that he'd win the war. Eisenhower was no more inclined to sanction a doomed Patton thrust than one led by Monty. He turned down his old friend, but placated him by giving him a little more gasoline.

Contrary to postwar myth, the most important element in Eisenhower's logistical problems was not a shortage of gasoline as such but a shortage of trucks to haul the gasoline from the rear to the front line. There were three reasons for this sorry situation, which was rapidly becoming critical. First, there was John C. H. Lee, known to millions of wartime soldiers as "Jesus Christ Himself." He was as inept a logistics chief as any major commander had to deal with anywhere in the world. During the buildup for Overlord, the Transportation Corps had forecast that Bradley and Patton would need 240 truck companies. Lee insisted on cutting the number to 160.[27]

The style of any organization is invariably established at the top, and Lee was determined to enjoy a comfortable war, an ambition in which he succeeded. So, too, did many of the officers assigned to his headquarters. Their greatest single coup was to move Lee's huge headquarters into Paris only a week after it was liberated. They commandeered more than three hundred hotels and made the city their playground, to Eisenhower's fury. He had intended to reserve Paris as a place for combat troops to enjoy a brief respite from living in the mud. Yet to move Lee's organization out of Paris was going to be time-consuming, would tie up hundreds of trucks and require tons of gasoline. Fuming but impotent, Eisenhower had to live with Lee's fait accompli and his incompetence.[28]

The second reason was that Transportation Plan bombings had devastated the French railway system. When Allied armies broke out from Normandy, there was a desperate need for trucks to keep them moving and there were nowhere near enough trucks, tires, spare parts and mechanics. To make matters worse, the British too were facing a truck crisis. American armies alone might just have managed to solve their logistical problems, but in September 1944, they were forced to carry those of the British, too, which cannot have come as much of a surprise to Eisenhower, because in North Africa American officers had discovered that British logistics were as quaint as British country pubs. In the course of a week, a U.S. Army truck hauled twice as much as its British counterpart.[29]

The situation in France wasn't any better; in some respects, it was worse. Monty's logistics depended heavily on a new three-ton British truck—or "lorry"—but hardly had they begun to roll on French roads than they broke down with cracked piston rings. The fourteen hundred that had been shipped to France by August 1944 were useless, as were thousands of replacement engines. The U.S. 26th, 95th and 104th divisions arrived in Normandy in early September ready to fight, and were instantly immobilized because all their trucks—and hundreds more—were needed to haul Monty's supplies.[30]

Finally, there was the huge supply burden that was Paris. Its entire four thousand tons of food and fuel per day came out of the allocation for the U.S. First and Third armies, whose divisions were fighting much farther from the ports than Monty's. A division could sit still and stay alive on 250 tons a day, but to move and fight it needed at least five hundred. Supplying Paris was the equivalent of keeping sixteen divisions immobilized. Eisenhower therefore sought to push those divisions still

able to move as far as he could and as fast as he could before the bad
weather arrived. American divisions were advancing with only one unit
of fire—that is, one day's supply of ammunition instead of the five that
was considered the minimum for units operating in the face of the
enemy.

At the end of August, Churchill had a long discussion with him on
how supply was affecting strategy. Eisenhower described to him how
American logistics were organized to provide maximum mobility and
were even now keeping alive a drive that the textbooks said was impossible. "Their high mobility could never be achieved by our methods," a
chagrined Churchill told Alexander.[31]

Following the meeting with Bradley and Patton in Chartres, high
winds grounded Eisenhower's B-25. He returned to Granville in an
L-5, a small spotter aircraft normally assigned to adjusting artillery fire.
Short of fuel, the pilot landed on the beach near Granville and Eisenhower unwisely tried to help pull the plane higher up the beach before
the tide came in. He wrenched his left knee severely and spent the next
few days mostly in agony and mainly in bed, trying to run the war while
flat on his back.

On September 3, with British troops advancing into the outskirts of
Antwerp, Ramsay informed Montgomery that Antwerp had to be in operation by September 15 before there could be any advance from the
Rhine to Berlin. SHAEF's planning staff had just completed a study to
decide whether it might be possible, given the rapid collapse of the German Army in France, to advance all the way to Berlin by the end of September. After that, rain and fog would rule out the possibility of any
rapid advance. Bad weather has the effect of doubling the strength of an
entrenched defender and halves the strength of any attack.

The planners concluded that it might be possible to push three army
corps (approximately ten divisions) all the way to Berlin by September 30, but only if five other corps (some fifteen divisions or there-
abouts) were completely immobilized and Antwerp and the ports of
the Pas de Calais were providing at least seven thousand tons a day by
September 15 and the weather allowed delivery of a further two thousand tons a day by air. The key was Antwerp, but taking the port was not
enough. Antwerp is fifty miles inland, connected to the sea by the
Scheldt estuary. The estuary would have to be cleared before the port
could be used.[32]

Antwerp fell into British hands so rapidly that the Germans did not have the time to blow up the docks and fill the harbor with wreckage. That was good, but not good enough. There was no attempt to envelop it. Not a single armored division was sent north to cut across the German rear and force a withdrawal. Instead, the Germans were able over the next week to improve their defenses, bring in reinforcements and stockpile ammunition—all of which was monitored by Ultra, and none of which was acted upon.[33]

Montgomery's indifference to Eisenhower's messages urging him to get Antwerp operating probably owed much to the advice of his chief supply officer, Lieutenant General Miles Graham, who assured him that with the Channel ports it had recently captured—Le Havre, Dieppe, Boulogne and Calais—the British 21st Army Group did not need Antwerp. It was only Hodges and Patton who needed it. Without it, they would be unable to advance into Germany.[34]

On September 4, Montgomery sent Eisenhower a message that ran, "I consider we have now reached a stage where one really powerful and full-blooded thrust is likely to get there and thus end the German war. We have *not* the maintenance resources for two full-blooded thrusts. . . . If we attempt a compromise solution . . . we will prolong the war. If you are coming this way, perhaps you would look in and discuss it. . . . Do *not* feel I can leave this battle just at present."[35]

There is no doubt that the rapid capture of Antwerp, which Eisenhower had expected the Germans to defend as furiously as they had defended Brest, had given him pause. For several days he thought a German collapse was possible. By the time he received Monty's latest message, however, he had returned to his earlier opinion—that there would probably have to be a big battle somewhere west of the Rhine before Allied armies advanced into Germany. Instead of accepting Monty's summons to lunch, he dictated a memorandum for the record that said Monty's recent operations reflected "his usual caution."[36]

Eisenhower could not put off seeing Montgomery indefinitely, however, and on September 10 he flew to Brussels in his C-47, still in agony from his twisted knee. When Montgomery and Miles Graham boarded Ike's plane, Monty was clutching a sheaf of top-secret cables. He sat down bristling. With Eisenhower was a British general, SHAEF's chief logistics officer, Sir Humfrey Gale, a man some American officers regarded as "practically a genius." Supply was going to be central to this discussion, but Montgomery imperiously demanded that Gale get off the airplane immediately, adding that his own logistics expert, Graham, would remain aboard. Eisenhower asked Gale to leave the airplane and Graham stayed put.

Monty then brandished the top-secret cables he was clutching. Had Eisenhower really dictated these messages, he demanded angrily, messages that rejected his plan for a single-thrust attack toward Berlin? Eisenhower said he had. "Well they're nothing but balls!" Montgomery retorted. "Sheer balls! Rubbish!"

Eisenhower leaned forward and touched Montgomery's knee. "Steady, Monty. You can't speak to me like that. I'm your boss."[37]

Calmly raising the question of whether Antwerp was "open," he eventually got Monty to acknowledge that it wasn't. For his part, Montgomery argued that he had not received the priority in supplies that he had been promised. Eisenhower replied that he had never meant "absolute priority."

"What you're proposing is this," he went on. "If I give you all the supplies you want, you could go straight to Berlin. Right straight to Berlin? Monty, you're nuts. You can't do it! What the hell! If you try a long column like that in a single thrust, you'd have to throw off division after division to protect your flanks from attack." Besides, he added, referring to the SHAEF study on a drive to Berlin, "The beachhead can't supply a thrust into Germany."[38]

On September 22, Eisenhower convened a high-level meeting at SHAEF's main headquarters, which had recently moved from England to the Trianon Palace Hotel in Versailles. The meeting confirmed Eisenhower's broad-front strategy, and he decided that despite the defeat at Arnhem, Montgomery's advance on the Ruhr would still have priority over the operations of Bradley's 12th Army Group. But he sent a stiff message to Montgomery: "I insist upon the importance of Antwerp. . . . I am prepared to give you everything for the capture of the approaches to Antwerp." It was another three weeks before Montgomery made a serious attempt to secure the Scheldt estuary. The port wasn't in operation again until November 28.[39]

During October and November, in some of the worst autumn weather of the century, both Bradley and Montgomery tried to bludgeon their way to the Rhine. Patton became so exasperated that he ordered the chaplains of the Third Army to pray to God to stop the rain.

Eisenhower, meanwhile, wrote to Marshall, "I am getting exceedingly tired of weather. Every day we have some report of weather that has broken records existing anywhere from twenty-five to fifty years."[40]

He made a tour of frontline units in early November, as much for his own morale as theirs. Being with combat infantry boosted his spirits, and they welcomed him like a friend and a brother. Enlisted men as a rule despised officers and they especially loathed generals; but they invariably made an exception for Eisenhower and ignored the stars. He felt equally attached to and at home with them. But everywhere he went, he heard the same complaint—not enough artillery ammunition. The U.S. Army had the best artillery in the world, yet it hardly ever roared as it should have done.[41]

Making a dismal picture even worse, rain and mist made close air support impossible across most of the front most of the time. Infantry battalions attacking modern defenses with little air support and only a few volleys of artillery fire paid a high price in blood for every yard gained. The British had faced a manpower crisis since July, and Bradley, too, was running out of manpower that fall. Many rifle companies were down to half strength.

Eisenhower was nevertheless determined to keep the pressure on the Germans, and on November 16, Bradley took advantage of a break in the weather to launch Operation Queen, which began with four thousand aircraft, including heavy bombers, trying to blow a hole in the Siegfried Line. Afraid of any repetition of friendly-fire losses, Bradley placed the bombing too far ahead of his troops. By the time the ground assault hit the German lines, the Germans had reestablished their position. Eisenhower informed the Combined Chiefs, "German morale on this front shows no sign of cracking . . . final victory can only be achieved by prolonged and bitter fighting."[42]

Shortly after this, Eisenhower received a message from Monty that said, "We have failed and we have suffered a strategic reverse. . . . We now require a new plan." Montgomery was trying to make the most of the failure of Queen. He revived his demand for a single thrust, and "if you should decide that I should do that work—that is O.K. by me." Eisenhower replied, strongly refuting the assertion that there had been a strategic reverse and refused to accept the demand for a new strategy.[43]

He received an early Christmas present from Ernie Pyle, an inscribed copy of his latest book, *Here Is Your War: The Story of G.I. Joe.* When Eisenhower reached the last chapter, he was arrested by Pyle's self-portrait as a one-man army out to present the truth about infantry soldiers in combat. On December 15, he wrote to Pyle, thanking him for the book and telling him, "I would like to authorize a hundred per cent increase in your army. . . . Let me join. I will furnish the 'brass' and you, as in all other armies, would do the work. . . . The difference between you and me in regard to this infantry problem is that you can express yourself eloquently upon it. I get so fighting mad because of the general lack of appreciation of real heroism—which is the uncomplaining acceptance of unendurable conditions—that I become completely inarticulate. Anyway I volunteer. You don't have to resort to the draft."[44]

As he wrote this, Allied soldiers were shivering in foxholes across three hundred miles of front and the snow was falling steadily.

25

Fog of War

In September 1944, as Allied armies thrust toward the Rhine, Eisenhower moved into an attractive villa near the Saint-Germain golf course, on the outskirts of Paris. He established SHAEF headquarters at the Trianon Palace Hotel in Versailles, a thirty-minute drive from the villa. The hotel was forbidding, if not depressing—huge, gloomy rooms with high ceilings and feeble lights. The anvil chorus of military typewriters sounded through the corridors.

Eisenhower placed his office in the annex of the hotel, the more modern and less pretentious part of the building, working in a relaxed, idiosyncratic way that belied the image of the Supreme Bureaucrat. The floor near his desk was covered with operations maps, which he studied for long periods, bent over in a chair. Kay, given a commission in the Women's Army Corps that October, worked out of sight, behind a high partition. Telek played and napped on the maps. When officers came to discuss current or future operations, Telek was unceremoniously dislodged. Using Eisenhower's captured German sword as a pointer, the visitors could talk strategy and tactics while he paced up and down behind the desk, smoking vigorously. When the visitors left, Telek returned to sprawl insouciantly over Belgium or France.[1]

Eisenhower was a world figure now, and his every action and every utterance was praised or damned. He managed to elude most of his critics—and some of his friends—because there were two Ikes, not one. The Eisenhower who got the world's attention was the Supreme Allied Commander. In this role the British, and many a war correspondent, saw him as an amiable, not exceptionally bright figure, a smiling man who presided rather than decided, a chairman-of-the-board type who got his way, but by negotiation and compromise, not by superior arguments cogently expressed—good at the "supreme" part of the job description—not so good at the "commander" part.

Then there was Eisenhower the commander of the U.S. Army in Europe. In this role, he sometimes seemed almost a different man. Acting as the senior American general in Europe, freed from the quasi-political constraints of his role as supreme commander, he was beyond any doubt a firm, confident, hard-driving general. What he offered was strong leadership—"aggressive, outspoken and sharply definite about what he wanted," was how one general described it.[2]

He had not risen to the top by accident. Eisenhower had chosen not to try to please everyone he dealt with. He concentrated his efforts on pleasing whoever happened to be his boss, hoping to make that person feel he was virtually irreplaceable. In this, he had nearly always succeeded. The great exception was MacArthur, but MacArthur had wanted something impossible—an assistant who could make the Philippine defense plan work. Eisenhower couldn't work miracles. He had learned much from MacArthur all the same, and adopted some of his techniques, such as initially criticizing proposals that he actually agreed with and sounding enthusiastic about ideas he didn't agree with at all. It was when Eisenhower's mind seemed made up that he was probably still open to new ideas, and when he sounded undecided, there was a good chance he had already made a decision. Many people found this confusing and, like Alan Brooke, concluded that Eisenhower was hopelessly indecisive. The effect, however, was that it reserved him his freedom of action while he went about picking other people's brains with the cold-blooded detachment of a professional burglar.[3]

Optimism was also one of his techniques, never more so than when things were going badly. He insisted on a calm and cheerful atmosphere at AFHQ and at SHAEF, and got it.

His old friend George Patton had become one of his fiercest critics, disparagingly calling him "Divine Destiny" and sneering at him as "the best general the British have got." Eisenhower would have been well aware of such remarks. The Army was as gossipy as an Elk's club. He tried to take such taunts as part of the job, but in fact he resented them. His observations on Patton after the war tended to be cutting and dismissive. For now, however, he had to make the best use of him he could, much as he was trying to do with Montgomery.[4]

To many people, then and later, it seemed obvious that he should simply issue direct orders and bend Monty to his will in good military fashion. In truth, though, he had no real power over Montgomery. He could not, for example, promote or relieve him. Monty was not, that is, a subordinate like Bradley or Patton. Besides, even within the U.S. Army, officers discover that as the chain of command goes up, there is more and more discussion and there are fewer direct orders. At the top, SHAEF, like the Pentagon, resembled a huge debating society. Eisenhower was praised during the war for his ability to get strong-willed generals of different nationalities to work together, and he deserves credit for that, but his command style was also a reflection of situational imperatives. Not only was Eisenhower unable to promote or fire British officers, he was not allowed to choose his senior commanders; otherwise, he would have had Alexander with him—not Montgomery—and he would never have picked Leigh-Mallory to command the Allied air forces.

MacArthur was in a comparable position in the southwest Pacific. He not only negotiated with rather than commanded the Australians, he even negotiated with his own army commanders, Walter Krueger and Robert Eichelberger. He did not give them direct orders. Instead, he and they would talk about what he wanted done. Once agreement was reached, that agreement was cast as an order. Eisenhower tried to operate in much the same way, as did Maitland Wilson in the Mediterranean and Mountbatten in Southeast Asia.

He also had a view on leadership that didn't involve desk pounding or confrontation. "In the hurley burly of a military campaign—or a political effort—loyal, effective subordinates are mandatory," he later explained to a member of his White House staff. "To tie them to the leader with unbreakable bonds one rule must always be observed—take full responsibility, promptly, for everything that remotely resembles failure. Give extravagant and public praise to all subordinates for every success."[5]

In the febrile days of mid-September, when the pursuers came, panting, to a sudden halt, Hitler's mind began moving to the offensive. The German Army in France was as good as destroyed, but there remained the million-man army in Germany. Supplemented with the conscription of able-bodied males from the ages of sixteen to sixty and more than a dozen divisions redeployed from Italy, the Balkans and the eastern front, it would increase its numbers by December to nearly 2.5 million.[6]

German weapons production, meanwhile, was still rising. It reached an all-time high in November 1944. Hitler lacked mobility and command of the skies, but there would be plenty of manpower and firepower for a potentially crippling attack if he waited until the weather grounded SHAEF's tactical air.

Eisenhower had repeatedly told people that fall that he wanted to bring the German Army to battle west of the Rhine and destroy it there. Once that was done, nothing could stop his double drive to envelop the Ruhr and the Saar. But on December 12, thinking that the chance of getting such a battle had gone now that winter had blanketed the front with snow, he told Brooke and Churchill that it would probably be May 1945 before he could encircle the Ruhr. They were appalled and told each other that here was the proof that Eisenhower had blundered.[7]

Hitler's plan was to launch a counteroffensive across the Ardennes to the Meuse River, then drive 110 miles northwest to take Antwerp. That would cut off Montgomery's forces from Bradley's. If he destroyed Monty's command, the Anglo-American alliance might fall apart.[8]

Hitler entrusted this operation to von Rundstedt, who was confident he could reach the Meuse but thought his chances of reaching Antwerp were more or less zero. All the same, Eisenhower's strategy had resulted in a three-hundred-mile front. He could not be strong everywhere, so a risk had to be taken somewhere, and he took it in the Ardennes. There, a one-hundred-mile stretch of forest was being held by the VIII Corps, consisting of just four divisions under Troy Middleton, one of Eisenhower's oldest friends.[9]

The Germans knew they could not assemble a huge attacking force without Allied intelligence monitoring it. They therefore generated signals traffic and began deploying their troops in a way that made senior

Allied intelligence officers think the blow would fall near Aachen. In fact, it was aimed at an area twenty-five miles south of Aachen. Montgomery was so complacent that on December 16, he disseminated an intelligence paper that concluded, "The enemy cannot stage major offensive operations."[10]

There was a message waiting for Eisenhower when he arrived at his office that morning: he was being promoted to the new five-star rank of General of the Army. He also received a letter delivered by courier from Monty. Could he go to England to spend Christmas with his son? To his request, Montgomery had attached a memo dated October 11, 1943: "Amount £5. Eisenhower bets war with Germany will end before Xmas 1944—local time." On the memo Monty had scribbled, "For payment, I think, at Christmas." How Eisenhower envied Monty the chance to spend Christmas with his son. If only he could do the same! He dictated a message granting Christmas leave, and promised to pay up, but "I still have nine days."[11]

Around midday, Eisenhower's orderly, Sergeant Mickey McKeogh, married WAC Corporal Pearlie Hargreaves, a member of Ike's office staff, in the chapel of Louis XIV at Versailles. Ike threw a party at his villa for the happy couple, gave them a one-hundred-dollar war bond and kissed the bride before slipping away for a meeting with Bradley on the shortage of combat troops.[12]

They had barely begun when SHAEF's chief intelligence officer, Major General Kenneth Strong, interrupted them—reports were coming in of a major German assault in the Ardennes. "A spoiling attack," said Bradley.

"That's no spoiling attack," said Eisenhower. There weren't enough American troops in the Ardennes to make a spoiling attack worthwhile, and the Germans knew it. He was now up against the fact that he, like Grant, fought with everything he had—no reserves. But near the northern edge of the Ardennes was the 7th Armored Division, which had been mauled in Holland. Its former commander had been fired and a new general had just taken over. And to the south, one of Patton's divisions, the 10th Armored, had been rotated out of the line a few days earlier. He told Bradley to send both divisions to Middleton at once. Bradley said Patton would object to losing an armored division. Eisenhower impatiently responded, "Tell him that Ike is running this goddamned war!"[13]

For twenty-five years the Infantry School had studied the German offensives of 1918 and taught an entire generation of officers the essential lesson: Hold the shoulders, and you limit the depth of the penetration. The movement of the 7th and 10th Armored divisions would help to do just that.

Next day, December 17, the picture of what the Germans were doing became clear: Hitler had assembled six hundred thousand men, nearly two thousand artillery pieces, fifteen hundred tanks and more than a thousand combat aircraft to mount this counteroffensive. He had struck when fog pinned Allied aircraft to the ground. The foggy weather was expected to persist for several days at least.

As Eisenhower studied the maps, the pattern of the battle ahead began taking shape in his mind. There were few roads in the Ardennes, and to break through to the Meuse, which was obviously their immediate objective, the Germans would have to take a crossroads town called Saint-Vith, near the northern shoulder. There was another important crossroads town, called Bastogne, not far from the southern shoulder. If the Germans wanted to prevent Patton from turning north and hitting them in the flank as they advanced, they would have to take Bastogne.[14]

Although Eisenhower had no strategic reserve to speak of, there were two uncommitted divisions—the 82nd and 101st Airborne. Both had taken a beating in Holland, where Montgomery had used them for two months as regular infantry following his failure at Arnhem. He had refused to release them until the weather ruled out all chance of another airborne operation. They were currently being brought back up to full strength. The 82nd was ordered to move toward Saint-Vith; the 101st, to head for Bastogne.

Eisenhower did not send a message to Marshall; he wasn't going to do that until he had some good news to offer, and any message to the Chief of Staff right now could be misconstrued as a sign of anxiety. Instead, he dictated a letter to Brehon Somervell, the head of Army Service Forces, knowing that Somervell would almost certainly show it to Marshall. The letter really didn't have a lot to say about anything, but toward the end, and in a casual way, he mentioned the German attack, before concluding confidently, "We should not only stop the thrust but should be able to profit from it."[15]

On December 18, with the shoulders holding firm and the Germans blocked at Saint-Vith, he called a commanders' conference at Verdun, the grim, gray town where a million French and German soldiers had died in the biggest battle of World War I. He arrived there in the Cadillac around midmorning on December 19, obviously tired, but as his generals assembled in their overcoats on the second floor of a bitterly cold French barracks, he said firmly, "The present situation is to be regarded as an opportunity for us and not a disaster. There will be only cheerful faces at this conference table."[16]

Everyone agreed that the Germans must not be allowed to get across the Meuse. Once the German attack had been stopped, Allied units would hit the enemy's long, exposed southern flank. Eisenhower turned to Patton. "I want you to command this move—under Brad's supervision, of course—making a strong counterattack with at least six divisions. When can you start?"

"As soon as you're through with me."

"When can you attack?" Eisenhower asked again, incredulous.

"The morning of December 21, with three divisions." Some officers gasped with disbelief. Tedder stifled a laugh.[17]

"Don't be fatuous, George!" said Eisenhower. It would be hard to pull off a feat like that in ideal conditions, but nobody engaged with the enemy could yank three divisions out of line and in forty-eight hours move them a hundred miles north over icy roads and difficult terrain and at a time of the year when there was daylight only between eight in the morning and four in the afternoon. "If you try to go that early, you won't have all three divisions ready and you'll go piecemeal. You will start on the twenty-second and I want your initial blow to be a strong one!"

This was the finest moment of Patton's military career. His intelligence chief, Oscar Koch, had not been fooled by the German moves prior to the Battle of the Bulge. Even before Hitler launched this offensive, Patton was preparing to move half his army to the northwest instead of continuing east. Gripping a cigar, Patton used it to point to a line drawn on the situation map with grease pencil. The line curved noticeably between Saint-Vith and Bastogne. "The Kraut's stuck his head in a meat grinder." He made a circular motion with his free hand. "And this time I've got hold of the handle."

As the meeting broke up, Eisenhower remarked wryly, "Funny thing, Georgie. Every time I get a new star, I get attacked." He was referring to Sidi-bou-Zid and Kasserine Pass, which had come only days after his promotion to four stars. Patton shot back, "And every time you get attacked, Ike, I pull you out!"[18]

While Eisenhower was in Verdun, Beetle's British deputy, Major

General "Jock" Whiteley, was at Montgomery's headquarters in Hasselt, a small town in Belgium roughly a hundred miles north of Luxemburg city, which was where Bradley had recently placed 12th Army Group headquarters. Eisenhower had told him he was moving too close to the front, but Bradley ignored him. Luxemburg city was a pleasant, prosperous place that had been spared the ravages of war. It was a congenial spot, that is, for a date with a superstar, Marlene Dietrich. Unfortunately, it was a bad place to be when the German offensive drove a huge wedge between Bradley's headquarters and Monty's, and as the Germans advanced, they were tearing up telephone circuits.[19]

The field marshal was appalled at the reports of German gains. He read a much greater menace in them than did Eisenhower. The day Whiteley visited him, he sent Brooke an account of the unfolding battle—"great confusion and disorder . . . full-scale withdrawal . . . lack of grip and control . . . great pessimism . . ." Whiteley returned to Versailles convinced that Montgomery had to take control of the First Army, because at present it seemed almost paralyzed. Although Whiteley did not know it, Courtney Hodges, commanding the First Army, was in a state of shock. When the Battle of the Bulge began, he was so demoralized by the scale and suddenness of the German attack that he took to his bed for twenty-four hours. Monty was right about the lack of grip at First Army headquarters.[20]

Back at SHAEF, Whiteley found that Strong, who had just returned from Verdun with Eisenhower, agreed with him. A little after midnight, they woke Beetle Smith from a deep sleep and told him the situation in the north was so critical that Montgomery had to be given control of the First Army. Smith was incensed. He barked at them, "You are no longer acceptable as staff officers to Eisenhower!" and told them to consider themselves fired.[21]

Eisenhower had endured an exhausting, worrying day when he returned to Versailles, but before going to bed, he went to the map room at SHAEF to study the latest situation map of the Ardennes. Taking a grease pencil, he drew a line more or less across the middle, from east to west. The best way to fight this battle would be to make a powerful attack from the north when Patton struck from the south. The only force available for a counterattack from the north was the rested-and-ready XXX Corps, the armored spearhead of the British Second Army. To get the XXX Corps into the battle, he would have to give Montgomery control of the northern half of the battle area. Doing that would also help resolve the communications problems between Bradley in Luxemburg city and First Army headquarters a hundred miles to the north, at Spa.

By the time Eisenhower returned to his office at nine A.M., Smith had changed his mind. He advised him to put the First Army under Montgomery. Communications were so bad, said Smith, that it was the only thing to do. Eisenhower said he agreed and put a call through to Bradley, who was predictably outraged. He had gone to a lot of trouble in recent months to prevent Monty from getting control of the First Army. Instead, he had reinforced Monty by giving him the U.S. Ninth Army, a much smaller formation.

"By God!" Bradley bellowed. "I cannot be responsible to the American people if you do this. I resign."

Eisenhower stamped on him hard. "Brad, I—not you—am responsible to the American people. Your resignation means absolutely nothing!"[22]

A few hours later, Montgomery arrived at First Army headquarters, oozing self-satisfaction. He would save the Americans from themselves. Behind the smugness, however, was a commander whose generalship was limited by an exaggerated idea of German military abilities, a limitation recently reinforced by the British defeat at Arnhem. Monty was always worried about what the Germans might do to him.

During the early days of this crisis, Eisenhower continued to exude calmness and confidence, but while he was in Verdun, more than a dozen English-speaking Germans had been captured wearing American uniforms. Rumors flew that the Germans were on a mission to assassinate Eisenhower. He considered all talk of assassination ridiculous, but to his irritation, Beetle Smith surrounded him with dozens of burly MPs and tried to dissuade him from leaving SHAEF headquarters, day or night. A lieutenant colonel who looked something like Eisenhower was put to work as a decoy and conspicuously driven between the Saint-Germain villa and SHAEF Main each day. Eisenhower was appalled to find he was a new kind of prisoner of war. He hated it, and complained bitterly about it.[23]

On December 22, Eisenhower issued one of his rare Orders of the Day. The enemy, he said, "is gambling everything [and] will completely fail. But we cannot be content with his mere repulse . . . destroy him!"[24]

The next day, the Saint-Vith defenders made a fighting withdrawal, just as the skies finally cleared, allowing Allied fighter-bombers to get into the battle. The fall of Saint-Vith nevertheless allowed the Germans to feed fresh divisions into the Bulge. They renewed their drive toward the Meuse.[25]

On Christmas Day, Eisenhower became so anxious about Bastogne that he fell into a deep depression. There were eighteen thousand men defending the town against sixty thousand Germans. By all rational calculations, Bastogne had to fall. Kay Summersby had never seen him in such low spirits. Patton was taking longer to reach it than Eisenhower had expected after the confident boasts at Verdun. But still the town held out. Here, without a combat jump, was the ultimate airborne operation as taught at airborne schools—"An entire unit, fighting in every direction at once and holding out until the linkup occurs."

The defense was so vigorous that despite amassing an advantage of better than three to one, the Germans still lacked the confidence to mount the all-or-nothing attack that was their best hope of taking the town. On December 26, the 4th Armored Division broke through and Bastogne was relieved. The one thing Eisenhower had truly feared might happen in the Bulge never did.

26

End of a Mission

While the fighting in the Bulge was at its height, Eisenhower was contemplating the fate of a single soldier—Private Eddie D. Slovik, 28th Infantry Division, sentenced to death for desertion. Slovik had run away before. Originally classified 4-F, he had been drafted in early 1944, when the Selective Service System, running out of manpower, suddenly became a lot less selective.

Eddie Slovik was the product of a harsh, impoverished childhood and various reform schools, a young man doomed to a marginal existence but not to a firing squad. The essential difference between someone absent without leave (or AWOL) and a deserter is intention. An AWOL intends to return . . . sometime; a deserter is a soldier who intends to return . . . never.

There was no evidence to show that Eddie Slovik ever formed an intention to desert. Unfortunately for him, his court-martial was held at a time when the 28th Division had just been mauled in the Hürtgen forest, fighting a pointless battle because Courtney Hodges worried too much, like Montgomery. The 28th's AWOL rate rose dramatically. The division commander, Norman Cota, wanted a scapegoat. Eddie Slovik, a repeat offender, was it.[1]

Years later, when author Bruce Catton interviewed Eisenhower and asked him why he had upheld Slovik's death sentence, Ike gave an account of the case that was almost completely wrong. He claimed, for example, that he had sent an officer to give Slovik one last chance while he was "on the gibbet," but the recalcitrant Slovik had rejected this, and shown no remorse, and therefore had to die. Slovik was shot, though, not hanged, and he had written to Eisenhower not only expressing remorse but saying that if his life was spared, he would be a good soldier, concluding, "I Remain Yours for Victory, Pvt. Eddie D. Slovik."[2]

He was the only American soldier during the war executed for a military offense; seventy others were shot for crimes such as murder and rape. The worst break in Eddie Slovik's hard-luck life was to have his case land on Ike's desk at a time when all of Eisenhower's energies and anxieties were focused on the Battle of the Bulge. Had the same paperwork come into SHAEF a month earlier or a month later, Eddie Slovik might have survived World War II.

As Bastogne was being relieved, Montgomery was telling Bradley that the First Army would be incapable of offensive action for at least three months. Monty was, meanwhile, trying to hold back the spearhead of the First Army, VII Corps, commanded by "Lightning Joe" Collins. The U.S. 2nd Armored Division, one of its elite formations, was poised to attack the 2nd Panzer Division, which was leading the German advance on the Meuse. Alarmed by such aggressiveness, Montgomery ordered Collins to withdraw thirty miles.

Had he carried out this order, Collins would have collapsed the right flank of the First Army and handed the Germans the roads they needed to reach the Meuse. Instead, he ignored it. The U.S. 2nd Armored Division was commanded by Major General Ernest Harmon, one of the most capable and aggressive commanders in the U.S. Army, and this was his hour. On December 26, he threw his division straight at the oncoming Germans. The result was an epic toe-to-toe, get-everything-shooting kind of battle, with dozens of fighter-bombers pitching into the fray.

In the space of twelve hours, the 2nd Panzer lost half its tanks and most of its self-propelled artillery. At dawn on December 27, the survivors withdrew, under unremitting pressure from Harmon. Von Rundstedt was wrong: Hitler's drive to Antwerp couldn't even reach the Meuse.

On December 28, Eisenhower got away from Versailles at last and headed for Monty's headquarters at Hasselt. He told Montgomery he wanted a counterattack that would first cut across the salient, then move east, along the roads the Germans had used to get into the Ardennes. With the strategic initiative firmly in Allied hands and the Germans abandoning all hope of reaching the Meuse, Eisenhower now wanted to make sure there was no repetition of the Falaise-gap mistake, where half the Germans had been able to escape. If Allied forces held the roads going east, the Germans could either flee into the forests, where they would die of hunger and hypothermia, or come out with their arms in the air, shouting, *"Kamerad!"*

Montgomery, however, didn't want to hear about that. He was convinced the Germans were about to mount another major attack in the Ardennes. There was no evidence for this—not from Ultra, not from Tac R, not from photo recon or FEBA (Forward Edge of the Battle Area) flights and not from German prisoners. On the contrary—there was a steady flow of decryptions showing that the Germans were withdrawing. They had hoped to renew their offensive, but could not even establish a start line from which to launch an attack. Every decryption that arrived between December 26 and December 31 told the same story: the enemy had shot his bolt.[3]

Eisenhower said emphatically that he wanted a counteroffensive under way no later than January 1. Montgomery just as emphatically said he had to receive the German offensive first, ride it out and only then would an Allied offensive be possible. "He's a tired little fart," said Patton when he heard of this meeting. Eisenhower returned to Versailles exasperated.[4]

The next day, he received a letter from Monty demanding that he be made the ground-force commander. Otherwise, "we will fail again." Eisenhower's patience finally snapped. Blazing with fury, he dictated a message to the Combined Chiefs of Staff, saying it was impossible for him and Montgomery to work together. One of them would have to be relieved.[5]

It may be that he was simply venting his anger and had no intention of sending this him-or-me ultimatum. But Major General Frederick de Guingand, who was at Versailles that day, heard about it from Smith, begged Eisenhower to wait twenty-four hours before sending it and flew through a snowstorm to tell Montgomery that he was going to be fired. Monty, convinced he was indispensable, brushed aside the threat. "Who would they get?" he said, unimpressed.

"Alexander," said de Guingand.

The blood drained from Monty's face. He'd forgotten about Alexander. "Freddy, what should I do?" De Guingand drew from his tunic a suitably groveling letter he had written for this moment. It contained a pledge of complete cooperation in the future and concluded, "Very distressed that my letter may have upset you and I would ask you to tear it up. Your very devoted subordinate, Monty."[6]

The renewed German offensive that Montgomery had spent many hours planning to defeat never materialized. Instead, the enemy continued to withdraw. Even now, Monty refused to mount a counterattack. Instead of cutting the Germans off, he pushed them slowly out of the salient, starting at the tip.

Meanwhile, he continued to yearn for past glories, but wisely let Brooke and the British press take the lead this time. Marshall, who by now despised Montgomery as comprehensively as any man he had ever met, sent Eisenhower a cable that ran, "Under no circumstances make any concessions of any kind whatsoever. There would be a terrific resentment in this country . . ." Eisenhower assured him, "You need have no fear . . ."[7]

On January 7, Montgomery held a press conference. He arrived dressed in warrior's garb, ready to jump into battle in a red beret and a paratrooper's harness. He swaggered and boasted, preened and pontificated. He was, he let the journalists know, the man who had saved the hapless Americans from their stupidity. "I took certain steps. . . . I employed the whole available power of the British Group of Armies. . . . Finally it was put into battle with a bang. . . . The battle has been most interesting; I think one of the most interesting and tricky battles I have ever handled." He had learned something about American troops, he conceded—they fought well when given strong leadership. The sense of anger and outrage that this press conference unleashed throughout the U.S. Army would be impossible to exaggerate, or even describe adequately. Churchill had to defuse the crisis by making a speech in the House of Commons that stressed this was an American, not a British, battle. Few British soldiers were involved.[8]

With Monty's help, the Germans made a well-managed withdrawal. It was late January before the entire Bulge had been erased from the situation maps. Eisenhower, interviewed about it after the war, described the battle as "an incident" in the war, but it was far more than that. He had hoped in the early fall of 1944 to fight a major battle west of the Rhine, after which crossing the river should be comparatively easy. When that failed to materialize, he feared he wouldn't be able to get across until May 1945.

The Bulge gave him the battle he wanted. In one month, the equivalent of twenty full-strength German divisions, including all their equipment, had been destroyed. The Wehrmacht's armor reserve of fifteen hundred tanks had been wiped out. More than two hundred thousand Germans soldiers had been killed, crippled or captured; at least a thousand artillery pieces had been lost. These men and this weaponry would have helped make the Rhine a daunting barrier. A destroyed tank or gun on this side of it was worth three on the opposite shore. And it was much easier to kill or wound a German who was out in the open, mounting an attack, than it would ever be to deal with the same enemy dug in east of the Rhine.

Nevertheless, the destruction would have been even greater had not Montgomery dithered and allowed his fears to dominate his actions. The battle did not, therefore, provide Eisenhower with the satisfaction of a job well done; it did not, that is, improve his opinion of Montgomery one iota. On the contrary, what had been dislike and irritation became contempt.

Before the Bulge, Patton's Third Army had been advancing toward the Saar while, at the right end of the Allied line, the U.S. Sixth Army Group, under Lieutenant General Jacob Devers, advanced up the valley of the Rhone and into Alsace. When, at Verdun, Eisenhower had moved Patton farther west to relieve Bastogne, the Sixth Army Group had been thinned out to cover the positions that Patton had held. Hitler took advantage of this to launch a January offensive in Alsace, aimed at the recapture of Strasbourg and the defense of Colmar.[9]

Devers had given the French First Army, commanded by Philippe de Lattre de Tassigny, the honor of liberating Strasbourg. In the long rivalry between France and Germany, possession of Strasbourg—the capital of Alsace—had been a political barometer, showing which nation held the upper hand.

Fifty miles south of Strasbourg stood Colmar, the industrial heart of Alsace, and de Lattre insisted on liberating Colmar, too. Devers acceded to his request, expecting a swift conquest, because Ultra showed it was defended by no more than fourteen thousand Germans. The French had the defenders outnumbered by six to one and possessed far more firepower, yet they settled down for a prolonged siege. Eisenhower was appalled.[10]

As the Germans thrust toward Strasbourg, Eisenhower ordered a general withdrawal. Strasbourg had no military value and would inevitably be retaken at some future date. It wasn't worth fighting a battle to hold on to it. However, that point of view, although perfectly logical, made no allowance for Gallic pride.

During the afternoon of January 3, Eisenhower was in his office at the Trianon Palace Hotel, talking to Churchill about Montgomery, when de Gaulle arrived, to protest the pullout from Strasbourg. Taking the German sword he used as a pointer, Eisenhower indicated the key terrain—the passes. *They* had to be held, not Strasbourg.[11]

"If we were at war college," said de Gaulle, "I might agree with you. . . . From a strategic point of view, this would simply be a maneuver. But for France, this would be a national disaster. To France, this is sacred ground."

"You are asking me to change military orders for political reasons," said Eisenhower.

De Gaulle responded angrily, "Armies are created to advance the policies of states. Anyway, no one understands better than you that strategy involves more than technical military questions. It is also a matter of morale. Losing Strasbourg would be a blow at French national morale."

Churchill said, "General de Gaulle is right."

De Gaulle then said he would order the French First Army to defend Strasbourg. Eisenhower was already exasperated by the mediocre performance of the French First Army, which had failed to launch a single assault on Colmar. The French loved to talk about how eager they were to drive the Germans out of their country, but they seemed remarkably unwilling to close with the enemy. He asked scornfully just how long the French would be able to fight without American arms and fuel.

De Gaulle indignantly raised the ante—if the Americans permitted the annihilation of the French First Army, just how, he demanded to know, would they manage to prosecute the war when the French people, in their fury, denied them the use of French railroads, airports, harbors, etc.?[12]

Relenting before a bad situation grew any worse, Eisenhower put a call through to Devers: the two American divisions defending Strasbourg would hold their present positions. Churchill said, "I think you've done the wise and proper thing." American troops secured key ground north of the city, and boundaries were redrawn so that the modest French force in Strasbourg could remain where it was and be reinforced by troops now near Colmar.[13]

Before he left Versailles, de Gaulle took tea with Eisenhower, and Eisenhower talked about some of his recent problems with Montgomery, describing him as "an acerbic critic and an untrustworthy subordinate."

De Gaulle told him not to let that bother him. "Military glory is its own reward and it is you who will be the victor in this war."[14]

Between April and August 1944, the strategic bombing of Germany was severely reduced by the need to aid Overlord, attack V-1 sites and mount carpet bombing missions to help the armies break out from Normandy. The Germans used those months to repair earlier bomb damage and put millions of slave laborers to work improving the defenses of the Siegfried Line. It was September before a sustained strategic bombing campaign against the German war economy was finally possible, and it was about time. German arms production had risen steadily since the summer of 1943 and advanced new weapons, such as jet fighters, Panther tanks and the V-2 rocket, were beginning to emerge from the factories.

Tooey Spaatz insisted that the primary objective had to be oil. Without fuel, even the best tank cannot move, even the best airplane cannot fly. Oil seemed at first glance to be an ideal objective for daylight precision bombing, the mission for which the B-17 Flying Fortress had been created. Unfortunately, German synthetic-fuel plants covered large areas, and the key elements within them were small and hard to hit. The Germans managed to produce enough aviation fuel to get their jet fighters in the air, and troops fighting in defensive positions did not need a lot of gasoline or diesel. Attacking oil targets crippled the Reich's offensive power, as the Bulge demonstrated, but left its defensive power almost intact.

While Spaatz was pushing for oil attacks, however, Tedder and Solly Zuckerman were urging Eisenhower to approve yet another transportation plan, this one aimed at crippling the Deutsche Reichsbahn, the German railroad. Eisenhower resolved this oil-versus-transportation argument by ordering Spaatz to use his B-17's to join the RAF's Lancasters in attacks on transportation targets when the weather ruled out oil targets.[15]

The British had developed airborne radar that permitted bombing through clouds and at night, provided the target was big enough. A sprawling marshaling yard or a large railroad bridge across a major river could be identified no matter how solid the cloud cover or how dark the night. The weather was so bad from October to February that the Reichsbahn was hammered day after day, night after night.[16]

By this roundabout, backdoor way, Eisenhower's airmen finally got their hands on the key to the destruction of the German war economy. Ninety percent of Germany's energy needs were produced by coal, and 90 percent of the coal was hauled by the Reichsbahn. The remaining 10 percent was moved from the coal-producing areas—mainly the Ruhr and Silesia—via an extensive river-and-canal network.[17]

Hitler gave railroad repair absolute priority, even over the repair of military defenses, but it made little difference. The signals and switching machinery in the marshaling yards were wrecked and irreplaceable. Repair crews were exhausted and lacked essential tools. In January 1945 rail traffic was down to 25 percent of the normal level. The Reichsbahn would grind to a halt in a month or so and arms production would, for all practical purposes, cease.

Eisenhower was deeply impressed and wrote to Spaatz and Sir Arthur Harris of RAF bomber Command, offering them both his congratulations and his gratitude. "The effect on the war economy of Germany has obviously been tremendous; a fact that advancing troops are quick to appreciate . . ." The end was finally near.[18]

☆ ☆ ☆ ☆ ☆

In the fall of 1944, Second Lieutenant John S. D. Eisenhower completed the Infantry School course at Benning. He was made a platoon leader in a rifle company in the 71st Infantry Division, which was slated to go to France in early 1945. The division was commanded by Major General William Wyman, an old friend of Ike's, and Mamie followed these developments with alarm. She thought she saw Ike's hand at work, thought he was pulling strings to get his son back to Europe, even if that meant exposing him to danger. The life expectancy of a second lieutenant leading a rifle platoon in combat at this stage of the war was so short it was almost a death sentence.

Eisenhower, meanwhile, was scrupulous about not getting involved. He was well aware of John's assignment, but he had no hand in it. He was therefore astonished, and deeply hurt, to get a letter in November 1944 in which Mamie berated him for what she called his "dirty tricks." He protested strongly. "So far as John is concerned, we can do nothing but pray. If I interfered even slightly or indirectly he would be so resentful for the remainder of his life that neither I nor you could be comfortable with him [and] please try to see me in something besides a despicable light . . . at least let me be *certain* of my welcome home when this mess is finished."[19]

While Eisenhower could not risk interfering in his son's assignment, Bradley could do so, and did. He had John assigned to a new kind of communications unit, one that provided higher headquarters with accurate, up-to-the-minute reports of what was happening at the front. John would get to see a lot of the battlefield without being in much danger of becoming a prisoner of war. Bradley also arranged for him to spend a few days with his father.[20]

"I cannot tell you how eagerly I am looking forward to seeing him," Ike wrote Mamie the day before John reached Versailles. "We'll probably talk ourselves to death."[21]

During the four days that his son was there, Ike did stay up into the early hours talking with John, yet there was still a barrier they could not overcome. It really never went away. Even after the war, one perceptive observer noticed, "Ike was a bit short with his grown son, a little inconsiderate of his feelings . . . here was John seeking his father's approval and waiting for a kind word [but] not quite getting it."[22]

Eisenhower was well aware of his inability to express openly and face-to-face the affection he felt for people. He blamed it on the Anglo-Saxon ideal of manly behavior—the stiff upper lip, the willed restraint, the stoicism in the face of pain and disappointment. In his letters, he could be warm, affectionate, express the sensitive side of his nature.

But he could never show it openly. To some people who served with him he seemed completely lacking in warmth, colder, even, than Marshall.[23]

He was undoubtedly constrained by this manly code, which reached a kind of apogee in military life. Yet there was another force at work, too—the long shadow of David Jacob Eisenhower, the overly strict, quick-to-whip father. Eisenhower never struck his son; Mamie would not have tolerated that. Instead, he imposed his will on his son in other ways, and was just as demanding as David Jacob and just as unforthcoming when it came to expressing his love for his son.

Eisenhower assured Mamie that they got along well. "He's lots of fun and we have a thoroughly good time when he is here. But I can't quite figure him out. . . . I must say I find him conservative and rather sedate. . . . He is terribly serious—I wish he'd have a bit more fun, or get more laughs out of life."[24]

Such comments are those of a father who longed almost desperately for his son to dare show *his* emotions, express what he was truly thinking and feeling. It did not seem to occur to Eisenhower that it was for him to take the first agonizing steps and risk failure or rejection in an effort to encourage his son to discover a different—happier—code. Yet even had that thought impinged on his mind, he could no more have done it than levitate.

Eisenhower planned to get all his armies up to the Rhine before attempting to cross it. A short pause would give Bradley, Montgomery and Devers a chance to bring their units up to full strength and make sure their logistics were in good working order before plunging into Germany for the last act of this epic drama.

Montgomery was still slated to make the main effort, and the offensive that he was planning to carry him to the Rhine, Operation Veritable, would begin on February 8. This was the first offensive effort the British had mounted for three months. It featured two converging attacks—no bold single thrust here—with a carpet bombing to provide a kick start.

The Germans cleverly flooded the area the U.S. Ninth Army—operating under Montgomery's headquarters—had to cross, impeding its advance, but on March 2, it smashed its way into Düsseldorf.

William Simpson, commander of the Ninth, began putting together an assault crossing of the Rhine, to strike while the Germans were still retreating. Monty ordered him to stay right where he was. He was planning a grand opera Rhine-crossing-cum-clambake-and-media fest. Nobody was going to rob Monty of his moment.[25]

Bradley, meanwhile, had launched his own drive. Both the First and Third armies reached the Rhine south of the Ruhr at about the same time that the British Second Army and Simpson's Ninth were closing on its northern end. And then, the evening of March 7, Bradley received a call from First Army headquarters: the 9th Armored Division, commanded by Ike and Bradley's classmate John W. Leonard, had just captured the Ludendorff railroad bridge that crossed the Rhine at Remagen![26]

Bradley was ecstatic, but SHAEF's chief planner, Major General "Pinky" Bull, happened to be visiting and he didn't like to see a good plan junked. "You're not going anywhere down there at Remagen," said Bull. "It just doesn't fit the plan."

Bradley put a call through to Eisenhower. "Brad, that's wonderful!" exulted Ike. Bradley told him that Bull said it didn't fit in with the plan. Eisenhower retorted, "To hell with the planners! Go ahead and shove over at least five divisions instantly, and anything else that's necessary to make certain we hold it."[27]

Remagen wasn't ideal for exploitation; the area was rugged and remote. But for an army as hooked on mobility and movement as Bradley's it might just be turned into a thrust deep into the belly of the beast. Remagen did not alter SHAEF's priorities, though. Monty would still be allowed to mount his huge set-piece crossing of the Rhine, Operation Plunder, on March 24.

And then, in the early hours of March 23, Patton pushed a division across the Rhine near Mainz, and had a second division cross later that day. As Monty launched Plunder, Patton was standing on the opposite side of the Rhine, urinating gleefully into the river, telling his staff that this was what William the Conqueror had done when he crossed the English Channel.[28]

Plunder, the biggest operation since D-Day, opened up with thirty-three hundred artillery pieces laying down the biggest barrage of the war. More than a million men lunged toward Germany, more than a hundred war correspondents scribbled eagerly and both Eisenhower and Churchill were on hand to watch it unfold. Two airborne divisions made a combat jump, just to add to the spectacle. By the time the paratroopers descended, their landing zones were in the hands of British troops.[29]

Meanwhile, to the south, the First Army tore out of the Remagen bridgehead and began to encircle the eastern half of the Ruhr. The Ninth Army, which was by far the most mobile part of Monty's command, was doing much the same, encircling the western half of the Ruhr. It was only a matter of time before the two armies linked up. At this point, Eisenhower informed Montgomery that the Ninth Army would be returned to Bradley's Twelfth Army Group.[30]

After Monty's famous Bulge press conference, Eisenhower had adopted a simple policy in regard to the field marshal. As he told Cornelius Ryan after the war, "Monty got so damn personal to make sure that the Americans—and me, in particular—had no credit, that I just stopped communicating with him. . . . I was just not interested in keeping up communications with a man that just can't tell the truth."[31]

That being so, Churchill and Brooke had been forced to abandon all hope of getting Monty reinstalled as Ike's deputy for ground forces. They tried instead to get Tedder sent to the Mediterranean, on the grounds that it was now "mainly an air theater," a strange claim in light of the huge ground offensive being prepared for the spring of 1945. With Tedder in the Mediterranean, they intended to get Alexander installed as Ike's deputy. Alexander was their last hope of being able to say that a British general had taken the ground war through to victory and Germany's surrender. With the end of the struggle in sight, there was an unseemly scramble for glory under way among both American and British commanders, and the attempt to push Alexander onto Eisenhower was a manifestation of that desire at the summit of the alliance.[32]

The British were contemplating a postwar future in which their empire was almost certain to fall away, and a war debt that was three times the size of their gross domestic product was going to hang around their necks for at least another generation. To them, the coin of prestige would have to substitute for the substance of power. They were not simply eager to amass all the prestige they could; they had a national duty to amass all they could. Eisenhower, sympathetic though he was to their needs and much as he liked Alexander personally, felt he had to say no.

That rejection had upset Churchill and Brooke profoundly, and his decision in late March to remove the Ninth Army from Monty's 21st Army Group drove them nearly to distraction. Churchill particularly seemed wounded, which in turn distressed Eisenhower, but he was acting, he insisted, on purely military grounds.[33]

The plan he had drawn up in May 1944 for encircling the Ruhr and capturing the Saar was coming to a successful conclusion. It was time to devise an endgame, beginning with the "Alpine redoubt." SHAEF planners seemed to be taking their cues these days from the newspapers, which had for months been producing stories that deep in the Bavarian Alps, the Germans had created the infrastructure of a defense network that could hold out for years, maybe indefinitely. Ike sent a message to Roosevelt, alerting him to a dismal, anticlimatic possibility—"that there will never be a clean cut surrender of the German forces on the Western Front."[34]

The other important reality was that Allied and Soviet forces were going to meet up somewhere in the heart of Germany. While it was obvious to some Allied leaders, such as Churchill, that the farther east this happened the better it would be, Eisenhower had no instructions from the Combined Chiefs to do anything other than destroy the German war machine and compel Germany's surrender.

On April 1, the First and Ninth armies linked up at Lippstadt. The Ruhr, which was roughly the size of Massachusetts, was completely surrounded. Some 320,000 enemy troops were taken prisoner in the biggest mass surrender of the war. This left the bulk of American forces massed near Kassel, meaning they were ideally placed to make a power drive across central Germany for a linkup with the Russians along the Elbe River. As they advanced, Eisenhower would be able to direct units to the north, if necessary, to keep the Red Army from thrusting into Denmark or south into Bavaria if it turned out there really was an Alpine redoubt.[35]

In mid-April, as American armies moved eastward across central Germany, the Red Army was fighting its way into the outer suburbs of Berlin. To Churchill, and to many of Eisenhower's critics in the Cold War years, it was obvious that at this point he should have set his sights on capturing Berlin before the Red Army did so. Certainly, he had the means to do it. The United States Army was by this time the ultimate expression of combined arms operations, seamlessly integrating air, ground, armor, artillery and modern logistics. It possessed more flexibility, firepower and mobility than any fighting force the world had seen. When it reached the Elbe—the river Eisenhower had chosen as the line where the two sides would meet—the First Army was still 150 miles from the capital of the Third Reich and the Red Army was only thirty miles away. But Eisenhower could still get there first and take the city.

In the end, he decided not to make a bid for Berlin—for various reasons, beginning with the human cost. When he asked Bradley for an estimate of projected U.S. losses, Bradley's answer was, "A hundred thousand casualties." That was enough to give any commander cause to think hard about the operation, because under the agreement made at Yalta in February 1945, Germany was going to be divided into zones of occupation. Berlin was deep within the Soviet zone. Eisenhower could take Berlin, but he could not keep the Soviets out of the city.[36]

His strategic outlook also played its part. As he informed Montgomery, who was panting to make a dash for Berlin, "That place has become, so far as I am concerned, nothing but a geographical location. . . . My purpose is to destroy the enemy's forces and his powers to resist." Churchill was indignant at this dismissal of Berlin as a worthwhile objective, but Eisenhower was following much the same strategy as Grant: Kill the enemy's army, and his cities will fall. When Lee surrendered at Appomattox, Richmond was still in Confederate hands. Grant never captured it. And Eisenhower was, by his own admission, one of Grant's greatest admirers.[37]

What's more, his personal feelings about the Soviets were ambivalent, as might be expected from a man who had viewed the New Deal as dangerously "socialistic." Eisenhower was guarded, however, in expressing his views. For one thing, he genuinely believed that soldiers shouldn't meddle in politics, even though at his level, the military and the political overlapped. For another, the policy of the United States government, as set by Roosevelt, was to look upon the Soviet Union in a positive light and to assume that relations with it in the postwar period would be good. It was not up to Eisenhower to challenge that policy. On the contrary, he went out of his way to make it seem that he agreed with it. So he told Harry Butcher, "The more contact we have with the Russians, the more they will understand us and the greater will be the co-operation." Long before this, he had discovered that anything he said to Butcher was likely to appear in the newspapers, which was why Butcher saw very little of Eisenhower in the last six months of the war. Ike no longer told Harry what he really thought; he told him only what he thought useful.[38]

He was more forthcoming with John. As American units moved forward to meet up with the Red Army along the Elbe River, for example, Eisenhower told his son that the Soviets were "arrogant," and, "I just don't know what our future is going to be with them. . . . I sure wish I had more of my divisions concentrated on the First Army front, ready to meet these people when they come in on the Elbe."[39]

His views on what the postwar would bring were expressed at length only once, and that was in a discussion with the American ambassador to France, Jefferson Caffrey, in October 1944. He told Caffrey, "If Europe is dominated by a single power, that would mean the postwar world will be divided between a superpowerful Europe, a weakened British Empire and the United States. In our case, would we maintain the adequate naval and air forces which that would imply?" Clearly, the dominant power that he saw taking over Western Europe was the Soviet Union. What worried him was the likelihood of a weak American response.

Shortly after this, he told Spaatz he anticipated a breakup of the Anglo-American alliance after the war ended, by which time the Soviets would have large ground forces in Germany. They agreed that the only way the U.S. would be able to secure its position following the inevitable demobilization of the U.S. Army was to keep a large force of heavy bombers in Europe. Even as Eisenhower spoke the Rooseveltian language of cooperation to those around him, expressing the urgings of an optimistic heart, his mind was listing in the opposite direction. His swift action to block any Red Army advance on Denmark hardly evidenced a great deal of trust.[40]

By this time, Eisenhower had moved his headquarters to the champagne capital, Reims, in northern France, where it was installed in an unprepossessing building that had formerly housed a trade school. Set next to the railroad tracks, it shook each time freight trains rumbled in or out of the station, half a mile down the line. He seemed to be going out of his way to find somewhere suitably Spartan. Even in his choice of a place to live he distanced himself from the large number of Allied commanders who lived in luxury, settling into a small château that was gloomy, decrepit and uncomfortable.

On May 3, Hitler committed suicide. The battle of Berlin ended the next day. The war ought, by rights, to have ended at this point, but the German high command was holding out until May 5—the anniversary of Napoleon's death. German generals arrived in Reims that day offering to surrender, but wanted the surrender to be phased over three days. That would permit many Germans now facing the Red Army to surrender to the Americans instead. Eisenhower turned them down, demanding immediate and unconditional surrender on every front.

Over the next thirty-six hours, the Germans made a pretense of negotiating, to buy time for their comrades to escape westward. Eisenhower had Smith, aided by Strong, who spoke German fluently, deal with the German delegation face-to-face. It was the early hours of May 7 before the Germans finally agreed to meet Eisenhower's demands. Eisenhower, with Tedder standing beside him, stood stern and unsmiling behind his desk as the head of the German delegation, General Alfred Jodl, was brought into his office. He warned Jodl that he and his colleagues would be held "personally and officially responsible for any violations of the surrender."[41]

After the Germans departed, Eisenhower and his staff debated just what he should tell the Combined Chiefs. His staff was looking for a rhetorical flourish, something sure to make it into the history books. They got nowhere. He would have to do it himself. At four in the morning, Eisenhower wrote out a laconic message that was almost Roman in its directness and vigor: "The mission of this Allied force was fulfilled at 0300, local time, May 7th, 1945."[42]

Occupation Duty

For years, Eisenhower had been telling people how glad he'd be when "this mess"—meaning the war—was over, but he soon found that victory in Europe could be as frustrating and exhausting as directing armies in battle. For the first couple of months after the German surrender, the amount of paperwork that flowed across his desk turned into a flood, the amount of mail reaching his office hit like a tidal wave and the SHAEF switchboard was overwhelmed with phone calls. Everyone wanted to congratulate him, half the world seemed to want to invite him to something or other, journalists clamored for interviews, politicians wanted to stop by and there were countless millions who simply wanted a glimpse of what he really looked like. Fame was a cage, and as the fame grew, the cage got smaller.[1]

He turned down nearly every invitation, and of those few he accepted, the one that meant most to him was an offer to be made a Freeman of the City of London and speak at the six-hundred-year-old Guildhall. This would be the first speech Eisenhower delivered on a public occasion and he worked conscientiously on getting it right. He wrote it out in longhand on a yellow pad, revising and polishing his text each night before he went to sleep, reading it out to Butcher in the morning. Although he had never given a speech in public, Eisenhower had written them for two secretaries of war, an assistant secretary of war and for Douglas MacArthur. And now he adopted MacArthur's technique of memorizing his speeches—holding only a slip of paper listing key words—when he spoke at the Guildhall on June 12.

Most of the British establishment seemed to be there, save for the royal family, but they were waiting for him at Buckingham Palace. He was listened to in a decorous silence, the Guildhall tradition. In the first part of his speech, Eisenhower spoke of his feeling of humility, calling it "the portion of any man who receives acclaim earned in blood of his followers and sacrifices of his friends." He expressed his heartfelt sympathy for those who had lost a child or a father, readily sharing their anguish. He had never stopped grieving over Ikky, and never would. There wasn't any readier access to Eisenhower's inner life than through his devastating sense of loss.

The main point of his speech, however, was not the cruel suffering of war but the need for the United States and Britain to remain as united in peace as they had been against Hitler. It was something he had spoken passionately about to Churchill and others before the war ended. Here, in the Guildhall, was the chance to talk openly about something that had been on his mind for months.

"To preserve his freedom of worship, his equality before the law, his liberty to speak and act as he sees fit, subject only to provisions that he trespass not on similar rights of others," Eisenhower declared, "a Londoner will fight. So will a citizen of Abilene . . . when two peoples will face the tragedies of war to defend those same spiritual values, the same treasured rights, then in the deepest sense those two are truly related."[2]

After the speech, Churchill took him onto the balcony, to greet the huge, adoring crowd filling the streets around the Guildhall. Grinning, buoyant, he bellowed that he was now a Londoner, too. After which he rode in a horse-drawn carriage through cheers of "Good old Ike!" to Buckingham Palace, where King George VI bestowed on him the Order of Merit, the only British honor that is entirely in the gift of the monarch. All the others are subject to approval by the government. Eisenhower treasured his O.M. above all the numerous foreign honors that came his way in World War II, having developed an affection for this shy and stammering but friendly and unaffected man, forced by duty to become king when his brother, Edward VIII, abdicated in 1936.[3]

Ten days later Eisenhower arrived in Washington, to address Congress and to meet the new President, Harry S Truman. Roosevelt had died shortly before the war with Germany ended and Truman was an unknown quantity. Mamie was at the bottom of the steps waiting for Eisenhower to descend when his airplane landed, and he hurried down to give her the passionate, lingering kiss of the warrior come home that was being demonstrated at airports and docks all over the United States in 1945.[4]

There was nothing memorable about Eisenhower's address to Congress, or his speech at City Hall in New York. There was no grand theme he was eager or ready to promote in his own country. For all the acclaim—and it was phenomenal—he said absolutely nothing that could be considered political. He stuck to bromides and platitudes; nobody did it better.

From New York, he flew to Kansas City. Ida, frail and not entirely lucid, had been brought to meet him. The excitement was too much for the old lady, and when Eisenhower boarded the train for Abilene, Ida took a sudden turn for the worse. Eisenhower spent the whole journey alone at the back of the train, engulfed in anxiety that his return might prove the death of his mother. She survived, though, and he responded warmly to the crowd waiting for him in his hometown. He told the throng, who had flocked into Abilene from all over Kansas, "Through this world it has been my fortune—or misfortune—to wander at considerable distances. Never has this town been out of my heart . . ."[5]

Before he left, Edgar, with whom the old sibling rivalry never really died, asked, "Are you going to make any more history, Dwight?"

"Ed, if I was interested in History, the best thing that could happen would be for my plane to fall into the Atlantic Ocean as I'm going back to Europe. I'm at the top of any reputation I could hope to build."

He and Mamie, along with John, had a week together at White Sulphur Springs, then he returned to Europe. Eisenhower was looking for a way of getting Mamie to join him in Europe, but Marshall vetoed that idea. It wouldn't be fair to the many thousands of servicemen who would be in Europe for a long time to come, he said, men who had done their duty but could not yet go home or bring their families to live with them. Eisenhower was too decent and fair-minded not to agree, much as he missed his wife.[6]

All the same, he had John for company. Two weeks after the war ended, SHAEF had moved to Frankfurt and Eisenhower established himself in a charming house not far away, in Bad Homburg. John was assigned to the SHAEF staff, but was champing at the bit to go fight the war in the Pacific. He had done nothing, he felt, to win the war in Europe and achieved nothing that would make him a better infantry officer. Eisenhower tried to talk him out of it, but John, with the idealism and fervor of youth, wasn't dissuaded. In the meantime, however, they saw each other daily and began to establish a closeness that had long eluded them.[7]

On July 15, Eisenhower met Truman in Antwerp, welcoming him to Europe. The President was on his way to Potsdam, to meet with Churchill and Stalin, and Eisenhower had something for him, a souvenir of the war. He gave Truman the large globe that had occupied a corner of his office, first in London, then in France, a globe that generals had clustered around and discussed strategy over. How Truman had yearned to live that kind of life! As a teenager, he had wanted desperately to go to West Point, become a great soldier, be a famous general, but his eyesight was too poor for him to pass the physical.[8]

Eisenhower had no major role to play in this, the last great summit conference of the war, but he went to Potsdam several times to meet with the President and his advisers. On one of these trips, he was riding in Truman's car, with Bradley, when Truman said, "There is nothing you may want that I won't try to help you get. That definitely and specifically includes the presidency in 1948. I'd be glad to serve as your Vice President."[9]

Truman was still slightly in awe of the office he held, an awe that would soon mellow into something more complex. Eisenhower may have sensed that whatever Truman said now, by 1948 he might well feel differently about standing aside, and it was hardly believable that he would ever hop onto a lower rung. Anyway, politics had never appealed to Eisenhower. "Many people seem astounded that I'd have no slightest interest in politics," he told Mamie. "I can't understand them." And, in truth, he had never expressed an interest in the White House, unlike MacArthur or Pershing. The life didn't appeal.[10]

Eisenhower was hoping the conference would give him a chance to convince the President and his advisers that the deal made at Yalta for the occupation of Germany was a bad one. Roosevelt, Churchill and Stalin had agreed to carve Germany up into American, British and Soviet zones. It was obvious to Eisenhower that such an arrangement would produce friction, yet there was no mechanism for dealing with the sources of that friction. There was only an Allied Control Commission, on which any one member could block the others on most issues. The ACC meant paralysis, not cooperation. Eisenhower argued for a joint occupation, run by a joint headquarters; to no avail.[11]

During the long and often frightening Cold War, there were endless disputes over who was to blame for it, but some kind of struggle was probably unavoidable. As early as 1835, Alexis de Tocqueville concluded the first volume of his masterpiece, *Democracy in America,* with this observation on the inevitability of American-Russian rivalry: "Their starting point is different, and their courses are not the same; yet each of them seems to be marked out by the will of Heaven to sway the destinies of half the globe."

It was Communism that turned that rivalry into a potential war and nuclear weapons that raised the prospect of mutual annihilation. Roosevelt, the first President to recognize the Soviet Union, had been blind to these dangers, having persuaded himself that he could handle Stalin, although to Churchill it seemed it was Stalin who was handling Roosevelt.

Things might have been different had it not been for Stalin, a man chillingly portrayed by his official, post-glasnost biographer, Major General Dmitri Volkogonov, as a sociopath and mass murderer. Stalin's criminality was not a secret, either. For those willing to look at the Soviet Union with an open mind in the 1930s, there was an abundance of evidence already available to draw upon. The problem was that before World War II, most people in the West chose to ignore it or simply refused to believe it. And once Hitler attacked the USSR, an undeserved halo seemed to descend on Stalin, the failed seminarist.[12]

By the time Truman reached Potsdam, however, there was a fresh indication nearly every day that Stalin intended to push the boundaries of the Soviet empire as far as he could. Tito was sending troops into southern Austria and northern Italy in the aftermath of the German surrender. Eisenhower advised Truman that the Yugoslavs were being encouraged by the Russians to violate the Yalta agreement and must be stopped.[13]

At Potsdam, Truman had been eager to get the Soviets into the war against Japan and wanted a commitment from Stalin to do that. Eisenhower told Truman emphatically that he was making a serious mistake. The Soviets had done nothing to defeat the Japanese empire, but Truman was putting them into a position where they could seize Japanese territory and would try to carve out a Soviet zone of occupation in postwar Japan. Truman ignored his advice, and Stalin declared war on Japan days after the conference ended.[14]

Nor should American wealth prop up Soviet power. Eisenhower urged Truman to be "flexible" about ending Lend Lease to Britain and France, but he said not a word about the Soviet Union, whose people were in worse straits than the British or French.[15]

In the months following the end of the war, Truman was unsure just how to meet the Soviet challenge. He began looking to the Joint Chiefs and Eisenhower to provide some hardheaded military advice. He told Eisenhower, "If you and General Marshall advise me to do something, I will do it." Eisenhower told him that was no way to arrive at a policy.[16]

Although he had no compunction about drawing the line at Soviet territorial ambitions, Eisenhower nevertheless hoped the United States would develop a good working relationship with the Soviets, and sought to prove to them that the U.S. was seeking a partnership, not a rivalry. When the Germans surrendered, there were tens of thousands of Allied troops in what would become the Soviet zone. Churchill and senior officers at SHAEF urged him to use this issue to negotiate better postwar arrangements for the Occupation. Eisenhower rejected their advice. He was not going to give the Russians a reason—or an excuse—to be difficult.[17]

The Yalta agreement called for the return of all 2 million Soviet citizens in the American and British zones in Germany. Some were deserters from the Soviet armed forces, others were former slave laborers and some were political refugees from Communism. Almost none wanted to go back to the Soviet Union, but Eisenhower was scrupulous about enforcing the agreement. He did not understand that tens of thousands would perish in the Gulag Archipelago or that thousands more would be shot for no greater crime than criticizing Stalin. And everyone was punished who failed to provide a satisfactory answer to NKVD interrogators demanding to know, "Why are you still alive?"[18]

Although Eisenhower remained wary about the Soviet Union's ambitions as a great power, he was resolutely optimistic about the Russian people. Many Americans who had the chance to meet ordinary Russians during the Cold War felt they possessed a warmth and generosity that was almost American. It was a sentiment profoundly reinforced in the course of his one visit to the USSR, in August 1945.

Eisenhower was flown to Moscow aboard Marshal Georgi Zhukov's airplane. He had seen the ruined cities of Germany but was stunned at the landscape of utter devastation that unfolded as the aircraft flew at low altitude across Poland and the Ukraine. Not a single dwelling stood undamaged for a thousand miles.[19]

The two generals got on well from the outset. Eisenhower saw Zhukov, who had led the Red Army all the way from Stalingrad to Berlin, as a great soldier and patriot, but more than that, he seemed to be an honest man of considerable charm. Eisenhower found his accounts of war on the eastern front enthralling, and he recognized in Zhukov a commander of extraordinary ability. When they attended a soccer game in Moscow and were introduced to the crowd, Eisenhower electrified the packed stadium by putting an arm around Zhukov's shoulders.

He was convinced that Zhukov would succeed Stalin, and by establishing a good personal relationship with him now, Eisenhower reasoned, the United States would reap a reward sometime in the future. Averell Harriman, the U.S. ambassador to Moscow, told him he was wrong. The Communist party had such a dread of "Bonapartism" that its leadership was organized to prevent any soldier from ever getting to the top, said Harriman. Marshall, however, considered Harriman—who had done nothing more demanding than play polo until he reached middle age—to be out of his depth, an intellectual lightweight. Eisenhower may have allowed Marshall's dismissive views of Harriman to cloud his mind to the truth in what the ambassador was saying. Far from having a great future ahead of him, Zhukov spent the rest of his life in fear of being purged, the fate of Soviet generals before him.[20]

After meeting Stalin in the Kremlin, Eisenhower described him as "benign and friendly." Benign Stalin, barely five feet tall, his white hair in a crew cut, smiling in a starched white jacket that made him look like an elderly sommelier, a man whose sigh could mean torture or death, raised a friendly toast, in vodka, to Eisenhower. Friendly Stalin, but "one may smile, and smile, and be a villain."[21]

On August 6, shortly before Eisenhower departed for Moscow, the first atomic bomb obliterated Hiroshima. Three days later, a second bomb wiped out much of Nagasaki. Eisenhower was dismayed. Things had changed dramatically, he told journalist Edgar Snow, an editor at the *Saturday Evening Post,* who was reporting on Ike's trip. "Before the atom bomb was used . . . I was sure we could keep the peace with Russia. Now, I don't know. . . . Everyone feels insecure again." The bomb was sure to trigger a nuclear arms race. The Soviet Union would feel it had to produce atom bombs of its own, while the U.S. would be just as determined to retain its advantage. Ike might have felt even worse had he known that the race had been under way ever since Soviet agents had managed to penetrate the Manhattan Project.[22]

When Eisenhower left Moscow, the war in the Pacific had ended. The Cold War had already begun.

Mark Wayne Clark, commanding the American zone in Austria, wanted to see his old friend again, and he thought he knew just how to do it. Among hunters, one of the great trophies was an Alpine chamois, an elusive and agile creature that few of them ever got into their sights. Austria also possessed some excellent trout streams. When Eisenhower returned to Frankfurt, there was an invitation waiting for him to have an Austrian vacation, shoot a chamois and catch a few trout. Irresistible.

They spent a week together at the end of August. Clark had arranged the chamois hunt with such expert help that Eisenhower had no trouble bagging one. A chamois was almost driven into range of his gun by expert hunters hiding in the woods. "I thought you said this was difficult," he said proudly, and Clark bit his lip. The trout were amazingly cooperative, fairly jumping onto his fishing line; Clark had taken him to the best-stocked trout stream in Austria, maybe in Europe. Eisenhower had a wonderful time, then he took Clark with him to Cannes, to enjoy a few days at a palatial villa rented by the U.S. Army from an American millionaire.[23]

The first morning in Cannes, Eisenhower came down to breakfast and found a large brown envelope on his plate, with TOP SECRET stamped in red. Opening it, he found a letter from the President and a report by the dean of the University of Pennsylvania Law School, Ernest Harrison, on the treatment of displaced persons—or DPs—in Germany. Harrison's report focused on the treatment of Jews, and it was damning. The condition of Jewish refugees in Germany, said Harrison, was inexcusably bad. They were herded into squalid camps, had little or no medical care, received a diet that barely kept them alive; their clothes were rags, their prospects miserable. Meanwhile, the Germans who had persecuted them and murdered their families were living in comfortable homes. How could this possibly be right?[24]

Eisenhower needed no lectures from anyone on the suffering of the Jews. In the last month of the war, American and British troops overran dozens of concentration camps and various death camps such as Bergen-Belsen and Buchenwald. The sights were heart rending; the stench, unendurable. Eisenhower forced himself to go into some of the death camps so that in years to come he would be able to challenge anyone who asserted that such places hadn't existed or that their horrors were being exaggerated. He also urged both the U.S. and British governments to send politicians and journalists to the camps at once, before evidence of their worst horrors was cleaned up.[25]

Harrison's report was, understandably, exceptionally sympathetic to Jewish DPs, and Eisenhower would have had no trouble sharing Harrison's feeling that people who had suffered so much deserved all the help that could be provided. Even so, there was not much he could do that wasn't already being done. What the Jewish DPs wanted was not to have the Germans forced from their homes so they could move into them but to be allowed to emigrate to Palestine, and that was beyond Eisenhower's power.

Nor could he resolve the food crisis. When the war ended, SHAEF found itself trying to care for 5.5 million German POWS, displaced persons and other refugees, instead of the 3 million it had planned for. Even before the war ended, Eisenhower was afraid the food shortage might be so severe that he'd have trouble feeding liberated Allied prisoners of war. Although he solved that problem, the desperate shortage of food meant that Germans in Allied hands received rations well below the levels stipulated by the Geneva Convention. DPs, too, went hungry, and given their poor health, many died as a result.

In 1991 a Canadian novelist, James Bacque, published a book titled *Other Losses* that accused Eisenhower of masterminding a conspiracy to punish captured Germans by starving them to death. According to Bacque, at least 1 million perished. In the mid-1950s, however, the German government made a thorough inquiry into the condition of Germans in Allied hands during and after the war. It concluded that out of the more than 5 million people SHAEF was responsible for, some 56,000 perished. This loss rate, roughly 1 percent, is almost identical to the death rate of Allied prisoners in German hands in World War II, and given the circumstances—the European food shortage, the destruction of the German railroads, the fact that the food-producing areas of Germany were in the Soviet zone—a death rate of 1 percent was an achievement, not an abject failure, still less calculated evil.[26]

There were other headaches, too, not the least of them Patton. The two most important Occupation policies were nonfraternization, which was usually unenforceable, and denazification, which was often farcical. Patton was openly critical of both policies. He believed that if Germany was going to be governed effectively, Germans would have to do it. Besides which, the United States needed to form a partnership with Germany as a barrier to the spread of Soviet Communism into Western Europe.

Exasperated at Patton's attitude, Eisenhower had seen him shortly before going off to hunt chamois and told him emphatically, "I demand you get off your bloody ass and carry out the denazification program as you are told instead of mollycoddling the goddamn Nazis!" In one ear . . .[27]

While Ike was still enjoying his Riviera vacation, Patton visited Garmisch-Partenkirchen, where there was a compound holding five thousand former Nazi officials. He got into a discussion with a German who protested that some of the people in the camp were, in effect, political prisoners. Patton more or less agreed, declaring in a booming voice, "It's sheer madness to intern these people."[28]

Eisenhower cut his vacation short and told Patton to meet him in Munich, where he asked Patton to start thinking about other possible assignments. It was obvious that Patton had to be sent back to the U.S. and put on a shelf somewhere. Patton said he wouldn't mind being head of the Army War College or commanding Army Ground Forces. Ike returned to Frankfurt thinking Patton was going to behave himself while a future assignment was worked out.[29]

Back in July, SHAEF had gone out of existence and Eisenhower was no longer the supreme commander. Instead, he had a new headquarters, U.S. Forces in the European Theater (USFET). He also had a new deputy, his old friend from the Philippines, General Lucius D. Clay. The USFET experts on the camps holding Jewish DPs reported that one of the worst was in Bavaria, and Eisenhower went to look at it for himself. Patton blustered when Eisenhower arrived, blaming the squalid conditions on the inmates themselves, who were "pissing and crapping all over the place," and said he was thinking of building his own concentration camp "for some of these goddamn Jews." Eisenhower told him, "Shut up, George," but Patton was as irrepressibly self-destructive in peacetime as he had been irrepressibly aggressive in war.[30]

At a press conference specifically arranged so that he could squelch the rumors that he was anti-Semitic and pro-Nazi, Patton began by saying, "I despise and abhor Nazis and Hitlerism as much as anyone." He seemed to have found the script, only to lose it. He rambled on about the need to make compromises, before announcing, "The way I see it, this Nazi thing is very much like a Democratic and Republican election fight."[31]

Eisenhower was outraged and sent a cable to Patton: "Fly up here on a good weather day and see me for an hour." Then he wrote a letter to Mamie: "That man is going to drive me to drink." The weather was so bad that Patton had to be driven to Frankfurt through torrential rains. Eisenhower met him with a smile, showed him into his office, then lost his temper. He could be heard clearly in the outer office. Kay Summersby was shocked; she had never known Eisenhower to be so angry or so loud.[32]

This time, Eisenhower relieved Patton of command of the Third Army, ordering him to take over the Fifteenth Army. The Fifteenth consisted of a small staff of drones diligently rounding up documents for the official U.S. Army history of what it had done in the war. Eisenhower said Patton could use his train to go back to Munich, then looked at his watch. "It's leaving in half an hour."[33]

To Eisenhower, firing Patton was but one of the many frustrations of his six months commanding the Occupation. Running a country, even a defeated one, was a task for the State Department, he told Truman, not the Army. The military role in the Occupation should be ended as quickly as possible. Besides which, the directions he had received from the JCS ignored the most important single problem the Occupation faced—revival of the German economy. Until that happened, the Occupation would achieve little.

Most of the time, Clay handled the day-to-day work of running the Occupation, although Clay had not been Ike's first choice for deputy. He would have preferred to see the assignment go to Beetle Smith, to whom it would be a command of sorts after years running a staff. Clay, however, turned out to be a great success in Germany, mainly because he was a much more sophisticated and thoughtful figure than the abrasive, desk-thumping Smith.[34]

George Marshall stepped down as Chief of Staff that fall, and Truman insisted that Ike take Marshall's place. "I just don't want the job," Eisenhower protested. He thought Bradley should have it instead, but Bradley had just been appointed to run the Veterans Administration. Reluctantly, he agreed to do as Truman wanted, on the condition he would be Chief of Staff for only two years, not the usual four. In those two years, he hoped to find a small liberal arts college that might be interested in taking on a retired five-star general who'd made a fair amount of history and would now like to teach some.[35]

Two things would make the Chief of Staff job tolerable. First, he was leaving the Occupation behind. And, second, he and Mamie would be together again. The bond of affection between him and Kay had frayed in the preceding months to vanishing point. That part of his life, like the war that had made it both possible and necessary, was over.

Out of Uniform

"I'm playing an awful trick on you, getting out so fast," Marshall admitted to Eisenhower as he handed over as Chief of Staff. "You're going to have an awful job. Everybody is going to want to get out right away, and you'll want to get them out, but you don't want to denude yourself. It's going to be very hard."[1]

The Army's plan for demobilization was based on surveys of what soldiers thought would be fair. They wanted demobilization as a matter of individual right, based on a points system: a point for every month of service, a point for every month overseas, a point for every campaign star, five points for a Purple Heart and so on. Marshall had organized it that way, and assumed the war with Japan would end sometime in 1946. The Japanese wrecked his plan by surrendering sooner than he'd expected. He had himself complicated matters by saying just before he stepped down as Chief of Staff that soldiers with two years of service would have priority, a statement that threw the points system into confusion.[2]

Eisenhower had hardly been sworn in as Chief of Staff when mass demonstrations erupted among disgruntled soldiers in Germany, Japan, London, Paris and Manila. Army discipline seemed about to collapse. Truman summoned Eisenhower to the White House and asked him what he intended to do about bringing this crisis under control.[3]

He explained to the President that getting men out of the Army wasn't the problem; getting them home was. A lot of shipping had to be sent to the Pacific to carry men home, and that would take time. Meanwhile, expectations had been allowed to rise far too high and had to be brought in touch with reality. The President agreed to cut the administration's stated goal of seven hundred thousand discharges a month to three hundred thousand a month and rescinded Marshall's promise of priority for those who had served two years.[4]

A few days after this meeting at the White House, Eisenhower explained the demobilization dilemma to a gathering of soldiers, congressmen and journalists at the Library of Congress auditorium. Using three huge charts and striding confidently about on a spotlit stage, while the rest of the auditorium was in darkness, he talked for an hour. When he had finished, Admiral Chester Nimitz took the stage and explained the shipping problem.[5]

The next day, Eisenhower testified before a Senate subcommittee, and when some senators began posturing as champions of the ordinary soldier, boldly challenging Army brass on behalf of G.I. Joe, Eisenhower nearly lost his temper. "If there is anyone in this world who has an undying interest in the enlisted men, it is I," he said, teeth gritted, cheeks flaming crimson, reading glasses tightly clenched. "Those fellows are my friends. I have commanded more American soldiers than anyone else in history. You cannot possibly have a greater interest in them than me."[6]

A couple of weeks later, an aide brought him opinion polls that showed a rise in public satisfaction with the speed of demobilization. "You should be happy, sir," said the aide.

"I can be truly happy now only if I can get completely out of official life," Eisenhower irritably replied.[7]

By the end of 1946, the Army that had won the war had been demobilized out of existence. Eisenhower now had to create a new kind of U.S. Army, one that was much smaller but still ready to fight. Although he spoke repeatedly about his hopes for peace and genuinely believed that the United Nations had the potential to prevent wars, Eisenhower was still a soldier, still bore the burden of the fighting man's pessimistic creed down the ages: "Only the dead have seen the last of war." Congress, however, was in no mood to continue the draft in peacetime to replace the wartime army. The White House, supported by many Republicans, favored Universal Military Training (UMT), which would take every male when he reached eighteen and give him up to a year in the military.

Because Truman was in favor of it, Eisenhower at first supported UMT, but as the Cold War took hold, he lost what faith he possessed in a lot of teenagers reluctantly playing at being soldiers. What he really wanted was an all-volunteer Army of professional soldiers, enlisted for a minimum of three years, but getting a volunteer force that was big enough for American's security needs now that it had global responsibilities might prove impossible.[8]

He was a lot more enthusiastic about another Truman policy, unification of the armed forces, something that he believed in as fervently as anyone in uniform. During 1945, he had told various people that he would gladly put everyone in the military into the same uniform once the war ended. His old friend—and Annapolis graduate—Swede Hazlett heard about it and wrote to accuse Eisenhower of harboring an infantryman's bias and plotting to get rid of the Marine Corps in the name of service unification.

Eisenhower wrote back: "You must remember that for the past three and a half years I have *not* been an infantryman! I have not even been a ground commander. . . . My viewpoint has been as much naval and air as it has been ground."[9]

It was obvious as could be to him that the war had taught one overriding lesson: Victory required a single commander with absolute authority to harness the power of ground, air and naval forces in a way that brought the strengths of each to maximum effectiveness. No duplication of effort, no untapped resources, no interservice squabbling and sulking. The supreme-commander system, having proven itself in both Europe and the Pacific, was his paradigm for postwar military reorganization.

The Navy, however, was too strongly entrenched and the Marine Corps had too much public support for Truman and Eisenhower to overcome. They had to settle instead for a Department of Defense under a secretary of defense who had little genuine control over the Joint Chiefs of Staff, a body whose members negotiated among themselves over roles and missions. The U.S. Air Force, which was separated from the Army in 1947, seemed in the ascendant, the Army in the shadows and the Navy in high dudgeon. Eisenhower's hopes for a truly unified military came to nothing. But he made an investment for the future by establishing the Armed Forces Staff College, where officers from all the services could learn to speak the same language and together discover the future of the military, the world of combined and joint.[10]

Mamie had Ike home at last, yet they had to get to know each other all over again. She had heard plenty of rumors about Kay and was brusque with the WACs on Eisenhower's staff who had been Kay's wartime friends and companions. The real problem, though, wasn't the long shadow of Kay Summersby; it was that Ike and Mamie had learned to manage without each other. He was also used to being looked after by a large staff. Eisenhower got more personal attention and devoted service from highly capable people—aides, pilots, drivers, secretaries— than mere money could ever purchase. The people on his staff had generated the kind of warmth around him that nearly every family strives for and many fail to achieve. He had also become used to having his word taken almost as law, his wishes treated as commands, his whims and foibles excused or ignored. To him, all of this seemed natural by now and Mamie was expected to accept it.

Not surprisingly, then, for a year or so there was an emotional distance between them—no hostility, but a lack of warmth and closeness. It was the kind of wound nearly every long relationship endures at some point, but it mended, as most do, because irritating habits apart, each accepted the other as a lifelong commitment. Even at the roughest times in their marriage, Ike and Mamie shared the same bed.[11]

They moved into Quarters No. 1 at Fort Myer, a large house with a breathtaking view, over the Potomac, of Washington and its gleaming monuments. The house was, if anything, too big, too grand, with huge, high-ceilinged rooms for formal entertaining. Ike and Mamie lived mainly on the second floor. Instead of eating in their imposing dining room, they ate in the breakfast nook next to it. There was a small library, and they took tea there. Other than that, they treated virtually the entire downstairs part of the house as a public space. Outside, Eisenhower dug up part of the garden and created a vegetable patch, where he got dirt under his fingernails and kept true to those Abilene roots.[12]

In September 1946, Ida died, at the age of eighty-four. At David's death in 1942, the Jehovah's Witnesses had taken over the arrangements, to the intense anger of Dwight and Milton, who felt they had really hijacked the occasion to generate publicity for their faith. During the war, there were newspaper stories from time to time that claimed the Supreme Allied Commander was—the irony of it!—the son of Jehovah's Witnesses. These stories infuriated Eisenhower, to whom they were an attempt to undermine the prosecution of the most righteous war in history. He made sure there was no repetition of what had happened with David. Ida's funeral service was held in the family home on South East Fourth Street, conducted by an Army chaplain from Fort Riley. All six brothers were there, as was Mamie.[13]

For several years, he and Swede Hazlett had exchanged letters on how marvelous it would be if they could only get John interested in Swede's fair-haired daughter. Nothing came of their hopes. Instead, John fell in love with an Army brat, Barbara Jean Thompson, a pretty and highly intelligent brunette. The daughter of an Army colonel, Barbara had seen a lot of the world and knew the ways of the Army. Both Eisenhower and Mamie were delighted when John married Barbara at Fort Myer in June 1947 and, if anything, felt even happier when, nine months later, Barbara gave birth to a son, Dwight David Eisenhower II.

Inevitably, as Chief of Staff, Eisenhower heard from any number of old friends who wanted him to get them promoted or assigned to important positions. Most of the time he turned them down, but now and then he helped out. Mark Clark wanted command of the Sixth Army, at Fort Ord, and got it. Eisenhower helped his old friend George Horkan become chief of ordnance, and when another friend, Tom Handy, wanted command of an Army group before he retired, Eisenhower made sure he was assigned one.

Eisenhower was nevertheless scrupulous about not being involved in his son's assignments. He did nothing on John's behalf—the ideal arrangement for them both. But when John talked about possibly resigning his commission, Eisenhower told him to think again. How could they justify the Chief of Staff's son quitting the Army? "You and I together would have a difficult time explaining your resignation." John stayed put, just like Ike.[14]

Truman always had problems with MacArthur. Even before he became President, Truman had found MacArthur's larger-than-life style irritating, but what was infuriating was the lordly disdain. Shortly after the

war ended, Truman asked MacArthur to come home, receive the acco-
lades of a grateful nation and address Congress. Much the same invitation had gone to Eisenhower, and Eisenhower had promptly complied.
A request from the Commander in Chief is really an order. Eisenhower
was running the Occupation of Germany at the time, but trusted his
staff to manage without him. MacArthur, however, had informed
Truman that he couldn't leave Japan just now. The Occupation there
might fall into disarray, he suggested, without his steady hand on the
controls.[15]

At this point Truman ought to have told MacArthur he *was* coming home, and wished him a happy retirement. That was what Roosevelt would almost certainly have done, and Truman's failure to call
MacArthur's bluff inevitably convinced MacArthur that the new President was weak and indecisive.

Eisenhower, meanwhile, retained a certain respect for MacArthur.
Much of his own approach to command bore the MacArthur stamp, and
his self-confidence had doubtless been richly nourished by the fact that
he had not remained at MacArthur's court but had broken free, rising to
outrank the courtiers who had preferred to live in another man's shadow
and fight among themselves for the best positions around the throne. As
Chief of Staff at a time when the Army was shrinking every day and
seemed in danger at time of losing its fighting spirit, Eisenhower appreciated as never before the magnificence of MacArthur's fight to save
the Army in the early 1930s.

Ostensibly, he was now MacArthur's boss, and it was nearly always
an uncomfortable arrangement for both parties when a former subordinate rose to command a man who had once commanded him. Yet it is
likely that Eisenhower never really thought of himself as MacArthur's
superior, and it is a near certainty that MacArthur never believed he had
to answer to Eisenhower.

As Eisenhower had expected, much of his time was spent in quasi-
political tasks, mainly wrangling with Congress. And some of it was
quasi-diplomatic, something inevitable in an unstable postwar world
where the United States had interests everywhere and military alliances
nowhere. He made numerous trips abroad, including one to China in
May 1946, where Chiang Kai-shek's corrupt Kuomintang government
was losing the long civil war to the Chinese Communist armies commanded by Mao Tse-tung. Truman had prevailed on George Marshall's

bottomless sense of duty to pressure Marshall into trying to mediate between the opposing sides. The Kuomintang needed a miracle and Truman thought Marshall, with his enormous prestige, might provide one.
In China, however, Marshall was virtually unknown and his prestige
counted for nothing with Mao and not much more with Chiang.[16]

Before he left for the Far East, Eisenhower was summoned to meet
with Truman aboard the presidential yacht, tied up at Quantico, Virginia. The secretary of state, James Byrnes, was planning to retire in a
few months, said Truman. Would Eisenhower ask General Marshall if
he'd be willing to take Byrnes's place? When Eisenhower met with Marshall in Chungking, he put Truman's question to him. The reply was a
weary yes. Like Eisenhower, all that Marshall really wanted these days
was to be allowed to retire.[17]

After leaving China, Eisenhower stopped off in Japan for two days
to see MacArthur. Most visitors got a lunch with the general and Jean
MacArthur, but Eisenhower was worthy of the supreme accolade—an
official dinner in MacArthur's residence at the American embassy, an
Art Deco treasure from the 1920s that the diplomats would not be getting the use of anytime soon. The food at the dinner was mediocre and
there was nothing alcoholic to drink, which dampened the conviviality
somewhat. But MacArthur had planned it that way, because he wanted
to get dinner over with quickly. As soon as it was possible to do so without being flagrantly discourteous to his guests, MacArthur dismissed
them and took Eisenhower to the embassy library.[18]

They reminisced for a while—mutual friends, old times, the War
Department under Hoover, making Roosevelt's Civilian Conservation
Corps a success, the turbulent times they had shared in the Philippines.
MacArthur said there was a rumor going around in Japan that the Navy
had gotten the President to agree to extra ruffles and bugle calls for
five-star admirals that were not going to be extended to five-star generals. Eisenhower wasn't much interested in military honors, and said
as much.

"That's all right, Ike," responded MacArthur. "Just so long as those
Navy sons of bitches don't get ahead of us, I don't care either!"

Finally, they got around to what was really on their minds. Eisenhower said, "General, you will surely be a candidate for the 1948 Republican party nomination."

MacArthur responded that it was obvious one of them was going to become President, the only question was which one, and he thought it would be Eisenhower. "I'm too old," said MacArthur. Besides, he could not walk away from a job as important as the Occupation of Japan.[19]

They debated the subject until one A.M. Eisenhower, growing weary of it, said he agreed with General Marshall, who had always preached a complete separation between the military and politics. Anyway, he added, "My country has given me everything I could possibly hope for or deserve. So I have no intention of running for the presidency."

The two men were seated in a pair of large chairs, and MacArthur suddenly leaned forward. He patted Eisenhower on the knee. "That's right, Ike. You go on like that and you'll get it for sure!"

When he told this story after he returned to the U.S., Eisenhower was still so angry his face went purple from rage.[20]

Eisenhower played only a small part in cementing the foundations of the Cold War. He did not see the Soviet Union as an inevitable enemy and was infuriated by people who talked about the probability of a U.S.–Soviet conflict. Nevertheless, as Stalin tested the limits of Western resolve, there were rumors from time to time of an impending Soviet attack. The first war scare came in April 1946 and Truman called the JCS and the secretary of state, Jimmy Byrnes, to meet with him at the White House. Byrnes confessed to being worried, but Eisenhower responded dismissively, "I don't believe the Reds want a war. What can they gain now by armed conflict? They've gained about all they can assimilate." Besides, they lacked even the logistical resources needed to defeat the U.S. forces based in Germany. The conclusion he drew from the current scare was that the U.S. needed better military intelligence. "It's very important that we be able to see behind the Iron Curtain, to detect activity preparatory to war," he told Truman and Byrnes. "We should concentrate on the first 100 miles behind the Russian line in Germany to see if they are piling up any supply dumps."[21]

Peace was offering Truman a world that seemed full, ironically, of danger. The United Nations was new and untried and had no military force of its own to impose its will on recalcitrant states. At the same time, there was a new world power, the Soviet Union, which boasted a huge and victorious army, proclaimed a revolutionary Communist creed and derided the "bourgeois morality" that people in the West called human rights and civil liberties.

At first, Truman wasn't sure how to respond, but only weeks after the April 1946 White House meeting, the head of the State Department's Policy Planning Staff, George Kennan, sent a sixteen-page telegram from Moscow that provided both an analysis and a prescription. Kennan saw Soviet power as a ruthless growth, inspired at least as much by fear as by ambition, with deep roots in the blood-drenched Russian past. The USSR's claims to political legitimacy were so fragile that over time, it was far more likely to fall apart than flourish. Given that prognostication, the right policy for the United States, said Kennan, was "containment," by which he meant that the political challenges the Soviet Union posed must be met with political responses, not military force. By containing the political power of the Soviets, the West, under American leadership, might outlast this inherently corrupt and brutal system and see it mellow over time into a modern state.[22]

Although the United States was rapidly demobilizing the Army at roughly the same time as Kennan was puzzling out how to deal with the Soviet Union, the Strategic Air Command had been activated. Its most likely target was the Soviet Union. SAC's commander, General George Kenney, estimated it would take two hundred atomic bombs to destroy the Soviet Union, yet the United States possessed no more than twenty atomic bombs in 1946 and only thirty in 1947. For some years, SAC was as much about atomic bluffing as atomic bombing, but even if the U.S. could not destroy the Soviet Union, it could inflict awesome retribution should Stalin miscalculate. From the outset, nuclear weapons gave containment a credibility that conventional arms alone could never have conferred.[23]

Containment provided the intellectual framework for American foreign policy throughout the Cold War. Yet because of SAC, this was not containment as Kennan had intended it. Far from limiting it to political responses to political threats, Truman made containment both political and military. Its machinery was a network of military alliances; its strongest card was American superiority in nuclear weapons.[24]

To help explain containment to a worried and at times bewildered public, which had assumed that the end of the war would usher in a long period of international tranquility, Kennan's cable was expanded slightly and published in July 1947 in *Foreign Affairs*. Abbreviated versions were later published in *Life* and *Reader's Digest*. Although there is no evidence that Eisenhower ever read Kennan's original telegram, it is hardly possible that he wasn't aware of it in some form. At a minimum, he would have been briefed on it by the State Department. He preferred briefings to documents; they took less time and a good briefer could provide context that a document was likely to skip.

Meanwhile, the British government had informed the U.S. that it could no longer afford to finance the Greek government's war against Communist insurgents. Stalin's followers were winning in their war against a Greek monarchy that had been imposed on Greece nearly a century earlier by the British. The monarchy had never managed to win the support of most Greeks. Even so, a Communist Greece would soon find itself at war with the fiercely anti-Communist Turks, destabilize the Balkans and create turmoil in the Middle East.

The White House and the State Department hurriedly worked out a statement of policy that would put limits on Communist expansion by force of arms. What Truman needed, and quickly, was to get an appropriation that would fill the void left by the termination of British financial support. The statement was so hurriedly pasted together and had such an attentive eye on the present that it even contained a deeply felt reference to the postwar poultry shortage. Presenting it to Congress, Truman declared that the United States would assist those countries that confronted Communist insurgents. The Truman Doctrine was the first public expression of the adoption of a containment strategy, and showed that it was not limited to containing political threats only: military actions would bring a military response. The United States sent military advisers to Greece and provided the Greek military with modern arms.

Eisenhower shared the public's growing dismay at the onset of the Cold War and the dark shadow of nuclear weapons. For a brief moment, it seemed that the shadow might lift. Shortly after Ike became Chief of Staff, his old friend Bernard Baruch was named to head a commission that would consider the future of both the atomic bomb and the development of atomic energy. The two were inextricably linked. The Baruch Plan, as it became known, proposed to put the atomic bomb under the control of the UN . . . eventually. For now, though, the U.S. would retain its monopoly while an inspection agreement was worked out with the Soviets. That was the deal. Stalin, not surprisingly, thought the American proposal was an attempt to stop development of the Soviet atomic bomb while overrunning the Soviet Union with American spies. To which there was a simple answer: *Nyet.*

The atomic bomb could no more be wished away than could the machine gun or the fighter-bomber. Eisenhower would gladly have seen nuclear weapons abolished, he assured Secretary of Defense James Forrestal, but the U.S. could agree to it only if there was an enforceable inspection regime. Any agreement short of that would put the country in serious danger. For now, he informed Baruch, "The existence of the atomic bomb in our hands is a deterrent to aggression in the world."[25]

Although Eisenhower wished the atomic bomb had never been invented and called it "this hellish contrivance," that was a personal and private reaction. Ike the soldier never allowed his repugnance for nuclear arms to deflect his attention from America's security needs. Amid the cooling ashes of the Third Reich, SHAEF had rounded up German rocket scientists, most notably Wernher von Braun, shipped them to the United States and put them on the Army payroll. Eisenhower had seen V-1's and V-2's pass over his head. He could read the writing in the sky.

Almost his first action as Chief of Staff was to sign a memorandum titled "Overall Effect of Atomic Bomb on Warfare and Military Organization." In it, he called for "rapid progress in the realm of rocket projectiles and missiles . . ." This was Eisenhower's view of the future—an America guarded by missiles carrying atomic warheads over huge distances. He foresaw the blunt instrument of containment before Kennan even wrote a line about containment.[26]

Harry Butcher was a journalist, so he should have been expected to act like one. To him, the war and his experiences at Eisenhower's headquarters were raw material, and he couldn't wait to turn them into a book. Eisenhower may seem in retrospect to have been astonishingly naive to trust Butcher as much as he did, but he had needed someone to chew the fat with, share jokes with, bring him gossip, listen to his opinions on people he liked, such as Churchill, and those he despised, such as Monty; someone to bounce ideas off, grumble to, express his doubts and worries to, remind him of home, reminisce about the good times before the war and play the role of fugleman pointing in a breezy, careless way to a future that would bring happiness and peace. So he had told Butch just about everything, and Butch had diligently written it all down in a diary that drew no clear distinction between what was official and what was personal.

Early in 1946, the Adjutant General informed Eisenhower that Butcher was writing a book. Eisenhower was appalled, but he brushed aside the AG's hints that maybe the Army ought to intervene. The diary that Butcher was using was not his property, but when Eisenhower decided not to do anything about it, he had no idea just how frank Butcher intended to be.[27]

The *Saturday Evening Post* ran excerpts, and Eisenhower was shocked. He managed to get some minor changes made before the book was published, and in fairness, it must be said that Butcher was scrupulous about deleting references to Ultra, to Ike's old friend Wayne Clark and to anything that was politically sensitive. Even so, the work was an eye-opener and it earned Butcher the small fortune he was hoping for. *My Three Years with Eisenhower* was one of the best-selling books of 1946.

It proved the death knell to Ike's friendship with Butcher, a relationship that had suffered serious damage even before the war ended, when Butcher spoke too frankly to a reporter about Eisenhower and Montgomery. Although Butcher was free to shrug off a dead friendship, Eisenhower was left to deal with the consequences of this betrayal. The worst offense Butcher committed was to hold Churchill up to ridicule and make Montgomery seem stupid.

It was as obvious to Eisenhower as a huge royalty check was to Butcher that the best guarantee of peace in the postwar world was a continuation of the Anglo-American partnership. By Eisenhower's standards, Butcher had done nothing to make the world a safer place. While Churchill was presently out of power, he was likely to come back (and did) and Montgomery had succeeded Brooke as Chief of the Imperial General Staff. Eisenhower sent placatory letters to Monty, assuring him that *My Three Years* did not present what he had actually said and did not portray his true sentiments. Monty, however, almost certainly knew better.[28]

There was another diarist Eisenhower had to worry about—Kay. She was, with Butcher, one of the two people he had completely trusted. His parting from Kay had been abrupt and had lacked warmth, although there was no acrimony, no scene. Shortly before leaving Germany, he had made an official request for a copy of the office diary she had kept during the war.

Kay herself typed it up from her notes, and when he received it, in January 1946, he sent a letter of thanks—"It will be the most tremendous help to me if ever I need to refresh my memory concerning those years when we were serving together"—and wrote an excellent reference for her, which went to Lucius Clay. But the diary that Kay had kept made worrying reading—more criticisms of Montgomery, disparaging remarks about the French, damning observations of high-ranking Army officers such as Jacob Devers . . . people he still had to deal with. Eisenhower was more than willing to help Kay stay in the Women's Army Corps and make the military her career. Better that than a book.[29]

Clay played his part, promoting her to captain, but to retain her commission, Kay would have to become an American citizen. She traveled to the U.S. in the spring of 1946 to file her application for citizenship, and in 1947, when the Air Force became a completely independent service, she transferred to it. The future of the Air Force in 1947 looked bright, and the Army's didn't.

None of which deterred her from writing a book, published in 1948 as *Eisenhower Was My Boss.* It was readable and filled with fascinating details about life at his headquarters during the war. Her memory was excellent, which put all Eisenhower biographers in her debt. As an intelligent, perceptive woman, she noticed telltale details that almost any man would have forgotten or ignored. There were only a couple of vague hints of an emotional relationship, but they were so indirect that other people who had served on the staff, including her WAC friends, didn't notice them. Even so, she made clear her distaste for Montgomery and there were strong hints that Eisenhower had felt much the same way. Kay's book earned her enough money to buy a small apartment on New York's Upper East Side. It also confirmed Eisenhower's belief toward the end of the war that Kay was an opportunist.[30]

It wasn't only his old friends who were rushing into print. Ralph Ingersoll, a well-known publisher and war correspondent, had published *Top Secret,* an account of SHAEF's operations from D-Day to VE-Day. According to Ingersoll, Eisenhower's weak leadership and faulty strategic ideas had prolonged the Second World War. Eisenhower was incensed by Ingersoll's book, telling old friends it was "a worthless book," but as Chief of Staff there was nothing he could do to rebut it directly.[31]

Bradford G. Chynoweth had an interesting war—too interesting. He and Eisenhower had served together in Panama in the early 1920s and again in the War Department in the early 1930s. Chynoweth was an able officer, almost an inevitable general, and in the fall of 1941 he got a star and a division, but it was a division in the Philippine Army. His men had no shoes or boots, were so short of weapons that he provided them with spears and bows and arrows, and when the Japanese invaded, they ambushed the enemy in the jungles of Visayan. Ordered to surrender in May 1942, Chynoweth had survived Japanese prison camps and emerged an excessively skinny brigadier general in 1945, eager to leave the Army and begin a second career as an educational reformer. He intended to lobby for the creation of a federal department of education. To help speed his exit from the Army, he wrote to his old friend Ike and told him why he was in such a hurry to get out. Eisenhower wrote back, "My immediate reaction is one of unalloyed envy."[32]

His old friend was going to pursue the kind of second career he wanted for himself. But not one college seemed interested in him, while Chynoweth had no trouble getting himself accepted at the University of California at Berkeley as an educational planner and reformer! Having one star was better than having five, because all anyone seemed interested in offering Eisenhower as a second career was the presidency.

The pressure didn't come only from the politicians. In the summer of 1946 he had attended the meeting of the Air Force Association in Dayton, Ohio. The principal speaker was a justice of the Supreme Court, Robert Jackson, currently representing the United States at the Nuremberg trials. No one seemed to take any interest in Jackson or what he had to say about Nazi war criminals. The huge room where the meeting took place was packed to the doors and people put ladders up to the windows just to get a glimpse of Eisenhower. The country's most famous aviatrix, Jacqueline Cochran, was introduced to him, and she was so astonished at the baying, gawping adulation that she blurted out, "Why don't you run for President?"

"Oh, no, no, no!"[33]

By the summer of 1947, Truman faced the depressing prospect of losing the 1948 election. The Republicans were in the ascendant and they dominated the Eightieth Congress, which was strongly right-wing and anti–New Deal. The prospect of handing the White House over to them made him squirm. So he renewed the offer he had made at Potsdam—Eisenhower for President; Truman for Vice-President. Eisenhower once again turned him down.[34]

At about the same time, the president of IBM, Tom Watson, offered him the presidency of Columbia University. It was an offer Watson had made a year earlier, but Eisenhower hadn't been interested then. As he told an old friend who was moving to York, Pennsylvania, "The prospect of work in New York is not half as pleasing as in York."[35]

He had never liked living in big cities. But after two years as Chief of Staff he was almost desperate to get out, and no small college had expressed the slightest interest in his services. His choices, then, were running Columbia, running for office or running a vegetable patch somewhere in retirement.

Eisenhower had no desire whatever to run for the White House. What he did have—and what people such as Truman hoped to exploit— was a strong sense of public duty, and with the Cold War becoming America's first order of business, he could hardly have refused an elevation to the White House if the people genuinely wanted a general for their President. That was what had happened with Washington. But running for office was beneath him. Party politics was too cynical and trawling for votes was too grubby to be endured. And at fifty-seven, he was too young for retirement. He accepted the job at Columbia.

That ought to have settled the matter, but it didn't. A group of Republicans ran in the January 1948 New Hampshire primary as Eisenhower delegates. They didn't have to ask his permission, and didn't. The most influential newspaper in the state, the Manchester *Union Leader,* endorsed him. The snowball had started down the mountainside.

Before it could turn into an avalanche, Eisenhower composed a letter to Leonard Finder, the publisher of the *Union Leader.* "It is my conviction that the necessary and wise subordination of the military to civil power will be best sustained . . . when lifelong professional soldiers, in the absence of some obvious and overriding reason, abstain from seeking political office. . . . My decision is definite and positive."[36]

No sooner had he sent it than he began agonizing. Maybe he'd given out the wrong signal. "There are a lot of youngsters who've more or less made me the symbol of both the obligations and the opportunities open to American youth," he told James Forrestal. "Have I just told them there's a limit to any man's conception of the obligation to the call of duty?" One thing he and Forrestal were sure of—this letter was going to take him out of the race.[37]

A month later, Bradley was sworn in as acting Chief of Staff, to Eisenhower's immense relief. Before taking up his duties at Columbia, however, he would write a book.

The President

Liberation day turned out to be February 7, 1948, when Truman came over to the Pentagon and swore in Bradley as acting Chief of Staff. He pinned Eisenhower's third Distinguished Service Medal on the famous Ike jacket, shook his hand, wished him luck, started to leave and suddenly remembered something. The President pulled out a silver cigarette case and handed it to Eisenhower—a gift to mark the end of more than thirty years of active duty. Truman's gesture ended this brief ceremony on a charmingly personal note.[1]

Within a day or two, Eisenhower realized something. Here he was, embarking on a civilian existence, and he didn't even own a decent suit or sports jacket. The only mufti he owned consisted of slacks and shirts for golf, with a few pairs of spiked shoes and a couple of caps to keep the sun out of his eyes. The first thing Eisenhower had to do as a civilian was get some suits made to match his new status.[2]

He also had a book to write, and not much time to do it. Even before the war ended, he got offers from publishers urging him to write his memoirs and make some money. He hadn't been seriously tempted until after he became Chief of Staff, when he talked to Richard Simon, of Simon & Schuster, and agreed to write about a couple of incidents, to see if he was capable of writing a book. Having read them, Simon naturally said Ike's efforts were marvelous, but by then he was swamped with Chief of Staff duties.

In the fall of 1947, with the great escape lined up, the chance to write a book finally appeared. He was already friendly with William Robinson, executive vice-president of the *New York Herald Tribune,* and Robinson urged him to start writing. The *Herald Tribune* was interested in the serial rights and would help find a book publisher, he said. The newspaper would put up $135,000 for the rights and Eisenhower should hold out for at least $500,000 from the book publisher. Eisenhower was flabbergasted—$635,000 for his memoirs? "I'm just a Kansas farm boy," he said, like a man in a daze. "These numbers are making my head spin!"[3]

But it wasn't the money that convinced him. He had been offered huge amounts to leave the Army and go on to the boards of major corporations and invariably said no. Right now, though, he was emotionally ready, and Robinson made the perfect pitch: Look at all the books being churned out these days, people rushing into print while interest in World War II is still hot, but almost none of them knows what really happened. These are books chasing a buck, or books by people with axes to grind, books that are stuffed with lies and errors, and unless they are challenged, this guff is going to be accepted as History, and once ideas take root, even wrong ideas, it is awfully hard to change them. A book by Eisenhower would be a service to truth, to America, to the people who had served in the war. Eisenhower agreed to write a war memoir.[4]

The money involved, though, frightened even major publishers. Simon & Schuster backed away. So did Harper & Row. Then Robinson phoned Douglas Black, the president of Doubleday. He was knocking now on the right door, because Black had met Eisenhower in February 1946, when Ike had received an honorary degree at Columbia and Black, as one of the trustees, had been introduced to him. He liked and admired Eisenhower enormously. Even so, Black had to think hard about putting up half a million dollars, but soon came around to it after meeting with Eisenhower at the Pentagon at the end of December 1947.

Eisenhower's attorney, John Davies, a highly respected and highly paid ornament of the Washington bar, proceeded to give him some of the most expensive advice he would ever get: Sell the book outright, Davies told him; treat it like a piece of property. As someone who had never received any income from writing and who had no intention of pursuing a literary career, Eisenhower could do that, because other people already had. By paying capital gains tax on $635,000, he would net $476,250. Eisenhower took Davies's advice, unable to imagine his book ever selling in the huge quantities needed to make it worth paying income tax instead.

He scrupulously did not write a word of his book before he handed over to Bradley, but in the evenings he reread two fat volumes titled *Memoirs of Lieutenant General Ulysses S. Grant.* They would be his model—vigorous, direct and simple, but not in the way that a primer is simple; rather, in a way that demonstrates that simplicity is ever the heart of elegance and the hallmark of sincerity.

On February 8, 1948, he set to work, having organized and planned his attack well in advance. Six officers and former officers who had served with him during the war beavered away as fact checkers and document hunters. The editor-in-chief of Doubleday, Kenneth McCormick, and Joe Barnes, foreign editor of the *Herald Tribune,* provided editorial guidance and support. One of the fastest and most accurate stenographers in the United States, the playwright Douglas Wallop, was hired to take down Eisenhower's dictation.[5]

Eisenhower rose at six, breakfasted with his staff at six-thirty and over coffee and eggs discussed progress so far and problems ahead, then at seven A.M. he began dictating, pacing restlessly while Wallop scribbled through a stack of steno pads. Apart from a short coffee break at midmorning, it went on for five hours. After lunch, he read the transcripts from the previous day's dictation session, covering nearly every page with comments, questions and criticisms that the six aides and assistants would deal with.

He readily took advice, including John's. Eisenhower had started with MacArthur and the Philippines. John told him to start with the Germans surrendering to him in Reims. A much better idea.[6]

By the middle of April, the book was almost finished. Eisenhower had, like Grant, stuck to things he was personally involved in and knew something about. He did not try to refight the whole war or comment on aspects of it that did not involve him. When he finished, he headed south, to enjoy a two-week vacation with Mamie at Augusta National Golf Course, where some of his newfound millionaire friends liked to relax. Its strange, fiercely willed perfection charmed and seduced him. Augusta National became more than a place to play golf. It wedged its way into Ike's life.

When *Crusade in Europe* was published later that year, it was an enormous success, both critically and financially, and its status as a contribution to history was enormous, much like Grant's memoirs. But one person wasn't impressed: Monty. He ridiculed it, saying Eisenhower's book "will not be read fifty years from now," but he proved to be a poor prophet. Although Monty's own memoirs were out of print by then, Eisenhower's *Crusade* was still selling steadily in 1998.[7]

Shortly before Christmas 1948, Eisenhower sent Truman a copy of *Crusade in Europe,* with a note that read, "This is the first volume that I have presented to anyone, except for those preserved for my immediate family." Truman, thrilled to get it, sent it right back. Would the general favor him with an autograph in the book? Eisenhower received hundreds of requests for his autograph every week. Even the President wanted one.[8]

With roughly 1.5 million books sold over those fifty years, *Crusade* would have netted Eisenhower, and his family, at least twice what he received for it had he rejected Davies's advice. For now, though, Eisenhower was launched into a new life with more money in the bank than he had ever dreamed of possessing.

Tom Watson was a kindly old gent who thought big, but was as unassuming and modest in manner as Eisenhower. Paternalistic and generous, he was famous for making IBM seem more like a family than a cutting-edge business. And although his company was without a serious rival in the world, he had one unfulfilled ambition—to get Eisenhower into the White House. That was why he persisted in offering the Columbia job to him even after Ike turned it down. And Eisenhower still loved the idea of becoming a college president. That was what one of his heroes, Robert E. Lee, had done when his military career ended. Eisenhower had a picture of Lee on display in nearly every office he ever occupied. He may have known Marse Robert's features even better than his own.[9]

The presidency of Podunk State—which was all Eisenhower had in mind—might remove him from the public eye, but that would have suited him down to the ground. The presidency of a major university in New York, on the other hand, would make Ike a big fish in a large and well-illuminated pond, and that was what suited Tom Watson. So he tried again, telling Ike what he'd already told him—that he had a lot to contribute to education, that his presence on campus would be an in-spiration to young people, that this was another form of public service, and Eisenhower, fed up with being Chief of Staff, finally relented.[10]

He laid down certain conditions, though: no fund-raising, no in-volvement in hiring and firing professors, no responsibility for the cur-riculum. What was more, said Eisenhower, "The trustees have to understand that I must convince myself, within a year, that I can be of real service. I must also have more recreation time than my average of the past twenty-five years. If either of these two conditions isn't met, I'll quit." Tom Watson said Ike's conditions were agreeable.[11]

Eisenhower took up his duties officially on July 1 and discovered that Columbia's situation resembled that of many a Kansas farmer: land-rich, cash-poor. Almost desperately so. Unlike Harvard, Yale and Princeton, it did not have a large endowment to finance improvements or better salaries. Despite what Watson had told him, the rest of the trustees had assumed all along that he was going to raise money, lots of it. They couldn't see any other reason for hiring him. Eisenhower's so-lution was to employ a full-time fund-raiser, Paul Davis, give him an en-ergetic staff and support him strongly. Davis raised tens of millions from Eisenhower's large and rapidly growing circle of millionaire friends and acquaintances, but the faculty disliked Davis intensely. In-stead of being grateful for the turnaround in the university's finances—and their own improved salaries—they criticized Eisenhower for appointing him.[12]

On October 12, 1948, he was officially installed as president of the university in an elaborate ceremony that attracted the presidents of more than two hundred colleges and universities, many of New York's political and social elite and members of his family. Milton, the presi-dent of Kansas State, adjusted the tassel on Ike's mortarboard before the ceremony began, and Ed wryly remarked, "Father would have liked this even better than seeing you as a general. He had more regard for college presidents."[13]

Walking each day from his residence at 60 Morningside Drive to his office in Low Library, Eisenhower soon became a familiar figure to Co-lumbia students, and he seemed to get off to a good start. Shortly after he arrived on campus, a group of students stopped him and one of them said, "We would like to raffle off something that's a part of you. Could we have one of your uniforms?"

"That's against regulations," said Eisenhower. "But I'll tell you what I'll do—I'll give you some of my underwear. Will that do?" He let them have an old T-shirt and a pair of shorts, a gesture that did a lot to dispel any idea they might have had that the new prez was as self-important as his predecessor, Nicholas Murray Butler, an educational innovator when young, a bloated ego when old.[14]

Shortly after this, Eisenhower gave a speech at the Waldorf-Astoria in which he decried the materialism that he claimed was undermining American values. "Maybe we like caviar and champagne when we ought to be working on beer and hot dogs." The next day the student newspaper, *The Columbia Daily Spectator,* editorialized: "We are willing to bet beer and hot dogs weren't on the menu at the Waldorf-Astoria last night." Eisenhower was so infuriated at being called a hypocrite that he threatened to boycott the forthcoming graduation ceremony.[15]

Although he did not follow through on the threat, his relationship with Columbia's undergraduate student body was never good again. Nor did he have much more success with the faculty, who were suspicious of him at the outset and came, in the end, to adopt an attitude that mingled pity with disdain. The poor man obviously hadn't a clue, they decided. He did not know, for example, the difference between Columbia College and Columbia University; was mightily impressed that the School of General Studies—which provided adult education—made a lot of money, while the rest of the university seemed to suck up cash; visited the football team during practice, and was almost boyishly excited to do so, but did not evince the velleity of an interest in scholarly research.

The faculty's scorn was based not so much on what it saw of Eisenhower as what it heard. He had brought an aide from the Pentagon, Major Robert Schulz, and got Columbia to hire a former Army officer who had served on his staff, Kevin McCann. These two assistants rapidly made themselves the two most detested people on campus, and much of the hostility they generated poisoned whatever chance there was of harmony between the president's office and the professors. They controlled his travel arrangements and his appointments. Jealous of their general's care, Schulz and McCann killed the request of virtually every faculty member who wanted a meeting with the university president. They deluded themselves that they were protecting him from people who just wanted to chew the fat, when what they were doing was cutting Eisenhower off from the freewheeling, endless discussion that is the lifeblood of any community of scholars. Eisenhower never really knew what was happening at Columbia, because only a handful of deans and administrators ever got a chance to talk to him.[16]

Schulz and McCann were not simply jealous, though; they were as possessive as paranoid lovers. Although Eisenhower had remarkable gifts as a military leader, he could—like MacArthur—be completely wrongheaded when it came to trusting people implicitly. Butcher was only one of those who, over the years, betrayed his trust, but Butcher had never spied on him. Schulz and McCann were a pair of shriveled souls who drilled a small hole in Ike's office door so they could spy on him as he sat at his desk, chain-smoking his way through a huge pile of correspondence, unaware that he was under constant surveillance even with his door shut.[17]

He had arrived at Columbia without any burning ambition to make intelligent young people into world-beating thinkers; what interested him was producing better citizens. He also devoted a lot of time and energy to establishing the American Assembly, a Columbia-run forum where businessmen and professors would get together and brainstorm major problems facing the nation. Averell Harriman provided a luxurious estate, Arden House, on the Hudson, forty miles north of the city, where these luminaries could cerebrate in a congenial, nonacademic setting. If even one original idea or important insight ever emerged from all the golf, dining and Havana cigar smoke that the American Assembly generated, no trace of it remains.

Another Eisenhower initiative was the Conservation of Human Resources program, run by the university's School of Business. He described it as a program "of immeasurable benefit to all the world in furthering the dignity of man as a human being [through] an exhaustive study into the ways and means of applying to every man's good, in today's intricate economy, all the resources of America, in such a way as to maintain and enlarge every freedom that the individual has enjoyed under our system." All of which sounds less like a program than good intentions out looking for a program. The faculty club probably laughed itself breathless as professors picked apart vapid pronouncements like this.[18]

He also told a friend, "I find it almost incomprehensible that no American university has undertaken the continuous study of the causes, conduct and consequences of war." Spurred by that conviction, he es-

tablished the Columbia Institute of War and Peace Studies. He was evidently unaware that Stanford already had the Hoover Institution on
War, Revolution and Peace. Moreover, the Hoover Institution was as-
siduously building up an important archive, which drew scholars from
around the world. Eisenhower's venture was based on kindly motives
rather than a well thought out idea. It would never enjoy the Hoover Institution's prestige.[19]

There is a simple test by which to tell what Columbia meant to
Eisenhower. Throughout his life, he kept in touch with people he liked
and he kept going back to the places that were important to him, or at
least talked about going back. After he left Columbia, he maintained
only sporadic contact with the university. It was an episode he seemed
almost happy to forget.

Mamie disliked New York intensely, but the house wasn't too bad once
it was fixed up. The presidential residence at 60 Morningside Drive was
a four-story town house of generous proportions. A confection of pink
brick and white marble built for Nicholas Murray Butler, it had a palatial interior and the slightly dead feeling of a place that was a showcase,
not a real home. Before the Eisenhowers moved in, the whole house was
remodeled, to make it more agreeable. A solarium was built on the roof,
where there had once been a huge water tank, and the upper two floors
became private quarters. The lower floors were devoted mainly to entertaining on behalf of the university—an arrangement, that is, much
like that at Quarters No. 1, which long remained Mamie's favorite
dwelling. She moved her piano into the solarium, along with the risible
porch furniture, bamboo shades and grass rugs they had used in the
Philippines.[20]

They entertained many old friends at 60 Morningside, but few faculty members or their wives ever entered during the Eisenhower years.
While most of the faculty was cool toward Eisenhower, faculty wives
scorned Mamie, something she was well aware of. Many of them were
highly educated, while Mamie had never been to college. Her middle-
brow tastes and interests were far removed from their intellectual and
artistic concerns. She did not for a moment see herself as having anything in common with them. Mamie was not only happy but proud to
consider herself a good Army wife, but to many a good faculty wife,

such women are dim-witted, downtrodden and faintly ridiculous. Her one pleasure in being in New York was that it was only an hour from West Point, where John was now serving as an instructor.[21]

Eisenhower had told Tom Watson that he expected more leisure time once he moved to New York, but he didn't get it. He soon discovered that all he could manage was golf one afternoon a week. That was not entirely Columbia's fault, however. He was spending almost as much time in Washington, as we shall see, as he was spending in New York.

What helped to make it bearable was that he had discovered painting. Years later, in *At Ease,* he recalled that he took up painting after he moved to New York, but it really began at Fort Myer. Shortly before Ike started work on *Crusade in Europe,* an Irish-born artist, Tom Stephens, was commissioned to paint portraits of Ike and Mamie. When Mamie fell ill with a strep infection in February 1947, only a few days before Eisenhower handed over to Bradley, Stephens, working from a paper palette, did a small picture of her hands as she lay in bed in Quarters No. 1. Eisenhower noticed the palette and asked Stephens what he would do with it. "Throw it away," Stephens replied.

"Don't do that," said Eisenhower. "Leave it here for me and I'll fool around with the paints." He got an orderly to bring him a piece of board, an old dust cloth and some thumb tacks. He had tried sketching during the war and had seen Churchill painting for relaxation on the ruins of Carthage. That evening, he attempted a portrait of Mamie. The result, she thought, was "the most awful looking thing!" Even so, she bought him paints and brushes for the anniversary of their engagement, St. Valentine's Day, February 14.[22]

In New York, he set up his easel in the solarium. When word got out that he was now a painter, he protested to his old friend Swede Hazlett that he was no such thing—"I am a deliberate dauber"—and disclaimed all artistic ability. "I was almost fired because of my deficiency at drawing at West Point and have nothing whatsoever of artistic talents. I simply get a bang out of working with colors . . ."[23]

His new passion was pursued late at night, almost as if it were a vice. Once everyone else had gone to bed, the house was quiet and that day's mountain of paperwork dealt with, it was nearly midnight. It was then that Eisenhower went into the solarium, got out the brushes and started to paint.

What helped, too, was the fantasy of escape. For a time he thought he might buy a place in Connecticut, a small farm perhaps. Then he toyed with the idea of somewhere in Colorado, but that was too far from Washington. His friend George Allen, a millionaire businessman and staunch Truman Democrat, a man whose gregariousness and abundant sense of fun knew no party limits, had a farm at Gettysburg and told Eisenhower that the adjoining property was coming up for sale. Would Ike be interested?

Eisenhower was only mildly interested, but Mamie, who'd become good friends with George Allen's wife, Mary, was enthusiastic about the chance to see more of her new friend. In 1950, Eisenhower acquired what would become, in time, the most famous small farm in America. Yet hardly had the ink dried on the deed of sale before he was pulled back into uniform and found himself on active duty again. It would be another decade before there was any escape to Gettysburg.

Eisenhower had told the trustees what he had told Mamie many years before: his country would always come first. And even before he took up his duties at Columbia, the Cold War took a definitive turn. In June 1948 Stalin blocked all road and rail access to Berlin. He intended to starve the city into the Soviet occupation zone by forcing the wartime Allies out. They frustrated him by mounting the Berlin airlift, which for more than a year flew in enough coal to keep the people of West Berlin from freezing to death and enough food to keep them from starving.

Only now did the United States fully, if reluctantly, accept that it was committed to leading the civilized world in a long, costly, potentially cataclysmic struggle against a new version of an old evil, tyranny. Eisenhower virtually commuted between Morningside Drive and the Pentagon. Typically, he worked all day at Columbia, caught a train to Washington that night, spent all the next day in the Pentagon, then caught a train back to New York, arriving home after dark. And so it went, for more than two years. He may not have been the most successful Ivy League president or the most ineffective, but he was undoubtedly the most absent.

Although there was now a Department of Defense, there were bitter fights over money and over unification. The Air Force was holding on to the most important mission—the nuclear deterrent—and it was demanding a force level of seventy groups, which would absorb half the entire defense budget. The Navy fought back with a proposal to build a force of supercarriers, vessels big enough, that is, to launch B-29's, flown by Navy crews, to strike deep into Soviet territory. Eisenhower considered this idea fantastic. The Navy's role was control of the sea, not strategic bombing. The United States already had one air force; it was wasteful and foolish to create another one, he argued.

He also strongly resisted the Marine Corps' plans to maintain twenty-thousand-man divisions. During the war, the Corps had built up to a force of six divisions. It was, in effect, almost an army in its own right. Eisenhower thought the United States needed only one army, not two. The marines, he insisted, should be organized in nothing bigger than brigades.[24]

The secretary of defense, James Forrestal, who had served as secretary of the Navy during the war, relied heavily on Eisenhower in these bruising struggles. The Joint Chiefs were of little help to either Forrestal or Truman. They spent most of their energies fighting each other.

Following his astounding victory in the 1948 presidential election, Truman asked Eisenhower to come to Washington and serve for a time as "Presiding Officer of the JCS." Eisenhower's ability to get people to work together as a team was desperately needed.[25]

Yet by now he was thoroughly disgusted with these foolish interservice squabbles, which could only damage the nation's security. He did not believe in a seventy-group Air Force or a fleet of supercarriers. What the United States needed, he was convinced, was a combined arms task force ready to move to any part of the world at short notice and intervene effectively to defend Western interests. The Pentagon was so bogged down in turf wars that no one paid any attention to Eisenhower's proposal for what would later be known as a rapid reaction force.

Only his loyalty to Truman and Forrestal made him accede to Truman's request to take a leave of absence from Columbia. Forrestal, he wrote in his diary, looked desperately ill, but, "He has a conscience and a sense of duty. These, coupled with his sense of urgency and his terrific, almost tragic disappointment in the failures of professional men to 'get together,' leads him to certain errors. . . . He gives his mind no recess and works hours that would kill a horse. Except for my liking, admiration and respect for his great qualities I'd not go near Washington, even if I had to resign my commission completely. To a certain extent these apply to Truman, but he does not see the problems so clearly as does Jim. . . . I like them both."[26]

In January 1949, just as Eisenhower arrived in Washington on temporary leave from Columbia, Forrestal was checked into Bethesda Naval Hospital. He had suffered a nervous breakdown. A few days later, he leaped to his death from a window. His successor, Louis Johnson, accepted the post only on the condition that Eisenhower be available for consultation at any time.[27]

Eisenhower returned to Columbia in March, but the strain of recent months soon laid him low with a bad attack of ileitis, or inflammation of the small intestine. Ileitis is both painful and exceptionally unpleasant, but some good came of Ike's illness—his doctor, Howard Snyder (who later became surgeon general of the Army), told Eisenhower to stop smoking. He did so immediately, and later admitted it was one of the hardest things he ever had to do. When asked how he did it, he said he had simply given himself an order to quit.[28]

Eisenhower recuperated at Truman's "Winter White House," a pleasant retreat in Key West. The Joint Chiefs came down to meet with him there. After several weeks, he moved to Augusta National Golf Course to complete his recuperation. The man who built Augusta National into one of the premier courses in the world, Cliff Roberts, was one of the richest men in the country and one of Eisenhower's greatest admirers. Out of this initial encounter grew a close friendship.[29]

After a month in Georgia, Eisenhower returned to Columbia and Louis Johnson was left the hopeless task of putting an end to interservice rivalry. Not that he achieved much. It was still tearing the JCS apart when, in June 1950, North Korea launched an invasion of South Korea, using battle plans drawn up in Russian.

Eisenhower headed for the Pentagon as soon as he heard the news. What he found in Washington dismayed him. Truman and Johnson seemed unable to think on their feet and face up to what was a clear act of aggression, one almost certainly provoked by Stalin. They assured him that MacArthur was getting everything he requested, but that wasn't true. He himself had no doubts that this was a new kind of war, one that demanded an immediate and robust response. "We must . . . be prepared for whatever may happen," he told himself. "Even if it finally comes to use of the A-bomb, which God forbid."[30]

Any hope the North Koreans had of driving U.S. forces out of the Korean peninsula ended on September 15, when MacArthur landed an Army division and a Marine division deep in their rear, at Inchon. By October, MacArthur's troops were advancing into North Korea.

Throughout that frightening summer, Truman and the National Security Council worried that the invasion of South Korea might be only a feint, a way of drawing the forces of the United States and its allies into a Far Eastern trap, before the real attack was mounted—an invasion of Western Europe.

During the Berlin blockade, the U.S. and Britain had organized the North Atlantic Treaty Organization (NATO), but the key to making it work was rearming Germany. The French balked at German rearmament, but the alliance could not wait indefinitely for the French to see reason. One way to maintain momentum was to appoint a military commander and Eisenhower was the obvious—really, the only—choice.

On October 28, Truman summoned him to the White House and asked him to accept the post. Eisenhower had told the press some months before that he would return to duty if ordered to do so, and now he drew the line at doing it as a favor to the President. He said he would prefer getting back into uniform "on an order and obey basis" and Harry S Truman obliged.[31]

30

Duty Calls

Swede Hazlett was appalled. It seemed to him that Ike had allowed Truman to exploit his sense of duty to talk him into accepting this new assignment. As soon as he heard that Eisenhower was going back to Europe, he wrote his old friend both to sympathize and to lodge a protest. Why should he have to go over to Europe and try to make this new organization work? Why couldn't the Europeans look after themselves?

Eisenhower replied immediately, to say he hadn't been "talked into" anything. On the contrary. This was a call he had to obey. "You do not attach the same importance to the success of the Atlantic Defense Pact as I do. I rather look upon this effort as about the last remaining chance for the survival of Western civilization. Our efforts in the United Nations have been defeated by the vetoes of hostile groups—but in the Atlantic Pact we are not plagued by the hostile groups and are simply trying to work out a way that free countries may band together to protect ourselves."[1]

Truman accepted that the U.S. was not going to persuade other countries to rearm unless it was willing to lead by example, but at present the Army had only two divisions stationed in Germany. He proposed to raise the number to six, but a man Eisenhower admired "extravagantly," former President Herbert Hoover, was demanding the withdrawal of American forces from Europe, an idea that many congressional Republicans endorsed.[2]

Eisenhower was dismayed at the new eruption of isolationism. Western Europe possessed the largest pool of skilled workers and the largest industrial capacity outside the United States. For Stalin to acquire such economic muscle, and combine it with the largely untapped natural resources of the Soviet Union, would produce a threat to American security that could only lead to disaster. "I am convinced," Eisenhower told the press, "that to retire into our own country to wait for the end would bring defeat."[3]

Just before Christmas 1950, he spent a day talking to Congress, trying to persuade isolationists from both parties that collective security was the only real security the U.S. possessed. He also held a private meeting in the Pentagon with Senator Robert A. Taft of Ohio, a man whose isolationist views were even more influential than Hoover's. Taft had not only voted against the NATO treaty but was trying to scotch Truman's plan to build up American forces in Germany by claiming the President did not have the authority to send troops overseas in peacetime without prior congressional approval. Taft was also the most likely Republican candidate for the presidency.

Eisenhower had nothing against Taft's views on domestic and economic policy. He agreed with virtually all of them. The issue between them was isolationism. But if Taft was prepared to support NATO, Eisenhower was prepared to help Taft. So before Taft arrived, Eisenhower scribbled a note in pencil that he intended to form the basis of a press release once their meeting concluded. It read, "Having been called back to military duty, I want to announce that my name may not be used by anyone as a candidate for President—and if they do, I will repudiate such efforts." He tucked this note into a jacket pocket.

What he hoped to get from this meeting was an overt commitment to the principle of collective security and explicit support for Truman's proposal to raise American ground-combat strength in Germany from two divisions to six, with the increase in air units that this would also entail. Taft, however, hemmed and hawed and, just like any ambitious politician, refused to commit himself to anything. Eisenhower felt slightly depressed. After Taft departed, he reached into his jacket pocket and tore up the statement that would have definitively taken him out of the 1952 presidential election. The meaning of this gesture isn't hard to read: if the only way to keep an isolationist out of the White House was to run for the presidency himself, he would probably do it. His duty in that instance would be clear.[4]

In January 1951, Eisenhower made an eighteen-day tour of the twelve NATO capitals to meet some of the politicians he would have to deal with and to talk to senior officers assigned to NATO headquarters. He returned to the U.S., reported to Truman on what he had learned, and shortly afterward he and Mamie boarded the *Queen Mary,* heading for France. The welcome they received when they landed in Cherbourg was warm only in its hostility. Walls throughout Cherbourg—and other French towns they passed through on their journey to Paris—were generously daubed with YANKEE GO HOME! or misspelled versions of same.[5]

Throughout Eisenhower's time in France, fiercely anti-American demonstrations erupted on the streets of Paris, orchestrated by France's large and influential Communist party, which had much of France—and nearly all French intellectuals—convinced that the threat to Europe came not from the Soviet Union but from the overbearing, uncultured Americans, whose rapacious capitalist instincts had made them rich and imperialistic. NATO was seen by millions of Frenchmen as a tool for subjugating Europe and denying it the workers' paradise that Communism offered. De Gaulle had created a national myth that the French, after four years of heroic resistance, had driven the Germans out of France. The tens of thousands of young Americans who had died to liberate France were almost never mentioned.[6]

Eisenhower was now the Supreme Allied Commander, Europe—or SACEUR—and he moved into his old digs, the Trianon Palace Hotel in Versailles. Not an arrangement that Mamie felt comfortable with. The Trianon Palace Hotel was where Ike and Kay had been together for seven months during the war. He and his staff took over one floor of the hotel. The fledgling NATO headquarters was set up in another hotel, the Astoria, in central Paris.

The French government offered the Eisenhowers the Petit Trianon, the charming fourteen-room villa built for Marie Antoinette within the grounds of the palace of Versailles. It had, until recently, been occupied by Lady Mendl, a major figure on the international social scene. Mamie took a look at it and said it wouldn't do. The house itself was delightful, but it was filled with eighteenth-century furniture, the kind serious collectors would drool over, but Louis the Something was not to Mamie's down-home tastes. The French press fulminated at the rejection of French sophistication and style by this ignorant woman from the American Midwest. Mamie couldn't wait to leave France.[7]

The French government offered another villa, at Marnes-la-Coquette, to the west of Paris. After some minor improvements, Ike and Mamie moved in. Most visitors thought it was a pleasant house, albeit one with Louis the Something plumbing.

Eisenhower was able to paint and to play golf, but for a time he seemed even more interested in the large pond at the back of the house. It was well stocked with ornamental fish, and there were two huge golden carp that chased the smaller fish around. Ever sympathetic to the underdog, he couldn't bear to watch the carp bullying the other fish. He spent hours standing on the rim of the pond agitating a fly rod. After many fruitless attempts, he realized that carp don't rise to flies. So he netted the carp out, striking a blow for justice.

The carp, however, were there for a reason—by chasing around, they kept both themselves and the other fish healthy. Two years later, when French premier Pierre Mendès-France visited the house, the first question he put to Al Gruenther, Ike's successor as SACEUR, was, "What's happened to the carp?" Before it turned into an international dispute, Gruenther restored the carp to their pond.[8]

Eisenhower had decided from the outset that the new headquarters should be a policy-making body, not an operational agency directing combat units. He had been told that his HQ would need nearly six hundred officers to operate effectively. One of his earliest decisions was to cut the number to two hundred.

Most were Americans, something that Eisenhower deplored. He was dependent, however, on the other countries in the alliance to assign some of their best officers to the new venture, which they were, at first, reluctant to do. For now, he consoled himself that there were some familiar faces from SHAEF days, and Brigadier Sir James Gault, his wartime British aide, was assigned as an aide once again. He also had Montgomery as his deputy, and this time he was happy about it. Montgomery shared his commitment to making NATO work and was highly regarded by senior officers in the NATO countries. He may have been a pain in wartime, but at Supreme Headquarters, Allied Powers Europe, or SHAPE, where there was no military glory to be pursued, he was a loyal and trusted subordinate.[9]

There was no doubt, though, that Eisenhower was NATO's strongest card. Most of his time was spent trying to get the various governments of the countries involved in NATO to support it by modernizing their forces. But he still loved to spend time with troops and never seemed so excited as when he visited units in the field. What he found was gratifying; the military was committed to NATO even in countries whose governments were halfhearted.

In May 1951, for example, he went to Italy, to inspect mountain troops—the Alpini—and an armored regiment holding maneuvers almost on the border with Austria (where there were dozens of Red Army divisions on occupation duty) and Yugoslavia. The Alpini astonished him with their offensive spirit, their skiing skills, their ability to move artillery rapidly through the mountains and their physical courage. "A wonderful show!" he exclaimed at the end of the maneuver. "I never saw anything like it before." He was equally impressed by the zeal and military bearing of the tank crews of the elite Bersaglieri.[10]

Eisenhower believed that Europe would have to be defended in the long run by the Europeans, and these visits convinced him it was possible. At the same time, however, German rearmament was implacably opposed by the French. They proposed instead a European Army, an idea that Eisenhower at first considered fantastic—"like something dreamed up by a dope fiend." The more he saw of troops in the field, though, the more he thought it might work. This was surely the innate Ike optimism coming into play again, because a European Army run by a committee of politicians couldn't fight its way out of a paper bag. It would be an open invitation to Soviet adventurism, not a barrier to Soviet ambitions.

NATO would succeed only if the United States provided strong leadership, something Eisenhower discovered when he met the Dutch general assigned to his staff. "Holland is a small country," the Dutchman lamented. "Her withdrawal from NATO would not hurt NATO much, and staying in won't help the Dutch much. It might even cost them heavily. Wouldn't Holland be better off staying neutral?"

Eisenhower told him, "If Holland drops out, the whole project will fail." It was obvious to him that if one member left, others would inevitably follow. His first task was to hold the budding alliance together.[11]

At no time as SACEUR did he think the Soviets were about to launch an attack. Although the Red Army and the forces of Communist satellites such as Poland, Hungary and Czechoslovakia were technolog-ically backward, Stalin had a troop advantage of roughly nine to one, something he might have found tempting were it not for American nu-clear weapons. NATO was a nuclear alliance from the start. Without nu-clear weapons, it would have died stillborn instead of becoming the only military alliance in history that its adversaries eventually sought to join. That was far in the future, however. For now, Eisenhower was try-ing to create a force of forty NATO divisions, able to make a conven-tional riposte to a conventional attack.[12]

The Red Army's offensive capability was based on its "tank armies" (in reality, about the size of a U.S. armored corps) at a time when sol-diers commonly remarked, "The best way to stop a tank is with another tank." Eisenhower got the British to move an armored division to Ger-many and pushed the Pentagon to provide NATO armies with thousands of new American tanks.[13]

He also worked on the French. Their problem with German rear-mament turned out to be not so much a case of opposition by the French government as a lack of political stability. During the 1950s, govern-ment in France was a revolving door, and sometimes the door got stuck and France didn't have a government for a week or two. No French gov-ernment was going to risk an eruption in the streets by welcoming Ger-many into NATO at America's behest. The most Eisenhower could hope for was a grudging, tardy French acceptance of the principle of German membership of NATO at some not too distant date, and that's just what he got. In a little more than a year, Eisenhower had achieved goals that he had thought would take up to four years.[14]

★ ★ ★ ★ ★

Back in July 1949, Thomas Dewey, governor of New York and twice-defeated candidate for the presidency, had asked for a meeting. Eisen-hower had agreed, on the condition that it be a strictly private encounter without any publicity. Dewey had met Eisenhower once before, briefly, at the end of the war. Since then, he had become convinced that Eisen-hower was the one man who could save the country from economic ruin and political chaos.

Dewey assumed Eisenhower was a Republican; he assumed, too, that he wanted to be President. Besides, he added, the people had such affection for Eisenhower that he really belonged to them now: "You are a public possession." The thing to do was to succeed him as governor of New York and use that as a springboard for the 1952 presidential election.

Eisenhower told him firmly, "I do not believe that anything can ever convince me that I have a duty to seek political office," but he could tell from the look in Dewey's eyes that the governor didn't believe him. As if to confirm it, Dewey told him that unless he got himself elected to something soon, he'd stand no chance in 1952. Eisenhower broke into a huge grin. "You've given me the best of reasons for doing nothing."

Dewey replied tartly, "Not if you want to save democracy!"[15]

In October 1950, Dewey tried again. He and Herb Brownell, his former campaign manager from 1944 and 1948, along with Ike's old friend and former deputy Lucius Clay, had lunch with Eisenhower at the Columbia men's faculty club. Dewey repeated what he'd said before—Eisenhower had a duty to run for the White House in 1952. Ike turned him down again.[16]

Other people were already at work trying to convince Eisenhower he ought to run, including Frank Carlson, a senator from Kansas. To all of them, he gave much the same reply: not interested. Any hope he had that things might be different once he was three thousand miles away soon evaporated. He got a regular stream of visitors from the United States while he was at Marnes-la-Coquette. Old golfing buddies, such as Cliff Roberts, came to play a few rounds on the fine course at Saint-Germain and try to talk him into running in the Republican primaries. Truman's court jester, George Allen, came and tried to get him to enter the Democratic primaries. Truman was convinced that Ike was really a Democrat at heart, and he had been—back in 1911. By 1948, however, Eisenhower had decided that if he ever ran for office, he would run as a Republican.

He still had never voted, though. Then a group of Kansans managed to get a special election called for a vote on the reintroduction of Prohibition. Eisenhower cast an absentee ballot, against the proposition, and registered as an Independent even though he had decided he was really a Republican.[17]

That decision, though, didn't give him any comfort. Now and then he met with Walter Lippmann, a highly respected political commentator. Eisenhower may have chosen to talk to him because Lippmann was considered not just a journalist but a moralist, even though in his private life Lippmann practiced the arts of dishonesty and deception. With the pressure mounting to seek the 1952 Republican nomination, Eisenhower said to Lippmann, "You don't suppose a man could ever be nominated by both parties, do you?"[18]

Meanwhile, he continued to ignore the pleas to declare himself from the steady stream of millionaires who crossed the Atlantic. People who could afford that kind of journey in 1951 were, he knew, *vox lucrum,* not *vox populi.* Politicians, too, were easily discounted. To Eisenhower, all politics was corrupt to some degree and the people who wanted him in the White House obviously had agendas of their own. Nor was he impressed by the hundreds of letters that arrived every week demanding that he run. It wasn't hard for a few people to organize a letter-writing campaign. What he wanted was a clear-cut call, and he wasn't getting it.[19]

Even so, Dewey hadn't given up and in September 1951 he, Brownell and Clay began to organize a campaign to get Eisenhower into the race. They organized a Citizens for Eisenhower movement to get his name on ballots in the primaries and set up a fund-raising committee to finance his campaign.

Lucius Clay, who had left the Army to become president of Continental Can Company, became their conduit to Ike, but their front man was Senator Henry Cabot Lodge of Massachusetts. Lodge had met Eisenhower back in the early 1930s, when he was a journalist and Ike was working on Army procurement. Lodge had served with distinction during the war and was a colonel in the Army reserve as well as a member of the Senate. He was also as convinced as Eisenhower that a Taft presidency would lead the entire world into another war.

Taft had given a two-and-a-half-hour speech on the Senate floor to demand the withdrawal of American troops from Europe and criticized Eisenhower for accepting the job as Supreme Allied Commander. America, said Taft, should commit itself to defending Europe if it was attacked by the Russians, and that ought to be all the reassurance the Europeans needed. Eisenhower may well have felt something close to despair at such naïveté.

Without NATO and a strong American commitment to Europe, politically unstable Italy would probably get a Communist government. During the 1950s, the Italian Communist party, which was controlled by Moscow, several times came within a whisker of winning power at the ballot box. If Italy went Communist, virtually the whole of Western Europe would slide into an accommodation with Moscow. The inevitable American and British reaction would lead to Communist parties across Europe demanding the protection of the Red Army, an invitation Stalin would find irresistible.

Lodge did not simply want to get Eisenhower elected; he was trying to stop Taft. On September 4, he had a long talk in Paris with Eisenhower, but when he tried to talk Eisenhower into running, Ike replied, "You are well known in politics. Why not run yourself?"

"Because I can't get elected," said Lodge. "You are the only one who can be elected by the Republicans."

Although Eisenhower wasn't persuaded, over time he began to see this visit as a turning point. He hadn't agreed to Lodge's plan to enter him in the upcoming primaries, but "I began to look anew—perhaps subconsciously—at myself and politics."[20]

For the time being, he referred his supporters to Army regulation 600-10, which read, "Members of the Regular Army, while on active duty, may accept nomination for public office, provided such nomination is tendered without direct or indirect activity or solicitation on their part." This regulation might almost have been written with him in mind, because it didn't take a Wall Street lawyer to see that if Ike's admirers could organize a movement to draft him, he would be able to respond positively and with a clear conscience.

A couple of weeks before Christmas, Ike had a visit from Cyrus L. Sulzberger, the principal foreign correspondent of *The New York Times.* Eisenhower and Sulzberger chatted for an hour and talked politics. Eisenhower was scathing about Taft. "A very stupid man," said Ike. "He has no intellectual ability nor any comprehension of the issues of the world." As for the political pressure on him to declare his candidacy, he told Sulzberger, "I do *not* want to run for President. I have never wanted the office." Yet if the country made it clear that it wanted him to run, he would feel compelled to oblige.[21]

At Christmas he got a visit from Bill Robinson of the *Herald Tribune,* who spent most of Christmas Day trying to talk him into declaring his candidacy. He also got a handwritten letter from Truman, who said he was still willing to back an Ike presidential bid, but, "if you decide to finish the European job (and I don't know who else can) I must keep the isolationists out of the White House. I wish you would let me know what you intend to do."[22]

On January 6, Lodge released the text of a letter to Governor Sherman Adams of New Hampshire, in which he stated unequivocally that Eisenhower was a Republican and would "consider a call to service by the party . . . to be the highest form of duty." He was declaring, in effect, that Eisenhower *was* a candidate.[23]

Livid with rage at Lodge's unauthorized action, Eisenhower issued a grudging, weasel-worded admission, conceding that Lodge's statement was "an accurate account of the general tenor of my Republican voting record." Many people then and later took this to mean he was now a candidate, but that was not the way he saw it. He was still a registered Independent and had voted Republican just once—for John Foster Dulles, in a special senatorial election in New York in 1950, but Dulles was hardly a politician.[24]

Meanwhile, John Hay Whitney, a millionaire socialite who was busy raising money for an Eisenhower campaign, decided that he could prove that the people really wanted Eisenhower. Whitney organized a midnight rally at Madison Square Garden for February 8. The Garden was packed; the streets around it heaved with humanity and the rally ran on until dawn. People screamed for Eisenhower until they collapsed from exhaustion. A film was made of these emotional proceedings, and Jackie Cochran flew to Paris with a copy.

Eisenhower watched it in his living room, with Mamie and his immediate staff. As she handed him the film, Cochran told him that the Garden held sixteen thousand people but forty thousand were there. He watched the film in rapt silence, his emotions playing across his face in counterpoint to the flickering screen. When the film clattered to a halt, he stood up and asked her if she'd like a drink. She accepted his offer, raised her glass and dramatically offered a toast—"To the President!"

Important wishes, desires that we can deny with every word even as our emotions yield to a sense of helplessness and inexorability, need to come to us in a pleasing way, or with the right smiling face, before we are weak enough, and strong enough, to surrender. For Eisenhower, the moment had come, in the dancing images of a black-and-white film of ecstatic strangers' faces, simple signs aloft forever in their grainy hands. This was no adman's lie, no huckstering commercial. The emotions on that screen were real; those tiny simulacra were real people.

Their love for him was undeniable—not that he would ever want to deny it.

As Jackie Cochran stood there, glass raised, Ike's self-control cracked. Tears flowed down his cheeks in a steady, pulsing stream. He brushed them away with those huge, clumsy hands, embarrassed but proud. Eisenhower reminisced for an hour about his childhood, his brothers, his father, but mostly about Ida—how much he loved her, how she had been the greatest influence on his life.

Cochran then talked about the rally and what it meant. It showed that people really did want him to be President, but "Taft will get the nomination if you don't declare yourself."

"Well, I think you're right." He told her he would return home but didn't say when.[25]

Five days later, he was in London for the funeral of King George VI. Lucius Clay was there, too, but not so much for the funeral as to bend Ike's ear. After the king had been buried, they went to Jimmy Gault's house, where Clay told Eisenhower that he had to declare he was a candidate for the nomination, immediately. There wasn't a day to waste, not even an hour. Eisenhower refused to budge. Each man restated his position until both of them were shouting. Eventually, Clay got up to leave. "Well, there's nothing more I can do," he declared.

Eisenhower followed him out of the room. "Let's don't leave things on this note," he pleaded. After wandering around the subject for the final time, he at last told Clay, "I'll run."[26]

Yet even now he couldn't bring himself to declare his candidacy. For one thing, there was an important NATO meeting he wanted to get out of the way before he announced he was quitting as SACEUR. The other, more fundamental reason was that if he was nominated for the presidency, he would have to leave the Army. As a five-star general, he was entitled to remain on the active list for the rest of his life. More than that, though, he was a soldier. Part of him would be a soldier forever. But when the moment came to resign his commission, he would embrace it without regrets. And by then, maybe it would be clear that the country as whole—not just the Republican party—wanted him to be President.

On March 11, New Hampshire held its primary and Eisenhower won, beating Taft into second place. That was gratifying, but it didn't prove much. The following week, however, Minnesota held its primary and Eisenhower got 108,000 write-in votes. He felt both humbled and overjoyed. More than a hundred thousand people had gone to the trouble of learning how to spell Eisenhower correctly just so they could cast a valid write-in ballot! This really was a call from the people.[27]

On March 24 Brownell arrived in Paris, at Eisenhower's request. Brownell had not only been Dewey's campaign manager in 1944 and 1948 but was a former chairman of the Republican National Committee. Eisenhower talked to Brownell for ten hours that day, not so much about whether he ought to run as about major domestic issues, such as the need for a balanced budget. Eisenhower had been shocked by the huge deficit that Truman had just proposed for the coming fiscal year.

Brownell presciently raised the issue of civil rights. Eisenhower described how he had promoted integration within the Army in the closing days of the war and made it plain where his sympathies were. He made plain, too, his doubts that this was an area for government intervention. Brownell had hoped for an overt declaration of Ike's candidacy to come from this marathon discussion, but still Eisenhower hesitated.

On March 29, Truman spoke at the annual Jefferson-Jackson day dinner, a blue-ribbon event for Democrats. During his speech Truman almost offhandedly said, "I shall not be a candidate for re-election." Eisenhower had felt uncomfortable at the prospect of running against Truman, after having told him in 1945 and again in 1948 that he would not do so. That hurdle had now collapsed. Yet still he hesitated.[28]

Clay was fed up, and Dewey feared Taft was building up an insurmountable lead, but he had a plan for pushing Eisenhower into declaring his candidacy. MacArthur had just been named keynote speaker at the Republican convention and was hoping this would lead to the vice-presidential nomination on a Taft ticket—after which he expected Taft to get elected, then die in a year or two, leaving MacArthur as President.[29]

Not that Clay was aware of MacArthur's confidence that he would outlive Taft (as he did), but MacArthur was the perfect decoy to get Eisenhower into the race, right now. Clay told Dewey that Eisenhower would never swallow having MacArthur as his Commander in Chief. The thing to do was to tell Eisenhower that MacArthur's speech was dynamite, so powerful that it would unleash a tide of emotion that would give him, not Taft, the nomination, and as everybody knew, this was a Republican year. Dewey wrote a longhand letter to Eisenhower telling him that MacArthur looked set to become President.[30]

The letter was then handed to the pilot of a TWA Constellation about to leave for Paris. By an interesting quirk of fate, the pilot's last name was Nixon, and the next day he handed the letter to Eisenhower, who read it, then destroyed it. Eisenhower promptly informed Truman that "circumstances in my personal life have markedly changed." He wished to be relieved from his present assignment and planned to resign from the Army.[31]

David and Ida Eisenhower, photographed shortly after their wedding in 1886. He seems slightly awed at finding himself facing the future with Ida, while she seems eager to see what tomorrow will bring.

Little Ike, second from the left in the front row, poses with his fifth-grade classmates in 1900.

Ike, looking like Huck Finn come to life, on a camping trip in 1904. He never lost his love of hunting and fishing and was adept at both.

Eisenhower stands in the back row in this photograph of the Abilene High School baseball team at the end of the successful 1909 season. Crazy about baseball, he was also crazy about football, yet here he looks poutingly sensitive, more thinker than jock.

He made the West Point football team, only to have his dreams of athletic glory shattered by a wrecked knee in his second year. That bum knee dogged him all his life, not least on the golf course.

Ike and Mamie shortly after their marriage in July 1916. They look confident and happy, a charming young couple.

Ikky, as Mamie called him, was a winsome tot, the kind of blond cherub many young couples long for. Eisenhower was unable most of his life to express his feelings freely, but with Ikky it was different. He plainly adored his infant son. Ikky's death in 1921 nearly drove Eisenhower into a nervous breakdown.

Eisenhower spent seven years working for General Douglas MacArthur, the most glamorous and controversial soldier of his time. Here, Eisenhower is shown on the right with MacArthur during the Army's operation to clear the Bonus Marchers from downtown Washington in August 1932. Eisenhower later claimed he had been opposed to MacArthur's direct involvement, but chances are his memory was faulty.

A reluctant Eisenhower traveled with MacArthur to the Philippines in October 1935. In an attempt to cope with the heat, Eisenhower shaved his head, to Mamie's horror. In Manila, his relationship with MacArthur became increasingly difficult. Eventually, Ike broke away and returned to the United States in the fall of 1939.

Following Pearl Harbor, Eisenhower was named Supreme Commander of the Allied landings in North Africa. There, Kay Summersby, a former model, became his assistant and driver. The nature of their relationship was probably less than she claimed, but more than he acknowledged.

On the evening of June 5, 1944, Eisenhower visited the airborne troops who would jump into Normandy in the early hours of June 6. The greatest regret of his military career was that he did not have the chance to lead men such as these into combat.

On June 5, 1944, as Eisenhower contemplated the invasion of France, his son, John S. D. Eisenhower, was graduating from West Point with a commission in the infantry. Eisenhower had tried, in vain, to persuade John to go into the (much safer) artillery. John stayed with the infantry and during the Korean War was awarded the Combat Infantryman's Badge.

Shown here with Ike following the breakout from Normandy are his three senior American field commanders: George Patton, Third Army; Omar N. Bradley, Twelfth Army Group; and Courtney C. Hodges, First Army. Of the three, the one he considered the most accomplished soldier was not Patton but Bradley.

Near the end of the war, Eisenhower was able to indulge his favorite pastime on sacred ground—Saint Andrews golf course in Scotland, ancestral home of the game.

Ida sits at her much loved ebony piano, holding a magazine that extols Ike's exploits. Still, when a journalist telephoned and said she must be proud her son, she gave the perfect answer: "Of course I am. Which one?"

President Harry Truman was so impressed with Eisenhower's character and accomplishments that he urged him to run for the White House in 1948. Truman even volunteered to be his vice-presidential running mate.

Eisenhower arrives at Columbia on May 3, 1948, to assume his new duties as president of the university. This, though, was second best. What he had really been hoping to do after he retired from the Army was become a history professor, but colleges seemed to think he was overqualified for that—apparently he'd made too much history to teach it.

Eisenhower returned to Abilene, Kansas, in June 1952 to launch his bid for the Republican presidential nomination. A thunderstorm left him struggling to make himself heard, and his speech, televised nationally, flopped.

Elected to the presidency, Eisenhower was sworn in by Chief Justice Fred Vinson on January 20, 1953, on the east steps of the Capitol. Seen here, left to right, are Harry Truman, Vinson, and Vice President Richard M. Nixon, who appears to be detached from these events, a member of the new administration but somehow apart from it.

During the election campaign, Eisenhower had pledged he would go to Korea, but his visit probably taught him little. He ended the war with a combination of implied atomic threats and overt appeals for a settlement.

Former presidents had gone from the White House into limbo. Eisenhower was the exception. He was consulted regularly by John F. Kennedy and, later, by Lyndon Johnson, especially on national security problems.

Bored much of the time following his departure from office, Eisenhower nevertheless continued his love affair with painting. He claimed he had no artistic ability, just a love of working with colors.

Ike and Mamie stayed in Palm Springs from Thanksgiving to Easter. Here they have been spotted in February 1965, looking like many another retired couple, watching the Bob Hope Desert Classic.

Eisenhower spent the last nine months of his life in Walter Reed Army Hospital in Washington, with Mamie living in a room next to his.

★★★★★

31

Moving On

It had all been so unlike him. This man, who exuded self-confidence and authority, someone capable of giving the order for D-Day, a man who even at his most charming seemed to live for the challenge of making decisions, had spent months agonizing instead of making up his mind and holding fast. Instead, he had tiptoed up to a Yes one day, only to tiptoe away from it the next morning. No wonder, then, that he began to feel his nerves were getting the better of him. "I think I'm heading for the psychoneurotic ward," he told Cliff Roberts three days before he got Dewey's letter. "I'm getting so I'm almost afraid to pass a doctor in the hall."[1]

Once he had made the commitment, the strain of prolonged prevarication was finally unleashed and he fell ill. A story was put out that Eisenhower was suffering a bad attack of conjunctivitis, but it was really a kind of nervous collapse, the release from months of accumulated psychological tension. After a few days of much needed rest, he bounced back.[2]

There was a longstanding agreement to attend the dedication ceremonies at the Eisenhower home and museum in Abilene on June 4, which gave him a good excuse to delay his return to the U.S. until June 1. He had no desire to start campaigning for the nomination; had no desire to campaign at all, in fact. He was nevertheless certain that he would be nominated.

What he was less certain of, even now, was whether he had accepted for the right reasons. "Is this really a call from the people? Maybe I'm just kidding myself," he told his chief of staff at SHAPE, Al Gruenther, and Gruenther would have understood what he was driving at. Both men understood the ambiguous nature of ambition in the military. Duty cloaks ambition, making it consistent with the ideals of service and self-sacrifice. What to a civilian is a clear choice is to the professional soldier a satisfyingly unfathomable mystery, and he cannot always be certain which is in the ascendant—the call of duty or the pursuit of personal ambition.[3]

Apart from the decision to kick off his campaign with a speech in Abilene, he had made one other decision: he would not base himself in New York, even though that was still his legal residence. Throughout his seventeen months at SHAPE he was, nominally at least, still president of Columbia, and still resided at 60 Morningside Drive. Dan Thornton, the Republican governor of Colorado, had urged him to make Denver his base if he did decide to run. Eisenhower followed through on Thornton's suggestion, probably because it would make the plunge into politics a lot easier for Mamie. In Denver, she would be among friends and family.[4]

On his way to Abilene from Paris, Eisenhower paid a courtesy call at the White House. He wasn't sure of how Truman would feel about him now that he was a Republican candidate, but Truman wasn't mad at him. On the contrary, what irritation he felt was reserved for Dewey and Lodge. "I'm sorry to see these fellows get Ike into this business," Truman told his staff. "They're showing him gates of gold and silver which will turn out copper and tin." So when Eisenhower told him how smears were already being circulated—that he'd been sleeping with Kay Summersby, that Mamie was a dipsomaniac, that he was really Jewish—Truman was sympathetic.[5]

The speech in Abilene turned out to be a washout, literally. Instead of addressing a huge throng of Kansans, he spoke to rows of empty seats as torrential thunderstorms lashed the plains. Eisenhower stood at a bank of microphones in a see-through plastic raincoat, pants rolled above his ankles, his few remaining strands of hair plastered across his forehead at one moment, whipped straight up in a spike the next. He spoke like a man depressed and doing his duty as he wrestled with the wind for possession of the pieces of paper that contained the text of his speech. Dewey, Lodge and Brownell could only groan as they saw this scene of their bedraggled hero swimming across their flickering TV screens. From Kansas, he moved on to Denver in a rueful mood and set up his nomination campaign headquarters in the Brown Palace Hotel.

With the primaries over and the Republican convention only a month away, Taft had roughly 525 committed delegates, to approximately 400 for Eisenhower. It would take 604 to secure the nomination, but although Taft was a lot closer to that figure than he was, the momentum was with Ike. Eisenhower told people around him, "I intend to fight like hell," and over the next few weeks worked hard at wooing delegates. He proved he could still master a press conference, seeming relaxed, affable, frank where Taft was increasingly tense and irritable. On a trip to Detroit, Ike was asked about the entry of generals into Republican politics. "Does it mean," said a reporter, "that you will bring the military into your administration if elected?"

"I think I should represent enough military for any administration with which I may be connected!" That brought a roar of pure delight.[6]

He was good with delegates, too, although he got carried away when he talked to the California delegation. It was reported he told them, "I am a true Republican. In Abilene, where I spent my boyhood, we used to look on the Democrats as the town drunks." Eisenhower had evidently forgotten that as a young man he'd been a Democrat himself.

Dewey and Brownell had just the right theme to stop any last-minute swing to Taft, a message emphatically supported by opinion polls and newspaper editorials: "Taft can't win." Even among registered Republicans, most preferred Eisenhower. There were also many Democrats who would vote for Eisenhower who would never vote for Taft. Ike also got the benefit of a composition by Irving Berlin, a song Eisenhower loved, called "They Like Ike." Long after people had forgotten the song, "They Like Ike" was lodged in the American consciousness with "Remember the *Maine*" and "Give 'em hell, Harry!" In the summer of 1952, I LIKE IKE buttons seemed to sprout everywhere.

As the convention drew near, interest focused increasingly on Texas, which had not one slate of delegates but two. The Republican party in Texas was divided into rival camps. One, firmly pro-Eisenhower, was under the control of H. J. "Jack" Porter of Houston, the party executive who managed its organization in the Lone Star state. Porter was the archfoe of Henry Zweifel of Fort Worth, who was chairman of the Republican party in Texas. Porter had organized county conventions throughout Texas and these had returned a slate of pro-Eisenhower delegates. Zweifel fought back with a slate of pro-Taft delegates he had handpicked.[7]

There were contested delegates from other states, such as Louisiana and Georgia, but Texas provided a blatant example of the antidemocratic, professional politics that Taft and his supporters had railed against as the kind of unspeakable corruption that characterized Truman Democrats. Taft said not a word against what had happened in Texas. He wanted and needed Zweifel's dubious delegates too much to take a principled stand on their provenance. Eisenhower fulminated indignantly at "those rustlers" in Texas, but to Dewey and Brownell, here was their best chance to stop Taft.

There was an eerie echo to all this. Back in 1912, Robert Taft's father, William Howard Taft, had clashed bitterly with Theodore Roosevelt over contested Taft delegates to the Republican convention that year, a convention that, by coincidence, was held in Chicago. The political pros were stealing delegates, TR thundered, and thwarting the will of the people. When the convention managers allowed contested Taft delegates to participate in the decision on whether they ought to be seated, TR saw he was going to lose and stormed out, bellowing grandiloquently, "We stand at Armageddon and battle for the Lord!" and formed his own party. This split in the Republican vote brought the election that fall of the Democratic candidate, Woodrow Wilson.

The rule allowing contested delegates to vote on their own qualifications had been adopted at every convention since 1912. But the nation's twenty-five Republican governors happened to be meeting in Houston in June 1952, and Dan Thornton and Tom Dewey got twenty-three of them—including several confirmed Taftites—to sign a manifesto that said the rule allowing contested delegates to vote on their own legitimacy was unacceptable.[8]

Even so, a Taft supporter was chairman of the convention's Credentials Committee and he had no intention of changing the rules. Eisenhower's handlers would have to wrest the decision away from the Credentials Committee and put it to a vote of the entire convention, excluding, of course, those with contested credentials. Brownell drew up a resolution, which he astutely called "the Fair Play Amendment," to change the rules.[9]

Seeing the danger, Taft offered to split Texas with Eisenhower. "That's swell," said Eisenhower, thinking Taft was making a sporting and gentlemanly gesture. It was, in fact, a trap. Right now Eisenhower had the moral advantage. More important, a deal with Taft would mean discarding the Fair Play Amendment. That would leave the Credentials Committee free to seat nearly fifty contested Taft delegates from southern states. The momentum on the floor would then swing to Taft. When Lodge, who was directing the Eisenhower forces on the convention floor, heard of Taft's offer to split Texas, he immediately contradicted Eisenhower, telling Taft's floor managers, "There will be *no* compromise."[10]

They responded by getting a television blackout imposed on the debate over the amendment. This farcically heavy-handed attempt at censorship only advertised to millions of outraged viewers that Taft had something to hide, and as the amendment came to a vote, attention was intently focused on California. Its seventy delegates were, under the state's unit rule, required to vote in a block. Ostensibly, they had arrived at the convention to vote for Governor Earl Warren, Dewey's 1948 running mate. Warren had declared his candidacy some months before, believing that the convention would be deadlocked between Ike and Taft, in which case, he might emerge as the compromise candidate.

Dewey, however, saw a different possibility. The California delegation would vote for Warren on the first ballot but then go over to Taft, and those seventy votes might just put Taft into the White House. Dewey was, moreover, a sternly unforgiving man, and he was still angry that Warren had failed to deliver California to the Republican party in the 1948 election. Dewey intended to undermine Warren's control of the delegation, both to hurt Warren and to block Taft. Mixed motives. His chosen instrument was the junior senator from California, thirty-nine-year-old Richard Milhous Nixon, who was obviously as ambitious as he was unscrupulous. Two months before the convention, Dewey and Nixon met at the Roosevelt Hotel in New York and Dewey offered Nixon the vice-presidential nomination. Nixon got himself, and twenty-seven of his followers, elected as delegates, and aboard the train that carried the California delegation to Chicago, Nixon circulated among the pro-Warren delegates, extolling the merits of Ike. He had kept his side of the bargain.[11]

Dewey, meanwhile, was going to keep his. During the convention, but before it chose its nominee, Brownell asked Eisenhower who he wanted for a running mate. "I didn't know I could do that," said Eisenhower, astonished. "I thought that was up to the convention." Dewey had told him several times what a good running mate Nixon would make, but Eisenhower hadn't grasped just what Dewey was driving at, or why. Under Brownell's prodding, however, he drew up a list of possibilities. Nixon's name was at the top, even though Eisenhower had never met him and knew almost nothing about him except that he was from California, was comparatively young and had made his name by exposing the perjury of Alger Hiss.[12]

By this time, the California delegation was split, with roughly twenty-five delegates supporting Warren, thirty supporting Eisenhower and the rest for Taft or undecided. If it came to a second ballot, Nixon and Dewey could be sure that California wouldn't go to Taft; it wouldn't even hold firm for Warren. It would swing to Ike.[13]

Warren, meanwhile, was troubled by what he was reading and hearing about Texas. Southern politics was notoriously corrupt and Warren was a man who, during his ten years as governor of California, had become passionate about integrity in public life. When the California delegation discussed how to vote on the Fair Play Amendment, Warren's role was crucial. From a purely selfish point of view, his best bet was to advise them to abstain, but he chose not to do that. Instead, he told them to look to their consciences. When this show is over, he told them, we'll all go home and we'll have to justify whatever we do here. Warren's conscience gave the Eisenhower supporters the votes needed to swing all seventy California votes behind the Fair Play Amendment.[14]

Taft's floor managers tried to alter the amendment, by removing the passages they objected to. When these proposed changes were put to a vote, they lost 654–548. This vote made it so plain that the amendment would pass, it was put to a voice vote and shouted into acceptance from the floor. Taft had been humiliated. Thirty-three Eisenhower delegates from Texas were seated, and only five of the Taft delegates made it.

Taft's only hope now was MacArthur's keynote speech. Since Truman had dismissed him from command in Korea and Japan in April 1951, MacArthur had become almost a god to the Republican right wing. He was also one of the most powerful orators of the age, yet his speech to the convention proved to be a meandering, yawn-inducing effort.[15]

On the first ballot for nominees, Eisenhower's tally was 595, to Taft's 500—nine short of victory. The Minnesota delegation then switched the nineteen votes it had cast for Harold Stassen, former "boy governor" of the state, over to Eisenhower, making a second ballot unnecessary.

During the preceding four days, Eisenhower had been holed up in a suite at the Blackstone Hotel, where he and his brothers followed what amounted to the first TV convention. He had been appalled at the fistfights on the convention floor and the hysterical atmosphere in which a nation's fate was hammered out. But with his nomination secure, sanity seemed to descend on the proceedings and he finally had a role to play. He got up and went into the bedroom, where Mamie was prostrated with an infected tooth, and told her it was finally over. Picking up the bedside telephone, he asked the operator to put him through to Taft, whose headquarters was in the Hilton Hotel, right across the street.[16]

Eisenhower was old enough to remember the 1912 election, when the split in the Republican party had delivered the White House to a Democrat who had won only 40 percent of the popular vote. He didn't need anyone to tell him there was no time to waste patching up an alliance with Taft.

After Taft said he could come over, Eisenhower collected his hat and his press secretary, James Hagerty, and with the two Chicago policemen assigned to protect him acting like pulling guards, he managed to force his way across a thoroughfare chockablock with people screaming, "*We Like Ike!*" and desperate for a glimpse of their hero. It took half an hour to walk fifty yards, and once inside Taft's headquarters, he found himself being led through a ballroom where dozens of women were crying, their permed hair a mess from their tugging at it, mascara streaks making black tire-tracks down their cheeks as they wept, while men stood around in small groups, hatred in their stony silence, anger blazing in their eyes. Eisenhower brushed past, clutching his hat, and stared intently ahead.[17]

He told Taft—who was so choked with emotion that he was almost incapable of speech—"This is no time for conversation on any matters of substance. You're tired and so am I, but I just want to say that I want to be your friend and hope you will be mine. I hope we can work together." Taft agreed to have some photographs taken of himself with Ike, but committed himself to nothing.[18]

The next morning, Brownell convened a meeting of the principal figures in the Dewey wing of the party in his suite at the Hilton and showed them Ike's list of possible running mates. Once the meeting was under way, he left, and Dewey took over. Various names came up, including Taft's, but Dewey rammed home Nixon's superiority over all the other possible candidates—youth, good war record, California, the man who exposed Alger Hiss.[19]

Eisenhower accepted Nixon without any enthusiasm. While much admired by party regulars, Nixon had a political reputation that was not exactly unblemished and some of Ike's golfing friends simply despised him. So when Nixon was summoned to the Blackstone to collect his prize, Eisenhower did not welcome him as a brother in arms. Instead, he launched into a little homily on the campaign ahead: it was going to be a moral crusade. "Will you join me in such a campaign?"

When he'd received the call to come and see Eisenhower an hour earlier, Nixon had reacted to the news that he was going to be Ike's running mate as if it was the last thing in the world he had ever expected. And now, playing to perfection the dark prince of Republicanism and looking suitably solemn, he told Eisenhower, "I'd be proud and happy to, General."[20]

Jim Hagerty was an owlish, bespectacled and rumpled figure whose suits always looked as if he'd been sleeping in them. He was a hard-bitten, hard-drinking, chain-smoking journalist who could have walked right out of the Ben Hecht–Charles MacArthur play *The Front Page.* Hagerty had been a reporter for *The New York Times,* like his father before him. In 1948, he had served as Dewey's press secretary, and during the Chicago convention, he became Ike's.

After a short break, he reported for duty at the Brown Palace Hotel, and when Eisenhower arrived for work, he said to Hagerty, "Come on. We're going to go out and play golf."

Hagerty had other things in mind. There were reporters clamoring for stories and interviews. "Oh, General," he said mildly. "I've got a lot of work to do."

"I don't want to play, really," Eisenhower replied. "I want to talk to you."

The issues that Republican politicians intended to campaign on were Communism—at home and abroad—corruption in Washington and the war in Korea. In truth, though, most people weren't greatly concerned about either Communism or corruption, taking a measured view of both. Nor was there a pocketbook issue. Two years of high defense spending to fight the war in Korea had banished all thought of recession. Ironically, though, Korea *was* the real issue in this election. People were happy to have the money but unhappy to have the war.

As they rode around in a little electric golf cart, Eisenhower told Hagerty, "If we don't get some settlement before I become President, I'm going to go over to Korea." Then he added, "Just keep that quiet."[21]

He launched his formal campaign for the White House immediately after Labor Day, and moved back to New York. His professional advisers had told him he could skip the Deep South. That was Democratic territory—not enough Republicans worth bothering about. But Eisenhower wasn't planning to be President only of the Republicans. He would launch his campaign, he told his advisers, with a whistle-stop tour through the South.

His nineteen-car campaign train looked like most other trains, except for a large round sign at the back in red, white and blue that had EISENHOWER SPECIAL emblazoned across the top and a cornball injunction across the bottom that would have seemed faintly ridiculous in Scarsdale but was downright friendly in small-town America. It read, LOOK AHEAD, NEIGHBOR. For two months, he crisscrossed the country aboard his train, clocking twenty-one thousand miles. But he left it at least once a week, to fly to major cities and give major speeches. All told, he covered an extra thirty thousand miles by air.

The train, however, got the attention, and the first trip was an eye-opener for his advisers. Huge crowds turned out to cheer him. This was the beginning of the end of the Democratic double nelson on the "solid" South.

Mamie, however, didn't want to be involved in campaigning, and at first said no to any idea of spending long periods on a train filled with politicians, speechwriters and journalists. What made it tolerable for her was that someone, possibly Eisenhower himself, thought to invite her eighty-year-old mother along. And this was no ordinary mother. Elivera Doud looked like a stereotypical old lady—rimless spectacles, gray hair, ghastly dark dresses and ugly shoes—but she played a lively harmonica and loved to shoot pool.[22]

Wherever the train stopped, day or night, huge crowds appeared and Eisenhower stood on the little platform at the back and delivered a brief speech. In one town, it might be about the declining power of the dollar (which he illustrated by holding up an egg and talking about the way its price had rocketed under Truman), at the next he might talk about the Democrats in Washington ("Too small for their jobs, too big for their breeches and too long in power"). Whatever the speech, though, he'd conclude, "Let me introduce my Mamie," which invariably brought a huge shout of approval. She emerged, waved, smiled, and the caravan moved on.

Exposed to the rough-and-tumble of a political campaign, Mamie was distressed. Eisenhower was portrayed by his right-wing opponents as a Communist appeaser, someone who had held back from taking Berlin in obedience to Stalin. His liberal critics accused him of being anti-Semitic and racist. After a few weeks on the train, she was begging him to renounce the nomination and quit, but it was too late for that.[23]

He loved greeting the crowds that turned out, especially in remote places. Yet it irritated him at times that they seemed to have come out just to get a look at him. There was no sign that they were there to listen to his ideas on what needed to be done. He was also getting fed up with the canned music endlessly pumped out from the train, with the frenetic atmosphere aboard it, with the lack of sleep and the tediously repeated campaign songs that enveloped him at every stop. When the Look Ahead, Neighbor special finally ground to a halt, Eisenhower was glad to get off.

In the course of campaigning Eisenhower made a discovery: the Republican right wing set the tone for the entire party. Twenty years of opposition had created a rump that was vociferous and almost completely negative. It had no positive ideas to advance. It wanted the U.S. out of the UN, American troops out of Europe, Commies out of government, Social Security out of retirement calculations and income tax out of existence. Such was the intellectual high ground of Republicanism circa 1952.

Even so, the Democratic party's candidate, Governor Adlai Stevenson of Illinois, never looked like winning that November. Virtually all of Eisenhower's political challenges came from the right wing of his own party, and he did his best to appease it. Any attempt to confront it could result in a split party and a President Stevenson. And there was no chance of being allowed to ignore it, which was what he almost surely would have preferred.

Gritting his teeth, Eisenhower made one of his first campaign appearances with Senator William Jenner, who was running for reelection in Indiana. Jenner's most famous utterance was to call George Marshall a "front man for traitors." The second most famous was to describe Marshall as "a living lie." Congressman Charles Halleck and others nevertheless demanded that Ike appear at a Jenner election rally in Indianapolis on September 9. This was Taft's heartland, the isolationist Midwest.

Jenner could hardly believe his luck. He was facing a tough fight, but here was Ike, the most popular man in the country. When Eisenhower finished a brief speech urging the election of Republicans in November, Jenner grabbed his arm and held it up. Eisenhower turned red, whispering angrily to Halleck, "Get me out of here." Back aboard the train, he was still fizzing with anger. "I have had to spend the entire day with that slimy skunk. If he'd grabbed my arm one more time I would have hauled off and slugged him."[24]

Several days later, Taft came to meet with him at 60 Morningside Drive. Taft brought with him a list of domestic policies that he wanted Eisenhower to sign up to, in exchange for his support—a smaller federal budget, more restrictions on organized labor and a stand against "creeping socialization."

Eisenhower was, by his own admission, both a conservative and a liberal: "I'm conservative where money is concerned, but liberal so far as human beings are concerned." This meant he could sign up to Taft's principles in good conscience and ignore them once he got elected if that seemed the right thing to do. On the big foreign-policy issues—the UN, NATO, the Marshall Plan, the principle of collective security—Taft made it easy for him, by leaving them alone. After two hours of discussion, Eisenhower said he would accept Taft's "guidelines."[25]

Much of the press ridiculed "the Morningside Surrender." Stevenson wittily observed, "It looks like Taft lost the nomination but won the nominee." Eisenhower shrugged the criticism off as an irrelevance.[26]

Even as he did so, however, the *New York Post* was about to run an

exposé of an eighteen-thousand-dollar fund set up by Nixon's admirers
to help pay some of his travel expenses and other bills not covered by
his senatorial salary. When the story broke on September 18, Eisenhower's immediate reaction was, "Get rid of that fellow, quick!" but he
soon had second thoughts.[27]

Eisenhower canvassed opinion on the train—which was crossing
the Midwest—and found it was sharply divided. Telegrams were delivered at every stop, most of them urging him to dump Nixon. Yet he
wasn't going to do anything in haste. For one thing, there was no proof
of wrongdoing, merely a sensational account in one of the most liberal,
pro-Stevenson newspapers in the country. For another, he hadn't heard
Nixon's side of the story. And, finally, Nixon was a hero to the party's
right wing. "If Nixon has to go, we cannot win," he told Sherman
Adams, the former governor of New Hampshire and one of the most
important political advisers riding the train. Even so, he told the press
that Nixon had to show he was "as clean as a hound's tooth."[28]

Dewey, meanwhile, had called Nixon, who was campaigning in
California. "I don't think Eisenhower should make this decision," said
Dewey. "I think you ought to go on television. . . . At the conclusion of
the program, ask people to wire in their verdict to you." If the result was
strongly negative, he should quit, but if it was in his favor, the crisis
would be over. "If you stay on, it isn't blamed on Ike, and if you get off,
it isn't blamed on Ike."[29]

That night, Eisenhower called Nixon from St. Louis. Nixon was
hoping for a message of solidarity, but Eisenhower offered not a word
of encouragement. "If I issue a statement now backing you up," he said,
"in effect people will accuse me of condoning wrongdoing." He told
Nixon he thought a television appearance would be a good way to resolve the issue. Becoming impatient, Nixon said he'd quit if that was
what the General wanted, but Ike ducked the question. Nixon then
asked when he could expect a decision on his future on the ticket.
Eisenhower wouldn't commit himself even on that. "Maybe after the
program we could tell what ought to be done."

"General, a time comes in politics when you have to shit or get off
the pot!" retorted Nixon, exasperated.[30]

The evening of September 23, when Nixon was scheduled to make
his TV appearance, Eisenhower was going to speak at the Cleveland
Public Auditorium. He, along with Adams, Hagerty, Brownell and a
gaggle of advisers and aides, wedged themselves into the office of the

auditorium manager to watch Nixon defend himself. Eisenhower sat clutching a yellow legal pad in one hand, a sharpened pencil in the other.

Nixon went on the attack, and stayed there. The previous day, the Republicans had revealed that a similar fund had been established for Stevenson's travel expenses. And now Nixon pointed out that Stevenson's running mate, a white-supremacist senator from Alabama, John Sparkman, had put Mrs. Sparkman into a well-paid position on the Senate payroll. Nixon went on to show how much he'd earned and how much tax he'd paid in recent years. He challenged Stevenson and Sparkman to do the same. Eisenhower stabbed his pad with his pencil. Nixon's ploy was going to force him to reveal his own finances. Not that he had anything to hide, but Eisenhower had an adamantine belief that money matters were nobody else's business.[31]

Having established his financial probity, Nixon shamelessly scraped the barrel of ordinary emotion until the hoops fell off. Sometimes defiant, sometimes struggling to contain the storm of obscure resentments that never ceased to rage within, he turned what people expected to be a dry, factual accounting of his office and travel expenses into a grippingly tacky defense of his life, his wife, his children and his children's dog, a black-and-white spaniel named Checkers. Poets and dramatists struggled throughout the twentieth century to reveal artistic significance in the banalities of everyday life. Not one surpassed Nixon's famous Checkers speech, which presented in a wife's cloth coat, the gift of a dog and the happiness of two small children the raw materials of History. It was the most compelling drama of stone-age TV, the earliest classic performance of the new medium. At its end, Nixon urged people to write to the Republican National Committee and decide his fate.

He was cut off before he could give the RNC's address, but the handful of people crammed into the auditorium manager's office knew even then what the result would be. Down through the floorboards came the sound of the thousands packed into the auditorium above. "We want Dick," they chanted as they stamped their feet. *"We want Dick!"* Eisenhower said to Hagerty, "I'm satisfied. Get me up a telegram that I can send to Dick," then he hurried upstairs to address the excited throng.

"I have been a warrior, and I like courage," he told them. "Tonight I saw an example of courage . . ." They screamed their agreement.

The telegram that Hagerty composed and dispatched over Eisenhower's name nevertheless had a slightly peremptory tone. "I feel the need for talking to you. . . . Tomorrow evening I shall be at Wheeling, West Virginia."

Nixon was so annoyed that even now Eisenhower was refusing to commit himself that at first he said he was going to Montana and to hell with Wheeling. Cooler heads finally prevailed. He flew to Wheeling the afternoon of September 24, but only after touching down in Montana.

Eisenhower was already at the airport when Nixon's plane landed. As Nixon stood in the doorway helping his wife, Pat, with her coat, Eisenhower was so relieved this whole sorry business was over that he did something completely out of character—he bounded up the steps like a teenager, put an arm around Nixon's shoulder and declared in a loud voice, "You're my boy!"[32]

Bad as this episode had been, the train would soon carry him on to the worst moment of the campaign. Dewey had urged him to stay out of Wisconsin, home of Senator Joe McCarthy. Earl Warren, too, had advised him to stay away. In his youth, Ike had read the entire Bible, so he would have come across, "He that touches pitch is defiled therewith," yet he foolishly and needlessly chose to go to Wisconsin. Even though Truman had carried the state in 1948 and it was next door to Stevenson's Illinois base, Wisconsin was going to vote Republican in 1952 whether Eisenhower visited or not. The proof was that McCarthy, who was up for reelection, was overwhelmingly and undeniably the most popular political figure in the history of the state. He didn't need Ike any more than Ike needed him.[33]

Two years earlier, by brandishing a piece of paper that he claimed bore the names of 205 "known Communists" in the State Department, McCarthy had put the federal bureaucracy under siege. Not only had he vilified Secretary of State Dean Acheson, but he had also produced a sixty-thousand-word account of Marshall's career that portrayed him as a Soviet agent and someone who "would sell his own grandmother for any advantage."[34]

Eisenhower was as eager as anyone to find and remove Communists and traitors from government. He knew such people existed, and the security of the nation demanded that they be found. What he couldn't stand was McCarthy's indifference to evidence, his eagerness to spread fear and his attacks on George Marshall. However much he supported McCarthy's avowed goals, Eisenhower despised the man, and as the train headed toward Wisconsin, he showed his speechwriters a paragraph in praise of Marshall that had been written by Arthur Sulzberger of *The New York Times*. He told them he was going to add this paragraph to the speech he gave in Appleton, McCarthy's hometown.

When the train stopped in Peoria, Illinois, and Eisenhower checked into the Pere Marquette Hotel, McCarthy appeared, as rumpled as ever and sporting a large stain on his tie. In the privacy of a hotel suite, the candidate berated McCarthy for his reckless accusations and his slurs against a great American, but McCarthy shrugged it all off. He was probably too drunk to care much what Eisenhower had to say. These rebukes would have sounded like little more than pathetic bleating as they entered the ever-thickening eighty-proof haze that was McCarthy's first layer of defenses. Afterward, when the press wanted to know how the meeting had gone, McCarthy told them equably it had been "a very, very pleasant encounter," which from his point of view was probably true, assuming drinks had been served.[35]

On October 3, when Eisenhower's train arrived in Milwaukee, the governor of Wisconsin, Walter Kohler, supported by the chairman of the Republican National Committee, a Michigan McCarthyite called Arthur Summerfield, managed to convince Sherman Adams that Eisenhower simply had to drop the paragraph praising Marshall. Rebutting McCarthy had nothing to do with the issues, they argued. Sherman Adams eventually agreed with them. The three men then told Eisenhower to drop the offending paragraph. He bristled. "You're telling me that I ought to take the reference out, to Marshall?"

"Yes I am," said Adams. "Not because you're not right but because you're out of context."

Eisenhower turned red, then purple, but they wouldn't budge. He could not attack McCarthy in his home state, they insisted. He'd be telling the Republican voters of Wisconsin that they had done the wrong thing when the elected him. And so it went, until Eisenhower finally yielded.[36]

The fact that he shared a platform with McCarthy and called for the election of all Republican candidates in the forthcoming election haunted him for the rest of his life. It haunted Adams, too. Yet if Eisenhower had delivered his speech as planned, he would have looked opportunistic and hypocritical—trying to get the benefits of associating with McCarthy while making a pathetic pretense of putting some distance between them by standing up for Marshall. He would have diminished himself, and McCarthy would have shrugged the whole thing off as the kind of cynical thing that happens in politics every day. Eisenhower had gotten himself into a situation where he could not emerge with any credit, whatever he did. His big mistake had been to reject the good advice to stay out of Wisconsin.

The Democrats tore into him, then and later, for his pusillanimous deletion of the paragraph praising Marshall, ignoring the fact that Stevenson was just as timid, and with less excuse. When he campaigned in Wisconsin, Stevenson did not offer a robust defense of the Truman administration, nor did he make an outspoken stand for civil liberties. Instead, he took refuge in opaque and ambiguous observations, such as: "Disturbing things have taken place . . . the voice of the accuser stills every other voice in the land." McCarthy responded by making a ferocious personal attack in a radio broadcast that brought Stevenson close to a nervous breakdown. Under McCarthy's brutal assaults, Stevenson talked about quitting the race.[37]

With the campaign entering the final straight, two of Eisenhower's speechwriters, C. D. Jackson and Emmet John Hughes, were working on a speech to be delivered in Detroit on October 24. Why not, suggested Hughes, have Ike say that he'd make a trip to Korea? The man was a five-star general, not just another politician. War was his business.[38]

Eisenhower had been thinking along the same lines for weeks. He didn't need persuading. In the course of the Detroit speech, Eisenhower talked about the current stalemate in the war and Truman's inability to bring the fighting to a close. "That job requires a personal trip to Korea. I shall make that trip. I shall go to Korea!" Here was the most electrifying utterance of the campaign. Without knowing it until they heard it, this was what most Americans wanted to hear. Once heard, it stood as a kind of promise, not that Eisenhower would tour the front—anyone could do that—but that Ike the soldier would find a way to end the war.

On election night, he won handily, with a huge margin in the electoral college. In the popular vote, however, he got 55 percent to Stevenson's 45 percent, which was more or less in line with the average split in presidential elections—a good result, but not a historic one. What mattered, though, wasn't the margin of victory but the fact of it.

Exhausted at the end of a long, trying, sometimes baffling campaign, he was fast asleep when Stevenson conceded. Cliff Roberts went and woke him up. Eisenhower emerged a few minutes later, beaming and alert. He thanked his supporters, made a short statement, then went back to the bedroom.[39]

Sprawled on the bed again, Eisenhower wearily picked up a hotel telephone and called the last Republican president, Herbert Hoover, living the life of an internal exile high in the Waldorf Towers. In their brief exchange of anodyne pleasantries, Eisenhower's past marched into the present, the memory of a younger, eager self stirred within the bald, tired man he had turned into as his destiny and his country's were placed once again on a single trajectory. It wasn't the presidency he had been seeking so much as a fate such as this, an extension of the life he had already lived.[40]

32

From Here to There

It was a ritual performed with a solemnity that testified to its importance, a routine that was bound to make a lasting impression on all the Eisenhower boys. At the end of each month, David Jacob Eisenhower received his modest wages from the Belle Springs Creamery, paid his outstanding bills with an alacrity that young Dwight considered exemplary, then handed over the few notes and coins that were left to Ida's care. She carefully counted the cash before putting it into the sugar bowl. The doctor was paid out of the sugar bowl, winter clothes came out of the sugar bowl, any unexpected expense came out of the sugar bowl. This fragile object, rattling with coins and rustling with notes, was all the financial security they had.

Ida's sugar bowl had been the young Dwight Eisenhower's introduction to the subject of economics, and what lessons did it teach? That banks couldn't be trusted—they might go bust at any time and take your savings with them. On the other hand, without interest to increase your savings, there was the threat of inflation, which might appear like a thief in the night and reduce the value of what was in the sugar bowl even as a family slept. Either way, the menace of penury was always near.

Of course, his understanding of economics had moved on since then. During his time at Columbia, and later in Paris, Eisenhower had sought out people who could educate him on the post-Depression "mixed economy," in which government was expected to play a major role. He began to read the financial pages every day, a habit he never lost.[1]

Besides the financial pages, Eisenhower read widely—far more widely than his detractors ever imagined—but he preferred to absorb some subjects through personal tutorials. He discussed the mixed economy at length with academic economists, with his millionaire golfing pals, such as Cliff Roberts, and with his old friend Bernard Baruch, renowned the length of Wall Street for making a fortune on the stock market before reaching thirty.

Intellectually, Eisenhower was a fiscal conservative, believing in a minimum of government and a maximum of private enterprise. Emotionally, however, he was almost an instinctive Keynesian. That was the legacy of Ida's sugar bowl. Eisenhower never forgot that out there, beyond the triumphant skyscrapers of New York, were millions of families for whom disaster was always only a few dollars away, no matter how diligently they paid their way. If the government had to provide a safety net, it should be one adequate to people's needs. One of the first things Eisenhower intended to do when he became President was increase Social Security, and he would create the federal Department of Health, Education and Welfare.

At the same time, he was worried about the high level of deficit spending that Truman had resorted to fight the war in Korea. War was waste of the worst kind, and increasing the national debt to finance death and destruction would eventually make America weaker, not stronger. A weak economy could not, over the long haul of the Cold War, provide strong defenses—of that, he was certain.

That was why, on election night, with the votes still coming in and in a state of eye-glazing exhaustion, he took a Detroit banker called Joseph Dodge aside for a few minutes and asked him how he'd like to be director of the Bureau of the Budget? That was Ike's first important action as President-elect.[2]

Dodge had been Lucius Clay's financial adviser in the Occupation of Germany, and the benefits of his advice were astounding. Germany was rising from the most comprehensive rubble Eisenhower had ever seen like a rocket-propelled phoenix. The deutschemark, long associated with the ruinous hyperinflation of the 1920s that had helped pave the way for Hitler's rise to power, was already one of world's strongest currencies. The German Bundesbank, created under Dodge's supervision and modeled on the Federal Reserve, was proving to be even better than the Fed at fighting inflation. Getting Dodge aboard the new team was Eisenhower's first move to secure a sound budget and, with it, sound defenses.

The next day, Eisenhower headed for Augusta, and a day or so later, when Brownell came to see him, he found him painting a picture. During the campaign, Brownell had mentioned several times that he didn't want a government job, but Eisenhower had no intention of losing his services. So now he asked Brownell to be White House chief of staff, a position that had never existed before. Brownell turned the idea aside. "My principal interest in life is to be a lawyer," he said. "I'd like to continue in the law."

Ike daubed at the canvas for a minute or so, then looked up. "How about being attorney general?"[3]

He asked Clay and Brownell to advise him on potential cabinet appointments, although he already knew who he wanted for his secretary of state—John J. McCloy, Wall Street lawyer and former assistant secretary of war, a man he knew, liked and trusted. Dewey and Brownell told him McCloy wouldn't do—nominally a Republican, he'd spent most of the past twelve years serving Democratic administrations. Not a real Republican, that is, but not a 100 percent New Deal Democrat, either.

That left John Foster Dulles, who was an inevitable possibility. Eisenhower knew and respected him as an important thinker on foreign affairs. Dulles had never made a secret of his desire to be secretary of state. One of his uncles had held the position and he, as a nineteen-year-old, had participated in the 1909 Hague Convention. Although there was a repellent self-righteousness about Dulles, he was nonetheless a highly paid, highly respected international lawyer and in 1950 Eisenhower had voted for him in a special Senate election in New York.

When he offered Dulles the position of secretary of state, Eisenhower was still hoping to get McCloy aboard as undersecretary of state. Dulles torpedoed that idea, unknown to Ike, by calling McCloy and describing the undersecretary's job in the new administration as being little more than an errand boy. Dulles was not about to help a potential rival stand close to the throne and not above lying to preclude it.[4]

On the recommendation of Sidney Weinberg, the biggest money

raiser in the Citizens for Eisenhower movement, Clay suggested that Ike appoint a Cleveland industrialist, George Humphrey, as his secretary of the Treasury. Clay, who knew Humphrey, knew too that he was a fiscal conservative with impeccable Republican credentials and a reputation for being exceptionally intelligent. Eisenhower accepted Humphrey without having met him.

His old friend, bridge partner and successor in command at SHAPE, Al Gruenther, urged him to appoint Dewey as secretary of defense. Eisenhower put it to Dewey, and Dewey said he didn't want the job. During the campaign, Eisenhower had grown so irritated by Dewey's arrogance and small-mindedness that it isn't likely he urged him to reconsider.[5]

Besides, he had a clear idea of just what was needed in the Department of Defense. Ike had been increasingly agitated at the success of generals and admirals who had used their powerful friends on Capitol Hill and their pull with influential journalists to undermine every secretary of defense and stop unification cold. He believed more than ever in a single armed service, with everyone in the same uniform but pursuing their various specialties—air war, ground war, naval operations, beach storming, whatever—within a unified framework. At present, the Army and the Marines duplicated each other's functions: the Air Force had an air force, the Navy had an air force, the Marine Corps had an air force and the Army flew its own helicopters. Each service bought its equipment and made its plans as if it could fight its own wars.

Nothing would change, Eisenhower was convinced, until there was a strong, head-cracking secretary. "We have tried two investment bankers [James Forrestal and Robert Lovett], a politician [Louis Johnson] and a military man [George Marshall]," he told Henry Cabot Lodge. "Maybe we should try an industrialist." And he knew just the man—Kaufman T. Keller, president of Chrysler. When he put this idea to Clay, however, Clay said, "If you are going into the business world, why not get the head of the biggest business we have?" Eisenhower accepted Clay's logic, and the appointment was offered to Charles E. Wilson, president of General Motors.[6]

Some appointments were almost routine. The party chairman usually got to be postmaster general, so that appointment went to Arthur Summerfield, an automobile dealer from Michigan. Similarly, the job at Commerce went to Sinclair Weeks, chairman of the Republican National Finance Committee. In both Summerfield and Weeks, mediocrity would be well represented in the new administration.

Agriculture went to Ezra Taft Benson of Utah, who was one of the twelve elders of the Mormon Church. Benson knew little about agriculture, but he was from the West and Taft was pushing him zealously. Besides which, Eisenhower liked Benson's high profile as a religious leader. After all, he'd described his campaign as "a crusade" that was going to "clean up the mess in Washington." Benson had solid crusader credentials.[7]

That made seven cabinet members chosen and one to go—secretary of labor—and Eisenhower wanted a Catholic and a woman in the cabinet. He offered the position to Clare Boothe Luce. It was a bizarre choice and one that she had the good sense to turn down. Eisenhower then decided to opt for a Catholic and a Democrat, but one with some knowledge of and interest in the subject. His choice fell on Martin Durkin, a Stevenson Democrat, head of the plumbers' union and a fierce opponent of the Taft-Hartley Act. Taft was having lunch in the Senate dining room when he heard about Durkin's appointment. He banged his fist on the table, agitating the flatware, and bellowed, "This is incomprehensible!" loud enough to spin gray and balding senatorial heads in his direction.[8]

No one ever did make sense of just why Eisenhower put Durkin into the cabinet. Even now, it might seem a quixotic choice, except in one respect: it showed that the new administration would play by different rules.

Truman had long admired Eisenhower and wanted to call him a friend, but there was never, in truth, much chance of that. During his service as Chief of Staff, Eisenhower had developed a strong antipathy to Truman. For one thing, Truman wanted him to drop by the White House at five each afternoon and join the presidential cronies in a drink, the kind of slightly louche behavior that Eisenhower, in his buttoned-up way, disapproved.

More than that, though, he blamed Truman for the Korean War. Although he had publicly supported Truman's defense budgets, in private he tried to tell Truman that the United States was reducing its military strength beyond the levels of safety. The final straw had been Truman's defense budget for 1950, which was only $13 billion. Eisenhower did not believe the United States could defend itself, its allies or its interests for anything less than $15 billion, but Truman ignored his advice. Even before Eisenhower got into politics, he considered Truman incompetent in the first task of government—the security of the state.[9]

Not surprisingly, then, his criticisms of Truman during the campaign were heartfelt. They represented Eisenhower's first and best chance to vent years of accumulated resentments. Truman was deeply wounded, never having expected Eisenhower to attack him so often or so forcefully. Nothing, however, offended Truman more than Eisenhower's pledge to go to Korea. He bitingly dismissed it as "demagoguery" and "patent medicine . . . a desperate attempt to get votes." Eisenhower, in turn, was infuriated by Truman's remarks.[10]

Once Eisenhower had been elected, he received a routine congratulatory telegram from Truman, with a pointed coda: "The *Independence* (the President's plane) will be at your disposal if you still desire to go to Korea." Eisenhower replied that he didn't care what plane he used—he was going.[11]

Before he left, he visited the White House to reassure himself that the transition was progressing—and would continue to progress—smoothly. On November 18, he met with Truman in the Oval Office, then spent half an hour in the Cabinet Room being briefed by Acheson and other senior officials on what he would find when power was transferred. It was a meeting that made him uncomfortable, given his deep irritation at Truman's scathing comments on his integrity during the election campaign. Eisenhower hadn't grown—and had no intention of growing—the extra layer of skin that professional politicians need.

With Truman and Acheson, he was taciturn to the point of seeming sullen and he fidgeted throughout the briefings he received. In truth, while Joe Dodge, his budget director, found it useful to get a preview of the budget that would go to Congress on January 15, five days before the inauguration, Eisenhower did not learn anything significant from this session. He wasn't told anything that a close reading of the newspapers would not have already afforded.[12]

Truman read into Eisenhower's discomfort a sense of anxiety at discovering the size of the challenges ahead. A few days later, at his desk in the Oval Office, with a sign reading THE BUCK STOPS HERE placed to face him, he mused aloud to his staff about what kind of president Eisenhower would make, and couldn't resist a little Schadenfreude. "He'll sit right here and he'll say do this, do that! And nothing will happen. Poor Ike—it won't be a bit like the Army. He'll find it very frustrating."[13]

When the Korean War began, Eisenhower's first thought had been that the United States should do whatever was needed to win it. He favored partial mobilization, authorization for MacArthur to attack North Korea and use of nuclear weapons, if that was what victory required. Since then, Eisenhower had become as frustrated as the rest of the country at Truman's inability either to win the war or bring it to a negotiated settlement.[14]

Shortly before he left for Korea, Eisenhower received a briefing from the JCS. They saw only two possibilities—to continue fighting indefinitely on the present scale of operations or to seek victory by conventional means, which would involve a bigger war and many more American casualties. Eisenhower dismissed both options as "intolerable." There had to be a better way.[15]

Departing for Korea on November 29—aboard a military airplane—he arrived in Seoul on December 2 and found that President Syngman Rhee was trying to get a war-winning offensive going to conquer all of North Korea. During the three days he spent in South Korea, Eisenhower saw Rhee twice, and then only briefly. The UN commander in the Far East, his old friend General Mark Clark, accompanied Eisenhower during his Korean visit and Clark was thinking along the same lines as Rhee. He kept Eisenhower up until three in the morning, arguing that a conventional victory was possible. Eisenhower advised him to forget it. "I know just how you feel, militarily," he said, "but I feel I have a mandate from the people to stop this fighting. That's my decision."[16]

Eisenhower spent most of his three days in Korea touring the front, talking to senior commanders and visiting combat units. He saw his son, John, currently serving with his old battalion in the Third Division, visited a Mobile Army Surgical Hospital and watched artillery batteries firing on enemy positions.

Eisenhower arrived at three conclusions. Even before he left for Korea, he believed that the brunt of the war would have to be borne by the South Koreans. They had not performed well when their country was invaded, but had improved greatly since then. Properly armed and trained, all they would need to continue the fight was American technical and logistical support. That was conclusion number one—the best way to fight the war was Koreans against the Chinese, not Americans against the Chinese.[17]

Conclusion number two was that victory could not be won by conventional means. The terrain was fearsomely rugged and the front more than three hundred miles wide. Hundreds of thousands of fresh troops would be needed, but Rhee had vetoed the offer of several divisions from Chiang Kai-shek, and it was politically impossible to send extra American divisions to Korea.

His third conclusion was this: "We cannot stand forever on a static front and continue to accept casualties without any visible results. Small attacks on small hills will not end this war." But what would?[18]

While Eisenhower was in Korea, MacArthur gave a speech to the National Association of Manufacturers and said he had a plan that would bring a swift end to the war. Eisenhower arranged to meet with him almost as soon as he got back to the United States. Knowing as he did how easily MacArthur could talk himself into an unshakable faith in an impossible plan, Eisenhower would not have had much trouble moderating his expectations when they met in Dulles's Upper East Side town house on December 14.

MacArthur at first proposed ending the war by delivering an ultimatum to Mao Tse-tung: Pull out of Korea, or see China's cities bombed and your country's tiny industrial base wiped out. Eisenhower said, "I'll have to look at the understanding between ourselves and our allies . . . because if we're going to bomb bases on the other side of the Yalu, if we're going to extend the war, we have to make sure we're not offending the whole free world . . ." This was a reference to the British, who he knew would never agree to an attack on China for fear that it might provoke a Chinese attack on Hong Kong.[19]

The other possibility, said MacArthur, would be to have the Air Force drop radioactive waste across North Korea, just south of the Yalu River. This radioactive belt would make it impossible for the Chinese to resupply or reinforce the three hundred thousand men they had deployed in Korea. It would also make it impossible for those three hundred thousand men to get out. They would be trapped. With the enemy demoralized and fixed in place, UN forces should make an amphibious assault on the east and west coasts of North Korea, while launching a major ground offensive from the south. The Chinese would be enveloped from three directions and wiped out.[20]

Eisenhower did not have to look deeply into this proposal to see that it was flawed. As Chief of Staff, and later as SACEUR, he had been closely involved in every aspect of nuclear weapons, from obtaining uranium ore to the final assembly of bombs. MacArthur had no more than an educated person's understanding of atomic weapons and had never been given control of them. Eisenhower knew enough to realize that handling radioactive waste was too complicated and dangerous for this plan to make sense. Even so—and possibly prompted by MacArthur's thinking—he began moving toward his fourth conclusion on the Korean War: nuclear arms were the key to a settlement.

Getting into politics forced Eisenhower to confront a question he had been avoiding ever since he got on the train to West Point: What kind of a Christian was he? There hadn't been enough religion in the family home—there had been an overwhelming surplus. The Bible was read, quoted and memorized, endlessly. What social life David and Ida had revolved around religion. But in the end, David never found a church that satisfied his yearning for some kind of absolute truth and Ida became a devout Jehovah's Witness, distributing pamphlets on the evils of war. Neither his father's spiritual restlessness nor his mother's pacifist certainties were for him, yet Eisenhower never doubted he was a Christian, albeit one with a lot of faith in God and very little in religion. That didn't change much.

Once he decided to seek the Republican nomination, however, Clare Boothe Luce, a convert to Catholicism—converted, that is, from casual unbelief and a life of promiscuity—told him he had to start going to church. Young people already consider you a role model, she said, and as President you will have to set an example to the nation.[21]

Eisenhower started going to church with Mamie, and Mamie was a Presbyterian, so he became a Presbyterian, too. But when Drew Pearson asked him about it, Eisenhower reached into his pants pocket, pulled out a coin and handed it to him. On one side was inscribed FREEDOM. On the other side appeared GOD. Eisenhower said, "That coin represents my religion."[22]

After he was elected President, he managed to convince himself that the government of the United States was based on religious belief, a conclusion that would have surprised the eighteenth-century men of the Enlightenment who had created it and considered faith a strictly private affair. He also developed an interest in prayer. The first manifestation that prayer would be part of the new administration came in a private dining room at the Commodore Hotel in New York on January 12, 1953.

Eisenhower had called his cabinet members, and Nixon, to meet with him there for two days to discuss various aspects of the transition, to finalize inaugural arrangements and to hear the draft of his inaugural address. As the waiters cleared the table after lunch, he asked Ezra Taft Benson to open what amounted to his first cabinet meeting with a prayer. A surprised and delighted Benson did so.[23]

Eisenhower wasn't happy with his speech. He had been working on it since Christmas, with the help of Emmet Hughes, but Hughes, a professional writer, tended to strive for high-sounding phrases while Eisenhower wanted to talk in a direct, down-to-earth way that almost anyone would understand. "My assistant is more enamored with words than ideas! I don't much care about the words if I can convey the ideas accurately," he told his diary. He wanted to talk about the need for increased labor productivity, for example, something that Hughes would have known was likely to set an inaugural-address record for yawning and scratching.[24]

Eisenhower plodded through his speech as his cabinet members, sunk into green leather armchairs, listened. His delivery of a set-piece speech on any public occasion was nearly always slightly stiff and self-conscious. This rehearsal was probably no different. Nevertheless, when he came to a halt, his cabinet applauded vigorously. "I think it is wonderful," said Wilson.

"I read it far more for your blue pencils than for your applause," Eisenhower responded, with a hint of asperity. "I wanted to read it now so you can think it over and be ready to tear it to pieces."

Various objections were raised. Humphrey thought there was too much about foreign aid, and Dulles said he thought there was too much about economics. Henry Cabot Lodge, who had been appointed ambassador to the UN, a post that Ike had elevated to cabinet rank, objected to a reference to Moscow as "the center of revolution in the modern world." Lodge said there were a lot of downtrodden people who were yearning for a revolution. "You are right," said Eisenhower. The passage was struck out.

The second day of the meeting at the Commodore was devoted to talks about how to end the wage and price controls imposed because of the Korean War. Eisenhower and Dodge wanted to lift them as soon as possible, bring in a tax cut and balance the federal budget by cutting government expenditure.

The morning of Inauguration Day, January 20, Ike and Mamie went to the National Presbyterian Church, where other Presidents, such as Ulysses S. Grant and Grover Cleveland, had worshipped. Back at their hotel room, Eisenhower hurriedly wrote out a brief prayer and put it into a coat pocket.

After a quick, early lunch, he was driven to the White House, to collect Truman. A couple of months earlier, when Truman had derided Eisenhower's trip to Korea as demagoguery, Eisenhower had raged, "I'll never ride down Pennsylvania Avenue with him! I'll meet him at the Capitol steps."[25]

He had relented, but not by much. Truman asked him to come in for a cup of coffee, and Eisenhower said he preferred to remain in the car. The ride to the Capitol was frosty, but Eisenhower couldn't resist asking who had thought to bring Major John S. D. Eisenhower home from Korea to witness his father's inauguration. "I did," said Truman. In fact, it had originated with Ike's old friend Omar Bradley, now Chairman of the Joint Chiefs of Staff.[26]

Eisenhower was sworn in as President by Chief Justice Fred Vinson, a sallow pachyderm of a man who clearly had not long to live. Having sworn to protect and defend the Constitution and after shaking hands with Vinson and Truman, he went over and gave Mamie a kiss. Returning to the rostrum, Eisenhower faced the huge crowd that had come out on an unseasonably mild and sunny day, and threw his arms aloft in the famous V sign, that radiant grin lighting up his face.

As the cheering and applause died down, Eisenhower reached into his jacket and pulled out the short prayer he had written two hours earlier. Having prayed that "our concern shall be for all the people, regardless of station, race or calling," he delivered his inaugural address. Most of it was as tedious and instantly forgettable as it had been back at the Commodore Hotel. It was important even so, for in its robustly international outlook there was an implicit rejection of the Republican right wing. The point of his speech was that all the important challenges to American life originated abroad, which meant that the Cold War not only had to be fought—it had to be won.[27]

The parade took six hours to pass the reviewing stand instead of the allotted four. To the consternation of the Secret Service, Eisenhower allowed a man dressed as a cowboy, riding a horse and twirling a lariat, to lasso him. Otherwise, the parade was an ordeal, something to be endured patiently and in good humor. But toward the end, a large, slow-moving object rumbled unsteadily past—a 280mm atomic cannon. This enormous weapon, the first atomic-artillery piece in the world, was both a triumph of miniaturization and the beginning of the end of the Korean War.[28]

The Organization Man

After countless meetings at 1600 Pennsylvania Avenue under three Presidents, he already knew the place well, including the residence upstairs. What the White House meant to Eisenhower was never home but duty, duty again and still more duty. To Mamie, though, the place was sheer enchantment and she loved living there. That did not mean, however, that she considered it perfect. From the day she and Ike moved in, she couldn't wait to change it, starting with the bedrooms.

Pink floral patterns on a pale green background—that was what Mamie had woken up to nearly every morning of her life. It was how her bedroom had been decorated as a child chez Doud and it remained her preference ever after. As an Army wife she had lived, she liked to say, "in everything from shacks with cracks to palaces." An ever-recurring bedroom decor represented stability and continuity. She found it comforting; what Eisenhower thought of it he seems to have kept to himself, but he wasn't President long before, once more, he found himself waking up to pink and green.[1]

Convinced as he was—or, rather, convinced as he needed to be—that he was here in response to the people's will rather than any desire of his own, he began his presidency with much the same optimism and determination to excel that he had brought to his previous assignments, excepting, of course, those two and a half depressing years as Chief of Staff. Besides, from his first day living in the White House, it wasn't just the place that seemed familiar. As he confided to his diary, "Plenty of worries and difficult problems. But such has been my portion for a long time—the result is that this just seems like a continuation of all I have been doing since July 1941—even before that."[2]

He was pleasantly surprised at how smoothly the transition had gone and had the grace to acknowledge Truman's contribution to its success. One of his first actions as President was to write to Truman: "The efforts you made to assure the orderly transfer of government, from your administration to this one, are largely a matter of public knowledge, but . . . you went to far greater trouble to accomplish this than almost anyone else could have known."[3]

His most urgent task was to change the antiquated working methods of the White House, methods that hadn't changed fundamentally since Hoover's day. Roosevelt hadn't bothered to modernize the way the executive branch did its work and neither had Truman. Much of Eisenhower's time his first few weeks as President was devoted to a complete overhaul.

There was a widespread supposition in the country that the first soldier-President since Grant would introduce a different approach to the presidency, something along military lines. Yet Eisenhower's leadership of the executive branch turned out to be less military than Emersonian. "An institution is but the extended shadow of a man," observed Emerson, and in Eisenhower's reorganization of the executive branch a unique, highly individualistic stamp was soon apparent, beginning with his mail.

There is a story that within hours of the inauguration, the chief usher handed him a sealed envelope. Eisenhower was annoyed. "Never bring me a sealed envelope," he said. "That's what I've got aides for." While it's a story that cannot be corroborated, it rings true.[4]

To Eisenhower, a sealed envelope would have been concrete proof of something he already believed—that this place was badly organized, badly run. Hundreds of letters addressed to him arrived each day. Just opening them would have been a chore. More than that, though, they had to be screened, so that only those that he had to read, whether to conduct government business or to keep old friendships in good repair, were placed before him.

Even after all but the most important items had been filtered out, he still had a large number of letters to answer. He also had huge numbers of official documents to sign. He groaned as he thought about the length of his name. "I wish I was A. Doe or something like that." He asked the attorney general's office if his initials would be considered a legal signature. To his relief, he was told that was acceptable. Thereafter, he rarely wrote out Dwight D. Eisenhower again, becoming DE instead, and when hurried, just E.[5]

Eisenhower was appalled to discover that Presidents were required by law to sign every presidential pardon, and there were more than a thousand pardons issued every year. He got the law changed so that he simply signed a single document listing the name of everyone receiving a pardon.[6]

Whatever changes he introduced, he knew he could not impose the military staff system. Military staffs are strictly hierarchical, something that would never be accepted by civilians. What Eisenhower did bring with him from the Army, however, was the military system of having two staffs. There was a small personal staff, which looked after him, paid his bills, handled his mail and generally made sure his time wasn't wasted on petty chores, and a much larger official staff, functioning under the direction of Sherman Adams. This personal staff/official staff system was adopted by all of his successors.[7]

Even so, it was not a complete success. Although Eisenhower delegated huge powers to Sherman Adams—powers that Adams exercised with a self-assurance that to less confident mortals looked like arrogance—the official staff still tended to bring things to him that he felt they ought to be dealing with. Eisenhower told his staff repeatedly that the only problems that crossed his desk should be the difficult ones— the ones that nobody else could resolve. "I shouldn't have to be my own sergeant major!" he protested.[8]

The root problem was the lack of a staff secretariat for the White House. Other great agencies of government—State, Defense—had staff secretariats, but not the executive branch. All it had was the executive clerk, an elderly gent whose functions hadn't changed since the days of McKinley. Eisenhower kept the executive clerk in employment, but also created a staff secretariat under an an able young brigadier general, "Pete" Carroll.

The staff secretariat provided coordination between the various offices within the executive branch. It also functioned as a buffer between him and a staff that would routinely push anything involving national security straight onto the President's desk. Carroll was not only an Army officer; he also sat in on National Security Council meetings. In effect, then, Eisenhower ended up with a chief of staff, Adams, who concentrated on domestic matters, and a staff secretary, Carroll, who ensured coordination in national security matters.[9]

One Eisenhower management technique became famous. His critics portrayed it as an example of his supposed indolence, tiredness or lack of intelligence. It was said that he had told his staff he would not read any memo longer than a single page. This was completely untrue. He had simply indicated a preference for one-page memos, a management technique pioneered by George Marshall. Yet he routinely received, and carefully read, memos that were six or seven pages in length. Many of the more important memos also had a detailed, authoritative report. Having read the memo, he then read as much, or as little, of the report as he felt necessary. Eisenhower thought nothing of reading budget reports running to more than a hundred pages, for example, and discussed them in detail with his economic advisers.[10]

He kept track of what was happening in government by getting a one-line summary of every letter received from a member of Congress. If the summary made the letter seem worth reading, he read it. He also got a daily summary of the thirty to forty most important actions undertaken by government agencies the previous day. Each action was covered by a brief descriptive paragraph. Here, too, if he wanted more information, it could be put in his hands immediately.[11]

Far from being the intellectual dead zone that some of his critics liked to imagine, Eisenhower was always interested in new ideas, another trait he shared with Marshall. He regularly told his staff, "I'm not the only person around here who gets ideas." He filled the White House staff with writers and college instructors and bright young lawyers, hoping they would provide the intellectual ferment that would drive the new administration into the future.

The way he had worked in the War Plans Division, at Allied Force Headquarters, at SHAEF, as Chief of Staff and at SHAPE had been to stimulate debates. He expected the White House staff to do what military staffs did—to present the boss with a choice of options and have the confidence to argue the merits and disadvantages of each with him, face-to-face. His civilian staff members were reluctant to engage in open debate. They were ready to follow his lead, to obey his orders, to explain his policies to others, but they preferred to argue by memo, not by fervent debates over his desk. His presence was a little too powerful, his personality a little too big for all but the toughest and most mature to challenge him man to man.[12]

At times, Eisenhower became irritated at their unwillingness to confront him, to tell him he was wrong. And, typically, his criticism could be scathing. "If I'd had a staff like this during the war," he once grumbled to his secretary, Ann Whitman, "we'd have lost it!"[13]

He was in the habit of making decisions quickly, and on a few occasions, when he was under severe pressure of time, he signed memos without bothering to read them, to the amazement of the staff. He took their word for it that what the memo recommended was the right course of action. He never acted that way with any major decision, but they were flabbergasted that he would do it at all.[14]

While he was quick with decisions, Eisenhower soon found that the federal bureaucracy acted with glacial slowness. It was a bureaucracy that had developed over twenty years under two Presidents who had their own styles. Naturally, when the bureaucracy frustrated Eisenhower, he blamed it on the thousands of Democratic appointees who filled the second-tier slots. "Almost without exception," he explained to Dulles, "these individuals reached these high administrative offices through a process of selection based upon their devotion to the socialistic doctrine and bureaucratic controls practiced over the past two decades." He was confident all the same that over time that would change.[15]

He had some minor management failings of his own to contend with. Eisenhower was too courteous and too sensitive to be able to get rid of a talkative visitor, for example. His secretary, Ann Whitman, or some other member of the White House staff would have to go into the Oval Office and rescue him. Even so, his long experience in the military had given him as good an understanding of the first law of political science as any politician: In a democracy, organization is power.[16]

Arthur Burns was a Columbia economics professor much admired by both business leaders and intellectuals, a rare feat. Eisenhower was so impressed that he appointed Burns to chair his Council of Economic Advisers. The esteem Eisenhower had for Burns was reciprocated in full. Near the end of a long life, during which he had rubbed shoulders with some of the most powerful men of the century, Burns decided, "Eisenhower was the best administrator I have ever known."[17]

There is no provision in the Constitution or in federal law for the cabinet. It simply evolved, born of presidential need and shaped by political logic. By the time Eisenhower was sworn in as the thirty-fourth President, government was unimaginable without it. Even so, he was convinced it had to be modernized, just like the White House. As Army Chief of Staff, he'd sat in on many cabinet meetings during the Truman administration. "They were the darnedest bores," he recalled. Worse, they achieved next to nothing, for lack of coordination. "Jim Forrestal at Defense never knew the action status of any Cabinet matter, except by getting up a special order, going in to the President and making him sign a specific piece of paper!" That had to change.[18]

Cabinet meetings became fixed, regular events: nearly every Friday morning for eight years, he met with the cabinet. Ezra Taft Benson urged him to have each meeting open with a prayer. Eisenhower said a prayer was a good idea and a silent one would be best. So each meeting began with a minute of silence, except for the morning when he launched straight into discussion. His assistant charged with civil rights issues, Maxwell Rabb, scribbled a short note and passed it to him. Eisenhower glanced down at the note, then looked up, slightly flustered. "Goddammit! We forgot the silent prayer!"[19]

He told his cabinet members he didn't expect them to come to the Cabinet Room to tell him what their departments wanted. They were there to advise him on what the country needed. They were to think like statesmen, not salesmen. "You," he told them, "are my operating lieutenants."[20]

As with the White House staff, he expected cabinet members to present him with options and to argue with one another, in his presence, about the superiority of one course of action over another. The cabinet was as slow to catch on as the staff. Eisenhower persisted nonetheless. He used these meetings for various purposes—coordinating policies, stimulating discussion, team building, but most of all for decision making.

As a rule, he didn't have a lot to say. He sat in silence much of the

time, head down, doodling on a piece of White House stationery, drawing his own hands or some cabinet member's nose or an abstract design
of circles or triangles. After a while he'd look up and point his pencil at
someone—Foster Dulles, say, or George Humphrey: "Well, what do
you think?"

After he'd heard enough, he might say, "I'd like to take a vote on
this." Within minutes, a decision was made, arrived at openly and dem-
ocratically. Most of the time, however—and always on key issues—
he simply thanked everyone for their contribution, then announced his
decision.

For every stimulating meeting, there were plenty more that were
deadly dull, partly because the meetings were too big and too democratic. It wasn't only cabinet members who participated. Eisenhower
would invite anyone he thought might have something to contribute to
the issues on that week's cabinet agenda. There might be as many as
fifty people crammed into the room, most of them ready to speak, but
few with anything significant to offer.

The pace also dragged because Eisenhower's secretary of defense,
Charles E. Wilson, loved to hear himself talk. Wilson was the most controversial of Eisenhower's cabinet appointments and the only one who
risked not being confirmed. General Motors did more business with the
Department of Defense than any other contractor, something that raised
obvious conflict-of-interest issues, seeing that Wilson was not only
chairman of GM but one of its major shareholders. When a question
was asked about this potential conflict at his confirmation hearing, Wilson foolishly replied, "I thought what was good for our country was
good for General Motors, and vice versa." This unthinking response,
easily transposed into "What is good for General Motors is good for the
USA," became his lasting contribution to modern American folklore.[21]

Wilson stubbornly resisted congressional pressure to put his stock
into a blind, irrevocable trust. Although Eisenhower had done that with
his own stocks and shares, he was reluctant to pressure Wilson into
doing the same. As head of GM, Wilson was making more than
$500,000 a year in salary and bonuses. As secretary of defense he
would earn $22,500. Eisenhower felt Wilson was already making a sac-
rifice so great it demonstrated a powerful commitment to public service,
not personal gain. Ike's old friend Bill Robinson told him a few days before the inauguration that the Senate didn't see it that way. It was going
to reject Wilson's appointment. During one of the inaugural balls,

Eisenhower had a word with Wilson and told him he'd have to put his share holdings into a blind trust. Wilson did so, and was confirmed.[22]

Eisenhower soon found out, thanks to cabinet meetings, what a bore Wilson was, talking much, saying little, but with an opinion on nearly every subject that came up. Not only was he boring; he could also be irritating.

At the very first cabinet meeting, Eisenhower extolled the virtues of free trade, including trade with countries that had fallen under Soviet control. "I am a little old fashioned," said Wilson sharply. "I don't like selling firearms to the Indians."

"Remember this," said Eisenhower. "The last thing you can do is begin to force all those peripheral countries—the Baltic States, Poland, Czechoslovakia and the rest of them—to depend on Moscow for the rest of their lives. How are you going to keep them interested in you? If you trade with them, Charlie, you have got something pulling their interest your way. You see, you immediately start talking guns and ammunition. I am not talking in those terms. . . . You can't just preach abstraction to a man who has to turn for his daily living in some other direction."

"I think I am going to be on the tough side on this one," Wilson obdurately responded.

"Charlie, I am talking common sense."[23]

Subsequent cabinet meetings brought forth similar homely pronouncements from the Wilson store of folk wisdom. Eisenhower found it tiresome. "Charlie fancies himself as a sort of homespun philosopher," he remarked wearily to Ann Whitman one day.[24]

The cabinet member with whom he got on best—and the only one who became a close personal friend—was George Humphrey. No one had been more reluctant to join the cabinet before finally saying yes. Humphrey was not a mixed-economy man. He believed in a maximum of free enterprise, a minimum of taxation and as little government as possible. "Taking this job is contrary to all my beliefs!" he protested as he yielded to Eisenhower's request.[25]

Humphrey was unapologetic about his strictly conservative, markets-know-best and government-knows-nothing approach to economic policy. On the contrary, he was proud of it. "I'm a hard shell, a non-progressive and everything else," he said, making gentle fun of progressives as "those more forward looking fellows."[26]

Eisenhower took short vacations at Humphrey's Georgia estate, where they would go on turkey shoots together and forget government business for a few days. Humphrey was a major figure in the cabinet—not because he was a financial fundamentalist, however, but because he was a highly intelligent and articulate man with a big personality. Being intelligent, he was amenable to persuasion. Over time, he did not, as many on the White House staff feared and expected, turn Eisenhower into a fiscal conservative. Instead, Eisenhower got Humphrey tilting—slightly—toward economic liberalism and converted him from hostility to the foreign-aid program into one of its most important defenders. Even the hard shell had its cracks, and Eisenhower found them.

Sherman Adams was an unsmiling man of medium build and strong features, and in middle age his gray hair was going white when Eisenhower made him the first-ever White House chief of staff. Adams's title was assistant to the President, but the chief-of-staff tag was applied more or less from the beginning, because it so obviously fit. Besides, the chief-of-staff system was an essential element in the modern military, and the White House staff expected he'd turn out to be a gray-suited version of the same but more emollient, more civilian, unlike Eisenhower's wartime chief of staff, Walter Bedell Smith, who had been famously blunt, decisive and tactless. But far from being a softer version of Smith, Sherman Adams made Beetle Smith look like an honors graduate of charm school.

Eisenhower never got around to spelling out Adams's exact duties. Both men assumed they knew what they were without having to hold a discussion. Certainly, Adams had a clear idea of what his task was from the outset. "The President does the most important things," he told a reporter one day. "I do the next most important things."[27]

Adams was not a Washington insider. He had served one term in Congress before becoming governor of New Hampshire. Blessed with abundant physical energy, he loved a good walk and during his White House years once briskly covered eighty-three miles in twenty-four hours. He was a man of simple tastes, befitting his Puritan roots and a distant kinship with John Adams, and his sole indulgence seemed to be classical music. He also enjoyed poetry and had developed a friendship with Robert Frost.

His wife, Rachel, was a strong personality in her own right, a woman with a Katharine Hepburn accent, thinness and poise. Adams had lunch at his desk each day, reaching into the brown paper bag that Rachel filled that morning with sandwiches. After a blistering row, in which she felt he'd been unjust, she gave him soap sandwiches the next day and he took a big bite out of one. Returning home that evening, the lingering souvenir of a mouthful of soap probably still tingling his palate, he didn't say a word about Lifebuoy for lunch—his way of admitting he'd been in the wrong.[28]

Somewhere along the way he had developed a severe politesse deficit. The words *thank you, hello* and *good-bye* seemed to have been excised from his vocabulary. One word he was good with, though, was *no*. His style as chief of staff was abrupt rather than brusque, but not everyone appreciated the difference.

Washington was filled with self-important people dreaming up excuses to see Eisenhower and hoping to have their picture taken with him. They had to go through Adams, and before long the city was buzzing, with the rejected ones moaning about what a son of a bitch that Adams guy was, and so *rude*. Nor did he show much respect for status. Here was a typical episode. Senator John Sherman Cooper of Kentucky went to see him one day and began explaining why it was important that he, Cooper, be allowed to choose the next federal district judge in Kentucky.

Adams grunted, "We'll make that appointment," and spun around in his leather chair, turning his back on the senator. End of conversation.[29]

Senator Prescott Bush of Connecticut had a very different experience. Bush decided to get to know Adams; he was curious to find out just what this man was like. Having decided to form a friendship with Washington's "Abominable No Man," he found that it was amazingly easy.[30]

The White House staff, with only a few exceptions, developed a strong liking for Adams. It took a while for people to get used to his abruptness, to having the phone ring, picking it up, hearing a voice at the other end say, "Go and see so and so. Tell him to do such and such, then report back to me." At which point there was a click and the line went dead.[31]

What the staff liked about him were his directness and honesty. There was no other side to Adams, no hidden agenda, no playing favorites, no office politics. Jim Hagerty, Eisenhower's press secretary, was impressed that if you went to Adams needing a quick yes or a fast no, you got it. Adams never tried to cover his back. He simply did whatever he thought was right.[32]

And that was what Eisenhower had been hoping for. "His quick mind is something I need so much around here," Eisenhower told other members of the staff. "He comes up with the kind of answers I can rely on."[33]

Adams also protected him from visitors who were going to waste his time. Although Eisenhower had an appointments secretary, it was really Adams who controlled the President's appointments. That was an important reason he was so unpopular with so many on Capitol Hill. On domestic issues, there wasn't much paperwork that got into the Oval Office without "O.K.—S. A." scrawled in a corner. It was also Adams, screening the memos, who tried to limit most of them to three hundred words and one page.

With the creation of a staff secretariat and the appointment of a decisive, confident chief of staff, Eisenhower had modernized the presidency, creating a system that allowed him to concentrate his time and energy on winning the Cold War by winning the peace.

34

Maximum Danger

He could hear them wailing against death in the winter darkness, their anguish carried on the freezing air. Night after night, people gathered in their hundreds near the Zero Milestone and clung—or chained themselves—to the railings fringing the South Lawn, where they sang Woody Guthrie songs, chanted the antique slogans of the left and demanded clemency for Julius and Ethel Rosenberg, who had betrayed atomic secrets to the Soviets. Both had been condemned to death nearly two years before Eisenhower became President and by January 1953 they had exhausted every legal avenue but one—presidential clemency.

Their guilt was not in dispute—not to him, anyway—and recent evidence shows that Julius was undoubtedly guilty. What haunted Eisenhower, though, was the punishment of the innocent. The Rosenbergs had two small boys. To execute their parents was to make these children orphans. Long before he became President he had fathered two sons himself. Yet treason is a different kind of crime, never more so than when a nation feels its very existence is at stake.[1]

It may well have been at Eisenhower's behest that two weeks after he became President, government lawyers told Ethel Rosenberg that if she submitted a separate plea for clemency she might be spared, because of her sex and because her sons would still have their mother. She told Julius she had rejected this suggestion, "in which I shall live without living and die without dying," and pledged, "No power on Earth shall divide us, in life or in death."[2]

This kind of spirit could only have made it harder for Eisenhower to do what he felt he had to do. With a heavy heart, he refused clemency. The Rosenbergs' crime, he said, "could well result in the deaths of many, many thousands of innocent citizens." On June 19, 1953, they died in the electric chair at Sing Sing.

The Rosenbergs were amateurish spies and the material they delivered to the Soviets had little value. Their punishment seems excessive compared to the crime, but these were fraught and anxious times, and would have been so even had Joe McCarthy succeeded in his adolescent ambition to become a successful chicken farmer and never sought fame beyond Wisconsin.

The national security strategy that Eisenhower inherited from Truman was an attempt to look into the abyss without blinking. Set out in a document known as NSC 68, it declared, "This Republic and its citizens [are] in deadly peril." It described the conflict with the Soviet Union as "a total struggle," which suggested that only one side would survive it. Negotiations with the Soviets on some issues might prove necessary, it conceded, but the fundamental conflict between the democratic, capitalist West and an illegitimate, aggressive Communist regime was too deep ever to be reconciled.

This inherent clash of antagonistic political systems combined with atomic arms to make a nuclear Armageddon likely, and NSC 68 offered a prophecy. By 1954 the Soviet Union would possess two hundred nuclear weapons, enough to embolden the expansionist and insecure Soviet leadership to attempt a surprise attack on the United States. NSC 68 said that 1954 would be "the year of maximum danger," the time such an attack was most likely to occur.[3]

Truman had been pondering this grimly pessimistic document when the Korean War broke out in June 1950. The Communist assault on South Korea was an act of aggression that seemed to justify both the martial tone and the alarming conclusions of NSC 68. In September 1950, Truman formally accepted this document as the basic national strategy for waging the Cold War. In doing so, he adopted the remedy to Soviet expansionism and adventurism advanced by NSC 68—the accumulation of "preponderant power," by expanding American forces—

nuclear and conventional—on a huge scale. The most important single step was a crash program to build a hydrogen bomb. The H-bomb was the only real hope of retaining America's nuclear advantage as the year of maximum danger approached. NSC 68 also brought the money for the Strategic Air Command to develop a large force of jet bombers and acquire a string of overseas bases from which it could reach deep into Soviet territory.[4]

The H-bomb project succeeded. At the beginning of November 1952, a thermonuclear device more than fifty times as powerful as the bomb that had obliterated Hiroshima was exploded on Elugelab, a tiny island in the South Pacific. The island vanished, its onetime existence marked on the ocean floor by a black scar two miles long and half a mile wide.

When Eisenhower was sworn in as President, the U.S. possessed roughly thirteen hundred nuclear weapons. At the same time, SAC had compiled a list of five thousand potential targets, of which roughly one thousand would have to be taken out in a first strike, but it did not yet have enough bombers, trained crews and forward bases to carry out a successful attack.[5]

The immediate needs of the Korean War and the overarching push to acquire preponderant power were driving the defense budget straight up—from $13 billion in 1950 to a projected $73 billion in 1953. Eisenhower refused to accept the strategic vision of NSC 68 or its astronomical price tag.

Two months into his presidency, he paced the Oval Office one afternoon thinking out loud about his hopes for a different national strategy and a less confrontational approach to the Soviet Union. "Look, I am tired and I think everyone is tired of just plain indictments of the Soviet regime," he burst out to an astonished Emmet Hughes, who had just brought him the rough draft of a speech to be delivered to the American Society of Newspaper Editors. "Just *one* thing matters—what have *we* got to offer the world? What are we ready to do to improve the chances of peace? If we cannot say these things—A, B, C, D, E—just like that— then we really have nothing to give, except just another speech.

"Here is what I would like to say—the jet plane that roars over your head cost three quarters of a million dollars. This is more money than a man earning ten thousand dollars a year is going to make in his lifetime. What world can afford this for long? We are in an armaments race.

Where will it lead us? At worst, to atomic warfare. At best, to robbing every people and nation on Earth of the fruits of their own toil.

"Now, there could be another road before us—the road of disarmament. What does this mean? It means for everybody in the world bread, butter, clothes, homes, hospitals, schools—all the good and necessary things for decent living. So let *this* be the choice we offer. Let us talk straight—*no* double talk, *no* sophisticated political formulas, *no* slick propaganda devices . . .

"What do we say about the Soviet government? The past speaks for itself. I am interested in the future . . . let us begin talking to each other."[6]

In his search for a new national strategy, he was even now expanding and strengthening the National Security Council. Under Truman, it had met intermittently, usually at moments of crisis. Under Eisenhower, it met every Thursday morning, and during the course of his presidency, he took part in almost every meeting. He created the post of special assistant to the President for national security affairs, and persuaded a Boston investment banker, Robert Cutler, to fill it.

Cutler possessed literary talents and interests, having been the class poet of his 1922 Harvard class and published three novels. He had also been active in the Army reserve. During the war he'd served on Stimson's staff and returned to civilian life with a brigadier general's star, a Distinguished Service Medal and one of the rarest things in the world, overt praise from Marshall, who called him "a rose among cabbages." Cutler had also served as a consultant to the NSC under Truman. His appointment provided a measure of continuity.[7]

Determined to keep the NSC from becoming too big to be truly effective, Cutler limited the permanent members to eight, plus the President and Vice President. To achieve what he liked to call "pow-wow," Cutler claimed you couldn't have more than twelve people involved in a discussion, and it was a good idea to make sure the table wasn't too big, either.

Eisenhower strengthened the NSC by putting the secretary of the Treasury, George Humphrey, and the chairman of the Atomic Energy Commission, Lewis Strauss, on it. He also began bringing outside consultants—the presidents of major businesses and universities—to meetings, hoping they would provide a completely independent view, but they undermined Cutler's small-size, modest-table theory, putting pow-wow in doubt. All we get from these outsiders, he told Eisenhower, is "ivory tower advice from people without operating responsibilities." Eisenhower got rid of them.[8]

At some point during any NSC meeting, Eisenhower was likely to say, "What's best for America?" Most of the time, he doodled while the discussion swirled around him, listening intently, head down, pencil busy. Dulles doodled, too, on a yellow legal pad, but with an air of simmering resentment. It galled him to be forced to tolerate outsiders—people such as Budget Bureau officials—treading onto the hallowed turf of foreign relations.[9]

With the NSC as with cabinet meetings, what Eisenhower was always looking for was lively, well-informed debate on compelling issues. Once a problem had been clearly identified, he expected Cutler and the NSC planning staff to present the meeting with potential courses of action. When he didn't get that, he became restless. One day his irritation got the better of him and he burst out in the middle of one of Cutler's expositions, "Damnit, Bobby, bring us issues and options so we can make some decisions here!"[10]

After any NSC meeting ended, Eisenhower was likely to continue the discussion in the Oval Office with Cutler, Dulles and a handful of others. Some of the White House staff complained to one another that he was spending too much time with the NSC, and a senior Pentagon official, Gordon Gray, became alarmed as he saw how intensely Eisenhower threw himself into national security problems. "We've got to do something," he told Cutler. "These NSC meetings are going to kill the President!"[11]

One Monday morning in May 1953, Eisenhower had barely gotten himself seated at his Oval Office desk when Cutler came in and started telling him what had happened the previous afternoon when he had gone to Dulles's house. Foster's brother, Allen Dulles, the head of the CIA, had been there. So, too, were Cold War propaganda director C. D. Jackson and Walter Bedell Smith, Ike's wartime chief of staff, whom Eisenhower had appointed undersecretary of state.

The meeting had been simply wonderful, said Cutler. Foster had spoken for ninety minutes, presenting a masterly overview of the entire world. The Soviets had managed to seize the initiative in the Cold War and the current national security strategy offered no hope of getting it back, but Dulles thought there were alternatives to NSC 68 that might regain it for the United States.

Cutler told Eisenhower he thought this discussion ought to be continued at the White House. "Let's say five-thirty P.M. on Thursday," Eisenhower replied. They'd meet in the solarium, up on the roof, where Eisenhower played bridge and painted.[12]

That Thursday evening, as Dulles began explaining alternative national security strategies, he was repeatedly interrupted by Mamie's canary, which seemed to be taking a lively interest. The canary was eventually banished, to trill in isolation behind ferns and canvases. Eisenhower heard Dulles out, then said he would create three task forces to explore the possibilities Dulles had presented.

Broadly speaking, Task Force A would take a fresh look at containment, regard the Soviet challenge as being more political than military and try to devise a containment strategy that wouldn't bankrupt the country. Task Force B would consider a strategy based on nuclear weapons and mutual deterrence. It would assume the Soviet threat was military, rather than political, demanding a strong military response. Task Force C was to look at the possibility of rolling back Soviet power. The idea was to force the Kremlin to consolidate what it had and stop trying to expand its influence. This strategy would be one of psychological warfare, economic pressure and covert operations, aggressively conducted, even at the risk of a Soviet military response.[13]

Setting up these task forces and appraising the results was called Operation Solarium and was typical of Eisenhower's style of Cold War management. The task forces worked throughout the summer, meeting at the National War College at Fort McNair. Task Force A was chaired by George Kennan, the intellectual fountainhead of containment. Kennan had been ambassador to Moscow until Dulles became secretary of state, when he was more or less forced out of the foreign service. But Eisenhower was not about to pass up the chance to exploit Kennan's mind and expert knowledge.

The chairman of Task Force B was an Air Force general who was both an expert on nuclear weapons and an experienced military planner. Task Force C was headed by the chief of naval operations, Admiral Robert W. Carney.

On July 16, Eisenhower had all three task forces report to him in person. Their presentations took an entire day and were made in the White House library. Each task force argued its strategy at length and in detail. It was late in the evening when Eisenhower stood up and began pacing the library carpet. Speaking for nearly an hour, without notes, he gave a clear synopsis of each presentation, then analyzed its strengths and weaknesses. Here was an Eisenhower that Kennan had never seen, did not even imagine existed. As the meeting broke up, Kennan remarked, astonished, "He has just asserted his intellectual ascendancy over every man in this room!"[14]

The result of Operation Solarium was NSC 162/2. Eisenhower took various elements from the task-force proposals and fashioned them into a new national security strategy. Where NSC 68 had postulated a year of maximum danger, Eisenhower was planning for the long haul. What lay ahead, he was certain, were many years of unrelenting struggle between Western societies based on the rule of law and Communist states based on the rule of fear. And where NSC 68 had anticipated a strong American response to every Soviet challenge, Eisenhower proposed to defend only America's "permanent interests," namely, Western Europe, Japan, Israel, Taiwan and South Korea.

Like Kennan, he believed that over time the Soviet Union would mellow. It therefore made sense to negotiate with the Russians. Even so, American forces not only had to be strong enough to deter Soviet aggression in Europe, or anywhere else of vital interest to the U.S.; if deterrence failed, the U.S. had to be ready to destroy the Soviet Union.

He intended to do this not after but before any attack on the United States could be launched. This was the most important single element in Eisenhower's Cold War strategy: he was not going to base American security on a strike from beyond the grave, on some radioactive fulfillment of an old Scottish ballad:

> I dreamed last night a terrible dream.
> Beyond the Isle of Skye,
> I saw a dead man win a fight—
> I think that man was I.

Eisenhower explicitly ruled out a preventive war, but not a preemptive strike. He began to create a strategic force capable of detecting any Soviet move toward a nuclear attack. Once detected, it might conceivably be possible to tell the Soviets to back down or else, but if a warning was tried and failed, or if there was not enough time even to warn the Kremlin, he was going to beat the enemy to the punch.

Any serious move toward launching a surprise attack would be interpreted as a casus belli. The bombs didn't have to explode first. At its most obvious and banal, it was the dramatic device of a thousand Westerns—at the climactic showdown, all the bad guy has to do is reach for his gun to justify the good guy's drawing quicker and shooting him dead.

"Our only chance of victory," Eisenhower told the NSC on December 3, 1953, "would be to paralyze the enemy at the outset of the war. . . . If war comes, the other fellow must have started it. Otherwise we would not be in a position to use the nuclear weapon, and we have got to be in a position to use that weapon . . ."[15]

Two days later, he told Churchill, "Anyone who holds up too long in the use of his assets in atomic weapons might suddenly find himself subjected to such widespread and devastating attack that retaliation will be next to impossible." And when senior congressional figures protested that his strategy ignored the requirement for Congress to declare war, he responded that if faced with "a gigantic Pearl Harbor, I *will* act to protect the United States."[16]

In January 1954, Dulles gave a widely reported speech in which he spoke of America's "massive retaliatory power." Eisenhower was repeatedly pressed to explain what "massive retaliation" meant, but he invariably took refuge in ambiguity, giving many people the impression that he hadn't thought clearly about how nuclear weapons would be used. In truth, he knew exactly what he had in mind. "When we talk about power and massive retaliation," he told members of the NSC, "we mean retaliation against an act that to us means irrevocable war!" On another occasion, he told his staff plainly, "SAC must not allow the enemy to strike the first blow."[17]

Right-wing Republicans damned the Roosevelt and Truman administrations as "twenty years of treason" and held up the Yalta agreement as proof of Democratic complicity with Soviet Communism. They had also been persuaded by MacArthur, by the Korean War and by genuine dismay at the triumph of Chinese Communism over the Kuomintang regime of Chiang Kai-shek that Asia mattered far more to American security than did Europe.

Eisenhower loathed the Republican right wing and deplored all talk of twenty years of treason. He also never doubted that a free, democratic and militarily strong Western Europe was more important to America's security than the Far East, whatever happened there. Yalta, though, had been a mistake. It more or less sanctioned the permanent Soviet occupation of the Baltic states and Eastern Europe.

Although he detested Asia Firsters and the right wing of his own party, he nevertheless offered them the crumbs of comfort, while denying them any real influence over his foreign policy. In his first State of the Union address, delivered only weeks after he became President, Eisenhower declared, "I shall ask the Congress at a later date to join in an appropriate resolution making clear that this government recognizes no commitment of any kind contained in secret understandings of the past with foreign governments which permit this [Yalta] kind of enslavement." Republicans of all persuasions, not just those on the right wing, were ecstatic. They read into this opaque utterance a promise that at some point the United States would repudiate the Yalta agreement. What they overlooked—but Eisenhower did not—was that the Democrats were never going to agree to any posthumous censure of Roosevelt or a repudiation of Yalta.[18]

That was crumb number one. Crumb number two was equally paltry yet was eagerly snatched up. When the Korean War began, Truman had deployed the Seventh Fleet to patrol the waters between Taiwan and mainland China. He did not intend to allow the Chinese to invade Taiwan. This only encouraged Chiang's forces to step up their raids along the Chinese coast. In 1952, these raids became increasingly frequent and grew much bigger. There was a risk that they might provoke the Chinese into an attack on Taiwan, even if that meant attacking the Seventh Fleet. The U.S. could find itself being dragged by Chiang Kai-shek into a wider war with China. Shortly before Truman left office, he and the JCS decided to remove the Seventh Fleet from the waters between Taiwan and the Chinese mainland.[19]

They did not, however, announce this decision. Truman did not want to seem to be appeasing the Chinese Communists. It was Eisenhower's good fortune that he was able to announce the redeployment of the Seventh Fleet in his State of the Union speech. Coming from him, it didn't seem like appeasement. Instead, the Republican party was thrilled, eagerly talking about this move as "unleashing Chiang" when it had exactly the opposite effect. Without the Seventh Fleet to worry about, the Red Chinese were able to do a more effective job of guarding their coastline and the number of raids dropped sharply.

On March 4, as Eisenhower sat down for breakfast, the chief usher said he had a message from Robert Cutler—during the previous evening Stalin had suffered a stroke. He was not expected to survive. When Eisenhower walked into the Oval Office half an hour later, Cutler, Dulles, Hagerty and C. D. Jackson were there. "Well," said Eisenhower, "what do you think we can do about this?"[20]

In fact, there wasn't anything substantial to be done. After meeting with the NSC, Eisenhower issued a statement of sympathy for the "multitudes of Russians [who] are anxiously concerned because of the illness of the Soviet ruler. . . . They are the children of the same God who is father of all peoples everywhere. And like all peoples, Russia's millions share our longing for a friendly and peaceful world."[21]

Stalin died the next day, making a settlement of the Korean War more likely but not certain. To many Republicans, Korea posed a simple choice: all-out or pull out. Eisenhower rejected both possibilities. What he wanted was a settlement, one that would last.

Talks had been going on, intermittently, since July 1951, first in Kaesŏng, then at Panmunjom. The fact that the two sides had agreed to talk that summer was a tacit acknowledgment of a battlefield stalemate. It wasn't long, though, before the talks themselves reached impasse, and when it proved impossible to agree where the truce line should be drawn, they had broken down. Even during the armistice talks, fighting continued. Talks were renewed, in the summer of 1952, only to break down in November 1952, this time over the issue of prisoner repatriation.

The crunch point was Truman's refusal to allow the forcible repatriation of North Korean and Chinese prisoners, even though this amounted to rejecting the Geneva Convention, which made no provision for the principle of voluntary repatriation. Eisenhower's first task in Korea was getting a resumption of the talks, but he happened to agree with Truman—there would be no forcible repatriation. "To force those people to go back to a life of terror and persecution is something that would violate every moral standard by which America lives," he declared at a Republican fund-raising dinner in New York. "It would be unacceptable to the American code, and it cannot be done."[22]

Shortly after Stalin's death, the new Soviet leadership began pushing a more emollient line, declaring there were no outstanding conflicts with the capitalist West that couldn't be resolved "on the basis of mutual understanding." And then, at the end of March, the Chinese suddenly agreed to a proposal made by Mark Clark that the two sides should exchange sick and wounded prisoners. They also sounded more amenable on the issue of forcible repatriation.

Eisenhower saw a glimmer of hope in these developments—not only for an end to the war in Korea, but for a fresh start with the Soviets. He used the speech he had been working on with Emmet Hughes to reach out to the new leadership in the Kremlin and to vent his rising impatience with the arms race. Delivered to the Society of American Newspaper Editors in Washington on April 16, it became known as his "Chance for Peace" speech, one of the finest public utterances of his life.

As he began his speech, Eisenhower had a sudden ileitis attack. Sweat ran in rivulets down his bald head as he gripped the lectern and willed himself to move from one sentence to the next. There was something here he was determined to say. Not even agonizing pain in his small intestine was going to stop him now.

After some ritual bashing of the Soviets—at Dulles's behest—he launched with pent-up passion into a plea for the nations of the world to change course. The Cold War had divided humanity and filled it with dread. "The worst to be feared and the best to be expected can be simply stated. The *worst* is atomic war. The *best* would be this: a life of perpetual fear and tension; a burden of armies draining the wealth and labor of all peoples; a wasting of strength that defies the American system or the Soviet system or any system to achieve abundance and happiness . . .

"Every gun that is made, every warship launched, every rocket fired signifies, in the final sense, a theft from those who hunger and are not fed, those who are cold and are not clothed.

"This world in arms is not spending money alone. It is spending the sweat of its laborers, the genius of its scientists, the hopes of its children. The cost of one modern heavy bomber is this—a modern brick school in more than thirty cities. . . . We pay for a single fighter plane with half a million bushels of wheat. We pay for a single destroyer with new homes that could have housed more than eight thousand people . . .

"This is not a way of life at all, in any true sense. Under the cloud of threatening war, it is humanity hanging from a cross of iron."[23]

He urged the new Soviet leadership to join the United States in seeking a different path. "The first great step along this way must be the conclusion of an honorable armistice in Korea." It should also include an end to the Communist insurgencies in Vietnam and Malaya, an end to the Soviet occupation of Austria and the creation of a free and united Germany.

It was a lot to ask—too much, in fact. But Eisenhower would have been well aware of that. The most he could realistically hope for was a gradual shift in direction, not an outpouring of miracles. He was looking to the slow workings of history, not an instant payoff.

His rhetoric about houses and schools, wasted talents and dashed hopes meant nothing to the men in the Kremlin. These slightly pathetic, uneducated figures in ugly serge suits had risen to the top as Stalin's lickspittles. To them, idealistic language was merely another tool, like the feculent huts of the gulag and the rusty stains on the cement floors of the Lubyanka, for keeping their people ignorant, impoverished and under control. This was a leadership that had not evolved sufficiently to understand the moral imperatives of civilized societies. They ignored Eisenhower's "Chance for Peace."[24]

It was nonetheless well worth giving, for it remains the most trenchant criticism ever made of the Cold War, its sincerity so obvious that no decent person could doubt it. Eisenhower was right to give this speech despite the heavy toll on his strength, for what he said that day needed to be said.

Even as he spoke, there were indications of an impending Chinese offensive in Korea, a matter in which he had a strong personal interest. John Eisenhower was serving in Korea and had recently been awarded the Combat Infantryman's Badge. Eisenhower told the cabinet that if the Chinese did mount a major attack, it would be possible for UN forces to counterattack and drive them a hundred miles north, pushing them well beyond the 38th parallel. Even so, it would be impossible to do this without the Chinese learning of the preparations for such an attack in advance, something that would make an offensive more costly in terms of casualties. It would also require sending more troops to Korea and would add about $4 billion to the defense budget.[25]

When the Chinese finally launched their offensive, it was aimed at the Republic of Korea divisions, who fell back in disarray. The rapid redeployment of American troops to plug the holes and shore up the weak spots brought an interesting development—the Chinese backed off. They were clearly trying to avoid a major fight with the Americans.[26]

Eisenhower was determined that one way or another, the murderous roundelay of offensive followed by counteroffensive, followed by another offensive and so on, was going to stop. Atomic bombs were shipped to Okinawa, the atomic cannon was test-fired in May and went into production, work was started on a battlefield missile with an atomic warhead and development began of nuclear weapons that could be dropped from fighter-bombers.

In May, Dulles went to India to spend three days with Nehru, during which he made it clear that the United States wanted a settlement, not a bigger war. A few days later, the Chinese were told by an Indian diplomat that if the war continued, Eisenhower was prepared to launch an atomic attack on China itself if there was not an armistice soon.[27]

Talks at Panmunjom had resumed in April, but the Chinese offensive had cast a cloud over them. In June, however, there was rapid progress toward an armistice agreement. Whether it was the carrot proffered to the new leadership in Moscow or the stick of atomic war proffered to the Chinese that brought the breakthrough has been debated ever since. In all likelihood, it was probably because he had used both the carrot and the stick that Eisenhower's tactics worked.

The final obstacle turned out to be in neither Moscow nor Peking but in Seoul. The aged South Korean leader, seventy-nine-year-old Syngman Rhee, informed Eisenhower bluntly that he would never accept any agreement that left Korea divided. Eisenhower responded that Rhee could have a mutual defense treaty and large amounts of economic and military aid if he relented, or an American pullout if he didn't. Rhee backed down.[28]

On Sunday, July 26, the last, fine details of the armistice were being worked out at Panmunjom and signing was nigh. Eisenhower waited in the residence upstairs at the White House, tinkering with a message he intended to broadcast once the agreement was signed. He wondered about adding Lincoln's noble phrase "With malice toward none; with charity for all" to his text. Would that seem pretentious? Picking up the phone, he called Hagerty, who said a Lincolnian passage would work nicely.

The long-awaited word from Panmunjom finally came through a little after nine-thirty in the evening. Eisenhower went downstairs to the Broadcast Room to deliver his message live at ten P.M. He sat at the huge oak desk that Queen Victoria had given Benjamin Harrison, a magnificent object fashioned from the timbers of a Royal Navy frigate from the days of sail. As Eisenhower fidgeted with his spectacles and his message, a photographer hovering nearby asked, "How do you feel, Mr. President?"

A relieved smile broke across Eisenhower's broad features as he looked up. "The war is over—I hope my son is going to come home soon."[29]

New Look

For most of his life he'd been a study in brown, garbed in every shade the Army provided, from the bitter chocolate of the heavy greatcoat to the good-taste beige of the light tropical worsted. Even after he resigned from the Army, Eisenhower retained a partiality for shades of brown in his hats, shoes, suits and overcoats. Yet apart from the way that brown had seeped into his dress sense—and he was a remarkably sharp dresser for a lifelong federal employee—he had no difficulty putting the Army to one side when it came to defense policy.

In retrospect, it isn't surprising that his relationship with the Army he loved would turn out that way. Eisenhower had been an outstanding soldier not because he was ever interested in refighting the last war—a common criticism of military men—but because he was always thinking about winning the next one. His national-security strategy, based first and foremost on developing a preemptive strike capability, meant that the Air Force was going to have priority. Second would come the Navy, which could project American power into the most remote parts of the world and might one day supplement SAC's preemptive attack.

To the Army, however, it was agonizing to be relegated to third place under a soldier-President. There was a lot of bitterness and muted grumbling in the O Clubs that Ike seemed to have forgotten where he came from.

Such criticism hurt, because Eisenhower never stopped identifying with the Army. He couldn't go to the Army-Navy game, for instance, because he knew he would never be able to seem impartial, as tradition required. He was likely to holler, "Goddammit!" if Navy scored, and it might take chains to keep him seated if Army got a touchdown.[1]

Shortly after Eisenhower became President, the Army had a new Chief of Staff, General Matthew B. Ridgway, and the Navy got a new chief of naval operations, Admiral Robert W. Carney. Neither man agreed with the new national strategy. There was also a new Chairman of the Joint Chiefs. At the end of his visit to Korea following the election, Eisenhower had spent nearly a week sailing to Hawaii aboard the cruiser *Helena*. During that voyage, he got to know the naval commander in the Pacific, Admiral Arthur W. Radford. A naval aviator, Radford was an enthusiast for new military technologies and strategies based on nuclear weapons. When Omar Bradley's service as Chairman of the Joint Chiefs came to an end in the summer of 1953, Eisenhower appointed Radford to take his place.[2]

One of Radford's earliest actions in his new post was to take Ridgway and Carney for a cruise aboard the Navy secretary's yacht, the *Sequoia*. Over the course of three days and nights, as the sights along the Potomac slipped gently past, he pressured them into signing a paper in which they said they supported the administration's defense policies.

Radford knew that both Ridgway and Carney were going to be deeply unhappy when they saw the cuts that Eisenhower and Charlie Wilson intended to make in the defense budget. The budget that would go to Congress in January 1954 for fiscal year 1955 proposed to reduce defense expenditures from the current level of $43 billion down to $37.5 billion. The Air Force would get roughly 45 percent of the defense budget, the Navy 30 percent and the Army only 25 percent.

During the winter of 1953, Wilson was busy selling the new-style military to the public and to Congress. He argued that by giving airpower a greater role in national strategy and relying more on technology than on manpower, huge personnel reductions were possible. This cheaper but more powerful force structure—based on nuclear weapons, advanced technologies such as missiles and a dramatic reduction in ground forces—became known as the New Look.

Eisenhower, too, was selling it hard, first in his State of the Union address in January 1954, and again a few days later in his budget message to Congress. Dulles, meanwhile, gave a speech to the Council on Foreign Relations in which he talked about the new strategy, presenting it as one based entirely on deterrence, but deterrence with a hair trigger. "The way to deter aggression is for a free community to be willing and able to respond vigorously and at places and with means of its own choosing. The basic decision was made to depend primarily on a great capacity to retaliate instantly, by means and at places of our choosing."[3]

This speech gave the impression that the United States would strike back, hitting the Soviet Union only after it had been attacked, which wasn't true. In fact, even as Dulles gave his speech, Curtis LeMay, the commander of the Strategic Air Command, was working—with what glow of satisfaction we can only guess at—on a report that spelled out in detail SAC's ability to fulfill its primary mission. There were finally enough bombers, trained crews, forward bases and nuclear weapons for SAC to take out all six hundred Soviet military airfields and most of the command-and-control centers in a first strike. Every major urban-industrial center, such as Moscow and Leningrad, plus important urban-military centers, such as Vladivostok and Murmansk, would be destroyed in the same attack. The Soviets might have enough military power remaining in Eastern Europe to strike the cities of Western Europe in retaliation, but they would be incapable of posing any significant threat to the United States. Eisenhower's national security strategy now rested on the firmest possible foundation—American invulnerability to nuclear attack.[4]

Dulles's speech was colored by that realization, making him seem more than confident in America's might. But he couldn't talk about that directly. Instead, he confused the issue by talking about deterrence, without talking about the first-strike capability that made deterrence credible. His abrasive smugness and self-righteousness further clouded public understanding because they stirred up considerable animosity toward him. Dulles came across to liberal professors and journalists as a slightly creepy, Manichaean Presbyterian preacher stalking the world stage, H-bombs in his hands and sticking out of his every pocket, itching for an opportunity to nuke the godless Reds. Yet the "massive retaliation" speech, Dulles's most famous utterance, was written in large part by Eisenhower and all of it had been approved by him.[5]

Perceptive people such as George Kennan had no difficulty piercing the deliberate fog of obfuscation that Eisenhower and Dulles generated around nuclear weapons and the new national security strategy. In one of the BBC's prestigious Reith lectures, Kennan declared bluntly, " 'Massive retaliation' is only another expression for the principle of first strike."[6]

Meanwhile, most Americans paid little attention to massive retaliation or paused to wonder what it might mean in practice. It was enough for them that Eisenhower was in charge of the nation's defenses. That provided all the reassurance they needed.[7]

Some criticism came from Capitol Hill, expressed by people such as Stuart Symington of Missouri and John F. Kennedy of Massachusetts, but on the whole, politicians accepted the New Look enthusiastically. Congress not only voted substantially more money for the Air Force than Eisenhower requested but cut the Army's money to provide even more.

The position of Chief of Staff at a time like this called for someone who had enough political skill to protect the Army from such public humiliation, damaging as it was to Army morale. Ridgway was completely unprepared for the political challenge, as he later ruefully acknowledged.[8]

He had created the 82nd Airborne Division, led it brilliantly in World War II and proved himself a true master of the battlefield in Korea after the Chinese entered the war and captured Seoul. It was Ridgway who had driven them back across the 38th parallel, and the staggering losses he had inflicted pressured the Chinese into armistice talks in July 1951. Handsome, intelligent and brave, Ridgway was one of the finest soldiers in American history, but nothing had prepared him for the sheer hell of being Chief of Staff. Not the least of his burdens was Wilson. Ridgway loathed him from the first and treated him with disdain thereafter. On a day when Wilson gave a speech extolling airpower, Ridgway chose to give a speech that declared, "The foot soldier is still the dominant factor in war and weakening our ground forces would be a grievous blow to freedom." In effect, Ridgway refused to abide by the pledge he'd given Radford aboard the *Sequoia*.[9]

Eisenhower admired Ridgway as a combat soldier but thought he was completely wrong about the future of ground war. He was also angry that Ridgway not only feuded with Wilson but disparaged the New Look on Capitol Hill. When Ridgway appeared before a Senate committee in March 1955 and opposed the next tranche of manpower cuts that Wilson had recommended, Eisenhower decided he'd had enough. He ended Ridgway's tenure as Army Chief of Staff after only two years—the normal tour for a Chief of Staff was four years. Eisenhower also pushed Admiral Carney into a premature retirement, because even though Carney had not been as outspoken as Ridgway, he too had publicly criticized the New Look.

Ridgway gone was not Ridgway silenced. On the contrary. Once retired, he published a frank and angry account of his time as Chief of Staff in the *Saturday Evening Post*. Eisenhower was outraged. He told Radford, "Maybe we could introduce a new kind of oath, to be taken by all military and civilian officials who serve in the Pentagon," so that after they left government service they would "disclose nothing that the Department of Defense determines is security information." What he wanted, in effect, was something like the British Official Secrets Act, but Congress would never agree to that.[10]

General Maxwell Taylor, wartime commander of the 101st Airborne Division and military intellectual, was slated to be the next Chief of Staff. Before he would send Taylor's name to the Senate for confirmation, though, Eisenhower was going to get a commitment from Taylor that he would support the New Look and the nuclear strategy it was based on. He told Taylor, "You must understand and wholeheartedly accept that your primary responsibility relates to your joint duties." He was also required to declare that he shared Eisenhower's views on strategy. Eisenhower knew that Taylor was so ambitious he would say almost anything to be made Chief of Staff and so egotistical he would expect to win the argument thereafter. So he bore down hard on Taylor, telling him, "Loyalty in spirit as well as in letter is necessary."[11]

Taylor promised to support the New Look and the new strategy, but it wasn't long before he tried to convince Eisenhower, Radford and Wilson to abandon first strike. In place of the New Look, he offered what he called Flexible Response.

Unable to find a way of fitting nuclear weapons into ground combat, Taylor argued that a future war between the U.S. and the USSR could be fought with conventional weapons. "That's fatuous!" said Eisenhower. Any war with the Russians would be nuclear. And when Taylor argued that the next war would probably be a limited one, more or less on the same scale as Korea, he was still wrong. "Anything of Korean proportions would be one for the use of atomics," Eisenhower told Radford, annoyed at Taylor's refusal to recognize that fact.[12]

As he pressed Flexible Response on a President who was inflexible in his rejection of it, Taylor kept lowering the threshold at which the United States might go to war. His grand theory became an infantryman's dream world, a future where wars would be fought by forces so thinly spread and lightly armed that there would be no place for nuclear weapons—wars, that is, where the infantryman would be "the dominant factor" again.

Eisenhower soon realized that in appointing Taylor, he had made a serious mistake. Taylor's view of the future of war was so fundamentally different from his own that the two could never be reconciled, but having cut short Ridgway's time as Chief of Staff, it would be too much an admission of failure for him to do the same all over again. That left Taylor free to argue the case for Flexible Response in NSC meetings, but no one paid any attention to him, because it was obvious that Eisenhower didn't take him seriously.[13]

It was self-evident to Eisenhower that in any conflict smaller than the Korean War—the kind that Taylor seemed obsessed with—the U.S. would provide only a few infantry and artillery battalions, to serve as military advisers and to protect American air and naval bases. Its military role would be to use its aircraft and ships to support a friendly government. He assumed that the friendly government would provide nearly all the ground troops, but if it lacked the troops or the will to defend itself, the United States should not try to make good their absence by shoveling its own infantry into the conflict. The kind of war Taylor was talking about under Flexible Response was not going to be fought by the United States Army, at least not while Ike was President.

The Republican right wing had for years used the "loss of China" to Mao's Communists as a stick to beat Truman and the Democrats. They had accepted entirely MacArthur's vision of an Asia that was the future of the world and the key to American security. To Eisenhower, this was all nonsense.

"I think we can reduce it to very simple terms," he told Drew Pearson. "The area where there is the greatest intelligence, the greatest skills, the greatest production, the greatest amounts of iron and steel . . . Europe fits these details. If an enemy [i.e., the Soviet Union] wants to go to the superhuman task of conquering Asia as a back door to Europe, well, that's something we have to reckon with. But personally I don't think we can send American troops into Asia to stop it."[14]

NSC 162/2 was based on his belief that there was no real security except in collective security, which would make strong defenses affordable and provide the overseas bases that were essential to a strategy of first strike. In December 1953, Eisenhower traveled to Bermuda to meet with Prime Minister Winston Churchill and the French premier, Joseph Laniel.

Eisenhower pressed the Frenchman on the creation of a European Army, while Churchill pressed Eisenhower for a resumption of the wartime Anglo-American agreement to share nuclear information, something that Eisenhower wasn't in a position to give them. What he could provide, though, was airburst atomic bombs. He did not want SAC to be forced to make a preemptive attack on the Soviet Union without the Royal Air Force sharing the risks. LeMay expected that only 15 percent of his bombers would be able to penetrate Soviet air defenses, strike their targets and survive the return to base if SAC had to make the attack on its own. So Eisenhower promised to provide nuclear weapons for British bombers and Churchill assured him that SAC would be able to use airfields in the UK to launch a nuclear strike against the USSR.[15]

That did not solve the problem of defending NATO from the Red Army, however. Unlike the continental U.S., Western Europe was too close to Soviet airfields for a strategy of preemptive attack to protect it. Nor were the NATO governments ever going to accept a strategy of liberation-after-defeat, a replay, that is, of the World War II scenario. What NATO adopted instead was a forward strategy, one based on the dubious assumption of a Soviet conventional assault; but this was the only assumption the Europeans would accept. This strategy provided for a fighting retreat to the Rhine, where the Red Army would be held by NATO forces. Eisenhower was still hoping at the time of the Bermuda conference that the European members of NATO would create a European Army, an idea the French had been pushing for years, without ever believing in it.

In the end, the French bluff was called. It was significant that Eisenhower, who had spent a total of five years in France, had never managed to penetrate the French psyche. Once the European Army idea vanished back into the smoke from whence it came, Eisenhower was deeply annoyed and his animadversions against the French became increasingly cutting. NATO's forward strategy would have to rest, then, on German rearmament and a force of at least twelve German divisions to help hold the line of the Rhine.[16]

Eisenhower often grumbled that the presence of large numbers of American troops in Europe had always been considered temporary, first during World War II, then following the Berlin blockade. No Pentagon planner, himself included, had ever foreseen an indefinite commitment of ground troops to defend the Old World. Every time he met with NATO leaders, he was likely to ask, "Why should 250 million Europeans be defended by 200 million Americans? You've got the skills, the wealth, the industrial capacity."[17]

Dulles warned him to tread carefully. Most NATO countries in the early 1950s had weak governments. War and occupation had shaken European democratic institutions to their roots. Any talk of reducing the American commitment would only help destabilize them and make them more vulnerable to Communist pressure. When Eisenhower started talking about his policy to bring the troops home, Brigadier General Andrew Goodpaster, his military staff secretary, corrected him: "Now, Mr. President, that's not *quite* our policy. That is the goal, but the timing of this matter remains open." It stayed that way.[18]

In August 1954, while the issue of German rearmament was still being thrashed out, Clare Boothe Luce, whom Eisenhower had appointed ambassador to Italy, drafted a thirty-six-page report on how the Cold War was going in Europe. The United States, Mrs. Luce wrote, had not only lost the initiative, but it was probably going to lose the war. According to her, most of Western Europe was becoming neutralist, thanks to the French. Worse still, Italy was on the verge of surrendering to Communism, and by 1959 more than half the countries presently in NATO would be under Soviet control.[19]

While Mrs. Luce was arriving at this alarming conclusion, the "neutralist" French finally agreed to German rearmament. Then, out of the blue, Admiral Radford was quoted in *The New York Times* as saying that the huge manpower reductions envisaged by the New Look would see the withdrawal of most American ground forces from Europe. The White House immediately denied the story in *The New York Times,* but the German chancellor, Konrad Adenauer, responded to it by complaining bitterly about American "undependability" and warned that if the U.S. pulled out, the Soviets might decide to make a nuclear attack on Western Europe.[20]

Radford's intervention, which was almost certainly a bluff and in all likelihood was discussed in advance with Eisenhower, had the desired effect—Adenauer wasted no time in creating a well-trained, well-equipped German Army. Meanwhile, the six American divisions in Germany remained where they were, a human shield to discourage Soviet adventurism. The Soviets could neither attempt to overrun Western Europe in a conventional assault nor attack it with nuclear weapons without killing thousands—probably tens of thousands—of young Americans. Their lives were the strongest possible guarantee that the United States would not abandon its NATO allies in the event of war.

Strangely, though, Eisenhower was deeply reluctant to accept that fact. He was still yearning to bring them home, and leave only American air and naval units to support European ground forces. It was an odd, almost illogical, outlook for someone who sternly told the chairman of the House Military Affairs Committee, Carl Vinson, "If we don't defend ourselves on the Rhine, we'll have to defend ourselves in New York."[21]

Besides the human shield of flesh and blood represented by American troops in Germany, most NATO countries wanted a nuclear shield and asked Eisenhower to provide nuclear weapons for their armies. He invariably turned them down. Battlefield nuclear weapons deployed to Europe remained under tight U.S. control.

He rejected criticism from Congress that it was too risky even to place them in Europe. What if some out-of-control colonel decided to use them? "If we got into a major war," Eisenhower conceded, "some field commanders *are* likely to blow the other fellow's big punch. [But] we've got to have them there or else we expose our own six divisions."[22]

The Soviets responded to German rearmament and NATO's forward strategy by creating the Warsaw Pact, but this inevitably turned into yet another instrument of state terrorism. They employed it to invade Hungary and murder Hungarians and to invade Czechoslovakia and murder Czechs.

With the collapse of the Soviet Union, virtually every Warsaw Pact member sought to join NATO, which the oppressed people of Eastern Europe ardently embraced as a guarantor of democratic freedoms and human rights. Eisenhower once described himself as "the most optimistic man in the world," but even he could hardly have foreseen NATO's moral and political victory.

One thing that made Americans uneasy about their alliance with the British in World War II was Churchill's all too obvious desire to maintain the British empire after the war ended. They needn't have worried. Britain would be too broke to hang on to its imperial possessions and too tired, in reality, even to cling to imperial dreams. For the first twenty years or so after World War II, the British were looking for ways to be rid of the empire, not excuses to hold it.

The French were a different matter. They had created a fiction that their overseas possessions were integrated into metropolitan France; that their colonies were not really colonies; that they were holding no one down. Children in remote villages in Africa and in tiny schoolrooms across Indochina solemnly recited aloud from French history texts, "Our ancestors, the Gauls . . ."

During his thirty months in command of NATO forces, Eisenhower was indignant at the determination of the French to hold on to their colonies. There was already a Communist-led guerrilla force taking root in Indochina. He urged the French government to grant independence to its Indochinese subjects, in vain. By the time he became President, the insurgency had turned into a small war. "A tragedy," he reflected. "An example of the stupidity of men."[23]

By early 1954, the French were under intense pressure from the ably led and tenacious Viet Minh, who drew their military strength largely from the support of the Vietnamese people, while the military strength of the French army of occupation was based largely on huge amounts of American weaponry and financial aid.

The French, however, were in no mood to be lectured by Eisenhower. The insurgency they faced and the war in Korea were both backed by China. The Korean armistice in July 1953 allowed the Chinese to devote even greater resources to the guerrillas of the Viet Minh, a development for which the French angrily blamed him. They argued that the U.S. should never have agreed to an armistice that applied only to Korea.

Eisenhower increased assistance to the French, but not even this stemmed the advance of the Viet Minh. The French installed a new commander in Indochina, General Henri Navarre, but Navarre promised to do no more than fight the Viet Minh to a standstill, which might produce a settlement comparable to the one in Korea.[24]

In the fall of 1953, the Viet Minh had advanced into northern Laos, and then withdrew. As they pulled back, Navarre created a huge fortified outpost in the mountainous jungles northwest of Hanoi, at a place called Dien Bien Phu, close to the border with Laos. He packed it with fifteen thousand troops, mainly Foreign Legionnaires, and proposed to block any new invasion of Laos—a bizarre plan for an area that had no roads to be blocked.

Dien Bien Phu depended on supply by air. In his memoirs, Eisenhower blandly recalled, "I instructed both the State and Defense Departments to communicate my concern as to the move." In private, he was scathing.[25]

The Viet Minh soon besieged Dien Bien Phu, hauling artillery over the mountains to pound the fortress. When the French tried to fly in reinforcements, the Viet Minh, well supplied with light antiaircraft artillery, had little trouble shooting down the slow, lumbering transports loaded with reinforcements on the way in, wounded men on the way out.[26]

As the siege progressed, the French made an urgent request for twenty-five obsolescent medium bombers and four hundred USAF mechanics to keep 'em flying. Eisenhower provided ten B-26's and two hundred mechanics. Senator John Stennis of Alabama was dismayed. "First we send them planes. Then we send them men. We are going to war inch by inch."

"Every move I authorize is calculated to make certain *that* does not happen," Eisenhower assured him.[27]

The token force of B-26's made no appreciable difference, and by April 1954 the French situation was desperate. Navarre had 250,000 French troops in Indochina plus 300,000 soldiers in native units yet was unable to relieve the beleaguered garrison. The French government begged for American help.

There were currently two U.S. Navy carriers in the Gulf of Tonkin. "We might have to make a decision to send in squadrons from the carriers to bomb the Reds at Dien Bien Phu," Eisenhower told Hagerty, but if that happened, "we'd have to deny it forever." There simply was no public support or congressional backing for American intervention in a colonial war.[28]

Dulles, however, delivered a speech to the Overseas Press Club on March 26 in which he argued that if the Communists won in Indochina, "they would surely resume the same pattern of aggression against other free peoples in the area," and went on to describe Southeast Asia as possessing "great strategic value. . . . Communist control of Southeast Asia would carry a grave threat to the Philippines, Australia and New Zealand, with which we have treaties of mutual assistance. The entire Western Pacific . . . would be strategically threatened." He called for "united action" to prevent the advance of Communism across Southeast Asia.[29]

Eisenhower approved this speech in advance, and "united action" was simply collective security in a new context. "The United States just can't throw its forces against the teeming millions of Asia," he told his staff. It would need local allies.[30]

Dulles's speech did nothing, though, to stem the chorus of voices in Congress, on the JCS and within the NSC for American intervention. During the last week in March and the first week in April 1954, every argument that would be used a decade later to justify the Vietnam War was urged on Eisenhower. He dismissed them all.

If the source of the problem was China—the one point on which everyone agreed—then the only logical strategy was to attack China. Otherwise, the United States would be committed to fighting one limited war after another on the periphery of Asia, he said, wasting its military strength and destroying its economy. It was clear to him, he added, that China was propped up by the USSR. In which case, the right strategy was war with the Soviets.[31]

Upping the ante into the stratosphere was one way to bring the debate to a close, but what really did it was Eisenhower's assertion that he would sanction intervention provided three preconditions were met: first, it would have to be an allied effort, with Britain and Australia committing ground troops; second, the French had to promise independence to the people of Indochina; and finally, Congress would have to declare war.[32]

He probably knew even as he spelled out these preconditions that there was no realistic way of their being satisfied in time to save Dien Bien Phu. And once Navarre's fortress fell, the case for intervening would fall with it.

Having shut off the path to intervention by raising the threshold too high for ardent interventionists such as Radford to get across it, Eisenhower proceeded to undermine his achievement. This was almost surely due to the fact that with the result now certain, he couldn't bring himself to accept a French defeat. At a press conference on April 7, he talked about the fate of Indochina. "You have the broader consideration of what might follow," said Eisenhower. "What you would call the 'falling domino' principle. You have a row of dominos set up, you knock over the first one, and what will happen to the last one is the certainty that it will go over very quickly." If the Viet Minh ejected the French, Indochina would come under Communist control, followed by Burma, Thailand and Malaya.[33]

He didn't go all the way to Australia, as Dulles had done, but like Dulles, he failed to see that Southeast Asia possessed little strategic value in itself. Eisenhower might have realized that but for the fact that he had spent four years in the Philippines in the 1930s. How many hours had he listened to MacArthur pontificating about how the Philippines was the most strategically important place in the western Pacific?

MacArthur was wrong. There were only two strategic points in the region—Singapore and Hong Kong—and the most important mineral resource, the oil of Brunei, was also under British control. Provided these three remained in the control of Western democracies, it hardly mattered who controlled Cambodia or Laos, Vietnam or the Philippines, impoverished places on the road between nowhere much and nowhere important.

There had been an implicit recognition of that fact in NSC 162/2, which had rightly identified America's vital interests as being the Western Hemisphere, Japan, South Korea, the Middle East and Western Europe. Not a word there about the nation's survival turning on who controlled the rice paddies of the Mekong or guarded the temples of Angkor Wat. But NSC 162/2 had been drawn up when the President and NSC were thinking coolly.

The measure of how little Eisenhower understood the strategic, political and military realities of Southeast Asia was illustrated by his anger at the British. Churchill resisted Eisenhower's repeated efforts to push Britain into sending its troops into Indochina. The British chose, instead, to concentrate their efforts on defending Hong Kong and Singapore, a strategy Eisenhower ridiculed as trying "to save a couple of miserable trading posts." This was an amazing judgment, seeing that

Singapore then, as now, controlled one of the five most important trade routes in the world, the strait of Malacca.[34]

Nor did he or Dulles ever see that the postcolonial upsurge of nationalism that Communists were presently exploiting would eventually turn Southeast Asian countries into anti-Communist strongholds. They assumed that a united Vietnam would be a compliant satellite, yet nearly all the heroes in Vietnamese history were men and women who had fought against Chinese domination, while the heroes of Cambodian history were those who had fought against Vietnamese domination, and so on. American ignorance of Southeast Asia was almost limitless.

As the siege at Dien Bien Phu drew to its ghastly conclusion, Eisenhower and Dulles's visceral anti-Communism was being stirred to such a feverish pitch that they began, as old men will, reciting a narrative of their youth—in this case, the ascent of Adolf Hitler. In a long letter to Churchill in which he described and defended American policy in Southeast Asia, Eisenhower reduced the case to terms he expected Churchill to understand more or less instinctively: "We failed to halt Hirohito, Mussolini and Hitler by not acting in time."[35]

Agitated by a flawed analogy with a remorseless Nazi state that had marched from conquest to conquest over the spineless backs of democratic governments, they became prisoners of the past. Eisenhower's domino theory made no more sense than his belief that Saigon was vastly more important than Hong Kong and Singapore.

Dien Bien Phu surrendered on May 7. The next day, a summit conference began at the old League of Nations complex in Geneva. The original purpose of this meeting of the Soviets, the Chinese, the Americans, the British and the French had been to talk about Korea, but the armistice was holding up well. The French turned the meeting into a conference on Indochina.

Eisenhower and Dulles urged the French to grant independence to Indochina but to remain there until the guerrillas were defeated. After Dien Bien Phu, however, all the French wanted from Indochina was a rapid exit. Laos and Cambodia would be established as independent states. Vietnam would be temporarily partitioned until elections were held north and south of the partition line in 1956 to form a government for the entire country.

The U.S. declined to sign the Geneva accords, because Eisenhower couldn't bring himself to be bound by them. He simply refused to accept the freely expressed will of the Vietnamese if it meant that they would choose a Communist government. With 60 percent of the Vietnamese living north of the partition line, such a result was likely, but the fact that the most admired figure in the whole of Vietnam was Ho Chi Minh made it a certainty.[36]

Dulles declared that the U.S. would be guided by the spirit of the Geneva accords, but Eisenhower did exactly the opposite. The United States treated South Vietnam as a new country, an impoverished domino with its own red-and-yellow flag and a government that, he himself admitted, lacked the support of its own people. Less a country, then, than a bluff.

To defend it, Eisenhower pressed ahead with "united action," and the Southeast Asia Treaty Organization was formed. From the way Dulles talked, Americans got the impression it was a Pacific version of NATO. It wasn't. If one member of NATO was attacked, there was little doubt that the rest would fight. But what had the members of SEATO agreed to do if one of them was attacked? They had solemnly pledged to consult one another. United action was, in reality, another bluff.[37]

Hidden Hand

It probably never occurred to John Foster Dulles as he peered into his shaving mirror each morning, Rolls Razor in hand, that the pallid, heavy features looking back at him represented an artistic leitmotif. The granite brow radiated a sense of the powerful intellect it fronted, and the blue-gray eyes were like those of a bird of prey, baleful but alert. The lower half of the face was all sagging flesh etched with deep lines, each seemingly carved by some disappointment or secret resentment, and the thin line of the mouth had a bitter cast. In his sour gravitas, Dulles resembled the angry sage down the ages—King Lear in a rumpled suit or Pope Julius II in spectacles—another somber addition to the parade of power-obsessed men who achieve a lifetime's ambition only to be greeted with scorn, not acclaim.

Valedictorian at Princeton and first in his class at Georgetown Law School, he had aimed almost from the time he was in rompers to be secretary of state. Dulles had been involved with international organizations since adolescence and had served Truman by negotiating the peace treaty with Japan. Even so, Eisenhower didn't hold Dulles in nearly as much regard as Dulles himself did.

As members of the board of the Carnegie Endowment for International Peace, the two men had been acquainted since 1946. In 1950

Dulles had asked Eisenhower to endorse him in the forthcom
York special election to fill a Senate vacancy caused by the dea
incumbent. Eisenhower turned him down, telling him that as p
of Columbia, it would be unseemly for him to give a political endorsement, but that didn't stop Eisenhower from voting for Dulles in the privacy of the polling booth.

At the Republican party convention, Taft had used his influence to
get Dulles appointed to write the foreign-policy plank of the Republican
platform in the 1952 election. Strident in tone and informed by a cru-
sading vision of rolling back the red tide of Communist advance, it was
the kind of fierce document, bristling and puerile, that Taft was sure to
like and Eisenhower was certain to deplore. During his campaign,
Eisenhower did not refer to his party's foreign-policy plank, did not
once seek Dulles's advice, did not even call him for a chat. He wanted
John McCloy as his secretary of state, not Dulles. It was only after Taft
vetoed McCloy that Eisenhower relented, and appeased Taft by offering
Dulles the post. That late summons was something Dulles never forgot;
it may have put another line in that sagging, prematurely aged face.[1]

Unlike Eisenhower, who played golf and bridge and dabbled with
paints, hosted stag dinners and went turkey shooting, Dulles did almost
nothing but work. The nearest thing he knew to relaxation was to have
a long chat in front of the fireplace in the library of his Georgetown
home, sipping Old Overholt rye while casually dressed—for him—in
an old tweed suit. Before he went to sleep each night, he read a detec-
tive novel for half an hour.[2]

Eisenhower didn't hit it off with Dulles as quickly or as completely
as he liked to pretend. It seemed logical to him to bring everything involving foreign policy under the secretary of state. Dulles, however, rejected that idea. It didn't fit with his conception of what the secretary
should do, which was to be more—a lot more—than a member of the
cabinet. He saw himself as the President's principal foreign policy adviser, more a minister without portfolio than the head of a major government department.

Dulles cared only about policy; administration was for lesser
minds, inferior talents. Nevertheless, he was so jealous of his domain
that he was reluctant to allow anyone else to manage the department.
Eisenhower eventually had to force him to accept an undersecretary for
administration. Dulles chose a Quaker Oats vice-president, Robert

Lourie, a wizard with a balance sheet. Unfortunately, the balance sheet was where Lourie's abilities ended. He hired Scott McLeod, a former FBI agent, to handle employee loyalty, a pressing concern in the heyday of McCarthyism.

Half the country seemed to think the State Department was riddled with Communist agents and sympathizers. Why else would China have been "lost" to the Communists? Acheson had been an inept defender of the foreign service, which included many of the most intelligent and able people in government, and there were hopes that Dulles would do better. Instead, he allowed Lourie to unleash McLeod on them, and McLeod was one of McCarthy's most fervent admirers. Dulles seemed content to wage the Cold War with a Department of State that was traumatized and demoralized.[3]

He added to the problem. When Ambassador George Kennan was declared persona non grata by the Russians, Dulles fired him, claiming Kennan lacked "positive loyalty." This, Kennan discovered, meant a kind of feudal loyalty to his master, Dulles, something that isn't normally—if ever—demanded of people on the government payroll. Yet even after he fired Kennan, Dulles still sought his advice on how to handle the Soviets![4]

Not only did Dulles frustrate Eisenhower's design for putting foreign policy formulation and operation on a more coherent basis, but he also turned out to be a poor performer at meetings of the cabinet and the NSC. "He is not particularly persuasive in presentation and, at times, seems to have a curious lack of understanding as to how his words and manner may affect another personality," Eisenhower informed his diary.[5]

He also discovered that not only did Dulles shun the task of running his department, but he was incapable of delegating authority to others and couldn't stand anyone else getting credit for any improvement in international affairs. Deeply religious and a former president of the World Council of Churches, he possessed a strong mystical streak. At times, Clare Luce got the distinct impression that Dulles believed he was in direct contact with God, who was *his* minister without portfolio.[6]

That religious conviction distorted his understanding of the Cold War. Certainly, it was absurd to pretend there was nothing to choose on moral grounds between freely elected democratic governments and rule by Communist oligarchs, always ready to send in the tanks. But Dulles convinced himself that neutrality was a sin. That wasn't a helpful policy position when many newly independent states were trying, for understandable reasons, to avoid being drawn into the Cold War. Ironically, Dulles's view was close to the Leninist dictum "Who is not for us is against us."[7]

During his first year as President, Eisenhower had Dulles come over at about five-thirty each afternoon for a talk about foreign policy. He developed a profound respect for Dulles's vast reading, a lifetime of book learning far greater than his own. Unfortunately, as Eisenhower discovered, Dulles couldn't resist hiding behind displays of knowledge to camouflage an aversion to risk. He was forever giving the NSC little lectures on the history of a current pressing issue instead of offering a firm recommendation on what to do about it. Dulles was far closer to the professor who wows graduate-school seminars than the hard-edged Cold Warrior ready to make tough decisions.[8]

Even so, when Dulles assumed his duties as secretary of state, Eisenhower had visited more countries than Dulles and knew far more of the major players, both military and political. That soon changed, because Dulles spent much of his time traveling. He covered roughly seventy thousand miles a year, and this was in propeller-driven planes that flew at half the speed of modern jetliners. During Dulles's numerous and prolonged absences, Eisenhower complained, "Nobody at State can make up their mind!" But given its recent traumas, what else could he expect?[9]

Over time, Eisenhower developed confidence in Dulles's ability to fathom the implications of complex events, an ability rooted in his grasp of modern diplomatic history. He told Sherman Adams, "I think I know the inside of Foster's mind almost as well as my own." To that extent, he forged an intellectual friendship with Dulles, but it never turned into the kind of personal affinity he had for George Humphrey.[10]

It was widely believed that in foreign policy, Eisenhower allowed Dulles to lead him by the hand, if not the nose. Dulles, however, was always careful to stay within the bounds of his—admittedly broad—remit. One of his aunts had been married to Robert Lansing, who had failed as Woodrow Wilson's secretary of state because he had lost Wilson's confidence. He resolved not to be like "Uncle Bob."

Eisenhower, too, helped him stay on the rails. When, for example, Dulles advised him that unrest against French rule in Algeria was going to produce another Indochina, a seedbed of Communism, Eisenhower told him firmly that he was wrong. He knew a lot more about Algeria than Dulles and reminded him of that fact.[11]

Eisenhower also rejected Dulles's advice that summit meetings were a waste of time. Nor did he care for Dulles's advice on how he ought to present himself as leader of the free world. "I sense a difference with Foster," Eisenhower told his staff one day. "His is a lawyer's mind, but we are trying to win friends and influence people." Dulles seemed to want him to be "a sort of international prosecuting attorney," something he had no intention of being. That big grin and the outflung arms were more his style.[12]

The Central Intelligence Agency had been created in 1947 on the basis of the Office of Strategic Services' wartime experience and personnel and modeled itself to some degree on the British Secret Intelligence Service, better known as MI-6. It would not have been possible to fight the Cold War effectively without a body such as the CIA, but there were many times when Eisenhower wasn't completely convinced that the CIA he had was really the CIA he needed.

When he became President, the director of central intelligence was his wartime chief of staff, Walter Bedell Smith. Eisenhower made an error in allowing Dulles to recruit Smith away to be undersecretary of state, because this had brought the swift promotion of Dulles's brother, Allen, from being deputy director to director of the CIA.

Nevertheless, Eisenhower was soon convinced he'd made the right decision. During the struggle for the leadership of the Soviet Union following Stalin's death, the principal contenders were Georgi Malenkov and Vyacheslav Molotov. Allen Dulles told Eisenhower that Malenkov would succeed. Once Malenkov established his ascendancy, Eisenhower's trust in his new director of central intelligence struck deep roots.[13]

Allen Dulles also got off to a good start with the new, reconstituted NSC. He opened most meetings, usually with some interesting intelligence information that grabbed everyone's attention, and followed up with a smooth presentation lavishly illustrated with maps, photographs and charts.

Despite his confidence in Allen Dulles, Eisenhower was irritated at the CIA's attitude that it was an independent body, the espionage equivalent of the Federal Reserve. Legally, it enjoyed no such position, but

Truman had allowed it to launch covert operations entirely on its own authority. One of Eisenhower's earliest actions was to change that. Covert actions were to receive prior approval from the National Security Council. He also required the CIA to report to the NSC every six months on all current and planned operations.[14]

Eisenhower asked General James Doolittle to conduct a review of the CIA's management and senior personnel. The problem with the CIA, Doolittle informed Eisenhower, was that it was badly run, and the main reason for that was Allen Dulles, who had no more administrative ability than his big brother, Foster. Doolittle also suggested to him that having brothers at the head of State and the CIA made it difficult to know what was really going on. Eisenhower brushed that aside. "It's a good thing they're related," he said. In fact, it undermined his efforts to control the agency.[15]

When, after several years, it became only too evident that the CIA was still resisting direct presidential control, Eisenhower created the Foreign Intelligence Advisory Board. The board conducted its own review and produced a scathing report. Again, Eisenhower balked. "To put in all the administrative improvements they propose," he told Cutler, "I'd have to fire Allen Dulles. And with all his limitations, I'd rather have him as chief of intelligence than anyone else I can think of. In that business you need a strange kind of genius."[16]

What he wanted most from the CIA was something it was never going to deliver. Under Truman, the agency had made repeated efforts to penetrate the security services of the Soviet bloc, trying to place agents behind the Iron Curtain and to recruit people already there. It failed miserably.

Although Foster Dulles seemed in awe of the agency, showing far more respect for its personnel than for his own foreign service officers, the military viewed the CIA with disdain. The intelligence mission it had tried and failed to do left a large gap. The military created the Defense Intelligence Agency to fill it, producing the kind of duplication and proliferation that Eisenhower rightly deplored.

By the time Eisenhower became President, the CIA was devoting 80 percent of its efforts to waging the Cold War and only 20 percent to gathering intelligence. It had carved out a role for itself in political warfare and propaganda. It ran Radio Liberty and Radio Free Europe and played an important part in persuading the French and Italians not to elect Communist governments. The area where it made its influence felt most, however, was in the impoverished Third World, where a little American know-how and plenty of cash could take covert operations a long way.[17]

Time magazine's Man of the Year for 1951 was Dr. Mohammed Mossadegh, prime minister of Iran, a politician who gave many of his most important speeches in his pajamas, a semi-invalid who appeared barely able to walk at one moment yet pranced about as sprightly as a robin the next. Mossadegh's eccentricities, such as bursting into tears whenever he was moved by joy or anger, made him seem baffling rather than endearing, but the reason he was on the cover of *Time* was that he was taking his country to the brink of disaster. One slip and Iran would probably tumble into the embrace of Stalin.

The British had created modern Iran in order to control its oil. They had also created the Iranian royal family to help continue that control into perpetuity. Mossadegh had come to power after World War II as an archnationalist, opposed to British hegemony and despising the young shah of Iran, Reza Pahlevi. In 1951 Mossadegh threatened to nationalize the oilfields. The British struck back—they closed their Iranian refinery and organized an international boycott of Iranian oil.

The British Secret Intelligence Service meanwhile began planning a coup to overthrow Mossadegh and asked its friends in the CIA if the U.S. would like to be involved. Beetle Smith, who was then head of the CIA, thought it was probably the best way of stopping Mossadegh, who was increasingly dependent on the Iranian Communist party for support. He briefed Eisenhower on the proposed coup shortly after the 1952 election, and days before Ike was inaugurated, he got an impatient call from Smith. "Damn it, Ike, when is our goddamn operation going to get under way?"[18]

Eisenhower also got a long letter from Mossadegh, pleading for increased American financial assistance. Because of the oil boycott, Iran was virtually broke. The American ambassador in Iran, however, had no time for the eccentric Dr. Mossadegh, who was flagrantly violating his country's constitution and resorting to street mobs to enforce his will. The shah was a virtual prisoner in his palace.[19]

Toward the end of June, Allen Dulles and Beetle Smith explained the proposed Iranian coup, Operation Ajax, to John Foster Dulles, who was thrilled. "So this is how we get rid of that madman Mossadegh!"[20]

The British proposed that Kermit Roosevelt, a highly experienced OSS veteran and grandson of Teddy Roosevelt, direct the coup. Returning to Tehran in July with a suitcase holding $1 million in rials, the currency of Iran, Roosevelt met with the shah, informed him of the broad outlines of the plot and began financing and directing the activities of pro-shah street mobs. The shah promptly departed for the safety, and comforts, of Italy.

Throughout August 1953, Tehran was brought to a standstill by street battles between the shah's well-financed rioters and the Communist-organized mobs of Dr. Mossadegh. With the capital city paralyzed and the country plunged into economic chaos, the Iranian Army, which had tried to stay aloof from politics, finally intervened and arrested the weeping Dr. Mossadegh in his pajamas. The shah returned from exile, eternally grateful for American help. Eisenhower never doubted that Ajax was rials well spent. Iran was the first American success at something the Soviets had done across Eastern Europe—oust a hostile government and install one more to its liking.

More important, the overthrow of Mossadegh showed Eisenhower that although the CIA was not much good at penetrating Soviet intelligence, it could mount covert operations successfully. This was its true calling. He personally decorated Kim Roosevelt with the National Security Medal and listened in rapt fascination to his account of the Iranian coup. "It seemed like a dime novel," Eisenhower wrote in his diary, enthralled.[21]

For all his great knowledge of international affairs, Latin America was virtually terra incognita to John Foster Dulles. It might seem strange, perhaps, that he had so little interest in "America's backyard," but the reason is simple: like most people, he tended to take Latin America for granted. But just as he was named secretary of state, the CIA warned the incoming administration of trouble ahead south of the border. There was, the agency claimed, a rising threat of "exaggerated nationalism" sweeping through Central and South America. Soviet Communism was poised to use this exaggerated nationalism to overthrow governments friendly to the United States.

Dulles had no illusions about the nature of these governments. Most were dictatorships, usually under military strongmen who'd seized power in a coup, and were propped up by bayonets. "Do nothing to offend the dictators," he told his staff. "They are the only people we can depend on down there."[22]

The most worrying situation, Allen Dulles informed Eisenhower and the NSC shortly after the inauguration, was in Guatemala. Several years earlier, an intelligent and idealistic young army officer, Jacobo Arbenz, had been elected president in the first truly democratic election in Guatemala for a generation. Once in power, Arbenz surrounded himself with left-wing advisers, some of whom were undoubtedly Communists. He also turned Guatemala into a place of refuge for Communist activists thrown out of other Latin American countries. Eisenhower's brother Milton was sent to take a look at Latin America and returned to inform the President that "the Guatemalan government has succumbed to Communist infiltration."[23]

What really frightened Guatemala's neighbors, however, wasn't the Communists in Arbenz's circle but his land-reform program. The biggest landowner was the United Fruit Company, and Arbenz more or less expropriated much of UFCO's property, offering compensation far below the land's true worth, but the Guatemalan government was too poor to offer substantially more.

The dictators who controlled Honduras and Nicaragua were horrified at these developments. Land reform was more of a threat to the existing order in most of Latin America than any political initiative short of arming the population. Arbenz was denounced as a Communist at the very moment McCarthyism reached its zenith.[24]

When, in the summer of 1953, the CIA began planning an operation to overthrow Arbenz, Eisenhower gave tentative approval, subject to his personal confirmation before any action was taken. Over the months that followed, he listened to numerous CIA briefings about Guatemala and the Communist threat, until he saw more dominoes wobbling, ready to topple. "My God, just think what it would mean if Mexico went Communist!" he told the cabinet.[25]

Dulles, meanwhile, was helping the CIA as strongly as he could. When it was pointed out to him that the present ambassador, although a fervent anti-Communist, was considered cautious, Dulles promptly replaced him with the ambassador to Greece, Jack Peurifoy, a loud, abrasive, overbearing character who was famously incautious and spoke only two words of Spanish—*muchas gracias.*[26]

After a six-hour interview with Arbenz, in which Señora Arbenz acted as interpreter and Arbenz gave answers that were false, evasive or disingenuous, Peurifoy cabled his conclusion to Dulles: "If Arbenz is not a Communist, he will certainly do until one comes along."[27]

Through the spring of 1954, the CIA continued planning and trained—more accurately, half trained—a force of roughly 150 Guatemalans for an invasion. A slightly disreputable and ineffectual right-wing Guatemalan colonel, Carlos Castillo Armas, was placed in command of this force, and it was equipped—in truth, poorly equipped—with World War II weapons, including three P-47 fighter-bombers flown by American pilots.[28]

By June, everything was in place. Eisenhower imposed a naval blockade to prevent arms shipments reaching Arbenz. Then the rebel air force swung into action, buzzing Guatemala City, dropping a few bombs, and when they ran out of bombs, the P-47 pilots hurled empty Coke bottles onto the streets, hoping they'd make a noise that would sound like exploding ordnance to terrified peasants huddled in their shacks. With this air support, Castillo Armas led his invaders across the border from their camp in Honduras. They advanced inland for six miles, then halted. The last thing they were looking for was a fight.[29]

In approving this operation, Eisenhower had gone backward, returning in a single bound to the heavy-handed interventionist polices that had poisoned American relations with Latin America from the Spanish-American War up to the New Deal. Roosevelt had put a stop to intervention and introduced the "Good Neighbor" policy in its place. Completely misjudging the nature and seriousness of the threat of Communism in Guatemala, Eisenhower had abandoned the Good Neighbor idea. The Guatemalan Army was firmly anti-Communist and it was the army, rather than Arbenz, that held power in Guatemala.

That same army now had to make a judgment: Should it stand by Arbenz and crush the small, inept, underarmed force commanded by Castillo Armas? While it was trying to decide, one of the P-47's slewed off a muddy runway and was totaled. Another was shot down by small-arms fire. The rebel air force was down to its last airplane, unless the United States was willing to supply more.

Allen Dulles informed Eisenhower of the loss of the two P-47's, and Eisenhower, who knew as well as any airman just how potent even a few airplanes could be, if only for the psychological effect, asked, "What do you think Castillo Armas's chances are without the aircraft?"

"About zero."

Eisenhower replaced the lost airplanes with P-51's. In their silver silhouettes was the sign the Guatemalan Army had been waiting for. The success of this operation depended on convincing Americans that their government was not involved in any way, while persuading Latin Americans that the Eisenhower administration backed it to the hilt. Even a decade later, Eisenhower continued to lie about his role in the overthrow of Arbenz. His memoir *Mandate for Change* provides an almost entirely fictitious account of what happened.[30]

The gift of a few P-51's flaunted American support from their slender and beautiful wings. Once Guatemalans realized that Castillo Armas had the power of the United States at his back, excited rumors spread across the country and shook Guatemala City—the Marines had landed on beaches in the north . . . the 82nd Airborne Division had just jumped into the fight. Demoralized and terrified at the prospect of a direct confrontation with American military power, the Guatemalan Army shrank from making even the appearance of putting up a fight for Arbenz. Learning that the army would remain in its barracks, Arbenz had no choice but to flee. He went into exile in Mexico.[31]

A week later, Jack Peurifoy imposed Castillo Armas on the people of Guatemala as their new *presidente,* having rejected various Guatemalan politicians who were far more popular with the people but possibly less pliable, and certainly less indebted to the United States. Dulles was greatly impressed by what Peurifoy had wrought and began worrying that maybe Guatemala was too small a place "for a man of his great talents."[32]

Eisenhower, meanwhile, was telling the nation about what had just happened in Central America. "The people of Guatemala, in a magnificent effort, have liberated themselves from the shackles of international Communist direction," he said. "They have reclaimed their right of self-determination."[33]

Congressional Business

As he settled into the White House, Eisenhower was annoyed. He would have to make another big speech in less than two weeks, the State of the Union address. "It is a mistake for a new administration to be talking so soon after the inauguration; basic principles, expounded in an inaugural talk, are one thing," he told his diary. "But to begin talking about a great array of specific problems is quite another. Time for study, exploration and analysis is necessary." Not surprisingly, then, during his first year in office he did not put much pressure on Congress to pass important legislation. He hadn't decided what he was willing to argue for, yet.[1]

Eisenhower also convinced himself that he was showing Congress more respect for its coequality with the executive branch than it had enjoyed since Hoover's day. Roosevelt had treated Congress with lordly disdain and Truman was feuding with it much of the time. Eisenhower intended to change all that.

Besides, the prospects of a good working relationship with Capitol Hill looked bright. Taft, after some hesitation, had agreed to be Senate majority leader. By a happy coincidence, Taft was also one of the few members of the Senate who played golf. Eisenhower and Taft forged a friendship with golf banter and small bets on tricky putts. He told Taft to call him on the phone at any time and to walk into the Oval Office whenever he wanted to see him, no appointment necessary.[2]

The first order of business for the new administration was to reduce government spending. As things stood, the deficit that would result from Truman's proposed budget for 1954 was going to smash through the $290 billion legal limit on the national debt. Eisenhower and budget director Joseph Dodge found ways to cut $10 billion from the 1954 budget, keeping under the ceiling—by a whisker—but he couldn't cut any deeper without taking chances with the nation's security.

Much of his budget agony was the result of the Republican party platform, which he treated at times almost as holy writ. Every senior member of the White House staff was told to keep a copy of the platform for ready reference. A promise was a promise was a promise. And one of those promises was a tax cut. Eisenhower couldn't find a way to do it.

When he presented the revised budget for 1954 to the cabinet, Taft was outraged. He pounded his fist on the gleaming mahogany surface. "With a program like this, we'll never elect a Republican Congress in 1954!" he bellowed. "You're taking us down the same road Truman traveled. It's a repudiation of everything we promised in the campaign!" Taft eventually came around, but Eisenhower remained sorely troubled by his failure to cut taxes. He opted in future years for a much more modest fiscal objective—the balanced budget. Even that would be a struggle.[3]

On April 20, 1953, Eisenhower shot a round of golf with Taft at Augusta National. Back at the clubhouse, Taft felt pain in his legs—the first sign of a cancer that would prove inoperable. In June he resigned as Senate majority leader and at the end of July 1954 he died. Sometime later, Eisenhower signed a bill that authorized the postal service to issue a stamp bearing Taft's portrait. As the ink dried, he mused to his secretary, Ann Whitman, "I honor Taft's memory, but I don't know how to evaluate his place in history."[4]

His feelings were probably colored by the fact that with Taft's unexpected departure, Eisenhower found himself with something he hadn't anticipated during his first two years in office—trouble with Congress. The Republicans had a tiny majority in the Senate and an even narrower one in the House, but this was the first time since Hoover's day that they had controlled both houses of Congress. Taft had exercised an effective grip on Capitol Hill, but his successor, Senator William Knowland, of California, was worse than ineffectual. A right-wing newspaper publisher, Knowland didn't like Ike and disagreed with his program.

Eisenhower tried to court him, as he'd successfully courted Taft, but Knowland proved not only too far to the right but too far from statesmanship to respond. After a year of having to deal with him as Senate majority leader, Eisenhower concluded, "Knowland is the biggest disappointment I've had since I've been a politician." There were a lot of contenders for biggest disappointment by then, but Knowland was a 20-gauge blank cartridge.[5]

In truth, some of Eisenhower's problems with Congress were due to the fact that he wasn't really a politician; not then, not ever. And he not only knew that, he was proud of it. For example, he despised the whole milieu of favors given and favors received that provided the architecture of a congressman's life and a lobbyist's income. Presidential counsel Bernard Shanley came into the Oval Office one day and told him that the head of Twentieth Century–Fox, Spyros Skouras, wanted to see him. Skouras was a major contributor to Republican party funds and a friend of the Greek shipping tycoon Aristotle Onassis, and Onassis was in trouble with the IRS. Eisenhower said, "Call Skouras. Tell him I would be delighted to see him. But if he raises the Onassis case, he will never come into this office again."[6]

He loathed the whole business of patronage, which involved not only allowing legislators to push forward people for positions great and small but extended to giving them a veto on major appointments within their states. Eisenhower was also astonished at the amount of string-pulling and log-rolling involved. "I just can't begin to connive the way you have to to get the best out of a congressman," he told his staff. It was one of those complaints that skirts the frontiers of boasting.[7]

The biggest problems he had with Congress those first two years were what to do about Joe McCarthy and how to stop the Bricker Amendment, the brainchild of Senator John Bricker of Ohio. This proposal represented a posthumous revenge on Roosevelt. At wartime summit meetings with Stalin, and especially at Yalta, Roosevelt had made agreements with Stalin that would normally be expected to be incorporated in a treaty, and that treaty would have to be ratified by the Senate. It is ratification that normally makes a treaty binding, by incorporating it into federal law.

Eisenhower would not defend what Roosevelt had done, calling him "indiscreet and crazy" in his dealings with Stalin. But he accepted the validity of Yalta and other agreements. They were, he argued, well within Roosevelt's powers as Commander in Chief in time of war. Besides, whatever the mistakes at Yalta, the Bricker Amendment was not the solution.[8]

The key provision in Bricker's proposal was that a treaty would become incorporated into American law "only through legislation which would become valid in the absence of a treaty." What this amounted to was that if Congress didn't ratify an agreement with a foreign power, the states would have to pass legislation that made it part of state law before it had any legal force anywhere in the United States. When the Bricker Amendment was presented to the Senate in January 1953, it had sixty-two cosponsors and looked certain to be adopted.

The vague language of the amendment allowed many senators to think it was fundamentally innocuous. After all, any President who disliked it would deal entirely with the Senate, in which case the Bricker Amendment wouldn't come into play. But Eisenhower saw that the amendment's vagueness was the core of the problem. In the hands of a Congress that was seriously antagonistic to the President, it could be used to undermine his dealings with foreign governments. It was already being pushed by the American Bar Association, whose leadership—including his brother Edgar—consisted of strict constitutional fundamentalists who thought federal power was tainted and that states' rights were the real basis of the Constitution. The ABA interpreted the amendment to mean that no treaty could be ratified except with the consent of all forty-eight states. Eisenhower was not about to risk the United States being reduced at some future time from being an above-the-title actor on the world stage to a being glove puppet in the hands of forty-eight legislatures.[9]

While deriding the Bricker Amendment in private—"A stupid, blind violation of the Constitution by stupid, blind isolationists"—he chose not to start his presidency by getting into a fight with Congress. Eisenhower preferred, instead, to have Dulles lead the administration's opposition to the Bricker Amendment and used his own influence with key congressmen to keep the proposal bottled up in committee.

By 1954, however, Bricker and his supporters were insisting on action and every effort Eisenhower made to get the amendment rewritten to make it completely harmless had failed. Most of the Republican members of the Senate were prepared to vote for it, and so were at least a dozen Democrats, including Senator Lyndon B. Johnson, one of its most effective cloakroom operators.[10]

A body of internationalist worthies calling themselves the Committee for the Defense of the Constitution sprang into life under the aegis of former associate justice Owen Roberts and the dean of Harvard Law School, Whitney Griswold, to alert the country to this lunacy. The key player, however, was bound to be Eisenhower, who had been astonishingly slow to wake up to the danger. He grimly remarked to Jim Hagerty one day in January 1954, "If it's true that when you die the name of the things that bothered you most are engraved on your skull, I'm sure I'll have there the mud and dirt of France during the invasion and the name of Senator Bricker."[11]

When the Bricker Amendment finally came to a decision in February, the last vote was cast by Harley Kilgore of West Virginia, who was probably drunk at the time. He mumbled something that the tally clerk heard as a nay. It may well have been a slurred version of aye. Whatever it was, the Bricker Amendment was defeated by a single vote.[12]

Thereafter, Eisenhower kept Congress busy with a steady stream of important legislation. During his first administration he managed to get better than 80 percent of it passed. No postwar president could boast a better record of success. Because for all Eisenhower's resistance to learning to think and act like a conventional politician, he possessed something that no one in Congress could match: he wasn't simply popular. The affection and esteem that people had for him went beyond mere popularity. He used that powerful hold on the trust of his countrymen to bend Congress his way.

It was odd, but the most popular man in the world was not a natural on radio and television. Eisenhower was, in fact, abysmal and never became any better than competent. In the privacy of the Oval Office he routinely dictated memos up to eight pages long that were models of intellectual clarity. They revealed a powerful mind, an excellent memory and a gift for language. He could be droll, commanding or reflective, as the occasion demanded. Yet he was also a stilted, platitudinous and overly earnest public speaker, almost painfully self-conscious and given to weird syntactical excursions that left people wondering exactly what it was he'd just said.

When he decided to run for the presidency, he allowed Edward R. Murrow, legendary war correspondent and a television pioneer, to interview him at 60 Morningside Heights for *See It Now,* a news program rightly famous in its day and a journalistic legend thereafter. Murrow admired Eisenhower but could hardly believe how discomfited he was by a film or television camera. After the interview ended, he told Eisenhower he was terrible on television. He needed professional help, and soon.[13]

Eisenhower paid no attention. His first televised speech for the nomination, in Abilene, was a coast-to-coast washout, as he wrestled with torrential rains and gale-force winds in a deserted open air stadium. The opening television appearance of the campaign that fall wasn't much better. Seated in a studio, he attempted to give a set-piece speech and to appear casual and relaxed by reading not from written notes but from a TelePrompTer, a new piece of TV technology. The text scrolling across the TelePrompTer moved jerkily, making it hard to follow. Eisenhower got redder and redder as he struggled to keep pace with it. Finally, he reached the last sentence and, the moment he finished, barked, in parade-ground style, "Turn the goddamn thing off!" It was an order heard in millions of homes.[14]

During his first nine months as President, Eisenhower appeared on television several times, never looking anything but awkward, never sounding anything but trite. Yet he felt keenly the need to communicate with the country. As Eisenhower fretted about public relations, Henry Cabot Lodge, the ambassador to the UN, was worrying about the same problem. He wrote to Eisenhower and gave him some good advice: "Become the T.V. President."[15]

When Eisenhower became President, 30 percent of American homes had a television set, and the number rose steadily from month to month. Truman had appeared on TV about a dozen times, but only a handful of people ever saw those broadcasts. Eisenhower was the first President to have the opportunity to use television as Roosevelt had used radio—to secure his own popularity and to advance his legislative program. Prodded by Lodge, he finally acted on Murrow's advice and sought help.

His television mentor was a movie star, Robert Montgomery, a good-looking, suave but fundamentally uninteresting actor of limited range. Montgomery, however, was an astute man who saw that Eisenhower could turn the possibilities of television to his advantage. He made Eisenhower rehearse his television appearances, use makeup and wear blue shirts and told Eisenhower's barber, Steve Martini, to improve the presidential haircut by letting it grow out more at the temples. When Eisenhower realized he wasn't getting his usual cut, he stared into the mirror. "What's this?"

"Mr. Montgomery told me to do it."

Eisenhower's neck turned red. "Never mind him. I don't want to look like a goddamn movie star. I'm just a G.I. So cut it that way!"[16]

Because Eisenhower found the presence of the cameras unsettling, Montgomery ordered that for both the rehearsals and the broadcasts they had to remain out of sight. What Eisenhower was actually looking at when he appeared to be staring directly from television screens was a black cloth. Holes had been cut in the cloth and camera lenses discreetly poked through them; their crews and other technicians were completely out of his sight.[17]

The first of the new-style broadcasts was made from the South Lawn on Christmas Eve 1953, with dozens of candles twinkling in the background and Christmas decorations in the trees and shrubbery. It was a low-key occasion, with the President asking people to join him in giving thanks for the good things that had happened in the past year, such as the end of the war in Korea.

His next two broadcasts weren't as successful. Then, on April 5, 1954, he finally got it right. Instead of sitting at his desk in the Oval Office reading from notes, he got up, walked to the front of the desk and half sat on it, folding and unfolding his arms, showing some of his natural animation. Next day, *The New York Times* led the applause, with a headline that read NEW FORMAT BRINGS OUT THE PRESIDENT'S WARMTH AND CHARM BEFORE THE CAMERAS. Eisenhower was jubilant. "That's what I've been telling you boys," he said when Montgomery and Hagerty came into his office. "Just let me get up and talk to the people. I can get through to them that way."[18]

Although this was a breakthrough, he never became as good on TV as Roosevelt had been on radio, but he improved greatly. There was about Eisenhower a distancing effect that the adoring crowds had never realized existed, a withholding of a part of himself that very few people, if any, ever managed to break down. He could not put it aside, assuming he ever really wanted to, and somehow nothing seemed to raise that barrier more readily than his awareness of an audience he could not see, one that he could not impose his personality upon directly. He almost never wanted to communicate anything about himself—which was what interested viewers most—but tried to offer dull information about legislation or collective security, the kind of information that interested them least. Yet in the end he did achieve the goal Lodge had set for him. He *was* the first television President. The formats he created, with the aid of Montgomery and Hagerty, were adopted by all his Oval Office successors.

While Eisenhower was coming to terms with the new medium, he relied even more heavily on an older one, the press. In Jim Hagerty he probably had the most effective press secretary of any President. Hagerty was a man with printer's ink in his veins and a three-pack-a-day smoking habit, and four martinis before dinner were inevitable. Hagerty was shrewd and hardworking and enjoyed Eisenhower's complete trust.

Hagerty convinced Eisenhower to hold press conferences every two to three weeks and he got him to liberalize them. Previous presidents had spoken to the press only on an off-the-record basis. The President could not be quoted directly and the press could quote only from an edited White House transcript of the conference.

Eisenhower allowed journalists to quote him directly. He also had his press conferences filmed, with Hagerty editing the film before it was released for television. Some journalists screamed, "Censorship!" but Eisenhower couldn't understand why. They had never protested at being allowed to quote only from an edited transcript.

The real problem was probably never put to him openly: he seemed aloof to the working press. Happy enough to have major publishers come to his stag dinners, he seemed uncomfortable around the scribblers—probably because they were more intensely curious than the millionaire publishers happy to bask in the glow of presidential acquaintanceship.

One way or another, however, Eisenhower's public relations was enough to make nearly all his successors envious. He took a keen interest in public opinion polls. His approval rating hit 75 percent early in his presidency, dipped now and then into the mid–60 percent range, but most of the time it remained above the 70 percent mark. His popularity was not simply a nice thing to have. It was Eisenhower's most important political advantage, because it helped keep the wild men of his own party in check and persuaded the Democratic party leadership not to give him a rough ride.[19]

To many Republicans, the most pressing business of government was tackling the Communist menace. No one was more determined than Eisenhower to root out subversives and traitors, a point he made in his first speech as a political candidate. Elect me President, he pledged, and "any kind of Communistic, subversive or pinkish influence will be up-rooted from responsible places in our government."[20]

Truman had unwisely tried to head off the Republican Congress in 1947 by creating the Loyalty Review Board, which heard appeals from people dismissed from government service as security risks or because of doubts about their loyalty. The FBI was required to run checks on all 2.5 million federal employees, and to help it shoulder this burden, a two-thousand-strong civil service investigative branch was created.

Loyalty being largely a matter of emotional commitment and security a question not so much of what someone had done in the past but what he might do in the future, the guidelines for the loyalty-and-security program needed to be clearly defined. They weren't. On the contrary, they were left as vague as could be and the result was inevitable—a reign of fear. What was taken as proof of loyalty and security was conformity.

Anyone who subscribed to *The New Republic,* collected recordings by Paul Robeson, read avant-garde literature, practiced yoga or showed an interest in modern Russian or Chinese history ran the risk of being denounced by someone wielding the coward's favored instrument, the poison pen. Thousands of careers were destroyed, many lives blighted, without any evidence whatever that this program made the U.S. any more secure.

Eisenhower, nevertheless, was convinced that it wasn't enough. Even before he got around to acting, Arthur Summerfield, his fervently McCarthyite postmaster general, announced that the great housecleaning was already under way. Summerfield, a Chevrolet dealer with an eighth-grade education, was proud to inform the nation that the administration was "rooting out the egg heads."[21]

In April 1953 Eisenhower issued Executive Order 10450, abolishing the Loyalty Review Board. Until now, dismissal had been based on "reasonable doubt." From now on, employment had to be "consistent with national security"—which meant whatever anyone in a position of authority wanted it to mean. An associate justice of the Supreme Court, William O. Douglas, doubted that even Eisenhower could meet such an exalted standard of proof.[22]

In his 1954 State of the Union message, Eisenhower announced that under the new program, more than twenty-two hundred "security risks" had been dismissed from government employment. Yet it soon became evident, as journalists pressed for details, that fewer than a hundred people had been dismissed for grounds remotely involving loyalty or security. The rest were alcoholics, people who didn't pay their bills, homosexuals, people with mental illness and the like. Executive Order 10450 was being used almost entirely as a quick way of getting rid of misfits formerly protected from dismissal by civil service regulations.[23]

In his memoirs, Eisenhower boasted about the effectiveness of his reform of the loyalty-and-security program. What he didn't mention was that roughly half those dismissed had been hired by his administration.[24]

In November 1953, to show that Republicans took security seriously and Democrats didn't, Brownell gave a speech in Chicago to denounce a dead man, former assistant secretary of the Treasury, Harry Dexter White, as a Communist. Worse, said Brownell, "Harry Dexter White was a Russian spy!" Yet even after Truman and Roosevelt had been informed of White's disloyalty, said Brownell, they ignored that information and promoted him.[25]

Truman promptly called Brownell a liar, although it now seems likely that White was indeed a Communist. Whether he was a spy is a different matter. Either way, Brownell's attempt to portray Truman as indifferent to Soviet espionage was disgraceful. Six months before White died, he had been suspended from his post because of doubts about his loyalty.

On December 2, Eisenhower assured a press conference that the new administration had subversion under control. "Fear of Communists actively undermining our government will not be an issue in the 1954 elections. Long before then, this administration will have made such progress rooting them out that this can no longer be considered a menace." When pressed to explain just what a security risk was under Executive Order 10450, however, he rambled around the issue instead of dealing with it, like someone hoping to stumble into an answer along the way. "If a man does certain things that, you know, well, make him a security risk in certain situations—and I don't care what they are—where he is subject to a bit of blackmail or weakness let's say."[26]

The point of Brownell's speech and Eisenhower's press conference was to prepare the ground for the 1954 midterm elections by showing that the Republicans had the Commies on the run. Eisenhower would have gladly outlawed the Communist party, but the Democrats had already drafted legislation that would do that. He was not going to allow them to claim credit for making Communism a criminal offense. Instead, he got the Democratic measure thrown out and substituted in its place the Communist Control Act of 1954. This made it a federal crime for a Communist to run for public office. He also submitted the Loss of Citizenship Act, which made it possible to revoke the citizenship of anyone found to be a Communist party member. Until now, loss of citizenship had applied only to treason. Eisenhower considered all of these measures right and necessary, and given what is known now about the controlling role of the Soviet Union over the activities of foreign Communist parties during the Cold War, there *was* a problem, but McCarthyism had made it as much a problem of public relations as one of national security.

A few hours after Eisenhower's December 2 press conference, Charlie Wilson called him to say he had received a report that the head of the wartime Los Alamos laboratory and discomfited holder of the title father of the atomic bomb, J. Robert Oppenheimer, was probably a security risk. The next morning, Eisenhower had the National Security Council and the chairman of the Atomic Energy Commission meet him at the Oval Office and said he wanted "a blank wall" between Oppenheimer and anything classified secret or top-secret. "I don't care how it's done, but it must be done immediately."[27]

Oppenheimer was as loyal to the United States as Eisenhower, but he had made the mistake of riling the Air Force. While LeMay was straining every nerve to acquire enough nuclear bombs to destroy the strategic power of the Soviet Union in a single preemptive strike, Oppenheimer committed the unforgivable sin of arguing that some of America's fissionable material be set aside to produce tactical nuclear weapons for the Army. The Air Force, moreover, was putting so much effort into SAC that it neglected to provide modern air defenses for the continental U.S. Oppenheimer supported the Army's efforts to develop antiaircraft missiles to fill that role. He also poured scorn on the Air Force's hopes of developing an atomic-powered bomber and opposed the atmospheric testing of nuclear weapons.[28]

As well as his critics in the Air Force, Oppenheimer had a powerful foe in the chairman of the Atomic Energy Commission, Lewis L. Strauss, a man almost consumed with jealousy for the admiration that Oppenheimer commanded among scientists throughout the world. In recent months Strauss had been urging J. Edgar Hoover to keep Oppenheimer under surveillance, something the FBI was delighted to do.[29]

What troubled the President, however, was Oppenheimer's opposition to developing the hydrogen bomb. Oppenheimer had raised both moral and practical objections. A bomb so powerful would not be used against military targets but against cities. Besides which, he argued, existing technology made it impossible to produce an H-bomb small enough for a B-29 to deliver. The first U.S. hydrogen explosion, in November 1952, was produced by a "device" as big as a two-story house. It was not a deliverable bomb.

In August 1953, however, the Soviets exploded a hydrogen bomb, not a device. This technological breakthrough created alarm in the Pentagon, but the U.S. was by then about to test its first true H-bomb. Edward Teller, long Oppenheimer's chief rival among nuclear scientists, had made an even greater breakthrough than his Soviet counterparts. His H-bomb would be much smaller, weigh considerably less yet produce an even greater explosion.

The Atomic Energy Commission was, nevertheless, in deep trouble. It had opposed development of the H-bomb on the same practical grounds as Oppenheimer, and Strauss was eager to deflect the new President's attention away from that fact. More important, the staff director of the congressional Joint Committee on Atomic Energy, William L. Borden, had given a friend of his an envelope filled with documents that described in detail Teller's technological breakthrough in designing an H-bomb and provided material relating to highly secret codes. The friend, who was a contract consultant to the AEC, lost the documents on the overnight New York-to-Washington train. The train was dismantled, but the documents were never found.[30]

Borden had not only shown himself to be a major security risk but had also brought the security procedures of the AEC into question. A distraction or a scapegoat was needed. Enter J. Robert Oppenheimer. The Air Force was already masterminding a campaign to discredit him. Articles had appeared in *Fortune* and *Time* portraying him as a security risk. Just as the Oppy-is-a-spy mood music reached full volume, Borden, forced to quit his post on the Joint Committee, was writing a letter to J. Edgar Hoover: "Based upon years of study of the available classified information, more probably than not, J. Robert Oppenheimer is an agent of the Soviet Union."

Borden had been trying for years to smear and humiliate Oppenheimer. His great hero was Edward Teller, Oppenheimer's fiercest scientific rival. When the H-bomb project was first mooted, Teller had claimed that a new laboratory, one under his control, was the only way of guaranteeing success. Oppenheimer argued, instead, that a new lab wasn't needed. Arguments over a new lab became central to the debate over developing a new bomb. Teller got his lab, but his bitterness toward Oppenheimer remained, as did Borden's.[31]

By 1953, Oppenheimer was so vulnerable to anti-Communist hysteria that he might as well have been a medieval leper trudging miserably through every town he came to ringing a handbell and shouting, "Unclean!" His first wife and brother had both been Communist party members. At Berkeley in the 1930s, he had mingled unconcernedly with Communist sympathizers, Socialist party activists, Trostkyites, anarcho-syndicalists and just about every kind of political thinker capable of making the men around the Eisenhower cabinet rub their balding pates with concern for the future of the Republic.

During World War II, while Oppenheimer was directing the Manhattan Project, a French friend, Haakon Chevalier, had tried to steer him into meeting Soviet intelligence agents, something he had rejected. Oppenheimer wasn't even sure Chevalier *was* trying to involve him with Soviet intelligence, and unwisely waited eight months before reporting this incident. Nor did he end his friendship with Chevalier.[32]

When Eisenhower's blank wall went up, Oppenheimer was director of the Institute for Advanced Study at Princeton, but since 1947 he had been a contract consultant to the AEC. That contract had barely six months to run; it would expire on June 30, 1954.

Eisenhower believed that Oppenheimer still posed a risk to development of the H-bomb; that he was encouraging other scientists not to work on the project even now. This was completely untrue. Oppenheimer had, in fact, offered to end his consultancy when the decision was made to develop the H-bomb, in case he was seen as an impediment or a rallying point for those who remained opposed to the bomb's development. If Eisenhower believed that Oppenheimer was using his prestige to slow progress on the H-bomb, the most likely source of this misinformation was Lewis Strauss.[33]

Oppenheimer demanded a hearing to establish his loyalty and restore his clearance, unconcerned about the contract, but determined to defend his honor. A hearing was arranged, and despite Eisenhower's attempts to keep the Oppenheimer case secret, the news inevitably leaked out. Eisenhower's old friend and wartime assistant secretary of war John McCloy tried to make Eisenhower see that he was making a terrible mistake, one that would damage him in the long lens of History. What was happening, said McCloy, was "somewhat like inquiring into the security risk of a Newton or a Galileo. . . . I cannot escape my conviction that this man, whatever the hearing may disclose, as much as any other—possibly more—was responsible for our preeminent position in the field of nuclear weapons."[34]

Oppenheimer faced twenty-four charges, twenty-three of which predated his involvement with the AEC. Number 24 was his opposition to the H-bomb project. The only purpose of the first twenty-three charges was to suggest a treasonable motive for number 24, because these twenty-three had already been investigated in depth, helping to produce a security file on Oppenheimer that filled four feet of shelf space. Borden did not offer a single new piece of evidence to add to this exhaustive file. The most important government witness was Edward Teller.[35]

On May 27, the three-man panel that Strauss had chosen to hear the case finally reported. It concluded unanimously that Oppenheimer was entirely loyal, yet by a two-to-one vote, it ruled that it would be in the national interest to revoke his security clearance. This recommendation went to the AEC, which spent more than a month making up its mind. Then, with less than two days to run on Oppenheimer's contract, Hagerty received a telephone call from Lewis Strauss. The AEC, said Strauss, had just voted four to one to accept the panel's recommendation. Hagerty then informed Eisenhower, who responded, "I'm very pleased" and called Strauss to congratulate him. When the news reached Capitol Hill, there was spontaneous applause on the floor of the House of Representatives. When the news reached the scientific community, there was anger and dismay.[36]

In his memoirs, Eisenhower produced an account that bore only a passing resemblance to what actually occurred. He portrayed the Oppenheimer hearing as being absolutely fair. In truth, it was little better than a kangaroo court. Oppenheimer's lawyers were not allowed to hear much of the testimony against him or to read all of the documentary evidence being employed to discredit their client. No restraints were placed on the prosecution. On the contrary, hearsay, malicious gossip, unsubstantiated allegations and the like were solemnly accepted as evidence, material that would be rejected by almost any federal district court. Edward Teller, "father of the H-bomb" and long known as Oppenheimer's rival, was the prosecution's star witness.

Not one member of the panel had any legal training. It consisted of Gordon Gray, a former secretary of the Army and a member of the NSC (a fact Eisenhower forgot to mention in his memoirs); a big-business tycoon whose company, Sperry Rand, relied heavily on Air Force contracts and a token scientist. The scientist was the only panel member who found in favor of Oppenheimer on both loyalty and security.

Eisenhower had few, if any, qualms about the injustice done to Oppenheimer, for three reasons. "This fellow Oppenheimer is sure acting like a Communist," he grimly informed Hagerty after reading the testimony on Oppenheimer's friendship with Chevalier. Second, he had to reassure the public that the administration was keeping its pledge to root out subversives, and the Oppenheimer case had become public knowledge. Finally, he was almost desperately afraid that McCarthy might grab hold of the Oppenheimer case and use it to terrorize American scientists the way he had terrorized federal employees. It was a race that Eisenhower won. He managed to humiliate J. Robert Oppenheimer before McCarthy could beat him to it.[37]

In the end, the reputations that suffered lasting damage were those of Lewis Strauss, Edward Teller and the AEC. Oppenheimer's standing dwarfs theirs. This gifted man was made a scapegoat for one of the biggest security lapses of the Cold War—top-secret documents lost on a train. The man who lost them was never punished.

There had never been a primary result like it in the history of Wisconsin, and possibly not in any state. McCarthy had been too ill to campaign in the six weeks leading up to the 1952 primaries. On polling day he nevertheless picked up more votes than the combined total of his Republican challengers plus all four contenders in the Democratic primary. With that kind of a send-off, his reelection in November was guaranteed. McCarthy's greatest strength was the same as Ike's—his overwhelming popularity.

Eisenhower knew better than his staff that however much he deplored McCarthy's tactics and regretted the damage they were doing to the country, he couldn't tackle him head-on. Truman had tried it, and how had that worked out? McCarthy had gotten as much news coverage as Truman, as if his words and actions were as important as the President's. Eisenhower complained in frustration to his old friend Bill Robinson, executive editor of the *New York Herald Tribune*, "We have here a figure who owes his entire prominence and influence in today's life to the publicity media of the nation."[38]

Besides, it was impossible to make an attack on McCarthy without splitting the Republican party. At least one third of it was right-wing and McCarthyite. As leader of a divided party, he would stand no chance of getting his legislation through Congress. The Republicans possessed a small majority in the House, and their majority in the Senate was one vote. Then Taft died, to be replaced by a Democrat.

Even if the prospect of GOP civil war didn't deter him, just how was he going to undermine McCarthy? No President has supervisory powers over a member of the Senate. Only other senators possess that, and when the Senate reconvened in January 1953, four members who had clashed with McCarthy the previous year were no longer there. On the Hill, challenging McCarthy looked like kissing your seat good-bye.

Eisenhower could not even present Congress with an executive branch that was united against McCarthy. His point man would have to be his congressional liaison, Major General Wilton B. ("Call me Jerry") Persons, an experienced operator on the Hill. Persons had been Marshall's congressional liaison during the war and was highly respected, but Persons was also a great admirer of Joe McCarthy. The Republican leadership in the Senate was pro-McCarthy, as were at least two members of the cabinet, Arthur Summerfield and Sinclair Weeks, and Nixon had risen to prominence by treading the same slimy path as McCarthy. An executive branch that was bogged down in debates over McCarthy, combined with a Republican party at war over McCarthy, would not destroy McCarthy's power. What it would do, though, was undermine Eisenhower's.

Unable to curb McCarthy, Eisenhower retreated into a posture of Olympian aloofness. When liberal members of his staff urged him to tackle Tail Gunner Joe (McCarthy had served in Marine Corps intelligence during the war but claimed that he had gone along on combat missions as a volunteer tail gunner and blasted Japanese planes out of the sky in his free time), he retorted, "I just will not—*I refuse to*—get into the gutter with that guy." He was waiting for McCarthy to stumble, and when that happened, he wouldn't hesitate.[39]

In the Congress that convened in January 1953, McCarthy became chairman of the Committee on Government Operations, which did not much interest him, and chairman of its Permanent Subcommittee on Investigations, which interested him profoundly. The subcommittee had the power to investigate all operations of the executive branch. Heretofore, he had been a freebooter, but now he could hire some staff.

His crucial pick was a young New York lawyer, Roy Cohn, to be chief counsel of the subcommittee. As an assistant U.S. attorney in New York, Cohn had participated in the prosecution of Julius and Ethel Rosenberg—lustrous Cold Warrior credentials. Cohn also possessed a lack of scruple equal to McCarthy's and knew something about living a secret life. McCarthy, always on the hunt for "faggots" in government, probably never suspected that Roy Cohn was a homosexual.[40]

At about the time he went to work for McCarthy, Cohn became besotted with one G. David Schine, whose father owned a chain of luxury hotels. Cohn made Schine an unpaid consultant to the investigations subcommittee. In search of something to investigate, and see some sights while they were at it, they chose to inspect the libraries set up in European countries by the State Department's information agency. Hearing that Cohn and Schine were on their way, frightened agency staff in Germany threw works by known lefties such as Howard Fast and Dashiell Hammett into the burn bag.

On June 14, 1953, Eisenhower arrived at Dartmouth College to give a graduation speech. Waiting for the commencement ceremonies to begin, he noticed John McCloy engaged in animated conversation with several professors.

"What's this, what's this?" said Eisenhower, his curiosity piqued.

"I was just telling them about the burning of State Department books abroad," said McCloy.

"Oh, they're not burning books," said Eisenhower.

"I'm afraid they are, Mr. President. I have the evidence."

Eisenhower was astonished, then he was angry. He forgot about the speech he'd come to Dartmouth to deliver. Instead, when he was called to speak, he gave an impromptu talk about intellectual freedom. "Don't join the book burners," he intoned. "Don't be afraid to go into your library and read every book [that] does not offend your own sense of decency. That should be the only censorship."[41]

This episode infuriated McCarthy, who began an investigation of John McCloy. Meanwhile, however, he hired a staff director for his subcommittee, a former missionary named J. B. Matthews, who had recently published an article in *American Mercury* called "Reds in Our Churches." Matthews claimed that no fewer than seven thousand Protestant clergymen had joined the Communist conspiracy to overthrow American democracy.[42]

Eisenhower paid no attention to this development, but Emmet Hughes and the assistant attorney general, William P. Rogers, got the National Conference of Christians and Jews to send a telegram to the White House protesting Matthews's outrageous assertions. Sherman Adams drafted a reply to the NCCJ that strongly repudiated Matthews, walked into the Oval Office and handed it to Eisenhower. The President must sign so it could be released at once.

There wasn't a moment to lose, Adams said, because McCarthy was about to announce that he was firing Matthews. Nixon had just buttonholed McCarthy in a Senate corridor and was trying to keep him talking long enough for the White House to issue this statement. Eisenhower scrawled his "DE." An hour later McCarthy announced he had fired Matthews, but the morning newspapers reported that McCarthy was only reacting to the President's message to the NCCJ.[43]

Apart from such initiatives, Eisenhower bided his time, knowing that even better opportunities would come. McCarthy was not only an alcoholic but was also in excruciating pain much of the time from an operation for a herniated diaphragm. He now carried a twenty-four-inch scar that ran from his navel, under his armpit, and up to the top of his left shoulder. The surgery had also left him with a spasmodic twitching of the head. McCarthy's drinking began at breakfast and he toted a briefcase clanking with brandy bottles.[44]

Once the Matthews episode passed, he started an investigation of the Signal Corps's radar research station at Fort Monmouth, New Jersey. During World War II, Julius Rosenberg had been employed at Fort

Monmouth. McCarthy demanded access to the loyalty-and-security files on the hundreds of civilian scientists and technicians employed there.

Eisenhower was in Denver in September 1953 when the secretary of the Army, Robert T. Stevens, a textile manufacturer from North Carolina but also a veteran of both world wars, came to see him. What should he do about McCarthy? "Admit any error. There's no use trying to cover it up," Eisenhower told him. "Show what you're doing, and then stand your ground."[45]

Stevens tried to follow Eisenhower's advice. The Army refused to give McCarthy access to the files, but in a futile gesture of appeasement, it hurriedly suspended thirty-seven employees on grounds ranging from the trivial to the risible. McCarthy bitterly denounced Stevens for obstructing the hunt for Reds.

Before matters got any worse, Stevens tried to make peace with McCarthy and, inevitably, failed. Eisenhower was dismayed at Stevens's weakness, but now he had a strong sense of the developing battle. McCarthy wasn't going to back away. He was on a collision course with the Army, Eisenhower's spiritual home. The President asked Brownell whether he had the power to order Army officers to ignore subpoenas issued by McCarthy's committee. Would the Constitution allow that? Brownell soon reported back that he could do it, because the subpoenas amounted to a senatorial limitation on the workings of the executive branch. With the answer he wanted, Eisenhower chose to wait for the right time to use it, like a sniper in hiding.

The other important development involved G. David Schine, who had been inducted into the Army in the fall of 1953. The loss of the object of his affections to the coarse embrace of the military had left Roy Cohn almost bereft. He tried to pressure the Army into giving Schine a commission, but the Army refused. In yet another gesture of appeasement, though, Schine was spared the hand-roughening chores of KP, the tedium of long marches, the muddy parts of basic training and other unwelcome intrusions into a soldier's life. Schine was also granted a three-day pass every week; his fellow soldiers might, if they were good, receive one a month. When McCarthy refused to call off his attacks on Stevens, the Army released its file on the untouchable Private Schine.

At roughly this point, one of the thousands of informants in McCarthy's "Loyal American Underground" told the senator there was an Army dentist at Camp Kilmer, New Jersey, one Captain Irving Peress, who was a member of the American Labor party. The ALP was Trotskyite rather than Communist, but such distinctions meant nothing to McCarthy, his informants or the vast majority of Americans. At the end of January 1954, McCarthy grilled Peress, but Peress repeatedly invoked the Fifth Amendment and a few weeks later was out of the Army, with an honorable discharge and a routine promotion to major before he left. McCarthy was incensed. "Who promoted Peress?"

Unable to savage the dentist, he humiliated the commanding officer at Camp Kilmer, Brigadier General Ralph W. Zwicker, a veteran of the Normandy campaign of 1944. Zwicker held both the Silver Star and a Purple Heart. That did not deter McCarthy from berating him: "You don't have the brains of a five year old . . . you are a disgrace to the uniform you wear."[46]

He'd just crossed the line. For the first time, sentiment among conservative Republicans shifted against McCarthy. The American Legion and the VFW issued public rebukes. Right-wing newspaper columnists deplored his attack on Zwicker. But not even this could make him call off his attacks on Stevens and the Army. "This guy McCarthy is going to get into trouble over this," Eisenhower told Hagerty. "I'm not going to take this one lying down."[47]

As he began looking for a way to destroy McCarthy, so did Edward R. Murrow. CBS executives were nervous about where Murrow was taking them, but he was forthrightly telling the CBS News staff, "We are going to be judged by what we put on the air. But we are also going to be judged by what we *don't* broadcast." In March 1954, he presented two editions of *See It Now* that showed McCarthy in action—bullying, blustering, out of control, a man without honesty or scruple. Eisenhower was thrilled. He invited Murrow to the White House and embraced him.[48]

McCarthy's already sliding popularity took a sharp downturn, but still he kept attacking Stevens, probably because Stevens seemed afraid of him. McCarthy and Cohn accused him and the Army of attempted blackmail by concocting a false story about favors sought for G. David Schine. McCarthy's Committee on Government Operations would hear the Army's case against McCarthy and McCarthy's case against the Army. Eisenhower intervened with the Senate leadership of both parties to ensure that McCarthy wouldn't chair the hearings. To his chagrin, McCarthy found he was going to be no more than a witness before his own committee.

The hearings began on May 11, and were shown live on television. At the end of the first week, it was obvious that Murrow had been right—the small screen could destroy Joe McCarthy. The print medium that had made him great couldn't bring him down, but Philco and Zenith could do it. A suicidally dissolute life had ravaged McCarthy's never-handsome features. If it is true that a man becomes responsible for his face as he grows older, McCarthy was the most villainous-looking realization of the true portrait of Dorian Gray that anyone had ever seen.

His only chance was to find a document or a witness he could use to distract attention from himself and put the Army back on the defensive. But when week two began, Eisenhower exploded the bombshell he'd been holding on to since January. He took Brownell's ruling that he could order the military not to respond to McCarthy's subpoenas and stretched it like a piece of rubber until it covered the entire executive branch.

Since the time of Andrew Jackson, it had been accepted that discussions between a President and his staff and his dealings with his cabinet were privileged. Congress could not insist on knowing what advice the President got or what instructions he gave. Eisenhower made a breathtaking claim that this privilege extended to the entire executive branch and thereby gave him the power to order everyone in it to refuse to testify or hand over documents.

It was a dubious interpretation of constitutional law, one that would not stand up a generation later. Eisenhower got away with it because McCarthy and Cohn were so dumbfounded that they did not even think to challenge it in the federal courts. At a stroke, Eisenhower destroyed McCarthy's power to intimidate the executive branch.[49]

When the hearings dragged to their close, toward the end of June, the Army was exonerated. McCarthy was physically and emotionally used up. He was drunk most of the time, drugged much of the time. His obnoxiousness had been underscored by the civility and obvious decency of the Army's leading counsel, a courtly, whimsical old-fashioned gentleman lawyer, Joseph Welch. Television made a villain of McCarthy and a hero of Welch.

Senator Ralph Flanders of Vermont demanded an investigation into McCarthy. Had McCarthy violated the rules of the Senate? Eisenhower invited Flanders to the White House. The Senate established a special committee, chaired by Arthur Watkins of Utah, to look into McCarthy's behavior. On December 2, the Senate formally "condemned" McCarthy by a vote of 67–22 for conduct unbecoming a senator. A delighted Eisenhower asked Watkins to come over to the White House and, when Watkins arrived, shook his hand warmly. "You handled a tough job like a champion."[50]

McCarthy struck back, offering an apology for having urged people to vote for Eisenhower in 1952. He had done that in the belief that Eisenhower would be a staunch anti-Communist. "I was mistaken."

At a stag dinner on December 6, Eisenhower's guests wanted to know just what he was going to do about McCarthy now. "Nothing," he said. "I think I'll just let the son of a bitch kill himself."[51]

Look Ahead, Neighbor

There wasn't much about the campaign that he'd actually enjoyed, apart from the plank and the saw. Getting up and speechifying wasn't interesting. Besides, the crowds that came out to welcome the train or to pack an auditorium seemed more interested in just looking at him—as if he were a movie star or a big-time gangster—than in anything he had to say. But if there was one thing Eisenhower hoped they'd remember, it was the economics lesson with the plank and the saw.

He was looking for a way to illustrate what had happened to living standards under Truman when somebody hit on the idea of having Eisenhower pick up a plank about six feet long, which had been cut partway through two feet from the top and two feet from the bottom. "This plank represents the buying power of a dollar in 1945," he'd say, raising it high enough for the crowds gathered around the campaign train to get a good look. Taking the saw, he'd cut off the top part. "And this is what has happened to it since then."

Placing the saw on a line marking the other partial cut, he said, "And here's what will happen if there is another eight years of Democratic policy." After a few passes with the saw, he was left with a piece of wood just two feet long, a stump compared to the plank he'd begun with. He held the stumpy bit of lumber over his head and waggled it. The crowd laughed and applauded.[1]

When Eisenhower reorganized the White House, Sherman Adams

persuaded him he ought to have a professional economist on the staff. Eisenhower appointed Gabriel Hauge, who had a Harvard Ph.D., had taught economics at Princeton, been editor of *Business Week* and served as a speechwriter during the campaign.[2]

This did not mean that Hauge would be his main adviser on economics. There was already a body called the President's Council of Economic Advisers, or CEA. Truman had failed to make much use of it and many Republicans on Capitol Hill thought the CEA was another New Deal excrescence, something to be gotten rid of. Eisenhower was planning to beef up the CEA, not abolish it. There was a risk of friction between any economist he put on the White House staff and whoever he appointed to be chairman of the CEA, but he avoided that by asking Hauge to recommend someone to be chairman.

Hauge said he thought Arthur Burns, of Columbia, would be a good choice. Eisenhower already knew and liked Burns, who was a world authority on the workings of the business cycle and one of the most highly regarded economists of the time. When Eisenhower offered him the appointment, he made it clear just what he was looking for. "I don't want my CEA to be political." It wasn't there to promote Republicanism; it was there to serve the country.[3]

Burns proved to be an able administrator, reorganizing and strengthening the CEA in much the same way that Eisenhower had done with the National Security Council. He also knew how to give interesting and persuasive briefings to the cabinet. Eisenhower was impressed. "Burns would have made a fine chief of staff overseas during the war," he told Adams.[4]

The appointments of Hauge and Burns worked out much as Adams had hoped they would. Burns provided the President the macroeconomic picture of government spending. Hauge educated him on the microeconomic—the effects of a particular policy decision on agriculture, on export markets, on business expansion and so on. Hauge also arbitrated when Burns and secretary of the Treasury George Humphrey disagreed over economic policy—Hauge nearly always supported Burns.

Humphrey was, by his own admission, a hard-shell conservative and he was said to have told Eisenhower shortly after the inauguration, "If anybody talks to you about money, you tell him to go see George." If so, he must have been a disappointed man, because he never had a free hand in setting economic policy.[5]

On the face of it, though, it looked like fiscal conservatism had risen triumphantly into power, because the budget director, Joseph Dodge, was just as conservative as Humphrey, and Burns was a zealot on the subject of inflation. And then there was the secretary of commerce, Sinclair Weeks. "He's so completely conservative in his views that at times he seems to be illogical," a dismayed Eisenhower wrote in his diary only three weeks into his presidency.[6]

Yet fiscal conservatism did not prevail, mainly because Eisenhower made the big economic decisions, just as he made the big foreign policy decisions. Few would have expected it, but he found economics interesting and followed policy debates closely, read economic reports carefully and had a good head for statistics.[7]

It may have come as a pleasant surprise to discover that he would not have to make a one-man stand against fiscal conservatism. Arthur Burns's anti-inflationary zeal was balanced by a strong belief in social harmony. When Humphrey opposed increased spending to fight a severe economic downturn in 1954, Burns argued for it. He later presented a report that said that although economic growth, Humphrey's chief goal, was important, so too was "the need of the people for a sense of security . . ." After Humphrey criticized his report, Eisenhower reassured Burns, "This is a magnificent document—even if some of our radical liberals will unquestionably call it a reactionary treatise, while the real reactionaries will call it 'a blueprint for socialism.' All of which probably proves that you are just about right."[8]

He came to feel that Burns and Hauge tended to think first of all of the impact on people of budget decisions, while Humphrey and Dodge tended to think of the impact of decisions on budget numbers. Humphrey was so closely attuned to the outlook of the business community that he was unable, without help, to detect the significance of anything bigger. Eisenhower had to push the larger issues under his nose.

At a cabinet meeting in the fall of 1954, Dulles reported some good news: the Japanese economy was reviving, making Japan more secure against Communist pressures. Humphrey then gave the bad news—this reviving Japanese economy was already posing a challenge to companies in Pennsylvania that produced electrical equipment.

Eisenhower said it would help if American businessmen accepted the need for sacrifice, considering the strategic importance of Japan to the U.S. "No," said Humphrey, shaking his big, bald head. "The American businessman believes in getting as much as he can while the getting is good."

"Maybe that's the trouble with businessmen," said Eisenhower.[9]

He found an unexpected ally in the chairman of the Federal Reserve Board, William McChesney Martin, a Missouri Democrat appointed by Truman. The Fed had been created in 1912 to supervise the banks and thereby protect the currency. During the Depression and World War II, it assumed another major role—selling government debt. After 1953, Martin made the Fed a partner in what was rapidly emerging as the principal objective of economic policy—national prosperity. Eisenhower twice reappointed him chairman.[10]

Martin, Eisenhower and Burns were agreed that the biggest threat to prosperity was inflation. They feared it so much that they didn't aim to control it but to kill it. In modern times, inflation had turned into a kind of economic zombie, never more than half dead, never less than half alive, continually coming back.

From mid-1952 until the late fall of 1953, there was an inflationary boom. Eisenhower's first priority was to stop that boom from leading to a crisis. In electing him, Americans had set aside one of their deepest fears—that Republican governments generated depressions. Economic failure would destroy his presidency faster than anything else he could imagine.

He took the steam out of the boom by slashing the budget, especially spending on defense. The Pentagon spent 70 percent of the budget in 1953, and the cost of wars past, present and future actually consumed close to 90 percent once interest payments on the national debt were included. Truman's last budget, for fiscal year 1954, anticipated revenues of $68.7 billion, expenditures of $78.6 billion and a deficit of nearly $10 billion. Eisenhower got the deficit down to $3 billion. The ending of the Korean War, however, brought a recession, and in his next budget, Eisenhower allowed the deficit to rise to more than $4 billion, to keep the downturn in check, but he also kept inflation low.[11]

During his presidency, the constant attention to inflation paid off. For the whole of Eisenhower's eight years in the White House, inflation averaged 1.5 percent. No President since has achieved such a figure. He also managed to produce three budgets that yielded a revenue surplus. No one has equaled that, either.

Most people, however, worried more about unemployment than inflation or balanced budgets. This was also a new generation. As living standards rose, it wasn't glad to settle for making more money, owning more stuff. The more people had, the more they wanted. For the first time in history, the federal government was under pressure to ensure a steady—even rapid—rise in the standard of living.[12]

Eisenhower recognized that desire, and saw in it more than two cars in every garage. Stalin continued to develop the USSR as a war economy, and the Soviet satellites did the same. The Korean War seemed to justify Stalin, because a war economy was what the United States had in 1953. Eisenhower pushed the transition to a peace economy almost as rapidly as other governments had mobilized for war. The West's remorselessly rising wealth would make possible a peaceful victory over Communism. Ronald Reagan saw through to success a strategy that began with Eisenhower.

As Eisenhower told his old friend and bridge partner Al Gruenther shortly after assuming the presidency, "We can only combat Communism in the long term if our economy is healthy." He was right. Possessions, not weapons, won the Cold War, because Eastern Europeans and Russians finally grasped the true nature of Communism—it not only made people poor, but would keep them in poverty forever.[13]

A flawed man but a kindly one, Warren G. Harding was the first President who believed the federal government had a duty to help the poor. There was plenty of poverty in the early 1920s. The World War I economic boom had been followed by a sharp economic downturn and Harding wanted a new department created to provide for the out of work and out of luck. Just as he began pushing this idea, he died.

Roosevelt wanted something similar to Harding's proposal, but despite the proliferation of New Deal agencies to fight the Depression, he couldn't get Congress to support a department of welfare. He settled instead for a body with much less status and power, the Federal Security Agency. Truman had presented legislation that would create a department of health, education and welfare to Congress, and it was thrown out.

Imagine the surprise, then, when Eisenhower dusted off Truman's bill, added a few refinements and asked the Republican-controlled Eighty-third Congress for what Truman had been denied. The Republican leadership told him the Constitution didn't say a word about the fed-

eral government being responsible for people's welfare or their education or their health. That was left to the states and localities. If he really
wanted to do this, he ought to push through an amendment to the Constitution first. He ignored that, insisted on the establishment of HEW
and got it, partly because he had already appointed Oveta Culp Hobby
to run the Federal Security Agency and she would be in charge of the
new department. Mrs. Hobby had organized the Women's Army Corps
during the war, was the publisher of the *Houston Post* and was a Democrat for Eisenhower, but she had the social outlook of Calvin
Coolidge.[14]

Eisenhower wanted to extend Social Security to elderly people who
had retired before the creation of Social Security in 1935, or shortly
after it came into existence—people, that is, with little or no record of
contributions. Mrs. Hobby criticized the proposed change as "a criminal raid on the Social Security Trust Fund," even though Eisenhower
was behind it. In the end, he brought another 10 million people into the
Social Security net.[15]

When Mrs. Hobby bungled the production of Jonas Salk's revolutionary antipolio vaccine, weakly protesting "no one could have
foreseen the demand," he had to get rid of her. Eisenhower promptly requested an emergency appropriation from Congress so he could ensure
that every child, even the poorest, would be vaccinated. Within two
years, polio was under control.

Although he shared the unease of most Republicans at the way the
federal government had grown in wartime and refused to shrink in
peacetime, Eisenhower didn't intend to try rolling back the New Deal.
What he offered was better management of the welfare state and, in critical areas, expansion, not contraction.

Truman had sent to Congress a bill to reform health insurance so
that everybody would be properly covered. He got into a shouting
match with the AMA, and his bill was defeated. Eisenhower tried to
achieve Truman's aim by avoiding a head-on collision. HEW presented
Congress with a health-reinsurance bill, guaranteeing the insurance
companies against loss if they just made sure that even the poor got decent health coverage. The American Medical Association rose up in
wrath, screaming, "Socialized medicine!" Republicans he'd counted on
deserted in droves. Eisenhower was angry and disgusted. He told the
Senate majority leader, William Knowland, "Listen, Bill, as far as I'm

concerned the AMA is just plain stupid. This plan of ours would have shown the people how we could improve their health and stay out of socialized medicine." Even so, he lost, like Truman before him, to the big battalions of the doctors' lobby.[16]

He had a major success elsewhere, though, with his approach to social welfare. Eisenhower promoted his reforms as "vocational rehabilitation" and stressed the fact that there were 2 million Americans with physical disabilities, yet only sixty thousand were rehabilitated each year. "Humanity and self-interest alike" justified better provision. Congress applauded. "Vocational rehabilitation" was such an ambiguous term that it was stretched over the following years to cover far more than people with physical disabilities. The indirect approach again— government by Leavenworth tactics.[17]

Eisenhower was convinced that increased national prosperity meant little unless everyone got a share in it. There wasn't much he could do to ensure that it happened, but where he had the opportunity to act, he took it. He tried to get Humphrey to support an increase in the minimum wage, but Humphrey resisted. In the end, Eisenhower not only raised the minimum wage by 33 percent but extended it to cover millions more workers.[18]

In the summer of 1954, Eisenhower got into a fight with the GOP leadership over his efforts to expand federal aid to public housing. Angrily pacing the Oval Office, hands on hips, he vented his frustration to Jim Hagerty: "I am convinced of one thing. The only right approach to take on all these domestic problems is a liberal approach." He cursed the "hidebound reactionaries in this party of ours." In the end, he got a bigger housing program.[19]

The housing program had an important part to play in a bigger scenario. In the 1950s, American cities were in crisis. Years of underinvestment, thanks first to the Depression, then to World War II, had coincided with the movement of millions of black people out of the South and into the North. Meanwhile, millions of whites moved up into the middle class and out into the suburbs. Cities across the country were blighted. Eisenhower had a clear view of what should happen to them: "We must use what we have or destroy it." In other words, the dead neighborhoods—the slums, that is—would have to be reborn. He became the President who launched urban renewal.[20]

Razing the slums and rebuilding the cities would help maintain full employment. So too would infrastructure projects that aided national defense. Shortly after the Korean War ended, he told Charlie Wilson at Defense, "I want a shelf of projects that could be activated quickly in the event of an economic recession."[21]

In 1954 the recession he had anticipated arrived, and when it ended in early 1955, he had a survey made of thousands of proposed state and local construction plans. After he had reviewed it, he told his staff, "I think it would be a good idea to have a considerable number of projects at all times under way, but at a slow rate of execution. We can step them up more rapidly than we'd be able to do with projects that hadn't been actually begun." Like a good general, he was preparing for the next battle even as the noise and fury of the last one died down.[22]

Eisenhower was not above taking a direct and personal interest in the unemployed. He saw a newspaper story one day about former paratrooper, James Lawrence of Brooklyn, who had served in Korea, was arrested and charged with stealing $24.50. Lawrence was unemployed and married and had three children. Eisenhower told a senior member of his staff to look into it. "If this story is true, there ought to be a job we could find for such a man."[23]

As Eisenhower struggled to push a liberal program through a Republican Congress, his staff wondered what it was that made him so interested in ordinary people and their problems. His secretary, Ann Whitman, was the one who asked him about it, and he started reminiscing about Ida. She had endured great discouragements, he said, yet she was the happiest person he had ever known. His mother's attitude to life, and to people, was exemplified by her last words.

Toward the end, Ida Eisenhower was nearly bedridden and blind, needed constant care and had a nurse-companion, Mrs. Robertson, sharing her bedroom. "Mrs. Robertson got up during the night to do something for my mother, but Mother heard her and said, 'You'd better get back into bed, Mrs. Robertson. It's cold.' A few minutes later, there was a slight rustling sound, and Mother was dead." What philosophy he had about life, he concluded, was there, in his mother's concern for other people, something that held good right to the end.[24]

In his youth Ezra Taft Benson had sought converts to Mormonism on the wet, dreary streets of towns in northern England. In maturity, he had been a county farm agent and had taught agricultural economics. His energetic salesmanship had made him the ideal public relations agent for the Idaho potato. And as old age approached, he was one of the twelve apostles of the Mormon Church, looking forward to a life of spiritual concerns. And then he received a summons to meet with Dwight D. Eisenhower, the President-elect.

Eisenhower intended to offer the post of secretary of agriculture to Benson for two reasons—because it would please Taft and because Benson was not a prisoner of the farm lobby. When they met, he told Benson, "I want you to help me to do a job of the utmost importance to the nation. I'm concerned at the growing control of agriculture by government."

Benson said he felt the same way. "Farmers should be permitted to make their own decisions on their own farms, with a minimum of government interference."[25]

What neither man was prepared to face up to was the blindingly obvious fact that agriculture was being transformed even as they met and the government wasn't any more responsible for that than it was for the shape of the clouds. Eisenhower's past made him a hostage to an almost Jeffersonian belief that America's best values were expressed in the lives of sturdy small farmers, that rural life was superior—more authentic, somehow—to an urban existence. He'd bought a Gettysburg farm for his retirement; he was the gentleman-farmer-in-waiting.

Yet farming was less a way of life these days than a business, and like businesses everywhere, the big outfits were squeezing out the little guys. Only 5 percent of all farms accounted for half of all farm acreage and more than half of agricultural output. Year after year, the big farms were growing even bigger. Large-scale farming wasn't driven by government but by new technologies, which in turn were driven by the voracious demands of agribusiness.

Only 10 percent of the nation now lived on farms, and the figure fell from year to year. Despite the dramatic decline in the number of American farmers, there remained a large surplus. With perfect logic, farm surpluses were blamed on surplus farmers. In practice, however, marginal farmers consumed all they produced. The surpluses were produced by superior organization and advanced technologies. To prise the bottom third of farmers off the land would have resulted not in less food but in longer welfare rolls.[26]

Eisenhower never faced up to such realities, lost as he was in the idealized world of his youth. When I was growing up, he told the cabinet, farmers in central Kansas made a good living without government help. Benson, too, was living in another world. There was as much religious fervor in Agriculture under Benson as there was in State under Dulles.[27]

The principal tool for propping up farmers was parity payments, which guaranteed them a fixed price at which the government would buy their surpluses. Under the New Deal legislation that Eisenhower inherited, the government would pay between 75 and 90 percent of market value on farm surpluses. During the campaign, Eisenhower had told a farm audience in Minnesota that he supported 90 percent of parity. That brought him a big round of applause from the work-gnarled hands of his audience. After he became President, however, he told Benson, "Our job would be easier now if I hadn't done that!"[28]

Benson saw parity for what it was—welfare for farmers—and was impolitic enough to say so. He talked about farmers "feeding at the public trough" and criticized farm-belt congressmen for encouraging them to push their snouts in ever deeper. Eisenhower repeatedly had to reassure those same congressmen that Benson wasn't going to get rid of price supports.[29]

He also gave Benson a lesson on tactics. Taking a yellow legal pad one day, he made a big black X at the top of the page. Then he drew a square at the bottom, explaining to Benson what he was doing. "Ezra, in the military, you always have a major objective. The X is our objective." He tapped the square he'd drawn. "Here are our forces. Now, it might seem that the simplest thing to do is to go straight toward the objective. But that is not always the best way to get there." He drew lines that went out to the edge of the page, came back again, made sudden twists and loops. "You may have to move to one side or the other. You may have to move around some obstacle. You may have to feint, to pull the defending forces out of position. You may encounter heavy enemy forces, and temporarily have to retreat. That may be the way you have to work at this farm problem."[30]

It was a lesson that Benson remembered but not one he chose to absorb. Nor would he play by the same rules as his cabinet colleagues. The cabinet could discuss a farm issue, get a decision from Ike, Benson would agree with it, only to go back to his department and think of ways to avoid implementing the decision he'd just said he'd support.

There was, for example, a decision to continue taking large amounts of Cuban sugar, because the U.S. had advised Cuba to become a major exporter of sugar. That was sure to be unpopular with western states that produced sugar beets, but Eisenhower felt the U.S. had an obligation to keep its word, that it would buy Cuban sugar. Benson, however, tried to get out of implementing the policy. Such things happened repeatedly, yet when it was put to him that Benson was untrustworthy, Eisenhower testily replied, "People may think he's a goddamn fool, but he's a man of integrity." He was convinced that anything Benson did, he did only because he was convinced God wanted him to act that way. Besides, Benson outperformed the rest of the cabinet in one important respect. Eisenhower determined agricultural policy, but it was Benson who was reviled. Farmers loved Ike and voted for him gladly, but they burned Benson in effigy and pelted him with surplus tomatoes.[31]

Eisenhower resented the unremitting pressure to provide 90 percent parity, fixed by law. The basic crops, the ones that got the most support, he cuttingly called "the political crops." Even so, he worried that if market forces *were* allowed to prevail, farm prices would collapse. The resulting depression in agriculture might spread from the farms to the rest of the economy, in much the same way that a fire can leap from one side of the street to the other. "Some investment now in our farming areas could be cheaper than to risk a farming collapse," he told Sherman Adams.[32]

As things turned out, "some investment" turned out to be a huge, if hidden, increase in welfare. Parity payments rose from roughly $800 million a year under Truman to more than $5 billion a year under Eisenhower. Washington provided more than half the net income of American farmers.[33]

He wanted to give the surpluses away, but Benson persuaded him to export them instead. The trouble was, years of subsidy had pushed the price of American farm products so high that they stood no chance on world markets. Egyptian cotton was cheaper; so was Canadian wheat and New Zealand butter and so on. To overcome this problem, in 1954 Eisenhower got Congress to pass Public Law 480. This provided generous compensation to American farmers for whatever losses they might suffer in export markets.

Dulles tried to educate Benson on what this exercise in agricultural dumping was doing to America's relationships, and not only with allied countries such as Britain, Australia and France. It was also crushing farmers in the countries of the Third World. But Benson, "enveloped in a kind of celestial optimism," in Sherman Adams's phrase, claimed PL 480 was providing "friendly competition [and] fair competition," and no doubt he believed it.[34]

The more Eisenhower learned about farm policy, the more worried he became about the environment, and what people were doing to it. "We've previously considered that a man's land, as well as his home, was his castle," he told Adams one day. "He was allowed to ruin it if he wished. Well, a nation cannot divest itself of an interest in its own soil and water."[35]

In 1955 Eisenhower was impressed—and troubled—after reading one of the earliest works promoting environmentalism, *Big Dam Foolishness.* It revealed how water was being wasted and soil eroded across much of the United States because of greed and ignorance. Farmland was being swept into the rivers, which then silted up much of the plains. He told the secretary of the interior, Doug McKay, "We must plan for the best use of water resources from the mountains all the way to the oceans." Eisenhower thought maybe the government should buy marginal land from the farmers, in order to save it, but Adams reminded him that the Republican party was against extending federal land holdings.

Eisenhower responded, "That's possibly true, but we want to protect the soil of America just as much as we want to protect free speech and the right to worship. We must think of the future." If things went on as they were, the day would come when American agriculture would no longer be able to feed the nation. It was for the government to stop that from happening and the best time to act was now.[36]

★★★★★

39

Spirit of Geneva

He had no doubt what was the best thing about being President. "At last I've got a job where I can stay home nights, and by golly I'm going to stay at home," Eisenhower gleefully informed his friends. Nor did it take him long to discover the worst thing. "I'm not unhappy in this job," he told his secretary, Ann Whitman, "but it *is* the loneliest job on Earth." And to his friend Bill Robinson, executive editor of the *New York Herald Tribune,* he confided, "Any man who wants to be President is either an egomaniac or crazy."[1]

One of the unpleasant discoveries was that old friends, such as Omar Bradley, would no longer call him Ike. They invariably called him Mr. President. That created a slight distance between him and them, which made them feel more comfortable, but it planted an unsettling feeling in him that he had not only moved up but away—from them, from his past, almost from his own life.[2]

There were ways of dealing with the loneliness, of course. The White House had plenty of guest rooms. He could have the whole gang—his golfing, bridge and fishing millionaire buddies—come and stay. They were happy, as most people would be, to have the chance to spend weekends at the White House. Not Eisenhower's big brother Edgar, though. A man proud to stand at the outermost right edge of the

Republican party, like the last crusader in a doomed cause, Edgar thought the White House still stank of Roosevelt. "The place hasn't been adequately fumigated," he told Eisenhower, rejecting his invitation to come for a short stay.[3]

Although he couldn't hope to remake the place to Edgar's satisfaction, Eisenhower nevertheless had reasons of his own for signaling a break with the past. He got rid of the presidential yacht, the *Williamsburg,* for example, and shut down the presidential winter quarters at Key West. "The very word 'yacht' created a symbol of luxury in the public mind," he told his old friend Swede Hazlett.[4]

Mamie was appalled; she wanted to hang on to the yacht. To mollify her, Eisenhower changed his mind about abolishing the presidential retreat in the Catoctin Mountains, Roosevelt's "Shangri-la." But he obviously couldn't keep the old name without reminding people of the New Deal, so he changed it to Camp David, renaming it for his five-year-old grandson. It was an astute ploy. Nobody could criticize Camp David without hitting a child. So nobody did.[5]

Mamie, meanwhile, was making some changes of her own. After having the bedroom painted her favorite shades of pink and green, she said she wanted to tackle the State Dining Room. It was too dark and heavy for her taste. Gold leaf and dazzling white would work nicely, she thought. Eisenhower said he thought it would cost a lot of money to do it up that way, but her mind was made up. "If I have to pay for this myself, it is going to change!" [6]

She also fussed over the furniture and the rugs. When a Weimaraner, a gift from the German government, cocked a hind leg over an Aubusson rug in the Diplomatic Reception Room while being presented to the President, Mamie nearly fainted. Even after it had been cleaned, the rug had a faint yellow stain. Repeated cleaning didn't seem to help much, and after each failure Mamie bemoaned the fact to Eisenhower, until he erupted impatiently, "Mamie, I've a few more important things to worry about than a rug!"[7]

What she liked most about living in the White House was that she and Ike could spend more time together. "I have my man right where I want him," she'd tell her friends, with a satisfied smile. As far as anyone could judge, he was more openly affectionate toward her than he'd ever been, often putting an arm around her shoulders and calling her Mrs. Ike.[8]

All the same, she remained frosty toward Ann Whitman, someone she had taken a dislike to during the campaign for various reasons, including the fact that Ann Whitman was fairly attractive. On one of her rare visits to the Oval Office, Mamie saw Ann Whitman holding a cup of coffee. Mamie thought it wasn't in keeping with the dignity of the setting. "Get rid of that," she snapped at Whitman. Eisenhower turned red. "Mamie, you take care of your part of the White House and I'll take care of mine!"[9]

Still an early riser, Eisenhower got up at six each morning, although chances were he'd been awake for at least an hour thinking about the most pressing problems he had to deal with. Once he'd shaved and dressed, he read a folder of intelligence reports that had arrived overnight, then skimmed three newspapers—the *New York Herald Tribune, The New York Times* and *The Washington Post*—before going to breakfast at around 7:15. Normally, he had at least one breakfast guest—Al Gruenther, say, or Lucius Clay. But the person who had breakfast with him most often was his brother Milton.

By eight o'clock he was at his desk, already working his way through letters, memos and reports. He continued working until it was time to go upstairs to the residence to have lunch with Mamie and a few guests, often congressmen. His doctor, Howard Snyder, urged him to take a nap afterward, but Eisenhower refused to do it.

Around 3:30 P.M., having seen the last of his scheduled appointments, he pulled on spiked golf shoes and went outside for half an hour to hit chip shots with a five iron. He had the Rose Garden ripped up to make way for a one-hole chip and putt course at the top of the South Lawn and the patient, keen-eyed tourist who was interested in doing so could catch a glimpse of the presidential swing through the fence down by the Zero Milestone.

Around six o'clock Eisenhower finished his work for the day and got up from a clean desk to go back upstairs and have a predinner cocktail, often with the two most powerful Democrats on Capitol Hill, Sam Rayburn and Lyndon B. Johnson, two people whose help he came to rely on after the 1954 midterm election gave control of both houses of Congress to the opposition.[10]

At seven o'clock, the Eisenhowers sat down to dinner. Ike had taken his bar and television set from Morningside Heights and put them in the solarium, which was where he and Mamie had dinner while watching

TV. The solarium was also where he played bridge and grilled steaks for the gang.

Eisenhower watched two or three movies a week in the movie theater in the White House basement, and his favorite films, like MacArthur's, were always Westerns. He famously got so involved during a screening of *High Noon* that when the bad guys thought they had trapped Gary Cooper in a burning building, Eisenhower shouted, "Run! Run!" Once Cooper made good his escape, Ike turned to Mamie, exhilarated but relieved. "I never thought he'd make it!"[11]

About once a month he held a stag dinner, for thirty to forty people. Many guests were only bare acquaintances; some were people he had heard or read about. All were people whose views he wanted to hear, across a wide range of topics. His guests found two small gifts next to each place setting. Eisenhower had personally placed there a small jackknife with a black handle and a lucky penny, to offset any bad luck generated by the gift of something sharp.[12]

He still read Westerns for half an hour before going to sleep, but he also had an appetite for serious reading, such as Eric Hoffer's *The True Believer,* a minor classic on political belief in the modern world. He read Hoffer's book carefully, annotated it extensively and urged his cabinet to read it.[13]

The Democratic press and some Democrats in Congress tried to beat him up with his golf clubs, suggesting he was neglecting his responsibilities for the sake of a better swing or smoother putting. Yet polls showed that most people didn't think he was spending too much time playing golf. It didn't bother them at all.

If anything, Eisenhower's interest in golf was breaking up the game's upper-crust image. Because Ike played it, golf was no longer the recreation of the stuffed shirt and the stockbroker. No one imagined he was much good at it, or that he was pursuing it for snobbish reason or to make business deals. As he teed up the endless supply of golf balls that Spalding provided—each one embossed with MR. PRESIDENT in gold letters—he had a nation's support from Burning Tree to the municipal links.[14]

Naturally, there were times when golf, painting, making vegetable soup or grilling some steaks didn't seem to make much difference, days when Eisenhower felt physically and emotionally exhausted. Yet he had a willed optimism, a gritty determination to be positive no matter what bad news, setbacks or criticism the day had brought. When he told the students at Dartmouth, "Don't join the book burners!" he had also told them something else: "Unless each day can be looked back upon as one in which you have had some fun, some joy, some satisfaction—that day is a loss. It is un-Christian and wicked to allow such a thing to occur."[15]

A month before he was sworn in as President, Eisenhower was briefed on the results of the first hydrogen-bomb test. The explosion had been much bigger than anyone expected, unleashing a force of ten megatons—equivalent to fifty Hiroshima-size atomic bombs. Eisenhower had left the briefing deeply troubled. Was such a weapon, as terrifying in its implications for those he was sworn to defend as for those he might unleash it against, going to move the world toward a more secure future? He had his doubts.

They surfaced in his inaugural address. "Are we nearing the light—a day of freedom and peace for all mankind?" he asked rhetorically. "Or are the shadows of another night closing upon us? . . . Science seems ready to confer upon us, as its final gift, the power to erase human life from this planet."[16]

Hardly had he been sworn in before he got another briefing, this time on the frightening and inexplicable loss of top-secret documents on the hydrogen bomb and vital codes. The AEC chairman was encouraged to resign and Eisenhower offered the post to Lewis Strauss.

The new chairman of the AEC had arrived in Washington in the early 1920s as Herbert Hoover's secretary. Quick-witted and ambitious, Strauss had soon learned how Washington operated. After Hoover's presidency ended, Strauss used his Washington contacts to land a well-paid job with a New York investment bank and became rich. Returning to Washington at the end of World War II, he became assistant to James Forrestal, the first secretary of defense, who provided him with something he coveted—a title. Forrestal made Strauss a rear admiral in the Naval Reserve, and ever after he loved to be known as Admiral Strauss. Among his numerous important acquaintances from his time working for Forrestal was General of the Army Dwight Eisenhower. To Eisenhower, Strauss seemed a good choice to head the AEC, not because he had any understanding of nuclear physics—he had none—but because he was so well versed in the ways of the federal bureaucracy and so decisive in his manner that it seemed a safe, if hardly inspired, appointment.[17]

As Strauss was settling into his new post, Eisenhower's adviser on Cold War strategy, C. D. Jackson, was trying to write a speech about nuclear weapons. Eisenhower hoped to use the speech to allay the growing national mood of anxiety about thermonuclear weapons. He may, without realizing it, have been seeking to allay some of his own anxieties, too. Jackson produced draft after draft, and Eisenhower rejected them all. They seemed unable to move beyond the obvious—mass destruction, incalculable suffering.[18]

Eisenhower, meanwhile, was asked at a press conference to say something about the Soviet H-bomb. He made a few anodyne remarks, then added, "Now, a word as to our own situation. We do not intend to disclose the details of our strength in atomic weapons of any sort, but it is large and increasing steadily." Far from calming people's fears, he appeared to be boasting about America's nuclear might.[19]

Jackson was still wrestling with the speech when Eisenhower headed for a vacation in Denver at the end of August 1953. Two weeks later, he had to cut it short when Chief Justice Fred Vinson died. On the flight back to Washington to attend Vinson's funeral, a thought came to Eisenhower: there was only a limited supply of uranium, and it could be used either for bombs or to provide energy. Suppose nearly all the fissionable material in the world were controlled by an international organization, which then made it available for use in atomic power plants or for medical research. That might head off proliferation of nuclear weapons, keep the number of weapons the nuclear powers controlled to a minimum and help calm people's fears.[20]

He put this idea to the NSC, which was enthusiastic, and had Strauss join with Jackson to produce a new speech. By the time Eisenhower headed for Bermuda to meet with Winston Churchill and French premier Joseph Laniel at the beginning of December, the speech was nearly finished. In Bermuda, Eisenhower told Churchill and his scientific adviser, Lord Cherwell, that nuclear weapons had "achieved conventional status" within the U.S. armed forces.

The British were thunderstruck. It seemed to them that Eisenhower was preparing the way to use atomic bombs in almost any circumstance. In fact, Eisenhower had already concluded that there was virtually no way to justify their existence except as a deterrent to Soviet nuclear weapons.[21]

From Bermuda he flew to New York, to address the United Nations. Arriving outside the UN in midafternoon on December 8, he got out of the presidential limousine, waved his hat at the crowd and shook hands with Dag Hammarskjöld, the secretary-general, who led him inside. On the way to the Hall of Assembly, he excused himself for a few minutes and strode briskly into the Meditation Room. For a few minutes Eisenhower was alone, with his speech, his conscience, his God and one Secret Service agent. However he formulated his desire within a silent prayer, what he was praying for was that he would not be the President who consigned humanity to oblivion by failing to get the H-bomb under control.[22]

His speech was listened to in rapt, almost reverential silence. What was at stake, he said simply, was "the very life of the world." People were afraid of the atom, but it could be controlled if the governments of the world were prepared to act. The existing atomic powers—the U.S., the Soviet Union and Great Britain—should place most of their fissionable material in the hands of an international atomic energy agency. He concluded, "The United States pledges before you—and therefore before the world—its determination to help solve the fearful atomic dilemma—to devote its entire heart and mind to find a way by which the miraculous inventiveness of man shall not be dedicated to his death but consecrated to his life."[23]

He finished in a strange silence, his audience still spellbound. And then, after nine or ten seconds, the General Assembly erupted as sober diplomats sprang to their feet, applauding so hard that their hands probably hurt the next day. Even the five delegations representing constituent republics of the USSR joined in. Over the months that followed there was . . . nothing.

There was a fundamental flaw in Eisenhower's rightly admired, much-vaunted "Atoms for Peace" speech. It was, on the face of it, generous in the extreme. He had declared he was willing to give five times as much fissionable material over to international control as the Soviets. The flaw was that even if the two sides ultimately achieved uranium stockpiles of the same size and possessed exactly the same number of weapons, it would leave the strategic disparity between the two sides intact. Thanks to SAC, the U.S. would still be able to destroy the Soviet

Union in a single, swift, unstoppable preemptive strike. That was one advantage that Eisenhower could not and would not bargain away. No President would, but least of all him. The Soviets knew that was so, and even as the fervent applause for his "Atoms for Peace" speech faded into history, his bold initiative was already trickling away to vanish like a dry creek. It would be 1957 before the International Atomic Energy Agency was established, but it had a small staff, a small budget and little real power over atomic research and development. No country that was truly determined to acquire nuclear arms would ever be stopped by the IAEA.

Besides, the United States itself did not seem in any hurry to bring the atom under international control. In March 1954, only three months after Eisenhower's speech, an explosion at Bikini atoll in the South Pacific cast a pall of radioactive dust over the Marshall Islands, a U.S. territory. More than 230 Islanders fell ill with radiation sickness. Strauss flew out to inspect the situation.

Before he returned, a news story flashed around the world that a Japanese fishing vessel, the inaptly named *Lucky Dragon,* had returned to port with its entire twenty-three-man crew suffering from radiation sickness caused by the Bikini explosion. Eisenhower held a press conference, intending to provide reassurance, but he stumbled. "It is quite clear," he declared, "that this time something must have happened that . . . surprised and astonished the scientists." It sounded uncomfortably close to an admission that the scientists in question were playing dice with the existence of the human race.[24]

A week later, Strauss returned and told Eisenhower the *Lucky Dragon* was not a fishing boat at all but a Russian espionage ship. Eisenhower personally escorted him into the Indian Treaty Room of the State, War and Navy Building for a press conference, expecting that the admiral would calm people's fears. The blast was twice as powerful as the scientists had expected, Strauss acknowledged, but, "at no time was the testing out of control."

He did not repeat for public consumption his assertion that the Japanese fishermen were Communist spies. Instead, he ridiculed their claims of radiation poisoning. Mere "chemical activity," he said dismissively, something caused by contact with coral. As for the Marshall Islanders, "the natives appeared to me to be well and happy."

Then, answering a reporter's question about the size of the H-bomb, he said proudly, "An H-bomb can be made large enough to take out a city."

The reporter responded, "Any city?"

"Any city!"

"New York?" asked another scribbling reporter.

"The metropolitan area, yes." There were gasps of astonishment.

As he walked out of the room with Strauss, Eisenhower said, "I wouldn't have answered that one that way, Lewis."[25]

It turned out that the Japanese fishermen were indeed suffering from radiation sickness, and one died. There was never any evidence to support Strauss's contention that they were spies, and hundreds of Marshall Islanders required medical treatment for radiation poisoning. Far from being a good choice as chairman of the AEC, the bombastic, egotistical Strauss was a public relations disaster. Fear of the Bomb rose dramatically during his stewardship.

The post-Stalin leadership of the Soviet Union was looking for ways to move away from Stalin's murderous legacy while holding on tightly to the Communist party's monopoly of power. To demonstrate their good faith, the Soviets agreed to withdraw their forces from Austria, on condition that the U.S., the UK and France did the same, and provided the Austrians committed themselves to a state of permanent neutrality. The occupation of Austria ended in May 1955.

Eisenhower did not simply welcome the Soviet withdrawal from Austria; he used it to argue that now was the time for a summit meeting. Dulles told him he was wrong. There was no point in having a summit, Dulles insisted, unless it would yield a major agreement. Eisenhower brushed that aside. Any treaty on disarmament, which was what Eisenhower wanted most of all, would require an atmosphere of trust, and a summit might generate just such an atmosphere. Besides which, the British and French were pressing hard for a summit.[26]

A meeting was set for Geneva, starting July 18, 1955, at the old League of Nations complex overlooking the lake and the spectacular *jet d'eau*. The Soviet delegation was headed by the elderly, white-haired Marshal Nikolai Bulganin, an old soldier with a white goatee, and the secretary-general of the Communist party, Nikita Khrushchev. The Soviet defense minister, Georgi Zhukov, whom Eisenhower had met several times at the end of the war and taken an instant liking to, would also be there.

Eisenhower arrived in Geneva carrying a wedding present for Zhukov's daughter, who had been married a few days earlier in Moscow. Zhukov embraced him in a crushing Russian bear hug, yet as they chatted and reminisced, it was evident to Eisenhower that Zhukov was ill at ease. Just why that was so, no one was certain, but it may well have been due to the fact that less than a year earlier, *The Memoirs of Marshal Zhukov* had been published. Zhukov had derided Eisenhower as a war-mongering capitalist lackey and enemy of the heroic Soviet people. It probably hadn't occurred to him when he wrote his book that he would ever meet Eisenhower again.[27]

In getting-to-know-you sessions with Bulganin and Khrushchev, Eisenhower was pleasantly surprised to find that they were eager to visit the United States. In fact, they eventually turned out to be more curious to see the outside world than any Russian leaders since Peter the Great. Eisenhower was tempted to say, "Good, come on over," but decided he'd better discuss it with Dulles first.[28]

Eisenhower and Churchill had arrived in Geneva hoping this summit might lead to an agreement to hold an all-German election, confident the result would be a united Germany within NATO. That was something the Soviets feared, so they refused to consider it. They proposed instead an end to the four-power occupation, a withdrawal of forces and a neutral Germany, much like Austria. Eisenhower and Churchill rejected that. NATO without Germans would never amount to anything, least of all a guarantor of European security.

The summit got nowhere on Germany, but Eisenhower had something else to propose. Some months earlier, Nelson Rockefeller and Harold Stassen had both suggested programs of aerial inspection of the U.S. and the USSR. Meanwhile, the NSC had established a small team of scientists and intelligence experts called the Committee on Meeting a Surprise Attack. A nuclear Pearl Harbor was never far from Eisenhower's mind.

Out of the discussions on surprise attack and the proposed programs of aerial inspection evolved the idea that Eisenhower presented to the Geneva conference on July 21. "My proposal is to give each other a complete blueprint of our military establishments," he said, looking directly at Bulganin and Khrushchev, as if addressing them personally. "From one end of our countries to the other . . . to provide within our countries facilities for aerial photography to the other country," including airfields, communications and maintenance. There would be no restrictions on where the aircraft could fly.

Just as he finished, a thunderstorm broke and the lights went out in the building. Eisenhower chuckled in the darkness. "Gee, I didn't think it would have that effect!"[29]

After the lights came on, the delegates made their way downstairs for tea and coffee, energized by the novelty and daring of Eisenhower's "Open Skies" proposal. The British and French were voluble in their enthusiasm, but the Soviets were poker-faced. Holding a teacup, Eisenhower turned around and saw Bulganin standing close by and asked what he thought. Bulganin said the proposal needed study.

Eisenhower then turned to Zhukov. "Wouldn't a system like this have helped prevent the last war, if each side had known with certainty what the other one had?" Before Zhukov could answer, Khrushchev broke in: "The trouble is, this proposal is just espionage. This would be fine for you, because it would give your strategic forces the chance to accumulate target information. You could then zero in on us with your strategic forces. Therefore it wouldn't be a contribution to peace or stability."[30]

By "strategic forces," Khrushchev meant SAC and, by implication, the American strategy of first strike. Eisenhower tried to assure Bulganin and Khrushchev that they had nothing to fear. The United States was not going to attack their country. "Let us remember this—the world's winds go east and west, not north and south," said Eisenhower. "If there is a war, both of us will be destroyed. Only the Southern Hemisphere will be left."[31]

What Khrushchev had said was nonetheless irrefutable. The strategic disparity between the two sides meant that the United States would gain far more from Open Skies than the Soviet Union ever could. Open Skies would improve SAC's target data while confirming something the Soviets already knew—that the United States enjoyed crushing, overwhelming strength in nuclear weapons and—crucially—in the ability to use them.

Eisenhower was personally affronted by Khrushchev's veto on Open Skies. Having offered a sincere attempt to make the world safer, he angrily dismissed Khrushchev's objections as "spurious." He never accepted that it wasn't only the U.S. that feared a surprise attack with nuclear weapons—so did the Soviet leadership. He read their fears as aspersions on his own integrity and on America's desire for peace.[32]

Had the strategic situations been reversed, however, and such a proposal been put to Eisenhower, he would have rejected it as robustly as Khrushchev did. Instead, he would have devoted every effort to achieving nuclear parity not just in numbers but in delivery systems. That was what the Soviets were already doing, and shortly before he left for Geneva, he had set in motion a plan to monitor their progress by means of a revolutionary reconnaissance aircraft, the U-2, which would fly through their skies with or without their consent.

40

Lifesaver

Bryce Harlow, the pint-sized former congressman from Oklahoma who had been hired to craft speeches and drink bourbon with the right people on Capitol Hill, thought he knew more than a little about bad language and fiery tempers, but he had never seen anything like Ike's. Behind the friendly grin there was another man, one who didn't simply shout and swear when he got angry but seemed almost on the verge of a sulfurous vanishing act, disappearing in the flames and smoke of spontaneous combustion. The first time it happened, Harlow had been explaining some changes he thought were needed in a speech draft that Eisenhower had written. He was astonished to see the President jump up from his chair, his face turning pink, then crimson, then purple as he paced the Oval Office carpet, arms thrashing like the branches of a tree in a hurricane, bellowing that he didn't want the goddamn speech changed!

As Eisenhower cursed his way through a lexicon of profanity acquired in more than thirty years of military service, Harlow was fascinated. "A Bessemer furnace," thought Harlow. "It's like looking into a Bessemer furnace." After a couple of minutes, the furnace door abruptly clanked shut. When Eisenhower sat down, the fierce red tones drained from his face. He was his normal, equable self again.[1]

Such Bessemer incidents might erupt at almost any time, triggered by trivial irritants more often than not. The longer Eisenhower was in the White House, the less control he seemed to have over his temper. By the time he set off for Geneva, he had reduced his secretary, Ann Whitman, to a nervous wreck. Special counsel Bernard Shanley often found her sobbing at her desk, wondering how much longer she could take such verbal abuse from a man she admired and sought only to serve. Shanley tried to comfort her and tell her not to take it so personally, that it was a form of therapy for an overburdened chief executive.[2]

Not even the summit seemed to make any difference. While newspaper editorials were hailing the "spirit of Geneva" and his approval rating in the Gallup poll reached 79 percent, Eisenhower continued raging just as before. Ann Whitman wasn't alone in her misery. He was berating others on the White House staff. Maybe, they told one another, he'll be better once he's had a vacation.

In mid-August, Eisenhower and Mamie set off for Denver. Over the next few weeks he fished in mountain streams and painted the Rockies. On September 23, he dropped a line to Lyndon Johnson, the Senate majority leader, who had recently suffered a heart attack and was convalescing in Texas. "I most earnestly hope for your sake that you will not . . . try to do too much too quickly."[3] Then he headed for Denver's most prestigious golf course, at the Cherry Hills Country Club, for a round of golf with a couple of old friends and the club pro, Ralph ("but everybody calls me Rip") Arnold.

The game was interrupted by phone calls from Dulles, wanting to discuss matters that Eisenhower thought could have waited until after he'd finished playing. After wolfing down a hamburger lavishly garnished with bermuda onions, he decided to shoot an extra nine holes with Arnold. Teeing up for the eighth hole, Eisenhower suddenly felt sick. "Maybe I can't take these onions anymore," he told Arnold. "They seem to be backing up on me."[4]

Back at the Doud home, Eisenhower painted for a while, had a light dinner, then went to bed at ten o'clock. At one-thirty in the morning, he woke up. There was a sharp pain in his chest. Those damn onions again, he told himself. He groaned, and moments later, Mamie appeared at his bedside. "Are you having a nightmare?" she asked.

"No, dear. But thank you."

She went back to bed, but instead of abating, the pain grew worse.

He went into her bedroom and pointed to his midriff. "I've got a pain in my lower chest." He asked her if there was any milk of magnesia.

Mamie found some and gave it to him by spoon. Eisenhower returned to bed, but Mamie was alarmed—he had complained about feeling unwell in the past, but he had never asked for medicine. She picked up the telephone and called Howard McCrum Snyder, the seventy-four-year-old presidential physician.[5]

A tall, white-haired general practitioner whose skills were rusty and knowledge outdated, Snyder had, over the years, become a friend of the family. Eisenhower had been urged by Lucius Clay and others to get a new doctor, but he wouldn't consider it. Besides, Mamie had boundless faith in Snyder, who had been treating her for a valvular heart condition since 1943.

Snyder arrived at three A.M., decided that Eisenhower was suffering from acute indigestion, and treated him accordingly. He didn't realize that what he was dealing with was a potentially fatal heart attack. Eisenhower developed a cold sweat, so Snyder asked Mamie to slip into bed with her husband to help keep him warm. Around dawn, Eisenhower got up and went to the toilet, came back and fell asleep at last. It was noon before Snyder came to his senses and called Fitzsimons Army Hospital and said he wanted to arrange an electrocardiogram. An hour later, Snyder was staring at an EKG printout that showed a hole the size of a dime in the anterior wall of the President's heart.[6]

Eisenhower awoke in the early hours of September 25 to find himself in a room at Fitzsimons, drenched in sweat. He was sweating so freely that his pajamas had to be changed. His sturdy constitution had allowed him to survive Snyder's incompetence, an incompetence that Snyder was already trying to cover up by fabricating a false medical record. Not that Eisenhower had any idea of that. He believed that Snyder had just saved his life. So, too, did Mamie. "I'm not worried about Ike at all," she told journalists after the heart attack was confirmed. "My gracious, nothing could happen to him [with] Dr. Snyder always poking at him."[7]

His doctors, who now included the nation's preeminent heart surgeon, Dr. Paul Dudley White, said it would be four months before they'd know if he was going to make a full recovery. He told them, "I'll be good," and willed himself to be quiet and calm to help his heart, although the fact that the hospital kitchen was feeding him eggs, sausage and bacon for breakfast and steak for lunch or dinner nearly every day was probably not doing it much good. As he stared at the crucifix now hanging from his sickroom door, the prospect of spending the rest of his life as a cardiac cripple was more than he could bear. "That would be just as good as being dead," he told Robert Cutler.[8]

A few weeks after the heart attack, Eisenhower was photographed on the roof of the hospital, seated in a wheelchair but looking tanned and healthy. On his shirt pocket was embroidered MUCH BETTER, THANKS, but he adamantly ruled out any return to Washington until he was strong enough to walk into the Oval Office and get back to work. No one wanted a disabled President.

In the meantime, Sherman Adams kept the executive branch busy and focused. Congress studiously refrained from creating difficulties. Nixon showed no signs of itching to get hold of the reins. No major foreign policy crisis erupted. The country seemed to put everything on hold.[9]

Eisenhower returned to Washington on Veterans Day, November 11, dressed in shades of brown. Before boarding the presidential aircraft— *Columbine III*—he made a short, gracious speech of thanks to all who had helped him during his illness, observing with obvious emotion, "Misfortune—and particularly the misfortune of illness—brings to all of us an understanding of how good people are."[10]

Arriving at National Airport, Eisenhower told the waiting crowd, "The doctors have given me at least a parole, if not a pardon." As his motorcade crossed Memorial Bridge and drove down Constitution Avenue, it passed under a huge banner emblazoned, WELCOME HOME, IKE!! while crowds lining the street applauded and cheered, relieved that the most popular man in the world had returned to them.

Cardiac specialists puzzled over his "heart history." No Eisenhower had ever suffered from heart disease. Both David and Ida had lived into their eighties. Ike had given up smoking back in 1949, watched his diet, maintained his weight at 172 pounds—only seven pounds more than when he'd graduated from West Point—and took regular exercise. The job was demanding—"It's pound, pound, pound," he'd told Field Marshal Sir Bernard Montgomery only ten months before the heart attack.

But the demands of the presidency did not, in and of themselves, explain why it had happened to him. After all, Roosevelt had survived them for twelve years despite suffering from polio. Snyder said he was baffled, too.[11]

The more Eisenhower reflected on matters, though, he ruefully concluded that he had brought it on himself. It was that volcanic temper that had nearly killed him. He resolved to get a grip on his anger from now on and not let minor irritants upset him.[12]

Besides, he did not intend to run again. All he had to do was survive another year. He had told his old friend Bill Robinson that he wouldn't run again only a few weeks after becoming President, and he had told Gabe Hauge the same thing in May 1955. "I just know that I could not again go through the campaign that I went through in '52. . . . It is a hard, bitter job, and I just have not got that much remaining energy." Anyway, he added, it was time for a younger man to take over.[13]

He still felt much the same way right up until he found himself in the hospital, because once he survived, the issue—which he had been ducking, not confronting—finally had to be faced. It became the subtext of his convalescence, given urgency by looming deadlines: the doctors would decide in February what his long-term prospects looked like, in July the Republican convention would meet in San Francisco, and barely a year later the 1956 election would be held. Deadlines had always been, for him, the guillotine of decision making—inescapable, unyielding, stark.

Back in the White House, Eisenhower wrestled with the possibility of running again, tempted at breakfast, disenchanted by dinner. He was torn as he had been torn in the agonizing months leading up to his first bid for nomination. Was this a call to duty? Did the people really want him? Wasn't he just kidding himself? What would he do if he retired?

Shortly before Thanksgiving, Leonard Hall, the chairman of the Republican National Committee, told him he had to say *something*. Stevenson had just declared he would be a candidate in 1956. Eisenhower replied that Hall could say whatever seemed right to him. No decision had yet been made. So Hall told a press conference shortly before Christmas 1955, "The ticket still will be Eisenhower and Nixon." The journalists, who had just decided among themselves by a nine-to-one margin that Eisenhower wouldn't run again, burst into mocking laughter.[14]

A few weeks later, William Knowland announced that he would be a candidate if Eisenhower chose not to run. Jim Hagerty asked him bluntly, "Mr. President, do you know what you're going to do yet in 1956?"

Eisenhower said the Democrats who might succeed him—Stevenson, Estes Kefauver or Averell Harriman—were all "crackpots." As for Knowland, he was "impossible." He had been hoping a younger leader might emerge from within the GOP, ready to succeed him in 1956, but all the likely candidates—including Nixon, George Humphrey, Sherman Adams and Herb Brownell—were deficient in some way. He hadn't made up his mind to run again. "I don't want to, but I may have to."[15]

A month later, on January 13, Eisenhower held a White House stag dinner that, for once, had a theme. Normally, the conversation at these affairs flowed wherever the mood of the moment and the personalities present wanted to take it. But this time there was a serious question to ponder: Should he seek reelection? Milton and John both said no. The majority, however, were clearly in favor, including Snyder, who believed activity was more likely to keep him alive than was going into retirement at Gettysburg.[16]

The country as a whole seemed to be moving the same way. During Eisenhower's hospitalization, polls had shown a majority against a second term, probably because people thought it would kill him. By January 1956, he seemed to be recovering his health and strength, and now a majority wanted him to run again. His own mind was more or less made up. On February 29, after being told he had made a complete recovery, Eisenhower announced he would run again.

He had been back at work for two months, pacing himself carefully, taking a nap after lunch and trying—without always succeeding—to keep his anger under control. He played golf more often, spent longer periods painting, went to his farm and Camp David more frequently. Then, in May, his old internal troubles returned to plague him, but this time he finally had a diagnosis. He was suffering from ileitis, or a partially blocked small intestine. Poorly digested food—a chunk of celery, for example—would complete the blockage, producing agonizing cramps.

On June 6, the twelfth anniversary of D-Day, the ileitis flared up again. He was taken to Walter Reed Army Hospital and nearly a dozen surgeons conferred—and hesitated. The responsibility of cutting the

President open rested with the commanding general of Walter Reed, Major General Leonard Heaton, who was some way short of being a great surgeon.

While Heaton and surgeons who had been brought in from across the country debated what to do, Eisenhower was vomiting dark green fluid—three pints of the stuff. His blood pressure was falling so dramatically that he was about to go into shock. His abdomen was becoming distended and giving him pain, and for some strange reason, so was the calf of his right leg. At one-thirty in the morning, the surgeons decided they couldn't procrastinate any longer. They had Eisenhower wheeled into the operating theater and told him they were sorry but they had to cut. "Well, let's go," he said. Heaton took up a scalpel and began an obsolescent and risky operational technique that modern surgeons rarely used for ileitis.[17]

Eisenhower survived his doctors once again. He left Walter Reed three weeks after his operation, feeling weak and looking it, with a well-tailored suit that seemed almost to fall off his gaunt frame. His recovery was slow, making him angry and depressed, but by August 21, when he boarded *Columbine III* and headed for San Francisco, he was a portrait of vigorous good health despite his sixty-five years. He looked, that is, like an Ike that Americans would want to keep in the White House for at least four more years, if not forever—an Ike who had never been sick.

In 1947, as Jewish survivors of the Holocaust struggled to push the British out of Palestine and make way for the creation of Israel, Harry Truman met with Chaim Weizmann. Both the State and War departments were strongly opposed to a Zionist state, but Weizmann urged Truman not to follow their advice. "God put you into your mother's womb so that *you* could be the instrument to bring about the rebirth of Israel after two thousand years," said Weizmann dramatically. Truman, a man with a deeply emotional nature, someone who had read the entire Bible twice, a man whose deep interest in history could make the past seem as real in his imagination as the present, burst into tears.[18]

When Eisenhower became President, the warm, emotional ties that Truman had forged with Israel and its leaders were abruptly replaced by what Dulles called "friendly impartiality." For three years, nothing much seemed to happen to put either the friendship or impartiality to the test. Then the Egyptian government, headed by a military strong-man who had forced Egypt's king into exile, Gamal Abdul Nasser, decided to build a huge dam at Aswan, on the upper Nile. The World Bank got the British and U.S. governments to agree to put up nearly $1.5 billion for the project.

Before the agreement was signed and sealed, however, Nasser placed a large arms order with Czechoslovakia. Eisenhower was incensed. Czechoslovakia was a Soviet satellite; its arms factories were outposts of the Red Army. In March 1956, he told Dulles that he wanted Nasser to know something: "He cannot cooperate as he is doing with the Soviet Union and at the same time enjoy most-favored-nation treatment by the United States."[19]

Nasser was not impressed. In May, he recognized the People's Republic of China. To Eisenhower and Dulles, that was almost as good as flashing a Communist party membership card. Congress, meanwhile, made it clear that it wasn't going to provide money for Nasser's dam. The project was as good as dead, but neither Eisenhower nor Dulles bothered to inform the Egyptians of that fact for another two months. When Dulles finally and formally withdrew the American offer of financial help, he trampled all over diplomatic protocol by telling the press before he informed the Egyptians. And when he did see the Egyptian ambassador, it was not so much to tell him anything he didn't already know as to insult and humiliate him. Shortly after this, Nasser seized the Suez Canal, which the British had built and which they owned and still operated. He also made it clear he was looking now to the Soviet Union to rescue the Aswan Dam project.[20]

For the British, the Egyptian seizure of the Canal was a national humiliation. Besides, the British relied heavily on the Canal for shipment of their oil supplies from Iraq, Kuwait, Saudi Arabia and Iran. Eisenhower received a letter from his old friend Anthony Eden, who had succeeded Churchill as prime minister. "We are all agreed that we cannot afford to allow Nasser to seize control of the Canal in this way. . . . We ought in the first instance to bring maximum political pressure on Egypt. [But] my colleagues and I are convinced that we must be ready, in the last resort, to use force to bring Nasser to his senses."[21]

Eisenhower warned Eden of the international outrage that would follow military action. There was also the risk of stirring up a guerrilla war, backed by the Soviets. "Initial military successes might be easy, but the eventual price might become far too heavy." He had Dulles carry this letter to London.[22]

Even as Dulles flew across the Atlantic, the French were putting an idea to the Israelis. Since the creation of Israel, Egypt had been the foremost member of the Arab coalition opposed to its existence. As for the French, they blamed the bitter and bloody war they were fighting to hold on to Algeria on Nasser's help to Algerian guerrillas. The French proposal was that Israel would attack across the Sinai Desert, toward the Canal, but before Israeli tanks reached it, French and British forces would make airborne and amphibious assaults to occupy key points along the Canal, ostensibly to protect it from being ruined in a clash between Israelis and Egyptians. Nasser would be humiliated, his military power destroyed. A new government, one more friendly to Israel and the West, would then be installed in Cairo. After thinking over the French idea, Eden agreed to take part.

From mid-September until late October, as Eisenhower campaigned for reelection, he received intelligence reports on the buildup of British forces in Malta and Cyprus, intense activity at French naval bases around the Mediterranean and the sudden appearance of sixty modern French fighters in the blue and white colors of the Israeli Air Force. The British and French governments, meanwhile, consistently lied to Eisenhower about what they were doing and preparing to do. Allen Dulles was also completely confused. He told Eisenhower that the Israelis were preparing to invade Jordan.[23]

On October 29, the Israelis attacked Egypt, sending a powerful armored column across the Sinai peninsula. Eisenhower cut short a campaign speaking tour and hurried back to Washington. When he walked into the Oval Office that evening, he was fizzing with rage. Both Dulles brothers were there, with Wilson from Defense and Radford representing the JCS. The Israeli thrust was, to his mind, an act of cynical and naked aggression. "Foster, you tell them, goddammit, that we're going to the United Nations. We're going to do everything that there is so we can stop this thing."[24]

Nothing, however, would deter Britain and France. They demanded that the Egyptians allow them to occupy positions along the Canal, certain that Nasser would never agree. They launched their attack on October 31. Eisenhower was incredulous. "I just don't know what got into these people. It's the damnedest business I ever saw supposedly intelligent governments get themselves into."[25]

When the United Nations debated an American resolution demanding a cease-fire, the U.S. was supported by the Soviets, while its erstwhile allies and key partners in NATO were reviled and berated. Eden had never imagined such an outcome. He had not expected the commitment of U.S. military forces, but he had expected Eisenhower to block or delay any action in the UN that would hinder the plot to get rid of Nasser. Dulles, too, wanted the operation to continue at least until Nasser was overthrown and only then impose a cease-fire. The Joint Chiefs wanted to go even further—they advised Eisenhower to provide enough landing craft so the British and French attack would quickly succeed.

When the UN voted for a cease-fire, Nasser didn't hesitate to seize the lifeline that Eisenhower had just tossed him, and with the U.S. so actively working against them, the British and French had little option but to halt their advance. So, too, did the Israelis. They were short of the Canal—but in possession of nearly the whole of the Sinai.

Eisenhower occupied the moral high ground throughout the Suez crisis, something the British and French could not have expected from someone who had enthusiastically supported the plots against Arbenz in Guatemala and Mossadegh in Iran. His motives were complex and not wholly consistent. He had been outraged to discover that the British and French had deceived him. More than that, though, he could not see any justification for their actions.

To him, they were merely using the seizure of the Canal as a pretext to send in the gunboats—former imperial powers chasing the shadows of imperial glory. In his last speech of the 1956 campaign, he spoke with evident emotion about how deeply he treasured America's friendship with Britain and France. "But this we know above all: There are some firm principles that cannot bend—they can only break. And we shall not break ours."[26]

His reactions had been impeccably moral, yet it is difficult to believe that had some Panamanian Nasser tried to seize the Panama Canal, Eisenhower would have clung so firmly to principle. Like most Americans, he was alert to the imperialistic behavior of other nations while remaining steadfastly convinced that the United States never acted the same way. His deeply held hope that Third World countries would admire America's moral lead over Suez came to nothing. Many—possibly most—still saw the U.S. as an imperial power.

Eisenhower accepted no responsibility for the inevitable consequences of what he had done. As British and French influence in the Middle East collapsed, the Soviets filled the vacuum. They became a major factor in the politics of the region for the next thirty years. The last vestiges of impartiality in dealing with Israel were abandoned, because Israel refused to withdraw from the Sinai without assurances of long-term military and economic support from the U.S. Fatally undermined, pro-Western governments from Libya to Iraq were toppled in the aftermath of Suez. Finally, in magnifying the power and prestige of Nasser, Eisenhower had ensured that the Middle East would be racked by more—and more dangerous—wars in years to come.

Eisenhower had a habit that went back to the Army of drawing up lists of names. In the Army they were lists of people suitable for promotion. Now, though, they were lists of the greatest men he'd ever known, or potential Republican presidents of the future. He never put Nixon's name at the top of any of his lists of presidential possibilities. Nor did he ever develop a close personal relationship with his Vice-President. During Eisenhower's time in the White House, Nixon was never invited to the private quarters. He cuttingly told Emmet Hughes and others, "Nixon is a born loser. He's just not presidential timber."[27]

Their relationship was strictly business, and as Eisenhower wrestled with the question of whether or not to run for reelection, his thoughts turned inevitably to Nixon. At Christmas 1955, he had a long talk with him in the Oval Office. What did Nixon want? How did he see his future? Nixon seemed vague and insecure. Eisenhower told him to think things over, then let him know what he'd decided. Months passed, with Nixon silent and reclusive.[28]

As he waited for Nixon to make up his mind, Eisenhower explained the Nixon problem to Secretary of the Interior Fred Seaton. "I don't know exactly what he wants to do, and I don't think he knows himself. I am not going to say he is the only individual I would have for Vice-President, but there is nothing to be gained politically by ditching him."

A few days later, Jim Hagerty returned from a trip he had made around the country, talking to Republican leaders. "Not one person was for Nixon for Vice-President for a second term," reported Hagerty.[29]

Ever since his decision to run again, Eisenhower had been hoping he might be able to persuade Nixon to stand aside. He would have loved to put Milton on the ticket, but that was obviously out of the question. For a while, he considered George Humphrey, only to conclude that Humphrey would never become liberal enough to be electable.

From time to time Eisenhower had mused aloud about the chances of remaking the GOP so it would be conservative on money issues and defense problems but liberal on everything else. Sometimes he even toyed with heretical thoughts about creating an entirely different party.[30]

Leonard Hall, the Republican party chairman, suggested he offer the VP slot to Frank Lausche, the governor of Ohio. Lausche was a Roman Catholic and a Democrat. "I'd love to run with a Catholic," said Eisenhower enthusiastically. Hall thought it would be easy to get Nixon not to run. He was wrong. Nixon would not even discuss it with him, but simply turned away and stared at the ceiling in his office until Hall departed.[31]

Eisenhower's number-one candidate was Robert Anderson, a brilliant young banker and former secretary of the Navy, and an idea began to form. If he could persuade Nixon to stand aside, he could possibly talk Anderson into becoming his running mate.[32]

On April 26, after Hall's unwelcome visit, Nixon finally went to see Eisenhower to talk about his future. He said he'd like to be the vice-presidential nominee again. Eisenhower was evasive. Selection of a running mate would have to wait until after the convention had chosen its presidential nominee, he said. He reminded Nixon that no one who had served as VP for eight years had ever been elected President. Wouldn't it be better for him to assume a major cabinet post—secretary of defense, for example—and establish his credentials as a powerful figure in his own right? That could only improve his chances of being the Republican nominee in 1960. Nixon brushed that idea aside. Taking a cabinet post after being Vice-President would look too much like a demotion, he said dismissively. With Nixon clinging like a limpet to the ticket, any lingering hope Eisenhower had of securing the slot for Anderson vanished.[33]

There wasn't the velleity of a doubt about Eisenhower's reelection. "Nothing could have stopped his nomination," wrote Drew Pearson when the convention ended. "Even if he had died en route to San Francisco, Len Hall would have stuffed him and run him anyway."[34]

Nor did anyone expect Eisenhower to campaign even half as vigorously as he'd done in 1952. On September 12, he kicked off his low-key campaign in a sagging, disreputable-looking tent that had been raised on a field near the Gettysburg farmhouse, surrounded by lesser tents for the press, the caterers and a medical team. Republican speakers from across the country stood at a bank of microphones and rambled excruciatingly. Nixon gave a short, rousing speech, Eisenhower posed for a thousand and one photographs, then gave a talk about the dangers of complacency, illustrating it by reminiscing about the Army's setbacks in North Africa in World War II.[35]

Adlai Stevenson's only real issue in the campaign was a proposal for a ban on nuclear testing in the atmosphere. Eisenhower ridiculed this as a "theatrical" gesture, hardly worth talking about. What he offered the people was more of the same, at home and abroad, for another four years.

That was precisely what most people wanted. His margin of victory, in both the popular vote and the electoral college, was greater this time than in 1952. Even so, both houses of Congress had solid Democratic majorities. While Eisenhower's supporters cheered their hero, he was dismayed at the result. He told Senator Styles Bridges, "If I'd known what the outcome would be, I would probably have refused to run."

As he took the oath of office once again, Eisenhower was not looking forward to the next four years.

Just Men

With sad panda eyes that suggested weariness of spirit and slow, deliberate movements that betrayed a lack of vitality, Chief Justice Fred M. Vinson led his fellow justices toward the elevated bench of the Supreme Court once a week to hear oral arguments. Dressed in the traditional flowing—and forgiving—black robes, Vinson swayed slightly, as if from the huge weight of responsibility that goes with being the ultimate wise man of the judicial tribe. In public, his jaded gravitas might seem fitting. Out of view, however, in the book-lined seclusion of his chambers or in the privacy of his dull, cluttered apartment at the Wardman Park Hotel, he acted like a man half in love with death, someone ready to flee the burdens of this life.

He was only sixty-three, but Vinson's breathing was labored, his face was a sickly gray and deeply lined, a vast paunch flowed over his belt and his hands were fidgety. Sixty times a day, the yellowed, pudgy fingers tapped and pulled a cigarette out of its brightly colored pack; sixty times a day he flicked a Zippo into living flame. He drew the narcotic smoke hungrily into an ever diminishing pair of blackened lungs. And for hours each night the free hand was curled around a glass filled with a little branch water and plenty of Kentucky bourbon, the amber nectar of his home state.

Only days after Vinson swore in Eisenhower as President in January

1953, Associate Justice William O. Douglas asked a doctor friend for a medical opinion on the Chief Justice. "He'll die soon," said the doctor.[1]

In June of that year the attorney general, Herbert Brownell, came to the White House and told Eisenhower that the Chief Justice was asking for an opinion on a case currently before the Supreme Court, *Brown* v. *Board of Education of Topeka.* This case was actually a consolidation of five legal actions, each of which asked the Court to reverse its decision in one of the most important cases in American legal history, *Plessy* v. *Ferguson,* which had been decided back in 1896. The Supreme Court at that time had ruled that state and local governments did not have to provide exactly the same services to black people as they provided to whites. Instead, they could provide services that were "separate but equal." Yet the attorneys in *Brown* v. *Board,* led by Thurgood Marshall of the National Association for the Advancement of Colored People, were arguing that this decision had been unconstitutional. What Vinson wanted to know was, What did Brownell think?

Eisenhower was perplexed. He thought the separation of powers was an absolute barrier between the executive and the judiciary. Besides, wasn't education the kind of issue that the Constitution had left to the states to decide? Why should school integration involve the federal government?

Brownell explained that *Brown* was based on an argument that the "due process and equal protection" clause of the Fourteenth Amendment made segregation unconstitutional. Marshall was arguing that separate schools were inherently unequal schools when race was the sole basis for separation. As for the Justice Department offering its opinion, this was completely proper given the nature of the case, and as a practicing attorney, Brownell was "an officer of the court." That, said Brownell, imposed a duty on him to respond and to file an amicus curiae ("friend of the court") brief.

A few weeks after this meeting, Brownell reminded the President that he was still searching for a new solicitor general. Six months into the new administration, the slot hadn't yet been filled. Eisenhower suggested Brownell offer the post to Governor Earl Warren of California. Shortly after the 1952 election, Eisenhower had told Warren he could have the first vacancy on the Supreme Court, partly out of respect for Warren, who seemed a model of moderate Republicanism, partly out of gratitude for Warren's principled stand on the Fair Play Amendment, which had been crucial to Eisenhower's nomination. It seemed a good idea to improve Warren's credentials for Supreme Court service by first providing him with some high-level legal experience. Warren agreed to become solicitor general.[2]

Before he could be appointed, however, Fred Vinson died, in the early hours of September 3, 1953. Eisenhower asked Dulles if he would like to take Vinson's place, but this was mainly a matter of courtesy. Dulles said he preferred to remain secretary of state, as Eisenhower almost certainly knew he would. He then tried to persuade Earl Warren to go ahead and become solicitor general and wait for the next Supreme Court vacancy. He had never anticipated that the first vacancy would be the Chief Justice slot. Warren, however, insisted that Eisenhower keep to the letter of his given word.[3]

On October 3, Warren was sworn in and Eisenhower, breaking with precedent, appeared at the Supreme Court, with Mamie, to watch this brief ceremony and to sign Warren's commission as Chief Justice. It was a gesture that touched Warren deeply.[4]

Over the next few months, Eisenhower and Brownell held several conversations about the amicus curiae brief that the Justice Department would submit on *Brown*. Brownell was certain that the decision in *Plessy* v. *Ferguson* had been a travesty of constitutional law. "If that is your opinion," Eisenhower told him, "you should state it."[5]

Eisenhower disliked having the *Brown* decision come during his presidency. Without ever being an overt liberal on race, in the context of the Army he had been a liberal of sorts. Eisenhower had never denigrated the fighting quality of black troops. In trying to create a Philippine army, he had been motivated in part by his conviction that Filipinos would make excellent soldiers if properly trained and armed. During the Battle of the Bulge, he had taken advantage of the infantry crisis to appropriate black volunteers from support units, hurriedly give them some retraining as riflemen, then put them into infantry platoons alongside white soldiers. This experiment soon gave the lie to the widespread belief in the Army that black soldiers wouldn't fight.[6]

As Chief of Staff, he had been trying to get the Army integrated, if only partially, when Truman issued an executive order, in 1948, aimed at imposing integration on the military. Eisenhower was working out ways to implement Truman's order when his service as Chief of Staff came to an end. Following Eisenhower's departure for Columbia, Truman's order was simply ignored. It took the Korean War to bring integration to a reluctant, conservative Army, which drew nearly half its officers from southern states.[7]

Eisenhower was, at best, willing to help move things along, but not at a pace or in a way that provoked riots, civil disobedience or lynchings. Where opportunities for action appeared, Eisenhower seized them. As President, he appointed the first black person ever to serve on the White House staff, Frederic Morrow. The District of Columbia was as segregated as almost any city in the South. Eisenhower forced the integration of theaters, restaurants and schools. His assistant secretary of labor, J. Ernest Wilkins, was black and, during his superior's absence, became the first black person to take part in cabinet meetings.

When he learned that the Navy was still resisting integration, Eisenhower ordered his secretary of the Navy to end that resistance immediately. He appointed a liberal lawyer, Maxwell Rabb, to the White House staff to serve as his civil rights adviser and cultivate contacts with black organizations and leaders. Eisenhower also told Rabb that he wanted ideas on how to advance integration, but they had to be serious and practical, not grandstand plays, unlike the antilynching legislation such as Truman had sent regularly to Congress knowing it would not become law. "I want something meaningful on civil rights or nothing," he told Rabb.[8]

Every step he took was governed, all the same, by a sense of how little room for maneuver he had. In anticipation of the *Brown* decision, the governors of Georgia, South Carolina and Mississippi publicly declared their intention of closing the public schools in their states if the Court found in favor of the plaintiffs. One of Eisenhower's deepest fears throughout the struggle to advance civil rights was that southern states would shut down all their public schools and allow those in middle-class white areas to reopen as private institutions, after which southern state legislatures would then adopt legislation to fund "private" education, leaving blacks and poor whites with no schools at all.[9]

He was well attuned to southern sensitivities, and liked to tell people, "I have lived in the South, remember." But there were limits to what Eisenhower would tolerate. When a southern politician at one of the stag dinners used the word *nigger*, Eisenhower jumped up from his chair, his anger visible. "You will not talk that way in my house again!"[10]

In February 1954, Eisenhower invited Earl Warren to attend a stag dinner at the White House. Among the other guests was John W. Davis, the 1924 Democratic candidate for the presidency and currently the leading attorney for the defendants in the *Brown* case. As the group made its way from the dinner table to an adjoining room for coffee, whiskey and conversation, Eisenhower took Warren by the arm.

Warren, with a cap of snow-white hair shining above a generous forehead, a pair of frank blue eyes that gazed out with an innocent air from behind rimless spectacles, a permanently rumpled appearance and benign mien, looked like a Norman Rockwell version of the ideal grandpa sprung improbably to life from the cover of the *Saturday Evening Post*—he was, that is, the kind of person Eisenhower was instinctively drawn to. Eisenhower was not in the habit of taking people by the arm. The fact that he did so now was telling.

"These are not bad people," said Eisenhower, referring to Davis and the various southerners among his guests. "All they are concerned about is to see that their sweet little girls are not required to sit in school alongside some big overgrown Negro bucks." This was only an indirect way of saying they were afraid that black teenage boys, many of whom became sexually active long before white teenage girls, would molest or seduce their daughters and granddaughters if allowed to attend school with them.[11]

Warren was outraged. To him, this was a blatant attempt to pressure the Court into rejecting *Brown*. That, though, seems unlikely, because when the government's amicus curiae brief went to the Court a week later, it asserted that the Fourteenth Amendment had established "a broad constitutional principle of full and complete equality of all persons under the law, and forbade . . . all legal distinctions based on race or color." What Eisenhower was probably hoping to get from Warren wasn't a rejection of *Brown* but an approach to enforcement that the South could live with.

As he later explained it to members of his staff, Eisenhower thought that integration should begin at the graduate-school level and move down, a year at a time. That would give high schools more than four years to prepare for it. Grade schools would have eight years or more to get ready. By the time integration reached the first grade, the U.S.—and especially the South—would have spent more than sixteen years adjusting to integration. He also thought it would be better for state courts, instead of federal courts, to take the lead in overseeing implementation, since state courts were much closer to the communities they served.[12]

On May 17, 1954, the Supreme Court handed down its decision. Warren, who had written the ten-page opinion, read it aloud in a stoic monotone. "We come then," he concluded, "to the question presented: Does segregation of children in public schools solely on the basis of race . . . deprive the children of the minority group of educational opportunities? We believe that it does." The judgment was 9–0.

Brownell was astounded. Under Vinson, the Court had split 5–4 on just about everything. That Warren had managed to achieve unanimity on what was almost certain to be the most important legal decision of the second half of the century seemed unbelievable. What the Court still had to decide, though, was how its ruling would be enforced.

Over the next year, Eisenhower and Brownell discussed how to secure a plan that would make resistance impossible and evasion difficult. They decided to recommend that the federal courts give school authorities ninety days in which to submit plans for school integration. Once a plan had been approved, the courts would ensure that it was implemented.

On a Saturday morning in April 1955, Eisenhower had the solicitor general, the able and highly admired Simon Sobeloff, bring the draft of the new amicus curiae brief over to the White House. Going through it line by line and word by word, Eisenhower sharpened the language and the argument. This revised draft was submitted to the Court during oral argument two days later.[13]

To his and Brownell's dismay, the Court did not compel school boards to present plans for desegregation within ninety days. Instead, it said desegregation must proceed "with all deliberate speed." This was largely the work of Hugo Black, who had advised his fellow justices, "Vagueness is not going to hurt. Let it simmer. Let it take time." Seeing that Black was a former Klansman and senator from Alabama, transformed into the leading liberal on the Supreme Court, his position as an expert on this matter seemed unassailable.[14]

The Court may have hoped that Eisenhower would now weigh in publicly in support of the *Brown* decisions, and Warren would criticize him severely for not doing so. He couldn't do it and shouldn't do it, he told Jim Hagerty and others. For a President to say whether he agreed or disagreed with any Court decision would amount to "executive review" of the Court. He'd be challenging the separation of powers and exceeding his constitutional authority. Whether he agreed or disagreed wasn't the point. His responsibility was to uphold the law. As far as *Brown* went, "I will enforce it."[15]

In the spring of 1955 a newly ordained black minister, Martin Luther King, Jr., arrived in Montgomery, Alabama, and within a few weeks was drawn into a boycott of the local bus service. Eisenhower followed the newspaper accounts from Montgomery with interest as the boycott dragged on through the winter and into 1956. The boycott triggered bombings and shootings, death threats and beatings, nearly all instigated by whites.

Meanwhile, across the South, segregationist organizations were springing fiercely into existence. There were the Association of Catholic Laymen, the Pond Hollow Segregation Club, the Virginia Defenders of State Sovereignty and Individual Liberties, the National Association for the Advancement of White People, and scores more. But far out in front were the White Citizens Councils. Beginning in July 1954 with fourteen members, the councils boasted 250,000 only two years later. Warren, Black and the other members of the Court were astonished and dismayed. They had never anticipated such a backlash, given the mildness of the ruling on implementation.[16]

Race was forcing its way on to the President's agenda by the time Eisenhower suffered his heart attack in September 1955. When he finally returned to Washington in December, he found that the Justice Department had drafted a civil rights bill and Brownell was seeking the cabinet's approval for it. Instead of rejecting it, as Eisenhower may have hoped it would, the cabinet approved it, with modifications. Faced with having to decide between killing the bill and submitting it to Congress, Eisenhower reluctantly agreed to send it up to Capitol Hill. This legislation was certain to be passed by the House, but no civil rights law had made it to the Senate floor since 1875.[17]

Brownell's bill was a four-part offering: Title I would create a national, nonpartisan civil rights commission; Title II would establish a civil rights division in the Department of Justice; Title III would authorize the department to intervene wherever civil rights were being violated or were likely to be violated; finally, Title IV would secure people's voting rights, by striking down state laws and practices that had long disenfranchised black people across much of the South.

This bill was passed by the House, by a large margin, just before the 1956 Republican convention. By this time, Eisenhower had been convinced by Brownell that the time was right and the bill would make a difference in civil rights. He pushed it enthusiastically during the campaign. And when the Eighty-fifth Congress convened in January 1957, Brownell was assured of the support of the senator who mattered most, Lyndon B. Johnson, the Senate majority leader. Johnson had long been opposed to civil rights legislation, but he had never said a word in public that was critical of blacks and in his campaigns had actively sought the support of Hispanics.

Yet as he set about making Brownell's legislation into the Civil Rights Act, Johnson had his eyes fixed less on justice than on the 1960 Democratic presidential nomination. To win it, Johnson had to break away from being typecast as just another southern senator—that is, a backwoods populist on many issues but on race a bigot.[18]

Eisenhower had Johnson and Sam Rayburn, the House majority leader, who was also a Texas Democrat, come over for drinks in the evening about once a week. Outspoken in his pride at being a Kansan in most circumstances, in talking to Johnson and Rayburn, he sometimes referred to his birth in Denison, Texas, before remarking, "There's no problem that three Texans can't solve."

At one of these sessions, in the summer of 1957, Johnson told him he could get the civil rights bill through the Senate provided it was amended—Title III, which could be used to speed the pace of school integration, would have to go. Eisenhower had a choice: a weakened bill or no bill at all. He reluctantly opted for the weakened bill, but in private referred to it as "a defeat." The more he thought about the ground he'd surrendered, the more unhappy he felt. When the bill was passed by both houses of Congress, he thought about vetoing it.[19]

When all was said and done, though, this was the first civil rights legislation to become law since Reconstruction. Nor was it gesture politics: it would put ballots into the hands of many thousands of black people for the first time. On September 9, 1957, while on vacation in Newport, Rhode Island, Eisenhower signed the bill into law.[20]

Virgil T. Blossom, the superintendent of the Little Rock schools, was a sensible, responsible man and the seven members of the school board were much the same. The day after the first *Brown* decision was announced, Blossom met with the board and there was immediate agreement on two points—the decision was regrettable, but there would be no attempt to resist or evade integration. A plan was drawn up to integrate the city's schools, starting with Central High, one of the best schools in the country as judged by National Merit Scholarship results. A federal court approved the plan. Blossom was voted Little Rock's Man of the Year in 1955.

Unfortunately, implementation of the plan was postponed from 1956 to 1957, to allow for construction of an extra high school. What Blossom hadn't foreseen was that delay would give the White Citizens Councils twelve months in which to organize protests against school integration, protests that cast a pall over the reelection prospects of the Arkansas governor, a pudgy and unprincipled character named Orval Faubus.

The governor wasn't a bad man, merely a hollow one. He had integrated the Arkansas Democratic party, his son was attending an integrated liberal arts college and Faubus had looked on with a certain indifference when school boards in Fayetteville and Fort Smith drew up integration plans. Little Rock was different. With the Citizens Councils poised to turn the capital of Arkansas into a potential battleground, Faubus opted for reelection over principle, the law, common sense and common decency. He was going to make a stand.

On July 17, the President was reminded at a press conference that he had the power to use force to ensure that the schools were integrated. Eisenhower said he was well aware of that, but added, "I can't imagine any set of circumstances that would ever induce me to send federal troops . . . into any area to enforce the orders of a federal court. . . . The common sense of Americans will never require it."[21]

This utterance may have played some small part in prodding Faubus toward confrontation. Whether it did or not, when Central High opened on September 3 for the fall semester, up to seventeen black teenagers were expected to enroll. The evening of September 2, Faubus ringed the school with green-clad Arkansas National Guardsmen, then made a television address, insisting that he had acted only to prevent bloodshed, not to block integration. Few people, in Little Rock or the rest of the world, believed that.[22]

Eisenhower sedulously declined to condemn Faubus's action. The President was counting on the federal courts to resolve the issue, and a hearing on the legality of the governor's intervention was scheduled for September 20. He may have also believed that Faubus, having made his gesture, would pull the Guardsmen out and let the black students in even before the court hearing, which was almost certain to rule he'd acted illegally.

It might have turned out that way, had not 250,000 letters and telegrams arrived at the governor's mansion, nearly all praising Faubus for defying *Brown*. He couldn't back down now without looking weak and stupid. Faubus left the Guardsmen where they were. Mobs gathered outside Central High to chant, "Two! Four! Six! Eight! We ain't gonna integrate!" The black students, fearing for their lives, stayed home. Local members of the NAACP were beaten up, their houses and businesses were firebombed, their telephones vibrated with death threats.[23]

The congressman for Little Rock, Brooks Hays, was meanwhile pleading with his old friend Sherman Adams to arrange a meeting between Eisenhower and Faubus to resolve the issue. One was arranged for September 14, at Newport. During the twenty minutes they spent alone in Eisenhower's tiny office at the Newport News naval base, Faubus told Eisenhower about his wartime service, protested that he was a loyal citizen and said he had nothing but respect for the law. Eisenhower told him he didn't have to pull the Guardsmen out; they could remain in place to maintain order while the black students enrolled.[24]

Back in Little Rock, Faubus did nothing. He waited for the federal court to rule on whether he'd acted illegally, knowing that was exactly what he had done. He was going to present himself to the people of Arkansas as their heroic defender, crushed by the federal steamroller. A glorious defeat. Sure enough, when the federal court issued its ruling on September 20, he ordered the Guard to withdraw. Then he went on television to say he would find other means of frustrating school integration. Challenged to explain his failure to keep his word to Eisenhower, Faubus scoffed, "Just because I said it doesn't make it so."[25]

On Monday, September 23, nine black students slipped into the school by a side door and enrolled. A riot erupted in the streets outside, and they had to be escorted out of the building by dozens of policemen.

The next day, Eisenhower received a telegram from the mayor of Little Rock, Woodrow Wilson Mann: IMMEDIATE NEED FOR FEDERAL TROOPS IS URGENT. . . . PEOPLE ARE CONVERGING ON THE SCHOOL FROM ALL DIRECTIONS. . . . MOB IS ARMED. . . . SITUATION IS OUT OF CONTROL.[26]

Eisenhower signed orders that federalized the Arkansas National Guard and put it back onto the streets. To stiffen its resolve, he also sent a thousand paratroopers from the 101st Airborne Division to Little Rock. Then he flew back to Washington to make a televsion address to the nation. He had not sent in the troops to enforce integration, he insisted, but to uphold the law. It was a distinction of almost theological subtlety, like the doctrine of transubstantiation. The paratroops stayed a year, during which time they foiled five attempts to blow up Central High. Eventually, the nine black students graduated from high school; all went on to college. In 1958, Faubus was reelected governor and Congressman Brooks Hays lost his seat to a Faubus supporter.

Eisenhower was criticized during his presidency and long after it for not taking a more activist approach to civil rights, and there was a widespread assumption that he sympathized with white southerners rather than blacks. This was not true. He remarked to Hagerty, a few weeks after the first *Brown* decision, "You know, Jim, I suppose nobody knows how they feel or how many pressures or insults they have to take. I guess the only way you can realize exactly how they feel is to have a black skin for a few weeks."[27]

Toward the end of his presidency, he wrote his friend Ralph McGill, editor of *The Atlanta Constitution* and outspoken advocate of racial equality, to justify his own more cautious approach to civil rights. "Until America had achieved reality in the concept of individual dignity and equality before the law, we will not have become completely worthy of our limitless opportunities. [But] coercive law is, by itself, powerless to bring about complete compliance when . . . the great mass of public opinion is in bitter opposition. This was true under the carpetbagging government of the South [and] under the Prohibition Amendment. . . . It is still largely true within four states in the deep South."[28]

After he left the White House, Eisenhower several times described Warren's appointment as "a mistake" and in conversation with Stephen

Ambrose he once called Warren "that dumb son of a bitch." The principal reason for his disenchantment with Warren was not *Brown* but
a handful of cases involving Communists who had successfully challenged the laws passed in 1954 that amounted to a ban on the Communist party and gave Communists fewer legal rights than other
Americans.[29]

As for *Brown,* what angered Eisenhower was not the 1954 decision
overturning *Plessy* v. *Ferguson.* In his memoirs, he came out emphatically in favor of it. What he didn't say was that the second decision, on
implementation, was about as bad as could be. By countenancing delay,
it offered a gift to the segregationists.

Given his troubled, increasingly tense relationship with the
Supreme Court, it was ironic, then, that after his heart attack, he told
George Humphrey, "My tenure here may not be too long. But there's
one thing I can do that will last beyond me. I can have the best Supreme
Court. I'm going to have the finest Court there ever was."[30]

This was one ambition Eisenhower realized, but without ever knowing it. He was blind to his own achievement. As the century ends, there
is a consensus among legal scholars and historians that the Warren
Court, as it has become known, was the greatest body of American ju-
rists since the early days of the Republic.

Eisenhower's failure to appreciate the Court's achievements owed
much to his failure to penetrate either the mind or the heart of Earl Warren, a man who was neither an intellectual nor a liberal. Warren's motive power was a passionate belief in justice, as distinct from a belief in
the legal process as the instrument of justice. He formulated no judicial
theory worthy of the name. Nor did he have a love affair with the Constitution. His mind moved quickly to a single point in deciding any case:
Is this the right result? Warren made only the most cursory attempts to
have his decisions conform with legal precedents or established judicial
doctrine. His approach to the law seemed to many lawyers and judges
to be quixotic, oxymoronic or untidy—maybe all three.

What Warren brought to the Court was, nonetheless, something it
needed badly—moral purpose. He provided a sense of direction and encouragement to move boldly. Had he been more of a lawyer or more of
a judge, he would have been less of a Chief Justice.

Even so, he could not have achieved what he did without the support of five other justices—William O. Douglas, Hugo Black, John

Marshall Harlan, William J. Brennan and Potter Stewart. Eisenhower appointed the scholarly Harlan (whose grandfather, in lodging the sole dissenting opinion in *Plessy* v. *Ferguson,* had memorably declared, "The Constitution is color-blind"), the equally scholarly Stewart and Brennan, a very liberal Democrat from New Jersey. The Warren Court was not, that is, entirely Warren's creation; it owed its very existence to Eisenhower's choices.

Under Warren, the Court was moved to do something it never before attempted: it brought the entire Bill of Rights (freedom of worship, right of assembly, right to petition for redress of grievances, etc.) within the due process and equal justice provision of the Fourteenth Amendment. In doing so, the Court made the states—which control more than 90 percent of the criminal justice system—at long last accept and implement most of the rights guaranteed by the Constitution. The result was not so much a different America as a better America.[31]

Sherman Adams was admired and held in deep affection within the White House and many on the staff were awestruck by the level of his managerial ability, which sometimes seemed almost inspired. "That man could run anything!" Gabriel Hauge told another staff member one day as they crossed West Executive Avenue.[32]

Which was why, when Adams cut short his European vacation after Eisenhower's heart attack and flew to Denver, he found Jim Hagerty waiting impatiently on the tarmac for him to descend from the airplane. Hagerty was so overjoyed he threw his arms around the phlegmatic but momentarily startled Adams and kissed him. Everything was under control. Sherm was back.[33]

As the staff was well aware, not only was Adams able and devoted to Eisenhower; he was a moderate counterweight to the conservative "gang" of golfing millionaires, to the influence in the cabinet of George Humphrey and to the mentally mediocre Senate minority leader, William Knowland. Adams thereby accumulated plenty of enemies—not only among the Democrats, who controlled Congress, but among powerful Republicans.[34]

For five years, Adams was nevertheless able to operate much as he wished, until his friend Bernard Goldfine found himself in serious trouble. Goldfine was a millionaire textile manufacturer who had saved three textile mills in New Hampshire from bankruptcy in the early 1950s, when Adams was governor. Out of this had developed a friendship.

Goldfine owned an apartment in a downtown Boston hotel, and invited Adams to use it anytime he wished. He also encouraged Adams to sign himself in as Bernard Goldfine for incidentals, such as room service. Adams gave Goldfine small gifts now and then, and Goldfine gave Adams a vicuña coat and a rug. All of which seemed harmless enough at a time when Eisenhower was enjoying the benefits of "Mamie's Cabin," a three-story building purposely erected for him by his rich friends at Augusta National at a cost of $450,000. At Gettysburg, there was a three-thousand-dollar putting green, paid for by the Professional Golf Association. From time to time, the White House refrigerators and freezers were filled with thousands of dollars' worth of prime steaks and other goodies provided by oil millionaire Sid Richardson. Eisenhower was able, too, to get such large tax write-offs for gifts he was passing on to the Eisenhower Library in Abilene that his net worth increased considerably during his presidency, to his surprise.[35]

In the spring of 1958, Goldfine was being investigated by the Federal Trade Commission and the Securities and Exchange Commission. Some of his business dealings were dubious, if not illegal. Goldfine suddenly began invoking Adams's name as if it were some kind of talisman that would stop the federal bureaucracy in its tracks. Instead, it infuriated the bureaucrats and aroused the interest of several congressional committees.

Adams might have invoked Eisenhower's blanket rule against anyone on his staff testifying before Congress, but he chose instead to appear before Congress, in June 1958, to admit that he might have been foolish in accepting the rug, the coat and the use of the apartment but that didn't make him a crook. Nor had he ever used undue influence to help Goldfine.[36]

To Eisenhower's relief, the Adams affair seemed to have petered out when Congress broke up for the summer. He himself had no doubts about Adams's honesty—various members of the gang had tried to do Adams favors, and he had invariably turned them down. Still, this was an election year, so Eisenhower asked the chairman of the Republican National Committee, Meade Alcorn, to poll the RNC members to see if they thought Adams had damaged the party's prospects. The poll results proved inconclusive. That might have been the end of it had not the gang closed in. Cliff Roberts, stockbroker and *genius loci* of Augusta National, wrote and told Eisenhower that Adams was hurting the party.

Eisenhower was vacationing at Newport when he got Roberts's note. He called Winthrop Aldrich, a major contributor to GOP funds. What did he think? "This man has to go or we are done," said Aldrich. Two days later, Eisenhower's golfing pals Cliff Roberts and Alton "Pete" Jones showed up, wanting to talk about Adams. He was a liability, Jones insisted, someone who'd drag the party down to defeat in November. "Well, you've made my mind up for me," said Eisenhower at last. Picking up the telephone, he placed a call to Meade Alcorn. "You've got to get Adams's resignation," said Eisenhower, adding regretfully, "It's the dirtiest political chore I could ask of anyone."[37]

Adams's ouster left Eisenhower feeling depressed. He sought to make amends by writing a generous letter of appreciation to Adams. Ironically, he also gave him a gift—an expensive sterling silver bowl, inscribed, "To SHERMAN ADAMS . . . from his devoted friend, Dwight D. Eisenhower."

With Adams's departure, all efforts within the White House to promote civil rights came to a definitive halt. Adams's place was taken by Major General Wilton B. "Jerry" Persons. A native of Montgomery, Alabama, conservative on every domestic issue and an archsegregationist, Persons was the kind of White House chief of staff the gang approved of. Yet there was no political gain from dumping Adams. The Republicans were trounced in the November 1958 elections, making Eisenhower the lamest of lame ducks on Capitol Hill.[38]

Rockets' Red Glare

Nikita Sergeyevich Khrushchev was almost desperate to beat the Americanskis at something. *Anything.* He boasted that communism would bury capitalism, later claiming he meant only by becoming richer and more productive, not by engaging in war. But how long might that take? Fifty years? A hundred? He needed something now. And in the summer of 1955, at about the time he returned from the Geneva conference, where Eisenhower had urged the Open Skies proposal on him, some of Khrushchev's scientific advisers informed him of an interesting development.

In the course of reading American science journals, they had learned that the United States had begun a project to put an artificial satellite into orbit in 1958, as part of its contribution to the International Geophysical Year. An orbiting satellite had obvious military possibilities, but the foolish Americans had decided not to make it a military project—they wanted it to be peaceful and scientific. We can beat them to it, the scientists told Khrushchev, because we're already developing the rocket.

The Soviet Union's hydrogen bomb was enormous, and in 1955 its engineers and technicians were working on the design of a huge liquid-fueled rocket powerful enough to carry it five thousand miles. With some modifications, said the scientists, we can use the rocket to put a small satellite into orbit long before it will be ready to carry an H-bomb. Khrushchev saw a possibility here that nobody in Washington had seen—the chance to score the propaganda coup of the century. The Soviet satellite, code-named *Sputnik* ("Fellow Traveler"), got his enthusiastic "*Da!*"[1]

In the summer of 1957, the Soviets made two test launches of their prototype intercontinental ballistic missile (or ICBM) and Khrushchev couldn't resist a little boasting. Bombers—by which he meant SAC's newest addition, the B-52—were now obsolete, he declared. When this instant obsolescence was put to Eisenhower at a press conference, he brushed it aside. Bombers would still be important for some years to come, he said emphatically. An ICBM wasn't a weapon until it had an accurate guidance system and could reenter the atmosphere without burning up. The Soviets were still working on those problems.[2]

Shortly after this, however, Allen Dulles told him there was one thing the Soviets could do with their ICBM—they could put a satellite into orbit, and there were signs they were preparing to do it. Eisenhower gave a metaphorical shrug. Any satellite they put up now would be a publicity stunt, nothing more. He wasn't interested in expensive publicity stunts.

The night of Thursday, October 3, 1957, Americans went to bed confident that their country was secure. Didn't they lead the world in science and technology? When they got up on Friday morning they heard, on the radio, a menacing *beep . . . beep . . . beep . . .* that cast doubt on the certainties of the night before. *Sputnik* was overhead, transmitting.

Eisenhower paid little attention to it. He headed for Gettysburg and did not come back until Sunday night. To his amazement, on Monday the Oval Office was virtually besieged. Generals were descending on him from the Pentagon to talk missiles, congressmen were rushing over from Capitol Hill insisting that he talk to them, diplomats from State were coming into the executive offices wanting to know what they were supposed to say to a dumbfounded world and reporters were clamoring for a press conference so that he could reassure a jittery nation. He remained calm, smiling, unconcerned, the man in charge, waiting for the fever to pass. Eisenhower had his usual prelunch rest and in late afternoon he went outside and spent nearly an hour hitting golf balls.[3]

On Tuesday, the National Security Council convened for its weekly meeting. Deputy Secretary of Defense Donald Quarles told the NSC that if satellites had been treated as a military hardware, the Army could have put one into orbit a year earlier, using its Redstone rocket. Even now, if the government was willing to stump up $13 million, the Army could put a satellite in orbit before the Navy's planned launch of *Vanguard,* the civilian satellite.[4]

Eisenhower said he wasn't interested in getting into a race with the Russians. "I want the satellite to remain a scientific project and keep it free as much as possible from weaponry."

Quarles wryly observed, "Maybe the Soviets have done us a good turn, unintentionally." When the U.S. did orbit a military satellite, neither the Soviet Union nor any other country could complain that it was violating its airspace. Not one country had protested being overflown by *Sputnik.*

Eisenhower asked Quarles to brief the NSC on the Air Force's current development of reconnaissance satellites. "Look five years ahead," Eisenhower told the NSC. That was what mattered, not that irritating *beep . . . beep . . .* overhead. This was the start of something, not the end.[5]

On October 9, Eisenhower walked into the most skeptical, if not overtly hostile, press conference of his presidency. He was the man from whom the entire country drew reassurance; with that reassurance now under a cloud, it was as if he had somehow let people down. No, he insisted repeatedly, there were no security implications. The government was already spending $5 billion on developing missiles. "Now, that isn't any weak, pusillanimous effort. That is a lot of money." The journalists weren't satisfied—how could America be as secure now as it was before? All he could do was insist, "The satellite imposes no additional threat to the United States."[6]

His claim that $5 billion a year was going into missiles went unchallenged, but it was more than a little misleading. The figure in the defense budget for missile research and development in 1957 was $1.7 billion. To produce a headline figure of $5 billion involved adding all kinds of ancillary expenses, such as the cost of cutting the grass at places where missile research was conducted, the salaries of typists and janitors at Cape Canaveral, the price of office equipment at Huntsville Arsenal, the maintenance of research ships out in the Pacific to monitor missile flights and so on.[7]

When the press conference broke up, he returned to his office and awarded the Medal of Freedom to Charles Wilson, who was stepping down as secretary of defense after nearly five years of frustration and fuming. Eisenhower had served, in effect, as his own secretary of defense. What he had wanted from Wilson was a firm, decisive manager, someone who would force the services to stop being so parochial and cooperate more closely. Wilson had dominated GM, but the Pentagon was a tougher and wilier beast than anything big business ever spawned. Wilson got the nation's highest civilian award not because he had succeeded but to cover abject failure. Besides, he had proven valuable in one respect—*he* took the flak for the Pentagon's wastefulness, inefficiency and interservice conflicts, not the President.

At his first NSC meeting following the orbiting of *Sputnik I,* Eisenhower was at his common-sense best. "When you have worked out a good, sound plan at a time when you were able to be calm, the soundest policy is to stand by it." That was what he proposed to do.[8]

On October 15, he met with the Science Advisory Committee, chaired by Nobel Prize–winning physicist Isidor I. Rabi of Columbia, to consider nonmilitary responses. This body had been created by Truman in 1951, but no one had ever figured out just what it was supposed to do, so it met rarely and never played a crucial role in anything. For Eisenhower in this crisis, though, it offered a chance to start a dialogue with experts from the world of science. "I can't understand why the American people have got so worked up over this thing," said Eisenhower. "It's certainly not going to drop on their heads!"

The discussion that followed did not focus on hardware; it was mainly about brains. Why did so many of the brightest high school students not go on to college? Why didn't scientists get the respect they deserved? "The need is more for leadership than money," said James Killian, the president of MIT. Eisenhower agreed.[9]

The *Sputnik* crisis seemed about to subside when the Soviets launched another satellite, on November 3. *Sputnik II* weighed more than half a ton and carried a dog named Laika, doomed to a fiery death in the atmosphere. Animal lovers were outraged. Eisenhower tried to dispel the sudden upsurge in fear with a televised address, assuring the nation, "Long-range ballistic missiles as they exist today do not cancel the destructive and deterrent power of our Strategic Air Force." And to show he was doing something, he announced the creation of the President's Scientific Advisory Committee, with James Killian as chairman.

Many people felt encouraged by that. It sounded as though a scientist were right there in the Oval Office, whispering constantly in his ear.[10]

What Eisenhower and the country needed more than anything else was a U.S. satellite in orbit. The first launch of *Vanguard* was brought forward three months, to December 6, 1957. While tens of millions sat glued to their television screens, fingers crossed, breath bated, *Vanguard* rose sedately from its Cape Canaveral launchpad, reaching a height of fifty feet, before falling back and blowing up in a spectacular fireball. FLOPNIK, DUDNIK, KAPUTNIK, screamed overheated headlines next day.

This national humiliation put Eisenhower under even greater pressure to pour money not only into missiles but into education, particularly scientific education. He wasn't persuaded, however, that cranking out more scientists was the answer to anything. Creating a tiny, pampered elite, entirely under the control of an even tinier, all-powerful political elite who directed them into military projects and publicity stunts—instead of educating an entire nation to live productive and constructive lives—was the kind of thing the Soviets did. James Conant, the former president of Harvard and himself a distinguished scientist, agreed with him: "Not more engineers or scientists but a people who will not panic and political leaders of wisdom, courage and devotion . . . not more Einsteins, but more Washingtons and Madisons."[11]

Even so, the pressure was too relenting to resist completely or indefinitely. Eisenhower reluctantly sanctioned a billion-dollar education program, spread over four years. This legislation, the National Defense Education Act of 1958, eventually developed into a program that enabled hundreds of thousands of bright college students to go on to graduate school, and was not limited to the study of scientific subjects.

The Navy tried again with *Vanguard,* on January 28, 1958. Fourteen seconds before ignition, technicians noticed a fuel leak and the launch was abandoned. Two days later, an Army Redstone stood on the launch pad, with a satellite called *Explorer,* which was crammed with scientific instruments. A few minutes before midnight on January 31, the Redstone was launched. Eisenhower couldn't bear to watch it. "Let's not make too great a hullabaloo on this," he told his staff. But shortly afterward, Andrew Goodpaster came in with a message from Cape Canaveral—*Explorer* was in orbit. The huge grin flashed. "That's wonderful! I sure feel a lot better now."[12]

$$\star \quad \star \quad \star \quad \star \quad \star$$

While Americans were still reeling from *Sputnik*, a belief was taking root that Soviet missiles now posed a threat to America's existence. There was, that is, a "missile gap." For the rest of his presidency, Eisenhower tried to scotch this idea, but belief in it only grew. Nothing he said or did seemed to make any difference. In vain did he remind the nation that when he became President in January 1953, there was no effort being made to develop an intercontinental ballistic missile, or ICBM. Spending on guided missiles then amounted to $3 million a year. It was the New Look that brought a magnitude leap in funding for missile research and development and an Air Force commitment to acquire a force of nuclear-armed ICBMs.[13]

When the New Look was implemented, Eisenhower recognized that for some years to come, SAC would carry the principal burden of deterring the Soviet Union if possible, and destroying it in a first strike if necessary. Whether SAC could do it in 1954 or 1955, even with a surprise attack, was open to question. But in November 1954 a Defense Department study assured him that from January 1956, SAC would possess so many bombers and H-bombs that it would be able to destroy the Soviet Union even if the Soviets struck first with a surprise attack, something they wouldn't have the capacity to do unless they built a huge force of strategic bombers, and there was nothing to show they were attempting to do so. What's more, SAC would retain its overwhelming margin of superiority well into the 1960s, even allowing for improvements in Soviet air defenses. Eisenhower noted at the top of his copy of this analysis, "Worthwhile—excellent."[14]

That left the United States six or seven years to develop 5,000-mile missiles that could take the place of the bombers. As ICBM research progressed, so did work on ballistic missiles with shorter range, and by the end of 1955, Eisenhower was convinced that they too had to be developed, and rapidly. "The early development of an effective ballistic missile in the 1,000–1,700 mile range would be of critical importance to the national security interests of the United States," he told the NSC. Eisenhower directed that both intermediate range ballistic missile (IRBM) and ICBM research and development programs would now have priority over all other military research projects.

Much as Eisenhower detested duplication of effort, he found himself pushing three IRBM projects: the Army's Jupiter, the Navy's Polaris and the Air Force's Thor. There were also three ICBM projects under way—Atlas, Titan and Minuteman. He was not going to tie himself to a single missile in either category and risk living with the consequences if it failed.[15]

Even though Eisenhower remained calm and confident throughout the *Sputnik* crisis, one thing did bother him: the Soviet ICBM was three times bigger than Atlas, the American ICBM that would be deployed in a couple of years. He asked one of his most trusted science advisers, George Kistiakowsky, "Why are our ICBMs so small?" like a man embarrassed by the size of his penis. "Why didn't you build bigger ones?"

"Because we concluded in 1953 that our megaton warhead would weigh hardly more than a thousand pounds, so we built the missiles to carry a megaton warhead, which was big enough for our purposes," said Kistiakowsky.[16]

While he was confident that the United States would remain secure into the 1960s, Eisenhower was increasingly worried about the effects of fallout. Suppose SAC made a first strike; the fallout would pose almost as great a threat to Americans as a Soviet attack. "If global war should break out," he remarked, "the northern hemisphere would soon become a desert." Was the solution a shelter program? In the spring of 1957 Eisenhower commissioned a study.[17]

The chairman of the committee that conducted this inquiry was H. Rowan Gaither, Jr., head of both the Ford Foundation and the Rand Corporation. That summer, Gaither fell ill with cancer. His place was taken, for all practical purposes, by another member of the committee, Robert C. Sprague, an industrialist who had served as an adviser on various missile projects.

During the course of his work, Sprague went to SAC headquarters at Offut AFB, Nebraska, to talk to LeMay. What would SAC do if the Soviets started massing their strategic bomber force for an attack? asked Sprague.

"I'm going to knock the shit out of them before they get off the ground," said LeMay.

"Is that national policy?"

"It's *my* policy," said LeMay.[18]

Contrary to Eisenhower's instructions, the Gaither report turned into a critique of nuclear strategy. When it was presented to Eisenhower and the NSC in November 1957, a month after *Sputnik I* was launched, it offered some startling conclusions. The report said the Soviets were probably ahead in development of ICBMs, and predicted a period of American vulnerability to a Soviet ICBM attack, beginning in 1959. The Gaither report called for a huge buildup of American ICBMs and IRBMs and up to $8 billion a year more on defense spending. The proposed fallout shelter program also carried a big price tag—$25 billion.

Sprague personally thought there were only four possible courses of action: first, to continue with the current national strategy and attack the USSR only if it posed an immediate threat; second, to launch a preventive war, beginning with a knockout blow against the twenty-seven Soviet installations where its strategic forces were based; third, to deliver an ultimatum that the U.S. would attack unless the Soviets agreed to disarm and fourth, "to place reliance in God to find a solution." Sprague said the more he had learned in the course of this inquiry, "my resort to prayer has substantially increased." On balance, however, he thought the best options were preventive war or a disarmament ultimatum backed up with a threat of preventive war.[19]

Eisenhower was appalled at any suggestion that he launch a preventive war. He was also annoyed at the nonchalant way members of the Gaither committee talked about spending billions of dollars on this, billions more on that. Nor did he agree that there was an imminent Soviet threat to America's existence. "We must neither panic nor become complacent," he told the NSC. "We should decide what needs to be done, and do it—avoiding extremes."[20]

The Gaither report remained problematic, even though he had rejected its conclusions. The report provided a clear, comprehensive review of American strategy, force structure and nuclear weapons. It contained too many important secrets to be published. Unhappy Gaither committee members then started leaking parts of it, which made the security on what remained even tighter. The result was that Washington was filled with people who thought the report showed a nation vulnerable to attack.

Then, like the other shoe dropping with an almighty *thump!* a Rockefeller Brothers Fund report on national security was published in January 1958. Its authors included Edward Teller and Henry Luce, and they had reached an alarming conclusion: "Unless present trends are reversed, the world balance of power will shift in favor of the Soviet bloc." This report called for another $15 billion to be spent on defense over the next five years.[21]

The growing alarm about a supposed missile gap was seized upon by Joe Alsop, a journalist with whom Eisenhower had once been on friendly terms. During his time as Chief of Staff, he had spoken with remarkable frankness to Alsop, and Mamie had developed a friendship with Alsop's wife. When Eisenhower became President, however, the FBI informed him that Alsop was not only a promiscuous homosexual but a man who had arranged a *mariage blanc* in order to camouflage his homosexuality. After that, he treated Alsop with disdain.

In the summer of 1958 Alsop wrote several articles for *The Washington Post* asserting that in 1960, the U.S. would have thirty ICBMs deployed, while the Soviets would have five hundred; in 1961, the figures would be seventy against a thousand. Democratic senator Stuart Symington—a former secretary of the Air Force—was, meanwhile, telling fellow senators much the same story. Symington's figures were based largely on Alsop's and were, therefore, just as fictitious. He claimed that the CIA accepted his figures, but Allen Dulles was only doing so to hide the fact that it knew they were false, as did the President.

U-2 reconnaissance aircraft and a National Security Agency listening post in Turkey had been monitoring Soviet missile tests since the summer of 1956. The Soviets lagged behind the United States in the development of IRBMs and ICBMs, but Eisenhower would not say anything that might jeopardize U-2 flights or NSA operations. The stark truth was that the United States would be able to destroy the Soviet Union in a single blow for years to come.

By the fall of 1958, SAC had eleven B-52 groups and twenty-five B-47 groups deployed. That would allow LeMay to attack with more than a thousand bombers, escorted by more than a thousand fighters, and with hundreds of reconnaissance aircraft acting as a decoy force. The first eight ICBMs had also been deployed. Thor missiles were being installed in the UK, and Jupiter missiles were being deployed to Turkey. A French newspaper headline aptly read, NATO + IRBM = ICBM.[22]

Before he left office, Eisenhower created a strategic nuclear triad that would deploy 650 B-52's, 810 ICBMs and 384 submarine-launched Polaris missiles long before the Soviets could create a credible ICBM force. His successor, whoever he was, would command a strategic force that was not only enormously powerful but also invulnerable. Attacking any part of it would unleash all of it, but its real role was deterrence.

The most important leg of the triad was Polaris, because if the Soviets ever managed to make a surprise attack, the U.S.S.R. would be obliterated by white titanium-alloy missiles trailing long spumes of salt spray as they rose like avenging wraiths from the depths of the oceans. Death to one superpower spelled the annihilation of both. The Soviets couldn't be prevented from achieving strategic parity, but once they attained it, they would find they had spent billions they couldn't afford on weapons they could never use.

In January 1955, the Chinese Communists began attacking various small islands held by the Chinese Nationalist forces of Chiang Kai-shek. Most of these outposts had no military significance, but there were two that did—Quemoy and Matsu, both within the range of heavy artillery based on the mainland. These pinprick attacks were a reminder that the Chinese civil war wasn't over.

"Those damned little offshore islands," Eisenhower said to Hagerty. "Sometimes I wish they'd sink." Chiang liked to imagine he could use them to mount an invasion of the mainland, but that was an illusion. Even so, he couldn't abandon them without damaging the still fragile morale of his army, which the Communists had defeated countless times before, forcing the remnants to flee to Taiwan. If Chiang was forced to quit Quemoy and Matsu, Eisenhower was afraid his army might simply desert.[23]

As the crisis unfolded, Eisenhower asked Congress to give him the authority to act militarily without first seeking a declaration of war. Congress provided it. Shortly after this, he had Dulles announce that the United States would use tactical nuclear weapons if it had to intervene over Quemoy and Matsu. And when he was questioned about it at a press conference, Eisenhower said the U.S. would probably make some use of small atomic weapons. "I see no reason why they shouldn't be used as you would use a bullet or anything else." Because tactical nuclear weapons produced little fallout, Eisenhower continued to believe they had a battlefield role, unlike H-bombs, which were useful only as a deterrent against other H-bombs.[24]

The Europeans, however, were deeply upset, convinced that any use of nuclear weapons would trigger a larger war. It didn't seem to the French that Quemoy was worth Paris, or to the British that seeing London laid waste was an acceptable price for the defense of Matsu. Nor was the Democratic leadership in Congress persuaded that Taiwan was worth starting an unwinnable war with China. As the protests mounted and Hagerty worried about what Eisenhower might say about using nuclear weapons at his next press conference, Eisenhower reassured him with a smile and a laugh. "Don't worry, Jim. I'll just confuse them." Which is exactly what he did, spinning out convoluted, unfathomable replies to simple, direct questions.[25]

In truth, though, Eisenhower had no intention of intervening unless the Chinese Communists seized Quemoy and Matsu and then used them to launch an assault on Taiwan. That meant trying to move tens of thousands of troops, their supplies and artillery across 150 miles of open sea in fishing junks, vulnerable to the weather, the Chinese Nationalist Air Force and the U.S. Seventh Fleet. It would be a suicidal operation. Instead of preparing for anything so unlikely, Eisenhower instead tried to persuade Chiang Kai-shek to redeploy most of the fifty-eight thousand men he had on the two islands and strengthen the defenses of Taiwan.

Chiang, however, kept pressing for an American commitment to defend Quemoy and Matsu. He was still hoping to drag the United States into war with China, something Eisenhower was determined to avoid. The Chinese, too, made it plain that they wanted a dialogue with the U.S., not a showdown. They released the last American prisoners they were still holding from the Korean War as a gesture of good faith. Talks between American and Chinese diplomats began in Geneva, the first direct contacts between the two sides since the establishment of the People's Republic of China. The crisis passed.

Nothing much happened for the next three years, during which time Mao Tse-tung tried to persuade the Soviet leadership that China and the Soviet Union must join in a war to the death with the capitalist West. "We shouldn't fear war," Mao told them. "We shouldn't be afraid of atomic bombs and missiles. No matter what kind of war breaks out— conventional or thermonuclear—we'll win." He laughed off the prospect that hundreds of millions might die. "So what? War is war. The years will pass and we'll get people fucking so they produce more babies than ever before."[26]

By the time Khrushchev visited China in August 1958, Mao was convinced that Soviet satellites, H-bombs and missiles had brought a unique opportunity to end the struggle between Communism and capitalism in an apocalyptic finale. Khrushchev was appalled, but for the sake of solidarity, he offered Soviet backing for any attempt to capture Taiwan.

Three weeks after Khrushchev's departure, the Chinese started shelling Quemoy and Matsu again. By this time, Chiang had pushed a hundred thousand men onto these small islands—one-third of his army. Dulles and the JCS urged Eisenhower to consider using nuclear weapons to prevent any Chinese invasion of Quemoy and Matsu. But Eisenhower's feelings about nuclear weapons had evolved over the past three years. He no longer talked about tactical nuclear weapons as being more or less the same as conventional armaments.

He made a televised address, to assure the nation on two essential points: "There is not going to be any appeasement. I believe there is not going to be any war." He tried once again to get Chiang to redeploy his troops and to concentrate on the defense of Taiwan, offering landing craft for up to twenty thousand men as an inducement. Assault shipping would restore mobility and flexibility to Chiang's forces, without which Chiang could never realize his dream of a return in force to the mainland when—or if—the Communist regime collapsed. Chiang wasn't interested.[27]

The Chinese launched an aerial campaign to win air superiority over the Taiwan strait, the essential first step in any attempted invasion. As Eisenhower studied U-2 photographs showing the buildup on coastal airfields, he stroked his chin. "Let's see what we can do about the dogfights." Sidewinder missiles were rushed to Taiwan and in the space of two weeks more than a hundred Chinese MiG's were shot down for negligible losses among Nationalist pilots.[28]

The Chinese aerial offensive halted abruptly. The shelling stopped. It gave way to a new dialogue. Talks began in Warsaw between American and Chinese diplomats. It turned out that what Mao wanted was American recognition of China, something that Eisenhower favored but Congress would never accept.

Following the Suez crisis in the fall of 1956, Eisenhower had characterized his disagreement with the British as "a family spat," one he was eager to resolve. In March 1957 he traveled to Bermuda to meet with an old friend, the half-American Harold Macmillan, who had succeeded the disgraced Anthony Eden as prime minister. Eisenhower returned home in a buoyant mood. It was, he said, "by far the most successful international meeting that I have attended since the close of World War II."[29]

Even so, it had done nothing to meet the challenge of Soviet influence in the Middle East or reduce Nasser's hostility to Israel. A year after the Suez crisis, Eisenhower ruefully admitted to his old friend Swede Hazlett, "Since Nasser announced the nationalization of the Suez Canal, I cannot remember a day that has not brought its major or minor crisis."[30]

With Soviet backing, Nasser's supporters were trying to bring down pro-Western governments in countries such as Iraq. In July 1958 an Iraqi Army coup by pro-Nasser officers culminated in the brutal murder of the Iraqi royal family. The Christian president of Lebanon, Camille Chamoun, was meanwhile trying to cope with Moslem street mobs protesting his attempts to remain in power by usurping his country's constitution. Exploiting the increase in tension following the Iraqi coup, Chamoun appealed for American help against what he claimed was an impending Syrian invasion.

After listening to General Nathan Twining, the chairman of the Joint Chiefs, who said troops could be put ashore in a matter of hours, and Dulles, who was all doom and gloom, Eisenhower swiftly made up his mind. "We've come to the point where we've got to make a decision. And that is, do we send in the Boy Scouts or do we send in the Marines?"

Dulles responded, "Mr. President, what do you mean?" That Boy Scouts remark sounded like a dig at the diplomats.

"What I mean is, we're going to send the Marines in," said Eisenhower. Thousands of Marines landed on the beaches of Beirut twelve hours later.[31]

The CIA had, meanwhile, warned him that a coup was brewing in Jordan to overthrow King Hussein. Eisenhower called Macmillan and urged him to send British troops there, to protect the Hashemite king. After all, the British had created the Hashemite monarchy. Two days later, a British parachute brigade landed in Jordan. At the same time, American naval forces were deployed to the Persian Gulf to protect Iraq's small, almost defenseless neighbor Kuwait, which produced so much oil that it could keep the whole of Western Europe supplied for decades.[32]

Not only was the Middle East intensely volatile, but areas that had never before posed serious problems were becoming increasingly restive. The defeat of Japan and the collapse of European empires had ignited an explosive nationalism throughout what was becoming known as the Third World. When Nixon visited Venezuela in May 1958, he was surrounded by a hostile mob that spat at him, threw stones and hurled curses. The situation seemed so dangerous that Eisenhower moved a thousand paratroopers to Puerto Rico and Cuba in case Nixon had to be extricated by force.

During Nixon's visit to Venezuela, an American-backed revolt in Indonesia was falling apart. In 1954, the city of Bandung announced it would host a conference of Third World leaders. Dulles concluded that the main purpose of the gathering was to berate the U.S. "Why the hell did we ever urge the Dutch to get out of Indonesia?" grumbled an exasperated Eisenhower.[33]

Indonesian nationalism was providing a wide range of opportunities for Soviet penetration. On a visit to the U.S. in the summer of 1956, the Indonesian leader, General Achmed Sukarno, spoke of his admiration for Lincoln and Jefferson. But on a visit shortly afterward to China and the USSR, he spoke even more enthusiastically about Lenin and Mao.

In 1957, the U.S. ambassador to Indonesia reported that the country was in danger of falling under Soviet control. The CIA produced a plan to foment a revolution and install a more pro-Western government, one led by disaffected colonels; it was an echo of the plot that had worked earlier in Guatemala.

A rebel force was raised, trained and armed in the Philippines. It was even provided with an air force, consisting of four World War II Mustangs and a small force of B-25 and B-26 medium bombers of the same vintage. The pilots were American, Filipinos and Taiwanese. In January 1958, the rebels began attacking government outposts on the islands of Sumatra and Sulawesi. To Dulles, they were "the patriots." Sukarno called them "the terrorists" and started buying arms, at discount prices, from the Soviet Union.[34]

Without any support from the local population, the rebels were doomed. The Indonesian Army drove them into the mountains, then hunted them down, to Eisenhower's dismay. In public, he repeatedly denied any and all U.S. involvement, and the press gave him the benefit of the doubt.[35]

Then, on May 18, 1958, a B-26 with an American named Alan L. Pope at the controls was shot down. Pope survived with little more than scratches and bruises, and in his pockets were U.S. Air Force identification, his Post Exchange card from Clark Air Force Base in the Philippines and his diary. The administration insisted that Pope was really a civilian, a "soldier of fortune." Put on trial and duly convicted, Pope was sentenced to death. The revolt fizzled out.

"At the moment we can do little more than remain alert," Eisenhower told an old friend, Paul Hoffman. In the meantime, he tried to secure Pope's freedom. Sukarno eventually pardoned him, but not before Eisenhower was out of the White House.[36]

Picture It

In the late 1950s, American parents looked at the milk carton sitting next to the cereal bowl at breakfast and wondered, Strontium 90? Were they poisoning their children with this dangerous radioactive isotope produced in atmospheric nuclear explosions and shown to be present in cow's milk?

The Soviets conducted a series of H-bomb tests in the atmosphere in the winter of 1957, then declared a moratorium in March 1958, just as a long-prepared series of American tests was about to begin. Khrushchev urged Eisenhower to cancel the American tests. Eisenhower had little choice but to decline. The new tests were designed to produce smaller, "cleaner" warheads for ICBMs and IRBMs. Even so, the fallout problem simply couldn't be ignored.[1]

Eisenhower was developing a passionate desire to get the two superpowers disarming before he left the White House—not only because he was thinking about his place in history, but because like any other parent or grandparent he, too, was worried by Strontium 90.

The road to disarmament, he decided, came in two parts: remove the risk of surprise attack, which would reassure the Soviets, and devise a sure way of detecting nuclear tests, which would reassure the West. Only then would both sides be prepared to stop the buildup of nuclear arms and end nuclear testing. So in January 1958 he wrote to Marshal Nikolai Bulganin, the Soviet head of state, proposing "that we begin progressively to take measures guaranteeing against the possibility of surprise attack . . ." The Soviet response was a demand for a summit meeting.[2]

Eisenhower wasn't ready for one. The Geneva conference of 1955 had been a huge disappointment. Its centerpiece—his Open Skies proposal—had come to nothing. Without dropping their demand for a summit, the Soviets eventually agreed to a meeting of technical experts in Geneva to talk about surprise-attack and test-ban-verification problems. These talks began November 10, 1958.

That same day, however, even as the experts in Geneva were shaking hands, posing for photographs and putting their briefcases next to their chairs, Khrushchev was torpedoing the conference. In a speech to a Soviet-Polish friendship rally in Moscow, he whipped up a war scare over Berlin. The occupation of Berlin had to end, said Khrushchev.

The timing of his speech was curious. Did it mean the Soviet leadership had decided not to talk about disarmament as a prelude to a summit conference? Were they now trying to get a summit conference first, with disarmament talks postponed to a later date? Or were they just trying to throw their weight around and seize the initiative? On November 27, while Eisenhower and Dulles were still trying to figure out what Khrushchev was up to, the Soviet leader delivered an ultimatum. He demanded that the Western allies get out of Berlin. "Only madmen can go to the length of unleashing another world war over the preservation of their privileges as occupiers of West Berlin," said Khrushchev in a brusque note to Eisenhower. The U.S., Britain and France had better leave soon, because the Soviet Union was going to recognize the German Democratic Republic.

The State Department began referring to May 27, 1959, as K-Day, the day when the ultimatum would run out and the Western powers could expect to find themselves blocked by the GDR from using the roads and railroads that connected West Germany to West Berlin. Obviously, though, the East Germans would be acting as puppets of the Soviet Union. No one in Western capitals believed the East Germans were remotely independent.[3]

The NSC had already anticipated a crisis over access to West Berlin, and the policy to meet it was clear. According to NSC-5727, if the Soviets once again tried to force the Allies out, as they had done in 1948, "there would be immediate and forceful action to counter the Soviet challenge, even though such counter-measures might lead to general war."[4]

Eisenhower was not going to abandon the 2.2 million West Berliners to Communist domination and intimidation. An obligation assumed in 1945 to occupy West Berlin had evolved, by 1958, into an obligation to defend it. "Shouldn't we make it clear," he wondered at an NSC meeting two weeks after Khrushchev's ultimatum, "that we consider this no minor affair? In order to avoid beginning with the white chips and working up to the blue, we should put them on notice that our whole stack is in this play." Even so, he added, all messages sent to Khrushchev "should be in a friendly tone."[5]

In late January, the NSC reviewed the options again. Dulles was by this time seriously ill, dying a painful death from stomach cancer. He had only a few months left to live, and Berlin would be his last chance to show a doubting world that he had been a great secretary of state. Dulles urged Eisenhower to prepare himself, the country and NATO for a showdown with the Soviet Union at the end of May, even if that meant a nuclear war.

The Joint Chiefs advised Eisenhower to test Soviet resolve by sending an armored division across East Germany to Berlin. Eisenhower said that was pointless. A division might provoke a fight but wouldn't be strong enough to win it. Reconnaissance flights showed Soviet tank divisions dug in along every route from West Germany to Berlin. There were only two possibilities if the Soviets blocked access to the city, he told the NSC: "We would have to decide [are] we going to put bombs on Moscow [or] withdraw from Europe."[6]

At a press conference shortly after this, he was asked, "Would you use nuclear war if necessary to free Berlin?"

Eisenhower replied tartly, "I don't know how you could free anything with nuclear weapons . . . nuclear war as a general thing looks to me a self-defeating thing for all of us . . ."[7] Encouraged by this, Khrushchev renewed his demand for a summit meeting, but Eisenhower still said no. Harold Macmillan flew to Washington on March 19 to urge Eisenhower to reconsider. American IRBMs were about to be installed in Britain, making it a primary target.

Eisenhower took Macmillan to Walter Reed Army Hospital, to talk to the dying Dulles. Macmillan said he could see only four potential outcomes to the impasse: Khrushchev would cave in, the Allied occupation would end, there would be a negotiated settlement over Berlin or there would be a nuclear war. The best way to end the matter peacefully was probably to hold a summit. But if the U.S. was moving toward war, he would like to know that was the policy, because he wanted to send as many English children as possible to Canada first. It would take only eight Soviet H-bombs to obliterate England and the English. Dulles was disgusted. "What is the use of our spending $40 billion a year or more to create deterrent power if whenever the Soviets threaten us we have to buy peace by compromise?"[8]

Eisenhower at first seemed to agree with Dulles. "I refuse to be dragooned into a summit," he told Macmillan as they left Walter Reed. Within twenty-four hours, however, he had second thoughts. He couldn't agree to a summit under pressure from Khrushchev, but if everything else failed, he might agree—grudgingly, of course—to a summit urged on him by his old friend Harold Macmillan, for the sake of NATO unity. A week after Macmillan's visit, Eisenhower informed the Soviets that a summit might just be possible after all. Even now, though, he wouldn't make a firm commitment. It was a characteristic Eisenhower performance where nuclear threats were concerned—he twisted and turned, striving to keep open as many options as possible, until the very last moment for decision. These were the matters he agonized over as he did over nothing else.[9]

On May 24, Dulles died. He was buried three days later, on K-Day. In Berlin, nothing happened. The crisis seemed to have passed. On June 23, however, Khrushchev had a visitor—Averell Harriman, America's wartime ambassador to the Soviet Union. In a typical display of synthetic rage, Khrushchev postured and blustered. "We are determined to liquidate your rights in West Berlin!" he ranted. "If you want to perpetuate or prolong your rights, this means war! We may die, but the rockets will fly automatically. Your generals talk of tanks and guns defending your Berlin position. *They will burn!*" Harriman informed Washington that Khrushchev was even more dangerous than Stalin.[10]

Eisenhower didn't believe it. He read this *opéra bouffe* performance as yet another crude and clumsy demand for a summit meeting. Khrushchev still didn't understand that the more stridently he clamored for one, the harder it was for Eisenhower to agree. How, then, to hold a summit without seeming to capitulate? And how to keep Macmillan on board?

As Eisenhower wrestled with this dilemma, Khrushchev let him off the hook by dropping a heavy hint to some visiting American governors that he'd like to visit the United States someday. The new secretary of state, the tall, gaunt, arthritis-crippled Christian Herter, had a suggestion—why not invite Khrushchev to visit the United States soon? The invitation was accepted only a week after it was extended. Eisenhower offered a meeting in August. Too hot, said Khrushchev. How about September? Perfect, replied Khrushchev. Eisenhower assured Macmillan, "This will take the crisis edge off the Berlin situation."[11]

The Tu-114 that flew Khrushchev from Moscow to Washington on September 15 was a huge bomber, with a fuselage much higher off the ground than any American aircraft, thanks to its enormous double-bladed propellers. It was a mediocre airplane, but the Russians were proud of it because it was so big. They were less happy to discover that because Andrews AFB didn't have a ramp high enough to reach the exit door, a long ladder would have to suffice.

From the doorway, Khrushchev was astonished at the sight of Eisenhower waiting near the bottom of the ladder to greet him. They had first met in Moscow in 1945, when Eisenhower was in uniform. After that they had met up again in Geneva in 1955, but Switzerland was neutral. Here in the American motherland, though, he was Commander in Chief as well as President, so why wasn't he in uniform now? Instead, he wore a suit, like an ordinary civilian. Turning around, Khrushchev proceeded to descend gingerly onto American soil, ample rump wobbling, knuckles turning white as he gripped the rungs of the ladder. He then stepped toward Eisenhower clutching his hat, hand outstretched, the three large medals—Order of the Red Star, Hero of the Soviet Union, Order of Lenin—pinned to the breast pocket of his tan serge suit shifting heavily from side to side, moon-shaped peasant's face beaming.[12]

During Khrushchev's second day in America, Eisenhower took him for a helicopter ride over Washington during the late-afternoon rush hour. The Soviet leader saw the torrent of cars pouring out of the city.

"Very inefficient," he grunted. "In our country the workers take buses or the metro." As the helicopter clattered north over Maryland, its passengers flew for mile after mile above single-family homes lining the roads below. Khrushchev grunted again. "Very inefficient. In our country the workers live in apartments."

"You know," said Eisenhower, "our people want to drive their own automobiles and they want to live in individual houses."

"Well, my people don't want private automobiles," said Khrushchev. "And they don't want private houses."

Eisenhower replied wryly, "If you really believe that, I don't know how long you'll keep your job."[13]

After two days in Washington, Khrushchev set off to see New York, Iowa and California. He was impressed by the United Nations Building, envious of the productivity of American farmers and appalled by Hollywood, because he—and his wife—were forced to witness the disgusting and immoral sight of scantily clad dancers rehearsing a can-can on a movie soundstage. After that shocking exposure to bourgeois degeneracy, he returned to Washington.

Weeks earlier, while Khrushchev's itinerary was still being planned, Eisenhower had thought the best way to show him America would be to take Khrushchev around the country personally—drive with him into the suburbs, take him into people's houses, let him talk to ordinary Americans and see how they lived. That was obviously impossible, but when Khrushchev returned from California, Eisenhower asked him to come up to Camp David.

No one believed in people-to-people exchanges between countries more than Eisenhower. His faith in them bordered on the mystical. And now he seemed to feel that if only he and Khrushchev got together, man to man, they could cut through the need for summits, for formal disarmament talks and discussions between technical experts. The two of them might cut a deal and leave it to the diplomats and scientists to fill in the blanks.

At Camp David, Khrushchev was open and friendly whenever he and Eisenhower were left alone with their interpreters. They reminisced about their experiences in World War II and agreed to call each other "friend." But Khrushchev became wary and dour whenever Soviet officials joined them.

Khrushchev asked how much a worker earned in a week. What did a suit of clothes cost? A house? A television set? This intense curiosity about everyday life made Eisenhower wish all the more that he'd been able to take his guest to meet ordinary Americans. He did the next best thing—he took Khrushchev to Gettysburg in the helicopter, to meet Mamie, John and the grandchildren.[14]

Khrushchev assured Eisenhower that the Soviet Union wasn't what it had been under Stalin, when it was ruled by terror. Communist rule, according to Khrushchev, was now based on popular support and the gulag had been abolished, an assertion that Eisenhower would have known was untrue.

The two principal items of discussion were supposed to be Berlin and nuclear arms control and when Eisenhower said disarmament was "the most important problem" in the world, Khrushchev emphatically agreed. That turned out to be the beginning and end of agreement, however. A comprehensive arms control plan wasn't possible, Khrushchev said, because the United States possessed an overwhelming strategic advantage. From its bases ringing the USSR, SAC could destroy the Soviet Union, but the Soviet Union could only destroy Europe. Agreement now would freeze America's strategic superiority. No Soviet leader could agree to that.

Eisenhower didn't address this fundamental point—not then, not ever. He always talked and acted as though both sides were roughly equal in military technologies and firepower, while Khrushchev only talked and acted that way in public. The Soviets never forgot their vulnerability to SAC. Even in his memoirs, published fifteen years after this meeting, Khrushchev was still bitter about it. And so long as the Soviets were behind in both ICBM development and warhead design, there would be no nuclear test ban.[15]

As a result, there was virtually no discussion of arms control. Instead, there was a lengthy plea from Khrushchev for better trading arrangements between the two countries. They even debated the merits of American chocolates versus Soviet chocolates. There was also a closely argued discussion of the American refusal to recognize the Peking regime as the government of China. "You accept a divided Germany," said Khrushchev, "yet you won't accept a divided China. You support a separate government on Taiwan."

Eisenhower acknowledged that was true. "But the essential element is that we seek a peaceful solution in both cases."[16]

The most divisive issue was Berlin. Khrushchev said he needed to know how long the Allies intended to occupy West Berlin. "There can be no fixed time limit," said Eisenhower, "and I would resign before I would accept any United States withdrawal from Berlin."

When Khrushchev again urged a summit meeting to resolve the issue, Eisenhower said that was impossible so long as the Berlin ultimatum still stood. Khrushchev told him the ultimatum was a dead letter, but there was not going to be any public announcement of that fact. However, he said emphatically, "We are not going to take unilateral action."[17]

For some weeks the world basked in what newspapers called "the spirit of Camp David." Eisenhower deplored the euphoria. No agreements had been reached, no real progress made. But Khrushchev had invited Eisenhower to visit the Soviet Union, and with the threat to Berlin finally removed, Eisenhower not only felt able to accept but finally agreed to the summit Khrushchev wanted so badly. They would meet again in Paris, in May 1960.

As Eisenhower forged the New Look following the end of the Korean War and SAC assumed a dominant role in American strategy, Curtis LeMay had to confront the fact that to identify major targets he was relying on outdated captured German reconnaissance photographs and the blueprints of Soviet plants built before World War II by Western engineers and technicians. He even had to rely on maps going back before World War I. LeMay asked for a new reconnaissance aircraft to be built, one that could fly over the Soviet Union too high for the Red Air Force to shoot it down. In the meantime, the U.S. Air Force started floating balloons equipped with cameras across the Soviet Union. Only a handful were ever recovered.

Eisenhower, too, was troubled by the veil of secrecy that cloaked the Soviet Union. What was the point of it? In July 1954 he established a committee to examine the problems of meeting a surprise attack. The committee recommended a program of aerial reconnaissance. At roughly the same time Lockheed offered the government a new type of reconnaissance aircraft, the U-2. The Air Force rejected the U-2 in favor of a modified version of an existing aircraft, the Canberra. The CIA, however, was so impressed by the potential of the U-2 that it was willing to spend its entire $22 million reserve fund to finance construction of twenty aircraft. In December 1954, Eisenhower approved the U-2 project. The aircraft would have a range of 5,500 miles and fly at 70,000 feet, four miles higher than any Red Air Force fighter.

Seven months after giving the go-ahead for the U-2, Eisenhower went to Geneva and offered his Open Skies proposal, hoping it would make the U-2 project unnecessary. Khrushchev's answer was, *"Nyet, nyet, nyet!"*

The first U-2 reconnaissance flights were made from England at the beginning of July 1956. They flew over Eastern Europe, and Eisenhower was shown photographs from these missions. On July 4, the first flight to penetrate Soviet airspace took off from a West German airfield, crossed Eastern Europe, flew over Red Air Force bomber bases in the western Ukraine, then up to Leningrad. The next day, another flight was flown, this time across the southern Ukraine and up to Moscow.

Arthur C. Lundahl, the CIA's principal expert on aerial photography, brought specially prepared briefing boards into the Oval Office a few days later. They showed clear, detailed pictures of the Leningrad shipyards, with submarines under construction. The two concentric rings of surface-to-air-missile sites being built around Moscow could be seen, but their SAM-1 missiles couldn't reach the U-2. The briefing-board photographs also included pictures of Soviet fighters rising to challenge the intruder, then flaming out at around fifty thousand feet and tumbling back toward Earth until their pilots could reignite their engines.

"What altitude was this one taken from?" asked Eisenhower, deeply impressed and highly gratified, as he studied the photographs. "How did you achieve this resolution?"[18]

On July 10 there came an angry blast from Moscow, protesting violations of its airspace. The State Department rejected the allegations, denying that any overflying had occurred. Each flight was, Eisenhower recognized, a provocative act, and there was a risk, even if a small one, that a U-2 mission could be misinterpreted as the prelude to an attack, which might trigger a Soviet attempt to strike SAC's overseas bases. He would personally authorize all U-2 flights.

The risks involved were justified by the quality and quantity of information being produced. Eisenhower had also been assured by the CIA that if the Soviets ever did shoot down a U-2, the pilot stood virtually no risk of surviving—the plane would be blown up by a self-destruction device and the surviving pieces would be pulverized on impact with the ground.

Nearly every mission began with a two-page memo from the CIA that explained why another flight was needed. If Eisenhower was persuaded, he had Richard Bissell, the deputy director of the CIA, bring the flight maps to the Oval Office, spread them out on the huge presidential desk and show him the proposed flight route. Eisenhower, himself a qualified pilot, would stand up, put on his reading glasses and motion to Bissell: "Come around here." Side by side, they studied the maps, Eisenhower wanting to know: "Aren't you getting a little too exposed over here?" Or, "Why not fly that leg by this route?" marking the map with his pen. To the first qualified pilot to work at this desk, flight maps were neither a novelty nor a mystery.[19]

The CIA had been anxious to purchase the U-2 because of sightings of Soviet jet bombers in the early 1950s. The Soviet Union appeared to be creating its own version of SAC. Stuart Symington, the Democratic senator who had at one time been Truman's secretary of the Air Force, was telling journalists and politicians there was a growing "bomber gap." One of the U-2's earliest successes was to prove Symington wrong.[20]

While scotching the bomber-gap myth, the U-2 unearthed the earliest evidence of what the Soviets were really trying to do—beat the U.S. in the race to develop and deploy ICBMs. The sole launch pad for testing ICBMs was at Tyuratam, only six hundred miles from northern Turkey. The National Security Agency already had a large and effective listening post on a mountain close to the Turkish border. With U-2's overflying the Tyuratam launch pad and the NSA monitoring the telemetry of its missile tests, Eisenhower may have known nearly as much about the success and failures of the Soviet ICBM program as Khrushchev.

During the *Sputnik* crisis, Dulles had urged Eisenhower to tell the country about the U-2, to assure Americans that they still had the edge over the Soviets. Eisenhower demurred. If he spoke about the U-2, he would come under intense Soviet pressure to stop the flights. They might even declare that the next flight would be an act of war. For now, they lodged their protests quietly, unwilling to announce their impotence in their own skies.[21]

In the summer of 1957, the Red Air Force began to deploy the

SAM-2, a missile that could reach 70,000 feet. U-2 flight routes were drawn so they avoided known SAM-2 sites by at least twenty-five miles, and Eisenhower approved a successor aircraft, one capable of flying at three times the speed of sound and flying at 85,000 feet, the SR-71 Blackbird. More than that, though, he was pinning his faith on reconnaissance satellites.

Back in 1955, Eisenhower had approved an attempt to build the WS-1171, the first photographic satellite. This project, called Corona, was highly secret and hidden inside a publicly announced project, Discoverer, which the Air Force developed to conduct medical and scientific experiments in space. The camera aboard the Corona satellite would not offer the one-foot resolution of U-2 photography. That was impossible given its distance from the earth, but that was compensated for by something revolutionary: a bundle of infrared sensors that detected heat and movement through clouds, walls, roofs and the blackness of night. The U-2 flew now and then; Corona would be on watch all the time.

In February 1959, the first Corona satellite was launched, but failed to go into orbit. Over the next eighteen months there were other launches, all of them ending in failure of some kind. Eisenhower could only hope the satellite project would succeed before the Soviets managed to shoot down a U-2, something his scientific advisers told him was going to happen if the flights continued much longer.[22]

On April 9, 1960, a U-2 flew over the Soviet Union in what was expected to be one of the last flights. There was no protest from Moscow. The CIA then proposed another flight. This one, Allen Dulles insisted, was of crucial importance—it would pass over Plesetsk, the only site built so far to handle operational ICBMs. It would show if the Soviets had finally overcome their problems with guidance systems, reentry and warhead design and possessed a weapon that could strike the United States. Eisenhower reluctantly okayed the flight, but said the mission would have to be flown no later than April 25. The Paris summit was due to start May 16. "We don't want to have that thing up there while the summit's on."[23]

Because of problems with the weather, the flight, which would cross the Soviet Union from Peshawar in Pakistan to Bodo in northern Norway, couldn't be flown within Eisenhower's time limits. He extended authorization until May 1, which turned out to be the day the weather finally cleared.

Stung to fury by an overflight on what amounted to the holiest day in a good Communist's calendar, May Day, the Red Air Force mounted a maximum effort, sending a MiG-19 to 50,000 feet to track the U-2 and firing fourteen SAM-2 missiles. One missile obliterated the MiG-19. Another exploded slightly behind and below the U-2. Shrapnel from this detonation cut through the fuel lines of the U-2. Its pilot, Francis Gary Powers, ejected.[24]

Four days later the Soviets announced they had shot down an American spy plane. The State Department announced that it was an unarmed weather plane that had flown off course "and accidentally violated Soviet airspace."

That night, the State Department told the White House that Powers appeared to have survived and been taken prisoner. Two days later, Khrushchev confirmed it. The State Department then issued a statement that the flight had not been authorized by the President. Allen Dulles offered to take the blame and be fired. Eisenhower was angry at Dulles for insisting on another flight so close to the summit, but when John Eisenhower said, "You ought to fire him," Eisenhower's temper erupted.

"I am not going to shift the blame to my underlings!"[25]

His anger may have been provoked by the memory of how MacArthur had once tried to make *him* a scapegoat back in 1938.[26]

On May 9, as Eisenhower walked with a long, gloomy face into the Oval Office at the start of what was sure to be a difficult week, he grumbled to his secretary Ann Whitman, "I would like to resign!" The next day, he held a press conference and read out a statement, accepting full responsibility for the ill-fated Powers flight. The justification for it was simple: "No one wants another Pearl Harbor." The choice was either a secret program such as the U-2 or the Open Skies program that he had offered at Geneva five years earlier. In rejecting Open Skies, the Soviets had left him little choice but to press ahead with the U-2.[27]

On May 14, Eisenhower departed for Paris, having convinced himself that Khrushchev's furious denunciations of American espionage, provocation and general bad faith were a theatrical performance, something that Khrushchev had to do to satisfy his critics at home. De Gaulle had, meanwhile, sent an emissary to Moscow to ask if there was any reason to cancel the summit. The Soviets assured him they still wanted to proceed. He assumed that meant they were serious about seeking a nuclear test ban and the U-2 furor was over.

At the very first session, however, Khrushchev demanded a personal apology from Eisenhower, which wasn't so much unreasonable as absurd, given the extensive and intensive ongoing Soviet espionage operations in the U.S. at the time. The Pentagon, the CIA, the FBI and the NSA were all targets. Every method was used, from blackmail to bribery to murder.[28]

Khrushchev also demanded that Eisenhower punish those responsible for the May Day flight. That meant Eisenhower would have to punish himself. Having clamorously said that nothing but the impossible would satisfy him, Khrushchev then walked out of the conference. Samuel Beckett was elsewhere in the city, hunched over a small table in a cheap hotel, writing his play *Happy Days*. The characters in *Happy Days* are desperately in need of certainty, but the harder they pursue it, the more elusive it becomes.[29]

Eisenhower consoled himself that the summit that never was had brought the U.S., Britain and France closer together. But he returned to Washington depressed. There would be no ban on nuclear tests, no end to Strontium 90 in the milk to crown his presidency. "There's nothing worthwhile left for me to do," he glumly told George Kistiakowsky.[30]

Three months after Powers was shot down, there were two important developments. First, the film and infrared data from a Corona satellite were recovered for the first time. Second, Oleg Penkovsky, a Red Army colonel who was an expert on the Soviet missile program, defected to American intelligence. Penkovsky told his handlers there was no Soviet photographic satellite and no operational ICBM. It would be years before the Soviets achieved strategic parity. Eisenhower could leave office knowing that the Soviet Union was still not able to attack America. The most important legacy Truman had handed to him was one he would pass intact to his successor.[31]

★ ★ ★ ★ ★

44

The Torch Is Passed

It is late afternoon on July 7, 1959, another hot, sticky day, typical of Washington in midsummer, and the sixty-eight-year-old President of the United States gazes through the tinted windows of his limousine as it makes its way slowly along Constitution Avenue. The rush-hour traffic is quickly building up as the President studies his people.

Usually, the limo travels up and down Pennsylvania Avenue. It has been some time since Eisenhower has traveled along Constitution. With the Museum of Natural History on one side and the National Archives on the other, the traffic is bumper to bumper most days during the summer, and tourists throng the sidewalks. Looking at them now—gathered in knots at the crossings or in long patient lines to see the Declaration of Independence—Eisenhower starts to feel uneasy. There is something different about these people, something that isn't right.

In the Army, he had learned to tell a lot from a little, to look at a company and judge the whole regiment, to inspect a few buildings and get a feeling for whether the commanding general deserved another star. What he sees now troubles him. Why are they so badly dressed? And why don't they stand up straight, walk with their shoulders squared? From the look of it, something bad is happening to Americans' self-respect.[1]

Some of the change, he may have reflected, could be put down to his advancing years. He was a lot older than the average American, and if he lived for another eighteen months, he would leave office as the oldest man ever to survive the presidency. That was quite an achievement, considering.

He knew, too, that he was out of touch with what was going on these days among the young. "As for 'beatnik,' I am not even sure what the word is supposed to mean," he had recently confessed to Mamie's niece. Still, what he is looking at this late afternoon from his limousine troubles him, even if he doesn't understand it. Maybe because he doesn't understand it. Either way, he feels something important is going on.[2]

And he's right about that, because it amounts to the end of the fifties, the last days of the Eisenhower era, an age whose conventionality flowed from the desperate experiences of a generation that had reached maturity in the Depression and survived that only to be thrust into World War II, and survived that, and then was dragged into Korea. Because their lives had been shaped so directly by struggle and strife, they had created an America that was peaceful, prosperous and slightly dull for their children to grow up in.

This was a clean and orderly country, where women wore dresses to cook dinner and men put on jackets and ties to visit the Washington Monument. The questing spirit of an earlier America had given way to the self-discipline imperative in battling depression, fascism and Communism. There were those, of course, who deplored the blandness, the smugness, the conformity of the fifties, but Eisenhower has never paid much attention to cultural critics. He considers them ivory-tower dwellers, cut off from the real life of the nation, talking only to one another.

As a result, much that has happened in America's cultural and intellectual life in recent years has passed him by. He deplores the exuberant lines and in-your-face chrome of American automobiles. Instead, he blames Detroit for creating inflation by producing overly expensive, overly desirable automobiles that people will pay far too much to buy. The result of Detroit's innovative automobile designs, he is convinced, was the 1957 recession. Like any good soldier, he has paid far more attention to function than form and does not understand the semiotics of modern industrial design.

Similarly, and despite his many happy hours with a brush in his hand and a canvas to paint, Eisenhower despises America's most important art movement, Abstract Expressionism. All he can see in it is a lack of discipline in technique and a vulgar desire to shock.

Rock 'n' roll means nothing to him, and if he's seen anything of Elvis Presley—and he probably has, because Elvis has appeared three times on *The Ed Sullivan Show*—he doubtless shares the conviction of millions of parents that this sullen-looking young man with that strangely sculpted hair and those burlesque-style gyrations is undermining the morals of the young. Eisenhower enjoys music and still occasionally bursts loudly into song, but always off key, and he goes at it with more gusto than style. He loves, too, to listen to popular songs, but they are invariably the ballads from his youth, such as "There's a Long, Long Trail a-Winding" and "Rose Marie." Most of all, though, he likes military music—"Army Blue," "Tenting Tonight," "Battle Hymn of the Republic" . . .

Without his really noticing it, the cultural dam has cracked wide open. The sudden outpouring of youthful energy, questioning and experimentation in the late 1950s is the inevitable reaction of a new, unscarred generation to the stifling suburban yearning for the safe and the same that their parents have been so determined to create. And on that summer evening on Constitution Avenue, the balance between the generations is shifting fast. That is what Eisenhower glimpses—the people who spurn ties, the people who won't stand up straight and square their shoulders. What he is looking at in these tourist crowds is a more youthful and restless America slouching toward the sixties, advancing on its own rendezvous with destiny.

Eisenhower was wary of the press, but there were a few journalists he liked and trusted—Arthur Krock of *The New York Times,* David Lawrence of *U.S. News & World Report,* almost anybody who wrote for the *New York Herald Tribune* and Kenneth Crawford of *Newsweek.* But then Crawford started writing columns that Eisenhower thought were unfair, and he asked a mutual friend, George Allen, how Crawford could write such stuff. "I've always regarded him as a friend," said Eisenhower.

"Well, he admires you and he *is* a friend," said Allen. "His trouble is he hates Republicans."

"He may have something there."[3]

Ever since his election in 1952, he had been trying to define his own political ideas, and the more he did so, the more obvious it was that he was not entirely at home in the Republican party. He described himself to Dewey as "a responsible progressive," and for a time wanted the GOP to change its name to the Progressive Republican party.[4]

That wasn't going to happen, but after his reelection in 1956, he declared, "America has approved of Modern Republicanism," which he later defined as "A type of political philosophy that recognizes clearly the responsibility of the Federal government to take the lead in making certain that the productivity of our great economic machine is distributed so that no one will suffer disaster or privation through no fault of his own." That concern for people over political ideology was what set him apart from much, if not most, of his own party.

It also helped to explain why he was so much more popular than the party and its other candidates. After the 1954 and 1956 elections, Eisenhower was indignant at the inconsistency, almost the perversity, of the voters. Before all three elections, most people told pollsters, "We like Ike. We'll vote for him," but having voted for him, they then elected a Democratic-controlled Congress.

From 1954 until he left the White House, the Democrats controlled Capitol Hill. Even so, he managed to get better than 80 percent of his proposed legislation enacted. The Democratic leadership, namely Lyndon Johnson, the Senate majority leader, and Sam Rayburn, the Democratic leader in the House, liked to pretend they went along with Ike because they admired him. The truth was they considered him a political lightweight. "He can't find his ass with both hands," said Rayburn. Eisenhower could be equally scathing about Rayburn and Johnson.[5]

The reason why Eisenhower got so much from a Democratic-controlled Congress owed much to his popularity, almost nothing to the brain-dead Republican leadership on the Hill and a lot to the fact that in foreign affairs, the Democratic party was more internationalist than the GOP. Some of Eisenhower's biggest battles in his second term, for example, were over foreign aid, and the strongest opposition came not from the Democrats but from within his own party. It was much the same story on domestic issues—the programs he supported were, in most cases, programs that Democrats would have pushed had they held the White House.

When he proposed something they disliked, however—such as making Lewis Strauss his secretary of commerce—he didn't stand a chance. Strauss was a public relations disaster, given to bluster, peevishness and self-importance. Such people don't have to appear before many congressional committees to create powerful enemies. Eisenhower was nevertheless incensed when Strauss's nomination was rejected. "This is the most shameful thing that has happened in the Senate since the attempt to impeach Andrew Johnson," he raged. "The second most shameful thing in Senate history!"[6]

On other issues, such as statehood for Alaska and Hawaii, he found himself pushing at an open door. The Democratic party had been promoting statehood for these territories since 1916, and when polls showed that 80 percent of the country favored statehood for both, it was hurriedly written into the 1952 Republican party platform.

What opposition he faced came from the conservative wing of the GOP, which was convinced that Hawaii was controlled—lock, stock and piers—by the West Coast longshoreman and their crypto-Commie leader, Harry Bridges. Southern Republicans weren't happy, either, at the thought of admitting a state where miscegenation was assumed to be commonplace.

Opposition to Alaska came from Eisenhower and fiscal conservatives. Most of Alaska was owned or occupied by the military. What remained did not seem economically viable. One Republican senator told Eisenhower he could just about accept statehood for Hawaii, "but I can't do it for Alaska. . . . It will be a tin cup state until all of us have humps on our back." Eisenhower responded, "You reflect my sentiments exactly."[7]

Eisenhower couldn't bring himself to ask for statehood for Alaska and Hawaii during his first term, but after his reelection, he finally relented. A pledge was a pledge was a pledge. In 1958 he submitted a bill for Alaskan statehood to Congress, and quickly got it. Hardly had flag makers begun turning out forty-nine-star flags before he asked Congress to make Hawaii a state.[8]

It was the right—apolitical—thing to do, because of the four new senators and three new representatives that admission of Alaska and Hawaii produced, at least three, and possibly all, of the senators would be Democrats and so would at least two of the representatives. At about this time Eisenhower informed his old friend Harold Macmillan, "In my present position I conceive of my responsibilities as being somewhat broader than those of a politician."[9]

Another project that many Democrats on Capitol Hill were happy to support was the Interstate and Defense Highways System. Eisenhower had been impressed by what he had seen of the German autobahns, and his interest in highway construction dated back to the intercontinental truck convoy of 1920. Few doubted that better highways were needed, but the states maintained that interstate highways were for them to build—or not. State highway departments were an important source of patronage. The idea of federal accountants examining the books was enough to make strong men in some state legislatures feel faint. He would get no support from the states.

Eisenhower did not let that deflect him. In 1954 he set up a high-powered presidential committee to give him the advice he wanted. The next year he submitted legislation to Congress for a forty-one-thousand-mile construction project with a price tag of $40 billion. Construction would be financed by the sale of federal bonds. Conservative Republicans didn't like the financing package, which looked like a way of increasing the national debt without admitting it (and they were right), and killed the bill in the Senate Roads Subcommittee.

That wasn't the end of it. Eisenhower came up with a better financing idea—a tax of four cents a gallon on gasoline. The federal government would use this money to pay 90 percent of the construction costs in any state willing to come up with the other 10 percent. Federal safety standards would be observed, otherwise the states could control the program. In 1956 the interstate highways program sailed through both houses of Congress. It was a major stimulus to the automobile industry, the trucking industry, the oil industry, hotel and motel chains and to construction. It was also the biggest public works project in American history, but almost nobody noticed that.[10]

The timing could hardly have been better, because in 1957 the economy took a nosedive and by April 1958 unemployment had doubled in a year, to reach 7.5 percent. Eisenhower assumed this recession would be like the 1954 downturn—short and shallow. He was wrong. It turned out to be deep and prolonged, partly because he was so slow to respond.

"To be conservative in this situation can well get me tagged as an unsympathetic, reactionary fossil," Eisenhower told the former chairman of the Council of Economic Advisers, Arthur Burns, but it was a price he was prepared to pay for reducing inflation, which had shot up to 4 percent. Where had this inflation suddenly come from? Eisenhower blamed it on the automobile makers, who in 1957 created something like mass lust for big cars with dazzling colors, leather seats, bigger engines, air-conditioning, power steering, huge fins and endless excuses to show chrome. The price of cars jumped as their desirability quotient doubled in magnitude.[11]

Eisenhower had been trying to control inflation throughout his presidency. He couldn't bear to see it increasing so rapidly. "If we just let prices go up," he told his budget director, Maurice Stans, "the day will come when the housewife will take a market basket full of money to the grocery store and bring back a pocket book filled with groceries."[12]

Both Burns and the present chairman of the CEA, Raymond Saulnier, wanted him to revive the economy by cutting taxes. They also suggested an investment credit for businesses, to stimulate growth. Eisenhower rejected both ideas, and the recession got deeper.

He was not only mishandling the problem; he was doing so for all the wrong reasons. For one thing, he was afraid of appearing to be doing favors to business. Having a gang of millionaire pals excited not only ridicule but suspicion, and he wasn't going to encourage any more suspicion. For another, he had installed Robert Anderson as secretary of the Treasury and was overly impressed by the man. Anderson was worried about maintaining the value of the dollar and refinancing the national debt.

Eisenhower spent long sessions with Anderson, who tutored him on economics in a way that George Humphrey had never attempted. Anderson was useful, too, as a liaison with fellow Texans Sam Rayburn and Lyndon Johnson. During their tutorials, Anderson convinced Eisenhower that if the price of a sound dollar was to put millions of people out of work, it was worth it in the long run.[13]

On issues like this, the Democrats in Congress were willing to fight Eisenhower tooth and nail, Lyndon Johnson most of all. The 1960 presidential election was within sniffing distance and that prominent proboscis was already twitching. Johnson and other Democrats began pushing antirecession programs. Some were pure pork, but others, such as extending unemployment benefits and extending federal financing for housing construction, made sense. Eisenhower vetoed the pork projects and belatedly submitted his own watered-down versions of the Democrats' antirecessionary measures.[14]

The recession was making the problems of America's farmers even more pressing and they screamed for relief. Eisenhower was advised that if he didn't do something to help them, such as putting parity payments at a rigid 90 percent, the Republicans faced a wipeout at the polls in the 1958 midterm election. It was advice that he determinedly ignored, at his and the GOP's cost.

The Congress that convened in January 1959 would consist of a Senate that was nearly two-thirds Democratic and a House that was nearly two-thirds Democratic. Eisenhower's chances of doing anything important on domestic issues during his last two years in office were now close to zero.

There was, nonetheless, one great battle to be fought and he intended to fight it. Come what may, he was going to go out of office with a balanced budget. He told the cabinet, "We're going to take hold of the bush, thorns and all. I'm tired of being liberal with other people's money." There wasn't much he could do about the budget for the fiscal year ending in June 1959—that would show a deficit of $12 billion. But in the budget ending in June 1960 there was a surplus of $200 million. That was the last budget over which he had control from beginning to end.

Eisenhower's parsimony saw federal spending decline in real terms by 2 percent a year from 1957 through 1960—at a time, that is, when spending most needed to be sustained. His zeal was as misplaced as it was admirable. When he became President in 1953, the national debt stood at more than 100 percent of GDP; by 1960 it had fallen to 60 percent. That was no small achievement. While debt was going down, living standards had been going up, despite the two recessions.

Nevertheless, he had pressed down too hard in his efforts to squeeze inflation out of the economy. Over those eight years it had operated well below its capacity, losing $200 billion in potential output—nearly as much as it had cost to fight World War II. Eisenhower's inept handling of the 1957–1958 recession was just the triumph of ideology over pragmatism that people might expect from a reactionary, unsympathetic fossil. But *he* wouldn't lose anything by it. Nixon would.[15]

The fundamental tragedy of postwar Latin America was that democracy made only one sustained appearance south of the Rio Grande, and that was in tiny Costa Rica. The rest of its countries were under the overt or covert control of the military or in the grip of brutal dictators who ruled by terror. Cuba fell into the terror category. Its strongman, Fulgencio Batista, a onetime Army corporal who had come to power in a coup, was as brutal as he was incompetent. But that hardly mattered so long as the mobsters who controlled Havana were happy and American tourists could flock to Havana to get drunk, gamble and feel like gods as they summoned beautiful Latina prostitutes to the happiness that only dollars could bring.

Ordinary Cubans were less happy. When, in the late 1950s, a handful of youthful idealists began to attack government outposts in the remote Sierra Maestra Mountains and called on their countrymen to revolt, hope swept through Cuba, where before there had been only bitter tears and despair. By December 1958 the revolution had reached Havana. Batista fled into exile and on January 1, 1959, the rebel leader, Fidel Castro, became the unchallenged leader of a liberated Cuba.

Eisenhower had followed Castro's rise to power with a degree of sympathy. "I was happy to see someone lead a movement that uprooted the old Batista dictatorship," he told an old friend. What worried him was what kind of man Castro would turn out to be once he had power.[16]

The omens weren't good. A report by a CIA agent in Cuba was forwarded to Eisenhower in February 1959 portraying a country that was falling into chaos under a revolutionary movement that didn't know how to function as a government. "The glamour of the Sierra Maestra and the straggly beards is rapidly wearing off . . ." claimed the unidentified agent.[17]

In consolidating its rule, the Castro regime couldn't resist paying off some old scores. Show trials were held of people who had supported Batista—or who were denounced by their neighbors as having supported Batista. It made little difference. They got brief, farcical trials that were like something out of Kafka in Spanish, followed by swift public executions that reeked of the abattoir. Trials and executions were televised live and were seen by millions in the United States.

For many Americans, the romance of the Cuban revolution turned to disgust and revulsion. The same was true elsewhere. When Eisenhower made a seven-nation trip to South America a year after Castro came to power, one head of state told him, "Castro the revolutionary enjoyed real prestige in Latin America. Castro the political leader has lost it all."[18]

Shortly after this, secretary of state Christian Herter sounded out the Organization of American States on its willingness to help oust Castro, but the OAS refused to oblige. It had no evidence that Castro was a Communist; nor had the CIA. Besides, Herter advised Eisenhower, it didn't make sense to act before there was a potential leader ready to take Castro's place. For the moment, the U.S. would have to content itself with generating anti-Castro publicity and try to create an anti-Castro opposition that would be ready to move "when and if coordinated OAS action is within our reach."[19]

Allen Dulles had recently brought Eisenhower some schematic drawings of a Cuban sugar refinery. Two trained saboteurs could destroy a plant like this, said Dulles, and sugar was the mainstay of Castro's economy. Attacking the refineries might destabilize the regime. Eisenhower wasn't impressed. It wouldn't take long to repair the damage, he pointed out. If the U.S. was really going to undermine Castro, it would need a much more ambitious effort than this. Dulles's deputy, Richard Bissell, took this as an invitation to create a force of guerrillas to topple Castro and look for people who might be groomed to form a new Cuban government. In March 1960, after returning from his South American trip, Eisenhower okayed Bissell's plan.[20]

With the relationship between the two countries becoming increasingly problematic, Castro decided to visit the United States. He intended to astound the "Yanquis" by not doing what they expected of him and all other Latin American leaders: he wasn't going to ask for a dime in American aid.

He arrived in April 1960. Eisenhower didn't meet with him, because he had not invited him to come. But Castro was guest of honor at a luncheon hosted by Herter, followed by a two-and-a-half-hour private discussion with Nixon. The Vice-President reported back to Eisenhower, "He's either very incredibly naive about Communism or under Communist discipline."[21]

Herter offered a different, more astute appraisal: "He does not have the same idea of law and legality as we have," he told Eisenhower. "He appears to confuse the roar of mass audiences with the rule of the majority . . ." Even so, "It would be a serious mistake to underestimate this man . . . he is clearly a strong personality and a born leader . . ."[22]

Relations nevertheless continued to deteriorate as the revolutionary government clamped down on dissent. Unlike the Batista regime, it was not corrupt, and it showed a passionate commitment to improving the lives of ordinary Cubans. Its contempt for those who owned property or disagreed with its philosophy, however, made it antidemocratic. It was also unpredictable. The United States had been instrumental in Cuba's independence from Spain in 1898, and the Navy and Marine Corps still held Guantánamo Bay. An unpredictable, revolutionary government was likely at some point to pose a threat to the security interests of the United States.

There was also the growing problem with Cuban refugees—they were arriving in Florida by the thousands every week. In the late fall of 1960, the total stood at roughly a hundred thousand, many of them people with professional qualifications or business or management experience. The middle class was fleeing Cuba.[23]

The CIA continued to talk about ways of weakening Castro, but it was slow to implement Bissell's plan. Eisenhower told Dulles and Bissell, "Boys, if you don't intend to go through with this, let's stop talking about it." Toward the end of 1960, the CIA finally began a military training program in Guatemala for anti-Castro Cubans. Once the training began, what had been sold to Eisenhower as a plan to insert small groups of saboteurs and guerrillas rapidly evolved into something else—an attempt to create a force capable of making an amphibious assault and breaking in, rather than sneaking in.[24]

The other foreign policy crisis in the making was Southeast Asia. The United States had supported South Vietnam's refusal to implement the Geneva accords, which had promised a nationwide election in 1956. Eisenhower's justification was that there could be no honest election in the north, which was probably true; but if he believed an honest election in the south was possible, he was deluding himself. When it came to crookedness and brutality, there was nothing to choose between Ho Chi Minh's Communists and the apparatus of state terrorism that kept Ngo Dinh Diem in power.

In May 1957, Diem visited the U.S. and had a long meeting with Eisenhower. What he wanted to talk about was the threat of subversion and American help to increase the size of his army. Eisenhower told him that SEATO was there to help him if the north attacked his country, but Diem was contemptuous of SEATO. What he wanted was an army made mighty by American training, American equipment and American money.[25]

Over the next few years, Diem got much of what he asked for. But Eisenhower made sure there was no blank check. Instead, he wrote to Diem and told him that continuing American assistance would depend on the implementation of basic reforms in Diem's government.[26]

Thwarted by the Saigon government's refusal to hold an election, North Vietnam launched a campaign to unify the country by force. In April 1960, the State Department informed Eisenhower that there had been "a marked intensification of subversive activities" in South Vietnam. At Diem's request, said State, American officials were working with the South Vietnamese on plans to defeat Communist insurgents. "These plans may call for increased U.S. assistance in counter-guerrilla training [and] expansion of the U.S. Military Assistance Advisory Group in Viet-Nam would not be contrary to the Geneva Agreements."[27]

The number of American advisers was increased, but there was no move toward a magnitude leap in the scale or nature of the commitment to South Vietnam. It was still Diem's war, not America's.

Gettysburg did not appeal. Never had. He had only bought the farm there because George Allen owned property nearby and Mamie was good friends with Mary Allen. If they had a house there, Mamie told him, she could see a lot more of Mary.

What Eisenhower wanted for himself was a third term, to stay in the White House. Not that he would or could admit to wanting to be President. But had there been no Twenty-second Amendment, he would have run again—and been elected again. It was, he'd have said, not something he actually wanted but only a response to another call to duty, and he would have meant it. We all turn our lives into narratives, into stories, and the narrative thread he wove for himself was life as a succession of duty calls, which was true enough. Yet they were also one man's ambitions, each drawing on a previous success.

Lacking the possibility of a third term, he had no desire to hand over to Nixon. He wanted Robert Anderson as his successor. After the 1958 election, Eisenhower told Anderson he had to seek the Republican nomination. "I'll quit what I'm doing, Bob. I'll raise money. I'll make speeches. I'll do *anything* to help." But Anderson turned him down. He wanted to go back to banking and make some real money. It was probably just as well, because Anderson was a complex and devious man who was not above a little white-collar crime if that was what it took to get rich. He spent the late 1970s in a federal penitentiary, doing time for tax fraud.[28]

That left Nixon the certain nominee in 1960, but several days before the Republican convention opened, Nixon met with Nelson Rockefeller, to secure the support of liberal Republicans. They issued a joint statement that was supposed to reflect the unity of the two wings of the party, but when Eisenhower heard what it contained, he was incensed. Nixon and Rockefeller had said that the nation's security required an extra $3.5 billion a year. Eisenhower read this as a criticism of his handling of the nation's defenses. Nixon couldn't retract the statement. The only thing he could do now was promise that Rockefeller's opinions on defense would not be reflected in the party platform.[29]

Eisenhower addressed the Republican convention, but he was still angry. He told his old friend Charles McAdam, "Charlie, we nominated the wrong man."[30]

On August 24, with the Labor Day kickoff to the campaign little more than a week away, Eisenhower was asked twice about Nixon's role in decision making. Each time, he explained that only one person made the decisions in the White House—the President. But the question came back for the third time as the press conference drew to a close. "I just wondered if you could give us an example of the major idea of his that you had adopted in that role, as the decider . . ." Eisenhower bristled. "If you give me a week, I might be able to think of one. I don't remember." Nixon was wounded, both personally and politically.[31]

In the campaign that followed, Eisenhower wasn't campaigning for Nixon so much as he was campaigning against Kennedy, whom he mockingly called "the young genius." "Motorcades kill me," Eisenhower told a friend before the 1960 campaign began. "But I'll do almost anything to avoid turning the country over to Kennedy."[32]

Meanwhile, Eisenhower told Nixon and his running mate, Henry Cabot Lodge, "You boys are in charge. It's your campaign and I'll do just as little or just as much as you want me to."[33]

That suited Nixon. He was almost desperate to prove he could win in his own right, a man no longer living in Eisenhower's shadow. Nixon was too astute not to know how little warmth Eisenhower felt for him, how measured was Eisenhower's judgment on his abilities. He was going to show the old man a thing or two and bring to the campaign something Eisenhower couldn't—the energy of youth. After Eisenhower told him it would be a mistake trying to do it all himself, that a modern campaign was too big for one man, Nixon announced he was going to campaign personally in all fifty states.

Eisenhower did what he could for Nixon behind the scenes, talking to small groups, but around the middle of October, he feared for the outcome of the election. His millionaire pals said Nixon was leading "a lost cause." Eisenhower called Nixon and offered once again to help. Nixon finally accepted the offer. Eisenhower prepared to hit the road. Yet even now Nixon was ambivalent. At a White House luncheon only a week before polling day, Eisenhower offered to add three more areas to his schedule—upstate New York, downstate Illinois and Michigan. All crucial, all too close to call. Nixon made a few anodyne, noncommittal remarks, evading the issue. After Nixon left, Eisenhower asked Len Hall, chairman of the Republican National Committee, "Why didn't Dick pay attention to what I was saying?"

"He was uptight, Mr. President."

"Goddammit, he looks like a loser to me!"[34]

Kennedy was waging an effective campaign. Making the most of the lingering recession—"Let's get America moving again!"—he pledged to get the economy growing at 5 percent a year. He repeatedly accused Eisenhower of putting the country in peril by allowing a "missile gap" to develop and insisted that America's prestige abroad was collapsing.

During those last two weeks before the election, Eisenhower barnstormed the country, seething at Kennedy's claims of his administration's incompetence at home and abroad. His popularity was plainly undiminished by these attacks. Huge, ecstatic crowds welcomed Eisenhower wherever he appeared. On Election Day, however, Kennedy defeated Nixon, by the narrowest of margins.

The first few days after the election were awful. Defeat hurt Eisenhower as nothing else did. "It's the repudiation of everything I've done for eight years," he told his staff. He was bitter about it, and that bitterness was focused, inevitably, on John Kennedy.[35]

Nevertheless, he was determined that the transition would be smooth, that the new administration would take over as effortlessly as possible from the old one. On December 6, Kennedy came to the White House. It was the first time they had met since Potsdam, when John Kennedy had been a Hearst stringer at the conference. It was an encounter Eisenhower didn't remember.

Kennedy wanted to talk about Berlin, the Far East, how the NSC worked, how the White House was organized and what de Gaulle, Adenauer and Macmillan were like. Eisenhower wanted to talk about Cuba, the place of nuclear weapons within NATO (in other words, command and control of the Bomb), the current balance-of-payments problem that was depressing the value of the dollar and the rapidly deteriorating situation in Laos.[36]

On January 17, 1961, Eisenhower made his farewell address. In November 1957 he had suffered a slight stroke. It left his intellectual faculties unimpaired, as his ability to dictate long, complicated letters and memos proved. At the same time, it made him more wary than ever in his televised press conferences, where he had always been so afraid of blurting out secret information that he had been deliberately vague much of the time. But after the stroke, his syntax became so convoluted, not to say weird, that no one expected him to say anything much in his farewell address.

It became one of the most famous speeches of the postwar era. Eisenhower was at last free to express one of the biggest frustrations of his presidency—his inability to stop the waste, duplication and parochialism of the military. Two new dangers had arisen to threaten liberty, he told his countrymen. The first was "the conjunction of an immense military establishment and a large arms industry." The entire country needed to guard against "the acquisition of unwarranted influence by the military-industrial complex." He had originally intended to include Congress in this indictment and deliver a blast at the "military-industrial-congressional complex." At the last minute, he struck out "congressional." It wasn't for a President to berate Congress any more than it was his business to berate the Supreme Court.

The second threat to liberty came from the federal government's domination of research. Free, disinterested inquiry was unlikely to flourish, he declared, "when a government contract becomes virtually a substitute for intellectual curiosity."[37]

On January 19, 1961, the day before the inauguration, Eisenhower and Kennedy met again, this time in the Oval Office. They were alone,

and Eisenhower showed Kennedy how to use the code book and the pro-
totypical laptop computer contained in the satchel, better known as "the
Football," that was never far from the President. Having fed a special
presidential identity card into the laptop, he would then look up the appropriate codes (which changed daily) to launch a nuclear attack and
tap them into the computer.

From the Oval Office, the two men stepped into the Cabinet Room,
where Christian Herter, Secretary of the Army Thomas Gates, Secretary of the Treasury Robert Anderson and three Kennedy appointees—
Dean Rusk, Robert McNamara and Douglas Dillon—were waiting for
them. The main subject of discussion was Laos. Eisenhower called
it "the cork in the bottle." If it fell to the Communists, it was only a
matter of time before South Vietnam, Cambodia, Thailand and Burma
fell, too.

Herter added that Laos was entitled to aid under the SEATO pact, to
which the U.S. was a signatory. There was a problem, however, with
Britain and France, said Eisenhower—they didn't want SEATO to intervene in Laos. But if the U.S. couldn't get the assistance of its allies,
"then we must go it alone." That was how important Laos was. Kennedy
wanted to know how long it would take to get an American division into
Laos. Gates said seventeen days from the U.S., less if forces in the Pacific were deployed.

Eisenhower was still nettled by the missile-gap charge, which
Kennedy had pursued even after the Pentagon had briefed him on the
true situation. Maybe Kennedy had doubted—or wanted to doubt—
what he'd been told, but there was something he needed to know and understand. As the meeting broke up, Eisenhower told Kennedy, "You
have an invaluable asset in Polaris. It is invulnerable."[38]

The next day, under skies of blue and with freezing temperatures
steaming his breath, Kennedy dramatically intoned, "The torch has
been passed to a new generation . . ." Eisenhower, fidgeting, was already bored.

★ ★ ★ ★ ★

45

The End

The road ahead ran straight now, all the way to the end. There were no bends left in it, no crossroads, no interesting detours. Life as adventure was over. The power he had grown as used to as breathing had gone, and with it vanished excitement. Eisenhower was depressed for the first few months of his dull new existence, but he snapped out of it. In old age and sickness, he remained what he had always been—generous, busy and adaptable.

Mamie had done everything a woman could to turn the Gettysburg farmhouse into a real home, a place where they could be happy. Starting in 1955, she had begun remodeling it. By the time she was finished, there was little of the original structure left. What she was striving for was a Georgian look in white brick and fieldstone under a slate roof. During the years that she pushed this project along, Eisenhower was too busy to get involved. He gave the contractor only one instruction: "For God's sake, just get her what she wants and send me the bill!"[1]

When it was finally ready for occupancy in 1958, the farmhouse had fifteen rooms and eight baths. Most rooms were decorated, inevitably, in Mamie's favorite shades of pink and green. Ike got an oak-beamed study and a small room upstairs where he napped, called the General's Room.

Near the end of his presidency, Eisenhower bought a derelict nine-teenth-century schoolhouse less than a mile from the farmhouse. The schoolhouse was extensively remodeled to provide a home for John, his wife and their children. Ike had a private road built connecting John's house and his own, making it possible to travel between the two homes without leaving Eisenhower property.

Eisenhower liked to sit in his glassed-in porch, sprawled on a white wicker couch, and watch his purebred Aberdeen Angus herd grazing contentedly on the other side of his rose garden, but privacy was a prob-lem in the early years. Guests at a nearby motel and people who parked their cars on the edge of the property could see him on the glassed-in porch. He had a lot more privacy after one of his rich friends, Alton "Pete" Jones, bought three adjoining farms, on which he planted hun-dreds of strategically sited trees.[2]

While Eisenhower eventually found Gettysburg tolerable in the spring and summer, he had no intention of spending winters there. Fol-lowing Kennedy's inauguration, he and Mamie headed for Palm Springs, for a house at El Mirador Country Club recommended to them by Jackie Cochran.

He immediately found that he preferred Palm Springs to Augusta National, which had lost much of its charm after the Little Rock crisis. On his first visit to Augusta National following the forced integration of Little Rock Central High, he and Mamie had been met with hostile glances, not spontaneous applause, by sullen silence instead of south-ern hospitality. Palm Springs, on the other hand, was just as warm and a lot more sophisticated. From that time on, he spent November to April in California and May to November in Pennsylvania, and visited Au-gusta National only once a year for a week or so.

In Gettysburg, he had an office at the college, where he arrived at eight each morning, ready for work. During 1961–1962, he worked on the first volume of his presidential memoirs, *Mandate for Change*. Dur-ing the next two years he worked on Volume Two, *Waging Peace*. John had taken retirement from the Army to help him with his memoirs, and he also employed a former White House speechwriter, Bill Ewald. The presidential memoirs were worthy but dull, accurate without being re-vealing. Then, with these quasi-official tomes out of the way, he wrote a book that really did provide insights into his life and personality, *At Ease*, which, on publication in 1967, proved a major best-seller. He also helped John write *The Bitter Woods,* an authoritative account of the Battle of the Bulge, drawing freely on his remarkable memory of both men and events.

Eisenhower dictated letters, magazine articles and book chapters from the time he arrived at his office until ten-thirty, when he stopped for tea. After another hour of dictation, he went home for lunch with Mamie. Following a postlunch nap, he returned to the college in midafternoon and called it a day at five o'clock. Before dinner he took a short walk and hit a few golf balls. After dinner he read voraciously, mainly history and biography. On the weekends he played golf and bridge, hunted small game and shot crows.[3]

Even before Eisenhower left the White House, he had gotten into the habit of going to church nearly every Sunday. Both during his presidency and later he asked Billy Graham whether he truly believed in the existence of heaven and whether people met up there again with those they had loved in this world. Graham told him that such was Christ's promise and he believed it implicitly. The terrors of death were undoubtedly assuaged for Eisenhower by the prospect of being reunited with Ikky and Ida.[4]

During the 1960 election campaign, he had developed a contempt for John Kennedy that had nothing to do with Kennedy's youth or glamour. Eisenhower had arranged for Kennedy to be briefed on the true state of the nation's defenses, yet Kennedy had continued to claim there was a missile gap with the Soviets. To Ike, that wasn't politics—that was dishonesty.

Even so, Eisenhower had been favorably impressed at their two preinaugural meetings. He also privately praised Kennedy's cleverness in getting three prominent Republicans to take on three of the most controversial jobs in government—McNamara at Defense, Dillon at the Treasury and John McCone as head of the CIA. It wasn't completely surprising, then, that at their second meeting Kennedy had asked if he would be willing to help the new administration from time to time. Eisenhower had replied that he'd do so gladly, provided he wasn't expected to travel.[5]

Previously, former Presidents had gone into a kind of postpresidential purdah. Eisenhower was the first to be consulted regularly by his successors on important matters of state. He was also prepared to take up matters with them. When, in the fall of 1962, he learned that the

Studebaker Corporation's best hope of averting bankruptcy was its bid for a major defense contract, Eisenhower placed a call to John Kennedy. "Look, I have two men here with me and they tell me that unless Studebaker can get that tank contract, South Bend is going to be a disaster area." Within days, Studebaker got the tank contract.[6]

On November 22, 1963, Eisenhower was in New York for a lunchtime meeting with a group of prominent internationalists called UN–We Believe. Lunch for these notables, many of whom were millionaires, consisted of soup and sandwiches. The chairman, New York property developer William Zeckendorf, was calling the meeting to order when he was abruptly called out of the room. He returned a few minutes later, looking much older. The blood draining from his flabby features, Zeckendorf shook his head, like a man emerging from a trance. "I have terrible news—our President has been shot."

Eisenhower broke the stunned silence. "Killed?"

"No," said Zeckendorf. "All I know is, he has been shot. I believe he is still living."

The meeting hurriedly broke up and Eisenhower headed for his suite at the Waldorf-Astoria. Shortly after he arrived came news that Kennedy was dead. Eisenhower sent a telegram to Jacqueline Kennedy, expressing his and Mamie's grief. Then he wrote out a statement for the press, went out to the lobby and delivered it to a handful of journalists.

The next morning, he flew to Washington and met with Lyndon Johnson in the Executive Office Building. The two men talked alone for an hour and a half. Afterward, he sent an invitation to Harry Truman to ride with him and Mamie in the Kennedy funeral procession.[7]

The *Saturday Evening Post* asked him for an article on presidential successions, something that might help reassure a shaken country. Eisenhower said he would try. He arrived back at Gettysburg in the late afternoon twenty-four hours after the assassination, in a torrential downpour. Walking into the house shaking water off his hat, he grumbled that he didn't think it was possible to meet the *Post*'s Monday deadline. He met it, if by a whisker. While he was working on it Sunday morning came news that Oswald had been shot. "Good God," said Eisenhower. "What's going to happen next?"[8]

Before the ride to Arlington Cemetery two days later, Ike and Mamie and Truman and his daughter, Margaret, met at Blair House for refreshments. Eisenhower, sitting on a sofa, began reminiscing about the way Truman had dragged him out of Columbia and gotten him back into uniform to run NATO. "And you did a hell of a fine job, too," said Truman, who was sitting in a winged chair halfway across the room. Eisenhower got up from the sofa, picked up a side chair, went over and sat next to Truman. They chatted like old friends for the next twenty minutes, until the limousine arrived.[9]

Some months later, as he was working on the manuscript of *Waging Peace,* Bill Ewald said that maybe Truman's name belonged on the list of the greatest men Eisenhower had known. Ewald had suggested Truman's inclusion several times, but Eisenhower had invariably declined. This time, he nodded and cleared his throat as Ewald added "Harry S Truman," in pencil.[10]

Two years after John Kennedy's death, Arthur Schlesinger organized a poll of American historians, asking them to rate the presidents. To Eisenhower, this was little more than a cynical, early bid to ensure Kennedy an honored place in the nation's history. He was dismayed when Schlesinger's poll showed that Roosevelt, whom Eisenhower had never trusted or admired, was considered a great President. Worse, though, was the high ranking given to Truman, whom he considered incompetent. Truman was rated just below the greatest Presidents, while Eisenhower was placed well below average, rubbing shoulders with the half-forgotten shades of Chester A. Arthur and Franklin Pierce.[11]

He brooded on this for a while, deeply hurt, then wrote to his old friend Bill Robinson, telling him, "The other day I dashed off, from memory, the following as a memorandum for my files. The new economists and members of the [Kennedy] personality cult belittle the achievements of the devoted men and women who guided the Executive Branch from 1953 to 1961. Yet consider these accomplishments:

— Statehood for Alaska and Hawaii
— Building of the St. Lawrence Seaway
— End of Korean War; hereafter no American
    killed in combat
— Largest reduction in taxes to that time
— First Civil Rights law in 80 years
— Prevention of Communistic efforts to dominate
    Iran, Guatemala, Lebanon, Formosa, South
    Vietnam

— Reorganization of the Defense Department
— Initiation, and great progress in, most ambitious
   road program by any nation in all history
— Slowing up and practical elimination of
   inflation
— Initiation of Space program with successful
   orbit in less than three years
— Initiating a strong ballistic missile program
— Conceiving and building the Polaris program,
   with ships operating at sea within a single
   administration
— Starting Federal Medical Care for the aged
— Desegregation in Washington, D.C.
— Defense Education Bill
— Using Federal power to enforce orders of a
   Federal court in Arkansas, with no loss of
   life
— Establishment of the Department of Health,
   Education and Welfare
— Initiating of plan for social program in Latin
   America (later called Alliance for Progress)
— Atoms for Peace proposal

All this done with a Congress controlled by the opposition party for six years . . ."[12]

For all that this was a list of solid accomplishments, Eisenhower's greatest satisfaction was not his presidency. It was his years as Supreme Commander in World War II. The wartime adventures and comradeships loomed larger—and meant more—with age. "As the years go by I think that today I feel closer to the individuals of the Allied Forces of World War II than even when we were all together," he told Lieutenant General Sir Frederick "Boy" Browning.[13]

It was a blow, even though long expected, when the greatest of these old friends, Winston Churchill, died in January 1965. Eisenhower was among the few people invited to Churchill's funeral as personal guests of the Queen, and Lyndon Johnson asked him to head the American delegation.

Churchill's funeral seems to have prompted Eisenhower to turn his thoughts toward his own farewell. Upon his return, he began to dispose of his herd of prize-winning cattle. "I think I should tidy up my affairs," he told Arthur Nevins, the retired general who managed the farm. He also began urging Mamie to deed the property to the government. It wasn't easy, but she finally agreed. The nation would get the farm after she, too, was dead.[14]

During his White House years, Eisenhower had expected to be buried with Mamie, and she already had a plot reserved next to her parents' grave in Denver. The creation of his presidential library created another possibility. Eisenhower decided in the winter of 1963, while he was in Palm Springs, that he would be buried not in Denver but in Abilene, where a chapel was going to be built almost within the shadow of the family home. The chapel was redesigned to provide enough room for him and Mamie—and one other. In 1966, Eisenhower and the Army finalized their plans: he would get two funerals—a state funeral in Washington and a military farewell in Abilene. His mortal remains would be interred in a standard eighty-dollar Army coffin.[15]

In June 1966, shortly after the chapel was finished, he flew to Denver and collected Ikky's body. Then Eisenhower flew with it to Kansas. Ikky was reburied, in the chapel. In the fall of 1967, he stopped off to visit Ikky's grave—now marked with a tiny plaque—on the way to Palm Springs. Grief for his dead son seemed as powerful now as it had been when the child died.[16]

His winter sojourn in Palm Springs was marred by yet another heart attack. Eisenhower had, in recent years, suffered agonizing pains from angina and took nitroglycerine regularly. Flown back to Walter Reed from California in April 1968, he was installed in its grandest suite, on Ward Eight. When, a few weeks later, Nixon declared his candidacy for the presidency, Eisenhower offered a strong endorsement.

Shortly after Nixon's nomination at the Republican convention in August, Eisenhower suffered his fourth heart attack. He survived again, but now a large pacemaker was strapped to his chest and his strength had been drained by the numerous electric shocks from the defibrillator that got his heart beating again. Al Gruenther came to see him several days later. Still groggy, Eisenhower looked up into the face of his old friend and favorite bridge partner. "Have I turned into a vegetable yet?"[17]

The night of the 1968 election, a victorious Nixon came to see

Eisenhower—still in Walter Reed—and receive his congratulations. Then Nixon headed for Florida. While he was there, he chose Henry Kissinger to head the National Security Council, and Kissinger went to consult Eisenhower on how to improve NSC procedures.

Having written two books that were scathing about the Eisenhower administration's foreign and defense policies and never having met him, Kissinger wasn't expecting much. What he found was a man who was physically weak but mentally strong. "He had not long to live. Despite this, his forcefulness was surprising. His syntax, which seemed so awkward in print, became much more graphic when enlivened by his cold, deep blue, extraordinarily penetrating eyes and when given emphasis by his still commanding voice."[18]

A few weeks before he died, Eisenhower received a visit from Lieutenant General Vernon Walters, the talented linguist who had often served as his interpreter. He said he did not expect to leave the hospital alive, but "how can I complain when all the daydreams of my youth have been fulfilled?"[19]

In March 1969, as Eisenhower's lungs began filling up with fluid, tubes were pushed up his nose to provide him with oxygen. His time now was very short. With death almost upon him and his strength nearly gone, Ike motioned to Milton, who was standing near the bed. Milton bent down, and Ike whispered huskily to his brother, "I want you to know how much you have always meant to me."[20]

On March 28, with his family clustered at his bedside and Mamie tenderly clutching his large right hand, Eisenhower gasped, "I want to go. *God, take me!*"

★ ★ ★ ★ ★
NOTES

Glossary of
Frequently Used Abbreviations

EL	Dwight D. Eisenhower Library, Abilene, Kansas
COHP	Columbia University Oral History Project
FDRL	Franklin D. Roosevelt Library, Hyde Park, New York
FRUS	State Department, *Foreign Relations of the United States*
GCMF	George C. Marshall Foundation, Virginia Military Institute
HSTL	Harry S Truman Library, Independence, Missouri
MD, LC	Manuscript Division, Library of Congress
PDDE	Albert D. Chander, et al., eds., *The Papers of Dwight D. Eisenhower* (Baltimore: 1970).
PPP	U.S. Government Printing Office, *The Public Papers of the Presidents*
USAMHI	U.S. Army Military History Institute, Carlisle, Pennsylvania
USMA	U.S. Military Academy, Special Collections and Archives

Chapter 1: D. Dwight Eisenhower

1. Merle Miller, *Ike the Soldier* (New York: 1985), 59.
2. Bela Kornitzer, *The Great American Heritage* (New York: 1955), 26.
3. Carry Nation, *The Use and Need of Carry A. Nation* (Topeka: 1908).
4. Ray I. Witter interview, EL.
5. Doris Faber, *The Presidents' Mothers* (New York: 1978), 66–69; Kunnigunde Duncan, *Earning the Right to Do Fancywork* (Lawrence, Kansas: 1957), 5.
6. Kenneth S. Davis, *Soldier of Democracy* (New York: 1945), 32–33.

7. Thomas Braniger, "No Villains, No Heroes," *Kansas History* (Autumn 1992).
8. Kornitzer, 108.
9. Davis, 42–43.
10. Abram Forney interview, EL; Miller, 60.
11. Kornitzer, 29; Duncan, 15.
12. John Witter, *Six Roads from Abilene* (Seattle: 1954), 31.
13. Kornitzer, 107.
14. Witter, 48.
15. Dwight D. Eisenhower, *At Ease: Stories I Tell to Friends* (New York: 1967), 36; Witter, 30.
16. *Abilene Daily Reflector,* Dec. 5, 7, 1896.
17. *At Ease,* 31.
18. There is a comprehensive inventory of the books found in the family home at the Eisenhower Library. The Eisenhowers owned seven Bibles, three of them in German, five copies of the New Testament and dozens of books with religious themes.
19. Duncan, 16–17.
20. Davis, 44.
21. Forney interview, EL.
22. File, "Fourth Street Home," EL.

Chapter 2: 201 South East Fourth Street

1. Kenneth S. Davis, *Soldier of Democracy* (New York: 1945), 11, 65; Bela Kornitzer, *The Great American Heritage* (New York: 1955), 195.
2. Kornitzer, 65.
3. John Witter, *Six Roads from Abilene* (Seattle: 1954), 44; Davis, 52.
4. Milton Eisenhower interview, EL; Kornitzer, 37; Witter, 45–46.
5. Kornitzer, vi, 27.
6. Witter, 69.
7. Davis, 73.
8. Doris Faber, *The Presidents' Mothers* (New York: 1978), 75; Davis, 52–53.
9. Milton Eisenhower interview, EL.
10. Kunnigunde Duncan, *Earning the Right to Do Fancywork* (Lawrence, Kansas: 1957), 11.
11. Witter, 63; Levi J. Asper interview, EL; Milton Eisenhower interview, EL; Kornitzer, 41.
12. Faber, 76; Duncan, 12; Witter, 58.
13. Dwight D. Eisenhower, *At Ease: Stories I Tell to Friends* (New York: 1967), 51–52.
14. Kornitzer, 193–194.
15. Nettie Stover Jackson interview, EL.

16. Orin Snider interview, EL; Witter, 35.
17. Duncan, 4; Roy I. Witter interview, EL; Davis, 72.
18. Davis, 67–68.
19. Witter, 80.
20. Levi J. Asper interview, EL; John H. Long interview, EL.
21. Davis, 69.
22. Witter, 76–77.
23. *At Ease,* 97.
24. Witter, 72–74; Davis, 78–80; Kornitzer, 47–48.

Chapter 3: Little Ike

1. See, Lawrence A. Cremin, *A History of Education in American Culture* (New York: 1953); Edward F. Denison, *The Sources of Economic Growth in the United States* (New York: 1962), and *Accounting for United States Economic Growth, 1929–1959* (Washington, D.C.: 1965).
2. Dwight D. Eisenhower, *At Ease: Stories I Tell to Friends* (New York: 1967), 94; Kenneth S. Davis, *Soldier of Democracy* (New York: 1945), 74–77; Bela Kornitzer, *The Great American Heritage* (New York: 1955), 49; Levi J. Asper interview, EL; Merle Miller, *Ike the Soldier* (New York: 1987), 89.
3. Miller, 87.
4. Davis, 81–82; Steve Neal, *The Eisenhowers: Reluctant Dynasty* (New York: 1967), 16.
5. Ibid.; Miller, 105.
6. *At Ease,* 80–81.
7. Kornitzer, 46.
8. Miller, 86.
9. Orin Snider interview, EL; Howard Funk interview, EL.
10. Abilene High School yearbook, *The Helianthus,* for 1909.
11. John F. McDonnell interview, EL.
12. Ibid.; Davis, 90–91.
13. *At Ease,* 100.
14. John F. McDonnell interview, EL; Davis, 94.
15. *At Ease,* 89.
16. Davis, 17, 83.

Chapter 4: The Appointment

1. Kenneth S. Davis, *Soldier of Democracy* (New York: 1945), 99.
2. John Witter, *Six Roads from Abilene* (Seattle: 1954), 92.
3. Davis, 100.

4. Robert H. Ferrell, "Eisenhower Was a Democrat," *Kansas History* (Autumn 1990).

5. John F. McDonnell interview, EL.

6. Orin Snider interview, Levi J. Asper interview and Mrs. Robert J. Long interview, all EL.

7. Davis, 106.

8. Bella Kornitzer, *The Great American Heritage* (New York: 1955), 129.

9. Ferrell, *loc. cit.*

10. Stephen Ambrose, *Milton S. Eisenhower* (Baltimore: 1986), 26–30.

11. Merle Miller, *Ike the Soldier* (New York: 1987), 114; McDonnell interview.

12. Daniel Holt and James Leyerzapf, eds., *Dwight D. Eisenhower: Prewar Diaries and Selected Papers, 1905–1941* (Baltimore: 1998), 9.

13. Davis, 114–116.

14. John H. Long interview, EL.

15. Abram Forney interview, EL.

16. Davis, 116–117; Kornitzer, 42–43.

17. Holt and Leyerzapf, 8.

18. Miller, 115; Dwight D. Eisenhower, *At Ease: Stories I Tell to Friends* (New York: 1967), 105–106. Ike's own account of how he got the appointment is not strictly accurate. Like most memoirs, it is an account of what he believed happened, not what the documentary record shows.

19. Holt and Leyerzapf, 9.

20. *At Ease,* 106.

21. Davis, 118.

22. Levi Asper interview, EL.

Chapter 5: The Cadet

1. Merle Miller, *Ike the Soldier* (New York: 1987), 14.

2. The number of cadets sworn in on June 14, 1911, is put at 247 in "Vital Statistics: The Class of 1915," in Ike's 201 File at the Eisenhower Library.

3. Dwight D. Eisenhower, *At Ease: Stories I Tell to Friends* (New York: 1967), 4.

4. Ibid., 8; Miller, 23.

5. *At Ease,* 7.

6. Ibid., 18.

7. *New York Times,* Nov. 18, 1912.

8. *At Ease,* 14.

9. Miller, 37; Kenneth S. Davis, *Soldier of Democracy* (New York: 1945), 26.

10. Dwight D. Eisenhower Vertical File, Special Collections, West Point.

11. Davis, 110.

12. Bela Kornitzer, *The Great American Heritage* (New York: 1955), 36.

13. John H. McDonnell interview, EL; Davis, 141–142.

14. Ibid., 143; Orin Snider interview, EL.

15. Letter, DDE to Dorothy Mills, March 27, 1915, Gordon Young papers, USAMHI Archives.
16. Unpublished mss. "Ike and Gladys—The Summer of 1915," by Cole Kingseed, Eisenhower Vertical File, Special Collections, West Point; Davis, 143.
17. Letter, DDE to Ruby Norman, Nov. 5, 1913, EL.
18. Letter, DDE to Ruby Norman, Nov. 20, 1913, EL.
19. Letters, DDE to Ruby Norman, Nov. 24, Nov. 30, 1913, EL.
20. *At Ease,* 16.
21. Davis, 118.
22. Letters, DDE to Dorothy Mills, Feb. 23, March 22 and 26, 1915, Gordon Young papers, USAMHI Archives.
23. Miller, 42–43.
24. *At Ease,* 25.

Chapter 6: Miss Mamie

1. Unpublished mss. "Ike and Gladys—The Summer of 1915," by Cole Kingseed, Eisenhower Vertical File, Special Collections, West Point.
2. As Julie Nixon Eisenhower recalled, "Ike, to his dying day, found it difficult to express his feelings." Merle Miller, *Ike the Soldier* (New York: 1987), 166.
3. Kenneth S. Davis, *Soldier of Democracy* (New York: 1945), 157–158.
4. Maud Hart Lovelace interview with Mamie in 1943, in Delos Lovelace Papers, EL; Miller, 138.
5. Alden Hatch, *Red Carpet for Mamie* (New York: 1954), 71.
6. Miller, 144.
7. Lovelace; John S. D. Eisenhower, *Strictly Personal* (New York: 1974), 12.
8. Lovelace.
9. Susan Eisenhower, *Mrs. Ike* (New York: 1996), 35.
10. Vivian Cadden, "Mamie Eisenhower Talks About Fifty Years of Marriage," *McCall's* (Sept. 1966).
11. Miller, 129.
12. Steve Neal, *The Eisenhowers: Reluctant Dynasty* (Philadelphia: 1977), 38; Lester David and Irene David, *Ike and Mamie* (New York: 1989), 18.
13. Dwight D. Eisenhower, *At Ease: Stories I Tell to Friends* (New York: 1967), 121–122.
14. Susan Eisenhower, 40.
15. Hatch, 89–90; David and David, 60–61.
16. Susan Eisenhower, 42.
17. David and David, 66; Miller, 158.
18. Arthur Nevins interview, EL; Miller, 161.
19. Susan Eisenhower, 51; Hatch, 110.

20. *At Ease,* 133.
21. John Leonard interview, EL.
22. Miller, 168.
23. Alden Hatch, *General Ike* (New York: 1945), 63.
24. Transcript of "Eisenhower on Lincoln as Commander in Chief," broadcast by NBC television Feb. 11, 1963.
25. Letter, DDE to Frederick Summers, Aug. 26, 1943, EL.
26. Hatch, *General Ike,* 64.
27. *At Ease,* 151.
28. Miller, 173.
29. Susan Eisenhower, 55–56.
30. Letter, Norman Randolph to DDE, June 20, 1945, EL.

Chapter 7: Ikky

1. There is a copy of *Tank Tunes* in Ike's 201 File at the Eisenhower Library.
2. Although nearly all accounts give the spelling as *Icky,* Mamie spelled her son's name *Ikky,* and she must be considered the ultimate authority on this point.
3. Efficiency Report, July 26, 1919: "As senior officer on duty in Tank Corps camps at Meade and Colt he had the duties and responsibilities commensurate with the rank of brigadier general. . . . I regard this officer as one of the most efficient officers I have known."
4. Letter, Ira C. Welborn to the AG, Jan. 30, 1919, Eisenhower 201 File, EL. He scribbled the note to his father across the bottom of his copy of Welborn's letter.
5. John E. Wickman, "Ike and the Great Truck Train—1919" *Kansas History* (Autumn 1990).
6. "Report on Transcontinental Trip," Nov. 3, 1919, Eisenhower Papers, EL.
7. Susan Eisenhower, *Mrs. Ike* (New York: 1996), 59.
8. Dorothy Brandon, *Mamie: A Portrait of a First Lady* (New York: 1954), 106–107.
9. "Great Moments in Construction History," *Constructor* (August 1973).
10. Dwight D. Eisenhower, *At Ease: Stories I Tell to Friends* (New York: 1967), 157–166.
11. Martin Blumenson, *The Patton Papers* (Boston: 1982), I, 479.
12. *At Ease,* 180.
13. This story was first related in Kenneth Davis's *Soldier of Democracy,* and located at Fort Lewis, Washington, in 1940. In the margins of Ike's copy of the book, however, he wrote, "Many years before." Ike's previous experience commanding troops was at Camp Meade.
14. Julie Nixon Eisenhower, *Special People* (New York: 1978), 199–200; Susan Eisenhower, 60.

15. Letter, Mamie Doud Eisenhower to John Sheldon Doud et al.; no date, but evidently October 1920, Barbara Eisenhower Papers, EL.
16. Susan Eisenhower, 62.
17. Lester David and Irene David, *Ike and Mamie* (New York: 1981), 73–74.
18. Mamie Eisenhower interview, EL.
19. *At Ease,* 181; John Gunther, *Eisenhower* (New York: 1952), 58; letter, DDE to Louis Marx, Jan. 27, 1948, Eisenhower Papers, EL.
20. Carlo D'Este, *Patton: A Genius for War* (New York: 1995), 291–292.
21. *At Ease,* 171.
22. Steve Neal, *The Eisenhowers: Reluctant Dynasty* (New York: 1978), 35; Alden Hatch, *Red Carpet for Mamie* (New York: 1954), 69–70; Stephen Ambrose, *Eisenhower* (New York: 1984), I, 71–72.
23. Dwight D. Eisenhower, "A Tank Discussion," *Infantry Journal* (Nov. 1920).
24. *At Ease,* 173.
25. Letter, DDE to the Adjutant General, June 17, 1921; Memo, Eli A. Helmick to the AG, Nov. 1, 1921, Eisenhower 201 File, EL.
26. *At Ease,* 178.
27. Memo, AG to Pershing, Nov. 16, 1921, Eisenhower 201 File, EL.
28. Memo, Helmick to the Chief of Staff, Dec. 14, 1921; the Asst C/S to the AG, Dec. 14, 1921, Eisenhower 201 File, EL.

Chapter 8: Number One

1. David McCullough, *The Path Between the Seas* (New York: 1979), 605–610.
2. Dwight D. Eisenhower, *At Ease: Stories I Tell to Friends* (New York: 1967), 184.
3. Alden Hatch, *Red Carpet for Mamie* (New York: 1954), 127; Merle Miller, *Ike the Soldier* (New York: 1987), 207.
4. Susan Eisenhower, *Mrs. Ike* (New York: 1996), 76–78; Steve Neal, *The Eisenhowers: Reluctant Dynasty* (New York: 1978), 65–66; Virginia Conner, *What Father Forbade* (Philadelphia: 1957), 120–121.
5. Susan Eisenhower, 77; Hatch, *Red Carpet,* 128.
6. Alden Hatch, *General Ike* (New York: 1946), 72.
7. Mamie Eisenhower interview, EL; Hatch, *Red Carpet,* 129.
8. Neal, 65–66.
9. Roscoe B. Woodruff interview, EL; letter, Mamie Eisenhower to John and Elivera Doud, no date, but written aboard ship in 1922 en route to Panama, Barbara Eisenhower Papers, EL.
10. Rosalind Massow, "Mamie and Ike Talk About 50 Years of Marriage," *Parade* (June 26, 1966).
11. Dwight D. Eisenhower, "What I Have Learned," *Saturday Review* (September 10, 1966).
12. Miller, 209.

13. Bradford Chynoweth memoir, "Army Recollections," USAMHI Archives.
14. Kenneth S. Davis, *Soldier of Democracy* (New York: 1945), 194. Ike's copy is at the Gettysburg farm.
15. *At Ease,* 195.
16. Letter, Ira C. Welborn to the AG, April 14, 1921; message, AG to Eisenhower, Oct. 11, 1922, both in Eisenhower 201 File, EL.
17. Efficiency Report, August. 31, 1924, Eisenhower 201 File.
18. *At Ease,* 198.
19. Ibid., 199.
20. Ibid., 201.
21. Carlo D'Este, *Patton: A Genius for War* (New York: 1995), 332.
22. Mark C. Bender, *Watershed at Leavenworth* (Fort Leavenworth, Kansas: 1992), 34.
23. Maureen Clark, *Captain's Wife, General's Lady* (New York: 1954), 49.
24. Roscoe Woodruff interview, EL. Woodruff's view may have been influenced by the fact that shortly before D-Day Eisenhower removed Woodruff from command of one of the corps that was training to make the assault.
25. "The Leavenworth Course," by a Young Graduate, *Infantry Journal* (June 1927).
26. John W. Leonard interview, EL.
27. Memo, "Class Standing," June 18, 1926, General Service Schools Fort Leavenworth, in Eisenhower 201 File, EL.

Chapter 9: Guidebook Ike

1. Kenneth S. Davis, *Soldier of Democracy* (New York: 1945), 215.
2. Ike's copy is in the Gettysburg home.
3. Alden Hatch, *Red Carpet for Mamie* (New York: 1954), 96–97.
4. Dwight D. Eisenhower, *At Ease: Stories I Tell to Friends* (New York: 1967), 203.
5. Edgar T. Collins to the Chief of Infantry, Dec. 10, 1926, Eisenhower 201 File, EL
6. Xenophon H. Price, Memo, "Assignment of Duties," Jan. 26, 1927, Eisenhower 201 File, EL
7. Efficiency Report, June 30, 1927, and Pershing memo to Robert H. Allen, Aug. 15, 1927, both in Eisenhower 201 File, EL.
8. *At Ease,* 205.
9. Dwight D. Eisenhower, "An Enlisted Reserve for the Regular Army," 1928, the Army War College; W. D. Connor, memo dated May 5, 1928, Eisenhower 201 File, EL.
10. Susan Eisenhower, *Mrs. Ike* (New York: 1996), 91–92, 151.
11. Robert L. Bullard, *Personalities and Reminiscences of the War* (New York: 1925), 114.

12. Unpublished memoir, "Army Recollections." Bradford G. Chynoweth Papers, USAMHI.
13. Rosalind Massow, "Ike and Mamie Talk About 50 Years of Marriage," *Parade* (June 26, 1966).
14. Merle Miller, *Ike the Soldier* (New York: 1987), 243; Geoffrey Perret, *Old Soldiers Never Die* (New York: 1996), 105–108.
15. Letter, George A. Horkan to DDE, Aug. 15, 1994, Eisenhower Papers, EL.
16. Eisenhower diary, Sept. 24, 1929, Eisenhower Papers, EL.
17. Ed Cray, *Marshall* (New York: 1991), 110; Steve Neal, *The Eisenhowers: Reluctant Dynasty* (New York: 1978), 76–77; *At Ease,* 208.

Chapter 10: The Flaming Pen

1. Albert Wedemeyer, *General Wedemeyer Reports!* (New York: 1958), 16–17.
2. Unpublished memoir, "One Soldier's Journey," George Van Horn Moseley Papers, Manuscript Division, LC.
3. Eisenhower diary, Nov. 9, 1929, Eisenhower Papers, EL.
4. Guayule trip diary, Eisenhower Papers, EL.
5. Dwight D. Eisenhower, *At Ease: Stories I Tell to Friends* (New York: 1967), 210–211.
6. "Brief History of Planning for Procurement and Industrial Mobilization Since the World War," Eisenhower 201 File, EL.
7. Eisenhower diary, Nov. 24, 1930; Efficiency Report, Jan. 6, 1931, Eisenhower 201 File, EL.
8. Letter, MacArthur to DDE, Nov. 4, 1931; Eisenhower diary, Dec. 1, 1931.
9. John S. D. Eisenhower, *Strictly Personal* (New York: 1974), 6.
10. See, Eisenhower diary, March 28 and April 27, 1931, Eisenhower Papers, EL; Daniel D. Holls and James Leyerzapf, eds., *Eisenhower: Prewar Diaries and Selected Papers, 1905–1941* (Baltimore: 1998), 115–116n.
11. Eisenhower diary, Feb. 15, 1932, Eisenhower Papers, EL.
12. Walter W. Waters, *The B.E.F.* (New York: 1933).
13. Moseley, "One Soldier's Journey," II, 138–139, MD, LC.
14. Waters, 90–102, 174–178.
15. Order, Patrick J. Hurley to MacArthur, July 28, 1932, Bonus March File, Herbert Hoover Library; Perry L. Miles, *Fallen Leaves* (Berkeley, Calif.: 1964), 307.
16. *At Ease,* 216.
17. Letter, Mamie Eisenhower to John and Elivera Doud, July 30, 1932, Barbara Eisenhower Papers, EL.
18. Miles, *op. cit;* letter, Miles to MacArthur, Aug. 28, 1952, MacArthur Memorial and Archives.
19. Edmund Starling, *Starling of the White House* (New York: 1948), 296–297.

20. *At Ease,* 217. Cf. Dwight D. Eisenhower interview, Herbert Hoover Library.

21. Eisenhower diary, Aug. 10, 1932, Eisenhower Papers EL; "Report from the Chief of Staff, United States Army, to the Secretary of War on the Employment of Federal troops in Civil Disturbance in the District of Columbia, July 28–30," Eisenhower 201 File, EL.

22. Memo, the AGO, Feb. 20, 1933, Eisenhower 201 File, EL.

23. Eisenhower diary, Feb. 28, March 10, Oct. 29, 1933, Eisenhower Papers, EL.

24. Unpublished memoir, "Army Recollections," Bradford G. Chynoweth Papers, USAMHI Archives.

25. Holt and Leyerzapf, 75; John R. M. Wilson, *Herbert Hoover and the Armed Forces* (New York: 1993), 122–130.

26. Kenneth S. Davis, *Soldier of Democracy* (New York: 1945), 240.

27. Letter, Mamie Eisenhower to John and Elivera Doud, Oct. 6, 1932, Barbara Eisenhower Papers, EL.

28. Stephen Ambrose, *Milton S. Eisenhower* (Baltimore: 1985), 46–48.

29. Steve Neal, *The Eisenhowers: Reluctant Dynasty* (New York: 1978), 75.

30. John S. D. Eisenhower, 8–9.

31. Merle Miller, *Ike the Soldier* (New York: 1987), 45.

32. *At Ease,* 220.

Chapter 11: The House on the Wall

1. Dwight D. Eisenhower, *At Ease: Stories I Tell to Friends* (New York: 1967), 111.

2. Letter, DDE to Dorothy Mills, March 27, 1915, Gordon Young Papers, USAMHI Archives.

3. Letter, Mamie Eisenhower to John and Elivera Doud, Feb. 13, 1936, Barbara Eisenhower Papers, EL; Susan Eisenhower, *Mrs. Ike* (New York· 1996), 133–134.

4. War Department Special Orders 220, Douglas MacArthur 201 File, MacArthur Memorial and Archives.

5. James Ord diary, Oct. 2, 1931, Eisenhower Papers, El; *At Ease,* 223.

6. Press release, "The Cradle of Philippine Defense," n.d., 1941, MacArthur Memorial and Archives.

7. Manuel Quezon, *The Good Fight* (New York: 1944), 155–156; Douglas MacArthur, *Reminiscences* (New York: 1964), 102.

8. Ricardo Trota José, *The Philippine Army, 1935–1942* (Manila: 1992), 32 passim.

9. Eisenhower diary, May 29, 1936, Eisenhower Papers, EL.

10. Eisenhower diary, February 15, 1936, Eisenhower Papers, EL.

11. Eisenhower diary, May 29, 1936, July 16, 1939, Eisenhower Papers, EL.

12. Letter, Mamie Eisenhower to John and Elivera Doud, Feb. 13, 1936, Barbara Eisenhower Papers, EL.

13. Letter, Malin Craig to Douglas MacArthur, Aug. 6, 1937, MacArthur 201 File, MacArthur Memorial and Archives.

14. Geoffrey Perret, *Old Soldiers Never Die: The Life of Douglas MacArthur* (New York: 1996), 206–207.

15. *At Ease,* 226; Peter Lyon, *The Hero* (Boston: 1974), 79.

16. Letters, Dwight D. Eisenhower to Emily Ord, Jan. 31, 1938, and to T. J. Spencer, March 26, 1938, Eisenhower Papers, EL; *At Ease,* 227.

17. "Sixty-Ninth Annual Report of the Graduates of the U.S. Military Academy," (Newburgh, N.Y.: 1938), 277.

18. Eisenhower diary, April 14, 1938, Eisenhower Papers, EL.

19. John S. D. Eisenhower, *Strictly Personal* (New York: 1975), 27; Cable, Adjutant General, Philippine Department, to Adjutant General, War Department, March 3, 1938; Memo, Adjutant General to Chief of Staff, March 17, 1938, Eisenhower 201 File, EL.

20. J. Earl Schaefer interview, EL.

21. John S. D. Eisenhower interview, EL.

22. Eisenhower diary, Nov. 5, 1938, Eisenhower Papers, EL.

23. Efficiency Report, Dec. 31, 1937, Eisenhower 201 File, EL.

24. John Eisenhower (Burg interview); Eisenhower diary, Sept. 3, 1939, EL.

25. William L. Lee (Burg interview) and Hugh A. Parker (Burg interview), EL; John S. D. Eisenhower, *Strictly Personal,* 22.

26. "Application for Pilot's License," July 1, 1939, Eisenhower 201 File. Daniel D. Holt and James Leyerzapf, eds., *Eisenhower: Prewar Diaries and Selected Papers, 1905–1941* (Baltimore: 1998), 141–144.

Chapter 12: Star Bright

1. Cable, Sykes to Eisenhower, Jan. 5, 1940, Eisenhower 201 File; Eisenhower diary, Sept. 27, 1940; letter, DDE to Leonard T. Gerow, Nov. 25, 1940, Eisenhower Papers, EL.

2. John S. D. Eisenhower interview and William Simpson interview, both in EL; letter, DDE to Everett Hughes, Eisenhower Papers, EL.

3. Dwight D. Eisenhower, *At Ease: Stories I Tell to Friends* (New York: 1967), 236.

4. Dwight D. Eisenhower interview, EL.

5. Maurine Clark, *Captain's Wife, General's Lady* (New York: 1954), 71.

6. Mark Clark, *Calculated Risk* (New York: 1950), 9–11. Cf. Geoffrey Perret, *There's a War to Be Won* (New York: 1993), 38–39.

7. Maurine Clark, 72.

8. John S. D. Eisenhower, *Strictly Personal* (New York: 1974), 28–29.

9. *At Ease,* 237.

10. Susan Eisenhower, *Mrs. Ike* (New York: 1996), 161–162; letter, DDE to Leonard T. Gerow, Nov. 25, 1940, Eisenhower Papers, EL.

11. Letter, DDE to Everett Hughes, Nov. 26, 1940, EL.
12. Memo from Major General Walter C. Sweeney, titled, "Commendation," June 19, 1940, Eisenhower 201 File, EL.
13. James Stack interview, EL.
14. Letters, DDE to Leonard T. Gerow, Aug. 23, 1940, and to Everett Hughes, Nov. 26, 1940, Eisenhower Papers, EL.
15. Martin Blumenson, ed. *The Patton Papers* (Boston: 1970), II, 15; letter, DDE to Patton, Sept. 17, 1940, Eisenhower Papers, EL.
16. Letter, Patton to Eisenhower, Oct. 1, 1940, Eisenhower Papers, EL.
17. Letter, DDE to Leonard T. Gerow, Nov. 18, 1940, EL.
18. Letter, DDE to Patton, September 17, 1940. EL.
19. Kenneth Davis, *Soldier of Democracy* (New York: 1945), 263.
20. Daniel Holt and James Leyerzapf, eds., *Dwight D. Eisenhower: Prewar Diaries and Selected Papers, 1905–1941* (Baltimore: 1998), 503–505.
21. Mark Clark interview, USAMHI Archives.
22. Geoffrey Perret, *Old Soldiers Never Die* (New York: 1996), 374–376, 392, 431–432, 440–442.
23. Richard Ketchum, *The Borrowed Years: America on the Road to War* (New York: 1984), 650.
24. Letter, DDE to P. A. Hodgson, November 4, 1941, EL; Mabel Lovelace interview with Mamie in 1943, in the Delos Lovelace Papers, EL.
25. Alden Hatch, *General Ike* (New York: 1945), 107.

Chapter 13: War Plans

1. Forrest Pogue, *George C. Marshall: Ordeal and Hope* (New York: 1966), 235, 337.
2. Dwight D. Eisenhower, *Crusade in Europe* (New York: 1948), 14.
3. Kenneth S. Davis, *Soldier of Democracy* (New York: 1945), 281–282; Alden Hatch, *General Ike* (New York: 1945), 108–109. In his account, Hatch changed Richardson's name, presumably at Richardson's request, to Bill Kittrell.
4. Samuel E. Anderson interview, Air Force Historical Agency, Maxwell AFB, Alabama.
5. Dwight D. Eisenhower interview, EL. This is a slightly different and, I believe, more accurate version than that better-known account based on *Crusade in Europe.*
6. Pogue, 339.
7. Robert Ferrell, ed., *Diaries of Dwight D. Eisenhower* (New York: 1981), 45.
8. Letter, DDE to Daniel Van Voorhis, Feb. 24, 1942, EL; Stephen Ambrose, *Eisenhower* (New York: 1984), I, 136.
9. Letters, DDE to Leroy Lutes, Dec. 31, 1941, and P. A. Hodgson, March 2, 1942, EL.

10. Ferrell, 51.

11. Dwight D. Eisenhower, *At Ease: Stories I Tell to Friends* (New York: 1967), 249–250; Pogue, 338.

12. Ferrell, 52; John S. D. Eisenhower interview, EL.

13. Eugene Beebe interview, Air Force Historical Agency, Maxwell AFB, Alabama. Beebe was Arnold's aide and was present at many of these sessions.

14. Maurice Matloff and Edward M. Snell, *Strategic Planning for Coalition Warfare* (Washington, D.C.: 1953), 32–62, 97–119.

15. Mark Clark, *Calculated Risk* (New York: 1950), 16–17.

16. Albert D. Chandler, ed., *The Papers of Dwight D. Eisenhower* (Baltimore: 1970), I, 62; Ferrell, 43. Hereafter, *PDDE.*

17. Ferrell, 44, 46.

18. Ibid., 49, 51.

19. *PDDE,* I, 220.

20. Donald Smythe, *General of the Armies* (Bloomington, Ind.: 1986), 88–94.

21. Pogue, 290–295.

22. Thomas Betts interview, EL.

23. James Stack interview, EL. Stack was a key figure in the creation of the OPD.

24. Ray Cline, *Washington Command Post* (Washington, D.C.: 1951), Chapter 1.

25. John E. Hull, "Autobiography," John Hull Papers, USAMHI Archives.

26. Arthur Bryant, *The Turn of the Tide* (London: 1957), 422–429.

27. Ferrell, 58.

28. *Crusade in Europe,* 49–50.

29. Charles Bolté interview, EL.

30. Ferrell, 59–60.

31. Mark Clark, 20.

32. *Crusade in Europe,* 50.

33. Hatch, 115; Chandler, I, 311.

34. This photograph appears in John S. D. Eisenhower, *Strictly Personal* (New York: 1974).

35. Maurine Clark, *Captain's Wife, General's Lady* (New York: 1954), 97.

Chapter 14: Change of Plan

1. Kay Summersby Morgan, *Past Forgetting* (New York: 1976), 41.

2. Kenneth S. Davis, *Soldier of Democracy* (New York: 1945), 314; Charles Bolté interview, EL, and Zoebelein interview, USAMHI Archives.

3. Butcher diary, July 8, August 10, 1942, EL.

4. Dwight D. Eisenhower, *Letters to Mamie* (New York: 1978), 34, 38.

5. Ibid., 25, 35.

6. Bolté interview, EL.

7. Davis, 315; Harry C. Butcher diary, Oct. 8, 1942, EL.

8. Dwight D. Eisenhower, *Crusade in Europe* (New York: 1948), 58–59.

9. Butcher diary, July 14, 1942, EL.

10. Mark Clark, *Calculated Risk* (New York: 1950), 27–28.

11. Thomas T. Handy interview, EL.

12. *Crusade in Europe,* 18–19.

13. Bolté interview, EL.

14. Events soon made Ike's calculations look optimistic. On August 17, the British landed five thousand Canadians plus a force of commandos and fifty American Rangers at Dieppe to test German defenses. Within twelve hours two-thirds of the attackers were killed or captured. The rest were hurriedly withdrawn. After the war, Ike admitted that the critics had been right and he had been wrong about Sledgehammer. See, *Crusade in Europe,* 71.

15. Butcher diary, July 23, 1942, EL.

16. John S. D. Eisenhower's "Commentary" in *Letters to Mamie;* Stephen Ambrose, *Eisenhower* (New York: 1983), I, 183.

17. *Crusade in Europe,* 79.

18. Winston S. Churchill, *The Second World War* (Boston: 1949), II, 236 passim.

19. Jacques Raphael-Leygues and François Flohic, *Darlan* (Paris: 1986).

20. Clark, 40.

21. Robert D. Murphy, COHP.

22. Henri Giraud, *Mes Evasions* (Paris: 1949).

23. *PDDE,* I, 562.

24. Jean Lacouture, *De Gaulle* (Paris: 1984), I, 602; Lucian Truscott, *Command Decisions* (New York: 1951), 78.

25. Clark, 72.

26. *Crusade in Europe,* 88.

27. Paul W. Tibbets, Jr., *The Tibbets Story* (New York: 1977), 108–109.

28. Geoffrey Perret, *Winged Victory* (New York: 1994), 245–246, 449; *Crusade in Europe,* 97.

Chapter 15: Ignition

1. Harry C. Butcher diary, Nov. 6, 1942, EL.

2. *PDDE,* II, 666; Robert D. Murphy, *Diplomat Among Warriors* (New York: 1959), 121.

3. Dwight D. Eisenhower, *Crusade in Europe* (New York: 1948), 103.

4. Mark Clark, *Calculated Risk* (New York: 1950), 96–98; "Memorandum for the American General Staff," Nov. 7, 1942, EL.

5. *PDDE,* II, 672, 677.

6. *Crusade in Europe,* 101.

7. Butcher diary, Nov. 8, 1942, EL.

8. Ibid.

9. *PDDE,* II, 680.

10. Butcher diary, Nov. 9, 1942, EL.

11. George F. Howe, *Northwest Africa: Seizing the Initiative in the West* (Washington, D.C.: 1957), 262–264.

12. Butcher diary, Nov. 10, 1942, EL.

13. Marc Ferro, *Pétain* (Paris: 1987), 419–439; Lucien Adès *L'Aventure Algérienne 1940–1944* (Paris: 1979), 144n.

14. Hervé Coutau-Bergerie and Claude Huan, *Darlan* (Paris: 1989), 618–623; Jacques Raphael-Leygues and François Flohic, *Darlan* (Paris: 1986), 199–202.

15. Dwight D. Eisenhower, *Letters to Mamie* (New York: 1978), 66.

16. *PDDE,* I, 691, 707–709.

17. Harold Macmillan, *The Blast of War* (London: 1967), 221.

18. Albert Kesselring, *A Soldier's Story* (London: 1954), 163; British Air Ministry, *The Rise and Fall of the German Air Force* (London: 1948), 145.

19. F. H. Hinsley, et al., *British Intelligence in the Second World War* (London: 1988), III, Part 1, p. 486.

20. Howe, 254–255; *PDDE,* 735n.

21. Stephen Ambrose, *Eisenhower* (New York: 1984), I, 210–211.

22. Michael Howard, *Grand Strategy* (London: 1972), IV, 265–266; *PDDE,* II, 701–702, 764

23. *PDDE,* II, 686.

24. George C. Marshall interview, George C. Marshall Foundation, VMI.

25. Howe, 299–321.

26. Butcher diary, Dec. 6, 1942, EL; *PDDE,* II, 811.

27. *PDDE,* II, 804; Geoffrey Perret, *Winged Victory* (New York: 1994), 184–187.

28. Howe, 335–337.

29. *Crusade in Europe,* 124.

30. Butcher diary, Dec. 26, 1942, EL.

31. *PDDE,* II, 861; Kay Summersby Morgan, *Past Forgetting* (New York: 1976), 88.

32. Ann Whitman diary, Jan. 15, 1958; "Memo for Jim Hagerty," June 10, 1958, James C. Hagerty Papers, EL.

Chapter 16: AFHQ

1. Dwight D. Eisenhower, *At Ease: Stories I Tell to Friends* (New York: 1967), 258, and *Crusade in Europe* (New York: 1948), 132.

2. Dwight D. Eisenhower, *Letters to Mamie* (New York: 1978), 69.

3. Inez G. Scott interview, EL; Kay Summersby Morgan, *Past Forgetting* (New York: 1976), 95–96.

4. *PDDE,* II, 797.

5. Marriage request, Richard R. Arnold to C. G., II Corps, March 22, 1943, EL.

6. *Letters to Mamie,* 83, 84, 93.
7. Sue Sarafian Jehl interview, EL. Marshall "had a boyfriend [and] was one of the girls. We loved him truly."
8. Harry C. Butcher diary, Dec. 23, 1942, EL.
9. *Crusade in Europe,* 135; Harold Macmillan *The Blast of War* (London: 1967), 240; Butcher diary, Jan. 19, 1943, EL.
10. George C. Marshall interview, USAMHI Archives.
11. Michael Howard, *Grand Strategy* (London, 1968), IV, 242.
12. Martin Gilbert, *Winston S. Churchill* (London: 1988), VII, 149–151; Gordon Harrison, *Cross-Channel Attack* (Washington, D. C.: 1958), 36–46.
13. *Crusade in Europe,* 137.
14. Butcher diary, January 20–21, 1943, EL.
15. *PPDE,* II, 1214; *At Ease,* 260–261.
16. Butcher diary, January 26, 1943.
17. *Letters to Mamie,* 62.
18. *PDDE,* II, 679.
19. Arthur Bryant, *The Turn of the Tide* (London: 1956), 454–455.
20. Nigel Nicolson, *Alex* (London: 1973), 172–173; Butcher diary, Aug. 4, 1942, EL.
21. *Crusade in Europe,* 89.
22. Lord Tedder, *With Prejudice* (London: 1966), 280–281, 288–317, 340–361, and *Air Power in War* (London: 1948); cf. Richard Davis, *Carl A. Spaatz and the Air War in Europe* (Washington, D.C.: 1993), 147.
23. Diary, Nov. 17, 1942, and letter to Beatrice Ayers Patton, Nov. 19, 1942, George S. Patton, Jr., Papers, MD, LC.
24. *PDDE,* II, 928.
25. Davis, 322.
26. Butcher diary, Sept. 23, 1942.
27. Lucian K. Truscott, *Command Missions* (New York: 1954), 129–130.

Chapter 17: Tunisgrad

1. Martin Gilbert, *Winston S. Churchill* (London: 1986), VII, 348.
2. Gordon Harrison, *Cross-Channel Attack* (Washington, D.C.: 1951), 143.
3. British Air Ministry, *The Rise and Fall of the German Air Force, 1933–1945* (London: 1948), 144–147.
4. Gilbert, 360.
5. Dwight D. Eisenhower, *At Ease: Stories I Tell to Friends* (New York: 1967), 258, and *Crusade in Europe* (New York: 1948), 132.
6. Geoffrey Perret, *Winged Victory* (New York: 1994), 191.
7. *Crusade in Europe,* 141.
8. George F. Howe, *Northwest Africa: Seizing the Initiative in the West* (Washington, D. C.: 1957), 419–423.
9. *PDDE,* II, 971.

10. Martin Blumenson, *Kasserine Pass* (New York: 1966), 212–217.

11. Harry C. Butcher diary, March 1, 1943, EL; Geoffrey Perret, *There's a War to Be Won* (New York: 1993), 158–160; Ernest Harmon, *Combat Commander* (Englewood Cliffs, N.J.: 1972), 114–119; B. H. Liddell-Hart, *The Rommel Papers* (London: 1953), 398–407.

12. *Crusade in Europe,* 145–146; *PDDE,* II, 1006–1007; Nigel Nicolson, *Alex* (London: 1973), 212.

13. *PDDE,* II, 951; *At Ease,* 260–261.

14. Omar N. Bradley and Clay Blair, *A General's Life* (New York: 1983), 131–132.

15. Marshall's fear of Spanish intervention was groundless. Although Franco was still hoping for an Axis victory, any move against the Allies was likely to bring the loss of the Canary Islands and, given the pro-Allied sentiments of many of Spain's senior generals, a military coup. See, José M. Doussinague, *España Tenía Razón, 1939–1945* (Madrid: 1949), 70 passim; Paul Preston, *Franco* (London: 1993), 460–480.

16. Butcher diary, Dec. 10, 1942; *PDDE,* II, 699.

17. Carlo D'Este, *Patton* (New York: 1995), 461.

18. *PDDE* II, 920–921; Perret, *There's a War to Be Won,* 150.

19. Kay Summersby Morgan, *Past Forgetting* (New York: 1976), 99–100; letter, George S. Patton to Beatrice Ayer Patton, March 11, 1943, Patton Papers, MD, LC.

20. Inez Scott interview, EL; Summersby, 99.

21. All of these worries—plus dozens more—are documented in *PDDE, Letters to Mamie* and the Butcher diary.

22. Ralph Bennett, *Ultra in the West, 1944–1945* (London: 1989), 210–212.

23. Eduard Mark, *Aerial Interdiction* (Washington, D.C.: 1993), 45–46; Williamson Murray, *Luftwaffe* (Annapolis: 1985), 157–158.

24. Lord Tedder, *With Prejudice* (London: 1966), 411; Vincent Orange, *Coningham* (Washington, D.C.: 1992), 146–147; D'Este, 480–483.

25. *PDDE,* II, 1083.

26. Ibid. *PDDE,* II, 117; Butcher diary, April 14, 17, 1943, EL.

27. *PDDE,* II, 1089; Omar N. Bradley *A Soldier's Story,* (New York: 1951), 94.

28. Siegfried Westphal, *The German Army in the West* (London: 1951), 161.

29. *PDDE,* II, 1124.

30. Harold Macmillan, *The Blast of War, 1939–1945* (New York: 1968), 324–325.

Chapter 18: Missed Chances

1. Cable, Truscott to Eisenhower, June 11, 1943, Eisenhower 201 File, EL.

2. Kay Summersby Morgan, *Past Forgetting* (New York: 1976), 105–106.

3. Ibid., 62.

4. Harry C. Butcher diary, July 14, August 10, 1942, EL.

5. Athan Theoharis, ed., *From the Secret Files of J. Edgar Hoover* (Chicago: 1979), 57–58.

6. Kay Summersby, *Eisenhower Was My Boss* (New York: 1948), 15–16; *Past Forgetting,* 31.

7. *Past Forgetting,* 153.

8. C.J.C. Molony, *The Mediterranean and the Middle East* (London: 1973), 3–14; Dwight D. Eisenhower, *Crusade in Europe* (New York: 1948), 162.

9. Ralph Bennett, *Ultra in the Mediterranean* (London: 1989), 220–230; *Crusade in Europe,* 163. In this account he says "more than two divisions," but the cable from AFHQ says two.

10. Martin Gilbert, *Winston S. Churchill* (London: 1986), VII, 379.

11. Albert N. Garland and Howard McGaw Smyth, *Sicily and the Surrender of Italy* (Washington, D.C.: 1965), 58–63.

12. For a good recent discussion of Montgomery's modern reputation, see, G. Patrick Murray, *Eisenhower vs. Montgomery* (Westport, Conn.: 1996).

13. Milton Silverman, "Three Men in a DUKW," *Saturday Evening Post,* April 20, 1946; Geoffrey Perret, *There's a War to Be Won* (New York: 1991), 110–112, 135.

14. Charles H. Bonesteel III (St. Louis interview), USAMHI Archives; Robert W. Coakley and Richard M. Leighton, *Global Logistics and Strategy, 1943–1945* (Washington, D.C.: 1968), 33–34; *Crusade in Europe,* 193–194.

15. Garland and Smyth, 435–437.

16. Summersby, *Past Forgetting,* 131.

17. Gilbert, VII, 422; cites the official minutes of this meeting. Forrest Pogue, *George C. Marshall: Organizer of Victory, 1943–1945* (New York: 1973), 216; blandly avers that Eisenhower "seemed to respond more favorably to the British proposals than did Marshall." Although there is no record of it, chances are that Marshall would have made it plain to Ike that he could not talk about a cross-Channel attack as being "unnecessary." It is telling, too, that in both *Crusade in Europe* and *At Ease,* Ike only recalls his rebuke to Brooke. Nowhere does he mention his "drop in the bucket" comment to Churchill.

18. Dwight D. Eisenhower, *At Ease: Stories I Tell to Friends* (New York: 1967), 264.

19. Butcher diary, May 30, June 23, 1943, EL.

20. Jean Lacouture, *De Gaulle* (Paris: 1984), I, 673–678.

21. Garland and Smyth, 66.

22. *Crusade in Europe,* 166.

23. Lord Zuckerman, *From Apes to Warlords* (London: 1978), 187–189; *PDDE,* II, 1196; Kit C. Carter and Robert Mueller, eds., *U.S. Army Air Forces in World War II: Combat Chronology* (Washington, D.C.), 1991, 143–144.

24. *At Ease,* 265.

25. Kenneth Strong, *Intelligence at the Top* (London: 1952), 96–98.

26. Wesley Frank Craven and James L. Cate, *The Army Air Forces in World War II* (Chicago: 1953), II, 423–430; Stephen Ambrose, *Eisenhower* (New York: 1983), I, 248.

27. Johannes Steinhoff, *The Straits of Messina: Diary of a Fighter Commander* (London: 1971), 189.

28. Butcher diary, June 29, 1943, EL.

29. Nigel Nicolson, *Alex* (London: 1973), 199.

30. Ewan Montague, *The Man Who Never Was* (London: 1954).

31. F. H. Hinsley, *British Intelligence in the Second World War* (Cambridge, England: 1986), Part 2, vol. 1, 78–79.

32. John Gunther, *D-Day* (New York: 1943), 57–62.

33. Butcher diary, July 10, 1943, EL.

34. Clay Blair, *Ridgway's Paratroopers* (New York: 1985), 100–101.

35. Patton diary, July 12, 1943, Patton Papers, MD, LC.

36. Gunther, 66–74; Butcher diary, July 13, 1943, EL.

37. Craven and Cate, II, 464–465.

38. *PDDE*, II, 1269; Geoffrey Perret, *Winged Victory* (New York: 1993), 214–217.

39. *PDDE*, II, 1186.

40. Butcher diary, August 14, 1943, EL.

41. S.W.C. Pack, *Cunningham* (London: 1974), 259–260; Lord Tedder, *With Prejudice* (London: 1966), 456–457. Tedder's account suggests he was so eager to attack targets on the Italian mainland that he paid virtually no attention to the ferrying operation.

42. Hinsley, 95–99.

43. Lucian K. Truscott, *Command Missions* (New York: 1954), 243.

Chapter 19: One Down

1. Patton file, Eisenhower Papers, EL; Carlo D'Este, *Patton: A Genius for War* (New York: 1995), 533–534.

2. Stephen Ambrose, *Supreme Commander* (New York: 1970), 228–229.

3. *PDDE*, II, 1190.

4. Ambrose, 230–231; Harry C. Butcher diary, August 21, 1943, EL.

5. *PDDE*, II, 1353.

6. Maurice Matloff and Edwin M. Snell, *Strategic Planning for Coalition Warfare, 1943–1945* (Washington, D.C.: 1956), 157–161.

7. *PDDE*, II, 1261–1262.

8. Albert N. Garland and Howard McGaw Smyth, *Sicily and the Surrender of Italy* (Washington, D.C.: 1965), 558.

9. Ibid., 297–298.

10. Ibid., Appendix C; Dwight D. Eisenhower, *Letters to Mamie* (New York: 1978), 125.

11. F. H. Hinsley, *British Intelligence in the Second World War* (London: 1986), III, Part 1, 104; David Hunt, *A Don at War* (London: 1966), 214–225; Garland and Smyth, 558.
12. Garland and Smyth, 556–557.
13. Kenneth Strong, *Intelligence at the Top* (London: 1952), 112–114; Butcher diary, September 3, 1943, EL.
14. David Cahn, *The Codebreakers* (New York: 1966), 556.
15. Clay Blair, *Ridgway's Paratroopers* (New York: 1985), 135–140.
16. Garland and Smyth, 501–502.
17. *PDDE,* III, 1402–1403.
18. Kay Summersby, *Eisenhower Was My Boss* (New York: 1948), 82.
19. *Letters to Mamie,* 146.
20. Butcher diary, September 14, 1943, EL.
21. Samuel E. Morison, *Salerno-Sicily-Anzio* (Boston: 1955), 280.
22. *PDDE,* III, 1428; Nigel Nicolson, *Alex* (London: 1973), 221–222.
23. Dwight D. Eisenhower, *At Ease: Stories I Tell to Friends* (New York: 1967), 267; *PDDE,* III, 1436; Geoffrey Perret, *There's a War to Be Won* (New York: 1991), 203–205; Martin Blumenson, *Mark Clark* (New York: 1984), 137–141. Marshall was never really sold on Clark and soon gave Dawley one of his stars back. By the time he retired in 1948, Dawley was a major general again.
24. Albert Kesselring, *A Soldier's Record* (London: 1954), 184.
25. *PDDE,* III, 1441; Butcher diary, Oct. 5, 1943, EL.
26. *PDDE,* III, 1469–1470; Garland and Smyth, 551.
27. Martin Gilbert, *Winston S. Churchill* (London: 1988), VII, 521.
28. *PDDE,* III, 1494–1495; Dwight D. Eisenhower, *Crusade in Europe* (New York: 1948), 191.
29. Butcher diary, Oct. 28, 1943, EL.
30. *PDDE,* III, 1507.
31. Butcher diary, Nov. 12, 1943, EL.
32. Oliver Pilat, *Drew Pearson* (New York: 1973), 176–177.
33. *PDDE,* III, 1571–1573.
34. Butcher diary, Oct. 5, 1943, EL.
35. Ibid., Sept. 16, 1943.
36. Ibid., Oct. 28, 1943.
37. Gilbert, VII, 565.
38. Summersby, 99.
39. Forrest Pogue, *Organizer of Victory* (New York: 1973), 321–322.
40. Butcher diary, Dec. 6, 1943, EL; Summersby, 106.
41. *Crusade in Europe,* 207.

Chapter 20: Time Out

1. Winston S. Churchill, *The Second World War* (Boston: 1952), V, 421.
2. Martin Gilbert, *Winston S. Churchill* (London: 1988), VII, 606.

3. Ibid., 607; Lord Moran, *Churchill: The Struggle for Survival* (London: 1968), 170–175; Richard Lovell, *Churchill's Doctor* (Guildford, England: 1993), 228–229. Moran only hints at the heart attack; Lovell describes it.

4. Dwight D. Eisenhower, *Crusade in Europe* (New York: 1948), 212.

5. Kay Summersby, *Eisenhower Was My Boss* (New York: 1948), 112–113.

6. *Crusade in Europe,* 211.

7. Harry C. Butcher diary, Dec. 19, 1943, EL.

8. Ibid.; Summersby, 109.

9. Summersby, 114.

10. *PDDE,* III, 1611.

11. Ibid., 1624.

12. Gilbert, VII, 622.

13. *PDDE,* III, 1633.

14. Alden Hatch, *Red Carpet for Mamie* (New York: 1954), 188; Merle Miller, *Ike the Soldier* (New York: 1987), 577.

15. David Eisenhower, *Eisenhower at War, 1943–1945* (New York: 1986), 60; Butcher diary, Jan. 16, 1944, EL.

16. *PDDE,* III, 1641; *Crusade in Europe,* 216.

17. Forrest Pogue, *Organizer of Victory* (New York: 1973), 330.

18. Thomas T. Handy interview, EL.

19. Miller, 579.

20. Stephen Ambrose, *Eisenhower* (New York: 1984), I, 279–280.

21. *PDDE,* III, 1660.

22. *PDDE,* II, 1326, 1396; III, 1593; David Eisenhower, 56.

23. Hatch, 189; Miller, 579.

24. Kay Summersby Morgan, *Past Forgetting* (New York: 1976), 199.

25. Kenneth S. Davis, *Soldier of Democracy* (New York: 1945), 456–457.

26. Dwight D. Eisenhower, *At Ease: Stories I Tell to Friends* (New York: 1967), 268.

27. *Crusade in Europe,* 218.

28. Hatch, 192.

Chapter 21: Craftsmanship

1. Gordon Harrison, *Cross-Channel Attack* (Washington, D.C.: 1951), 60–63; James A. Huston, *The Sinews of War: Army Logistics 1775–1963* (Washington, D.C.: 1966).

2. George C. Marshall interview, George C. Marshall Foundation, VMI.

3. Frederick E. Morgan, *Overture to Overlord* (New York: 1950), 135–157; General Staff, SHAEF, "History of COSSAC," Walter Bedell Smith Papers, EL.

4. Francis de Guingand, *Operation Victory* (New York: 1947), 343. Cf. *PDDE,* III, 1653n.

5. Forrest Pogue, *The Supreme Command* (Washington, D.C.: 1954), 107.

6. Nigel Hamilton, *Monty: Master of the Battlefield* (London: 1983), 487.

7. Harrison, 64n.

8. Minutes of Meeting at Norfolk House, Harry C. Butcher diary, Jan. 21, 1944, EL.

9. *PDDE,* III, 1674; Butcher diary, Jan. 23, 1944, EL.

10. Butcher diary, Minutes of Meeting, February 2, 1944.

11. Pogue 111–113; Harrison, 168–170; "Memorandum," Butcher diary, Feb. 7, 1944, EL.

12. *PDDE,* III, 1783.

13. Thomas Betts interview, EL; James M. Robb interview, USAMHI Archives; Pogue, 66–97.

14. Arthur Nevins and Ray M. Barker interviews, both EL.

15. Butcher diary, May 21, 1944, EL.

16. Barker interview; Betts interview.

17. James H. Doolittle, with Carrol V. Glines, *I Could Never Be So Lucky Again* (New York: 1991), 328, 349.

18. Minutes of Supreme Commander's Conference, Jan. 24, 1944, in Butcher diary, Feb. 2, 1944, EL.

19. *PDDE,* III, 1754.

20. Lord Zuckerman, *From Apes to Warlords* (New York: 1978), 233 et seq.; Bill Newton-Dunn, *Big Wing: The Life of Trafford Leigh-Mallory* (Leicester: 1996), 97–101.

21. Martin Gilbert, *Winston S. Churchill* (London: 1988), VII, 727, 784.

22. David Irvine, *The War Between the Generals* (New York: 1981), 79.

23. *PDDE,* III, 1781–1782, 1802, 1820.

24. David Eisenhower, *Eisenhower at War* (New York: 1986), 185–190.

25. Geoffrey Perret, *Winged Victory* (New York: 1993), 295.

26. Richard Davis, *Spaatz and the Air War in Europe* (Washington, D.C.: 1993), 391.

27. Eduard Mark, *Aerial Interdiction in Three Wars* (Washington, D.C.: 1994), 232–242, 256–257; provides an excellent and authoritative account of what the Transportation Plan achieved.

28. Butcher diary, Feb. 7, March 3, 1944, EL; Kay Summersby, *Eisenhower Was My Boss* (New York: 1948), 138–143.

29. Butcher diary, Feb. 26, 1944, EL.

30. J. Lawton Collins, *Lightning Joe* (Baton Rouge: 1974), 179; Roscoe B. Woodruff, "The World War II of Roscoe B. Woodruff," Woodruff Papers, USAMHI Archives.

31. Butcher diary, April 28, 1944, EL.

32. David Eisenhower, 218.

33. Kay Summersby Morgan, *Past Forgetting* (New York: 1976), 194.

34. Butcher diary, May 12, 1944, EL.

35. *PDDE,* III, 1848–1849; Pogue, 163–164.

36. Butcher diary, Jan. 27, Feb. 11, 1944, EL.

37. Ralph Bennett, *Ultra in the West, 1944–1945* (London: 1989), 52–53.

38. Carlo D'Este, *Patton: A Genius for War* (New York: 1995), 585–586.

39. Omar N. Bradley, *A Soldier's Story* (New York: 1954), 231.
40. *PDDE,* III, 1840.
41. Ibid., 1841.
42. D'Este, *Patton,* 589–590.
43. *PDDE,* III, 1841n; Martin Blumenson, *The Patton Papers* (Boston: 1974), II, 452.
44. Dwight D. Eisenhower, *Crusade in Europe,* 225; *PDDE,* III, 1846. In *At Ease: Stories I Tell to Friends* (New York: 1967), 270–271, Eisenhower not only claims that he told Patton on May 1 he was not going to fire him but that Patton was so moved by emotion that tears streamed down his cheeks and his chrome-plated helmet fell off. The tears and helmet details are too vivid not to be true, but this incident probably occurred the next time they met.
45. Carlo D'Este, *Decision in Normandy* (New York: 1983), 83.
46. Hamilton, 560–566; Omar N. Bradley and Clay Blair, *A General's Life* (New York: 1981), 234.
47. Gilbert, VII, 771; Blumenson, 456.
48. Stephen Ambrose, *The Supreme Commander* (New York: 1970), 399.
49. This is reconstructed largely from Leigh-Mallory's notes on the conference, reproduced in Dunn, *Big Wing,* 109–111. These notes, dictated hours after the conference ended, provide the only detailed contemporaneous account. All other accounts are postwar recollections.

Chapter 22: The Day

1. Harry C. Butcher diary, May 23, 1944, EL.
2. Robert Wright, *Dowding and the Battle of Britain* (London: 1969), Chapter 11; Derek Wood and Derek Dempster, *The Narrow Margin* (London: 1961), 400–402.
3. Minutes of Supreme Commander's Conference, Jan. 21, 1944, in Butcher diary, February 2, 1944, EL; Leigh-Mallory's written objections are in Butcher diary, May 30, 1944, EL; Dwight D. Eisenhower, *Crusade in Europe* (New York: 1948), 246–247; Clay Blair, *Ridgway's Paratroopers* (New York: 1985), 187–188.
4. Winston S. Churchill, *The Second World War* (Boston: 1951), V, 619–620.
5. Kay Summersby diary, June 2, 1944, EL.
6. Kay Summersby, *Eisenhower Was My Boss* (New York: 1948), 144.
7. *PDDE,* III, 1904.
8. John M. Stagg *Forecast for Overlord* (New York: 1971), 104–109; Thomas Betts interview, EL.
9. Nigel Hamilton, *Monty* (London: 1983), II, 611.
10. Lord Tedder, *With Prejudice* (London: 1966), 545.
11. Charles De Gaulle, *Mémoires de Guerre* (Paris: 1959), I, 289–293.
12. Kenneth Strong, *Intelligence at the Top* (London: 1952), 136–137.

13. Stagg, 115–116.
14. Stephen Ambrose, *Eisenhower* (New York: 1984), 308; Chester Wilmot, *The Struggle for Europe* (New York: 1952), 225.
15. Summersby diary, June 4, 1944, EL.
16. Stagg, 120.
17. Jean Lacouture, *De Gaulle* (Paris: 1984), I, 763–766.
18. Butcher diary, June 8, 1944, EL.
19. Summersby, *Eisenhower Was My Boss,* 147; Summersby diary, June 6, 1944, EL.
20. F. H. Hinsley, *British Intelligence in the Second World War* (Cambridge, England: 1984), III, Pt. 2, 64.
21. Butcher diary, June 6, 1944, EL.
22. Martin Gilbert, *Winston S. Churchill* (London: 1988), VII, 796.

Chapter 23: Blitzkrieg, American-style

1. Geoffrey Perret, *There's a War to Be Won* (New York: 1993), 303–305.
2. Omar N. Bradley and Clay Blair, *A General's Life* (New York: 1981), 257.
3. John Stagg, *Forecast for Overlord* (New York: 1966), 114.
4. Harry C. Butcher diary, June 8, 1944, EL.
5. Kay Summersby diary, June 9, 1944, EL.
6. Dwight D. Eisenhower, *Letters to Mamie* (New York: 1978), 190.
7. Bradley and Blair, 259.
8. Butcher diary, June 12, 1944, EL.
9. John S. D. Eisenhower, *Strictly Personal* (New York: 1974), 72.
10. Diary, June 15, 1944, Carl A. Spaatz Papers, MD, LC.
11. Kay Summersby Morgan, *Past Forgetting* (New York: 1976), 221–222.
12. Author interview with John S. D. Eisenhower, Aug. 17, 1998.
13. Martin Gilbert, *Winston S. Churchill* (London: 1988), VII, 839–841.
14. Roy Lamson interview in Omar N. Bradley Papers, USAMHI Archives; Perret, 349–350.
15. Butcher diary, July 1–5, 1944, EL.
16. Thomas Hughes, *Over Lord: General Pete Quesada and the Triumph of Tactical Air Power in World War II* (New York: 1995), 173–176; Letter, Thomas Hughes to author, March 6, 1998; *Letters to Mamie,* 196.
17. Arthur Bryant, *Triumph in the West* (London: 1959), 179–183.
18. Henry L. Stimson and McGeorge Bundy, *On Active Service in Peace and War* (New York: 1948), 445.
19. Forrest C. Pogue, *The Supreme Command* (Washington, D.C.: 1954), 188.
20. L. J. Ellis, *Victory in the West* (London: 1962), I, 332–354.
21. Wesley Frank Craven and James L. Cate, *The Army Air Forces in World War II* (Chicago: 1948), III, 232–235.
22. Omar N. Bradley, *A Soldier's Story* (New York: 1951), 349.

23. Lord Tedder, *With Prejudice* (London: 1966), 572.
24. Russell Weigley, *Eisenhower's Lieutenants* (Bloomington, Ind.: 1981), 155–169.
25. John W. Leonard (Burg interview), EL; Bradley and Blair, 281.
26. Martin Blumenson, *Breakout and Pursuit* (Washington, D.C.: 1961), 317 passim; Carlo D'Este, *Patton: A Genius for War* (New York: 1996), 626–628.
27. Gilbert, VII, 823; cf. F. H. Hinsley, *British Intelligence in the Second World War* (Cambridge, England: 1988), III, 316, 318.
28. Arthur Bryant, 254–255.
29. Butcher diary, Aug. 2, 1944, EL.
30. *PPDE,* IV, 2050.
31. Pogue, 225; Butcher diary, Aug. 10–11, 1944.
32. *PDDE,* IV, 2065.
33. Roland G. Ruppenthal, *Logistical Support of the Armies* (Washington, D.C.: 1953), II, 50–51.
34. Winston S. Churchill, *The Second World War* (London: 1950), VI, 100.
35. David Eisenhower, *Eisenhower at War* (New York: 1983), 413–414.
36. Hinsley, III, 238.
37. Tedder, 575; Pogue, 208–209; Dwight D. Eisenhower, *Crusade in Europe* (New York: 1948), 275.
38. *PDDE,* IV, 2068; Butcher diary, Aug. 14, 1944, EL.

Chapter 24: Broad Thrust

1. Forrest C. Pogue, *The Supreme Command* (Washington, D.C.: 1954), 240; Dominique Lapierre and Larry Collins, *Paris, Brûle t'il?* (Paris: 1964), 285–286n.
2. Chester Hansen diary, Aug. 20, 1944, USAMHI Archives; F. H. Hinsley, *British Intelligence in the Second World War* (Cambridge, England: 1988), III, Part 2, 371–372; Lapierre and Collins, 237–238; Martin Blumenson, *Breakout and Pursuit* (Washington, D.C.: 1961).
3. This note, written with a blunt pencil, was later retrieved by First Army G-2 officers and is in the Courtney Hodges Papers, EL.
4. Jean Lacouture, *De Gaulle* (Paris: 1984), I, 761–762.
5. Charles de Gaulle, *Mémoires de Guerre* (Paris: 1957), II, 626.
6. *PDDE,* IV, 2089.
7. Pogue, 230n; Maurice Vigneras, *Rearming the French* (Washington, D.C.: 1962), 171–172, 182.
8. Omar N. Bradley, *A Soldier's Story* (New York: 1951), 392.
9. Omar Bradley and Clay Blair, *A General's Life* (New York: 1984), 309; Dwight D. Eisenhower, *Letters to Mamie* (New York: 1978), 209.
10. Chester Hansen diary, Aug. 25–26, 1944, USAMHI Archives.

11. *PDDE,* IV, 2108.
12. Walter B. Smith, *Eisenhower's Six Great Decisions: Europe, 1944–1945* (New York: 1956), 156–159; *PDDE,* IV, 2323.
13. Letter, DDE to Hastings Ismay, Dec. 3, 1960, EL.
14. SHAEF G-3 Division, "Post-Neptune Courses of Action," Record Group 331, National Archives.
15. Harry C. Butcher diary, Aug. 15, 1944; *New York Times,* Aug. 16, 1944.
16. Nigel Hamilton, *Monty: The Field Marshal* (London: 1986), 27.
17. Letter, Eisenhower to Marshall, May 28, 1943, EL. These remarks do not appear in the version of this letter published in *PDDE.*
18. *PDDE,* IV, 2121; Hamilton, III, 33.
19. Chester Wilmot, *The Struggle for Europe* (London: 1952), 460; Bernard Law Montgomery, *Memoirs of Field Marshal Montgomery* (Cleveland: 1958), 242–243.
20. Martin Gilbert, *Winston S. Churchill* (London: 1986), VII, 930n.
21. *PDDE,* IV, 2129.
22. First Allied Airborne Army headquarters diary, Sept. 2–3, 1944, Floyd Parks Papers, USAMHI Archives. Parks, an officer Eisenhower had known and admired since Camp Colt days, was the FAAA chief of staff.
23. Cornelius Ryan, *A Bridge Too Far* (New York: 1974), 93. Eisenhower later told the editors of his papers, "I not only approved this operation, I insisted on it. What we needed was a bridgehead over the Rhine. If that could be accomplished I was quite willing to wait on all other operations." *PPDE,* IV, 2135n.
24. Hinsley, II, Part 2, 383–387; Ryan, 88–90; Hamilton, III, 71 et seq. Cf. the obituaries of Williams in the London *Times,* June 29, 1995, and the *Independent,* June 30, 1995. Williams had been expected to become one of the great scholars of his generation, but on returning to Oxford after the war, he spent the rest of his life as a dull, gray academic bureaucrat.
25. Lionel F. Ellis, *Victory in the West* (London: 1968), II, 45–50.
26. Martin Blumenson, *The Patton Papers* (Boston: 1970), II, 568.
27. Roland G. Ruppenthal, *Logistical Support of the Armies* (Washington, D.C.: 1953), I, 553–557.
28. *PDDE,* III, 2021–2022; Pogue, 268.
29. Lucian K. Truscott, Jr., *Command Missions* (New York: 1954), 188. Cf. diary, Nov. 15, 1943, John P. Lucas Papers, USAMHI Archives—"Now I am stopped, not by the enemy but by the British inability to move. Their transport is so inferior . . ."
30. Geoffrey Perret, *There's a War to Be Won* (New York: 1991), 371.
31. Gilbert, 930.
32. John Major and Robert Love, eds., *Year of Decision—The Diary of Admiral Ramsay* (Hull, England: 1991), 135; Pogue, 254.
33. Hinsley, II, Part 2, 119–122.
34. Sir Humfrey M. Gale and Walter B. Smith interviews, both in USAMHI Archives.

35. *PDDE,* IV, 2120n.
36. Dwight D. Eisenhower, *Crusade in Europe* (New York: 1948), 304; *PDDE,* IV, 2122.
37. G. Patrick Murray, *Eisenhower vs. Montgomery: The Continuing Debate* (New York: 1996), 84.
38. Ryan, 85–86.
39. *PDDE,* IV, 2175.
40. Ibid., 2296.
41. Perret, 92–93, 372.
42. Charles B. MacDonald and Sydney T. Matthews, *Three Battles: Arnaville, Altuzzo, Schmidt* (Washington, D.C.: 1957), 413–414; *PDDE,* IV, 2312.
43. *PDDE,* IV, 2323–2325.
44. Ibid., IV, 2349.

Chapter 25: Fog of War

1. James M. Robb interview, USAMHI Archives.
2. Chester Hansen diary, Aug. 12, 1944, USAMHI Archives; Lucian K. Truscott, Jr., *Command Missions* (New York: 1950), 25; Lewis Brereton, *The Brereton Diaries* (New York: 1946), 309.
3. Geoffrey Perret, *Old Soldiers Never Die* (New York: 1996), 231; David Eisenhower, *Eisenhower at War* (New York: 1984), 640.
4. Martin Blumenson, *The Patton Papers* (Boston: 1970), II, 411; Carlo D'Este, *Patton* (New York: 1995), 445, 486 et seq.
5. Memo, DDE to Emmet John Hughes, December 10, 1953, EL.
6. Hugh M. Cole, *The Lorraine Campaign* (Washington, D.C.: 1950), 552.
7. Arthur Bryant, *Triumph in the West* (London: 1958), 351–355.
8. Charles B. MacDonald, *A Time for Trumpets* (New York: 1984), Chapter 1.
9. Hugh M. Cole, *The Ardennes: Battle of the Bulge* (Washington, D.C.: 1965), 33–35; Geoffrey Perret, *There's a War to Be Won* (New York: 1991), 397–398.
10. F. H. Hinsley, *British Intelligence in the Second World War* (Cambridge, England: 1988), III, Part 2, 438.
11. Letter and enclosures, Montgomery to Eisenhower, Dec. 15, 1944, Eisenhower Papers, EL. The bet was made in January 1944, when Eisenhower—and Monty—expected Overlord would be mounted on or about May 1. See, letter, DDE to Hastings Ismay, Dec. 3, 1960, EL.
12. Harry C. Butcher diary, Dec, 16, 1994, EL.
13. Dwight D. Eisenhower, *Crusade in Europe* (New York: 1948), 342; Omar N. Bradley and Clay Blair, *A General's Life* (New York: 1983), 355–356; John S. D. Eisenhower, *The Bitter Woods* (New York: 1969), 215.
14. Eisenhower, *The Bitter Woods,* 279.
15. *PDDE,* IV, 2355.
16. *Crusade in Europe,* 350.

17. Diary, Dec. 19, 1944, George S. Patton, Jr., Papers, MD, LC; Kenneth Strong, *Intelligence at the Top* (London: 1952), 163; Charles R. Codman, *Drive!* (Boston: 1957), 231–233.
18. D'Este, 680–681; Martin Blumenson, 599–601.
19. Dietrich told her daughter that Bradley was "scared of her" and couldn't wait to get her out of his headquarters: Maria Riva, *Marlene Dietrich* (New York: 1993). The diaries maintained by Bradley's aide, Chester Hansen, nevertheless show that Dietrich visited Bradley over a period of several months and stayed for up to three days at a time. Dietrich was a fantasist. She told her daughter she was at Bastogne when it was surrounded—a story on a par with her repeated claim that *The Blue Angel* was her first movie, when it was really her eighteenth.
20. Perret, *There's a War to Be Won,* 407.
21. Bryant, 270–273; Strong, 224–225; D.K.R. Crosswell, *Chief of Staff* (New York: 1987), 285–286.
22. Stephen Ambrose, *Eisenhower* (New York: 1984), I, 368. Bradley and Blair, 363–364, make no mention of Bradley's threat to resign at a time of crisis, nor of Eisenhower's sharp rebuke.
23. Kay Summersby diary, Dec. 25–26, 1944, EL; Mickey McKeogh, *Sergeant Mickey and General Ike* (New York: 1946), 154–155.
24. *PDDE,* IV, 2370.
25. Bruce C. Clark interview, USAMHI Archives; Eisenhower, *The Bitter Woods,* 378–379.

Chapter 26: End of a Mission

1. William Bradford Huie, *The Execution of Private Slovik* (New York: 1970).
2. Ibid., 180.
3. F. H. Hinsley, *British Intelligence in the Second World War* (Cambridge, England: 1988), III, Part 2, 449–450.
4. Nigel Hamilton, *Monty* (London: 1984), II, 269–270. Hamilton's explanation for this, and other, disagreements is that Eisenhower suffered from "delusional insanity," a term commonly applied to schizophrenics who claim to be hearing, and obeying, strange voices.
5. G. Patrick Murray, *Eisenhower versus Montgomery: The Continuing Debate* (New York: 1996).
6. Francis W. de Guingand, *Generals at War* (London: 1964), 110–111; Bernard Law Montgomery, *The Memoirs of Field Marshal Viscount Montgomery of EL Alamein* (Cleveland: 1958), 286.
7. *PDDE,* IV, 2387n, 2390.
8. Martin Gilbert, *Winston S. Churchill* (London: 1986), VII, 1144–1145.
9. Jeffrey J. Clarke and Robert Ross Smith, *Riviera to the Rhine* (Washington, D.C.: 1993), 505–526, 533–551.
10. Russell Weigley, *Eisenhower's Lieutenants* (Bloomington, Ind.: 1981), 580; *PDDE,* IV, 2431, 2491.

11. Kay Summersby diary, Jan. 1–3, 1945, EL.

12. Charles de Gaulle, *Mémoires de Guerre,* (Paris: 1959), III, 179–180; Jean Lacouture, *De Gaulle* (Paris: 1984), II, 67–74.

13. Dwight D. Eisenhower, *Crusade in Europe* (New York: 1948), 362–363.

14. Forrest C. Pogue, *The Supreme Command* (Washington, D.C.: 1954), 402.

15. Lord Tedder, *With Prejudice* (London: 1966), 610, passim; Lord Zuckerman, *From Apes to Warlords* (New York: 1978), 300–305.

16. *PDDE,* IV, 2247–2249.

17. Allen C. Mierzejewski, *The Collapse of the German War Economy: Allied Air Power and the Collapse of the German Railway* (Chapel Hill, N.C.: 1990), 83 passim.

18. *PDDE,* IV, 2506.

19. Ibid., IV, 2267n; Dwight D. Eisenhower, *Letters to Mamie* (New York: 1978), 220.

20. John S. D. Eisenhower, *Strictly Personal* (New York: 1974), 83.

21. *Letters to Mamie,* 234.

22. Merle Miller, *Ike the Soldier* (New York: 1987), 219. The observer was Herbert Mitgang.

23. Jacob Devers interview, EL.

24. *Letters to Mamie,* 241, 244, 247.

25. Charles B. MacDonald, *The Last Offensive* (Washington: D.C.: 1973), 178–179n.

26. William M. Hoge interview, USAMHI Archives; cf. Ken Hechler, *The Bridge at Remagen* (New York: 1957).

27. Kay Summersby diary, March 8, 1945, EL; *Crusade in Europe,* 380; Omar N. Bradley and Clay Blair, *A General's Life* (New York: 1983), 407.

28. Carlo D'Este, *Patton: A Genius for War* (New York: 1995), 712.

29. Lionel F. Ellis, *Victory in the West* (London: 1968), II, 288–292.

30. *PDDE,* IV, 2562–2563.

31. Cornelius Ryan, *The Longest Day* (New York: 1974), 82n.

32. *PDDE,* IV, 2480–2482, 2494.

33. Kay Summersby diary, April 1, 1945, EL; Gilbert, VII, 1275.

34. *PDDE,* IV, 2566.

35. John Ehrman, *Grand Strategy* (London: 1956) 147–148; Hinsley III, Part 2, 733–736; *PDDE,* IV, 2551.

36. Letter, DDE to Hastings Ismay, Dec. 3, 1960, EL; David Eisenhower, *Eisenhower at War, 1943–1945* (New York: 1984), 727; Bradley and Blair, 419. Eisenhower's feelings about this decision came out during the 1952 election campaign, when he responded vehemently to criticism of his decision not to take Berlin. None of his critics, he noted bitingly, had offered "to go out and choose the ten thousand American mothers" whose sons would have been killed capturing "a worthless objective." *New York Herald Tribune,* June 16, 1952.

37. *PDDE,* IV, 2568; Gilbert, VII, 1273–1275.

38. Harry C. Butcher diary, May 25, 1945, EL.

39. John S. D. Eisenhower interview, EL.
40. U.S. Department of State, *Foreign Relations of the United States, 1944* (Washington, D.C.: 1948), III, 742–743; *PDDE,* IV, 2242–2243.
41. *Crusade in Europe,* 426.
42. *PDDE,* IV, 2696. Beetle Smith's WAC secretary, Rush Briggs, corrected the time to 02:41 before this message was transmitted.

Chapter 27: Occupation Duty

1. Dwight D. Eisenhower, *Letters to Mamie* (New York: 1978), 255, 258, 259.
2. Dwight D. Eisenhower, *At Ease: Stories I Tell to Friends* (New York: 1967), 388–390.
3. *PDDE,* VI, 161.
4. Alden Hatch, *Red Carpet for Mamie* (New York: 1954), 200.
5. Levi J. Asper interview and Earl Endacott memoir, both in EL; Steve Neal, *The Eisenhowers: Reluctant Dynasty* (New York: 1978), 224.
6. *PDDE,* VI, 134–135, 150.
7. John S. D. Eisenhower, *Strictly Personal* (New York: 1974), 112–114.
8. Margaret Truman, *Harry S Truman* (New York: 1973), 47, 55.
9. Dwight D. Eisenhower, *Crusade in Europe* (New York: 1948), 444; Douglas Black, COHP. The remark about the vice-presidency does not appear in Eisenhower's book, but he told Black, his publisher, about it.
10. *Letters to Mamie,* 256.
11. Eisenhower claimed that during the conference, he had urged Truman not to use the atomic bomb against the Japanese—"They're licked, and they know it." There is no mention of this, however, in either Truman's diary or Stimson's.
12. Robert C. Tucker, *Stalin in Power* (New York: 1990), 474–478.
13. *PDDE,* VI, 57.
14. Walter Millis, ed., *The Forrestal Diaries* (New York: 1951), 78–79.
15. *Crusade in Europe,* 442.
16. John S. D. Eisenhower interview, EL; Robert D. Murphy, COHP.
17. Stephen Ambrose, *Eisenhower* (New York: 1983), I, 428–429.
18. Cf. Georgi Zhukov, *Memoirs of Marshal Zhukov* (London: 1971), 666.
19. *Crusade in Europe,* 469. Eisenhower says he did not see "a house standing," but many photographs from the time clearly show houses still standing in eastern Poland and western Russia. All, however, are terribly damaged.
20. W. Averell Harriman and Elie Abel, *Special Envoy to Churchill and Stalin, 1941–1946* (New York: 1975), 502–503.
21. *New York Times,* August 15, 1945.
22. Edgar Snow, *Journey to the Beginning* (New York: 1958), 360–361.
23. Mark Clark interview, USAMHI Archives.
24. Peter Lyon, *Eisenhower: Portrait of the Hero* (Boston: 1974), 358–360, 362–363; PDDE, VI, 267n, 417n.

25. Martin Gilbert, *Winston S. Churchill* (London: 1986), VII, 1305.
26. The most thorough treatment of this controversy is in Günther Bischoff and Stephen E. Ambrose, eds., *Eisenhower and the German POWs* (Baton Rouge: 1993).
27. Ladislas Farago, *The Last Days of Patton* (New York: 1981), 146.
28. Carlo D'Este, *Patton: A Genius for War* (New York: 1995), 761.
29. Letter, George S. Patton to Beatrice Ayers Patton, Aug. 18, 1945, Special Collections, West Point.
30. D'Este, 763; Lyon 360.
31. Farago, 196–197.
32. Kay Summersby, *Eisenhower Was My Boss* (New York: 1948), 278.
33. George S. Patton diary, September 29, 1945, Patton Papers, MD, LC.
34. John J. McCloy, COHP.
35. Dwight D. Eisenhower interview, EL.

Chapter 28: Out of Uniform

1. Dwight D. Eisenhower interview, EL.
2. Dwight D. Eisenhower, *At Ease: Stories I Tell to Friends* (New York: 1967), 316; John C. Sparrow, *History of Personnel Demobilization in the U.S. Army* (Washington, D.C.: 1952), 64–97.
3. Sparrow, 244 et seq.
4. *PDDE,* IX, 599–605, 611–612, 670–672, 753–755.
5. *New York Times,* Jan. 17, 185; *Washington Post,* Jan. 17, 1945. These charts are reproduced in *PDDE,* VII, 601–602, 606.
6. Notes, Jan. 17, 1948, Frank McNaughton Papers, Harry S Truman Library.
7. Kevin McCann, *Man from Abilene* (New York: 1952), 136.
8. Letter, Eisenhower to MacArthur, Sept. 20, 1946, MacArthur Memorial and Archives; Dwight D. Eisenhower, *Ike's Letters to a Friend* (Lawrence, Kansas: 1986), 80.
9. Eisenhower, *Ike's Letters to a Friend,* 28.
10. Townsend Hoopes and Douglas Brinkley, *Driven Patriot: The Life and Times of James Forrestal* (New York: 1992), 325–349.
11. Susan Eisenhower, *Mrs. Ike* (New York: 1993), 235.
12. Alden Hatch, *Red Carpet for Mamie* (New York: 1954), 204–205; Dorothy Brandon, *Mamie: A Portrait of a First Lady* (New York: 1954), 256–258.
13. Robert Bolton interview and Ray I. Witter interview, both EL.
14. *PDDE,* VII, 1164.
15. Geoffrey Perret, *Old Soldiers Never Die* (New York: 1996), 498.
16. Tang Tsou, *America's Failure in China* (Chicago: 1963), 371–377; 392–399.
17. Memo for Record, May 29, 1959, Ann Whitman File, Diary Series, EL.
18. Peter Lyon, *Eisenhower: Portrait of the Hero* (Boston: 1974), 372.
19. Perret, 501.
20. Joseph Alsop, *I've Seen the Best of It* (New York: 1980), 338.

21. *Ibid.,* VII, 1106n.
22. George Kennan, *Memoirs, 1925–1950* (Boston: 1967), 547–559. Equally prescient was the Clifford-Elsey report, prepared six months before Kennan's long telegram, which no one but Truman saw: Clark Clifford, *Counsel to the President* (New York: 1991), 124–128.
23. Harold Borowski, *A Hollow Threat: Strategic Air Power and Containment Before Korea* (Westport, Conn.: 1982), 145–147, 166–171.
24. John Lewis Gaddis, *Strategies of Containment* (New York: 1982), 54–88.
25. Walter Millis, ed., *The Forrestal Diaries* (New York: 1953), 327; *PDDE,* VII, 1127.
26. *PDDE,* VII, 575.
27. Ibid., VI, 327–328, 348.
28. Ibid., VII, 825, 853.
29. Cable, Clay to Eisenhower, Sept. 20, 1946; letters, DDE to Kay Summersby, Jan. 15 and March 11, 1946, EL.
30. Author interview with John S. D. Eisenhower, August 17, 1998; Cliff Roberts, COHP.
31. *PDDE,* VII, 1070, 1072, 1121.
32. Bradford G. Chynoweth memoir, "Army Recollections," USAMHI Archives; *PDDE,* VII, 903.
33. Jacqueline Cochran (Wickman interview), EL.
34. McCann, 140–141.
35. Letter, DDE to John C. H. Lee, March 8, 1948, EL.
36. *PDDE,* IX, 2011.
37. Memo to the President from James Forrestal, Jan. 22, 1948, Harry S Truman Library. Many commentators interpreted the remark about "the absence of some obvious and overriding reason" as a slap at MacArthur's political ambitions, something Eisenhower strongly denied. Forrestal was the only person with whom he discussed this letter, and neither man mentioned MacArthur; nor did Forrestal when he forwarded this memo to Truman.

Chapter 29: The President

1. Susan Eisenhower, *Mrs. Ike* (New York: 1996), 248.
2. Robert Schulz interview, COHP.
3. Douglas Black interview, COHP.
4. Dwight D. Eisenhower, *At Ease: Stories I Tell to Friends* (New York: 1967), 324–326.
5. Arthur Nevins interview and Craig Cannon interview, both EL; Schulz, loc. cit.; Black, loc. cit.
6. John S. D. Eisenhower interview, EL.
7. Nigel Hamilton, *Monty: The Field Marshal* (London: 1986), 736.
8. Letters, DDE to Harry S Truman, Nov. 1948, and Harry Vaughn to DDE, Dec. 2, 1948, HST Library.

9. William H. Rodgers, *Think: A Biography of the Watsons and IBM* (New York: 1967), 202–201.
10. Travis Beale Jacobs, "Eisenhower Comes to Columbia," *Columbia Library Columns* (Autumn 1997).
11. Susan Eisenhower, 250; Black op. cit.; Dwight D. Eisenhower, *Ike's Letters to a Friend* (Lawrence, Kansas: 1984), 40.
12. Albert Jacobs interview, COHP; Grayson Kirk, COHP; Black, op. cit.
13. Bela Kornitzer, *The Great American Heritage* (New York: 1955), 96.
14. Louis M. Hacker interview, EL.
15. Lester David and Irene David, *Ike and Mamie* (New York: 1981), 172–173.
16. Grayson Kirk interview, EL; Jacobs; Hacker.
17. Helen King interview, EL.
18. *New York Times,* March 24, 1950.
19. *PDDE,* XI, 950n, 1403–1404.
20. Robert Schulz interview, COHP; Alden Hatch, *Red Carpet for Mamie* (New York: 1954), 214–215.
21. Susan Eisenhower, 252.
22. *At Ease,* 340–341.
23. *Ike's Letters to a Friend,* 61.
24. Townsend Hoopes and Douglas Brinkley, *Driven Patriot: A Biography of James Forrestal* (New York: 1990), 347–348; *Ike's Letters to a Friend,* 59.
25. Letter, Harry S Truman to DDE, Jan. 8, 1949, EL.
26. Robert H. Ferrell, ed., *The Eisenhower Diaries* (New York: 1981), 152–153.
27. *Ike's Letters to a Friend,* 72.
28. Clare Boothe Luce interview, COHP.
29. Cliff Roberts interview, COHP.
30. Ferrell, 175–176.
31. Ibid., 179.

Chapter 30: Duty Calls

1. Dwight D. Eisenhower, *Ike's Letters to a Friend* (Lawrence, Kansas: 1984), 82.
2. Richard Norton Smith, *An Uncommon Man* (New York: 1984), 390–393.
3. *New York Times,* Jan. 21, 1951.
4. Dwight D. Eisenhower, *At Ease: Stories I Tell to Friends* (New York: 1967), 371–372.
5. Robert Schulz interview, COHP; Thomas Handy interview, EL.
6. Cf. Simone de Beauvoir, *Les Mandarins* (Paris: 1958), for an incisive picture of the ardent Stalinism of most French intellectuals after World War II.
7. Lester David and Irene David, *Ike and Mamie* (New York: 1981), 175.
8. Alfred Gruenther interview, COHP.
9. *PDDE,* XII, 222.
10. Kevin McCann, *The Man from Abilene* (New York: 1952), 220–221; letter, DDE to Averell Harriman, May 4, 1951, Harry S Truman Library.

11. "Minutes of a Meeting with General Eisenhower in the Cabinet Room of the White House, Nov. 5, 1951," HST Library.

12. *PDDE,* XII, 629–630, 806.

13. "Minutes of a Meeting," op. cit.

14. Only six months after he left NATO, he had second thoughts; see, *PDDE,* XIII, 1457–1458.

15. Robert H. Ferrell, ed., *The Eisenhower Diaries* (New York: 1981), 161–162.

16. Herbert Brownell, *Advising Ike* (Lawrence, Kansas: 1993), 94; Richard Norton Smith, *Thomas E. Dewey and His Times* (New York: 1989), 555.

17. Cliff Roberts interview, COHP; Memo, Frank McNaughton to Don Bermingham, June 4, 1948, HST Library; Jean Smith, *Lucius D. Clay* (New York: 1993), 587. McNaughton informed Bermingham, a rich Alabamian who was trying to get Eisenhower into politics, that at the Army and Navy Club on June 2, a former *Washington Post* staffer, John F. Gerrity, was introduced to Eisenhower and asked if he would seek the Democratic nomination. Eisenhower replied, "I'm a Republican."

18. Ronald Steele, *Walter Lippmann and the American Century* (New York: 1980), 481. Lippmann was the author of a highly admired book, *A Preface to Morals,* published in 1929.

19. Kevin McCann interview, COHP.

20. William J. Miller, *Henry Cabot Lodge* (New York: 1969), 216–217; Dwight D. Eisenhower, *Mandate for Change* (New York: 1962).

21. C. L. Sulzberger, *A Long Row of Candles* (New York: 1969), 700–705.

22. Letter, Harry S Truman to DDE, Dec. 18, 1951, HST Library.

23. Miller, 228–229; *New York Times,* Jan. 7, 1952.

24. *New York Times,* Nov. 15, 1949, Jan. 8, 1952.

25. Jacqueline Cochran interview, EL; *PDDE,* XIII, 974–976.

26. Lucius D. Clay (interviewed by Jean Smith), Clay Papers, MD, LC.

27. Kevin McCann interview, COHP.

28. David McCullough, *Truman* (New York: 1992), 893.

29. Geoffrey Perret, *Old Soldiers Never Die* (New York: 1996), 575–576.

30. Jean Smith, *Lucius D. Clay* (New York: 1994), 582, 595.

31. *PDDE,* XIII, 1154–1156.

Chapter 31: Moving On

1. Letter, DDE to Cliff Roberts, April 4, 1952, EL.

2. Kevin McCann interview, COHP.

3. Arthur Nevins interview, EL; Alfred Gruenther interview, COHP.

4. Letter, Dan Thornton to DDE, March 24, 1952, EL.

5. Marquis Childs, *Eisenhower, Captive Hero* (New York: 1958), 134; David McCullough, *Truman* (New York: 1992), 889.

6. *New York Times,* June 16, 1952.

7. James Patterson, *Mr. Republican: The Life of Robert A. Taft* (New York: 1972), 539–540.

8. *New York Times,* July 3, 1948.

9. Herbert Brownell, *Advising Ike* (Lawrence, Kansas: 1993), 111–116.

10. Richard Norton Smith, *Thomas E. Dewey and His Times* (New York: 1982), 589, 595–596; William Miller, *Henry Cabot Lodge* (New York: 1969), 248.

11. Richard Norton Smith, 584; Jean Smith, *Lucius D. Clay* (New York: 1994), 601–602. Dewey was so confident that Nixon would be on the ticket he was putting bets on it long before the convention; Jack Bell interview, COHP.

12. The other names were William Knowland (senior senator from California and Warren's campaign manager); congressmen Charles Halleck of Indiana and Walter Judd of Minnesota and Governor Dan Thornton of Colorado.

13. Earl Warren, *The Memoirs of Earl Warren* (New York: 1977), 251.

14. Ed Cray, *Chief Justice* (New York: 1997), 232. There is no mention of this episode in Warren's memoirs, probably because it put Eisenhower deeply in his debt and played a crucial role in his eventual appointment as Chief Justice of the Supreme Court.

15. Geoffrey Perret, *Old Soldiers Never Die* (New York: 1996), 575.

16. Brownell, 120; Jean Smith, 599.

17. James Hagerty interview, COHP.

18. Dwight D. Eisenhower, *Mandate for Change* (New York: 1963), 45.

19. Herbert Brownell interview, EL.

20. Herbert Parmet, *Eisenhower and the American Crusades* (New York: 1974), 100.

21. Hagerty interview, COHP.

22. Rachel Adams, *On the Other Hand* (New York: 1963), 85.

23. Susan Eisenhower, *Mrs. Ike* (New York: 1996), 270; Stephen Benedict interview, COHP.

24. Charles Halleck interview, COHP; Benedict interview, COHP.

25. Leonard Hall interview, COHP.

26. William S. White, *The Taft Story* (New York: 1954), 187–189.

27. Benedict interview, COHP.

28. Sherman Adams, *Firsthand Report* (New York: 1961), 37; Richard Nixon, *Six Crises* (New York: 1962), 93.

29. Richard Norton Smith, 600–601.

30. William B. Ewald, Jr., *Eisenhower the President* (Englewood Cliffs, N.J.: 1981), 3; Earl Mazo, *Nixon* (New York: 1959), 121; Garry Wills, *Nixon Agonistes* (Boston: 1970), 104.

31. Eisenhower's close friend and stockbroker Cliff Roberts prepared Eisenhower's financial statement. To Ike's surprise and delight, it showed that he was not as rich as Stevenson: Cliff Roberts interview, COHP.

32. Earl C. Behrens interview, COHP. Behrens, a journalist from San Francisco, was standing behind Richard and Pat Nixon.

33. David Oshinsky, *A Conspiracy So Immense: The World of Joe McCarthy* (New York: 1984), 243–245.

34. Joseph McCarthy, *America's Retreat from Victory* (New York: 1951), 143.

35. Kevin McCann interview, EL; Ewald, 60.

36. Sherman Adams and Gabriel Hauge interviews, both COHP.
37. Porter McKeever, *Adlai Stevenson* (New York: 1989), 236–237; John Bartlow Martin, *Adlai Stevenson of Illinois* (New York: 1979), 744.
38. Emmet John Hughes, *Ordeal of Power* (New York: 1963), 32–35.
39. Cliff Roberts interview, COHP.
40. Clare Boothe Luce interview, COHP.

Chapter 32: From Here to There

1. Cliff Roberts interview, COHP.
2. Jean Smith, *Lucius D. Clay* (New York: 1993), 607.
3. Herbert Brownell, *Advising Ike* (Lawrence, Kansas: 1993), 132.
4. Smith, 609; Kai Bird, *The Chairman* (New York: 1991), 386–387.
5. *PDDE,* XIII, 1436.
6. Henry Cabot Lodge, *As It Was* (New York: 1976), 47–48; Smith, 610.
7. Ezra Taft Benson, *Cross Fire: The Eight Years with Eisenhower* (New York: 1962), 11–12.
8. Prescott Bush interview, COHP.
9. *PDDE,* IX, 2255; Cliff Roberts interview, COHP.
10. *New York Times,* Nov. 1, 1952.
11. Dwight D. Eisenhower, *Mandate for Change* (New York: 1963), 85.
12. Lodge, 31–35.
13. Margaret Truman, *Harry S Truman* (New York: 1973), 551–552.
14. Diary, June 28, 1950, Matthew B. Ridgway Papers, USAMHI Archives.
15. Lodge, 39; Carl M. Brauer, *Presidential Transitions: Eisenhower Through Reagan* (New York: 1986), 24.
16. Mark Clark interview, COHP. There is no mention of this meeting in Clark's memoir, *Calculated Risk* (New York: 1955). On the contrary, in *Calculated Risk,* Clark says he never presented his plan to Eisenhower, a claim that is simply incredible.
17. *PDDE,* XIII, 1416.
18. *Mandate for Change,* 95.
19. Dwight D. Eisenhower interview, Mudd Library, Princeton University.
20. Memorandum of Conversation, Dec. 14, 1952, Ann Whitman diary, EL.
21. Clare Boothe Luce interview, COHP.
22. Tyler Abell, ed., *The Drew Pearson Diaries, 1949–1959* (New York: 1974), 211.
23. Cabinet Minutes Series, Jan. 12, 1953, EL.
24. Robert H. Ferrell, ed., *The Eisenhower Diaries* (New York: 1981), 225; Robert J. Donovan, *Eisenhower: The Inside Story* (New York: 1956), 3–4.
25. William Bragg Ewald, Jr., *Eisenhower the President* (Englewood Cliffs, N.J.: 1981), 32.
26. Memo, Bradley to Truman, December 4, 1952, HSTL; *Mandate for Change,* 101.

27. *Public Papers of the Presidents: Eisenhower, 1953* (Washington, D.C.: 1958), 1–8.
28. Andrew J. Goodpaster interview, COHP.

Chapter 33: The Organization Man

1. Susan Eisenhower, *Mrs. Ike* (New York: 1996), 282–283.
2. Robert Ferrell, ed., *The Eisenhower Diaries* (New York: 1981), 225.
3. *PDDE,* XIV, 9.
4. Carl Brauer, *Presidential Transitions from Eisenhower Through Reagan* (New York: 1986), 33.
5. Edward Beach interview, COHP.
6. Nat Hentoff, *A Political Life* (New York: 1969), 59.
7. Bryce Harlow interview, COHP.
8. Ann Whitman diary, Sept. 28, 1953, EL.
9. Andrew J. Goodpaster interview, COHP.
10. Bryce Harlow and Percy Brundage interviews, both COHP.
11. Brauer, 33.
12. Memo, July 8, 1953, C. D. Jackson Papers, EL; William Bragg Ewald, Jr., *Eisenhower the President* (Englewood Cliffs, N.J.: 1981), 165–166.
13. Ann Whitman diary, May 19, 1955, EL.
14. Stephen Benedict interview, COHP.
15. Brauer, 42–43.
16. Homer Gruenther interview, COHP.
17. Andrew J. Goodpaster interview, EL.
18. Cabinet Minutes Series, April 18, 1957, EL.
19. Herbert Parmet, *Eisenhower and the American Crusades* (New York: 1978), 176.
20. Andrew J. Goodpaster interview, EL.
21. *New York Times* Jan. 21, 1953; E. Bruce Geelhoed, *Charles E. Wilson and Controversy at the Pentagon, 1953–1957* (Detroit: 1979), 49–51.
22. Cliff Roberts interview, COHP; Memo, Jan. 24, 1953, William E. Robinson Papers, EL.
23. Robert Donovan, *Eisenhower: The Inside Story* (New York: 1956), 10–11.
24. Ann Whitman diary, Jan. 30, 1957, EL.
25. Stewart Alsop, "The Man Ike Trusts with the Cash," *Saturday Evening Post* (May 23, 1953).
26. Parmet, 183.
27. Richard Strout, "The Administration's Abominable No Man," *New York Times Magazine,* June 3, 1956.
28. James C. Hagerty interview, COHP.
29. Ewald, 161–162.
30. Prescott Bush interview, COHP.
31. Edward Beach interview, COHP.

32. James C. Hagerty interview, COHP.
33. Ralph Cake interview, COHP.

Chapter 34: Maximum Danger

1. Allen Weinstein and Alexander Vassiliev, *The Haunted Wood: Soviet Espionage in America—The Stalin Era* (New York: 1999), 197–202; author interview with John S. D. Eisenhower, Nov. 13, 1998.
2. Michael Meeropol, ed., *The Rosenberg Letters* (New York: 1994), 591. In *Mandate for Change* (New York: 1963), 225, Eisenhower himself called Ethel "the strong one" and made no mention of the offer to spare her life.
3. *Foreign Relations of the United States, 1950* (Washington, D.C.: 1977), I, 234–292; Ernest May, ed., *American Cold War Strategy: Interpreting NSC 68* (Boston: 1993), 104–107.
4. Harry S Truman, *Years of Trial and Hope: 1946–1953* (New York: 1956), 323–331.
5. Stephen Zaloga, *Target America: The Soviet Union and the Strategic Arms Race, 1945–1964* (Novato, Calif.: 1993), 78–79; Memo, "SAC: Progress Analysis 1 Nov. 1948–31 Dec. 1956," Curtis LeMay Papers, MD, LC.
6. Emmet John Hughes, *The Living Presidency* (New York: 1974); 15–16; Robert R. Bowie and Richard H. Immerman, *Waging Peace: How Eisenhower Forged an Enduring Cold War Strategy* (New York: 1998), 115–119.
7. Robert Cutler, *No Time for Rest* (Boston: 1966), 241.
8. John Prados, *Keepers of the Keys* (New York: 1991), 75.
9. George V. Allen interview, COHP.
10. Elmer Staats in group interview, EL.
11. Prados, 71.
12. Cutler, 307–309.
13. Bowie and Immerman, 128–136.
14. Kenneth W Thompson, ed., *The Eisenhower Presidency* (Lanham, Md.: 1984), 71.
15. *Foreign Relations of the United States 1955–1957* (Washington, D.C.: 1990), XIX, 26.
16. Diary, Dec. 5, 1953, Eisenhower Papers, EL; *Congressional Record,* 83rd Congress (Washington, D.C.: 1954), C, 1782–1783.
17. Memorandum of Conference with the President, July 20, 1954; Ann Whitman diary, November 9, 1957, EL.
18. *Public Papers of the Presidents: Dwight D. Eisenhower, 1953* (Washington, D.C.: 1960), 16.
19. Robert J. Watson, *History of the JCS and National Policy* (Washington, D.C.: 1986), V, 256.
20. Robert J. Donovan, *Eisenhower* (New York: 1956), 41.

21. *PPP, Eisenhower, 1953,* 75.
22. *New York Times,* May 8, 1953.
23. *PPP, Eisenhower, 1953,* 182.
24. Vladislov Zubok and Constantine Pleshakov, *Inside the Kremlin's Cold War* (Cambridge, Mass.: 1996), 156–157.
25. Cabinet Minutes Series, May 5, 1953, EL.
26. Walter G. Hermes, *Truce Tent and Fighting Front* (Washington, D.C.: 1965), 462–470.
27. Stephen Ambrose, *Eisenhower* (New York: 1984), II, 101–105.
28. Cabinet Minutes Series, June 26, 1953, EL.
29. Donovan, 128–129.

Chapter 35: New Look

1. Ann Whitman diary, July 20, 1954, EL.
2. Stephen Jurika, Jr., *From Pearl Harbor to Vietnam: The Memoirs of Admiral Arthur W. Radford* (Stanford, Calif.: 1978), 303–305.
3. *New York Times,* Jan. 13, 1954.
4. Lecture, "Strategic Air Command," Jan. 28, 1954, Curtis LeMay Papers, MD, LC.
5. Robert R. Bowie and Richard H. Immerman, *Waging Peace: How Eisenhower Forged an Enduring Cold War Strategy* (New York: 1998), 199–200.
6. George Kennan, *Memoirs* (Boston: 1970), 246.
7. Dwight D. Eisenhower, *Waging Peace* (New York: 1965), 365.
8. Matthew Ridgway, with Hal Martin, *Soldier* (New York: 1958), 272.
9. *New York Times,* Nov. 11, 1953.
10. Memo of Conference with the President, May 14, 1956, EL.
11. Memorandum of Conference with the President, Feb. 24, 1955, EL; Maxwell Taylor, *The Uncertain Trumpet* (New York: 1961), 36–46; John Taylor, *General Maxwell Taylor* (New York: 1989), 191–194.
12. Memoranda of Conferences with the President, March 30 and May 24, 1956, EL.
13. Robert R. Bowie interview, COHP.
14. Tyler Abell, ed., *The Drew Pearson Diaries, 1949–1959* (New York: 1974), 210.
15. *Foreign Relations of the United States (FRUS) 1952–1954* (Washington, D.C.: 1978), II, 535.
16. *Waging Peace,* 180.
17. Vernon Walters interview, EL.
18. Andrew J. Goodpaster, in group interview, EL.
19. Memorandum, "Russian Atomic Power and the Lost Revolution," Aug. 21, 1954, C. D. Jackson Papers, EL.

20. James G. Hershberg, *James B. Conant* (New York: 1993), 694.
21. Ann Whitman diary, July 31, 1957, EL.
22. Bi-Partisan Leaders' Meeting, March 22, 1956, James Hagerty Papers, EL.
23. Ann Whitman diary, May 25, 1955, EL.
24. Bernard Fall, *Hell in a Very Small Place* (New York: 1964), 169 et seq.
25. Dwight D. Eisenhower, *Mandate for Change* (New York: 1963), 339.
26. Stanley Karnow, *Vietnam* (New York: 1983), 189–191.
27. *PDDE,* XV, 886–887; William Bragg Ewald, Jr., *Eisenhower the President* (Englewood Cliffs, N.J.: 1981), 107.
28. Sherman Adams, *Firsthand Report* (New York: 1962), 118.
29. *FRUS, 1952–1954* (Washington, D.C.: 1093), XIII, 1198.
30. Ewald, 109.
31. *FRUS 1952–1954,* XIII, 1419–1428, 1431–1445.
32. Melanie Billings-Yun, *Decision Against War: Eisenhower and Dien Bien Phu, 1954* (New York: 1988), 82 et seq. For a different view, see, James R. Arnold, *The First Domino* (New York: 1992), 172–189. James claims that Eisenhower wanted to intervene but Congress stopped him.
33. *Public Papers of the Presidents: Eisenhower, 1954* (Washington, D.C.: 1954), 383.
34. Stephen Ambrose, *Eisenhower* (New York: 1984), II, 205.
35. *PDDE,* XV, 1004.
36. Author interview with General Andrew J. Goodpaster, Feb. 22, 1999.
37. Fall, 393–394; Karnow, 218–119.

Chapter 36: Hidden Hand

1. David Horowitz, *The Rockefellers* (New York: 1982), 271n; Townsend Hoopes, *The Devil and John Foster Dulles* (New York: 1973), 135–136.
2. Hoopes, 144; Robert Donovan, *Eisenhower: The Inside Story* (New York: 1956), 264.
3. Ann Whitman diary, July 20, 1954, EL; letter, John Foster Dulles to Scott McLeod, Dec. 28, 1953, Dulles Papers, EL; David Oshinsky, *A Conspiracy So Immense* (New York: 1983), 261–163.
4. Sherman Adams, *Firsthand Report* (New York: 1962), 456; Carl Brauer, *Presidential Transitions from Eisenhower Through Reagan* (New York: 1989), 46.
5. Robert Ferrell, ed., *The Eisenhower Diaries* (New York: 1981), 237.
6. Clare Boothe Luce interview, COHP.
7. Andrew J. Goodpaster interview, EL.
8. George V. Allen interview, COHP; Stephen Ambrose, *Eisenhower* (New York: 1984), II, 469.
9. Ann Whitman diary, Nov. 21, 1956, EL.
10. Adams, 46.

11. Robert H. Ferrell, ed., *The Diary of James C. Hagerty* (Bloomington, Ind.: 1983), 73.

12. Ann Whitman diary, July 20, 1954, EL.

13. Peter Grose, *Gentleman Spy: The Life of Allen Dulles* (New York: 1994), 350.

14. John Prados, *The Presidents' Secret Wars* (New York: 1978), 109–111.

15. Ann Whitman diary, Oct. 19, 1954, EL; *PDDE*, XV, 1213–1215.

16. William Bragg Ewald, Jr., *Eisenhower the President* (Englewood Cliffs, N.J.: 1981), 266.

17. Thomas S. Powers, *The Man Who Kept the Secrets* (New York: 1975), 95.

18. Kermit Roosevelt, *Countercoup* (New York: 1979), 115.

19. *PDDE*, XIV, 337–340; Barry Rubin, *Paved with Good Intentions: The American Experience and Iran* (New York: 1980), 71–87.

20. Roosevelt, 1–19.

21. Ambrose, II, 129.

22. Diary, Feb. 8, 1955, Adolph A. Berle Papers, FDR Library.

23. Richard Immerman, *The CIA in Guatemala* (Austin, Texas: 1982), 137–138.

24. Piero Gleijeses, *Shattered Hope: The Guatemalan Revolution and the United States* (Princeton, N.J.: 1991), 228–230.

25. Cabinet Minutes Series, Feb. 28, 1954, EL.

26. *New York Times Magazine,* July 18, 1954.

27. *Foreign Relations of the United States, 1952–1954* (Washington, D.C.: 1983), IV, 1093.

28. Immerman, 133.

29. Richard Bissell interview, COHP.

30. Dwight D. Eisenhower, *Mandate for Change 1953–1956* (New York: 1963), 425–426.

31. Gleijeses, 343.

32. Ann Whitman diary, July 20, 1954, EL.

33. *New York Times,* July 1, 1954.

Chapter 37: Congressional Business

1. Robert H. Ferrell, ed., *The Eisenhower Diaries* (New York: 1981), 226.

2. James Patterson, *Mr. Republican: The Life of Robert A. Taft* (New York: 1972), 585–587; Sherman Adams, *Firsthand Report* (New York: 1961), 24.

3. Adams, 21.

4. Ann Whitman diary, July 25, 1956, EL.

5. Ibid., June 15, 1954, EL. The case for Knowland—failed politician, bankrupt publisher, and successful suicide—is put in George B. Montgomery and James W. Johnson, *One Step from the White House* (Berkeley and Los Angeles: 1998).

6. Bernard Shanley interview, COHP.

7. Ann Whitman diary, May 25, 1955, EL.

8. Stephen Ambrose, *Eisenhower* (New York: 1984), II, 155.

9. Herbert Brownell, *Advising Ike* (Lawrence, Kansas: 1994), 265–268; Robert H. Ferrell, *The Diary of James C. Hagerty* (Bloomington, Ind.: 1983), 7.

10. Duane Tannenbaum, *Eisenhower and the Bricker Amendment Controversy* (Ithaca, N.Y.: 1988), 216–219; William Bragg Ewald, Jr., *Eisenhower the President* (Englewood Cliffs, N.J.: 1981), 48–49.

11. Ferrell, *Diary of James C. Hagerty,* 14; *PDDE,* XV, 74–76, 282–283, 848–849.

12. Brownell, 270.

13. Joseph Persico, *Edward R. Murrow* (New York: 1989), 315. Cf. Tyler Abell, ed., *Drew Pearson Diaries, 1949–1959* (New York: 1974), 209.

14. Gabriel Hauge and Charles Halleck interviews, both COHP.

15. Letter, Henry Cabot Lodge to DDE, Oct. 30, 1953, EL.

16. Lester David and Irene David, *Ike and Mamie* (New York: 1981), 202.

17. Craig Allen, *Eisenhower and the Media* (Chapel Hill, N.C.: 1993), 32–34.

18. *New York Times,* April 6, 1954; Ferrell, *Diary of James C. Hagerty,* 41.

19. George H. Gallup, *The Gallup Poll, 1935–1972* (New York: 1972); Allen, 39–40.

20. *New York Times,* June 6, 1952.

21. *New Republic,* March 30, 1953.

22. William O. Douglas, *The Court Years* (New York: 1976), 69.

23. Jeff Broadwater, *Eisenhower and the Anti-Communist Crusade* (Chapel Hill, N.C.: 1992), 91–94.

24. Dwight D. Eisenhower, *Mandate for Change* (New York: 1963), 308–310; Earl Latham, *The Communist Controversy in Washington* (Cambridge, Mass.: 1966), 314–315.

25. Brownell, 236–242.

26. *New York Times,* Dec. 3, 1953.

27. Ann Whitman diary, December 3, 1953, EL; Lewis L. Strauss, *Men and Decisions* (New York: 1962), 268; Richard Pfau, *No Sacrifice Too Great: The Life of Lewis L. Strauss* (Charlottesville, Virginia: 1984).

28. Joseph and Stewart Alsop, "We Accuse!" *Harper's* (Oct. 1954).

29. Richard G. Hewlett and Jack M. Holl *Atoms for Peace and War, 1953–1961* (Berkeley, Calif.: 1992), 80.

30. Ibid., 35–41.

31. Philip M. Stern, *The Oppenheimer Case* (New York: 1969), 1.

32. On the repeated Soviet attempts to recruit Oppenheimer, see, Allen Weinstein and Alexander Vassiliev, *The Haunted Wood: Soviet Espionage in America* (New York: 1999), 198 *passim.*

33. Hewlett and Holl, 78.

34. Letter, John J. McCloy to DDE, April 16, 1954, EL.

35. John Major, *The Oppenheimer Hearing* (New York: 1971), 175–176.

36. Ferrell, *Diary of James C. Hagerty,* 80–81; James Hershberg, *James B. Conant* (New York: 1992), 680–681; Gerald Piel, *Science in the Cause of Man* (New York: 1961), 130.

37. Ferrell, *Diary of James C. Hagerty,* 61.

38. Letter, DDE to William Robinson, March 23, 1954, Robinson Papers, EL.

39. Emmet John Hughes, *The Ordeal of Power* (New York: 1963), 81.

40. Nicholas von Hoffman, *Citizen Cohn* (New York: 1988), 188–190; Sidney Zion, *The Autobiography of Roy Cohn* (Secaucus, N.J.: 1990), 91–95.

41. *New York Times,* June 15, 1953; Kai Bird, *The Chairman* (New York: 1992), 408.

42. J. B. Matthews, "Reds in Our Churches," *American Mercury* (July 1953).

43. Hughes, 83–84; Brownell, 256; Zion, 100–101.

44. David Oshinsky, *A Conspiracy So Immense* (New York: 1983), 231; Thomas J. Reeves, *The World of Joe McCarthy* (New York: 1991), 401–402.

45. Ann Whitman diary, December 4, 1954, EL.

46. Oshinsky, 375–377.

47. Hagerty diary, Feb. 25, 1954, EL.

48. Fred Friendly, *Due to Circumstances Beyond Our Control* (New York: 1967), 51.

49. Zion, 13–14.

50. Ann Whitman diary, Dec. 4, 1954, EL.

51. Earl Endacott memoir, EL.

Chapter 38: Look Ahead, Neighbor

1. *New York Times,* September 10, October 3, 7, 21, 1953; Dwight D. Eisenhower, *Mandate for Change, 1953–1956* (New York: 1963), 127.

2. Sherman Adams, *Firsthand Report* (New York: 1961), 54–55; William Bragg Ewald, Jr., *Eisenhower the President* (Englewood Cliffs, N.J.: 1981), 60–61.

3. Karl Brandt interview, COHP.

4. Adams, 156.

5. Peter Lyon, *Eisenhower: Portrait of the Hero* (Boston: 1974), 467.

6. Robert Ferrell, ed., *The Eisenhower Diaries* (New York: 1981), 227.

7. Percival Brundage, COHP; Erwin C. Hargove and Samuel A. Morley, eds., *The President and the Council of Economic Advisers* (Boulder; Colo.: 1984), 106–108, 117.

8. Letter, DDE to Burns, Jan. 14, 1955, EL

9. Memorandum of Conversation, Oct. 12, 1955, Ann Whitman diary, EL; Adams, 457–458.

10. Michael J. Rossant, "The Growing Power of William McChesney Martin," *The Reporter* (Oct. 17, 1957).

11. Iwan W. Morgan, *Eisenhower versus "The Spenders"* (New York: 1992), 61–70; Harold G. Vatter *The U.S. Economy in the 1950s* (Westport, Conn.: 1984), 90–97.

12. John W. Sloan, *Eisenhower and the Management of Prosperity* (Lawrence, Kansas: 1993), 151–154.

13. Memo, DDE to Charles E. Wilson, in *PDDE,* XVI, 1488–1491.

14. Stephen Bennett interview, COHP.
15. Robert J. Donovan, Eisenhower (New York: 1956), 173.
16. Ferrell, 94.
17. *Public Papers of the Presidents, Eisenhower: 1954* (Washington 1960), 62; Edward Berkowitz and Kim McQuaid, *Creating the Welfare State* (Lawrence, Kansas: 1990), 179–181.
18. Ann Whitman diary, Oct. 26, 1955, EL.
19. Ferrell, 106.
20. Ann Whitman diary, July 21, 1954, EL; Prescott Bush, COHP.
21. Ann Whitman diary, Oct. 26, 1953, EL.
22. Memorandum of Conversation, March 1, 1955, Ann Whitman diary, EL.
23. Ann Whitman diary, May 17, 1955, EL.
24. Ibid., May 2, 1955, EL.
25. Ezra Taft Benson, *Cross Fire* (New York: 1962), 11.
26. John D. Kendrick, *Postwar Productivity Trends in the United States, 1948–1969* (New York: 1973), 78–79; Edward C. Higbee, *Farms and Farmers in the Urban Age* (New York: 1963), 99.
27. Stephen Ambrose, *Eisenhower* (New York: 1984), II, 160.
28. Ezra Taft Benson interview, EL.
29. Edward L. Schapsmeier and Frederick H. Schapsmeier, *Ezra Taft Benson and the Politics of Agriculture* (Danville, Ill.: 1977), 45.
30. Memorandum of Conversation, Oct. 21, 1953, Ann Whitman diary, EL; Benson, 203.
31. Memoranda of Conversations, June 1 and Oct. 12, 1955, Ann Whitman diary, EL; Ewald, 66–68.
32. Benson interview, EL; Memorandum of Conversation, Oct. 12, 1955, Ann Whitman diary, EL.
33. Congressional Quarterly, *Congress and the Nation, 1945–1964* (Washington, D.C.: 1965), 699–701; Geoffrey Perret, *A Dream of Greatness: The American People, 1945–1963* (New York: 1979), 536–547.
34. Adams, 173; Schapsmeer and Schapsmeer, 100–102.
35. Elmer T. Peterson, *Big Dam Foolishness* (New York: 1954); Memorandum of Conversation, Oct. 12, 1955, Ann Whitman diary, EL.
36. Memoranda of Conversations, Oct. 1 and Nov. 5, 1955, Ann Whitman diary, EL.

Chapter 39: Spirit of Geneva

1. Lester David and Irene David, *Ike and Mamie* (New York: 1981), 194; Ann Whitman diary, Sept. 25, 1955; Robinson Notes, William Robinson Papers, EL.
2. George Allen, *Presidents Who Have Known Me* (New York: 1965), 283.
3. *PDDE,* XIV, 497–498, 625–626; XVI, 1607–1608.
4. Dwight D. Eisenhower, *Ike's Letters to a Friend* (Lawrence, Kansas: 1986), 111.

5. Edward Beach interview, COHP.
6. Robert Schulz interview, COHP.
7. David and David, 201.
8. Susan Eisenhower, *Mrs. Ike* (New York: 1996), 276.
9. Merle Miller, *Ike the Soldier* (New York: 1985), 152.
10. Beverly Smith "A Day in the Life of the President," *Saturday Evening Post,* Feb. 6, 1954; Rachel Adams, *On the Other Hand* (New York: 1963), 125; Bryce Harlow, COHP.
11. Miller, 72.
12. Sherman Adams, *Firsthand Report* (New York: 1961), 427.
13. Ann Whitman diary, April 1956, EL.
14. Herbert Warren Wind, "World's Most Exclusive Golf Course," *Sports Illustrated,* Jan. 24, 1955.
15. *New York Times,* June 15, 1954.
16. *Public Papers of the Presidents, Eisenhower, 1953* (Washington, D.C.: 1960), 2.
17. Richard G. Hewlett and Jack M. Holl, *Atoms for Peace and War, 1952–1961* (Berkeley, Calif.: 1992), 30–31.
18. Kevin McCann interview, COHP.
19. *PPP, Eisenhower, 1953,* 645.
20. Dwight D. Eisenhower, *Mandate for Change* (New York: 1963), 252; Lewis L. Strauss, *Men and Decisions* (New York: 1962), 356–357.
21. Martin Gilbert, *Winston S. Churchill* (London: 1986), VIII, 923–924.
22. *New York Times,* December 9, 1953.
23. *PPP, Eisenhower, 1953,* 813–822.
24. Robert H. Ferrell, ed., *The Diary of James C. Hagerty* (Bloomington, Ind.: 1983), 40.
25. Ibid., 36; *New York Times,* April 1, 1954.
26. Dillon Anderson interview, COHP.
27. Georgi Zhukov, *The Memoirs of Marshal Zhukov* (London: 1971), 659 passim; Robert Bowie interview, COHP; John S. D. Eisenhower, *Strictly Personal* (New York: 1974), 178.
28. Minutes, Meeting with Legislative Leaders, July 25, 1955, EL.
29. Department of State, *Foreign Relations of the United States, 1955–1957* (Washington, D.C.: 1988), V, 426 passim, and XX, 163–164; Vernon Walters interview, EL.
30. Robert Bowie interview, COHP.
31. Minutes, Meeting with Legislative Leaders, July 7, 1955, EL.
32. *Mandate for Change,* 522.

Chapter 40: Lifesaver

1. Kenneth Thompson, ed., *The Eisenhower Presidency* (Lanham, Md.: 1984), 148.
2. Bernard Shanley interview, EL; Leonard Hall interview, COHP.

3. Letter, DDE to LBJ, Sept. 23, 1955, EL.

4. Robert J. Donovan, *Eisenhower: The Inside Story* (New York: 1957), 360; Dwight D. Eisenhower, *Mandate for Change 1953–1956* (New York: 1963), 536.

5. Cliff Roberts interview, COHP.

6. Charles G. Lasby, *Eisenhower's Heart Attack* (Lawrence, Kansas: 1996), 97–102.

7. Robert H. Ferrell, ed., *The Eisenhower Diaries* (New York: 1981), 288; *Washington Post,* Oct. 16, 1955.

8. Robert Cutler, *No Time for Rest* (Boston: 1961), 340.

9. Sherman Adams, *Firsthand Report* (New York: 1961), 182–186; Homer Gruenther interview, COHP.

10. Report of Special Agent in Charge, Nov. 11, 1955, EL.

11. Ann Whitman diary, Nov. 24, 1954, EL.

12. Dillon Anderson interview, EL.

13. Ann Whitman diary, May 25, 1955, EL.

14. C.A.H. Thomas and F. M. Shattuck, *The 1956 Presidential Campaign* (Washington, D.C.: 1960), 19; Richard Nixon, *Six Crises* (New York: 1962), 155.

15. Robert Ferrell, ed., *The Diary of James C. Hagerty* (Bloomington, Ind.: 1983), 241.

16. Susan Eisenhower, *Mrs. Ike* (New York: 1996), 294–295; Lasby, 248–257.

17. Ann Whitman diary, June 9–12, 1956, EL.

18. Merle Miller, *Plain Speaking* (New York: 1974), 218.

19. Memorandum of Conversation, March 28, 1956, EL.

20. Cole C. Kingseed, *Eisenhower and the Suez Crisis of 1956* (Baton Rouge, Louisiana: 1995), 38–39.

21. Letter, Anthony Eden to DDE, Aug. 31, 1956, EL.

22. *PDDE,* XV, 2263–2265.

23. Stephen Ambrose, *Eisenhower* (New York: 1984), II, 353.

24. Memorandum of Conversation, Oct. 29, 1956, EL; Donald Neff, *Warriors at Suez* (New York: 1981), 365.

25. Emmet J. Hughes, *The Ordeal of Power* (New York: 1963), 210–220.

26. Dwight D. Eisenhower, *Waging Peace, 1956–1961* (New York: 1965), 83.

27. Billy Graham, *Just as I Am* (San Francisco: 1996), 200; Emmet John Hughes, *The Living Presidency* (New York: 1973), 22.

28. Ann Whitman diary, Jan. 11, 1956, EL; Leonard Hall (Parmet interview), COHP.

29. Ann Whitman diary, March 13 and March 17, 1956, EL.

30. Adams, 28.

31. William Bragg Ewald, Jr., *Eisenhower the President* (Englewood Cliffs, N.J.: 1981), 184–186, 199–200.

32. Ann Whitman diary, May 25, 1955, EL.

33. Richard M. Nixon, *Memoirs* (New York: 1978), 169–173; Arthur Krock, *Memoirs* (New York: 1968), 321.

34. Tyler Abell, ed., *The Drew Pearson Diaries* 1949–1959, (New York: 1974), 366.

35. Ann Whitman diary, Sept. 12, 1956, EL.

Chapter 41: Just Men

1. William O. Douglas, *The Court Years* (New York: 1980), 227.

2. Herbert Brownell, *Advising Ike* (Lawrence, Kansas: 1995), 166–168.

3. Ed Cray, *Chief Justice* (New York: 1997), 251.

4. Earl Warren, *The Memoirs of Earl Warren* (New York: 1977), 280; Ann Whitman diary, March 3, 1954.

5. Brownell, 193.

6. Ulysses Lee, *The Employment of Negro Troops* (Washington, D.C.: 1966), 688–705.

7. *PDDE,* VII, 830; VIII, 1514 1515; Richard Dalfiume, *The Desegregation of the Armed Forces* (Columbia, Mo.: 1969), 148–174.

8. Maxwell Rabb interview, EL; William Bragg Ewald, Jr., *Eisenhower the President* (Englewood Cliffs, N.J.: 1981), 204–207.

9. Robert H. Ferrell, ed., *The Diary of James C. Hagerty* (Bloomington, Ind.: 1981), 54.

10. Ann Whitman diary, July 10, 1957; Susan Eisenhower, *Mrs. Ike* (New York: 1996), 280.

11. Warren, 291–292; Cray, 292.

12. Ewald, 84–86.

13. This draft, with Eisenhower's changes written on it, is in the Simon Sobeloff Papers, MD, LC.

14. Roger K. Newman, *Hugo Black* (New York: 1984), 439.

15. James Hagerty, COHP; Arthur Krock, *Memoirs* (New York: 1968), 300.

16. Warren, 290.

17. Sherman Adams, *Firsthand Report* (New York: 1961), 337–338.

18. Robert Dallek, *Lone Star Rising* (New York: 1991), 517–528.

19. Ann Whitman diary, August 7, 1957.

20. Letter, DDE to William Knowland, Aug. 2, 1957, EL.

21. *Public Papers of the Presidents, Eisenhower, 1957* (Washington, D.C.: 1958), 546–555.

22. Roy Reed, *Faubus* (Fayetteville, Ark.: 1997), 207–213; Tyler Abell, ed., *The Drew Pearson Diaries, 1949–1959* (New York: 1974), 471.

23. Daisy Bates, *The Long Shadow of Little Rock* (New York: 1962), 52 passim; Anthony Lewis, *Portrait of a Decade* (New York: 1964), 47–49.

24. Ann Whitman diary, Oct. 8, 1957; Adams, 348–353.

25. Reed, 219.

26. Cable, Woodrow Wilson Mann to DDE, September 24, 1957, EL.

27. Ferrell, 66.

28. Letter, DDE to Ralph McGill, Feb. 26, 1959, EL.

29. Stephen Ambrose, *Eisenhower* (New York: 1984), II, 190.

30. George Humphrey (Parmet interview), COHP.

31. Cray, 530–531.

32. Author interview with Henry Roehmer McPhee, Nov. 12, 1998; letter, William Robinson to Robert W. Woodruff, June 25, 1958, Robinson Papers, EL.

33. James C. Hagerty interview, COHP. Hagerty also remarks in this interview, "I don't know anybody on that staff that didn't love Adams second only to the President."

34. Ewald, 163; Prescott Bush interview, COHP.

35. Jack Bell and Cliff Roberts interviews, both COHP.

36. Adams, 439. A potentially greater scandal was Adams's acceptance of thousands of dollars from Eisenhower admirers. They hoped to help Ike by helping Adams live better than a hand-to-mouth existence in Washington. The full story features in the forthcoming Adams biography by Professor Michael Birkner.

37. Ann Whitman diary, Sept. 4, 1958; Cliff Roberts and Meade Alcorn interviews, both COHP.

38. Persons had no desire to include Adams and did his best to avoid having it thrust on him. He also acknowledged in later years that he had been a poor substitute for Adams: William B. Persons interview, COHP.

Chapter 42: Rockets' Red Glare

1. Leonid Vladimirov, *The Russian Space Bluff* (New York: 1971), 52–58.

2. *Public Papers of the Presidents, Eisenhower, 1957* (Washington, D.C.: 1958), 811.

3. Ann Whitman diary, October 8, 1957, EL.

4. Constance M. Green and Milton Lomask, *Vanguard: A History* (Washington, D.C.: 1970), 185–212.

5. Robert A. Divine, *The Sputnik Challenge* (New York: 1993), 6–7.

6. *PPP, Eisenhower, 1957* (Washington, D.C.: 1958), 728–729.

7. Michael Armacost, *The Politics of Weapons Innovation: The Thor-Jupiter Controversy* (New York: 1969), 173n.

8. Charles J. V. Murphy, "The White House Since Sputnik," *Fortune,* (Jan. 1958).

9. Memorandum of Conversation, Oct. 16, 1957, DDE Diary Series, EL.

10. James T. Killian, *Sputnik, Scientists and Eisenhower* (Cambridge, Mass.: 1981) 20–24.

11. James G. Hershberg, *James B. Conant* (Boston: 1991), 92.

12. Ann Whitman diary, Jan. 31–Feb. 1, 1958; Memorandum of Conversation, Feb. 1, 1958, DDE Diary Series, EL.

13. Jacob Neufeld, *The Development of Ballistic Missiles in the United States Air*

Force, 1945–1960 (Washington, D.C.: 1990), Chapter III; Trevor Gardner, "How We Fell Behind in Guided Missiles," *Airpower Historian* (Jan. 1958).

14. Ann Whitman diary, Nov. 1954, EL.

15. Armacost, 70–81, 106–111; Harvey M. Sapolsky, *The Polaris System Development* (Cambridge, Mass.: 1972), 9–21; Neufeld, 133–134, 164–167.

16. George B. Kistiakowsky interview, EL; cf. George B. Kistiakowsky, *A Scientist at the White House* (New York: 1976).

17. Letter, DDE to Carl F. Marsh, Feb. 2, 1957, EL.

18. Divine, 40. It was, in fact, national policy. As Eisenhower bluntly expressed it, "SAC must not allow the enemy to strike the first blow." Ann Whitman diary, November 9, 1957, EL.

19. Department of State, *Foreign Relations of the United States, 1955–1957* (Washington, D.C.: 1984), XIX, 3–4, 638–661.

20. Dwight D. Eisenhower, *Waging Peace* (New York: 1963), 222. For a recent vindication of Eisenhower's criticisms of the Gaither Committee's conclusions, see, David L. Snead, *The Gaither Committee, Eisenhower and the Cold War* (Columbus, Ohio: 1999).

21. Rockefeller Brothers Fund, *Prospects for the Republic* (New York: 1961), 104.

22. Memo, "Bipartisan Leaders Meeting, Jan. 5, 1959," James C. Hagerty Papers, EL.

23. Robert H. Ferrell, ed., *The Diary of James C. Hagerty* (Bloomington, Ind.: 1981), 197; *PDDE,* XVI, 1662–1663, 1673–1674.

24. *PPP, Eisenhower, 1955* (Washington, D.C.: 1956), 332–333.

25. Dwight D. Eisenhower, *Mandate for Change 1953–1956* (New York: 1963), 478.

26. Strobe Talbot, ed., *Khrushchev Remembers* (Boston: 1974), 255.

27. *PPP, Eisenhower, 1958* (Washington, D.C.: 1959), 700.

28. Dino A. Brugioni, *Eyeball to Eyeball* (New York: 1994), 39.

29. Memo, "Bermuda Conference, March 21, 1957, Ann Whitman diary, EL.

30. Letter, DDE to Edward Everett Hazlett Jr., Nov. 18, 1957, EL.

31. James C. Hagerty and Bernard Shanley interviews, both COHP; Robert Cutler, *No Time for Rest* (Boston: 1961), 362–364.

32. Dwight D. Eisenhower, *Waging Peace* (New York: 1965), 269–280.

33. William Bragg Ewald, Jr., *Eisenhower the President* (Englewood Cliffs, N.J.: 1981), 295.

34. Audrey and George T. McKahin, *Subversion as Foreign Policy* (New York: 1993), 167–172; Richard Bissell interview, EL.

35. *New York Times,* May 9, 1958.

36. Letter, DDE to Paul Hoffman, June 23, 1958, EL; Department of State, *FRUS, 1958–1960* (Washington, D.C.: 1993), VI, 1140–1141; Memo, Christian Herter to DDE, Dec. 21, 1960, EL.

Chapter 43: Picture It

1. Richard G. Hewlett and Jack M. Holl, *Atoms for Peace and War, 1953–1961* (Berkeley and Los Angeles: 1991), 472–483.
2. Letter, DDE to Bulganin, January 12, 1958, EL; Jeremi Suri, "The Surprise Attack Conference of 1958," *Diplomatic History* (Summer 1997).
3. *Department of State Bulletin* (Jan. 19, 1959), 88.
4. Campbell Craig, *Destroying the Village: Eisenhower and Thermonuclear War* (New York: 1998), 91.
5. Department of State, *Foreign Relations of the United States, 1958–1960* (Washington, D.C.: 1993), VIII, 173–175.
6. Ibid., 302–303, 424–425; Dino A. Brugioni, *Eyeball to Eyeball* (New York: 1994), 40.
7. *Public Papers of the Presidents, Eisenhower, 1959* (Washington, D.C.: 1960), 245. He told his secretary, Ann Whitman, that if the Berlin crisis ended in a nuclear war, "You might as well go out and shoot everyone you see—and then shoot yourself." Ann Whitman diary, March 5, 1959.
8. *Public Papers of the Presidents,* 515; Alastair Horne, *Harold Macmillan* (London: 1989), II, 117 *et seq.*
9. William Burr, "Avoiding the Slippery Slope," *Diplomatic History* (Spring 1994).
10. *FRUS, 1958–1960,* X, Part 1, 269–281.
11. Letter, DDE to Harold Macmillan, July 28, 1959, EL.
12. Strobe Talbot, ed., *Khrushchev Remembers* (Boston: 1974), 375–376.
13. Henry S. Aurand and James C. Hagerty interviews, both COHP; Vernon Walters interview, EL.
14. Sherman Adams, *Firsthand Report* (New York: 1962), 454–455; Hagerty interview, COHP.
15. Talbot, 388–389.
16. Dwight D. Eisenhower, *Waging Peace* (New York: 1965), 442–447; Memorandum, "President Eisenhower's Talks with Chairman Khrushchev at Camp David," EL.
17. *FRUS, 1958–1960,* X, Part 1, 459–483.
18. Brugioni, 30–31.
19. Richard Bissell interview, COHP.
20. Allen Dulles, *The Craft of Intelligence* (New York: 1967).
21. Ann Whitman diary, Jan. 9–10, 1958, EL.
22. Curtis Peebles, *The Corona Project: America's First Spy Satellites* (Annapolis, Md.: 1997), 63–85; Dwayne A. Day et al., eds., *Eye in the Sky* (Washington, D.C.: 1998), 52–59.
23. Michael Beschloss, *Mayday!* (New York: 1987), 9.
24. Francis Gary Powers, with Curt Gentry, *Operation Overflight* (New York: 1970).
25. Beschloss, 271.
26. See pages 131–132.

27. Ann Whitman diary, May 9, 1960; *PPP, Eisenhower, 1960* (Washington, D.C.: 1961), 403–414.
28. John Barron, *KGB* (New York: 1974).
29. *FRUS, 1958–1960,* X, Part 1, 511–513.
30. Letter, DDE to Harold Macmillan, May 24, 1960, EL; George B. Kistiakowsky, *A Scientist at the White House* (Cambridge, Mass.: 1975), 375.
31. Jerrold L. Schechter and Peter S. Deriabin, *The Spy Who Saved the World* (London: 1995), 66–79.

Chapter 44: The Torch Is Passed

1. Ann Whitman diary, July 8, 1959;
2. Letter, DDE to Mamie Moore, July 29, 1960, EL.
3. Kenneth Crawford interview, COHP.
4. Ann Whitman diary, Dec. 1, 1954, EL.
5. William Bragg Ewald, Jr., *Eisenhower the President* (Englewood Cliffs, N.J.: 1981), 29; C. Dwight Dorough, *Mr. Sam* (New York: 1962), 379.
6. Ann Whitman diary, June 19, 1959.
7. Robert Ferrell, ed., *The Diary of James C. Hagerty* (Bloomington, Ind.: 1981), 30.
8. Jack Z. Anderson interview, EL.
9. Letter, DDE to Macmillan, Nov. 11, 1958, EL.
10. Prescott Bush interview, COHP; Jean Smith, *Lucius D. Clay* (New York: 1993), 617–619.
11. Letters, DDE to Arthur Burns, March 12, 20, 1958, EL.
12. Maurice Stans, *One of the President's Men* (Washington, D.C.: 1995), 73.
13. Ewald, 199, 291.
14. Iwan Morgan, *Eisenhower Versus "The Spenders"* (New York: 1992), Chapter 5.
15. Harold G. Vatter, *The U.S. Economy in the 1950s* (New York: 1963), 48.
16. Letter, DDE to Walter Marsh, March 26, 1960, EL.
17. "Report to the Director, CIA," Feb. 4, 1959, EL.
18. Letter, DDE to Macmillan, July 20, 1960, EL.
19. Memo, Herter to DDE, March 17, 1960, EL.
20. Gordon Gray interview, EL; Memo, Douglas Dillon to DDE, Dec. 2, 1960; *FRUS, 1958–1960,* VI, 1058, 1123–1131; Trumbull Higgins, *The Perfect Failure* (New York: 1987), 61–65.
21. Jeffrey Safford, "The Nixon-Castro Meeting of 19 April 1959," *Diplomatic History* (Fall 1980).
22. Memo, Herter to DDE, April 23, 1959, EL.
23. Memo, Herter to DDE, Dec. 23, 1960, EL.
24. Peter Wyden, *Bay of Pigs* (New York: 1979), 24–25, 31; Thomas G. Patterson, *Contesting Castro* (New York: 1994), 219 et seq.

25. White House Central Files, "Visit of Ngo Dinh Diem, May 8, 1957," EL.
26. Letter, DDE to Ngo Dinh Diem, Aug. 29, 1959, EL.
27. Memo, John A. Calhoun to DDE, April 21, 1960, EL.
28. Ewald, 199.
29. Dwight D. Eisenhower, *Waging Peace* (New York: 1965), 595–597.
30. Charles McAdam interview, EL.
31. *PPP, Eisenhower 1960–1961* (Washington, D.C.: 1961), 658; James Hagerty interview, COHP.
32. Ewald, 310.
33. Cliff Roberts interview, COHP.
34. Ann Whitman diary, Oct. 21, EL; Ewald, 312.
35. Letter, DDE to George Murphy, Nov. 20, 1960, EL; Ewald, 314.
36. *Waging Peace,* 712–716; Memo, "Informal List of Subjects to Be Discussed at Meeting of President Eisenhower and Senator John F. Kennedy," no date, EL.
37. Andrew J. Goodpaster interview, EL; Hagerty interview, COHP; *PPP, Eisenhower, 1960–1961* (Washington: D.C.: 1961), 657–658.
38. Memorandum of Conversations, Jan. 19, 1961, EL: Memo, Clark Clifford to LBJ, Nov. 29, 1967, Harry S Truman Library; Wilton B. Persons interview, COHP.

Chapter 45: The End

1. Lester David and Irene David, *Ike and Mamie* (New York: 1985), 218.
2. Arthur Nevins interview, COHP.
3. Nancy Jensen McCarty interview, EL; Nevins interview, COHP.
4. Billy Graham, *Just As I Am* (San Francisco: 1997), 204.
5. William Miller, *Henry Cabot Lodge* (New York: 1969), 335.
6. Kevin McCann interview, EL.
7. Robert Schulz interview, COHP.
8. John Bird interview, EL.
9. David H. Stowe interview, Harry S Truman Library.
10. William Bragg Ewald, Jr., *Eisenhower the President* (Englewood Cliffs, N.J.: 1981), 37.
11. William B. Ewald, Jr., interview, EL.
12. Letter, DDE, to William Robinson, Sept. 12, 1966, EL.
13. Letter, DDE to Sir Frederick Browning, Dec. 10, 1958, EL.
14. Nevins interview, COHP.
15. Unpublished memoir by Earl Endacott, EL.
16. Merle Miller, *Ike the Soldier* (New York: 1987), 192–193.
17. Ewald, 252.
18. Henry Kissinger, *The White House Years* (Boston: 1979), 43.
19. Vernon Walters interview, EL.
20. Stephen Ambrose and Richard Immerman, *Milton S. Eisenhower, Educational Stateman* (Baltimore, Md.: 1981), 160.

★★★★★
INDEX

A

ABOUT THE AUTHOR

GEOFFREY PERRET grew up in an Anglo-American theatrical family. Reared as a transatlantic commuter, he attended twenty-three schools before graduating from high school in Wheaton, Illinois. He served for three years in the U.S. Army and was educated at Harvard and the University of California at Berkeley. Both of his previous biographies—*Old Soldiers Never Die: The Life of Douglas MacArthur* and *Ulysses S. Grant*—were selected as Notable Books by *The New York Times*. *Eisenhower* is his tenth book. He is currently working on a biography of John F. Kennedy.

ABOUT THE TYPE

This book was set in Times New Roman, designed by Stanley Morrison specifically for *The Times* of London. The typeface was introduced in the newspaper in 1932. Times New Roman has had its greatest success in the United States as a book and commercial typeface rather than one used in newspapers.